Contemporary British Society

A New Introduction to Sociology

Nicholas Abercrombie and Alan Warde

with
Keith Soothill, John Urry and Sylvia Walby

Second Edition
Completely revised and updated

Polity Press

Copyright © Nicholas Abercrombie, Alan Warde, Keith Soothill,
John Urry and Sylvia Walby 1994

First published in 1994 by Polity Press
in association with Blackwell Publishers Ltd
Reprinted 1995 (twice), 1996

Editorial office:
Polity Press
65 Bridge Street
Cambridge CB2 1UR, UK

Marketing and production:
Blackwell Publishers Ltd
108 Cowley Road
Oxford OX4 1JF, UK

ISBN 0 7456 1066 8
ISBN 0 7456 1067 6 (pbk)

A CIP catalogue record for this book is available from the British
Library.

Typeset in 11 on 12½pt Times
by Photoprint, Torquay, Devon
Printed in Great Britain by Hartnolls Ltd, Bodmin, Cornwall

This book is printed on acid-free paper.

Contents

Acknowledgements

In preparing the second edition of this book the authors wish to thank those people who advised on revisions or who read sections of it: Bob Burgess, Brian Longhurst, Paul Gilroy, Colin Hay, Stephen Hill, David Morgan, John Scott, Beverley Skeggs, Roger Walters. Joe Abercrombie, Liz Bamford, Maeve Conolly, Karen Gammon, Chris Quinn, and Catherine Fletcher were very patient in typing parts of the manuscript and we owe them a special vote of thanks. Debbie Seymour of Polity Press has been inexhaustibly friendly, helpful, and efficient and Hilary Frost, Brian Goodale, Sarah McKean, and Pam Thomas between them converted an unruly manuscript into this printed text with admirable professionalism.

The authors and publishers wish to thank the following for permission to use copyright material:

Philip Allan Ltd. for Box 12.2 from Ivor Crewe, 'Why Did Labour Lose (Yet Again)?', *Politics Review*, Sept. (1992); and Fig. 2.6 from Alan Warde, 'The Future of Work', *Social Studies*, 5, 1 (1989).

David Austin for the cartoon from *The Guardian* (11.10.91) on page 409.

Ashgate Publishing Ltd. for Fig. 5.3 and Table 5.3 from C. Brown, *Black and White Britain* (1984), Gower; Table 5.2 from A. Bhat et al., *Britain's Black Population* (1988), Gower; and Table 5.5 from Hesse et al., *Beneath the Surface: Racial Harassment* (1992), Avebury.

Blackwell Publishers for Table 2.6 based on R. Bailey and J. Kelly, 'An index measure of British trade union density', *British Journal of Industrial Relations*, 23, 1 (1990); Box 2.2. from Hales, 'What do managers do?', *Journal of Management Studies*, 23, 1 (1986); Fig. 2.11 adapted from R. Pahl, *Divisions of Labour* (1984); Fig. 10.5 from E. Barker, *The Making of a Moonie* (1984), reprinted 1993 by Gregg Revivals; Gif. 6.7 from J. Gershuny, 'Change in the Domestic Division of Labour in the UK' in N. Abercrombie and A. Warde, eds. *Social Change in Contemporary Britain* (1992), Polity; Fig. 5.2 from H. Joshi, *The Changing Population of Britain* (1989); Tables 3.19, 3.20 and Fig. 3.7 from J. Scott, *Who Rules Britain?* (1991), Polity; and Fig. 2.4 in J. Scott, 'The British upper class' in Coates et al., *A Socialist Anatomy of Britain* (1985).

Cambridge University Press for Table 12.2 adapted from I. Crewe, N. Day and A. Fox, *The British Electorate* (1991); Table 3.6 from A. B. Atkinson and A. J. Harrison, *Distribution of Personal Wealth in Britain* (1978).

Christian Research Association for Fig. 10.2 from P. Brierley, *Christian England* (1991).

Commission for the New Towns for Fig. 3.4 for 'Stevenage Master Plan' (1966).

Dartmouth Publishing Company for Tables 2.8, 2.9, 2.10 from N. Millward et al., *Workplace Industrial Relations in Transition* (1992).

Express Newspapers plc for an extract from M. Atchinson, 'Save us from The Ravers', *Daily Express* (1991).

Guardian News Service Ltd. for Fig. 10.3 extracted from M. Kennedy, 'Carey says riots linked to poverty', *The Guardian*, 9.9.92; Box 10.1 from *The Guardian*, 6.4.92; Table 12.9 from *The Guardian*, 12.3.92; and extracts from *The Guardian*, 13.5.86 and 29.1.86.

The Controller of Her Majesty's Stationery Office for Crown copyright material.

The Journalist for Fig. 10.1 from their September (1989) issue.

King's Fund Institute for Tables 9.2, 9.3 and 9.7 from A. Harrison, *Health Care UK 1992: An Annual Review of Health Care Policy* (1992).

Macmillan Ltd. for Tables 3.1, 3.3, 3.4 and 3.9 from G. Routh, *Occupations of the People of Great Britain 1801–1981* (1987); Figs. 3.5 and 3.6 from Stewart et al, *Social Stratifications and Occupations* (1980); Box 3.3. from Crompton and Jones, *White-Collar Proletariat* (1984); for

Fig. 12.1 from Butler and Sloman, *British Political Facts, 1900–1979* (1980); for Tables 3.17, 3.18 from Price and Bain, 'The Labour Force' in A. H. Halsey, *British Social Trends Since 1900* (1988).

Methuen & Co. for Tables 2.2, 2.3 adapted from L. Hannah, *The Rise of the Corporate Economy* (1983).

David Morley, for Box 10.2 from D. Morley, *The 'Nationwide' Audience* (1980), British Film Institute.

Open University Press for Box 10.4 from P. Willis, *Common Culture* (1990).

Oxford University Press for Fig. 3.1, and Tables 3.21, 3.22 from Goldthorpe, Llewellyn and Payne, *Social Mobility and Class Structure in Modern Britain* (1980); Figs. 5.1, 6.2, 6.4 and Box 6.1 from *The British Population* (1992).

Penguin Books Ltd. for Fig. 11.5 from John Lea and Jock Young, *What is to be Done about Law and Order?* (1984). Copyright © 1984 John Lea and Jock Young.

Pergamon Press Ltd. for Tables 12.1, 12.4, 12.5, 12.6, 12.7, 12.8, and Box 12.1 from Health et al., *Understanding Political Change: the British Voter 1964–87* (1991).

Population Studies for Table 6.4 from J. Haskey, 'Social class and socio-economic differentials in England and Wales' (1984), *Population Studies*, 38.

Policy Studies Institute for Fig. 2.13 from W. Daniel, *The Unemployed Flow* (1990).

Random Century Group for Fig. 4.4 from Hanmer and Saunders, *Well Founded Fear* (1984), Hutchinson.

Routledge for Fig. 7.1 from Budd and Whimster, *Global Finance and Urban Living* (1992); Table 2.4 from J. Scott, 'Corporate control and corporate rule: Britain in an international perspective' (1990), *British Journal of Sociology*, 41, 3; Table 2.1 from A. Phizacklea, *Unpacking the Fashion Industry* (1990); tables 10.4, 10.5 adapted from Gershuny and Jones, 'The changing work/leisure balance in Britain, 1961–84' in Horne, Jary and Tomlinson, eds., *Sport, Leisure and Social Relations* (1987), Routledge and Kegan Paul; Fig. 10.3 from R. Wallis, *The*

Elementary Forms of the New Religious Life (1984), Routledge and Kegan Paul; Table 6.7 from Young and Willmott, *The Symmetrical Family* (1973), Routledge and Kegan Paul; Table 6.2 from Rapoport, Fogarty and Rapoport, *Families in Britain* (1982), Routledge and Kegan Paul; *Tables 6.6* 3.13 from P. Saunders, *A Nation of Home Owners* (1990), Unwin Hyman; Table 6.3 from S. Edgell, *Middle Class Couples* (1980), Unwin Hyman; Table 7.1 from P. Cooke, *Localities: The Changing Face of Urban Britain* (1989), Unwin Hyman; and Tables 3.14, 3.15 from Marshall et al, *Social Class in Modern Britain* (1988), Unwin Hyman.

Sage Publications Ltd. for Box 10.3 from K. Roberts, 'Great Britain: socioeconomic polarisation and the implications for leisure' in A. Olszewska and K. Roberts, eds., *Leisure and Lifestyle* (1989); and Table 2.11 from J. Allen and D. Massey, eds., *The Economy in Question* (1988).

Scarlet Press for Table 4.9 from Snyder, *European Women's Almanac* (1992).

Every effort has been made to trace all the copyright holders but if any have been inadvertently overlooked the publishers will be pleased to make the necessary arrangement at the first opportunity.

How to Use this Book

We have tried to write an approachable and accessible textbook on contemporary British society that looks at the society, rather than debates within sociology, and reviews relatively recent work rather than sociological classics. The following points may help you to get the best out of this book.

1 The book is divided into *chapters*, which are further subdivided into *sections*. We have assumed that many people will read only one section of the book at a time. Each section is therefore designed to stand on its own as a review of a particular topic, although in many chapters there is also an argument that connects sections.
2 In general we have avoided cluttering up the text with academic references. Where we do refer to a book or article we use the author-date system, that is, the reference appears as the name of the author or authors, followed by a date. You can find the full details by looking in the references at the back of the book under the author and date.
3 At the end of each section you will find a summary of the topic and, often, a list of other sections which contain other relevant material. You will also come across references in the text to other parts of the book which are especially relevant.
4 At the end of each chapter, there is a brief list of books (further reading) that explore in more detail the issues raised in the chapter.
5 There are illustrations of various kinds throughout the book. Courses in sociology now often include exercises in interpreting social statistics presented in various ways. We suggest that you use our tables, diagrams and graphs to find out information that is not discussed in the text; a close reading of a table can often tell you more, or suggest more interesting problems, than pages and pages of text.

6 We have found that people often have a very hazy idea of the geography of the British Isles. To help all our readers we have included maps of Britain and London, with all the places mentioned in the book marked on them.

7 Lastly, enjoy reading our book!

Maps

Map 1 Britain, showing places mentioned in the text

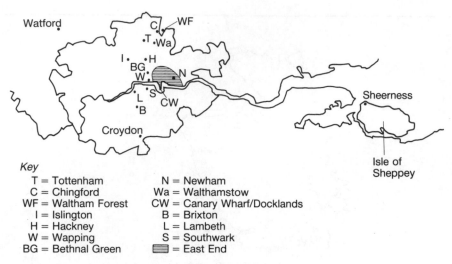

Key

T = Tottenham   N = Newham
C = Chingford   Wa = Walthamstow
WF = Waltham Forest   CW = Canary Wharf/Docklands
I = Islington   B = Brixton
H = Hackney   L = Lambeth
W = Wapping   S = Southwark
BG = Bethnal Green   ▤ = East End

Map 2 London, showing places mentioned in the text

List of Plates

1 Introduction

This book is both an introduction to sociology and an outline of the structure of contemporary British society. Our approach to introducing sociology is through a detailed analysis of one society. Its principal message is that Britain is an extremely complex society, its various social groups having very different social experiences. Our sociological description and explanation seek to portray the extent of this social diversity, and to respect the complexity of social life. At the same time, we try to account for its distinctive features in terms of underlying social-structural mechanisms which produce experiences in the social world. What any individual experiences, and what any social group shares, are significantly constrained by the way in which the society as a whole is *structured*. There is *both* diversity *and* structure.

1.1 Approaching Sociology

There are many ways in which sociology may be introduced. One way is via the grand questions of how societies in general cohere or change, questions classically addressed by social theorists such as Marx, Durkheim, Weber and Parsons. A second way is by examining and defining concepts that belong to the sociological vocabulary – concepts like *role, status, network, authority, community* – which are related to one another and have more specialized and restricted meanings than they do in ordinary language, and through which it becomes easier to talk about and understand social processes. Or, one could show what sociologists do, the methods they use to investigate the social world and the problems that arise in interpreting the data they collect. Yet another way is to present some of the findings about social practices and social relations in particular societies. This is the approach we adopt.

Runciman (1983) claims that sociology, and all other social sciences, consist of four distinct and separable activities: reportage, explanation, description and evaluation. Sociologists, first, report on what happened, on the events, processes or situations. Second, they try to explain *why* those events or processes happened, what were the reasons or causes for their occurrence. Third, sociologists attempt to describe what it was like for people who experienced these events or processes: how did it feel? How did the participants understand and interpret what was going on? Finally, sociologists may evaluate events or processes, declaring them to be good or bad, desirable or not. In practice these four activities tend to become intertwined, but in principle they are separate and different. Thus a reader is able, say, to accept explanations for gender inequalities offered in this book without sharing the evaluations; or facts reported may be seen as accurate without the reader necessarily agreeing with the descriptions of what it is like to be a woman in contemporary Britain. As Runciman (1983, p. 38) puts it:

> It takes little familiarity with the writings of sociologists, anthropologists and historians to be aware how often and how intricately the four are intertwined. In any full-length account of a complex event, process or state of affairs, the writer's purpose is likely to encompass reportage, explanation, description and evaluation alike. He is likely, that is, to want not only to persuade the reader that the events, processes or states of affairs which he has chosen to report came about as he reports them and for the reasons or causes which he has put forward, but at the same time to convey to the reader his idea of what it was like for the participants and to bring the reader round to his view of them as good or bad. But however intricately the four are connected in his account, it will always be possible in principle for the reader to disentangle them. In practice, the disentanglement is often made more difficult than it need be by the language and style in which the work is couched. But the distinction between them is no less fundamental to the methodology of social theory simply because a particular author obscures it, whether deliberately or not.

Sociologists, of course, disagree among themselves and all the elements of sociological inquiry are open to controversy. One sociologist can dispute the accuracy of another's *report* or offer a different *explanation*. But this is a feature of all kinds of knowledge: debate and argument, trying out competing explanations, confronting one report with another are, it is often said, the basis for the development of knowledge. In recent times, textbooks of sociology have tended to introduce sociology in terms of apparently mutually exclusive theoretical 'traditions' – functionalist, structuralist, interactionist, Marxist, for example. There are, of course, theoretical disagreements among sociologists, and theories affect explanations, descriptions and evaluations. But the significance of such theoretical disputes for understanding change in contemporary Britain is easily exaggerated. *In practice*, sociologists tend to use techniques, concepts, explanations and interpretations which draw on many, if not all, theoretical traditions. Concepts are taken from a number of competing theoretical positions, referring to action, meaning, structure and function when discussing social relations and today's societies. Sometimes from reading textbooks one gets the impression that understanding and analysing the social world is complicated because sociologists make it so, unnecessarily, by adopting obscure and mutually exclusive theoretical positions. Rather, to our way of thinking, the difficulties of sociological analysis arise *because the social world is extremely complex*. We have, therefore, set about giving a concrete sociological analysis of one society, Great Britain, respecting its complexity rather than focusing on sociologists' perceptions of societies. We have tried to write a book about British society, not about sociologists.

1.2 Modern Societies

Modern industrial societies are probably the most complex of those known in human history. This is partly reflected in their *density*: relatively large populations are maintained in a comparatively limited space. What is now Britain supported a population of around 3 million in 1600, 6 million in 1800, but 56 million in 1991. This expansion of population was made possible by two developments: an increasing division of labour and urban growth. The division of labour, through which more specialized work tasks were divided between different firms and individuals, increased the efficiency with which those things necessary to support the growing population could be produced (food, clothes, tools, houses, etc.). The expansion of cities provided a physical environment which helped the organization of the division of labour in production and a new social environment for the larger population. Perhaps the major cause of the complexity of contemporary British society is, however, the speed of social change: Britain (like all modern societies) is a *dynamic* society. This dynamism originated from and is sustained by *capitalist social relations*.

Britain is fundamentally a capitalist society. By this we mean that:

1 there is private ownership of the 'means of production' (property, plant, machinery, etc.);
2 economic activity is geared to making profits;

3 profits go to the owners of the means of production;
4 workers generally do not own productive property but work for
   wages;
5 the processes of production and sale of goods and services are
   organized into markets; everything is *commodified*.

These economic processes produce a social structure, one of whose main characteristics is a division between the owners of the means of production and the waged workers.

To define capitalism in such a way does not, of course, mean that it has remained unaltered since its origins in the seventeenth and eighteenth centuries. Quite the contrary: as we show in this book, there have been drastic changes in capitalism. The pattern of ownership of the means of production, changes in the distribution of income and wealth, the increasing complexity and fragmentation of the class structure, and the growth of the welfare state are but a few of the changes that have radically altered capitalist society. Indeed, capitalism by its very nature is an economic system that produces changes and diversity and this is one of its main features. It produces a self-propelling, ever accelerating sort of society.

Max Weber, among many others, noted how early capitalists of the seventeenth and eighteenth centuries used what he considered a peculiar logic – devoting their lives to accumulating wealth, or capital, but without spending it. He described this as the development of a 'Protestant ethic' which forbade the use of wealth and encouraged 'asceticism'. At the same time, the Protestant ethic promoted hard work and made worldly success a positive religious virtue. Manufacturers, farmers and merchants of the Protestant faith thus sought business success which was then, as now, measured by profit-making, but had no way of spending their increasing wealth other than reinvesting in their businesses. This process of profit-making and reinvestment, when seen in the light of competition between private enterprises, led to constant innovation. Firms cannot stand still. They must reinvest and reorganize their operations continually, otherwise their competitors will put them out of business.

The most simple example of this process is that of the introduction of new machinery. If firm A buys machines which make it possible to produce goods more cheaply than firm B, then B will be unable to sell its products and will go out of business, unless it responds. To purchase the same, or better, machinery is one response, but there are others – getting workers to work harder, making new products, or buying out firm A, for instance. The point, however, is that this innovation and change is self-perpetuating, inevitably built into an economic system where individuals and firms are free to produce any goods they choose, how they choose, constrained only by profitable competition. This 'logic' can be seen quite clearly in contemporary economic life: machinery becomes obsolete very quickly; there are frequent mergers, takeovers, and closures; new firms are continually being set up; and new generations of products appear increasingly rapidly.

Rapid economic change, inherent in capitalist social relations, is closely linked to cultural change. Partly because of continual economic development, British people are used to change. Though not always welcoming it, many people positively *seek* change. This may occur at the personal and individual level: moving to another town, joining a new religious movement, buying new types of goods, taking a different job. It also occurs collectively, in the political sphere and in the neighbourhood: radical political parties and new social movements are associations of people who collectively set about changing the social world. Britain is an 'active' society: people act as if they can alter the circumstances under which they live, to improve their own conditions and those of others.

This constant change and innovation generates a distinctive kind of social experience which some contemporary sociologists refer to as 'the experience of modernity'. Rapid change leads to uncertainty about the future, feelings of insecurity and anxiety, a sense of lost bearings in negotiating everyday life. Yet, at the same time, it brings a restlessness with permanence, a seeking after new experiences in pursuit of self-development, and selfish concern with personal well-being. The 'modern experience' generates particular personality types. At the same time, it threatens social instability as norms and behaviour change, old values and practices are discarded, new kinds of fads and fashions emerge, and traditional institutions become obsolete or are transformed. The experience of modernity is, thus, contradictory. On the one hand, it is exciting, bringing new and diverse experiences and fresh horizons. On the other hand, it removes all certainties, leaving people groping around in a social world without any established norms or guidelines. This, the paradox of modernity, is neatly summed up by Berman (1983, p. 1):

> There is a mode of vital experience – experience of space and time, of the self and others, of life's possibilities and perils – that is shared by men and women all over the world today. I will call this body of experience 'modernity'. To be modern is to find ourselves in an environment that promises us adventure, power, joy, growth, transformation of ourselves and the world – and, at the same time, that threatens to destroy everything we have, everything we know, everything we are. Modern environments and experiences cut across all boundaries of geography and ethnicity, of class and nationality, of religion and ideology: in this sense, modernity can be said to unite all mankind. But it is a paradoxical unity, a unity of disunity: it pours us all into a maelstrom of perpetual disintegration and renewal, of struggle and contradiction, of ambiguity and anguish. To be

modern is to be part of a universe in which, as Marx said, 'all that is solid melts into air'.

Britain is a capitalist society with a 'modern' culture. It has the 'paradoxical unity' Berman describes. Some of the possibilities for new experience and social experimentation are to be welcomed, others not; the paradox is that we tend to get both the beneficial and the detrimental consequences at the same time. For example, family relationships are changing: new laws and new attitudes to divorce permit women, especially, to escape miserable marriages, but that often leaves them in situations of social and economic insecurity, with heavy responsibilities for their children. The growth of youth subcultures, like punk, is equally typical of modernity. Unconventional styles of dress, language, music and entertainment alter frequently as young people pursue distinctive, and new, group identities. Such styles are tied up with a capitalist commercialism which, in seeking to persuade people to buy more, encourages changes of fashion.

In an important sense the experience of modernity is an *urban* phenomenon, an experience that is strongest in the largest of cities. In the city, social relations are relatively impersonal, impermanent, varied and unpredictable. Of course, not all social relations are like that. There are urban communities that are tightly knit and long established, where everyone knows everybody else and where there are collectively enforced rules of behaviour. A sense of community survives within a more general culture of modernity, and this shows the complexity of modern social experience. Complexity involves a multiplicity of experiences, and an enormous diversity.

Diversity can also generate inequality and thus, possibly, conflict. Key themes of sociological enquiry concern inequalities between classes, sexes, ethnic groups, status groups and age groups. Such differences need not produce conflict but they often do, particularly when difference is *interpreted* as inequality. The pursuit of equality, along with the pursuit of liberty, have been fundamental bases of actions to promote social change in Britain throughout the capitalist era. Social groups seeing themselves as unequally treated have organized together to improve their position. The struggle over the franchise (who should be able to vote), waged first by middle-class men, then by working-class men, followed by women, is a well-known example of the pursuit of one aspect of political equality – the right of equal citizenship.

The mechanisms of capitalist social relations and the division of labour combine to reproduce economic inequalities. Some employers make more profit than others, and some people, having no capital, make no profit at all but work for wages. And the circumstances under which people work for wages vary widely too: some employees have well-paid, secure jobs, have a lot of control over what they do, and work in pleasant conditions, but for others the experience of work is quite different. These inequalities, between employers and employees, and between different groups of workers, are perpetual sources of conflict in capitalist societies. In most cases, though, conflict is *institutionalized*, that is to say there are channels or institutions which resolve conflicts peacefully, by negotiation, without recourse to the use of force or violence. Thus, parliamentary democratic procedure, bargaining procedures in industrial relations, or regulation of competition between firms, are all ways of institutionalizing conflict. Of course, these are not always effective: internal war in Northern Ireland, riots in the inner city, policemen confronting striking miners, are all contemporary instances of conflict escaping from institutional regulation. But the point is that diversity generates conflict, fuelling experiences of instability, encouraging people to act to re-establish stability, which in turn produces further change.

Diversity, complexity and change are, then, features of contemporary British society. Any individual will know of, or shape, only a very small proportion of the variety of experiences that make up the social mosaic of the modern society. That, indeed, is one of the fascinations of reading good sociological reportage and description: it allows some access to the range and pattern of the experiences of social groups other than those to which the reader belongs. Sociology, however, also seeks to connect together context and experience, to show how certain social mechanisms or structures constrain and shape experiences. For all the diversity and complexity of everyday life, there are patterns to social action and interaction. The social world is *structured*. Just as the mosaics of the floors of Roman houses are made up of hundreds of pieces which, nevertheless, make a complete design, the patterning of social relations cannot be seen by looking at the individual elements. The mosaic has to be examined in terms of the *relative* positions of its different pieces, how they stand in relation to one another.

One of the outstanding features of societies is the way in which component parts are highly interrelated, or *interdependent*. This interdependence is often expressed in technical language in terms of a social *system*. Or, sometimes, the social system is described as an 'organism', societies being likened to animal bodies in which the various organs – heart, liver, lungs – all work together to keep the animal alive. Like most analogies, the model of the organism can be misleading if used too literally. There *is*, however, something system-like about social organization, with one institution affecting many of the others. Thus, for instance, the social organization of work affects the way education is organized, changes the role of the family in bringing up children, and results in the unequal distribution of income and wealth. It is this, the interdependence of social institutions, which makes sociological explanation so difficult and complicated. If one part of the mosaic changes then the whole pattern is altered, making it difficult to pin-point a single cause of any particular event, process or change.

The concepts that we have discussed above are ones which we will use in our analysis of change in British society. We stress that Britain is a diverse, changing and complex society. At the root of that diversity is a capitalist economic system and a 'modern' culture. These are fundamental bases of social change, generating sometimes order and harmony, at other times disorder and conflict. They are the structures behind everyday life with all its variety, ambiguity and contradiction.

1.3   Contemporary Britain

Some of the implications of the preceding remarks on the sociological interpretation of modern capitalist societies are briefly illustrated in the following thumb-nail sketch of key structures and changes of contemporary British society which we discuss in greater detail in the chapters that follow.

Our understanding of contemporary Britain begins by recognizing the process of industrial change which the country has experienced since the mid 1970s. In the context of an international recession, the British economy has declined more than most other nations in a comparable position in the world economic system. Many British firms have lost out in competition with foreign equivalents, though it has to be recognized that, increasingly, the most important firms are multinational corporations anyway. In response to this harsh external environment many firms have undergone restructuring, with changes in ownership as a result of takeovers, and changes in their internal organization. This restructuring has serious effects upon employees, partly as new machinery is introduced making workers redundant, and partly as jobs are redesigned so as to save money by making each worker more productive. In fact, British workers increased their productivity very considerably during the 1980s, but this has not improved the relative competitiveness of British industry. One of the most significant effects of the economic restructuring in Britain has been the decline of employment in manufacturing industry. Though some of the workers displaced from traditional manufacturing industries have found jobs in the so-called 'service sector', many have joined the expanding ranks of the unemployed. The British state has, in the 1980s, been either unwilling or unable to improve the situation, preferring to allow the cold winds of capitalist competition to reshape the economy rather than intervening directly.

Another effect of industrial change has been to moderate industrial conflict. Industrial disputes reached a post-war high in 1979 but since then, with the marked exception of the bitter miners' strike in 1984–5, industrial conflict has been muted. A number of factors account for this. High levels of unemployment, the decline of the traditional heavy manufacturing industries such as shipbuilding and steel, which were bastions of trade unionism, and more determined anti-unionism by government and employers, have combined to weaken the trade union movement. Changes in the division of labour and the industrial structure thus have contained conflict in the workplace, though there is no reason to imagine that the workers feel any less resentment about pay and working conditions.

Industrial change inevitably affects class relations and the class structure, because occupation is a fundamental basis of class position. The shape of the occupational structure has been changing in recent years, the numbers of manual workers declining, and the numbers of professional and semi-professional jobs increasing. A debate rages about the effects of this on class relations. In the twentieth century, the working class, through the organizations of the labour movement (primarily trade unions and the Labour Party), has exerted much political pressure for social reform. The main supporters of the labour movement were, however, manual workers, who were the majority of the working population and whose social situation was visibly distinct from that of the upper and upper-middle class.

The changing size and composition of British classes have, arguably, reduced the strength of the working class as a force for change. The future of class conflicts depends also on classes other than the workers. In many respects the incomes and work situations of routine clerical workers have become more like those of manual workers, though in the past they have often had distinct political commitments. Other elements of the middle classes are also experiencing change, and the future of British political life will be strongly affected by their reactions. Despite the flux at these lower levels of the class structure, there is very great continuity and permanence among the upper class, that network of property-owning families whose power and influence continue to structure social life in Britain. The very top positions remain within the grasp of hereditary upper-class families.

Women have played a critically important part in the redefinition of the social division of labour in the last 20 years. For instance, there are more married women in paid work today than there have been at any time in the last 100 years. However, the jobs women have tend to be relatively poorly paid and carry little authority. The segregation of men's work from women's work, which is the way that gender differentials are maintained, is increasingly a source of frustration and annoyance to women, who have organized to improve their position. This is to be expected since, apart from education where opportunities for girls and women have improved markedly in recent years, the inequalities between men and women have not been reduced. The disadvantages women face cannot be entirely explained by the mechanisms of capitalist social relations. Because of this we have to look for different mechanisms and different sets of relations in order to explain the position of women. These *patriarchal* relations coexist with the logic of capitalist inequalities, producing the particular structure of inequalities between men and women in Britain.

Patriarchy is a concept which recognizes inequalities of power between men and women, inequalities which can be seen, for instance, in the unequal distribution of housework, in stereotypes of femininity which describe women as helpless and passive, and in male violence against women. One of the more significant new developments since 1970 has been the revival of the feminist movement trying actively to promote change in the typical forms of gender relations in our society. Women have become more aware of their oppression; 'sexism' and 'male chauvinism' are expressions which have entered everyday language; groups of women have organized themselves to contest political issues which particularly affect women.

In a similar way, we can see the intersection of capitalist social relations and cultural stereotypes creating a further social division which is a source of social conflict – that between ethnic groups. Many members of ethnic groups, particularly those of Caribbean and Asian descent, even if many of them have been born in Britain, suffer social and material deprivation when compared with white people. The very presence in Britain of many different ethnic groups is one mark of the diversity of culture and experience among different sections of the population. Family forms and religious experience distinguish ethnic groups, and some of the most vital of contemporary cultural products – food, music, oriental religions – are the result of the presence of people with different cultural traditions. These differences are, however, frequently turned into bases for much resented inequalities. There can be no doubt that black people tend to get poorer jobs than whites do. What is more, they tend to suffer the consequences of white racism, the hostile or deprecatory attitudes and behaviours which are directed at them merely on the basis of their skin colour. Again, one can see an intersection of mechanisms of the labour market, in which black people get the poorest of working-class jobs and suffer the highest rates of unemployment. And, once again, we see signs of active resistance, of attempts by the disadvantaged groups to express their dissatisfaction and collectively to alter their circumstances.

This discussion of the generation of inequalities between classes, genders and ethnic groups in terms of income and employment has mainly been concerned with the impact of capitalist relations of production on different sections of the population. We should emphasize yet again that this is insufficient, on its own, as an explanation of why such inequalities exist. There are many features of the particular inequalities between the sexes and between ethnic groups that are not satisfactorily explained by economic processes alone. We need to refer, in addition, to both patriarchal relations of male domination, and racial prejudice and discrimination (racism), in order to explain how it is that women and ethnic minorities find themselves in a disadvantaged position. Separating out these mechanisms and weighing them against one another is extremely difficult but absolutely essential in the course of sociological explanation.

The next aspect of the contemporary social structure and change that we deal with is more directly concerned with the cultural experience of modernity. The family is one institution which exemplifies the degree of variety and complexity that characterizes social experience in Britain, and one which illustrates the insecurity and instability of social relations in the contemporary world.

One of the most striking features of the contemporary British family is the variety of forms it assumes. Besides distinctive household patterns of ethnic minorities, which are often adapted from their particular religious and cultural traditions or the need to provide accommodation for newly arrived immigrant kinsfolk, there is a remarkable diversity of household forms among other sections of the population too. There is a dominant image of what a 'normal' family is in contemporary Britain – a small, nuclear family of parents and dependent children. In reality, this is not normal at all, and only a small proportion of households are like this. Various social changes, including the facts that people live longer than they used to, that many more people are getting divorced, and that people expect more from marriage than before, have meant a rise in the numbers of single-person households, of one-parent families and of families formed by remarriage and step-parenting. Such changes may produce stress and anxiety within marriage as well as satisfactions.

Many of the contradictions of contemporary British society, and some of the points of tension between the organization of economic life and the culture of modernity, are reflected within the education system. Educational institutions both express and create social divisions. Current emphasis upon making education relevant for work – training for economic life – typifies these contradictions. On the one hand, educating people for future work roles always entails selection and differentiation: some people are made into successes, others into failures. Schools create inequalities between individuals by preparing their pupils differently by class, gender and ethnic group. On the other hand, schools are expected to transmit a common or dominant culture – to educate young people for citizenship and to be full members of a national community. To what extent schools actually do either of these things very effectively is open to debate. However, the complicated role that educational institutions play gives some indication of the complex interdependencies between institutions in British society: they are intended to fit in with the entire industrial and occupational complex, with the family, and with the dominant political institutions. What schools do is relevant to, and interdependent with, all other major institutions in contemporary Britain. Small wonder, then, that schools fail in some respects to satisfy the demands of all the groups who have an interest in their activities.

We have talked about the way that people in a modern, diverse, and rapidly changing world may set about trying to change it. To do this, people have to have a way of seeing the world, a way of understanding both what is wrong with it from their point of view and what is needed to effect a change. These ways of seeing we call *culture*. The modern world has enormous diversity of cultures, each appropriate to the multiplicity of social groups we described earlier. So, the working-class way of looking at the world is different from that of the middle class; the culture of women is very different from that of men. However, there also exists a general set of cultural themes, perhaps to do with morality, the importance of nation and so on, that prevail in modern Britain. These are dominant, both in the sense that they are the themes most available in the educational system and the mass media, and in the sense that they reflect the interests of dominant social groups. The intriguing sociological question concerns the relationship of the multiplicity of cultures to the dominant one. Are the many cultures subordinate or resistant to the dominant one? Is the dominant culture effectively transmitted through the mass media, for instance?

The same sorts of questions, concerning diversity and change in modern society and domination and resistance, also arise when considering politics. They are, indeed, the very stuff of politics. In parliamentary democracies people have the power, even if it is rather restricted, to change things. The most obvious way is through voting. Here too the social world is becoming more diverse and complex. Generally speaking, voters seem to be abandoning their traditional political loyalties, especially those formed along class lines. Also the *means* by which people seek to change their situation have become more diverse. Voting is, after all, only a periodic expression of opinion. British society is also characterized by a multiplicity of social movements and pressure groups. Women, ethnic groups and the peace and environmental movements are but four voices represented in new social movements which express their specific grievances and wishes.

It has to be recognized, however, that the capacity to change society, either by voting or by involvement in pressure groups, is limited. The powers of the state have very greatly increased in the twentieth century, especially since the Second World War. This is partly because the state has come to intervene in citizens' lives in a number of different ways, and partly a result of the vast resources the state can deploy. It is also a matter of the ultimate capacity to control. In this last respect, the growth in numbers of the police in Britain, and of their powers, is of significance. The character of the police force is changing: it is becoming more professional and technologically sophisticated. Some of these changes have been brought about in response to the fear of a rising rate of crime. Others are introduced because of the civil disturbances which, as we indicated earlier, have to be seen as elements of a rapidly changing society showing symptoms of strain.

Contemporary British society, as we have argued, is increasingly diverse and complex and is, furthermore, changing very quickly. Underlying this complexity are some basic structuring elements, two of the most important of which are capitalist social relations and a culture of modernity. The rest of this book looks at these issues in much greater depth.

2 Work and Industry

2.1 Introduction

The organization of work is the most basic element of modern social structure. Many of the most important institutions in British society – the education system, the family, the law, and politics – are tailored to meet the requirements of work. Work is also a fundamental determinant of the experience of individuals. There is a strong connection between the kind of work people do and many other aspects of their existence. How long you live, whom you marry, how much money you have, where you live, and how your children will fare, are all affected by your work.

Work is central to social existence because of the intensive division of labour in modern societies. Labour, or work, is a feature of all human societies. Personal survival, and the reproduction of the species, require always that work is done to provide food, shelter, security, and the like. That work is always *socially organized*, though the pattern of organization varies enormously between societies. Peasant households typically produce for themselves most of what they need. Most modern Britons, by contrast, do a very *specialized* job, for which they receive wages, with which in turn they buy many of the things they require. This specialization, this complex division of labour, requires a very high degree of social organization. Just think of how many people are required to behave regularly and reliably in a huge range of different tasks in order to operate British Rail. The degree of coordination required between 130,000 men and women employees is immense, though we now take it for granted.

In capitalist societies, the division of labour derives from the pursuit of profit by those who own the means to produce goods and services which can be sold, usually to satisfy needs. Workers are paid wages to bring them to work to produce commodities. The parts played by individual workers in the production process are very varied and the rewards and satisfactions obtained from work are correspondingly different. From this phenomenon of differentation derives social inequalities, social divisions and social conflicts.

Many of the inequalities deriving from work are well-known to everybody. In 1991, weekly earned incomes for workers in full-time employment ranged from £120 per week on average for women workers in hairdressing to £34,865 a week for the chairman of SmithKline. The very rich do not have earnings from employment, but rather have unearned incomes, for example from dividends from shares; the very poor may have somewhat different unearned incomes, perhaps from income support. Again, some jobs have more prestige than others. Prestige is usually related to income and to the nature of the work done. Some jobs offer more freedom than others. Some work is creative, much more is very routine. Perhaps most important, some jobs give *authority* to their occupants: managerial and supervisory positions carry with them some degree of power. In all these respects, the division of labour produces social inequality.

Unsurprisingly, then, conflict arises. Individuals and social groups attempt to alter the social organization of work to their own benefit. Firms, their owners and managers, try to organize work to pursue the goals of profit, growth, efficiency and control. This generates competition between firms and conflict with workers. In the 1980s, the reassertion of managerial prerogatives – the so-called 'right of management to manage' – has been a central strategic objective of these groups. This implies the existence of other groups who contest those goals and whose interests are served by a different manner of work organization.

Both trade unions and professional associations are bodies which seek to influence rewards and working practices. Thus we have the conditions for industrial conflict, primarily between workers and management, but also between groups of workers. Sometimes these conflicts become generalized. Class struggles are those based on the shared interests of many groups of workers against many managements. Gender struggles are those based upon a recognition of generalized, antagonistic interests between women and men. This second kind of struggle appears both in employment and in other spheres of work.

Money mediates between capital and labour: employees get paid. But it must be recognized that much work is unpaid. Housework is the most outstanding example. A sample of housewives with pre-schoolchildren, interviewed by Oakley (1974), did an *average* of 77 hours of *domestic* work per week (i.e. routine household tasks and child-care). That is surely work, but not employment. The distinction is very important. Employment is the kind of work classified as an occupation and paid for in wages. It is employment which produces the inequalities of power and income which are part of the sphere of industrial relations. Trade unions and professional associations, wage negotiations and job demarcation disputes, are expressions of employment relationships.

Other kinds of work are subject to different principles of organization. Domestic work is also divided between people, usually so that women do more of it than men. This unequal distribution of tasks is underpinned by the institutions of marriage and the family, producing conflicts between men and women (gender divisions). The link between these two different ways of organizing work is a matter of great dispute (see also section 4.3).

The division of labour in society as a whole is constantly changing. Some industries expand while others contract. Within industries the nature of tasks changes, as new machinery is introduced and new working practices are imposed. The spread of occupations is altered at the same time: currently, for instance, the proportion of manual workers in the labour force is declining. Demarcations between men's and women's jobs change too. There is also a geographical aspect to the division of labour, in the sense that where firms choose to locate their factories and offices has significant social consequences. Increasingly, the largest international corporations are locating their factories in the developing countries where labour is cheap, and their headquarters, when in Britain, are in the south-east of England. Divisions of labour outside formal, paid employment also alter. The domestic division of labour is changing. The availability of domestic machinery and the virtual disappearance of domestic servants have changed tasks and social relationships within households.

Changes in the division of labour have consequences for many other aspects of life. For instance, educational reforms since the mid 1970s have been directed towards preparing children better for new employment opportunities. Vocational training, youth training schemes, the expansion of engineering and information technology in universities are all justified in terms of providing a more efficient social organization of work (see section 8.3).

Some of the effects of a changing division of labour are illustrated in figure 2.1. This diagram does not exhaust all the effects, but nevertheless suggests that the division of labour has consequences for everyday life, family structure, community, class and politics. The connections between changes in the division of labour and other aspects of social life are not, however, necessarily direct or simple. The division of labour is not the only cause of, for example, political change; indeed, political action itself may alter the division of labour. The connections are complex.

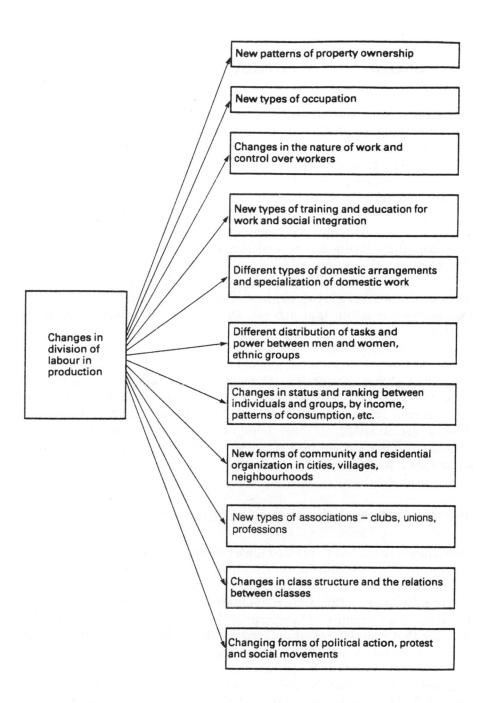

Figure 2.1 Some social effects of changes in the division of labour in modern Britain.

2.2 Economic Restructuring

Capitalism is an extraordinarily dynamic economic system (see chapter 1). Firms pursue profit in a competitive environment, devising strategies that will make their products more desirable than those of other producers. The reasons why products become desirable to consumers are many: goods may be relatively cheap, uniquely distinctive, particularly efficient and reliable, protected by tariffs or patents, etc. Firms must constantly choose among strategies for enhancing their profitability. The combined effect of many economic actors simultaneously new ways of organizing their businesses is sometimes called *economic restructuring*. This refers to the whole series of uncoordinated economic decisions made by firms – what to produce, what machinery to use, how to organize the workers involved, how much to pay and what to charge. Restructuring is a constant process, though it may be more intense at some times than others. One of the most consequential aspects of restructuring since the 1970s has been its extended *international* scope. The most powerful economic agencies today are large capitalist firms controlling global operations. Throughout the twentieth century they have grown in size and in the scope of their operations. So-called multinational corporations (MNCs) and transnational corporations (TNCs) are responsible for a significant portion of all industrial production. This section begins by describing some aspects of economic activity on a world scale.

The international division of labour

International trade has flourished under capitalist auspices for centuries – first through the activities of merchants, subsequently through colonialism and imperialism, as metropolitan nation-states secured immense economic benefits for the populations of the developed world. Moreover, the capitalist economic order has always been international in the sense that people moved in large numbers between countries, much migration being oriented to improving the economic prospects of individuals and families. It remains the case that international migration is extensive, though Britain has received very few new permanent settlers since 1972. The distinctive feature of the late twentieth century is that *firms* now operate on a global platform,scarcely seeming to belong to (or to feel responsibility towards) any nation-state. We now live in a world of multinational and transnational corporations. Employment in Britain is now increasingly affected by decisions taken by companies that are headquartered elsewhere and calculate the comparative advantages of producing goods in different locations throughout the world.

Multinational and transnational corporations

Some of these corporations have enormous turnovers – much greater in fact than those of many countries. For instance, MNCs control considerable proportions of the world's production capacity and account for a considerable amount of employment. They are both 'multi-plant' and 'multi-product' organizations. That is to say, they have many factories and offices in different places around the world, and they operate in many different industrial sectors producing a vast range of commodities. Operation on an international scale creates many strategic options. In the first place, they are able to benefit from the varied social and economic conditions in different nation-states. For example, analyses of the so-called 'new international division of labour' have shown how the MNCs make use of differential wage rates. Operations which are labour intensive (i.e. wages rather than machines or raw materials are the major cost to the enterprise) tend to be undertaken in less developed countries where wages are very low. Their headquarters and their research and development outfits remain in or near to the financial centres of the advanced societies. The result is that the MNCs are altering the geography of industry on a world scale in the competitive pursuit of profit. Though less spectacular, something similar happens within Britain, where the 'higher-order functions' of research, finance and corporate planning in the big corporations are being shifted to the south-east of England, with lower-level managerial work and routine branch-plant production being concentrated in the north and west of Britain.

Another strategic advantage arises from MNCs being free from the control of any single government. It is possible to evade pollution-control laws, which may be very expensive to accommodate, by locating dirty processes in countries with no environmental legislation. It is also possible to reduce tax liability by shifting financial assets from country to country, but still keeping them internal to the corporation. Moreover, governments give concessions and privileges to MNCs to persuade them to invest and, thus, to bring employment and money to their countries. Such incentives include tax concessions, rent-free premises, grants towards installing new machinery, etc. Recent British experience includes some well-publicized deals attracting Japanese car manufacturers to Wales and north-east England. These relationships are signs of the power of these global corporations and the impossibility of individual

governments exercising control over them. The decisions of the
corporations, made with a view to their own profitability, profoundly
affect local, regional and national economies. When it is no longer
profitable to produce motor vehicles in Britain, the MNC cannot be
prevented either from moving car production to, say, West Germany, or
from redirecting its investments to one of its other products – televisions,
cardboard boxes, or whatever. National governments have fewer
effective regulatory powers.

Global competition in manufacture

MNCs are leading agencies in the process of uneven geographical
development. International competition between firms intensified during
the recessions of the 1970s and 1980s. Global competition is especially
fierce in manufacturing, for goods can be transported and stored more
easily than many service activities (although financial, scientific and
tourist services are internationally highly competitive). British manufacturing firms did not perform well and, as more goods were imported,
jobs declined. Impacts varied between industrial sectors (i.e. depending
on what type of product was sold), as the examples of the chemicals and
fashion clothes industries show.
   Imperial Chemical Industries Limited (ICI) was created by the merger
of four British companies in 1926. It always operated abroad to some
degree, though in its early days primarily in the countries of the British
Empire – thus the title 'Imperial'. By the 1980s it was a massive
corporation with operations truly global, having factories in more than 40
countries and offices in more than 60 (Clarke, 1982). Its factories
produce a vast range of products which include organic chemicals, fibres,
general chemicals, industrial explosives, oils, paints, pharmaceuticals
and plastics. In response to the world recessions since the 1970s the
company rationalized its production, often by closing down British
operations. Figure 2.2 shows both how the number of workers in ICI has
fallen since 1971 and also how the proportion working in Britain has
declined. Whereas, in 1971, 72 per cent of ICI employees were in Britain,
by 1981 they were a mere 51 per cent. To take just one example of the
way this happens, ICI in 1981 opened a new plant in Wilhelmshaven in
West Germany, manufacturing exactly the same product (chlorine) as it
was already producing in Cheshire and on Teesside. This was done
primarily because electricity, which accounted for 80 per cent of the cost
of producing chlorine, was cheaper by half in Germany (Clarke, 1982).
What is economically rational for ICI is ominous for the employment
prospects of the population of northern England.
   Chemicals is an industrial sector dominated by large companies. Other

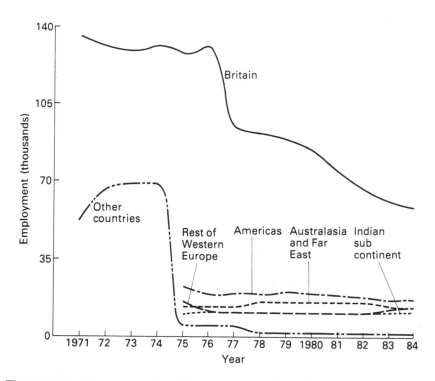

Figure 2.2 Employment in ICI world-wide, 1971–1984.
Source: Beynon et al., 1986, p. 72.

sectors consist of enormous numbers of separate firms, but they too are much affected by internationalization. Phizacklea's (1990) study of the fashion clothes industry is instructive. Clothing used to be mostly made in Britain, textiles being one of the staples of the industrial revolution. Since the early 1970s, a considerable amount of all clothing sold in Britain has been manufactured overseas. The primary reason for this is that wage rates are considerably lower in South East Asia and assembling clothes is a labour-intensive process. Table 2.1 indicates the relative cost per hour of labour in different countries. Products for which there is stable demand, like underwear and men's shirts, are likely to be made by young women workers in less developed countries. Fashion goods, by definition, are characterized by the very rapid turnover of styles which require fast response to new demands and short production runs. In the women's fashionwear section of the market, much of current manufacture still takes place in Britain.

For expensive fashion clothing, advanced technologies, especially computer-assisted design and manufacture (CAD/CAM), are profitable for some British firms, as they more obviously are also in Germany and Italy. Phizacklea points out that in terms of money value a significant

Table 2.1   International variations in wage costs per direct employee, 1984

Country	Hourly wages incl. piece-work incentive (£)	Social costs (%)	Wage costs total per hour (£)
West Germany	2.75	70	4.68
Egypt	0.48	52	0.73
England	1.90	27	2.41
Greece	1.21	85	2.24
Hong Kong	0.83	29	1.07
Haiti	0.30	32	0.39
Ireland	1.49	27	1.89
Italy	2.18	105	4.46
Ivory Coast	0.48	80	0.86
Malta	1.50	25	1.88
Morocco	0.30	10	0.33
Portugal	0.68	25	0.84
Spain	1.50	42	2.14
Sri Lanka	0.19	25.8	0.24
Switzerland	3.38	40	4.74
Tunisia	0.40	19.5	0.47
USA	2.82	33	3.75

Source: Phizacklea, 1990, p. 60; research by Kurt Salmon Associates reported in *Apparel International*, 1984, February

proportion of British imports comes from Italy and Germany, whose competitiveness depends on design and quality rather than cheap labour. Less expensive fashion items are also sourced in Britain, but these are usually produced by a vast number of small operators, typically in the inner cities and especially the East End of London, who are engaged as subcontractors to cut cloth and assemble articles for the retail chains. The position of small entrepreneurs is highly unfavourable for there is severe competition, partly because it requires very little capital to set up such a business. Consequently, working conditions in some businesses resemble the sweat-shops of the nineteenth century, with workers very poorly paid, casually employed and rarely unionized. In addition, home-workers, typically married women from ethnic minorities, are extensively used and their conditions are even more degrading, with pay likely to be less than £1 per hour and with neither job security nor social benefits. Using skills learned in the home, and excluded from more attractive labour markets by racist and patriarchal mechanisms, ethnic minority women produce many of the fashion clothes available in the high-street stores. Their low wages permit small British businesses to survive without introducing expensive and advanced machinery.

The effects of restructuring

The social consequences of economic restructuring on an international scale have been momentous. The manner of producing goods changes as influential competitors are imitated. The global success of Japanese corporations led to their widespread admiration in Britain in the 1980s, for instance. More generally, external competitive pressure came to justify the reform of working practices in the UK. Job opportunities were affected, Britain losing many manufacturing jobs as more goods (cars, clothes, ships, etc.) were made overseas. International production arrangements altered migration flows. For, while people are still crossing national borders in search of work, now the corporations can disperse jobs to wherever a suitable pool of labour exists. Companies, large and small, can more easily take advantage of ethnic and gender divisions in labour markets to keep wages as low as possible, the threat always being that the firm will not be able to compete with other producers in low-wage, less developed countries. The MNCs grew in size partly by taking over small companies, thereby extending their capacities in new markets across the globe. Meanwhile, government management, regulation and planning became difficult as world markets and foreign companies increasingly determined economic outcomes. Intense reorganization accompanied the new international division of labour.

Summary

1 Transnational corporations now operate on a world scale and they have become very powerful economic actors.
2 Their decisions about investment affect local areas throughout the world, yet governments have limited control over their behaviour.

2.3 Ownership and Control

Economic power, in terms of control over physical assets, is apparently responding to a centripetal force, tending more and more to concentrate in the hands of a few corporate managements. At the same time, beneficial ownership is centrifugal, tending to divide and sub-divide, to split into even smaller units and to pass freely from hand to hand. In other words, ownership continually becomes more dispersed; the power formerly joined to it becomes increasingly concentrated; and the corporate system is thereby more securely established. (Berle and Means, 1932)

It is a familiar argument that, in the twentieth century, the whole structure of the ownership and control of British industry has changed. A series of factors contribute to this: firms have grown larger by merger and takeover; increasingly, businesses are owned not by single entrepreneurs or their families but by many shareholders; and large financial institutions have gradually assumed ownership of significant sectors of British industry. These changes, and others, raise the issue of ownership and control which is posed in the quotation above from Berle and Means. If ownership is no longer concentrated in the hands of a single entrepreneur, but is spread among a number of shareholders who may have different interests, where does control of the enterprise lie? Do shareholders get together to dictate decisions? Or do professional managers take effective control? There are, in fact, a number of different issues raised by these questions and we start by considering the way in which the ownership of firms has become more concentrated.

Concentration and control

British industry might appear to be composed of a mass of competing firms. As consumers, when we wish to buy something, we are often faced with a welter of brand names. In the supermarket, for instance, a large number of manufacturers are represented, offering a wide range of different types of product. On the other hand, newspapers, radio and television throughout the 1980s were full of reports of a 'merger boom' – attempts by one large company to takeover another. This led to takeover battles in which large companies struggled with each other to gain control of another firm which was often in quite a different area of business.

Are firms typically independent or are they, perhaps, linked together? What then are the relationships of ownership *between* firms? Do the many apparently competing brands, for example, conceal the fact that a few firms manufacture them all? The general answer to these questions is that in the twentieth century there has been a concentration of ownership in British industry.

Concentration and the corporate economy

In Britain today, there are fewer and larger firms taking a larger

We, the Imperial Board, strongly recommend immediate acceptance of the United Biscuits offer.

(This is the form it should take.)

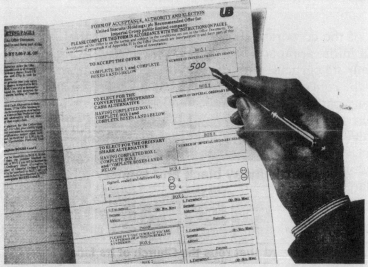

If you are an Imperial shareholder, the unanimous advice of your Board, fully supported by its financial advisers, Hambros Bank, is that you should accept the offer made by United Biscuits.

In order to do this you should complete the white United Biscuits acceptance form immediately. All forms should be returned by 3.00pm on Friday, 21st March 1986.

This is the way to "stay with Imperial."

By accepting the UB offer, you will help create a major new British group, United Imperial, which will ensure Imperial's businesses continue to prosper.

It is most important that every UB form of acceptance is despatched without delay. That is the best way of repelling the unwelcome Hanson bid.

If you need advice on how to complete the UB acceptance form, please telephone 0272-666961.

IMPERIAL GROUP

The directors of Imperial Group plc (including those who have delegated detailed supervision of this advertisement) have taken all reasonable care to ensure that the facts stated and opinions expressed are fair and accurate. The directors accept responsibility accordingly.

Plate 2.1   Take-over battles, with large companies competing with each other to gain control of another firm, were often quite public.
Source: Imperial Tobacco Limited

proportion of sales. The British economy is increasingly dominated by large corporations; it has become a 'corporate economy'. As Hannah (1976, p. 1) says:

> It is a commonplace that in the course of the present century British industry has witnessed a transformation from a disaggregated structure of predominantly small, competing firms, to a concentrated structure dominated by large, and often monopolistic, corporations. The 100 corporations which now occupy the dominant positions account for something approaching one half of total manufacturing output, whilst at the turn of the century the largest 100 firms accounted for barely 15 per cent of output.

The rise of the corporate economy can be investigated in a number of ways. An initial approach is to look at the degree to which a few large firms dominate particular industries. The conventional way of measuring this is by the *concentration ratio*, which usually refers to the proportion of sales in any particular industry accounted for by the five largest firms in that industry.

Hannah (1983) shows substantial degrees of concentration in 1969 in a whole range of manufacturing industries (table 2.2). The table shows that in several industry groups, roughly three-quarters of sales are taken by the five largest firms, and in tobacco the proportion is 100 per cent. Even

Table 2.2 Concentration in industry groups, 1957 and 1969: shares of the largest five firms

Industry	1957 firms (%)	1969 firms (%)
Food	41.3	52.7
Drink	32.7	69.5
Tobacco	96.5	100.0
Chemicals	71.0	73.7
Metal manufacture[a]	45.7	59.5
Non-electrical engineering	29.8	25.3
Electrical engineering	47.2	68.0
Shipbuilding	62.1	74.2
Vehicles	50.4	71.0
Textiles	44.2	65.1
Clothing and footwear	63.8	78.4
Building materials	53.1	51.1
Paper and publishing	47.5	63.2

[a] Excluding the nationalized British Steel Corporation and its constituents.

Source: adapted from Hannah, 1983, p. 144

in the industry group with the lowest concentration ratio – non-electrical engineering – the five largest firms account for one-quarter of the sales. The degree of concentration in manufacturing also shows a steady increase over time, with the largest five firms taking a larger and larger proportion of sales. In most industry groups there were fairly substantial increases in the five-firm concentration ratio in the period 1957–69, as can be seen from table 2.2.

Evidence of the degree of concentration in non-manufacturing industries is less easy to come by. In the financial sector in 1971 the four largest banks controlled 92 per cent of total deposits, while the four largest life insurance companies took 31 per cent of their market. In retailing generally, being a service industry that is localized and segmented, there is not much concentration. But in certain retail sectors, there can be considerable concentration. In 1984, the five largest store groups accounted for 44 per cent of footwear sales, 42 per cent of domestic appliances, and 36 per cent of men's and boys' clothing. In 1988, the top five multiples controlled 70 per cent of food sales (Gardner and Sheppard, 1989). At the other end of the scale there are service industries with minimal levels of concentration. The three largest hotel groups, for instance, control only 8 per cent of the total number of beds available.

The way in which a few firms dominate particular industries or markets is not necessarily the most sociologically interesting thing about the concentration of British industry. We also need to look at the economy as a whole and the way in which relatively few firms dominate it. This is particularly important as businesses have grown larger by absorbing other firms that operate in quite different areas of industry. The result is the increased importance of *conglomerates* with diversified interests in a very wide range of products.

The growth of conglomerate enterprises

In the early part of this century the largest 100 firms produced about 16 per cent of output, but the proportion had jumped to some 45 per cent in 1970 and it is still rising. Figure 2.3 makes clear that there have been two spurts of concentration, from 1910 to 1930, and from the later 1940s onwards, tailing off somewhat in the 1970s. An alternative way of showing concentration is to consider the proportion of assets held by the largest manufacturing firms. Table 2.3 shows that even in the short period from 1957 to 1965 there were substantial increases in the proportion of assets owned by larger firms. In 1965, the largest 200 firms had 86 per cent of assets, 13 per cent more than in 1957. The five largest firms own one-fifth of manufacturing industry.

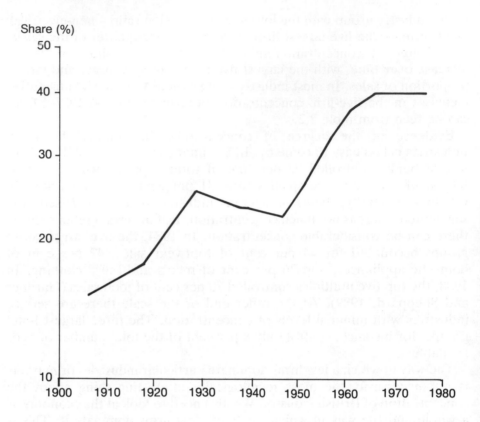

Figure 2.3 The share of the largest 100 firms in manufacturing net output, 1907–1978 (semi-logarithmic scale).
Source: Hannah, 1983, p. 92.

Table 2.3 Proportion of assets in UK manufacturing held by large firms, 1957 and 1965

	1957 (%)	*1965 (%)*
Share of largest 5 firms	17.0	20.1
Share of largest 50 firms	48.4	60.9
Share of largest 100 firms	60.1	74.9
Share of largest 200 firms	73.0	86.2

Source: Hannah, 1976, p. 166, reproduced with permission

The most important single cause of concentration in the British economy is merger, or the acquisition of one firm by another. During the 1960s and 1970s most of the disappearances of firms quoted on the Stock Exchange were due to mergers with other firms. One index of the importance of concentration by acquisition is the proportion of investment in the acquisition of other companies. Firms might grow either by investing in plant, machinery, or workers, or by acquiring other companies. Hannah (1983) shows that, during intense merger activity in the economy, the proportion of investment expenditure in manufacturing industry going to acquisition can rise to 50 per cent, as it did in the 1960s and 1970s.

We have been using manufacturing industry as the main example in the discussion so far. Indeed, it is this sector that has led concentration, although other sectors, in finance and property for example, are following suit. Related to this is a point that we made earlier about the diversification of large firms. Firms grow bigger often by the acquisition of other firms not trading in their sector of the economy. In 1955 only 12 per cent of all mergers were of this diversified or 'conglomerate' type, while by 1972 over half were (Campbell, 1981). Furthermore, this diversification is often on an international scale.

In sum, there is an increasing domination of the British economy by large firms, many of which are growing larger by extending their interests into new and different areas of the economy. As the takeover battles of 1986 seem to indicate, it is the already large firms that are most involved in merger activity, giving themselves an ever faster rate of growth.

Interlocking directorships

This process of concentration, the rise of the corporate economy, gives a certain unity to the British economy. Industry and commerce are no longer made up of a multiplicity of competing firms with little connection with each other but are dominated by relatively few firms. The evidence that we have presented so far actually rather *understates* the degree of unity. This partly arises from the fact that firms may own only relatively small parts of other firms, less than that required to give total control. These smaller overlaps in ownership do not count as a merger, yet they clearly do represent a considerable degree of cooperation and interdependence between firms. Equally as significant is the phenomenon of interlocking directorships. The ease of communication between firms is very much enhanced by the fairly common practice of having directors of one large company sitting on the boards of other similarly powerful firms. As J. Scott (1985, p. 44) says: 'These "interlocking directorships" tie together the diverse capitalist interests and provide a basis for some degree of coordination in their activities.'

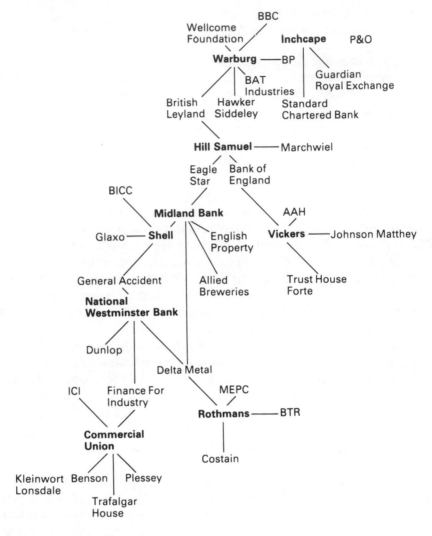

Figure 2.4   Networks of interconnecting shareholdings in a number of large companies, 1976.
Source: Scott, 1985, p. 45

Figure 2.4 shows part of the network of interlocking directorships by portraying the directorships held by a small number of people. In the study from which this illustration is taken, 11 people had a total of 57 directorships in the top 250 companies, and many others in subsidiaries of these companies and in smaller companies. The directorships of 9 people linked together 39 very large companies. This is clearly only a section of a large network but one which is, nevertheless, held together nationally, at least in the larger firms, by a remarkably small number of people. Scott (1985) argues that at the heart of this network are those companies which dominate the capital market and are able to provide finance for investment. The banks, particularly, are organized into cliques and clusters which occupy a central position. But this centrality should not be seen as bank control over the non-financial sector as a whole; rather it simply reflects the banks' importance as providers of capital. Besides providing capital, the network of interlocking director-ships also makes for a more efficient flow of information between firms. The coordination and unity of the economic system, which we have argued are characteristics much more pronounced now than even 50 years ago, are thus partly facilitated by the personal contacts between directors. Interlocking directorships are, however, not the only vehicle by which personal relationships unify British industry. Of some con-tinuing importance is the persistence of family and kinship relationships – ran issue we take up in more detail in section 3.6 on the upper class. Kinship connections are important because of the continuing significance of the personal ownership of shares, and it is to this issue we now turn.

Ownership and control

The quotation from Berle and Means given earlier argues that there has been a progressive separation of legal ownership from effective control. The discussion here applies mostly to large companies with multiple shareholdings; in small firms there may be no separation of ownership and control but, as we saw in the previous section, the British economy is increasingly dominated by large firms. In such companies, shareholders each own only a relatively small proportion of the shares. With ownership diversified in this way, it *appears* that real control passes to the professional managers who, working in the company full-time, have a much better idea of the company's business than do shareholders. J. Scott (1990) points out that the terms 'ownership' and 'control' are rather misleading and he proposes replacing them with the terms 'ownership', 'control', and 'rule'. *Ownership* simply refers to the right to receive an income. *Control* is the capacity possessed by a particular group of owners to determine policy and strategy by a number of means including having representatives on the board of directors. *Rule* describes actual involve-ment in decision-making. Essentially, then, the question is: what is the relationship between ownership, control, and rule?

The first point to decide here is who does actually own shares in British companies. Figure 2.5 presents some data on this issue. In 1990 the proportion of shares held by individual persons amounted to 20 per cent while pension funds held 31 per cent and insurance companies about 20 per cent. The balance between these two kinds of shareholder has been

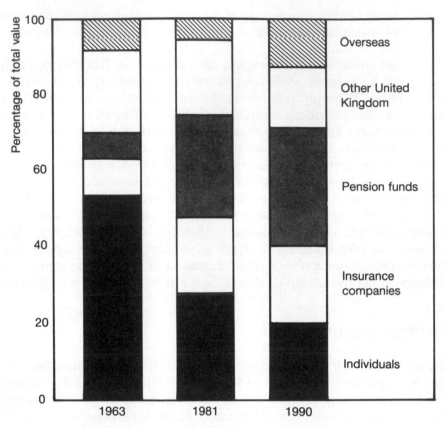

Figure 2.5   Who own's Britain's shares?
Source: *Social Trends*, 1992, p. 103. Crown copyright.

shifting. In 1963, personal shareholders held 54 per cent of all shares
while these financial institutions held only about 13 per cent.

There has, therefore, been a move away from the personal ownership
of shares towards ownership by large financial institutions. This is a
depersonalization of ownership, in that individual people no longer own
companies. It is worth noting that this depersonalization does not mean
that wealth in the form of company shares is more evenly spread among
the population. What has happened is only that the minority of wealthy
families no longer hold their wealth in a single company but spread it
more widely by buying shares in a number of companies (see section 3.3
for a discussion of the distribution of wealth and section 3.6 for an
account of the upper class). The shift in share ownership has given great
power to the largest financial institutions. For example, the ten largest
institutions are responsible for investing £100 billion, about one-quarter
of the total value of the stock market.

The depersonalization of wealth might, however, seem to imply a separation of ownership, control, and rule. If individual persons are less involved in ownership, perhaps managers can acquire more influence? In order to answer this question it is helpful to distinguish between different *types* of control. Scott (1990) identifies four types that are of particular note. First, there is control by a single institution or family interest – wholly owned. Second, a single institution or family may have majority control simply by owning the bulk of the shares. Third, a minority interest may have control because, although it owns only a relatively small number of shares, all the rest are dispersed among a large number of shareholders, each of whom has an even smaller stake. Lastly, companies may be controlled by a *constellation of interests*, a loosely associated group of shareholders, each of whom will have only a very small holding. The associations within these constellations are shifting and often temporary. As Scott says: 'A constellation . . . is not a cohesive controlling group, but those who seek to participate in the decision-making powers of the board must take account of the wishes and interests of the constellation of leading shareholders' (p. 358). One way in which a constellation of interests may be formed is by the mechanisms of interlocking directorships and of mutual shareholdings. For example, a study of Burmah Oil showed that no single investor held a substantial proportion of the shares. Yet six of the largest institutional shareholders were, on more detailed examination, closely linked via the holding of shares in each other's companies and interlocking directorships. Burmah's

Table 2.4 Modes of control of companies in Britain, 1976 and 1988

	Companies			
	1976		*1988*	
Mode of control	*Industrial (no.)*	*Financial (no.)*	*Industrial (no.)*	*Financial (no.)*
Public corporations	13	0	11	0
Wholly owned	34	4	47	7
Other majority control	30	10	14	1
Minority control	39	12	32	13
Non-proprietary[a]	0	8	0	12
Constellation of interests	84	16	96	17
Total	200	50	200	50

[a] Refers to building societies and mutual insurance companies which have no share capital *per se* and are controlled by their depositors and policy holders.

Source: J. Scott, 1990, p. 362

six non-executive directors, for example, held six other directorships in four of the institutional shareholding companies.

Table 2.4 shows the proportions of different types of control in the 250 largest companies in Britain. A large proportion are controlled by constellations of interest, the next most common category being wholly owned companies. There has been some movement between 1976 and 1988 with an increase in the proportion controlled by constellations or wholly owned at the expense of other majority control.

The argument so far points to the importance of financial institutions in the ownership and control of large British firms, particularly where they are able to form alliances with each other in a constellation of interests. How then are the financial institutions – banks, pension funds, unit trusts and insurance companies – themselves owned and controlled? The short answer to this question is that the process of the depersonalization of ownership applies to financial companies as well as to other branches of the economy. Banks, for example, have substantial shareholdings in each other. Institutions like pension funds, unit trusts, building societies and insurance companies are in rather a different position, however, for they are 'owned' not by shareholders but by the very large number of individuals who have pension rights, insurance policies and unit trusts. This form of ownership seems to approximate much more to the Berle and Means model, for it is impossible for, say, holders of insurance policies to control the policy of even small insurance companies, and this would appear to leave strategic control in the hands of management. In a sense this is correct. There is a divorce between ownership, control, and rule in these so-called 'mutual' companies. However, the evidence does not show that the managers of these mutual companies have a free hand. Their boards of directors contain the directors of other mutual companies and financial institutions. In other words there is, here too, a substantial degree of interlocking directorships. The result is that control of these companies may well pass to constellations of interests represented by the directors of other companies, although, importantly, these interests are not those of ownership.

Summary

1   The British economy is dominated by relatively few large companies whose dominance is becoming more pronounced as firms merge with one another.
2   Not only is there a concentration of ownership by merger and takeover, but companies are also bound together in a network of interlocking directorships.
3   There has been a depersonalization of ownership of British com-

panies, with the financial institutions taking a larger proportion of the shares of large companies.

4 The bulk of British companies are still effectively controlled by owners, often through a 'constellation of interests'.

5 The mutual institutions have increasing importance and they tend to be controlled by boards of directors that overlap with one another.

Related topics

All these elements give a certain unity to the British economy. Large companies are bound together in a network of greater coherence than, say, 50 years ago. One question raised by this is whether the coherence of the network also gives a coherence to an upper class which is centred around the people who control British industry and commerce. This question is explored in section 3.6. Another question, dealt with in section 2.4, is how operational rather than strategic management is accomplished, and what effect that has on the structure of economic organizations.

2.4 Economic Organizations and Management

In the previous section we presented evidence showing that *strategic* control of the major, privately owned economic enterprises in Britain is concentrated in the hands of a relatively small number of socially interconnected people – the large shareholders, directors and top executives. The principal aim of strategic control in private enterprises, which is also a condition of the enterprises' survival, is the making of profit. Achieving that goal is not automatic: firms go bankrupt, unprofitable ventures close down, boards of directors get removed. There are real problems in transforming the decisions and directives of strategic controllers into the efficient, profitable production of goods and services for which there is a demand. The difficulties include adequate use of financial resources, the coordination of many different stages in the design, production and sale of commodities, and the integration of supervision of the varied activities of often thousands of employees. The various ways of linking strategic objectives with the daily operations of production are studied by organization theory.

Organizations are concerned with the coordination of human efforts, on a regular basis, through the deliberate and formal establishment of a set of positions, with a view to achieving certain specified goals. Parties, trade unions and churches, as well as armies, hospitals and firms, are organizations. *Economic organizations* are those concerned with the production of goods and services. There are many types of economic organization, each with different goals: besides privately owned capitalist enterprises there are state agencies, cooperatives, charitable bodies, etc. In contemporary Britain, most production of goods and services, and most paid employment, is achieved through private enterprises, though state agencies also play a very significant, if recently declining, role.

In this section, we first examine some features of the internal organizational structures common to both private enterprises and state agencies. *Organizational structures* are deliberately created with a view to achieving the specified goals of the people exercising strategic control. Organizational structure has been defined by Child (1972, p. 3) as 'the formal allocation of work roles and the administrative mechanism to control and integrate work activities'. The structure of organizations has been a focus of attention (for the sociology of organizations and organization theory) because it is believed that this partly determines their effectiveness.

Next, we examine *management*. Management is part of the organizational structure and at the same time is responsible for the maintenance, operation and modification of that structure. In the classic small firm, management is nothing other than the directives of the owner: the owner will personally supervise the implementation of his or her own strategic decisions. As economic organizations grew larger from the end of the nineteenth century, managerial jobs became more common. In the large economic organizations of contemporary Britain, whether private enterprises or public agencies, management is a complex network of interdependent roles and activities, hierarchically structured and itself requiring coordination.

The internal structure of economic organizations

The sheer scale of the activities of large corporations creates enormous organizational problems. To plan, coordinate and control on a global scale, as do the multinational corporations, is a remarkable achievement which raises questions about how strategic control (discussed in section 2.3) is exercised and is transformed into the everyday operations of making and selling commodities. However, similar problems, even if on a smaller scale, face any economic organization. Large corporations are, increasingly, adopting a multi-division pattern of organization, in which a head office takes strategic decisions but control over everyday matters is decentralized to management in smaller operational units (usually referred to as establishments or branch plants).

Strategic control is secured through strict and centralized financial discipline exercised at head office, the 'independent' plants being monitored closely in terms of their financial performance. This type of arrangement is a fairly recent development and is particularly prevalent in Britain. Large expenditures are vetted by headquarters on the basis of regular, detailed reports and sophisticated budgetary information systems. This has permitted a reduction in the average size of workplaces since the 1970s.

There are, however, alternative ways of structuring organizations. The design of organizational structure depends partly on the overall purpose or goal of the organization. Not all economic organizations are primarily oriented towards profit-making. The National Health Service, for instance, does not sell its services to its patients; rather they have a *right* to treatment. This means that hospitals and clinics must provide *satisfactory* service on a *fair* basis (i.e. to all citizens who are entitled to it, without discrimination by class, gender or ethnicity) rather than on a purely commercial basis. Goals constrain the choice of organizational structure. Thus cooperatives, which seek to be democratic, require internal organizational arrangements consistent with the fact that all workers share in ownership and have collective control over policy and practices. It remains the case, however, that the majority of British economic organizations have primarily commercial goals – to sell goods or services for more than they cost to produce.

Bureaucratic organization

Fundamentally, organizational structure is a concept of describing *the exercise of authority associated with the coordination of (work) tasks*. It is no accident that the founding father of the sociology of organizations, Max Weber, began from a theoretical concern with power and authority. Weber analysed the most widely recognized and most commonly maligned form of organizational structure – the bureaucracy. The key characteristics of Weber's *ideal type* of bureaucracy are listed in box 2.1.

In reality, almost all complex organizations are *to some degree* bureaucratic, but few approach the 'pure' type. Most important in considering contemporary economic organizations are two features, hierarchy of authority and formal rules.

1 In the ideal type of bureaucracy, *authority* can be represented as a pyramid. Higher offices have authority over lower offices: subordinate officials are directly responsible to the official immediately above in the hierarchy. The result, in principle, is a single line of authority (see figure 2.6). This provides an integrated vertical chain of

Box 2.1   Key features of bureaucratic organization

1 A specialized division of tasks, undertaken by officials, each
   with his or her own duties.
2 A hierarchy of authority – 'a clearly established system of
   super- and sub-ordination in which there is a supervision of
   the lower offices by the higher ones' (Weber, 1968) – and a
   clearly demarcated system of command and responsibilities.
3 A formal set of rules governing operations and activities
   which coordinates behaviour in a predictable, uniform and
   impersonal fashion.
4 A body of officials who are permanent, full-time workers,
   appointed by superiors, trained in a specialized task, paid a
   salary according to rank in the hierarchy, and to whom a
   career is open on the basis of ability and seniority.

command, but prohibits horizontal communication between officials
of the same rank.
2 The tasks and the decisions made in the course of operations are
   governed by *rules* in the sense that officials have limited discretion in
   dealing with cases. Their activities are closely prescribed, which
   encourages predictability and impartiality.

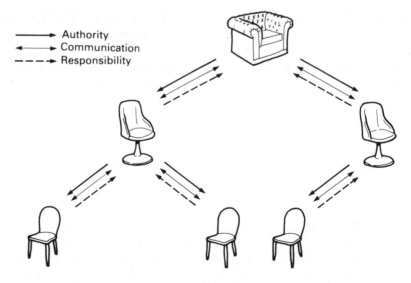

Figure 2.6   Authority, responsibility and communication in a bureaucracy.

Such a bureaucratic organization thus has a highly *centralized* structure of authority and a highly *regulated* set of activities.

Weber thought the bureaucracy was a more technically efficient mode of organization than any other previously developed. Its virtues, relative to earlier modes, included 'precision, speed, unambiguity, knowledge, continuity, discretion, unity, strict subordination, reduction of friction and of material personal costs' (Weber, 1968, p. 973). However, bureaucratic organizations also have widely acknowledged potential disadvantages for clients, officials and organizational efficiency alike. For example, clients of the Department of Social Security (DSS) frequently complain of impersonality, inflexibility, the incapacity of officials to make firm decisions, and excessive rule-following. Studies of the behaviour of officials in such organizations tend to show either a creeping timidity in decision-making by officials closely bound by both formal rules and responsibility to higher authority, or a tendency to subvert the organizational structure by developing informal and unauthorized practices. The difficulties experienced by the people involved with a bureaucracy *under certain circumstances* may reduce the effectiveness of the organization. Hence some organizations are designed to be less centralized than these.

Less centralized organizations still have some bureaucratic features, but they are more flexible and less hierarchical. In such firms, rules are less formal and less encompassing, authority and responsibility are less direct, jobs and tasks are less tightly defined, and communication is more varied and not restricted to hierarchical channels. Such organizational structures demand more initiative and personal responsibility from officials. Outcomes are less predictable but may be more inventive and problem oriented.

Contingent factors affecting organizational structure

Sociologists have tried to isolate what affects the degree of centralization in organizational structures. A number of factors influence centralization, but none determine it. It partly depends on the purposes and the circumstances of the particular organization. State agencies – the DSS, the army, the Inland Revenue – tend to be more bureaucratic. They value the predictability of their officials' behaviour and impartiality in treatment of clients, which bureaucratic forms sustain. It is considered important that soldiers *obey* orders, and that supplementary benefit claimants are treated *fairly* (i.e. get those benefits to which they are entitled, but none other). Private manufacturing firms, being concerned with profitable production, are less likely to put up with the inefficiencies of bureaucracies, which tend to be slow in decision-making. Nevertheless, where production processes are highly mechanized – in assembly-

line production for instance – predictability and obedience are considered of the highest value and may support bureaucratic forms. But for
many firms, the dysfunctions of the bureaucratic mode are considered
too great and they have, thus, developed less centralized organizational
structures.

Three contingent factors in particular constrain the selection of
organizational structure: the size, the technology and the external
environment of the enterprise.

Size   It is generally agreed that there is a statistical correlation between
size and bureaucratization. With small firms there is scarcely a problem
of organization. Coordination is maintained through face-to-face contacts,
and control is likely to be exercised directly by an owner-manager. Very
large units, by contrast, require methods of *impersonal* coordination and
control, which is a key aspect of the bureaucratic mode. There is
currently some tendency to designate semi-autonomous operating units
or profit centres: the design department may 'sell' its designs to the
production department, which will in turn charge the sales department
for the finished goods, so that each department has a separate measure of
its performance. In other words, the size of operating units may be
reduced if it is felt that this will benefit performance.

Technology   Machinery and equipment also set limits to alternative
organizational structures. Mass production on the assembly line involves
a different form of supervision to homeworkers on piece-rates. Where
mass production occurs in large factories, thus benefiting from economies
of scale, there is usually a very specialized and standardized division of
labour and, hence, a tendency to be bureaucratically organized. In this
sense, technology and size are related.

Environment   Firms do not exist in a vacuum; they are affected by
competition, by markets, by the state, etc. Certain environmental
conditions dispose firms to adopt different structures. One outstanding
example of this concerns adaptation to rapid *change*. In a classic study of
electronics firms in Britain in the 1950s, Burns and Stalker (1961) argued
that decentralized structures (they called them *organic* management
systems) were more amenable to changing external circumstances. In the
electronics industry, knowledge, techniques, design and products were
all changing quickly. Those firms in which responsibilities and tasks were
not rigidly defined, and where information passed openly regardless of
status in the organization, tended to be more effective at innovation (at
solving new problems). More centralized and bureaucratic organizations
seemed to work best in stable environmental circumstances.

The complexity of the environment, particularly with respect to information, also affects structure. The more sources of information, and the more difficult the information is to interpret, the more likely is decentralization. This happens because of increased specialization in the process of handling information, people with specialized knowledge often being able to obtain some degree of independence from their superiors. (This is one basis of the power of the professions – see section 2.7.)

One other feature of the environment, the presence of a serious threat to the organization, also has consequences for structure. In periods of crisis, strategic controllers tend to centralize decision-making and exert tighter controls.

In conclusion, it should be noted that the factors of size, technology and environment do not *determine* organizational structure. One of the powers of people exercising strategic control is that of making choices about organizational form, and those choices are one element in the processes of competition between firms and of conflict between controllers and their staff.

Management

'Management' is a rather loose concept. At its broadest, it refers to all people in positions of authority over others within a firm – from the managing director at the top to the supervisor on the shop floor. It is, therefore, essential to distinguish between different types of managerial position: executives, who exercise *strategic* control, should be distinguished from middle management with *operational* control, and also from supervisory workers. Though these categories are blurred at the edges they reflect important differences in power, prestige and function. In this section we are primarily interested in *middle management* – managers who are neither in a position of strategic control nor directly supervising workers on the shop floor. They are employees of the firm, but they exercise *authority* and *discretion* at plant or office level.

The purposes of management

Management has a number of purposes or functions which include liaison, filtering and transmitting information, allocating resources, directing subordinates, and planning and handling disruptions of work. Managers generally combine some specialist, technical activities and some general, administrative work, the proportion varying considerably from one manager to another. For example, an accounts manager may well work more or less alone on the specialized activity of accountancy, while some other managers, so-called line management, are largely concerned with directing and monitoring the performance of other workers. The principal purpose of modern middle management is to plan, coordinate and control operations in the everyday running of the firm.

Management practices

As in many social processes, the fit is weak between the formal aims of roles like management and the actual behaviour of the people who fill those roles. Studies of what managers actually do when at work suggest that, with the exception of some specialist functions, the job of manager is a very fluid and indefinite one. Hales (1986) summarizes the literature on managerial behaviour, isolating ten widely agreed attributes of managerial work (see box 2.2). The daily activities of management seem fragmentary and unpredictable: 'little time is spent on any one particular activity.'

It seems that for many managers, work entails little decision-taking. This is particularly the case at the lower levels where the degree of discretion is very limited. Thus, for example, Crompton and Jones, in *White-Collar Proletariat* (1984), a study of workers in a bank, an insurance company and a county council, observed that there were a considerable number of people who were described as having managerial or administrative jobs who exercised very little or no control or discretion in their own work. Moreover, they had no power with respect to the recruitment and disciplining of workers or to the organization of work. In many cases these people, better described as supervisory workers, did the same kind of work as their subordinates, though they would be called in to sort out practical problems or advise on difficult cases.

Scase and Goffee (1989) surveyed and interviewed managers in six large organizations spread across public and private sectors. Work had become more intensive during the 1980s: '84 per cent of the 323 men and 88 per cent of the 51 women managers claim they work an average week in excess of fifty hours and almost all state that this has increased significantly over recent years' (p. 23). However, the rewards anticipated from their work – independence of thought and action, security, status and promotion – were not forthcoming for most. Scase and Goffee saw this as part of a growing divide between senior executives, who make significant decisions, and junior and middle management, who express frustration with their jobs. This has reduced middle managers' loyalty and commitment to their firms. Nevertheless, careers are closely bound up with the success of the enterprise. Because managerial expertise tends

Box 2.2 Key features of managerial work

1 It combines a specialist/professional element and a general 'managerial' element.
2 The substantive elements involve, essentially, liaison, man management, and responsibility for a work process, beneath which are subsumed more detailed work elements.
3 The character of work elements varies by duration, time span, recurrence, unexpectedness and source.
4 Much time is spent in day-to-day trouble shooting and *ad hoc* problems of organization and regulation.
5 Much managerial activity consists of asking or persuading others to do things, involving the manager in face-to-face verbal communication of limited duration.
6 Patterns of communication vary in terms of *what* the communication is about and with *whom* the communication is made.
7 Little time is spent on any one particular activity and, in particular, on the conscious, systematic formulation of plans. Planning and decision-making tend to take place in the course of other activity.
8 Managers spend a lot of time accounting for and explaining what they do, in informal relationships and in 'politicking'.
9 Managerial activities are riven by contradictions, cross-pressures and conflicts. Much managerial work involves coping with and reconciling social and technical conflict.
10 There is considerable choice in terms of *what* is done and *how*: part of managerial work is setting the boundaries of negotiating that work itself.

Source: Hales, 1986, p. 104, reproduced with permission

to be organization specific, personal futures are always somewhat precarious. Hence involvement in 'politicking' is significant: managers are frequently concerned to promote their own departments and to advance their personal careers, which may detract from the rational pursuit of organizational goals. Ultimately, however, managers' decisions are constrained and judged by the criterion of the profitability of the branch in which they are employed. The company's successful performance determines the value of its managers' principal, personal asset – their position in the organizational hierarchy.

Managers are not a uniform or unified group of workers. Another
sample survey of 1058 currently practising members of the British
Institute of Management in 1980 (Poole et al., 1981) confirmed this. The
managers contacted were found in a wide variety of different
circumstances, with different degrees of seniority, a wide range of
incomes, and in different types of organization. They were also a
heterogeneous category with respect to their social backgrounds and
their qualifications. Managers are not from especially privileged backgrounds, and nor are they necessarily highly educated. Of this particular
sample, one-third had a degree and another third had a technical
qualification (e.g. OND or HND). Managers are neither a socially
distinctive nor a cohesive group.

Summary

1   The internal organizational structures of firms vary. Bureaucracies
    are characterized by the centralization of authority and the rigid
    application of rules that govern activities within the organization.
    Many private sector firms have a comparatively *decentralized* power
    structure.
2   The degree of centralization of authority in an organization depends
    on contingent factors, among which are the size of the enterprise, the
    technology it uses, and the economic environment within which it
    operates.
3   Management is a rather loose concept which refers both to the
    exercise of strategic control and to the supervision of routine
    activities. Most managers have limited powers.

Related topics

Questions of authority and control are dealt with in other sections. In
section 2.3 strategic control is discussed. In section 2.5 the methods of
control by managers and supervisors over other workers are analysed in
terms of managerial strategies. The class position of managers is
explored in section 3.5 on the middle classes. The tendency for men
rather than women to be in positions of authority at work is examined in
section 4.2.

2.5 The Labour Process

The experience of work

Consider this description, given by a man who works on the assembly line at Ford, fixing the trim on to motor cars:

> It's the most boring job in the world. It's the same thing over and over again. There is no change in it, it wears you out. It makes you awful tired. It slows your thinking right down. There's no need to think. It's just a formality. You just carry on. You just endure it for the money. That's what we're paid for – to endure the boredom of it.
>
> If I had the chance to move I'd leave right away. It's the conditions here. Ford class you more as a machine than men. They're on top of you all the time. They expect you to work every minute of the day. The atmosphere you get in here is so completely false. Everyone is downcast and fed up. (Beynon, 1973, p. 118)

For many people, the factory symbolizes a debased work environment. A woman employee cooking meals on a large community-centre site with several canteen and snack-bar outlets observed of the kitchens she worked in:

> It's just like a factory making radios. It *is* a factory. When we prepare the food, we don't think that someone is going to sit down and enjoy it. As long as it looks right we are not making any effort to improve the quality. There is no variety . . . Everything by the book, always the same way. (Gabriel, 1988, p. 58)

Boredom, lack of variety and the absence of opportunity to make decisions about how to set about work tasks are typical complaints.

But not everyone finds work as unpleasant as this. Another woman working in a small snack-bar on the same site said:

> I like working in this small bar better than anywhere else; you get to know the students who come here, we have a laugh and a chat. The bosses leave us alone; it's a first-rate job. (Gabriel, 1988, p. 70)

Many people derive intrinsic satisfaction from their work. A study by Newby (1979) of agricultural labouring found that 93 per cent of those

interviewed in East Anglia considered their job either 'mostly interesting' or 'interesting all the time'. Most workers like some part of their
work and dislike others. This was true of the sample of agricultural
workers who appreciated the variety of their jobs, enjoyed using farm
machinery, and liked seeing crops and animals grow, but disliked aspects
of the hours and conditions under which they had to labour.

Workers' reactions to their jobs are understandably mixed. The
deprivations resulting from not having a job – poverty, social isolation
and low social status (see section 2.9 on unemployment) – are sufficiently
severe to persuade people that any work is better than none. In this sense
people want to work. Similarly, most people will say that they are
satisfied with their job, partly because the realistic alternatives are not
much better. Previous experience, qualifications and the local availability
of other employment all severely limit any individual's choice of work.
On the other hand, employees usually feel that their talents and skills are
poorly utilized in work which they perceive as dull and monotonous. As
one study of unskilled work in Peterborough observed, 95 per cent of the
workers used more skill driving a car to work than they exercised on their
job (Blackburn and Mann, 1979). Variation in the experience of work is
considerable. Most people accept, instrumentally, the financial necessity
of having a paid job. But they also expect to derive other benefits – self-
satisfaction, self-actualization, performance of a duty and companionship
among them – from their employment.

Adults typically spend a lot of time working, so that the actual quality
of the experience of work deeply affects both personal and social
relationships. Sociologists have, therefore, examined closely the precise
content of jobs and the kind of relationships established between
employers, supervisors and employees. These are elements of the so-
called *labour process*.

In order to chart the consequences of work experience, it is necessary
to compare the qualities of jobs. Since there are thousands of jobs, each
distinctive, we need to reduce differences to a few, important dimensions. For sociological purposes, jobs may be grouped in terms of:

1 the range of tasks involved;
2 the degree of discretion given to the worker to decide how to
   accomplish those tasks; and
3 the mode of control used by managers and supervisors to try to ensure
   that those tasks are completed satisfactorily.

In these respects, the workers in the Ford assembly plant of Halewood
and a schoolteacher are involved in very different types of labour
process. Assembly work in car production entails that a single task be

repeated, in a tightly prescribed manner, under the close surveillance of a foreman. The schoolteacher, by contrast, undertakes a wider range of tasks; the way of working is left to the teacher's initiative, i.e. *how* teachers teach varies from one person to the next; and supervision is distant, headteachers interfering infrequently in what happens in the classroom. Sociologists have spent much time exploring what determines the quality of different labour processes. Why is it that, for example, schoolteachers are given more control over their work than assembly-line workers? The answer to such a question has been approached in the debate on 'deskilling'.

Deskilling

Sociological analysis of the quality of work has been much influenced by Braverman (1974), who examined the history of work in the USA. He argued that the labour process had become more fragmented and specialized since the 1890s and that the skill required at work was reduced for most jobs: a process of 'deskilling' had occurred. Braverman argued that this was the consequence not of technological innovation but of a conscious managerial strategy to increase control over workers' behaviour. Control was achieved by widespread introduction of the techniques of scientific management of the kind advocated by F.W. Taylor. 'Taylorism', as it came to be known, sought to break production tasks into their smallest possible units, to control the fashion and the speed with which each separate operation was completed, and to coordinate these operations as efficiently as possible. Characteristic of Taylorism is the 'time-and-motion study'. Wherever possible, the workers' autonomy was restricted and jobs were redesigned to transfer discretion and control from workers to management. As a result, according to Braverman, old political distinctions between skilled and unskilled workers, and between manual and non-manual workers, would disappear. The real nature of work for almost all the labour force would become similarly routine, fragmented, deskilled and controlled by management. This would happen in offices as much as in factories. Braverman saw this as the basis for the development of the kind of working-class political consciousness anticipated by Marx. This argument has been extensively criticized and, as a result of the ensuing debate, we are clearer about the changes in work in Britain.

One pertinent line of criticism of Braverman is that his analysis is not readily applicable to countries other than the USA. In Britain, it is clear that the transition to modern management occurred much later than in the USA, not happening here until the mid 1920s. Moreover, it had less of an impact in Britain. In this respect, Braverman ignores the considerable range of strategies employed by managements in order to control their workers. Taylorism is but one possible strategy.

The extent of deskilling is also disputed. Undoubtedly some jobs, like those of the workers at Ford mentioned earlier, are as Braverman describes. But it is debatable whether jobs which have disappeared or been degraded in the last 50 years outnumber those new, skilled and professional jobs that have been created. The expansion of the welfare state has increased professional and semi-professional occupations, and new technology certainly generates some jobs for highly skilled technicians. Indeed, the uncertainty of the consequences of the introduction of new technology is underlined by Jones (1982), who examined the effects of the introduction of numerical control on engineering workers in south Wales and south-west England. He found no consistent effect resulting from the implementation of identical computer-assisted techniques in different factories: whether the machine operators' jobs improved or deteriorated appeared to depend on other factors. Certainly people do not *perceive* their jobs to have deteriorated recently. Marshall et al. (1988, p. 116) on the basis of a national survey said: 'Asked to report on whether their present jobs required more, less, or about the same amount of skill as when they first started to do them, more than 96 per cent of all employees claimed that their work had not been visibly deskilled.'

Resolving the question of the degree of deskilling partly depends upon obtaining an acceptable measure of skill. This is difficult, however. All occupational groups would like to be called skilled, since that is grounds for demanding high wages and is a source of social status. The very label 'skill' is a valuable resource which does not *necessarily* reflect the technical difficulty of a given job. It is significant that few occupations filled predominantly by women are called 'skilled'. For example, some of the intricate and dextrous work done by women, in electronics assembly or in the garment-making trades, clearly requires special aptitudes and a lengthy learning process, but is not considered as skilled and is poorly paid. This suggests that trade union organization is at least as important as knowledge or aptitude in establishing work as skilled. If this is the case, if skill is primarily socially constructed, then evaluation of Braverman's thesis becomes impossible. It is for this reason that earlier we described jobs not in terms of the skill required, but in terms of tasks, discretion and control.

Furthermore, the political consequences anticipated by Braverman have not transpired. Even if there had been a general tendency for workers to become deskilled, it does not follow that they will act as a politically united class. It seems that workers are today no less divided and fragmented than at other times in the last half century. In fact, Braverman paid little attention to the political consciousness of workers.

The omission led him to underestimate the importance of workers' resistance to deskilling. Workers struggle against losing control over the labour process, against management intervention, and against new technologies. These struggles must be borne in mind when assessing changes in the nature of work.

In conclusion, Braverman probably generalized too widely from one kind of transition which occurred in the USA. He also focused his attention rather too narrowly on the process of production, without sufficient consideration of other political and economic constraints that also determine the quality of work. Subsequent reflection suggests that an adequate explanation of the quality of work experience requires that we look more carefully at individual enterprises and at particular occupations. The place of the firm in a market for its products affects both the kind of managerial strategy it can employ and the kind of technology it can use. Management's control over workers is maintained by wage payments as well as by supervision on the shop floor. The level and method of payment are themselves constrained by the firm's market position. The quality of work seems to be the effect of a number of forces, none of which *alone* determines the nature of work, but which together, in different combinations, account for much of the variety of work. As Braverman argued, the kind of managerial strategy used for disciplinary purposes is important, but so too arc thc nature of the organization, the kind of technology employed, and the capacity of the workforce to resist management.

Organizations, technology and the quality of work

The nature of work is partly dependent upon the organization of the enterprise providing employment. Generally, large firms are more complex, rules and procedures are formally specified, and the element of administrative authority is more prominent. Thus there is a tendency for work to be more specialized and authority relations more impersonal than in small firms. Work may then be more fragmented, with less discretion left to the worker. However the effect of size should not be exaggerated, for, as we saw in section 2.4, there are differences between large firms, some being more bureaucratic, others more flexible, depending upon the economic environment in which they operate.

The type of technology (equipment and machinery) used by an enterprise is obviously one important cause of the quality of work experience. A teacher's work might be much altered by the introduction of new electronic technology. In higher education, the Open University offers an instructive example. The use of television means that

Plate 2.2 A typing pool.
Source: Network

Plate 2.3 A production line in a chocolate factory.
Source: Michael Ann Mullen/*Format*

proportionately little of teachers' time is spent personally teaching students. The same lesson can be broadcast to thousands of students simultaneously. Teachers thus become relatively specialized: as writers of the course materials, as presenters of programmes, or as tutors corresponding with students about their work. Indeed, it is conceivable, with developments in communication technology, that in the near future people will be educated mostly at home, using televisions, microcomputers and direct-link telephones. Under such circumstances, the work of teachers would be transformed. Similarly, the tedium of assembly work in automobile manufacturing is a direct result of a decision to use production-line techniques to make cars. There are, however, other ways of manufacturing cars: some are still effectively hand-built by craft workers. But, among mass manufacturers, Volvo, for example, launched a well-publicized and successful experiment in the 1970s to abandon assembly-line production. Instead, flexible work-groups were created, each collectively responsible for a wide range of tasks, which were rotated frequently among members of the group. The results, according to the firm, were lower levels of turnover and absenteeism, reflecting greater work satisfaction, without any loss of efficiency.

It is important to realize that enterprises have a degree of choice about what technology to use. Such choices are not purely technical matters. Of course, there are economic constraints over the choice: goods have to be sold at competitive prices, privately owned firms insist on making profits, and workers demand adequate wages. Nevertheless, as the Volvo example illustrated, there is often a choice. What determines the decision? Some sociologists have argued that employers and managers, when selecting technology, are especially concerned with establishing and maintaining *control* over the work force. Decisions about technology are an aspect of so-called managerial *strategies*.

The effects of technology should not be exaggerated. It used to be thought that work satisfaction was directly determined by the technology used: manual workers on assembly lines were likely to be bored and discontented, while those involved in craft work or in automated-process production would derive more satisfaction from their work. In turn, it was argued, greater work satisfaction would lead directly to a reduction in industrial and political conflict. Reality, however, is more complicated. Not merely the machinery but also the social organization of the workplace and the general political culture beyond the factory strongly affect workers' attitudes.

One analysis which demonstrates that technology itself does not determine people's experience of work or their political attitudes is that of Gallie (1978; 1983). Gallie compared the attitudes of workers in four oil refineries, two in France and two in Britain. All the refineries used advanced, automated, continuous-process technology; to all intents and purposes the technological situation was identical in each. But the industrial and political responses of the British and French workers differed sharply. The French workers identified strongly with the working class, expressed greater resentment of class inequality, were more hostile towards the management and believed that redress of their industrial grievances required political action. The British workers, by contrast, whilst recognizing the existence of class inequality, showed significantly less resentment about it, and were more likely to seek remedies for their dissatisfaction at the local level, within the plant, through trade union representation. This shows that the same technology can have quite different effects on workers in different contexts. The greater radicalism of the French workers, Gallie thought, derived from the interaction of a high level of work grievance and the exposure over time to the radical messages of the parties of the French left. It was particularly important that trade unions were unable effectively to redress grievances in France, collective bargaining procedures being very weakly developed. As Gallie (1983, pp. 258–9) says:

> The most striking difference in the work situation of French and British workers lay in the structure of managerial power. French employers had retained virtually intact their traditional rights to determine unilaterally both the terms of payment and the organization of work with the firm. It was an institutionalized system in which the representatives of the work-force were given minimal influence over decision-making. In other terms, it was a system in which there was a very low level of institutionalization of industrial conflict. In Britain, on the other hand, the employers had made much more substantial concessions to the trade unions. Traditional conceptions of managerial prerogative had been considerably eroded and issues relating to both salaries and work organization had become subject to procedures for joint regulation . . . The British cases had seen a deliberate attempt on the part of employers to develop procedures for institutionalizing industrial conflict.

Gallie, then, demonstrated that technology alone determines neither the nature of the experience of work nor the character of the workers' responses. Rather, national political culture is important, as are, especially, the strategies which managers use to control their workforce.

Managerial strategies and control at work

Managerial strategies are ways of getting workers to spend their hours at work in a fashion which advances the economic goals of management.

Plate 2.4 An industrial kitchen.
Source: Camera Press

Given that much work is unpleasant, management has a problem of motivating workers to complete their allotted tasks quickly and effectively. Care and effort on the part of workers are not guaranteed merely by their presence at work. A major source of industrial conflict is the so-called 'effort bargain', the negotiable definition of what constitutes a 'fair day's work'. Management has two, intertwined, resources at its command – payment and authority.

Management's control is based ultimately on the threat to stop paying wages to ineffective workers, i.e. if the worker's effort falls beneath a certain acceptable minimum, he or she can be sacked. There are, however, more subtle ways in which payment can be used to generate effort. Payment by piece-rates, for example, whereby a worker gets a certain amount for each article completed, means that wages are directly related to work effort. The productivity deal is the equivalent system in large-scale manufacturing industry where, since no individual completes any particular product, collective financial incentives are provided to encourage high output. The other main way of regulating effort by financial incentive is by constructing promotion ladders within companies. If promotion can be made to depend upon performance then workers have an incentive to work hard and obediently.

The other major managerial resource is authority, which is exercised in association with payment. By and large, workers accept that management has some right to instruct them what to do. The presence of managers and supervisors watching over workers is, thus, legitimate. At the same time, though, in practice that authority is frequently resented and challenged by workers. The concept of managerial strategy refers to the various ways of exercising authority at work, of making managerial control effective in the face of resistance. A considerable number of strategies have been identified. Here we will consider four pure (or 'ideal') types of strategy – those based upon direct control, technical control, bureaucratic control and responsible autonomy. These rarely exist in pure form: in most firms elements of more than one strategy coexist.

Direct control

The employer or manager in small establishments, and the supervisor in larger enterprises, may watch over the worker, threatening to stop part of the worker's payment, or dismiss the worker, if he or she is not working sufficiently quickly or accurately. This is a method of direct control, sometimes called 'simple control' because it is the most basic way to ensure effort. Such a method unsurprisingly tends to cause extensive resentment on the part of workers. This strategy is probably used less than it used to be, thought it still characterizes small firms and firms where workers are relatively poorly organized. It is less effective in large establishments, partly because workers organize collectively to resist the authority of supervisors, and partly because supervisory workers and lower-level managers are not necessarily as enthusiastic about disciplining workers as an owner might be. Many occupational groups succeed in regulating their own work effort by taming supervisors.

Technical control

This is associated with scientific management and Taylorism. Taylorism maintains that, for industrial efficiency, jobs should be broken down into the smallest possible component tasks and the labour process redesigned so that each task is completed in the fastest way possible. This has often involved time-and-motion studies, the time taken for each element of a task being precisely measured in order to specify a minimum rate of working for each task. This has had three distinctive consequences:

1 Jobs have been fragmented into a very narrow range of tasks or, ultimately, a single, simple task.
2 The appropriate way of doing that task has been decided by the work study consultant on behalf of management, so that workers have no longer any discretion over how to go about their work. (This

principle is often called the separation of conception from execution.)
3 The design of the job, and the speed at which it has to be done, have
been justified as 'scientific' because they are the result of the
application of standardized measurement techniques.

These principles of Taylorism are widely applicable. The classic example
still remains the operation of the assembly line, where tasks are few,
discretion is absent, and the speed of work is determined by the line
itself. The worker on the line is compelled to keep up the same pace of
work as the machine. The rate of work is determined directly by the
technology – thus the term 'technical control'. Of course, management
chooses the machinery and the speed at which it operates. The attraction
for management of technical control is great. Partly, it defuses
interpersonal conflict between supervisor and worker because the
process is deemed 'scientific'. Partly, it makes output predictable and,
hopefully, quick. But technical control also generates worker resistance.
Since such methods are generally only applicable in large enterprises, lots
of workers, equally bored, are likely to be gathered together. Such
workers are relatively easy to organize in unions and are likely to refuse
to cooperate willingly with management. The kinds of resistance offered
in such situations vary from 'soldiering', that is working slowly when the
work study expert comes to assess the rate for individual tasks, to active
sabotage, such as throwing a spanner in the works to gain a rest.
Managerial control is often strongly contested in such situations.

Bureaucratic control

This is the normal staple form of control in the civil service, though it is
now common in advanced sectors of industry, especially among large
corporations. Basically, the worker's approach to the job is governed by
formal rules and policed by a minutely differentiated hierarchy of
authority. From one angle this hinders solidarity among workers:
resentment is dispersed as each rank complains about its immediate
superiors rather than about the organization as a whole. Furthermore,
because it is hierarchical, a bureaucracy offers promotion prospects.
Promotion is used as a reward for obedience and loyalty, thus suppress-
ing resistance. This strategy is used to control manual workers in industry
through the operation of 'internal labour markets'. Companies recruit
new workers from the outside only at a very few levels and always
promote workers from inside the company. Thus a worker's future
depends upon a satisfactory performance within that company, which
may make her or him reluctant to oppose management. Work in a
modern bank is a good example of bureaucratic control. The cashier does

a fairly wide range of tasks – dealing with customers, checking records, exchanging money – but has little discretion in the design of work and, being at the bottom of a hierarchy, has no authority.

Responsible autonomy

Under this mode of control, the worker is given a much greater degree of discretion and is less subject to supervisory authority. The classic case is the craft worker – skilled engineers, printers and the like. Such workers are typically left to design and organize their own working time, largely because they have more knowledge than management about the work itself. Craft workers are trained apprentices, who build up a knowledge of tools and techniques, and apply that knowledge and experience in the course of work. This raises problems of control for management, since the quality of work and the effort expended lie largely in the hands of the workers themselves. This may often not matter, since such workers frequently develop a kind of self-policing system whereby standards of work are collectively guaranteed. Besides, craft workers usually work efficiently because they derive satisfaction from the use of their skills, which are a source of personal pride. Nonetheless, management have to pay relatively high wages as part of the bargain to persuade craft workers to be 'responsible', and discontented craft workers can easily reduce the quality and quantity of their labour because it is not kept under close surveillance. There is, thus, a strong temptation for management to try to reorganize work to by-pass such crafts. This is, of course, a principal objective of Taylorism. If a craft task can be broken into simple operations, or machines can be introduced to replace craft workers, then management can wrest control from labour. It was Braverman's contention that jobs characterized by responsible autonomy are increasingly being replaced by ones subject to technical control. However, recent accounts have argued for the very opposite process, a shift away from the rigidities of technical control towards more flexible arrangements in the workplace.

Trends and tendencies: towards flexibility?

There is currently extensive debate about the ways in which increased competition between firms during the protracted and repeated economic recessions since the mid 1970s has affected industrial organization and work practices. A difficult economic climate has encouraged enterprises to adopt new arrangements to suit trying circumstances. The adaptation most discussed has been the pursuit of greater *flexibility*. Atkinson gave an influential specification of what this has meant for labour in British industry:

> Under the combined influences of profound economic recession, uncertainty about market growth, technological change in both products and production methods, and reductions in working time, British employers are beginning to introduce novel and unorthodox formations in their deployment of labour. They mark a signficant break with the conventional, unitary and hicrarchical internal labour markets which dominate UK manpower management both in theory and in practice. These innovations are intended to secure greater flexibility from the workforce, in terms of its responsiveness both to the level of economic activity (numerical flexibility) and to the nature of that activity (functional flexibility). (Atkinson, 1985, pp. 13–14)

A general tendency for increased flexibility has been identified in four aspects of industrial production: changes in technology, products, jobs and employment contracts.

Technology   New technologies provide new opportunities for organizing production. Recent technological advances include: computerized control of manufacturing processes; computer-aided design and computer-aided manufacture (CAD/CAM); and the use of robots alongside computer control. In association with social reorganization on the factory floor, these developments permit more efficient small-batch production. On old-fashioned assembly lines of the sort described by Braverman or Beynon, it was very difficult to change from producing one product to another. The machinery was 'dedicated' to producing a very large volume of identical products which could, by virtue of the economies of scale that underlay mass production, be sold fairly cheaply. Microelectronics allows machine tools to be reprogrammed very quickly in order to shift between products.

Products   It is therefore possible to produce small quantities of much more specialized products, sometimes called 'customized production', for particular market niches, whether these be specialist chemicals or fashionable clothes. The phenomenon of the 'Third Italy' has attracted much attention (see for example Scott, 1988). Here, there is a growing concentration of small firms in the textile, clothing, pottery and engineering sectors, based on use of the latest technology and craft labour, producing for quickly changing consumer tastes in world markets. The franchised Benetton chain supplies such clothing in Britain which is produced in this flexible way in north-east Italy.

Jobs   This new organization of production needs more versatile workers. The routinized and fragmented jobs disappear along with the old
dedicated assembly lines; fewer workers are employed to carry out more
tasks; and the new processes work most efficiently where workers are
responsible for programming and maintaining the machines themselves.
These developments are referred to as increasing 'functional flexibility',
which may mean the removal of demarcation barriers between different
crafts and hence the 'multi-skilling' of workers. This is most evident
within Japanese industry but is still unusual in Britain. It entails a mix of
the two managerial strategies of responsible autonomy and bureaucratic
control.

Contracts   One final way of achieving flexibility is by reducing the
number of workers doing nothing at any point in time, thus saving on
labour costs. 'Functional flexibility' describes the ways in which workers
are moved around from job to job within the factory as required. An
alternative is what is called 'numerical flexibility'. Here firms employ on
a permanent and full-time basis only those workers who can be fully
occupied for 40 hours per week. Extra capacity is achieved by other
means. Either firms employ workers on a temporary, part-time or casual
basis, thereby avoiding paying wages for wasted time. Or they subcon-
tract out certain activities for which there is insufficient demand on a
permanent basis. It may be cheaper and more efficient, for instance, to
use external firms of designers or caterers than to employ such people
directly. Similarly, specialist parts may be bought in from another firm.
Such firms will typically be relatively small, and in some cases large
companies set up their own ex-managers in small businesses with
guaranteed contracts for a period of time in order to establish networks
of subcontractors.

Towards post-Fordism?

Some authors consider the growth of flexible organization and working
practices so significant as to constitute the basis for a major new phase in
the development of capitalist societies. Various terms are used to
describe the new phase: 'flexible accumulation', 'neo-Fordism' and 'post-
Fordism' all imply slightly different scenarios (see Wood, 1989), but each
identifies a transition away from Fordism, as described by Braverman, to
a more flexible *system* of production, the ideal-typical characteristics of
which are listed in table 2.5. As can be seen, the characteristics of
Fordism are precisely those that Braverman argued were becoming more
general in the late twentieth century. Fordist production describes a
system of mass production in mechanized workplaces (including offices)

Table 2.5 Ideal types of production system

	Fordist	*Post-Fordis*
Technology	Fixed, dedicated machines	Micro-elec controlled machines
Product	For a mass consumer market Relatively cheap	Diverse specialized products High quality
Labour process	Fragmented Few tasks	
		Many tasks for versatile workers
	Little discretion	Some autonomy
	Hierarchical authority and technical control	Group control
Contracts	Collectively negotiated rate for the job Relatively secure	Payment by individual performance Dual market: secure core, highly insecure periphery

Source: Warde, 1990, p. 88

where work is routinized and closely supervised and where deskilled workers come to share a common proletarian condition.

Post-Fordism offers a different prospect. If the new scenario is accurately identified, then it certainly sweeps away many of the industrial conditions identified by Braverman. In some cases it entails the return of the craft worker: the pattern of work in the 'Third Italy' is one in which craft workers use their experience and very advanced technology to work in small, quasi-domestic workshops. In all instances, flexible organization and working practices entail the abandonment of the technical control that contributed to the degradation of labour on the dedicated assembly line. It means the contraction of mass production and, some authors suggest, a significant change in patterns of consumption as new products, designed to suit special tastes or needs, are made available. Also it signifies the end of secure full-time employment for a substantial portion of the labour force.

These accounts of new flexible practices identify *tendencies*. Flexible production describes the leading edge of industrial innovation on a world scale. Scarcely anyone thinks that mass production has yet been superseded; it is, rather, that this is the way things are developing. Employment figures show a decline in unskilled manual work and an increase in white-collar occupations. Subcontracting has increased somewhat. There has also been a considerable increase in the number of small businesses: self-employment comprised about 12 per cent of total employment in 1992 (see section 3.2). A growing proportion of jobs are part-time and there are more temporary jobs than there used to be.

However, there are two kinds of objection that may be raised about this view of the future of industry. First, there is an empirical problem of how many people are being affected by these changes. Second, there is an explanatory problem: do these things have anything in common? Are they a unified set of changes with a common cause, or is the apparent power of this trend more a function of sociologists' concepts?

The extent to which these tendencies have developed in Britain remains doubtful. Relatively few firms have introduced a complete flexible package on the model of the Japanese, for example. B. Jones (1988, p. 453), studying the engineering industry, argued

> that British industry has not yet made a systematic shift to flexible automation. The systems that have been implemented have not yet been accompanied by a corresponding revolution in work roles, or the functional and authority aspects.

This may be an indication of Britain being somewhat backward, since comparative studies show far more examples of integrated flexible production systems in Germany and Japan. In all countries there can be no doubt that mass production survives in many industries, for instance in food processing. In addition, the new international division of labour has seen some of the most routinized of mass production processes developed in factories owned by the Western multinational corporations but located in the less developed countries.

Nor is it entirely clear that these changes are part of a coherent or unified system of manufacturing production, still less that they are the harbinger of a new age. In Britain, conditions of employment have altered in the last ten years, with some functional flexibility and many more insecure jobs. However, these features may have other causes than attempts by firms to move towards flexible accumulation. Part-time work has been increasing since the early 1960s, before flexible production had been thought of, and has more to do with the movement of more low-paid women workers into the labour force. Moreover, most part-time work is not in manufacturing industry, where it has been declining recently, but in the service industries. Agency work, a form of flexible contract, is largely restricted to a couple of occupations – nursing and secretarial work. Temporary contracts are more prevalent in the public sector than in the capitalist sector, contrary to the logic of competitiveness that lies behind flexible accumulation. This suggests that changes in employment conditions may have more to do with state policy than capitalist reorganization. Indeed, it might be proposed that, in Britain at least, what we have seen in the last ten years is a consequence less of advanced technology and new products than of a change in the balance of power between employers and unions. Declining membership, the loss of legal immunities, unemployment, and fewer jobs in traditional manufacturing industries with high union density, have swung the balance of industrial power significantly in favour of employers (see section 2.6).

Both the deskilling argument of Braverman and the new writings about flexible specialization and post-Fordism overstate the coherence of trends in the organization of work and production. Plenty of examples of the processes described can be found. But overall, management always has a variety of options and there is no 'best' way of organizing all types of production: the conditions for profitability in the garment trade are not like those in petrochemicals. Firms try to secure competitiveness by using particular combinations of technology, control strategies and payment systems, subject to the pressures of their external environments. Of course not all such combinations are effective; possibilities are limited. But the economic environment tends to be so volatile, the internal workings of organizations so complex, that it is unlikely that companies will alight on common solutions to the problems of job design.

Summary

1 Different jobs give different rewards and satisfactions. Jobs in which the worker does a variety of tasks and has discretion over how to carry out those tasks tend to give most satisfaction.

2 Many jobs have been deskilled in the twentieth century as work has been reorganized to give management more control by reducing the workers' range of tasks and degree of discretion. At the same time, however, new occupations requiring technical capacities and specialized knowledge have emerged. Whether there has been an overall trend towards deskilling is disputed.

3 Too much emphasis should not be placed on technological innovation in explaining changes in work, because technology can be used in many different ways. The manner in which technology is deployed reflects power relations between management and workers.

4 The experience of work is strongly affected by the way in which management tries to control workers in the process of production. There are many types of managerial strategy, of which direct control,

technical control, bureaucratic control, and relative autonomy are important variants.

5   During the 1980s management talked a lot about increasing flexibility in the workplace. Various changes were made in the organization of the labour process and in employment contracts, but it is debatable whether this constitutes a major transition in production in Britain.

Related topics

Some discussion of the effects of new technology on work patterns occurs in section 2.9. The characteristics of modern office work are discussed in section 3.5, and managers' work is examined in sections 2.4 and 3.5. Aspects of worker organization and consciousness are dealt with in section 2.6 and at length in section 3.4.

2.6   Trade Unions and Industrial Relations

Trade unions are the most important and visible organizations for the protection of employees' interests in the workplace. The study of industrial relations is primarily devoted to the relationship between unions and management.

The image of the unions, and the popular ambivalence towards them, result from their structural role. Unions are well established. Together they have a vast membership: 10.2 million in 1989, or two out of every five employees. And generally they are organizations which support and protect their members against powerful adversaries, employers. This inevitably involves them in a degree of conflict with management. There is a general conflict of interests between employer and employee concerning both control at work and payment. At the same time, however, that conflict is usually covert and limited. Mostly, in practice, unions accept private ownership, profit-making, managerial authority and market mechanisms. They seek not to undermine employers so much as to secure, within the existing framework, a 'fair' deal for the members – a customary and adequate wage, some security and some dignity. For their part, employers seek usually not to destroy unions but to secure satisfactory levels of output and profit.

Bargaining and negotiation are the normal forms that the relationship takes. Worker representatives negotiate with management about the so-called 'wage–effort bargain'. Occasionally negotiation breaks down and open conflict emerges. Strikes and lock-outs are the most publicized forms of conflict, but there are other forms of industrial action by means of which workers collectively resist managerial authority. Overtime bans and working to rule are common forms of industrial action. Labour may, alternatively, organize politically to reduce the power of management generally, as for example by implementing wider consultation procedures or workers' control. Another important mode of resistance is individual: sabotage, work limitation and absenteeism may all be used by individual workers as ways of expressing hostility towards management. Such means may be the only ones available for non-unionized workers, but they are not restricted to such workers.

Arising from the inequality of power between management and workers, industrial relations are always ones of potential conflict. As Fox described it, industrial relations are relations of 'low trust'. There are, however, considerable costs for both sides in engaging in sustained open conflict. Management generally seeks a cooperative workforce, for strikes, work limitation, sabotage and the like reduce the productivity and income of the enterprise. Management therefore tends to seek to reduce the arena of mutual conflict. This may be achieved in a number of ways: refusing to recognize trade unions, persuading employees that there are no grounds for hostility, and establishing procedures for negotiations over issues which cause grievance to workers. Trade unions usually have no wish to escalate conflict either. Unions exist primarily to protect the economic interests of their members by securing satisfactory conditions for workers within a firm or industry. They are thus concerned with the exchange bargain, under which workers sell their labour power: pay, hours, security of employment and safety at work are their immediate concerns.

Over a long period of time, a range of procedures have developed in many industries whereby such matters are negotiated routinely by union representatives and officials. Often these officials are as committed as management to those peaceful and routine procedures: unions themselves play a central part in what is referred to as the *institutionalization of industrial conflict*. Most industrial relations activity is institutionalized. Unions rarely use the ultimate sanction at their disposal, the strike. The point at which unions are prepared to cease negotiating and call upon their members to withdraw their labour depends on a number of factors – the strength of the union, the economic position of affected firms, the rate of unemployment, the law, etc. Given popular prejudices, it is worth recording that most workers have never been on strike, and that in 1989 only 4.1 million days were lost through disputes, an average of 0.2 days per worker. Even in 1979, the year in which most days were lost through strikes since the Second World War, only 1.2 days per worker were lost. In any year much more time (in 1989, about 7 days per worker) is lost through illness.

Unions, politics and the law

Trade unions have always caused political controversy and the recent period has been no exception. Political parties and governments have a stake in industrial relations because the balance of power between employers and workers is a pivot of British political life. Trade unions are connected to the Labour Party, through direct affiliation of members and indirectly through the Trades Union Congress (TUC). Employers individually, and through their collective organizations like the Confederation of British Industry (CBI), are closely identified with the Conservative Party. Because this political alignment exists, economic policy and the laws concerning industrial relations alter with changes of government.

Conservative governments between 1979 and 1992 attempted to alter the balance of political and industrial power in favour of capital and employers. Three means were used: reducing the national political influence of unions; introducing legislation to diminish the operational effectiveness of unions in workplace disputes; and exerting much tighter discipline over its own, state employees.

The unions played a prominent and direct role in national politics in the 1960s and 1970s. The TUC was widely involved in routine consultation about economic and social policy and was for a time responsible for delivering wage restraint in exchange. Moreover, individual unions had used industrial action in order to influence government policy. First, then, TUC involvement was severely curtailed by the Conservative governments. They, also sought to reduce direct state involvement in bargaining procedures, refusing to intervene in issues like plant closures and leaving the determination of wages and conditions in the private sector entirely to negotiation between managers and their employees. Other legislative and disciplinary measures also served to eliminate the use of industrial action for political ends.

Second, various pieces of legislation regarding the organization and activities of unions reduced their operational effectiveness. Kelly (1990, p. 55) sums up the changes:

> Four major pieces of anti-union legislation were passed, with more in the pipeline, in order to outlaw the closed shop, curb the number of pickets, narrow the definition of a lawful trade dispute, outlaw political and solidarity strikes, impose the use of secret ballots in union decision-making and reduce individual employment rights by the extension of qualifying periods, abolition of protective machinery and exemptions for small firms. Above all trade unions have been given a 'legal personality' and can be sued for a wide range of unlawful activities.

These measures made recruitment and the conduct of disputes more difficult.

The government's third line of attack on union power was to exert influence over decisions made by public agencies. Since the public sector was highly unionized, intervention in the levels and processes of pay settlements was a means of directly confronting unions. In addition, the privatization of some nationalized industries, the closure of parts of others, such as coal-mines, and the restructuring of welfare services like the NHS, all impacted on unions. Industrial relations in the public sector became increasingly 'adversarial' as unions reacted against government policies. The bitter, year-long, miners' strike of 1984–5 demonstrated that unions were unable to match through industrial action the concerted power of the state: a resolute government had limitless resources for sitting out the conflict and was able, also, to deploy considerable physical force through the policing of the dispute. The public sector was the scene of most of the industrial conflict in the 1980s, but the defeat of the miners was symbolic. Subsequently collective bargaining rights were withdrawn from some groups of public employees, including nurses and teachers.

Plate 2.5 Police confronting miners during the strike of 1984–5.
Source: Network

Government encouraged the reassertion of managerial prerogatives in the public sector generally. Wages continued to decline relative to the private sector, and by the early 1990s government was imposing wage controls on state employees. Nevertheless, union density in the public sector declined little and bargaining procedures remained broadly intact.

At the beginning of the 1980s many opinion polls recorded a widespread conviction that trade unions had too much power. By the end of the decade this belief was much less commonly held and trade unions were more popular than at any time since the 1950s – suggesting that people thought the government had been successful, and perhaps over-zealous, in its policies. There were many indications that the trade union movement was significantly weaker by 1990.

This was not, however, simply the effect of state legislative measures, which had mixed consequences. For *economic conditions* – including high unemployment and industrial restructuring – were so unfavourable to workers that, even if the new legislation had been completely ineffective, unions would still have been in a weak position. Academic controversy revolves around two questions concerning the severity and the permanence of changes. Some argue that the industrial relations system in Britain has been fundamentally altered and that unions are unlikely to recover their former strength. Others see the set-backs for the union movement in the 1980s merely as part of a recurrent cycle in which the power of unions ebbs and flows, depending on prevailing economic conditions. We will consider various aspects of union activity relevant to assessing the extent of change.

Trade union organization and membership

There were, at the end of 1989, 309 trade unions in Britain, representing 10.2 million members. Only 74 of these unions were affiliated to the TUC, its total affiliated membership being 8.2 million. Mergers have resulted in unions being fewer, and larger, than before: in 1960 there were 650 unions; by 1980, 438. The largest ten unions in 1989 represented 61 per cent of all union members.

Unions are basically voluntary associations which seek to represent *democratically* their membership. Most officials, especially senior ones, are elected and the policies of unions are determined at conferences of delegates. However, problems arise in attempting to organize large numbers of people. Some characteristics of bureaucratic organization (see section 2.4) emerge: large unions are staffed by permanent, salaried officials, who are distributed in a hierarchy of posts, the most influential of which are located at central headquarters. Because officials are supposed to represent the membership, tension may develop between the central officials and the members. Conflicts may also arise over issues of union policy.

Writing as long ago as 1915, Michels noted that it was difficult to maintain democratic procedures within a bureaucratic organization. On the face of it, unions, despite their bureaucratic characteristics, are one of the few institutions in British society which make any attempt to be democratic. They have procedures of direct democracy (elections, meetings, etc.), making leaders responsive to members, which are completely absent in schools, the army, the monarchy, or the House of Lords. Some unions are, however, more democratic than others. Also, the extent of democratic control varies historically. Overall, the biggest British unions are now more democratic than they were in the 1950s. Recognizing that participation by lay members in union affairs was essential to a thriving and effective organization, powers were intentionally devolved to the workplace, especially during the 1970s. Since then, however, there has been a significant decline in membership.

The size of trade union membership is one measure of strength. In 1979, 53 per cent of the working population were members of a trade union or a staff association. That figure, referred to as union *density* (i.e. the proportion of people eligible for membership who actually join), was higher than at any time in British history. Changes in union membership and density are presented in table 2.6. This shows that the number of union members increased slowly between 1954 and 1969, whilst density remained constant at a little above 40 per cent. In the next decade, 1969–79, membership and density grew significantly. Since 1979 there has been an annual fall in membership. In 1979 there were about 12 million employee members in Great Britain. By 1987 the number had fallen to just over 9 million, about the same number as in 1969. Major gains of the 1970s have been lost.

Explanation of the varying volume density of union membership may be considered from two points of view. First, why in general do people join unions? Second, what factors operate to produce variations in membership for different groups of workers?

Why join trade unions?

People join unions primarily because collective action is the most effective way for workers to defend and promote their occupational interests. Unions try to modify and regulate the conditions under which labour is sold by using their collective organizational strength to offset the power of employers. Individual workers have few effective sanctions at their disposal: when faced by an employer a worker alone cannot

Table 2.6   British trade union membership and density, 1954–1987

Year	*1* Union membership, GB (000s)	*2* Employees in employment, GB (000s)	Union density GB: col.1 ÷ col.2 × 100 (%)
1954	8,609	20,961	41.1
1959	8,661	21,565	40.2
1964	9,071	22,344	40.6
1969	9,423	22,135	42.6
1974	10,579	22,297	47.4
1975	10,966	22,213	49.1
1976	11,138	22,028	50.6
1977	11,561	22,114	52.3
1978	11,801	22,246	53.0
1979	11,960	22,611	52.9
1980	11,652	22,432	51.9
1981	10,895	21,362	51.0
1982	10,434	20,896	49.9
1983	10,112	20,556	49.2
1984	9,895	20,722	47.7
1985	9,739	20,995	46.0
1986	9,485	21,079	45.3
1987	9,427	21,388	44.1

Source: Bailey and Kelly, 1990, p. 269; various statistical sources

prevent wages falling, insist on improving working conditions, or protect jobs during an economic recession. The market situation of most occupational groups depends upon collective solidarity.

Strength of numbers is important, since the larger the organization of workers, the more difficult it is for employers to replace the labour force. Unions are generally weak in small firms because, unless the workers are very highly skilled, the replacement of a handful of them is relatively easy. Unionization is effective in the sense that better-paid employees are generally well organized. Organization does not guarantee high rewards, but is an important contributory factor. Not only do unions improve the financial situation of their members among other things, but they also help to maintain workers' control over the labour process. This is sometimes part of the same process as obtaining high financial rewards: in the engineering industry and in printing, traditionally, control over the job strengthened the union's bargaining position. In addition unions may offer legal and political representation and social benefits.

What affects trade union membership?

If it benefits workers to be union members, it might be asked why there are many occupations with very low levels of unionization. There are several factors which affect levels of membership besides government policy, which we look at briefly in turn, including:

1 the general economic environment;
2 the size, ownership and economic position of the employing establishment;
3 the typical social characteristics of the labour force;
4 employers' attitudes to unionization;
5 union bargaining and recruitment policies.

Unions tend to decline in size in periods of high unemployment and when real wages are increasing. Both conditions were true of the 1980s.

The size of an enterprise is important. Small firms are weakly unionized; large, bureaucratically organized firms, especially those with centralized personnel management, can scarcely function in the absence of unions to transmit grievances and bargain on behalf of employees. This size-cum-organization effect is one reason why state-owned industry, where most employment is in large organizations with centralized management and centralized bargaining procedures, has higher levels of unionization. Union density is over 60 per cent in the public sector, but less than 30 per cent in the private sector. Large firms in the private manufacturing sector are, however, also subject to the same pressure of size. In private services, by contrast, firms are smaller, and densities in hotel and catering and the distribution sectors are very low (less than 10 per cent). This is in part because such firms operate in a competitive environment where wages comprise a substantial proportion of costs. During the 1980s industrial structure has changed in such a way that establishments where high levels of unionization were normal (private manufacturing and public agencies) have become less prevalent. Workplaces have tended to become smaller. More important, employment contracted most sharply in manufacturing industry and public bodies after 1979, which meant that jobs in enterprises with high levels of unionization disappeared fastest. A larger proportion of remaining jobs were in privately owned firms in the service sector of the economy.

The composition of the labour force is a third important factor. Full-time workers are more likely to be members than part-time, and associatedly, as table 2.7 shows, men are more likely to be members than women. About 44 per cent of male employees, compared with 33 per cent of women, were members in 1989. This is not because men and

Table 2.7 Membership of trade union and/or staff association, Great Britain, spring 1989

	All (000s)	(%)	Men (000s)	(%)	Women (000s)	(%)
Employees and self-employed:[a]	25,482	100.0	14,474	100.0	11,008	100.0
Member	8,804	34.9	5,422	37.8	3,382	31.0
Not a member	16,454	65.1	8,919	62.2	7,535	69.0
Employees:[b]	22,049	100.0	11,862	100.0	10,187	100.0
Member	8,491	38.8	5,167	44.0	3,324	32.9
Not a member	13,368	61.2	6,586	56.0	6,782	67.1
Self-employed:[b]	3,425	100.0	2,607	100.0	819	100.0
Member	313	9.2	254	9.8	58	7.2
Not a member	3,086	90.8	2,333	90.2	753	92.8

[a] Includes some who did not state whether they were employee or self-employed.
[b] Includes those who did not state whether they were a member of a trade union and/or a staff association.

Source: *Employment Gazette*, April 1990, p. 206. Gower copyright.

women behave very differently when in the same industrial situations. As will be shown in sections 3.2 and 4.2, women crowd into certain occupations, and many of them are employed in private services. Only in one sector of manufacturing industry – textiles – do women comprise a majority of the workforce, and there union density is high. Though an increasing proportion of members are in white-collar occupations (in 1979, 40 per cent of all union members were non-manual workers), manual workers are more likely to join a union. Again this is less because of the attitudes of workers, more because white-collar workers are typically found in smaller work units and because of greater employer resistance to recognizing white-collar unions.

Employer recognition of a union for the purposes of collective bargaining is the primary precondition for attracting and retaining members. Some employers are more ready to offer recognition than others. During the 1960s and 1970s state industries positively encouraged unionization and their membership remains very high. In private services, by contrast, employers are more reluctant to recognize unions. During the 1980s very few employers actually withdrew recognition from unions, but new firms, particularly in the early 1980s, proved very hesitant to grant recognition to any union. Employers, sensing government encouragement and a new balance of power in industry, avoided making agreements with unions. Simultaneously, other establishments sought to use new human relations management techniques which they

imagined might circumvent the need for union represer
fostering the cooperation and commitment of individual emp

Trade unions as organizations thus faced a range of adverse
circumstances in the 1980s. In response, they revised their r
strategies, devoting effort to trying to attract new people in
job areas, including women in part-time work. As yet, the union
movement has not halted the decline. Its task is difficult. There is a
constant turnover of members, as people leave jobs and move workplaces: for example, 25 per cent of members of USDAW, the
shopworkers union, are new every year. Such unions thus need to recruit
heavily even to maintain membership levels. Nevertheless, some unions
(in the public sector and in telecommunications in particular) grew
during the 1980s.

Workplace bargaining

Unions' main function is to bargain about wages. Bargaining occurs at
various levels in Britain. In some cases bargaining over pay and other
matters takes place at *national level*. Basic wages and conditions are
negotiated between all employers and relevant unions for all workers in a
given industry throughout Britain. This occurs most commonly in state-
owned industries (workers in higher education and on British Rail have
the same contracts wherever they work), but it also occurs in the private
sector. In other cases bargaining occurs at the *company level*: all people
employed by the same company in the same job have identical
conditions. Alternatively, bargaining may occur at *plant level*. That is to
say, negotiations cover only those people working on a single site.

National bargaining had replaced local and workshop bargaining
between 1920 and 1970, both increasing the sense of solidarity of union
members (because the outcome of a wage claim is binding for workers in
London, Lancaster and Llandudno) and preventing employers deserting
high-wage regions for lower-wage regions. Centralized bargaining
became almost universal in state administration and services. However,
one of the main trends in the last 20 years has been the re-emergence of
workplace bargaining in manufacturing industry, especially in private
firms. Localized agreements between management and workforce,
concerning productivity and bonus payments for instance, have become
increasingly prominent. This in turn has made union representation *in the
workplace* more necessary – a development which initially led to an
enormous increase in the numbers of shop stewards. Estimates of the
number of shop stewards put the figure at 90,000 in 1961, 175,000 in 1968
and over 250,000 by 1978. In favourable circumstances in the 1970s this

shift to workplace bargaining probably advantaged labour; in the 1980s it has been enthusistically adopted by management, as employers have increasingly become its beneficiaries.

A large Workplace Industrial Relations Survey (WIRS), the third of its kind, was carried out in 1990 (Millward et al., 1992). Evidence was collected for just over 2000 workplaces, all of which had 25 or more employees; 2550 questionnaires were completed by senior management, mostly from personnel departments, and 1466 by worker representatives. Questions were similar to those asked in the previous surveys of 1980 and

Table 2.8 Proportion of employees covered by collective bargaining, 1984 and 1990

	All establishments		Establishments with any recognized unions	
	1984 (%)	1990 (%)	1984 (%)	1990 (%)
All establishments	71	54	89	80
Sector:				
Private manufacturing	64	51	82	76
Private services	41	33	82	78
Public sector	95	78	96	84
Union density, all sectors:				
Non	1	–	–	–
1–24%	30	15	52	29
25–49%	63	54	67	62
50–74%	87	75	88	80
75–89%	92	84	93	87
90–99%	97	91	97	93
100%	98	94	99	99
Base: all establishments				
Union density, private sector only:				
None	–	–	–	–
1–24%	27	12	51	27
25–49%	58	47	64	55
50–74%	80	77	82	80
75–89%	86	84	88	88
90–99%	94	94	95	94
100%	93	(100)	97	(100)
Base: all private sector establishments				

Source: Millward et al., 1992, p. 94

1984. Together these surveys offer systematic evidence of trends in industrial relations over a decade.

The 1990 study throws further light on declining union membership by reporting a significant fall in the proportion of workers covered by collective bargaining arrangements. In 1990, 36 per cent of all the workplaces surveyed contained not a single union member. The proportion of employees who were union members in all the workplaces surveyed fell from 58 to 48 per cent between 1984 and 1990, partly spurred by legislation to abolish the closed shop. It is possible to be a union member employed in a workplace where one's union is not recognized for bargaining purposes; and, conversely, it is possible for a worker to be covered by a collective bargaining agreement without being a union member. As table 2.8 shows, in the establishments surveyed the proportion of workers covered by collective bargaining fell from 71 per cent in 1984 to 54 per cent in 1990. Decline in the public sector was almost entirely due to the withdrawal of bargaining rights for school-teachers. Union density in private manufacturing declined in particular sectors in engineering (especially among small firms) because industry-wide bargaining involving many employers ceased in 1989. Low union recognition was most characteristic of firms in the private services sector.

WIRS (Millward et al., 1992) confirmed that the presence of trade unions improves relatively both pay and working conditions. Table 2.9 indicates the factors affecting the incidence of an employer paying very low wages (less than £3.28 per hour in 1990). The more employees covered by union recognition, the fewer there were who were badly paid. The table also shows that the smaller the firm, and the more part-time and women workers in the workforce, the more prevalent is low pay. Influences considered relevant to determining the last pay settlement by personnel managers are shown in table 2.10. A cost-of-living calculation is the most important factor in all establishments. However differences are apparent between the public and private sectors and between unionized and non-unionized firms. In the public sector, limits imposed by higher authority (i.e. primarily the government) are particularly germane, whereas economic performance is considered more relevant in the private sector. Within the private sector, non-unionized firms reward people much more widely on the basis of individual performance. The extent to which this makes possible the exercise of arbitrary managerial power is indicated by Millward et al.'s (1992) summary of the characteristics of 'union-free' workplaces in 1990 (see box 2.3).

Generally, workplace procedures themselves did not change radically during the 1980s. Where collective bargaining arrangements were already established, little altered, though there is evidence that discipline is becoming more strict and employees are working harder. Rather, the main change was the declining coverage of employees by collective

Table 2.9 Proportion of establishments with any lower-paid employees in the private sector, 1990

	Any lower-paid employees (%)	Unweighted base	Weighted base
All private sector:	27	1346	1306
Manufacturing	22	618	418
Services	29	728	888
Number of employees at establishment:			
25–99	28	473	1021
100–499	25	501	261
500–999	10	169	17
1000 or more	15	203	7
Percentage of workforce part-time:			
41 or more	49	165	191
6–40	32	338	447
0–5	17	832	662
Percentage of workforce female:			
71 or more	46	174	221
31–70	29	453	444
0–30	17	563	561
Ownership:			
Independent establishment	30	228	391
Branch of larger organization	26	1019	858
Head office	13	99	57
UK owned	28	1086	1160
Foreign owned	13	214	133
Union representation:			
No recognized union	32	576	809
1 or more recognized unions	19	770	497
Coverage where recognized unions:			
1–49 per cent	32	122	113
50–79 per cent	26	173	114
80–99 per cent	13	297	142
100 per cent	9	178	129
Number of competitors:			
None	27	113	76
1–5	22	376	347
More than 5	31	590	702
Capacity utilization:			
Full	26	465	414
Somewhat below full	27	434	339
Considerably below full	24	64	54

Base: private sector establishments reporting typical pay and hours for at least one of five occupational groups

Source: Millward et al., 1992, p. 244

Table 2.10 Factors influencing the size of the most recent pay settlement according to managers, 1990

	Manual employees			Non-manual employees		
	Private sector		Public sector (%)	Private sector		Public sector (%)
	Union[a] (%)	Non-union[b] (%)		Union[a] (%)	Non-union[b] (%)	
Cost of living	56	47	50	57	47	44
Labour market	29	39	13	40	30	25
Recruitment, retention	6	11	1	6	8	9
Economic performance:	36	36	12	38	35	9
Economic performance, ability to pay	32	34	7	34	34	5
Productivity increases	5	3	5	6	2	4
Linked to other settlement	15	14	13	8	12	13
Other influences:	13	29	32	17	39	41
Limits set by higher authority	3	1	15	5	2	15
Individual performance	2	23	4	4	32	4
Strike threat, union bargaining power	2	–	6	2	1	13
Not stated	6	4	16	11	4	10
Unweighted	701	511	433	507	859	565
Weighted	403	708	345	260	1075	464

Base: establishments with employees named in column heads where most recent pay settlement determined at establishment or higher in the organization

[a] Establishment with recognized unions for employees named in column heads.
[b] Establishments with no recognized union for employees named in column heads.

Source: Millward et al., 1992, p. 238

Box 2.3   The characteristics of 'union-free' workplaces compared with unionized, private sector establishments

Without the constraint of union negotiations, pay levels were set unilaterally by management, generally managers at the work-place. In a minority of cases management at head office or some other level in the enterprise took responsibility for setting levels of pay for a group of workplaces. Only in rare cases was pay set by statutory minima. However, managements in around a fifth of non-union workplaces claimed to consult employees or their representatives about pay increases. Labour market and com-mercial and financial considerations dominated managements' thinking on the size of pay settlements to a much greater degree than in the unionized sector. Pay was more a matter of individual performance, with formal job evaluation being rare. Again reflecting the lack of union influence, differentials between the highest and lowest earners in non-union workplaces tended to be relatively wide. Lower-paid employees were more common.

Managers generally felt unconstrained in the way they organized work. Opposition from employees to changes in working methods was rare, and the lack of skills which managers in unionized workplaces often cited as a problem was also rare. Greater use of freelance and temporary contract workers was another aspect of the greater flexibility of labour in the non-union sector. Work-force reductions were no more common, but they were much more likely to be achieved by compulsory redundancies than by less painful measures such as natural wastage. Dismissals (other than those arising from redundancy) were common, nearly twice as frequent per employee as in the union sector.

Source: Millward et al., 1992, pp. 363–4

bargaining agreements. For these, an increasing proportion of workers in the private sector, employment conditions were often inferior and more precarious than for the rest.

Industrial conflict

Strikes are the aspect of industrial conflict which receives most publicity. The strike is the ultimate sanction available to a union in a dispute with an employer; the possibility of workers collectively withdrawing their labour is fundamental if unions are to have any influence over the behaviour of employers. But resistance may take many forms. High rates of absenteeism and lack of effort, for example, both present themselves as problems for management, and thus may be used by workers as ploys in negotiation. Especially in establishments where unions are not recognized, these may be the only possible ways of registering dissatisfaction. At the same time, it cannot be assumed that every instance of, say, absenteeism amounts to workers' resistance. Moreover, it should be realized that some of these practices are much less effective in applying pressure upon management than others. Although high rates of labour turnover may create difficulties for management – new workers have to be trained, worker morale is likely to be low, etc. – quitting a job is a weak form of 'resistance'.

The first Workplace Industrial Relations Survey (Daniel and Millward, 1983) enquired about the frequency and type of industrial action which occurred during the 12-month period between mid 1979 and mid 1980. This was a period of intense industrial conflict, as is shown in figure 2.7 which gives the number of days lost by strikers each year between 1969 and 1989. Levels of conflict are volatile, and much of the variance is due to isolated, occasional, very lengthy, industry-wide strikes.

Daniel and Millward demonstrated that where no trade union existed, industrial action was, unsurprisingly, rare. In establishments which were unionized the likelihood of industrial action grew under the following five conditions:

1 the more manual workers there were at the establishment;
2 the higher the density of union membership;
3 the greater the proportion of workers who were men;
4 the greater the proportion of workers employed full-time;
5 the more the establishment itself was the main place of collective bargaining.

The final condition proved important. Where bargaining was decentralized, industrial action was more likely to occur. This was partly because this degree of decentralization often coincided with the use of a system of payment by results (PBR). Almost half the manual workforce is on some kind of piece-work system or productivity bonus scheme. They get paid according to output. This, however, gives considerable scope for conflict at the workplace over the price paid per item, the speed at which tasks have to be accomplished in order to get a bonus, etc. Ten years later, in 1990, these factors were still relevant. Conflict was, however, less prevalent. Industrial action had declined sharply since 1984–5. There

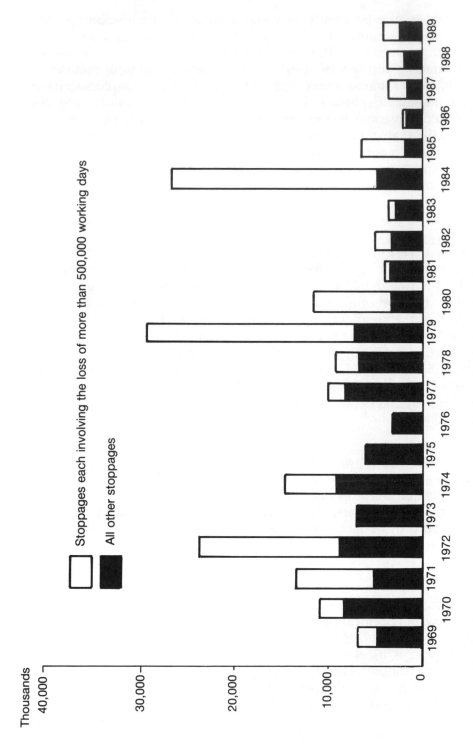

Figure 2.7 Working days lost due to stoppages through industrial disputes.
Source: Bird, 1990, p. 339

were both fewer strikes and fewer other sorts of industrial action. Strikes were almost entirely about pay, with the issue of manning and work allocation the most common source of non-strike activity. Most industrial action occurred in the public sector, with a significant number of white-collar workers involved, many for the first time. Lower levels of action seem to have arisen neither from a change of attitudes among employees nor from structural alterations in the organization of bargaining, but because of the uncongenial economic and political environment.

Summary

1 Industrial relations are mostly a matter of routine negotiation and bargaining between trade union representatives and management: industrial conflict in Britain is *institutionalized*.
2 Currently about 40 per cent of all workers are members of a union, density having fallen from a peak of 55 per cent in 1979. People join a union because collective organization is necessary to protect their occupational interests. The rate at which workers join unions is affected by a number of factors including the macro-economic climate, the nature of the workplace, the character of the workforce, employers' attitudes towards unions, government policy and union recruitment strategies.
3 Conflict between workers and management is endemic to industrial relations, taking many forms and occurring unevenly in time and across industries. Among the factors which affect strike rates, for example, are the level of union organization, the social characteristics of the workforce, the bargaining system in operation, as well as the general economic and political climate.
4 In the 1980s the political influence of trade unions subsided dramatically. Where they still maintained collective bargaining agreements, workplace industrial relations were little altered. However, unions experienced a severe decline in membership and industrial coverage during the decade. It is debatable whether this represents a permanent shift to a narrower range of operation or whether it is just a low point in a cyclical process.

Related topics

One important issue concerns the links between industrial behaviour and class formation. Material on industrial and class attitudes and behaviour can be found in section 3.4 for manual workers and in section 3.5 for routine white-collar workers. Further information on women workers is in section 4.2. Material on media presentation of unions and industrial relations can be found in section 10.2. Further discussion of government economic policy and its connections with political and class conflict appears in sections 12.3 and 12.5.

2.7 Professional Occupations and Associations

All professions are conspiracies against the laity.
George Bernard Shaw, The Doctor's Dilemma

Government statistics refer to some occupations as professional. Among the 'higher' professions are included doctors, solicitors, judges, university teachers, architects and top-ranking civil servants. The 'lower' professions include schoolteachers, nurses, librarians, physiotherapists and social workers. People in these occupations are relatively privileged. Professionals on average earn more than most other groups of employees. Professional jobs also carry a considerable degree of prestige: people may scorn bureaucrats, trade unionists and shopkeepers, but professionals are rarely considered anything but worthy. Given the financial and status rewards associated with being a 'professional', it is unsurprising that many occupational groups attempt to get themselves recognized as professional. (There are parallels with the strategies of manual workers to have their jobs described as 'skilled'.) Since practising a profession is merely taking part in some of the tasks generated by the complex modern division of labour, the question arises: what is distinctive about these jobs which makes them so well rewarded?

It is impossible to list a set of characteristics which will determine unambiguously whether or not an occupation is a profession. Various sociologists have tried to identify the distinctive 'traits' of a profession, but they have not agreed upon which should be included; nor have such approaches helped in the explanation of professional privileges. This is partly because professions, like other occupations, change over time. The classic model of a profession is an ideal type based on the nature of a few elite occupations in the nineteenth century. The 'classic' model, contrasted with the model of proletarian occupations, is illustrated in box 2.4

It should be stressed that these are ideal types and that rarely has any occupation had all these characteristics. Moreover, today, very few professionals work under the conditions described in the ideal type. People at the higher levels of legal, medical and architectural occupations

Box 2.4 Two ideal types of occupation: proletarian and professional

The following summary is of *ideal types*, that is artificial constructions of characteristics which do not always occur together in reality. The classic professional model finds its closest approximation in reality among lawyers, doctors and the clergy in the later nineteenth century.

	Classic model of a proletarian	*Classic model of a (collegiate) profession*
System of reward	Wages paid by employer: workers are wage-labourers	Paid fees, by a client, in exchange for services; are self-employed
Training and recruitment	No credentials required and very limited training	Has higher-education qualifications (usually a degree) and special practical training
Content of work	Routine, mindless and fragmented work	Specialized theoretical knowledge: combines conception and execution
Authority relations at work	Subordinate in a hierarchy of authority: no control over work.	Self-regulating and self-directing: controls own work
Occupational organization	Organized, if at all, by a trade union which bargains with employers on behalf of members	Organized by professional association, of which membership is compulsory and which regulates entry and standards of practice and which is a body of equals
Status situation	Low	High
Ideological image	Casual, irresponsible	Expert, responsible, altruistic

approximate most closely to this type: barristers and consultant doctors in private medical practice, for example.

Occupational control

The basis of professional privilege is power to shape and influence the social organization of work. That power is maintained through collective organization in professional associations. Power derives from high degrees of *occupational control* – control by practitioners themselves over various aspects of the occupation, including payment, recruitment and working practices.

Consider, for example, doctors. Medical doctors are one of the highest-paid occupational groups in Britain. They derive their income from two sources, salaries paid by the National Health Service and fees paid by private patients. Though some doctors are entirely reliant on one of these sources, most have some income from both. Private practice is more lucrative, NHS work more secure.

The main professional association for doctors is the British Medical Association (BMA). It had 78,000 members in 1985. Specialists – surgeons, physicians, and the like – have their own associations, the Royal Colleges. The professional associations negotiate salaries with the state and establish levels of fees. They are in a powerful position regarding levels of payment because entry into the profession is highly restricted. All doctors have to be registered with the General Medical Council (GMC). The GMC officially licenses doctors on behalf of the state: it is illegal to practise medicine unless you are on the register of the GMC. While some members of the GMC are lay people nominated by the state, the majority are doctors. The GMC thus maintains a monopoly in the market for medical services, and monopolies, of course, can easily inflate charges. In order to become a member it is necessary to obtain certain qualifications: a degree and a period of practice in hospital are required, taking seven years of training in all. Medical education is largely controlled by the GMC and the Royal Colleges, and they decide on the content of education and how many doctors should be trained in any given year. The GMC and the professional associations are also responsible for controlling working practices. The GMC and the BMA discipline doctors, dealing with complaints about malpractice. So groups of doctors effectively decide among themselves both what is good and what is bad medicine. The professional associations are thus very powerful, being exclusive, self-recruiting and self-policing. The professional associations exercise a high degree of control over the occupation on behalf of their membership.

Doctors as individuals in the work situation also exercise control, both over patients and over other workers in health services. Doctors lay claim to expert knowledge, which is inaccessible to patients, and they decide on treatment. Both of these conditions give doctors considerable power over their patients. In hospitals, doctors also exercise power over other workers. Nursing staff, radiographers, pharmacists, etc., themselves lower professionals, are subordinate in the hierarchy of authority to doctors. The question which this raises is: how have doctors achieved such a powerful occupational position, from which their privileges flow?

Doctors themselves would probably justify their own privileges in terms of training, knowledge, responsibility, the importance to their clients of good health, the inconveniences of the job or the public service which they provide. Others would argue that these are merely self-legitimating reasons, a claim supported by the fact that far less privileged occupations have these qualities too. Rather the doctors' advantages derive from their overall high degree of occupational control. That control is achieved by collective exploitation, through an effective association, of characteristics of the work situation and the market position which, in turn, reinforce the power of the association. In other words, market position, work situation and collective organization are the mutually supporting props of occupational control.

Professionalization as an occupational strategy

> Professionalism . . . [is] an occupational strategy which is chiefly directed towards the achievement of upward collective social mobility and, once achieved, it is concerned with the maintenance of superior remuneration and status. (Parry and Parry, 1976, p. 79)

The rewards are such that many occupational groups aspire to be recognized as professional. Implicit in the medical model is a lesson for other occupations: professionalization is an *occupational group strategy*, a way of achieving collective upward social mobility, as Parry and Parry (1976) describe it. If successful, all workers in a particular occupation improve their social and material positions.

The strategy has been attempted by many groups. Key elements in the strategy include setting up an association, getting universities to provide courses which all practitioners must attend and pass, and establishing a set of tasks unique to the occupational group and from which all other workers are excluded by law. The degree of success of such strategies is one thing which separates the lower from the higher professionals.

A number of factors determine the success of professionalization strategies. First, success depends on when, historically, the strategy is embarked upon. Because exclusiveness is a basis of control, profession-alization is competitive between different occupational groups. If doctors have exclusive rights to sign death certificates or sick notes (both important prerogatives), then nurses are barred from those tasks. Indeed, the rise of the modern medical profession was at the expense of groups like nurses and midwives whose opportunities for collective upward social mobility were blocked.

Second, the origins and characteristics of the personnel of occupational groups are important. One reason why the older professions were invested with considerable exclusive powers (like the BMA monopoly) was because they were originally recruited from among the sons of the upper and upper-middle class. Such men were considered reliable and could be given state-guaranteed powers. The higher-class origins of judges, army officers and doctors remain strongly visible even today.

Similarly, it is not accidental that many of the higher professions are staffed by men. In 1981 there were 12 male self-employed professionals for every one woman. Witz (1991) shows that patriarchal power was used both to exclude women from the higher professions and to ensure that occupations filled by women were rendered subordinate. In the late nineteenth century, women were not permitted to take university degrees in medicine in Britain, and hence were ineligible for professional accreditation. Instead, women, who traditionally had been principal carers for the sick, were forced into auxiliary and lower professional occupations like nursing and midwifery, where they could obtain training. Collusion between groups of upper-class men, in hospitals, universities and state departments, operated a process of *occupational closure* against potential women doctors.

The history of medical professionalization also demonstrates the central role of the state. It is the state that grants the monopoly to practise. The British state has probably been more sympathetic to professional claims than its continental counterparts, and consequently professional men have had more influence in British society than in some others. By the same token, governments can rescind the powers of professionals and in the 1980s some attempts were made to reduce occupational monopolies.

Third, professionalization strategies are likely to meet with resistance from potential customers. Generally speaking, professional occupational control is against the interests of the purchasers of services. Where there are few potential customers, or where the customers are organized, professionalization is difficult to secure. For example, as almost the only employer of teachers, the state has the power to oppose the extension of occupational control. Indeed, many of the lower professions are almost entirely dependent upon the state for employment – social workers, nurses, executive grade civil servants, etc. By contrast, the higher professions are generally those where potential customers are many and there are opportunities for the professional to be self-employed in private practice. Generally, being an employee, whether of the state or of a large corporation (company lawyers and accountants, etc.), tends to reduce the professional's control.

Professional knowledge

In many respects, then, both established and aspiring professions behave like most other occupational groups. They organize to promote their members' interests regarding pay and control at work in the same way as do trade unions. Similar processes produce a hierarchy of rewards among all occupational groups: professions are closed-shop occupations, with effective organization and control at work. There does, however, seem to be one distinctive feature of existing professions which marks them out from other occupational groups, and that is the role of their special knowledge in securing occupational control.

It has often been pointed out that professions try to prevent the general public gaining access to their expert knowledge by making it incomprehensible to an outsider. This is partly achieved through universities which give qualifications on the basis of the student's receptivity to a theoretical knowledge which is not made available to anyone else. But while protected knowledge is undeniably part of professional strategies of exclusivity, that knowledge is also necessary for successfully carrying out the job. Where there is no need for the flexible use of expert knowledge in the course of doing the job, workers are unlikely to be able to maintain high levels of occupational control. Where work can be subdivided or routinized, professionals, like skilled manual workers and managers (see section 2.5), must expect that employers *will* rationalize their activities. But the one feature which survives in common among the occupations described as professions today is the high degree of discretion, or control, over work tasks retained by the worker. It is the mixture of expert, abstract knowledge and practical experience, which can be neither rationalized nor quickly acquired, that protects 'educated workers' from proletarianization.

The body of knowledge upon which a profession is based tends to have several distinct characteristics:

1   Professional knowledge must generally be considered true, which today usually means that it has scientific legitimation. The status of

the clergy in twentieth-century Britain has fallen as theological knowledge has become less credible.

2   Professional knowledge must be applied successfully to practical problems and must be useful to some substantial section of the community.

3   Professional knowledge must not be too narrow nor be too easily expressed as practical rules for application. This is because the exclusiveness of the occupational group is hard to maintain if untrained people can quickly master the techniques involved. At the same time, however, professional knowledge has to be specialized and coherent in order to be accepted as true, effective and capable of being transmitted during a professional training course.

4   The key feature of professional knowledge, perhaps, is that it allows the professional to exercise his or her judgment in applying abstract knowledge to the client's particular case. The services of the higher professionals usually take the form of giving advice to clients in a situation of *uncertainty*, where the professional's knowledge and experience gives his or her judgment an authority which can scarcely be challenged by the client. Judgment in circumstances of uncertainty cannot be routinized or expressed as rules, thus providing an exclusive knowledge base for the professional's control in work. Occupational control is extended by preserving space for informed judgment. One of the principal reasons why many occupations fail to achieve professional status is because they cannot carve out an exclusive sphere of activity in which they make important judgments.

The dividing line between trade unions and professional associations is now difficult to draw. Once there was a difference based upon the ways in which each sought to promote their members' interests, professions for instance rejecting tactics like going on strike. However, in recent years, professionals working in the state sector – doctors, university teachers, schoolteachers, nurses, etc – have held strikes to support demands made to their employers for improved conditions. It also used to be the case that the social class background of recruits to the higher professions was very exclusive, though that too is less marked now. In general, for sociological purposes, it is sufficient to note that occupational groups exert different degrees of *occupational control*, and that professions have high degrees of control.

Summary

1 Professions are relatively privileged occupations, being well rewarded, prestigious and having autonomy at work.
2 Professions exercise high degrees of occupational control through exclusive professional associations. In the higher professions the extent of occupational control is very considerable, the members setting the level of their fees, being subject only to internal discipline, controlling recruitment, etc.
3 Many occupational groups seek to be recognized as professions though this is not easy to achieve. Other groups of workers and clients try to prevent this. Furthermore, only certain sorts of occupations – partly characterized by the giving of advice on the basis of knowledge inaccessible to the client – seem able to establish claims to professional status.

Related topics

Fruitful comparison can be made with the work situation of other kinds of employees (section 2.5) and their mode of organization in trade unions (section 2.6). The class position of professionals is discussed in section 3.5 on the middle classes. The role of the medical profession is examined, in passing, in chapter 9.

2.8 Deindustrialization

Services and the changing industrial structure

In the nineteenth century, Britain acquired the reputation of being 'the workshop of the world'. The growth of Britain's manufacturing industries was the basis of the world's first industrial revolution. Today, relatively few people are employed in these manufacturing industries. Vast numbers of jobs in textile manufacture, shipbuilding, steel production and the like have disappeared recently. Greater numbers of people now work in shops, in financial services (banking, insurance, etc) and in the provision of human services like health care and education (see also section 3.2).

The decline of employment in manufacture has been an issue of great concern. Decline has been rapid and dramatic. In 1966, 8.6 million people were employed in manufacturing industry; by 1992 there were only 4.4 million. One reason for this has been the replacement of human labour by machines. The production of goods for mass consumption is particularly susceptible to mechanization and automation. In such cases, like motor vehicles, output may increase while the number of jobs falls owing to the replacement of people by robots. Another reason is the declining demand for some manufactured products, like cargo ships and steel, during the world recessions of the 1970s and 1980s. A further reason is the declining competitiveness of some British manufacturing industries in the world market. This has affected both labour-intensive industries like textiles, where low wages in less developed countries reduce costs, and capital-intensive industries like motor manufacturing, where other advanced economies display higher rates of capital investment. The overall process of falling employment in the manufacturing sector is called 'deindustrialization'.

Deindustrialization describes a particular shift in the *industrial structure*. Industrial structure refers to all businesses engaged in producing or selling goods or services in the formal economy. The nature of what is for sale obviously changes over time, as does the amount of labour needed in the production of goods or delivery of services. Thus, for example, until 1851 over 50 per cent of the British working population was engaged in agriculture. By 1981, however, only 2 per cent of the workforce were either farmers or agricultural labourers. Improved transport facilities, permitting more imported food, and an increased productivity of labour have meant that far fewer workers are required to feed a much larger population in 1981 than in 1851. One way in which the general shift in the industrial structure has been described is in terms of three *sectors*:

1   the primary sector, referring to those industries which either extract minerals from the ground or grow and harvest food;
2   the manufacturing sector, containing industries which *make* commodities;
3   the service sector, in which industries mostly do not produce a final, tangible object, but either *circulate* commodities, as in retailing and banking, or *provide a service direct to clients*, as in education and domestic service.

Over the last 200 years there has been a change in the proportion of people who have been employed in each of these sectors, as is shown in figure 2.8. The proportion of workers in the primary sector diminished steadily as more people entered manufacturing employment. Thereafter the tertiary sector started to increase its share, so that around 65 per cent of all workers are now in service industries.

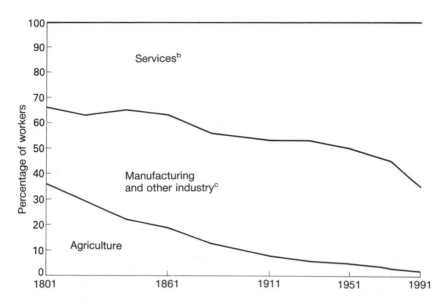

Figure 2.8 Approximate[a] proportions of workers in different economic sectors, 1801–1991.
[a] Estimates of proportions vary considerably; this figure gives only a rough and rather unreliable impression of the situation, especially in the nineteenth century.
[b] Refers to transport, distribution, commerce, professional, personal and government services.
[c] Includes mining, construction and utilities (gas, electricity etc.).
Source: Lee, 1984; Deane and Cole, 1967; Rowthorn, 1986

Services and employment

There is considerable disagreement about the importance of this process of industrial sector shift. Economists argue over whether deindustrialization is a cause or an effect of Britain's poor economic performance. Others doubt whether the shift is meaningfully described because the concept of 'services' is so difficult to define precisely. Originally, a service was thought of as something intangible, not a thing that one could handle; it was contrasted with a manufactured product like a handbag. However, some activities that we call services, or see as being provided by service industries, are entirely tangible: a take-away meal or a video, for example. It thus came to be appreciated that 'services' is a residual category of official statistics, defined negatively as those economic activities that neither extract products from the earth nor mass manufacture goods. There are many kinds of service industries.

Table 2.11 Employment change in the service industries, Great Britain, 1959 and 1981

	Employment 1959 (000s)	1981 (000s)	Change 1959–1981 (000s)	(%)
Public passenger transport (roads and railways)	705	393	−312	−44.3
Goods transport and storage (road haulage, warehousing, wholesale distribution)	1,030	1,269	+239	+23.2
Sea and air transport	317	218	−99	−31.3
Private motoring services (garages)	339	482	+143	+42.2
Retail distribution	1,844	1,846	+2	+0.1
Post and telecommunications	334	430	+96	+28.7
Financial services (insurance, banking, finance)	458	779	+321	+70.0
Other business services (property, advertising, business services, unallocated central offices, law, accountancy, research and development, other business-related professions)	464	1,070	+606	+130.7
Leisure and recreation services (including broadcasting and gambling)	238	334	+96	+40.2
Hotels and catering	665	928	+263	+39.6
Other personal services (hairdressing, laundries, dry cleaning, shoe repairers, private domestic services[a])	268	157	−111	−41.3
Public administration (central and local government)[b]	1,255	1,400	+145	+11.6
Health and education	1,616	3,124	+1,508	+99.3
Welfare services (social services, voluntary organizations, religious organizations)	259	675	+416	+160.6
All service industries (000s)	9,797	13,105	+3,308	+33.8
Share of total employment (%)	44.79	61.48		

[a] Private domestic service is not included in figures based on Department of Employment sources.
[b] Population census figures for this group include the armed forces. They are not included in Department of Employment figures.

Source: Allen and Massey, 1988, p. 99; from Buck, 1985

	Producer service	Consumer service
Intermediate service	Warehousing Management consultancy	Retailing
Final service	Auditing of accounts	Package holidays Medical treatment

Figure 2.9   Different types of service industry.

Table 2.11 lists what are conventionally described as service industries. Considered all together, they have little in common. Nevertheless, it is probably useful to make two distinctions: between producer and consumer services, and between intermediate and final services (see figure 2.9). Intermediate service industries are involved in circulating money, commodities or information. Banking, retailing, goods haulage and telecommunications are all intermediate services. All these services may be rendered to firms (including those in the manufacturing and primary sectors) in which case they would be called producer services. Alternatively they might serve individuals – for example, private citizens with a personal bank account – in which case they are (intermediate) consumer services. Final services are offered by institutions like hospitals, where the patient receives treatment directly and immediately from medical staff. In medicine, as with education or legal advice, there is no tangible product and the service is consumed completely at the same time as it is provided.

Service industries have grown at different rates. In recent years, intermediate services dealing with money and information provided to other industries (producer services) have expanded quite rapidly as big manufacturing firms, for example, have found need for specialized financial, legal and administrative expertise. Those intermediate services more concerned with the distribution of goods – shops, warehouses, etc. – have also increased their turnover, but they have not generated much new employment. This is because the rationalization which affected employment levels in manufacturing industry has also had an impact on distribution. So, for example, big shops have reduced the number of shop assistants and, instead, employ staff mainly to stack shelves or collect money at check-outs.

The human services have been a principal source of new employment since the Second World War. The expansion of health, education, and social services provided many new jobs, a significant proportion of which

professional and semi-professional positions. However, some
nal consumer services have contracted during the same period,
s have closed, laundries have shut, and the public transport
s contracted.

Social consequences: a post-industrial society?

Sociologists are uncertain about the social consequences of these changes
in the industrial structure. Clearly, such changes have *some* implications
for the nature of work and the institutions and activities we have been
considering in this chapter. Daniel Bell (1973), and other exponents of
the *post-industrial society thesis*, argued in the 1970s that this process
would generally improve the quality of life and work in the Western
world. It was anticipated that unpleasant, dirty and routine jobs in
factories would be eliminated. Instead, a greater proportion of workers
would be dealing with people, doing more rewarding work, in better
surroundings, providing assorted services to clients. The post-industrial
society thesis assumed that full employment would be maintained as new,
more desirable, jobs in services multiplied.

However, the realities of deindustrialization in Britain have turned out
rather differently. First, since the service industries are so heterogeneous, no straightforward generalizations are possible about the
changing quality of employment. Many occupations in the service
industries, like cleaning or working in a fast food outlet, are no more
attractive, and are less well remunerated, than traditional manual factory
jobs. Second, as we will see in detail in section 2.9, the main recent effect
in Britain of the decline of employment in manufacturing industry has
been exceptionally high levels of *un*employment. New jobs have not
emerged in sufficient quantity to replace those lost in manufacturing (see
figure 2.10). This may be due partly to the economic recession, but it is
also, importantly, a consequence of changes in people's patterns of
consumption since the early 1960s.

Gershuny (1978) argued that the contraction of some final consumer
services is especially significant. He maintained that the reason why
cinemas, laundries and passenger transport have declined is because
many people now have personal access to machines which provide the
same service, i.e. TV and video, washing machines and motor cars. It
used to be the case that as people's incomes increased they spent more
money on personal services and less on basic necessities like food. (This
observed regularity is usually called Engel's law.) However, Gershuny
noted that while people in Britain had become better-off since the 1950s
and did spend less on food, they did not tend to increase expenditure on
final services. Rather, he claimed, they tended to buy the machinery with

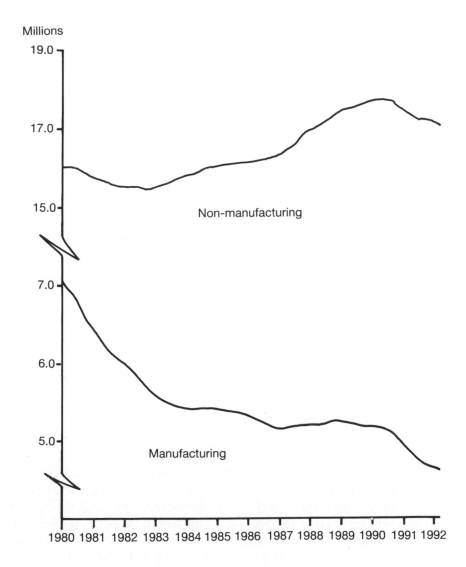

Figure 2.10 Manufacturing and non-manufacturing employees in employment, United Kingdom, seasonally adjusted, 1980–1992.
Source: *Employment Gazette*, January 1993. Crown copyright.

which they could service themselves: a 'self-service' economy was emerging. A clear instance of this is the proportion of average income spent on transport goods (cars, bikes, etc.) as opposed to transport services (trains and buses) over the last quarter century. As table 2.12 shows, people are spending more of their incomes on goods. The economic impact of this is to boost the car manufacturing industry, but to reduce employment in public transport. Since the manufacture of cars is less labour intensive than public transport, jobs have been lost overall. The preference for self-servicing is itself partly due to cost – labour-intensive services are expensive – but is also a matter of personal convenience and new lifestyles based on aspirations to own mass consumption goods.

Table 2.12 Buying goods rather than services: shifts in household expenditure on transport, 1953–1991 (percentage of total household expenditure)

	Purchase and maintenance of vehicles (%)	Fares (%)
1953–4	3.5	3.5
1958	5.1	2.9
1963	8.6	2.6
1968	10.5	2.1
1973	11.2	1.9
1978	11.0	1.8
1985	13.0	2.1
1991	13.5	1.9

Source: Gershuny, 1978; *Family Expenditure Survey*, various years

There has been considerable debate about how widespread are the tendencies outlined by Gershuny. If he were correct, Bell's (1973) post-industrial society thesis would have to be dismissed in so far as prospects for employment in existing service industries would be poor. Evaluation of his case may best be achieved by appreciating the alternative ways that services can be delivered and discovering how households decide whether or not to purchase services.

Modes of service provision

There are several ways in which services can be obtained. For example, if the interior of your house gets painted, you have consumed a service. The painting could be done: (1) by paying a decorating firm; (2) by getting the state to provide a decorating service; (3) by arranging for a friend or neighbour to do it; (4) by you (or another member of your household) doing it yourself. In each case someone does the *work* of

Table 2.13 Four ways in which services may be obtained

Mode of provision	Manner of obtaining service	Who does work	Who pays (if anyone)	Principle upon which service is obtained
Market	Commercial purchase	Paid employees	Consumer	Market exchange
State	State provision	Paid employees	State	Citizenship right
Communal	Personal connections	Neighbours or acquaintances	No money involved	Reciprocal obligation
Domestic	Household do-it-yourself	Members of household	No money involved	Family obligation

painting, but only under modes (1) and (2) will someone be *employed* as a painter. This repeats the distinction made in section 2.1 between employment and work: employment is paid activity registered in the formal economy, but much work is done outside the formal economy. There is some evidence that the proportion of services produced outside the formal economy is growing. This would prevent the benign process anticipated by Bell (1973) of deindustrialization leading to more employment in services.

Table 2.13 illustrates the four different means of obtaining a service. In the past, there have been significant shifts in the type and quantity of services obtained in the different modes. The balance in the quantity of services provided in each mode will affect both employment opportunities and social life. The prospects for the expansion of those modes generating employment are not very encouraging. We will examine each in turn.

The market mode

Many human services, and virtually all intermediate services, are bought in the market place. A meal in a restaurant, a visit to the cinema, attendance at a private school, are all bought at a price set by the market. Access to such services depends upon income: you can buy only those services you can afford. Money is the medium of exchange. Most workers in the market sector are in legal paid employment, though some transactions occur informally (see below). Demand for many marketed services has, as Gershuny noted, remained stable over time, partly as a result of the growth of self-servicing. Use of marketed services is severely restricted among poorer households. Expansion of these services may be expected to continue increasing slowly.

The state mode

Many human services are provided by the state. Access to state services is a matter of rights, established through political channels and exercised by virtue of being an eligible citizen. All citizens have a right to state health care at no (or minimal) cost; all citizens with appropriate qualifications are entitled to free higher education. A large number of people are employed to provide education, health and social services. Since the Second World War, state services have been responsible for the growth of professional and administrative jobs. Such services are paid for ultimately from taxation. Conservative governments since 1979 have been particularly concerned to reduce the cost of state-provided services, to cut public expenditure (see also section 12.5). The consequences include both a reduction in state employment and a curtailment in public services. Deterioration in the quality and quantity of services is more difficult to estimate, but if this trend continues (and it seems likely that it will owing to the problem of financing state services from a declining tax base) then this will become a less important source of human services. Demand may, perhaps, increase in other modes of service provision in response. Those who can afford to may buy private health care, for example. Those who cannot will suffer.

The communal mode

An alternative way to obtain a service is by exchanging services. A baby-sitting circle is arranged on the basis that if you look after my children I will do the same for you another time. But equally you might baby-sit for me and in exchange I will mend your car. Significantly, money is not involved. Access to these services is through personal contacts and social networks. Evidence suggests that not much work gets done this way, but it remains an alternative mode, though one which does not entail employment.

The domestic mode

The fourth alternative is to provide services yourself, for your own household's consumption. Such domestic services range from repairing your own house, through child-care, to cooking and cleaning. All are services you could obtain in other ways – by employing domestic servants, for instance – but which many people do themselves. No money is involved. This sector accounts for a considerable amount of all work done. It is this, the domestic provision of services, which Gershuny believes is increasing and which may prevent any great expansion in the market mode. Growth in the domestic mode of provisioning is a major source of sociological interest, affecting as it does employment opportunities, lifestyles and gender relations.

Service provision on the Isle of Sheppey: a case study

A recent investigation by Pahl and Wallace (1985) of the Isle of Sheppey on the north Kent coast gives reason for deep concern about the social implications of the decline in manufacturing employment. Pahl (1984) explores the ways in which households organize their time and resources in order to 'get by' in present economic circumstances. The central questions he examined were: what services did households consume, and by what means were those services provided?

The Isle of Sheppey has a population of about 33,000. Most jobs on the island used to be in the Admiralty dockyard at Sheerness until it was closed in 1960. Between 1960 and 1981 there was work in the private docks (used for importing cars), in some manufacturing industries (steel and pharmaceuticals), and in the holiday trade. Wages were mostly low and opportunities for women were very limited. Jobs were also precarious and unemployment was above 20 per cent by 1983. The island is rather isolated, which partly accounts for the existence of relatively cheap owner-occupied housing. Although most households were working class, 77 per cent were owner-occupiers.

Pahl (1984) started his study with a concern for how people adapted to recession and unemployment. There had been considerable speculation about the extent of informal paid work. Some people work for money but without declaring their earnings to the Inland Revenue, in order to evade tax. Estimates of the value of such informal paid (and illegal) activity are as high as 7.5 per cent of the national income. It is imagined that the unemployed are specially prone to such behaviour, using their 'free' time to work for an undeclared income. The availability of domestic durable goods like power drills, paint brushes, aluminium ladders, etc. were thought to be a factor permitting people to make a partial or total livelihood from doing odd jobs for neighbours, outside the formal economy. Pahl explored these issues and found these popular beliefs to be almost entirely unfounded. There was very little evidence of the existence of an informal, paid sector. What he did discover, though, was an enormous amount of work being done in the *domestic* mode of provision. To his surprise, he found that it was not the unemployed who did a lot of domestic self-provisioning, despite the time they had available. Rather, the more people in a household who were in formal,

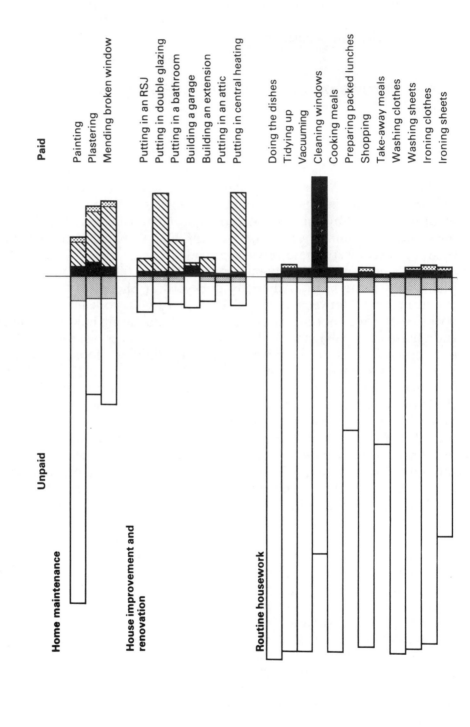

Paid

Home maintenance
Painting
Plastering
Mending broken window

House improvement and renovation
Putting in an RSJ
Putting in double glazing
Putting in a bathroom
Building a garage
Building an extension
Putting in an attic
Putting in central heating

Routine housework
Doing the dishes
Tidying up
Vacuuming
Cleaning windows
Cooking meals
Preparing packed lunches
Shopping
Take-away meals
Washing clothes
Washing sheets
Ironing clothes
Ironing sheets

Unpaid

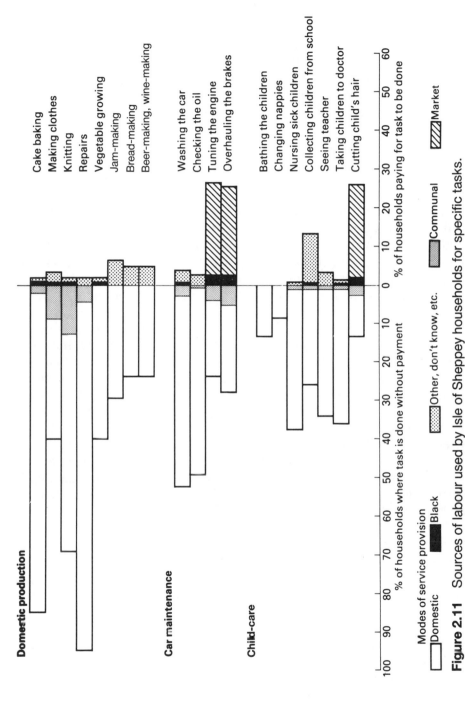

Figure 2.11 Sources of labour used by Isle of Sheppey households for specific tasks.

Source: adapted from Pahl, 1984, pp. 218–19, with permission

Domestic production

Cake baking
Making clothes
Knitting
Repairs
Vegetable growing
Jam-making
Bread-making
Beer-making, wine-making

Car maintenance

Washing the car
Checking the oil
Tuning the engine
Overhauling the brakes

Child-care

Bathing the children
Changing nappies
Nursing sick children
Collecting children from school
Seeing teacher
Taking children to doctor
Cutting child's hair

% of households where task is done without payment

% of households paying for task to be done

Modes of service provision

Domestic   Black   Other, don't know, etc.   Communal   Market

paid employment, the more work they did at home. This was the basis of a social *polarization*. Households with more than one wage earner had relatively high incomes but they also produced more services for themselves – house maintenance, car repairs, home cooking, etc. As a result their standard of living was substantially higher than that of households with little or no paid employment. In other words, extra time available because of unemployment was not used to improve living standards.

The evidence for Pahl's argument came from asking people about the services their households consumed and who did the work to provide those services. He asked his sample of 730 respondents which services, from a list of 41, their household obtained, and then who did that work. Figure 2.11 shows the list of tasks and which mode of provisioning was used. The only service widely obtained from the black economy was window cleaning. Neither the communal mode of provisioning nor the market mode was much used (supporting Gershuny's argument). But households did a vast amount of work themselves in car repairs, house maintenance and domestic production, as well as in routine housework and childcare.

Pahl then proceeded to examine which types of household did which tasks. The pattern was partly as expected. Stages of the life cycle explained some variations: households without children obviously do not change nappies. Income was also important: poorer households cannot afford cars and therefore do not need car maintenance services. Variations in income on the Isle of Sheppey were very largely the result of the number of household members in paid work: social class differences mattered very little. Being in employment increased the degree of self-provisioning even among those activities that might appear to be available to all households regardless of age or income – baking, or decorating. From this, Pahl drew the important conclusion that the capacity to engage in domestic modes of provisioning (and communal or paid informal ones too) is dependent on being in employment as well. Without paid work, people lack the resources and the contacts to engage in unpaid work. The idea that the unemployed can get by through substituting time for money is simply wrong, because they cannot obtain the materials or tools with which to provide services, for themselves or anyone else.

The study of Sheppey corroborated some of Gershuny's speculation about the limited expansion of marketed services and the extensiveness of domestic provisioning. New machines – whether cars or vacuum cleaners – were purchased by households which could afford them, and they were used to undertake more tasks than before in the home.

Pahl also explored how tasks were divided up within the household. He confirms that women do more domestic work than men. The proportion of domestic work done by a married woman depends on whether she also has paid employment and on her age and the stage of the family cycle. Women do the most unequal proportion of domestic labour when young and with small children. (This corresponds to the time when there are most tasks needing doing!) Domestic tasks are less unequally shared after children have left home and when the wife is in full-time paid employment.

Pahl, then, gives reasons for believing that recession and deindustrialization will have socially divisive effects. Those households with members in paid employment do relatively well, particularly as they use their resources through self-provisioning to further enhance their standards of living. Households without employment subside into a state of deprivation and are unable to do much to improve their position. Both kinds of households spend lots of time at home, the former vigorously pursuing a comfortable domestic lifestyle, the latter virtually imprisoned in a deteriorating domestic environment. Domestication and home ownership are highly unattractive without the resources which are still only obtainable at a satisfactory level through regular employment. Thus life without employment, or a society 'beyond employment', looks bleak. Pahl and Wallace (1985, p. 224) sum the situation up:

> On the Isle of Sheppey, beyond employment most likely means poverty, isolation, little opportunity for informal work, involuntarily home-centred, with deteriorating dwellings and capital goods. Multiple earners bring prosperity, however short-lived: no earner brings a downward spiral of economic and social detachment.

Summary

1   A growth of employment in service industries has partially compensated for severe job loss in British manufacturing since the mid 1960s, but there is a considerable shortfall which is registered in increasing rates of unemployment.

2   There is considerable debate over the implications of the increased proportion of workers in the service sector.

3   There are several ways in which people may obtain services: we have distinguished the market, the state, the communal and the domestic modes of service provision. The social relations involved in each are different. Only the first two provide employment.

4   There may be a tendency for more work to be done in the domestic mode, especially as part of a move to *self*-servicing. Since domestic

and informal service provision require resources – materials, tools, etc. – households without one or more members in paid employment are prevented from engaging in such 'do-it-yourself' work and, hence, tend to grow relatively more poor.

Related topics

More material on occupational change can be found in section 3.2. Regarding the domestic mode of service provision, discussion of gender differences occurs in sections 4.3 and 6.4 on households and housework, respectively. The state's role in providing services is discussed in sections 12.4 and, especially, 12.5. A more detailed study of one largely state-provided service – health care – is to be found in chapter 9.

2.9 Unemployment

Unemployment is a condition suffered by a considerable proportion of the British population. It is persistently perceived as the most important political issue in Britain (table 2.14): only in 1990 was unemployment not deemed the single most pressing issue (when the cost of living and the poll tax were given priority). It is an unenviable condition because it entails both material hardship and loss of social status. Lack of money is one reason why people seek to avoid it, but there remains a motivation to work beyond mere income, as evidence from many surveys have shown.

Table 2.14   Percentage of people answering 'unemployment' to the question 'What would you say is the most urgent problem facing the country at the present time?', 1981–1992

Year (July)	%	Year (July)	%
1981	69	1987	67
1982	70	1988	41
1983	80	1989	21
1984	60	1990	12
1985	79	1991	35
1986	75	1992	46

Source: *Gallup Political Index Reports*, each July from 1981 to 1992

Current trends in unemployment are, therefore, most disturbing. Demographic change and economic restructuring are likely to keep levels high throughout the next decade unless political strategies change dramatically.

The rate of unemployment

One of the objectives of the political settlement after World War II in Britain was to achieve full employment and thereby eliminate the insecurity and hardship associated with unemployment. Since then, levels of unemployment have fluctuated from month to month and year to year. However, between 1945 and 1975 the overall level was negligible, the mean being about 3 per cent. Subsequently there was a rise, and a much higher plateau was reached during the 1980s when levels approached those of the slump of the 1930s. This is partly the result of the Conservative governments of the period having other priorities.

Figure 2.12 shows the numbers officially unemployed between 1982 and 1992. These are hard to compare directly with earlier years because the method of calculation was adjusted by the government so that fewer persons would be recorded as unemployed. The new method of compiling the figures counted only those claiming benefit and seeking full-time work, instead of those 'registered for work', thereby excluding, from October 1982, those seeking part-time work, married women ineligible for benefit, and the formerly self-employed. In 1983, people over 59 were effectively removed from the count, as were those under 18 after 1988 when they became ineligible for benefit. The figures are thus conservative estimates. Many people who want and are seeking a job are not counted as unemployed.

Personal and social consequences of unemployment

The unpleasant consequences of unemployment have been demonstrated in many studies. A substantial proportion of the unemployed live in poverty, surviving only on minimal state benefits. The longer unemployment lasts, the deeper the poverty. This is illustrated by the expenditure patterns of the unemployed. Households whose head has been unemployed for less than a year are clearly poorer than the average household, but a fair amount better-off than those whose head has been out of work for a longer period. Shortage of money is the most pressing problem associated with being unemployed. Figure 2.13 compares levels of

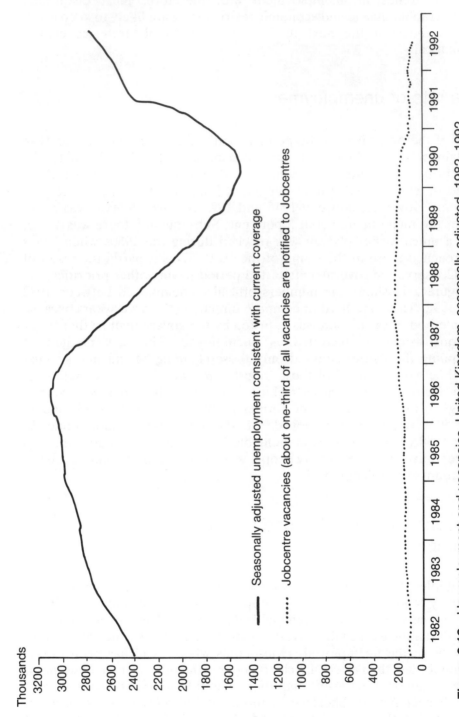

Figure 2.12 Unemployment and vacancies, United Kingdom, seasonally adjusted, 1982–1992.

Source: Employment Gazette, September 1992. Crown copyright.

Seasonally adjusted unemployment consistent with current coverage

Jobcentre vacancies (about one-third of all vacancies are notified to Jobcentres

Mean score

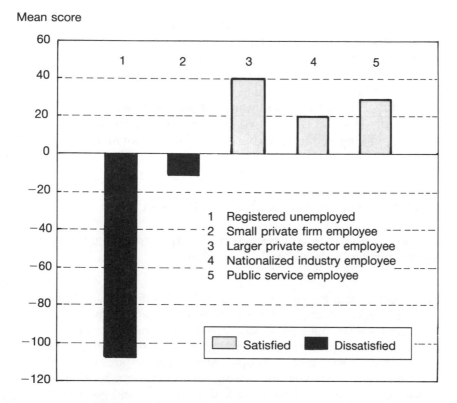

Figure 2.13 Levels of satisfaction with family income: aggregate of scores ranging from +200 for 'very satisfied' to −200 for 'very dissatisfied'.
Source: Daniel, 1990, p. 89. Crown copyright.

satisfaction with household income between the unemployed and various categories of employees. This derives from a large survey in the early 1980s, reported by Daniel (1990), which demonstrates unequivocally both that state benefits provide the most meagre levels of support to families and that most people of working age are desperate to avoid unemployment and, if unfortunate enough to lose a job, make strenuous efforts to find another quickly.

Besides financial hardship, the unemployed are likely to suffer many other misfortunes. They are less healthy than the employed. They are also more likely to get divorced: increased conflict between husband and wife is regularly reported by the unemployed, quarrels arising partly because of worries about money, partly because of the demoralization of unemployed men in particular. Boredom, sickness, sleeplessness, isolation, anxiety and loss of self-confidence are among the main complaints normally associated with a period of unemployment. It used to be thought that these conditions became worse the longer a person was unemployed, but the recent research of Daniel (1990) suggests that these distressing features take effect immediately and do not intensify. The intensity of these complaints varies. The impact is greater for men than women, greater for married than single men, but greater for single than married women.

It remains a source of dishonour, for married men especially, to be unemployed. Thus, consider two men made redundant in Newcastle upon Tyne, talking about the experience of unemployment (see box 2.5).

Box 2.5   The experience of unemployment

A man, in his fifties, reflecting on his experience of unemployment after having been made redundant, said:

> It affected me a lot when I was unemployed. I didn't think I was going to get another job. It was very depressing and got worse the longer I was unemployed. It wasn't so much the money or the way I felt. It was degrading – in the dole office or when people asked me what I was doing. People would say – 'are you still unemployed?' 'Are you not looking for work?' I was looking. It was very degrading. I have worked all my life and got angry. People who have never been unemployed don't know what it is like; they have never experienced it . . . When you are unemployed you are bored, frustrated, and worried, worried sick: at least I was. Of course it is worse for the man who has got a family: he has got responsibilities. So you worry for the wife and the bairns. (Sinfield, 1981, p. 41)

Another man in similar circumstances, who had later found himself another, but inferior, job:

> When I was unemployed I was very worried: I thought that was it, I didn't expect to get another job. I slept in late until about 11 a.m. I got very bored. Hours in the early afternoon were the worst – hours when I thought that I used to be working. I wasn't ready for retiring yet: I can still work, I wanted to work. I got very jealous of those who were working. My wife is right when she said it affects me *as a man*: it isn't the money so much as the feeling men have. (Sinfield, 1981, p. 41)

Even though, in July 1992, there were 26 people unemployed for each vacancy notified to Jobcentres, stigma remains.

Unemployment is least distressing to the young, but they too suffer significantly. Allatt and Yeandle (1992) demonstrated this in their study of the effect of youth unemployment on working-class families in north-east England. Unemployed young men and women described their experience in the language of illness. They felt sick, fed up and depressed. Also, like invalids, they withdrew from family situations, often to bed. Ironically, one of the main sources of irritation among other family members was that those without work stayed in bed in the mornings. While kin felt pity for the unemployed and offered, in many cases, generous economic and emotional support, the lowly status associated with unemployment was inescapable. As Allatt and Yeandle observe, getting a job is a basis for the renegotiation of positions within families, part of a transition from childhood dependence to adulthood. To be employed enhances personal autonomy, gives some financial independence and opportunities for consumption and carries some positive, moral virtue associated with earning a living. It also brings extra power within the household in negotiations with parents, conveying additional rights. The personal effects of unemployment are distressing.

The social costs of unemployment are, not surprisingly, considerable. Besides the expense of unemployment benefits and the wasting of people's skills, illness, crime and family breakdown create severe social problems. Given how unpleasant it is to be unemployed, more resistance to the rapid increase in unemployment in the 1980s might have been anticipated. For three decades after 1945 it was believed that no government could survive with employment rates much above 3 per cent because neither the electorate, nor the unemployed themselves, would tolerate mass unemployment. Yet, despite unemployment being seen as the principal political issue, and notwithstanding the inner-city riots of 1981, 1985 and 1991, the political response has been negligible.

Political consequences of unemployment

The absence of political unrest may be attributed to a number of factors, which themselves tell us more about unemployment.

First, there has been a significant, and apparently successful, campaign by government to reduce popular expectations about what can be done to alleviate the situation. Unemployment has been presented as an inevitable outcome of recession. Opinion polls suggest that many people, though deeply concerned about the problem, believe that no government policy can make any difference. Fatalism prevails.

Second, the unemployed have not, at least since the 1930s, organized themselves to protest. This is partly because unemployment is, for almost everyone, a temporary condition. In the 1980s at least, people were unlikely to identify themselves as belonging to a permanent social category with a common political interest. Most people flow on to the unemployment register and off again quite quickly. Relatively few people are unemployed for a long period of time. Older people become discouraged, defining themselves as ill or settling for early retirement. Young people shift in and out of casual and temporary jobs. Those with family responsibilities spend their time urgently seeking a new position rather than considering their political options.

   Third, those most susceptible are likely to have had repeated experience of unemployment. Risk varies depending on previous job. The chances of unskilled manual workers being unemployed at any time, or for long periods of time, are higher than for any other group. People lacking skill are most vulnerable. As Daniel (1990) shows, in periods of recession, if skilled workers lose their jobs, they reason that any job is better than none and are therefore mostly prepared to accept less skilled and poorer paid employment. In competition for available work they are

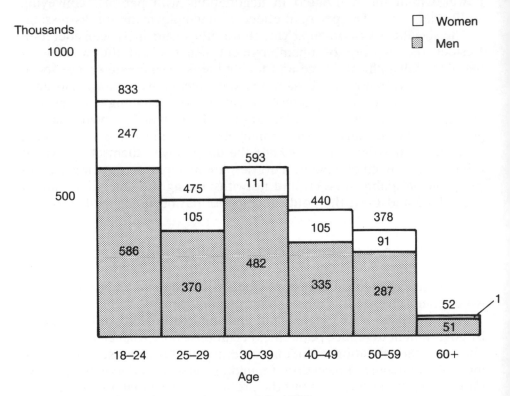

Figure 2.14 Unemployment by age, July 1992.
Source: *Employment Gazette*, September 1992. Crown copyright.

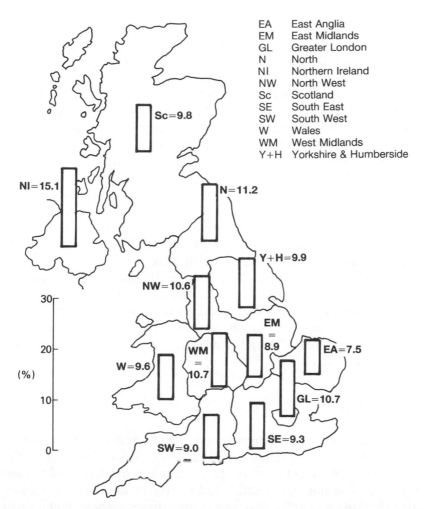

Figure 2.15   Regional variations in unemployment, July 1992 (per cent): for official data collection and planning, Britain is divided into 12 standard planning regions which vary in their demographic, economic, social and political characteristics.
Source: *Employment Gazette*, September 1992, table 2.3. Crown copyright.

preferred by employers, making it extremely difficult for the less skilled to find any sort of job. What are customary problems of irregular and temporary work for the less skilled are exacerbated, but not changed in nature, at times of high unemployment.

Risk also varies with age and gender. The young and older men are most likely to be unemployed. Figure 2.14 shows the numbers among different age groups in July 1992. One in five young people aged 18–19 were unemployed; and the rates for those under 25 were higher than for any other age group. The group next most at risk are those aged over 50.

There is also variation by gender, but this is a statistical artefact of the refusal to count married women. There is reason to believe that women suffer from enforced unemployment just as badly, though no worse, than men.

Fourth, the impact of unemployment is uneven regionally and locally. As the map in figure 2.15 indicates, the rate of unemployment in East Anglia is less than half that of Northern Ireland. There are even more extreme variations *within* regions. In Scotland, Aberdeen had a rate of 3.8 per cent whereas in Cumnock and Sanquhar it was 18.6 per cent. In Wales, Newtown had a rate of 4.6 per cent, Holyhead one of 14.4 per cent. The worst area of all in the UK was Strabane, in Northern Ireland, where 23.9 per cent of the workforce was without a job. The geographical concentration of unemployment does find some political expression, in that areas of high unemployment often elect Labour MPs. But regional differences do tend to be divisive.

Thus, despite some attempts to organize the unemployed during the 1980s, their responses tend to be limited because they comprise a diverse set of people who consider their condition temporary and who pursue a personalized solution of finding another job. For most this is attainable, though the experience of being unemployed, no matter for how short a period, is very upsetting.

The end of work?

Many writers doubt that unemployment can be reduced in the foreseeable future. As figure 2.16 shows, by 1991 the civilian labour force (those in or seeking employment) was about 27.5 million people, 2 million more than in 1981. The number is estimated to rise by another 0.5 million in the decade up to 2001. At the same time, many technological developments already under way are designed to reduce labour requirements. The gap between the demand for labour and its supply which has increased in recent years may get even greater. Whether this will be the case depends partly on the effects of new technology, and partly on political decisions.

New technology

Micro-electronics is one, and perhaps the most spectacular, area of technological development at present. Its potential capacity is enormous for creating new products, changing production techniques and altering employment patterns. The development of 'microchips' – pieces of silicon, the size of fingernails, on to which are imprinted very complex electrical circuits – has reduced the size and price of electronic

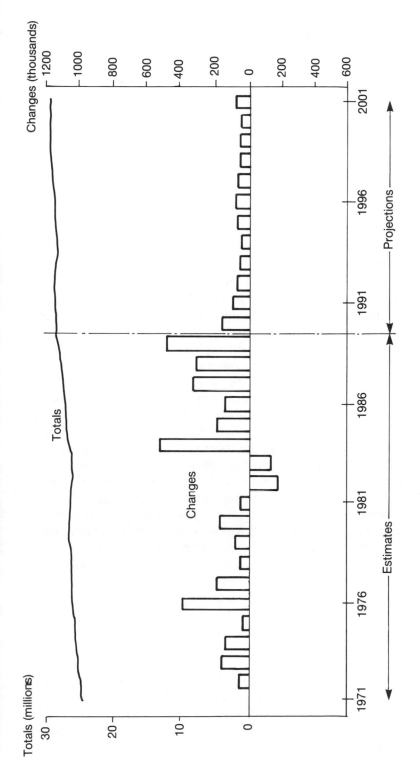

Figure 2.16 Estimates and projections of the civilian labour force, Great Britain, 1971–2001. *Source: Employment Gazette*, April 1990. Crown copyright.

equipment, at the same time increasing its flexibility and power. The home computer is just one, rather mundane, example. Today's desk-top computer costing £500 has greater computational power than mainframe machines from 20 years ago which cost 1000 times more and required a room the size of a gymnasium to house. The possibilities of the new cheap machines in the field of, say, communications are remarkable: shopping from home, individualized packaged educational programmes, programmes for medical self-diagnosis, electronic postal services, and participation in political decisions by computer, are but some of the uses envisaged today. We can do no more than guess about the likely social consequences. For example, it might make for yet more home-centred lifestyles, with clerical, technical and managerial work being done in the front room and the output being transmitted as computerized messages to co-workers and customers. The consequence which is probably most debated is its effect on employment.

Pessimistic interpretations observe the many current jobs which are threatened by the new technology. Robots in factories, stock control systems in warehousing, computerization in the office can all be expected to replace considerable quantities of human labour. In many cases, human skills will be rendered obsolete and work will be further degraded. Optimists point to the creation of new skilled jobs and the abolition of old, routine, unpleasant work. They also argue that technological innovation in the past has not reduced employment overall, because new and previously unimagined products and processes get developed. To date, microtechnology has probably had a limited impact on available employment; it has, in the short run, created as many jobs as it has destroyed. Current unemployment rates are primarily due to other causes. However, little of this technology is yet in use in Britain, owing partly to low levels of investment and partly to worker resistance. When it becomes widespread – which may take a few years yet – it might be expected to have a massive impact. Because it tends towards greater ease of centralized control through improved communication, it will almost certainly reduce discretion at work, even where it does not abolish jobs altogether. We tend to be pessimistic, but it seems entirely safe to predict that the new technology will not *reduce* unemployment.

Political remedies

It is equally difficult to predict the direction of political interventions. It would seem, however, that new radical policies are necessary if unemployment is to be reduced. Recovery by private industry after economic recession alone will have little effect, since increased competi- tiveness probably entails less, rather than more, employment. Changes in people's patterns of work seem essential. Shorter hours, fewer working weeks per year, etc. could share available work out more evenly but, since these too would entail lower wages, they are unlikely to be welcomed in the absence of a sharp change in attitudes to work. The outlook is bleak for those unable to get a job in a society where paid employment remains the basis of a tolerable standard of living. For, even if the unemployed were treated more generously – and there would be more popular support for this now than in the 1970s – their situation would only improve in the context of other broad social changes.

Government training packages have also been introduced in the belief that national economic performance would be improved if the British labour force was, as a whole, better qualified, more flexible and therefore better able to respond to new opportunities. By 1992 there were 325,000 people on work-related government training schemes. Most of these were on Youth Training (YT), introduced as the Youth Training Scheme (YTS) in 1984. YTS guaranteed all school-leavers a place on the scheme, which involves a mixture of work experience and further education, for which minimal wages are paid. Since 1988 young people, aged 16–18, have been denied any form of unemployment benefit, so that participating in YT has been the only source of income for the under 18s without a paid job. This illustrates some of the limitations of the British solution to training.

The scheme arose to deal with two different problems: to improve the general skill levels of entrants to the British labour force and to reduce the number of young people who are unemployed. As Raffe (1990) points out, these two objectives are in tension with one another. To the extent that YT experience is seen as a way of mopping up youth unemployment, then it will have low status, employers will not be very keen to recruit its trainees, and therefore young people will pursue other avenues to employment if they have other opportunities. This reduces the status of the scheme. Therefore it will fail to achieve its other objective, to expand the pool of high-quality, transferable skills perceived necessary for economic development. For, regardless of the quality of the skills training offered by YT, young people shun it. They will prefer other options which improve their personal employment prospects, regardless of whether these make any contribution to enhancing the skills of the British workforce as a whole. The collective benefits of a more skilful national labour force are thereby forgone. This contradiction is to some degree attenuated because there are, in fact, several different types of programme within YT. Those schemes which lead directly to a job for the trainee at the end of the course, or which pass on skills in short supply in a local labour market, do attract applicants and persuade employers that they are recruiting valuable new workers that could not be acquired from any other source.

Another problem is that training schemes cannot compensate for the lack of available jobs. Since the only reason for an individual to attend a training scheme is to get a more desirable job than would otherwise be available, any scheme must improve job opportunities. Completing training does improve a trainee's chances of getting a job, but many fail to find employment afterwards. YT can make no perceptible short-term contribution to creating new, permanent jobs. This is not to say that government schemes for unemployed youth are a bad thing; rather, such policies are not a short-term solution to high levels of unemployment.

Summary

1 Unemployment is a major social and political problem, the numbers registered being greater than at any period in the past.
2 Unemployment is unevenly spread. Age, class, previous occupation, gender and region are all bases of variation in unemployment rates.
3 The personal and social consequences of long-term unemployment are distressing and wasteful.
4 There is a debate about likely future levels of unemployment. The effects of technological change and political intervention are unpredictable, but do not seem likely to reduce unemployment levels in the near future.

Related topics

Some of the problems faced by young people in gaining access to employment are discussed in section 8.3. On the relationship between unemployment and poverty see section 3.3, and on the relationship between unemployment and health see section 9.5.

Further Reading

The topic of ownership and control is surveyed by Scott (1991). Reed (1989) offers a general introduction to the literature on managers and their activities. A good summary of the labour process debate is Thompson (1989). Evidence about flexibility is advanced by Allen and Massey (1988), especially Richard Meegan's chapter 4 on the end of Fordism in the motor industry. Wood (1990) contains an interesting set of essays on the same topic. The major recent survey giving general information about workplace industrial relations is Millward et al. (1992). Johnson (1972) remains the best short overview of professions.

For a brief review of the debate about professions and a discussion of the general link between knowledge and control, see Turner (1985). Kumar (1978) offers a good critical appraisal of versions of the post-industrial society thesis. Gershuny (1978) and Pahl (1984) both contribute considerably to understanding what kinds of services people produce and consume. A good survey of sociological issues surrounding unemployment is White (1991).

3 Class

3.1 Introduction

Social class is the most debated concept in sociology. There are two important and connected issues with regard to class that will concern us in this chapter. First, there is the problem as to whether the class structure is simple or complex. Are the boundaries between classes fuzzy or sharp? Does our society consist of a number of discrete, separate classes or is it just a set of continuously graded layers? Second, we have to ask if social class is as important in social life as it once was. Have other forms of social differentiation, like gender or ethnicity, become as important as class or, perhaps, even more important?

Class structure: simple or complex?

One way of illuminating this first issue is to consider two extreme models of the class structure. Although it is actually a very misleading account of his work, Marx is often credited with the idea that modern, capitalist societies have two social classes – a large proletariat or working class, and a small bourgeoisie or capitalist class. Some of Marx's followers may have adopted a theory like this, although even they generally argue that the two significant classes have smaller groups between them that do not properly belong either to the proletariat or to the bourgeoisie. More recent sociologists working within a Marxist framework have suggested that there is a fairly large, permanent, and socially significant middle class between the working and capitalist classes. Even with the recognition of a middle class, however, most Marxist theories propose relatively simple models of the class structure with a few, fairly well-defined classes organized around the antagonistic relationship between capital and labour.

In terms of simplicity or complexity, the opposite of Marxist theories are those accounts that argue that there are a multiplicity of social classes. A theory of this kind is proposed by Roberts et al. (1977). Here the class structure is seen, not as a set of relatively few, coherent groupings but rather as a collection of fragments. The authors argue that the middle-class/working-class, manual/white-collar divide does represent a significant break in the class structure. But this does not mean that one can treat either class as a unified block. The middle class, especially, is much more fragmented than unified and it is difficult to speak of it as a class at all.

Most sociological theories of class fall somewhere between a simple two-class model and a multi-class or fragmentary model. It is usually argued that there are three classes, the middle class being created by the growth in new white-collar occupations since the beginning of the century. These classes, however, are not coherent entities but are themselves divided. It is conventional, for example, to see the distinction between skilled and non-skilled workers as representing an important division within the working class. There may also be intermediate groupings not clearly attracted to any social class: self-employed workers, for instance.

The salience of class divisions

It is often proposed that social class is no longer as important as it was even 30 years ago (the 'decline of class' thesis). Such a proposition is based on a variety of arguments. The ownership and control of capital have moved away from families and towards pension funds and investment trusts. The relative 'decline' of the manufacturing sector and growth of employment in government and the service sector has meant a greater diversification of work and has increased the differences between different groups of workers. Variations in economic performance have sharpened the boundary between those in relatively secure occupational careers and the unemployed or sub-employed. Some of these changes are also affected by gender. For example, the shift from the manufacturing sector to the service sector has been associated with a decline in relatively skilled male manufacturing jobs and an increase in less skilled, lower-paid female jobs in the service industries. These processes, amongst others, it is agreed, are creating a greatly more diverse class structure. Their net effect 'is to fragment traditional "bourgeois" and "proletarian" groupings and redraw the boundaries of common interest in new ways not specifically reducible to established differences of class. The "new middle" and "new working" classes have been created,' (Marshall et al., 1988, p. 4).

The 'decline of class' thesis does not simply propose that increasing complexity and diversity have made the definition of class a much more difficult matter. It also argues that class *identity* has become a less straightforward matter, that is, people do not identify themselves with a particular social class as strongly as they used to.

The most important recent study of the British class structure (Marshall et al., 1988), to the contrary, has provided evidence that class identity remains strong. They interviewed 1770 people of working age in England, Scotland and Wales during 1984. They conclude:

> There is no obvious lack of class awareness among the population of modern Britain as a whole. Sixty per cent of our sample claimed that they thought of themselves as belonging to one particular social class, and well over 90 per cent could place themselves in a particular class category. The proportions who refused to do so, or stated that they did not know to which class they belonged, were very small. Almost three-quarters (73 per cent) of the respondents felt class to be an inevitable feature of modern society; 52 per cent thought that there were important issues causing conflict between social classes (only 37 per cent actually disagreed with this); and, perhaps most strikingly of all, half of the sample agreed with a question . . . which was formulated so as to invite respondents to disagree with the judgment that today, as in the past, there is a dominant class which largely controls the economic and political system, and a lower class which has no control over economic and political affairs. (p. 143)

Sociologists usually understand the class structure as a system of inequality. In Britain, people in the working class tend to earn less money than those in the middle class, for example. Of course, class is not the only source of inequality between people. Gender or ethnic differences also provide a basis for unequal access to resources, or unequal treatment. We demonstrate in other chapters in this book (especially chapter 4) that, for example, women are paid less than men, even for the same kind of work. Women also suffer other disadvantages. They are, for instance, treated radically differently from men in public places. It seems very likely that factors such as gender have become more important. They are certainly more significant as sources of social conflict; women are more aware of their inequality of condition and opportunity. Our argument in this book is, however, that social class membership remains an important determinant of life chances – the benefits of all kinds that an individual may have in life. For example, chapter 9 shows that the chances of remaining in good health vary with social class, chapter 8 discusses the relationship between social class and educational attainment, and chapter 12 reviews the evidence on the influence of social class on political behaviour. We thus share Marshall et al.'s (1988) conclusion that although some elements of the 'decline of class' thesis are plausible, Britain is still largely a class-divided society: 'Britain remains a capitalist *class* society, and the various attempts to identify "post-industrial" (and post-capitalist) features in the developments of recent years are not at all convincing' (p. 11).

One's view of the complexity of the class structure or the significance of class clearly depends partly on what definition of social class is adopted. In this chapter we will largely follow Lockwood's (1958) celebrated definition of class membership in terms of market situation and work situation. Market situation refers to 'the economic position narrowly conceived, consisting of source and size of income, degree of job security, and opportunity for upward occupational mobility' (p. 15). Work situation comprises 'the set of social relationships in which the individual is involved at work by virtue of his position in the division of labour' (p. 15) and refers to such matters as the degree of independence or control that a worker has over his or her work or the degree of skill that is deployed. Lockwood also mentions status situation, or position in the hierarchy of prestige, in connection with the determination of class. Although we will discuss questions of status, we do not see them as entering into the determination of class but rather as effects of class position. People do, or do not, have status because they occupy particular class positions.

The most obvious characteristic of Lockwood's definition is that it refers to occupations; class position is dependent on the market and work situations of occupations. We start this chapter, therefore, with an account of the occupational structure. The following section, on the distribution of income and wealth, discusses the most important element of market situation, namely income. The subsequent three sections deal with the three major social classes, and we conclude with a discussion of social mobility – the movement of people from one class to another.

3.2 Social Class and Occupational Structure

Occupational position does not encompass all aspects of the concept of class, but it is probably the best indicator of it . . . The hierarchy of prestige strata and the hierarchy of economic classes have their roots in the occupational structure; so does the hierarchy of political power and authority . . . The occupational structure also is the link between the economy and the family, through which the economy affects the family's status and the family supplies manpower to the economy. (Blau and Duncan, 1967)

For most people in modern Britain their occupation, and the occupations of other members of their household or family determine the resources available to them. Occupational position is a central determinant of inequalities in income, lifestyle and class relations.

Most empirical measures of 'objective' class position depend on manipulating answers to questions about occupations. Occupation is what a worker does and is identified by the label given to a particular job: radiographer, crane driver, typist, etc. There are thousands of such jobs. Notice that the occupation refers to what a person is described as doing at work; no reference is made to the 'industrial sector' in which the person is employed. One can be a crane driver at the docks or in the construction industry, for example. ('Industry' is defined by the final product or service.) For most purposes of sociological analysis, it is desirable to group occupations together to talk about aggregates of people who have roughly similar occupations, and thus similar material resources and working conditions. There are many ways to group occupations together: official statistics use several different techniques.

Reid (1989, pp. 52–74) provides an extensive list of the ways in which different social surveys (conducted by sociologists and by government departments) have combined occupational groupings into social classes. Advertising agencies and opinion poll surveys use a scale whereby a person is allocated to a category (A, B, C1, etc.) largely on the basis of estimates of the prestige of her or his occupation. British official statistics use a class schema that is built on a combination of employment status and occupation (sometimes in terms of the Registrar-General's social class categories, sometimes as socio-economic groups). Sociologists scrutinize such categories closely because of the need for precision in describing the class structure. Formidable technical problems are associated with the questions of how many classes are there and where their boundaries lie.

Employment status and occupational class

The *employment status* of workers refers to two conditions. First, it denotes whether a person is an employer, self-employed, or an employee. Second, it distinguishes between people with authority (i.e. in managerial and supervisory positions) and those who are in a subordinate position. Data on employment status tell us about features of the labour force relevant to issues of ownership, managerial control and authority at work (see sections 2.3 and 2.5).

Table 3.1 Occupational class and industrial status by sex, 1981

	Employers (000s)	Own account (000s)	Managers (000s)	Foremen (000s)	Other employees (000s)	Unemployed (000s)	All (000s)
Men							
Higher professions	89.0	52.7	33.7	–	686.3	23.5	885.2
Lower professions	21.8	63.5	117.6	25.1	913.4	46.0	1,187.4
Employers, proprietors	443.1	231.9	–	–	–	–	675.0
Managers, administrators	–	61.9	1,652.0	–	332.3	102.1	2,138.3
Clerical	–	7.8	–	100.8	733.5	45.1	887.2
Foremen, inspectors	–	0.6	–	604.8	150.9	54.4	810.6
Skilled manual	–	361.0	–	–	3,176.6	421.0	3,958.6
Semi-skilled manual	–	150.7	–	–	2,852.6	395.5	3,398.9
Unskilled manual	–	47.0	–	–	864.1	674.5	1,585.6
All men	553.9	977.0	1,803.3	730.7	9,699.7	1,762.0	15,526.7
Women							
Higher professions	5.9	10.5	4.2	–	79.3	3.3	103.2
Lower professions	11.5	36.3	73.5	73.4	1,309.2	45.0	1,548.9
Employers, proprietors	131.1	98.1	–	–	–	–	229.1
Managers, administrators	–	28.3	413.3	–	47.8	19.9	509.3
Clerical	–	23.7	–	113.6	2,632.4	104.1	2,873.8
Foremen, inspectors	–	0.2	–	135.6	110.1	15.8	261.7
Skilled manual	–	10.0	–	–	463.9	37.0	510.9
Semi-skilled manual	–	20.6	–	–	2,535.9	165.4	2,721.9
Unskilled manual	–	7.2	–	–	775.8	337.1	1,120.1
All women	148.5	235.0	491.1	322.6	7,954.4	727.4	9,878.9
Total men and women	702.4	1,212.0	2,294.4	1,053.3	17,654.1	2,489.4	25,405.6

Source: Routh, 1987, pp. 42–3

Table 3.1 identifies employment status in 1981. It shows that, in all, 1.9 million people were either employers or self-employed (own account), some 8.4 per cent of all people in work. The majority (about two-thirds) of the self-employed are without employees. Working on their own account, without paid help (though some may use family labour: section 2.3), this proportion of the population might properly be termed *petit bourgeois*. They are workers with very small businesses, a group which Marxists thought would disappear with the growth of organized capitalism, and the same group which recent Conservative governments have encouraged to expand in the hope that they would generate economic growth and reduce unemployment. In fact during the twentieth century until 1981, there was little change in the size of this group. In 1911, there were some 1,207,000 self-employed, 6.2 per cent of those in employment; by 1981 there were 1,212,000, or 5.3 per cent. Evidence from the *General Household Survey* indicates a striking increase since 1981. Table 3.2 shows the changing rate of self-employment since 1975, suggesting that 12.5 per cent of all economically active people were self-employed by 1988.

Returning to table 3.1, in 1981 91.7 per cent of workers were employees, selling their labour power for wages. There are, however,

Table 3.2 Composition of the labour force: economic activity and employment status for men and non-married and married women (economically active persons aged 16 or over), Great Britain, 1975–1988

Economic activity and employment status	1975 (%)	1979 (%)	1981 (%)	1983 (%)	1985 (%)	1986 (%)	1987 (%)	1988 (%)
Men:								
Employees	86	85	79	75	77	74	75	75
Self-employed	10	10	11	12	12	14	15	17
Unemployed	4	5	10	13	11	11	10	8
Base = 100% (no.)	9302	8486	8914	7052	7071	7218	7391	6999
Non-married women:								
Employees	91	90	84	80	82	84	85	85
Self-employed	3	2	2	3	3	4	3	4
Unemployed	5	8	13	16	14	12	11	11
Base = 100% (no.)	1843	1871	2107	1628	1792	1828	1842	1771
Married women:								
Employees	93	91	88	86	87	86	86	87
Self-employed	5	6	6	7	7	8	8	8
Unemployed	3	3	6	6	6	6	6	4
Base = 100% (no.)	4318	3999	4052	3254	3271	3515	3701	3574

Source: General Household Survey, 1988, HMSO, 1990, p. 195

distinctions within the category of employees. A substantial proportion of people were in managerial, supervisory or professional roles, thus exercising some authority or control at work. While most such people are far from being powerful, they are above the bottom rank in hierarchies of authority at work. In total, 77 per cent of all workers were without any degree of authority, though this does not necessarily mean that they were without discretion at work (see section 2.5).

There are significant differences between men and women with respect to employment status. For example, 11 per cent of men but only 4 per cent of women were self-employed. More striking still, only 70 per cent of men were in positions without *any* authority attached, whereas 87 per cent of women were in such a situation. The general point that women tend not to get positions of authority is borne out strongly by these figures. In fact, of some 6 million occupational positions which had some degree of control or authority, only 1.2 million (23 per cent) were filled by women.

Occupational Change

Table 3.3 Occupational classes: 1981 as percentage of 1951

Higher professions	227.6
Lower professions	258.4
Employers and proprietors	80.9
Managers and administrators	212.5
Clerical workers	156.4
Foremen, inspectors, supervisors	181.7
Skilled manual	79.6
Semi-skilled manual	86.2
Unskilled manual	91.8
All	112.8

Source: Routh, 1987, p. 37

The occupational structure changes over time, a result of the constant restructuring of economic organizations and the changing demand for products and services. The principal trends between 1951 and 1981 in size of occupational classes are summed up in table 3.3. This table shows fastest increases in the number of professional jobs, particularly owing to the expansion of employment in the health and welfare services in that period. There has also, though, been a growth in the numbers of scientists and engineers. There was also a significant growth in

Table 3.4 Occupational classes by sex, 1951, 1971 and 1981

	1951			1971			1981		
	All	M	F	All	M	F	All	M	F
Higher professions (000s)	434	399	36	824	774	50	988	885	103
(%)	1.93	2.56	0.52	3.29	4.87	0.55	3.89	5.70	1.04
Lower professions (000s)	1059	492	567	1946	946	1000	2736	1187	1549
(%)	4.70	3.16	8.18	7.78	5.95	10.94	10.77	7.64	15.68
Employers etc. (000s)	1118	894	223	1056	805	251	904	675	229
(%)	4.97	5.74	3.22	4.22	5.07	2.75	3.56	4.35	2.32
Managers etc. (000s)	1246	1056	189	2054	1733	321	2648	2138	509
(%)	5.53	6.78	2.73	8.21	10.91	3.51	10.42	13.77	5.15
Clerical (000s)	2404	990	1414	3479	1013	2466	3761	887	2874
(%)	10.68	6.35	20.40	13.90	6.38	26.99	14.80	5.71	29.09
Foremen etc. (000s)	590	511	79	968	801	168	1072	811	262
(%)	2.62	3.28	1.14	3.87	5.04	1.84	4.22	5.22	2.65
Skilled manual (000s)	5616	4733	884	5410	4647	763	4470	3959	511
(%)	24.94	30.37	12.76	21.62	29.25	8.35	17.59	25.50	5.17
Semi-skilled manual (000s)	7098	4294	2805	6162	3285	2877	6121	3399	2722
(%)	31.53	27.55	40.48	24.63	20.68	31.48	24.09	21.89	27.55
Unskilled manual (000s)	2949	2215	733	3125	1882	1243	2706	1586	1120
(%)	13.10	14.21	10.58	12.49	11.85	13.60	10.65	10.21	11.34
All (000s)	22513	15584	6930	25021	15884	9138	25406	15527	9879
(%)	100	100	100	100	100	100	100	100	100

Source: Routh, 1987, p. 38

managerial and supervisory positions. As firms and plants got bigger, more managerial staff were recruited to coordinate operations, buy and sell, deal with workers, plan production etc. Routine clerical work continued to increase, while there was a substantial decline in the number of people involved in manual work.

Many of these changes are the continuation of longer-run trends which have been apparent throughout the twentieth century. Professional and managerial positions have been expanding steadily since the late nineteenth century. So too has clerical work, especially for women. Meanwhile manual employment has remained about constant in absolute numbers, whilst declining as a proportion of all jobs. In 1911 80 per cent of workers were in manual occupations, compared with just over 50 per cent in 1981. Agricultural employment has declined both absolutely and proportionately.

More detailed information about change in the occupation structure in Britain since the Second World War, including a breakdown by gender, is contained in table 3.4, which allows comparison between the results of the 1951, 1971 and 1981 censuses. This shows that the rate of increase of professional and managerial employment has been more or less the same for men and women, but that clerical work has continued to become more feminized. Intermediate and routine office jobs have grown at a great rate during the twentieth century. In 1911 there were four men for every woman in clerical work; by 1981, the ratio was four men to twelve women. In parallel with feminization, there was a decline in the rewards and the status of office work. After 1951, the number of men in semi-skilled manual work also fell quite sharply but that for women remained more or less constant.

Women are crowded into three occupational classes: lower professional, clerical and semi-skilled manual. This process of occupational *segregation* is considered at length in chapter 4. The persistent pattern of segregation of men and women between 1951 and 1981 suggests that women did not improve their position in the occupational structure. Moreover, although there are far more women in employment, a great many are in part-time work: in 1992, 45 per cent of women employees were part-timers, compared with 10 per cent of men.

Satisfactory data are not available to describe thoroughly the changes during the 1980s. However, the rapid growth of self-employment apart, most post-war trends have persisted. The *General Household Survey, 1988* (table 9.52) shows that, of men in employment, 55 per cent were in manual jobs. The comparable figure for women (if personal service workers are counted) is 48 per cent (*General Household Survey, 1988*, table 9.56).

Mapping the class structure

Class structure refers to the architecture of class *positions*. Occupational change is an important consideration when describing the class structure, since it affects the size of different classes. There are many technical problems involved in deciding what criteria to use in order to allocate

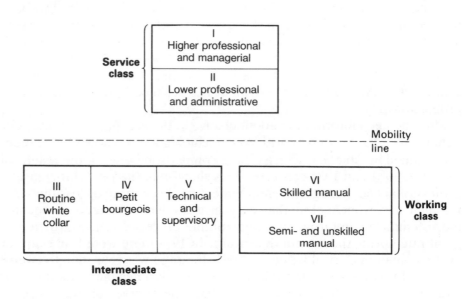

Occupational classes

I   Higher-grade professionals; higher-grade administrators and officials; managers in large establishments; large proprietors.

II   Lower-grade professionals and higher-grade technicians; lower-grade administrators; managers in small establishments; supervisors of non-manual workers.

III   Routine non-manual workers (largely clerical) in administration and commerce; sales personnel; other rank-and-file employees in services.

IV   Small proprietors, including farmers and small-holders; self-employed artisans; other 'own account' workers (except professionals).

V   Lower-grade technicians; supervisors of manual workers.

VI   Skilled manual wage-workers.

VII   All manual wage-workers in industry in semi-skilled and unskilled grades; agricultural workers.

Figure 3.1 Goldthorpe et al.'s (1987) model of the British class structure (Nuffield Mobility Study)
Source: Goldthorpe et al., 1987, pp. 39–41, reproduced with permission

individuals and households to an 'objective' class position. Basically, the aim is to isolate the least number of classes consistent with the proviso that the behaviour of members of each class is internally similar in relevant respects, whilst being distinct from that of other classes.

On *any* model of the class structure it is possible to show a statistical relationship between class position and various aspects of social privilege and disadvantage. Government statisticians first began to collect data in class terms (the Registrar-General's class scheme was first used in the 1911 census) because it threw light on morbidity and mortality. It is still the case that the higher one's class position the longer one lives on average. It is interesting that friends are very likely to belong to the same social class. Equally, a child's likely educational achievement remain strongly class-based (see chapter 8). The strength of the statistical association between class and other social behaviour depends in part on how class is measured. Official statistics classify a household by the occupation of its head, and the division between white-collar and blue-collar workers remains a key distinction. Marxists place more stress on the relationship with ownership of means of production. However, the currently dominant way of measuring class in British sociology is Weberian, based *primarily* on occupation.

The study of class structure by Marshall et al. (1988), the electoral studies of Heath et al. (1985; 1991) (see section 12.2) and the study of educational opportunity by Halsey et al. (1980) (see section 8.4) all use a version of the class model developed by Goldthorpe for the investigation of contemporary social mobility (see section 3.7). It operates with seven occupational classes, as listed in figure 3.1. For many purposes, these seven classes are grouped into three – the service class, the intermediate class and the working class. The service class includes higher and lower professionals and middle management; the intermediate class comprises routine white-collar workers, small proprietors and supervisory workers; and the working class is defined as manual workers without positions of authority. Goldthorpe's conception of class structure is shown diagrammatically in the figure.

Problems with occupational class measures

The backbone of the class structure, and indeed of the entire reward system of modern Western society, is the occupational order. Other sources of economic and symbolic advantage do coexist alongside the occupational order, but for the vast majority of the population these tend, at best, to be secondary to those deriving from the division of labour. (Parkin, 1971)

Box 3.1   Class structure: the effects of using men's and women's occupations

The following shows the class composition of a random national sample of men and women separately, allocating them to socio-economic groups according to their own most recent occupation. This puts most women into intermediate and junior non-manual and semi-skilled manual groups – which, of course, provide most of the jobs for employed women.

Socio-economic group based on own current job or, for those not working, last job, 1988 (adults aged 16 or over: full-time students separately identified)

	Men (no.)	Men (%)	Women (no.)	Women (%)	Total (no.)	Total (%)
Professional	585	6.3	110	1.1	695	3.5
Employers and managers	1,889	20.3	799	7.7	2,688	13.6
Intermediate non-manual	779	8.4	1,544	14.8	2,323	11.8
Junior non-manual	616	6.6	3,103	29.8	3,719	18.9
Skilled manual and own account non-professional	3,276	35.2	853	8.2	4,129	20.9
Semi-skilled manual and personal service	1,294	13.9	2,413	23.2	3,707	18.8
Unskilled manual	409	4.4	773	7.4	1,182	6.0
Armed forces	61	0.7	23	0.2	84	0.4
Full-time student	308	3.3	352	3.4	660	3.3
Never worked/no answer/inadequate description	90	1.0	439	4.2	529	2.7
Total	9,307		10,409		19,716	

The next table shows how the appearance of the class structure alters if all married women are allocated to their husbands' socio-economic group. This is the approximate consequence of using head of household to define class position, the effect being that women become much more evenly spread across the class structure. This happens because women in general marry men in superior occupational positions.

Socio-economic group based on own current job or last job, with married women classified to their husband's occupation. 1988 (adults aged 16 or over: full-time students classified according to their last job or as never worked).

	Men		Women		Total	
	(no.)	*(%)*	*(no.)*	*(%)*	*(no.)*	*(%)*
Professional	604	6.5	500	4.8	1,104	5.6
Employers and managers	1,895	20.4	1,841	17.7	3,736	18.9
Intermediate non-manual	801	8.6	1,094	10.5	1,895	9.6
Junior non-manual	679	7.3	1,525	14.7	2,204	11.2
Skilled manual and own account non-professional	3,295	35.4	2,651	25.2	5,946	30.2
Semi-skilled manual and personal service	1,346	14.5	1,786	17.2	3,132	15.9
Unskilled manual	444	4.8	535	5.1	979	5.0
Armed forces	61	0.7	60	0.6	121	0.6
Never worked/no answer/inadequate description	182	2.0	367	3.5	549	2.8
Total	9,307		10,409		19,716	

The conventional measure, using head of household, describes best the class structure of a society where households derive their incomes almost exclusively from a male breadwinner wage. In Britain, where married women's participation in employment has expanded rapidly since the 1960s, occupation of head of household becomes an increasingly problematic index of class position.

Source: tables from *General Household Survey, 1988*, HMSO, 1990, p. 272.

All forms of measurement have some disadvantages. Although occupation structure may be the backbone of the class structure, using occupational position as an indicator of class membership has some problems. Class position should be thought of as related to, but not the same as, occupation. Social class position refers to both the ownership of property and authority relations. There are several reasons why occupation is unsatisfactory as a sole indicator of class position.

First, common occupation does not itself produce a common consciousness or perceived common interests. Although trade unions and

professional associations are organized on the basis of shared, occupational interests, people in identical occupations can have differing values,
attitudes, loyalties and allegiances. Some occupations generate more of a
common outlook than others, though it is hard to decide whether it is
aspects of the labour process, or of trade union organization, or of the
kind of communities in which they live, that make coal-miners more
uniform in their political behaviour than, say, clerks.

Second, a person's present occupational place does not sum up his or her
entire work experience. Some people experience mobility between
occupations during their own lifetime. The term 'career' refers to the way
in which people often pass through several different occupations in their
lifetimes. Where these are structured or predictable (as in the transition
from apprentice to journeyman to master craftsman; or from junior
hospital doctor through registrar to consultant), reactions to work and
politics are often conditioned more by expectations of the final position
to be reached than by the lowly position taken up on entry to the career.
The importance of this is shown by recent findings on male clerks
discussed at length in section 3.5. Young male clerks tend to get
promoted into managerial occupations, whereas the prospects of
promotion for a female clerk are extremely poor. Hence, though male
and female clerks share the same 'occupation', it is not clear that the
political and class interests of women in clerical work coincide with those
of their male colleagues.

Third, not all persons have occupations. If you consider the number of
people too young and too old to hold jobs in the formal economy, the
number of unemployed, and the number of full-time housewives,
probably more than half the population is without an occupation. These
different groups of the 'non-employed' are, nevertheless, normally
considered as being in the class structure.

Most women work full-time as housewives for part of their lives, but
that work is not included in occupational classifications. In the past, that
has been one reason for using the occupation of heads of household
(mostly male) as the indicator of the class position of the whole
household. However, now most married women work; there are many
households where women bring in the only wage; and in a small
proportion of households women earn more than their male partners.
There is thus a technical problem (not to mention sexist distortion) in
conventional measures of household class position. Some indication of
the different effects of classifying women by their own occupation as
opposed to that of head of household is shown in box 3.1.

Some authors, Goldthorpe prominent among them, defend the
conventional approach, arguing that the family household is the most
important unit of class analysis. This is because men's incomes, being
larger, are a stronger index of material position and because not a lot of

information specifically relevant to class analysis is lost by ignoring the employment of other household members. Critics argue that this obscures systematic patriarchal power which allocates privileged occupational positions to men and implausibly ignores the cultural and material resources that women bring to households.

Summary

1   Sociologists have various ways of constructing models of the class structure on the basis of information about employment status and occupation.
2   The occupational structure is the backbone of the class structure and thus very important in understanding the formation of social class. However, a social class is more than a mere category of people in similar occupations. Members of a social class take part in common cultural activities and political organizations as well as having similar jobs.
3   The most important changes in the occupational structure since the Second World War have been the growth of professional and managerial jobs, the decline of manual work and the feminization of clerical work. The increase in part-time work, mostly for women, is also important.
4   Occupations are segregated so that certain categories of person – women and ethnic minorities especially – obtain inferior rewards from their jobs.

Related topics

The ways in which people experience work and organize together on the basis of their occupations are examined in sections 2.5, 2.6 and 2.7. More on deindustrialization and the decline of manual work in manufacturing industry can be found in section 2.8. Employment for women is surveyed in much greater detail in section 4.2. The employment prospects of ethnic groups are explored in section 5.3. Links between education and occupation are examined in section 8.3.

3.3   Income, Wealth and Poverty

Usually class categories are based on occupational characteristics. However, a prior step in an examination of the class structure is a consideration of how income and wealth are distributed in the population.

The distribution of income

Although it might seem a relatively straightforward matter to measure an individual's income, it is not so. Do we, for example, count individual or household income? Is it to be measured before or after tax? Is it just that derived from a job or should it include welfare payments of various kinds? One solution to these problems of measurement is to present data on income calculated in different ways. We can, for example, differentiate original income, gross income, disposable income, post-tax income and final income. Original income refers to the initial total income

---

Box 3.2 Redistribution of income through taxes and benefits, United Kingdom, 1988

This table uses a method of showing how any characteristic is distributed throughout a population. In this case, the population (of households) is divided into five equal groups called quintiles, starting with those households with the highest income and going down to those with the lowest. It is like arranging all the households in order of their income and then drawing lines at one-fifth, two-fifths, and so on down the distribution. You can then see how much of the total national income goes to any one quintile. So the richest quintile, or 20 per cent of households, had almost half of the total amount of original income in 1988.

Income measures: average per household (£ per year)[b]	Quintile groups of households ranked by equivalized disposable income[a]					All house- holds
	Bottom fifth	Next fifth	Middle fifth	Next fifth	Top fifth	
Earnings of main earner	740	3,090	7,400	10,830	19,500	8,310
Earnings of others in the household	90	470	1,940	3,830	6,200	2,500
Occupational pensions, annuities	160	500	790	830	1,300	720
Investment income	160	260	480	590	1,950	690
Other income	70	120	140	170	220	140
Total original income	1,210	4,440	10,750	16,260	29,170	12,360

add Benefits in cash:						
Contributory	1,640	1,640	960	640	430	1,060
Non-contributory	1,580	1,150	800	440	280	850
Gross income	4,430	7,240	12,500	17,340	29,880	14,280
less income tax[c] and NIC[d]	200	740	1,920	3,220	5,990	2,420
Domestic rates (gross)	470	480	530	570	700	550
Disposable income	3,760	6,020	10,050	13,540	23,190	11,310
Equivalized disposable income[a]	3,840	5,740	8,230	11,420	21,320	10,110
less indirect taxes	1,080	1,470	2,410	2,900	3,710	2,320
Post-tax income	2,680	4,540	7,650	10,640	19,480	9,000
add Benefits in kind:						
Education	790	790	960	810	420	760
National Health Service	1,120	1,060	980	820	720	940
Housing subsidy	100	100	50	30	10	60
Travel subsidies	40	50	50	50	70	50
School meals and welfare milk	60	20	20	10	10	30
Final income	4,800	6,570	9,700	12,360	20,700	10,830
Number of households in sample	1,453	1,453	1,453	1,453	1,453	7,265

[a] Equivalized disposable income has been used for ranking to contruct the quintile groups. The average equivalized disposable income for each group is shown below disposable income, but all other income values are unequivalized.
[b] Rounded to the nearest £10.
[c] After tax relief at source on mortgage interest and life assurance premiums.
[d] Employees' national insurance contributions.

Source: *Social Trends*, 1992, p. 98; from the *Family Expenditure Survey*.
Crown copyright

received by households from employment, occupational pensions, investments and other households. Additions to this original income of cash benefits from the state, retirement pensions or income support, for example, give gross income. Disposable income consists of gross income minus income tax, national insurance contributions and council tax. Deducting indirect taxes such as VAT yields post-tax income. Final income reflects more concealed additions to or subtractions from post-tax income, particularly various benefits from the state in the form of health and education services, for example, which have a cash value.

Box 3.2 shows the values of these various income categories for one year, 1988, and the effect the tax–benefit system has. There are large differences in original income: the bottom quintile has £1210 per household on average, while the top quintile has an average income of £29,170 per household, a ratio of 1:24. The tax–benefit system does

Table 3.5   Shares of household income, United Kingdom, 1977–1988

	Quintile groups of households ranked by equivalized disposable income				
	Bottom fifth (%)	Next fifth (%)	Middle fifth (%)	Next fifth (%)	Top fifth (%)
Equivalized original income					
1977	4	10	18	25	43
1979	2	10	18	27	43
1981	3	9	17	26	46
1983	3	8	17	26	47
1985	2	7	17	27	47
1987	2	7	16	25	50
1988	2	7	16	25	50
Equivalized gross income					
1977	9	13	18	24	37
1979	8	13	18	24	37
1981	8	12	17	23	39
1983	8	12	17	23	39
1985	8	12	17	24	40
1987	8	11	16	23	43
1988	7	11	16	23	43
Equivalized disposable income					
1977	10	14	18	23	36
1979	9	13	18	23	36
1981	9	13	17	23	38
1983	10	13	17	23	38
1985	9	13	17	23	38
1987	8	12	16	23	41
1988	8	11	16	23	42
Equivalized post-tax income					
1977	9	14	17	23	37
1979	10	13	18	23	37
1981	9	13	17	22	39
1983	9	13	17	22	39
1985	9	13	17	23	39
1987	8	12	16	22	43
1988	7	11	16	22	44

Source: *Social Trends*, 1992, p. 100; from the *Family Expenditure Survey*. Crown copyright

produce *some* redistribution, however, because final income ranges from £4800 to £20,700, a ratio of 1:4.3.

Table 3.5 shows the changes in the income categories (with the exception of final income) over the years 1977–88. In 1988, the top quintile took half of all original income. Although post-tax income is more equal, the top quintile took 44 per cent of all income, twice as much as the next quintile. More striking still, however, is the fact that incomes are becoming more unequal. In the 11 year period from 1977 to 1988, the richest quintile's proportion of post-tax income has risen from 37 to 44 per cent, while the proportions taken by the rest of the population have fallen.

Households in the top group have, in effect, taken income from all four of the other quintiles, most particularly from the poorest two. This relatively rapid growth in inequality constitutes a reversal of a historic trend towards greater income equality, as we shall see in the next section. It is not just inequality by income quintile that is noticeable. There are also substantial inequalities over the life cycle, as figure 3.2 shows. Household income rises sharply for married couples before they have children, falls while they have young children and rises to its peak when the children are between 16 and 24. From that peak income falls steeply towards retirement. Taxes keep final (post-tax) income below original income until just before retirement.

So far, we have been discussing relatively recent and short-term movements in the distribution which show an increase in inequality. What of longer-term trends?

Changes in distribution of income since 1949

The Royal Commission on the Distribution of Income and Wealth (1979) showed an apparent increase in the equality of the distribution of pre-tax *personal* income in the years 1949–77. The share taken by the top 1 per cent was more than halved and that accruing to the top 10 per cent was also reduced. This was not, however, reflected in any significant increase in the share taken by the bottom 50 per cent. What had happened, therefore, was that there had simply been a redistribution amongst those individuals in the top 20 or 30 per cent of income earners. As a whole, the income distribution showed a remarkable stability from year to year. As far as personal income *after* tax is concerned, there was a small increase in the degree of equalization in the late 1960s and early 1970s. However, there are small movements in both directions from year to year and there has been a reverse in the process of equalization in the 1980s.

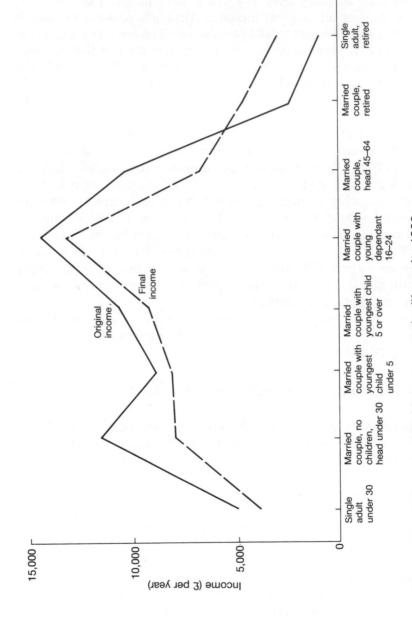

Figure 3.2 Original and final income over the life cycle, 1983.
Source: Social Trends, 1986, p. 91. Crown copyright.

The distribution of wealth

In many ways, wealth is more important than income from employment. Wealth often includes assets which can yield income in the future and it can be a more secure form of income than that which is earned. Even more than income, however, wealth is difficult to measure.

Problems of measurement

One may readily think of someone's wealth as comprising stocks and shares or building society accounts. But should one include his or her house or valuable personal possessions, or even the capital value of his or her occupational pension scheme? The best way of dealing with these difficulties is to investigate the distribution of the different kinds of wealth. In particular, we should distinguish marketable from non-marketable wealth. The first refers to those assets that could potentially be sold, like houses or shares. The second includes assets, such as pension schemes, which cannot be sold but which represent significant future income.

Another difficulty in measurement is that wealth is rather more concealed than income. People do, after all, have their income assessed on an annual basis by the Inland Revenue, but there is no equivalent set of procedures for wealth. There are two main methods for determining how much wealth someone holds. First, the size of an individual's estate may be estimated from the account of their assets that has to be made for probate purposes when they die. Second, one can conduct a survey and determine the distribution of wealth simply by asking a randomly chosen set of people what they own. There are clear difficulties with both of these methods. The first, in that it only deals with wealth left behind by individuals when they die, tells us nothing directly about the distribution of wealth amongst the living. Furthermore, rich individuals tend to distribute their assets among members of their families precisely to avoid the higher taxes payable on death. The estates method may thus seriously underestimate the extent of the wealth of the rich. Lastly, many people do not leave enough to qualify for taxation at probate and the Inland Revenue does not therefore provide very good data on the poorer members of the community. The second method, which depends on questionnaire survey, also has its drawbacks. Most importantly, many people will refuse to reveal details of their wealth to interviewers and a high level of non-response calls the representativeness of such surveys into question. It is also, clearly, very difficult to check that answers to a questionnaire of this kind are accurate.

The changing distribution of wealth

It is important to bear these difficulties of measurement in mind when assessing the evidence of the distribution of wealth. In presenting data, we will try to show the effects of different assumptions about what wealth is and different ways of measuring it. Some recent figures are presented in table 3.6. These are derived from the estate duty method and show distributions for different types of wealth.

Looking at marketable wealth, the proportion owned by the richest 1 per cent has declined very slightly since 1976, although there has been little change through the 1980s. Any redistribution that has taken place has not therefore benefited the poorer half of the country. We should

Table 3.6 Distribution of wealth for population aged 18 and over, United Kingdom, 1976–1989[a]

	1976	1981	1986	1989
Marketable wealth				
Percentage of wealth owned by:				
Most wealthy 1%	21	18	18	18
Most wealthy 5%	38	36	36	38
Most wealthy 10%	50	50	50	53
Most wealthy 25%	71	73	73	75
Most wealthy 50%	92	92	90	94
Total marketable wealth (£ billion)	280	565	955	1578
Marketable wealth less value of dwellings				
Percentage of wealth owned by:				
Most wealthy 1%	29	26	25	28
Most wealthy 5%	47	45	46	53
Most wealthy 10%	57	56	58	66
Most wealthy 25%	73	74	75	81
Most wealthy 50%	88	87	89	94
Marketable wealth plus occupational and state pension rights				
Percentage of wealth owned by:				
Most wealthy 1%	13	11	10	11
Most wealthy 5%	26	24	24	26
Most wealthy 10%	36	34	35	38
Most wealthy 25%	57	56	58	62
Most wealthy 50%	80	79	82	83

[a] Estimates for 1976, 1981 and 1986 are based on the estates of persons dying in those years. Estimates for 1989 are based on estates notified for probate in 1989–90. Estimates are not strictly comparable between 1989 and earlier years.

Source: *Social Trends*, 1992, p. 101; from Inland Revenue statistics. Crown copyright

also note that the wealthiest 10 per cent still owned more than half of the marketable property in 1989. There is, therefore, a certain circulation of wealth amongst the wealthiest, as measured by property possessed at death. As we have already pointed out, there is also a circulation of wealth before death, away from individuals to their families, a process which may be accelerating but which is not shown up in these figures. A large proportion of the nation's wealth is in the value of homes. If one takes out these assets, and looks at marketable wealth less the value of dwellings, the inequalities of wealth appear even more sharp. In 1989, the proportion of wealth of this kind taken by the most wealthy 1 per cent is 28 per cent.

If one defines wealth as including occupational pension schemes and state pension rights, which cannot be sold but which do constitute an asset of a kind, then the inequalities of wealth distribution are less sharp, with the top 1 per cent and the top 50 per cent taking less than they did when marketable assets were counted. Nonetheless, this measure *also* shows an *increasing* inequality, with the most wealthy 50 per cent gradually increasing their share.

What view one takes of these data depends at least partly on the definition of wealth and, specifically, whether or not pension rights are included. Townsend (1979), for example, argues that occupational pensions should be included on the grounds that they usually have some cash value even if surrendered early, but state pensions should not since they cannot be cashed. Trends for the different types of wealth show some increase in equality during the 1970s, at least amongst the top 50 per cent, followed by a flattening out in the 1980s. These conclusions reached by the estates method are roughly confirmed by studies based on the survey method (Townsend, 1979). However one defines wealth, it is very unevenly distributed, and more so than income.

These are relatively recent changes. A more long-run perspective is provided by table 3.7. This does not include any adjustments for partial inaccuracies of valuation or of wealth understated in estate duty returns, and it is very difficult to allow for changes in the way that people give away their property before they die. Inclusion of these would increase the share taken by the richer groups. Between 1938 and 1972, the share of the top 1 per cent declined significantly from about 55 per cent to 32 per cent. As we have noticed before, greater equality of this kind does not necessarily mean greater equality throughout the whole population, for wealth is largely being reallocated from the very richest to the not quite so rich. Thus, the share in total wealth of the top 20 per cent has only declined 10 per cent in the same period. The diffusion of wealth does not, in other words, extend very far.

The twentieth century has seen attempts to redistribute both income and wealth. The evidence suggests that these attempts have not been

Table 3.7 Shares in total wealth, 1938–1972

	England and Wales				Britain			
	Top 1% (%)	Top 5% (%)	Top 10% (%)	Top 20% (%)	Top 1% (%)	Top 5% (%)	Top 10% (%)	Top 20% (%)
1938	55.0	76.9	85.0	91.2	55.0	77.2	85.4	91.6
1950	47.2	74.3	–[a]	–[a]	47.2	74.4	–[a]	–[a]
1951	45.8	73.6	–	–	45.9	73.8	–	–
1952	43.0	70.2	–	–	42.9	70.3	–	–
1953	43.6	71.1	–	–	43.5	71.2	–	–
1954	45.3	71.8	–	–	45.3	72.0	–	–
1955	44.5	71.1	–	–	43.8	70.8	–	–
1956	44.5	71.3	–	–	44.0	71.1	–	–
1957	43.4	68.7	–	–	42.9	68.6	–	–
1958	41.4	67.8	–	–	40.9	67.7	–	–
1959	41.4	67.6	–	–	41.8	67.9	–	–
1960	33.9	59.4	71.5	83.1	34.4	60.0	72.1	83.6
1961	36.5	60.6	71.7	83.3	36.5	60.8	72.1	83.6
1962	31.4	54.8	67.3	80.2	31.9	55.4	67.9	80.7
1963			not available[b]				not available[b]	
1964	34.5	58.6	71.4	84.3	34.7	59.2	72.0	85.2
1965	33.0	58.1	71.7	85.5	33.3	58.7	72.3	85.8
1966	30.6	55.5	69.2	83.8	31.0	56.1	69.9	84.2
1967	31.4	56.0	70.0	84.5	31.5	56.4	70.5	84.9
1968	33.6	58.3	71.6	85.1	33.6	58.6	72.0	85.4
1969	31.1	56.1	67.7	83.3	31.3	56.6	68.6	84.1
1970	29.7	53.6	68.7	84.5	30.1	54.3	69.4	84.9
1971	28.4	52.3	67.6	84.2	28.8	53.0	68.3	84.0
1972	31.7	56.0	70.4	84.9	32.0	57.2	71.7	85.3

[a] Dashes denote that the information is outside the range of estate data.
[b] The estate data were not available by country for 1963: this means that we could not calculate a figure for Britain comparable with those for other years.

Source: from Atkinson and Harrison, 1978, p. 159, reproduced with permission

very successful. Wealth is still very concentrated and it is still relatively easy, especially with good professional advice, for a wealthy person to pass it on to other members of his or her family. An unequal distribution of income and wealth is not achieved by accident; it requires active social processes to create and maintain it. As Townsend (1979, p. 365) argues:

> Riches are not only inherited or made: to be riches, they have to be unavailable to the vast majority of the population. A theory of riches

depends not only on theories of acquisition – how much wealth is inherited, accumulated by entrepreneurial effort or by the exercise of scarce skills. It depends also on theories of denial of access to wealth – through selective succession, testamentary concentration, limitation of entry to the professions, monopolization of capital and property or at least severe restriction on the opportunity to acquire land and property.

Poverty

So far we have argued that changes in the distribution of income and wealth are confined largely to the richest 20 per cent. We turn now to look at what that might mean for the bottom 50 per cent and, specifically, at the incidence of poverty in contemporary Britain. It seems reasonable to say that there is a difference between being relatively deprived by being in the lower half of the income distribution, and being in actual poverty. There is an apparent distinction, in other words, between being badly-off by comparison with others and having a standard of living below some fixed level.

So a measure of relative poverty might be where people receive an income substantially less than the average for the society as a whole. Absolute poverty might be assessed by reference to a level of income

Plate 3.1   Poverty in the 1990s. Living conditions and especially accommodation remain highly problematic for some households.
Source: Network

deemed to be the minimum necessary for survival, a sort of Plimsoll line
conception of poverty. Measures of relative poverty are often objected to
on the grounds that they ignore the possibility that the whole society is
affluent and, hence, even the poor are well-off by comparison with, say,
Third-World countries. The difficulty with absolute measures, on the
other hand, lies in deciding where the Plimsoll line is to be drawn. In
practice, any definition of poverty depends on the values of the society
concerned and on its view as to what counts as the necessities of life.
Consequently, there is room for a great deal of disagreement about
where to put the poverty line. Government ministers, especially those of
recent Conservative governments, have a tendency to put the line very
much lower down than do, say, ministers in the Church of England. In
practice, therefore, the difference between absolute and relative measures of poverty is very blurred.

By almost any measure, poverty in Britain in the 1990s is widespread.
Furthermore, over the last ten years or so it has been becoming worse
and more visible. A recent study by Oppenheim (1990) used two
measures of poverty: the level of income at which supplementary benefit
used to be paid, and the level equivalent to 50 per cent of average
income. He calculated the number of people below these levels (who
were in poverty) and also the numbers of people at the margins of
poverty since, over time, people's income fluctuates and they may slip in
and out of poverty. Those in marginal poverty were defined as those with
incomes equal to between 100 and 140 per cent of supplementary benefit
or between 50 and 60 per cent of average incomes. He concluded that, in
1987, 5 per cent of the population were living below the supplementary
benefit level. In 1979 the corresponding figure was 4 per cent. However,
if you take the population living *at or below* the supplementary benefit
level, the changes are more dramatic. In 1987, 19 per cent were at or
below this level, while in 1979 the figure was 6 per cent. This represents a
very rapid spread of poverty. Similar results are given in figure 3.3, which
shows that 30 per cent of the population are within the margins of
poverty in 1987 compared with 20 per cent in 1979.

Hardship Britain: a case study

It is a very depressing thought to think we might have to spend maybe the
next five years on Social Security. It is a very disheartening, depressing
thought, to bring your new baby into the world, because when I had him,
do you know one of my first thoughts was 'Isn't he beautiful . . . oh I'm so
happy, oh God, how am I going to manage to bring him up and keep him
fed and clothed decently?' That sums it up for me. (quoted in Cohen et al.
1992, p. 59)

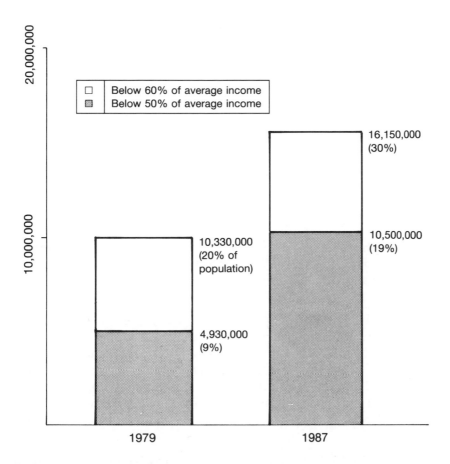

Figure 3.3 Numbers and proportions of the population living in or on the margins of poverty (defined as below 60 per cent average income) in 1979 and 1987.
Source: Oppenheim, 1990, p. 28

Many studies of poverty use quantitative or survey evidence on which to base their conclusions. The book *Hardship Britain* (Cohen et al., 1992), on the contrary, is a study that relies on in-depth interviews with people who live in poverty and claim income support on what their *experience* of poverty is like.

The book concentrates on changes to the social security system since 1988 which replaced supplementary benefit by income support and introduced the social fund which provided loans (rather than a grant) for large items. In the view of many of the interviewees this new system makes an already intolerable system worse. They had to cut down on food, reducing or forgoing such things as sweets, cakes, biscuits, and fresh fruit and meat. As one interviewee said of her husband, who suffered from stomach ulcers:

> The doctor has told him he needs fish and chicken regularly but we can't afford it . . . We seem to live off chips and potatoes . . . He should have low-fat meat every day . . . when we cook anything we have to use twice the gas . . . We only have a cooked meal three times a week to cut down on gas. (p. 89)

Heating has to be reduced, whatever the consequences. As one mother said:

> With him [the child] being asthmatic we should have the electric heating on in the bedrooms . . . we can't do it which is why he is like he is now . . . he's chesty all the time. (p. 16)

The lack of food and heating are but two consequences of too limited a budget. The result is a constant battle to make the money stretch, a battle often lost, with the consequence of going into debt. Some of these debts are commercial, to shops for instance, and would place a further burden on the weekly budget. Families or friends might help, which impose other sorts of burdens. A mother borrowed money from her mother for children's shoes:

> As long as she took back the money it'd be okay but my ma tends to say sometimes it doesn't matter and I feel guilty, with her being a pensioner, I feel I'm taking it out of my ma's pocket, you know what I mean, she needs it herself. But I'd need to be really desperate before I'd go. (p. 46)

Living in poverty is clearly in itself stressful. As one man in the study said:

> I think that the real problem of being on the dole is it destroys your self-esteem, you know, and your ability to provide for yourself . . . I feel a great lack of self-esteem and I think I'd really like to have a job where I could go out and come back and Lorraine as well could go out . . . where we could go out and earn some money and have a sense of achievement at the end of the day. (p. 70)

Poverty can also be destructive of relationships. Their lack of money makes many parents, for example, feel inadequate in their care of their children who are deprived of many of the things, like new clothes or toys, that those from better-off families take for granted. One mother complains:

> I have actually had to swallow my pride 'till it hurts . . . It makes me feel like a complete failure because I had such high ideals . . . I wanted to give my children the best, not to the point of spoiling them, but just so they could, you know, have confidence in themselves. So when I can't do that it makes me feel I'm failing. (p. 72)

Who is poor?

Some sections of the population are much more vulnerable to poverty than others, in particular the low-paid, the unemployed, the disabled, one-parent families and the elderly retired. These minorities are represented in the population in poverty out of all proportion to their numbers in the general population. Clearly, these groups are vulnerable simply because they have low incomes and are largely dependent on benefit payments of various kinds from the state. Furthermore, various social trends and aspects of government policy are likely both to increase the numbers of people in poverty and to alter the distribution between the various groups at risk. For example, the age structure is changing in such a way that not only is there an increasing proportion of the population aged 65 or over, but also the numbers over 85 are increasing rapidly (see section 6.3). Government policy affects the rates of benefit, which in turn affects the standard of living of vulnerable people who are in very low-paid jobs. The recent, very steep, increase in unemployment is also a consequence of government economic policy.

Poverty is a function of the distribution of income. As common sense would indicate, people are in poverty because they have a low income. The distribution of poverty is, therefore, explained by reference to those groups that are most likely to have low incomes. Any overall account of poverty, however, is dependent, in turn, on an explanation of how society is divided into *social classes* and how the mechanisms that sustain class divisions keep a large number of adults and children below an acceptable standard of living.

Summary

1 Since the beginning of the twentieth century, there has been some redistribution of income in Britain, but the distribution has not

changed much since the Second World War. In the period from 1945
to the present, there has been a small degree of equalization, but this
appears to have involved only those households in the top half of the
income distribution.
2 Wealth is more unequally distributed than income. As with income,
   what redistribution there has been has involved only the more
   wealthy half of the population.
3 However one measures poverty, a substantial proportion of the
   population are in poverty.

Related topics

Questions of poverty are discussed at a number of points in this book.
Section 6.3 on the elderly and section 6.5 on single-parent families are
especially relevant. The rest of this chapter contains data on comparisons
of income and wage rates. Section 3.6 gives some account of how the
upper class has preserved its favoured situation.

3.4 The Working Class

Debates about the working class

The future of the working class remains a contentious issue in
contemporary sociology. The debate is hard to appreciate without
recalling Marx's view of the revolutionary role of the working class in
capitalist society. Marx thought that the logic of capitalist accumulation
would turn the vast majority of the population into proletarians, i.e.
workers who relied on wages for their subsistence because they lacked
any other means of livelihood. Lacking property and increasingly
deprived of control over their own labour, the working class would come
to share a common (homogeneous) economic position. Uniformly
degraded work and poor pay would characterize the workers and
distinguish them from a small, privileged social class of property owners.
In such circumstances, Marx expected the workers to unite politically, on
the basis of their common class position, to abolish capitalist domination.
   The working classes of the Western world have rarely been revolutionary. For the last 150 years, however, the main force behind social and
political change has come from organizations of the working class – trade
unions and socialist parties. Such organizations have been 'reformist':
they have pressed successfully for improvements in pay and working
conditions, for the extension of political rights like the vote, and for

social rights like health care, education and social security benefits. These are achievements of labour movements on behalf of the working class, but they have not undermined capitalist economic relations. Since this reformist politics is universal in Western societies, except where it has been suppressed by dictatorships, it might be anticipated that it will continue as a form of working-class opposition to capitalism.

Some commentators believe, however, that the British working class is beginning to abandon even its reformism. They suggest that the working class is no longer an oppositional, never mind a revolutionary, force. It is argued that, since the Second World War, the working class has become thoroughly integrated into society. Standards of living have risen, welfare services have expanded, trade unions and the Labour Party have become accepted parts of the political system, with the result that the working class is no longer a marginal, excluded or deprived class. There is now one nation rather than two, with the working class committed to the perpetuation of welfare capitalism.

Differences over the way in which class conflict might be expected to develop have formed the background to sociological debates in the last 30 years, and have revolved around interpretations of how social changes have affected manual workers. Two issues have been central. The first is whether the position of the working class has changed relative to other classes, and particularly whether manual workers remain a *distinctive* class. The second concerns changes in the internal structure of the working class, especially whether or not it is becoming more *internally divided* and hence less prone to acting politically in a united, or 'solidaristic', way.

Sociological interpretations

A distinctive class?

Two main positions exist concerning the distinctiveness of the working class. One says that there has been a *convergence* between manual and other workers and that there is no longer a perceptible difference between the working class and the middle class. The other asserts that the boundary remains significant: the working class remains distinct, even though its characteristics may have altered to such an extent that it constitutes a *new working class*.

These two positions were clearly presented in the famous debate, still a base-line for discussion, about the effect of affluence on the working class. Proponents of the 'embourgeoisement thesis' detected convergence; their critics (Goldthorpe et al., 1968a; 1968b; 1969) denied convergence, but identified a class of workers with new characteristics.

The embourgeoisement thesis, crudely stated, maintained that since workers had become better off during the post-war boom, and their patterns of consumption thereby altered, they had begun to adopt the lifestyle and social values of the middle class. Convergence was occurring between manual and non-manual workers: it was to be expected that manual workers would become 'bourgeois'. Thus, the working class would become indistinguishable from other classes.

Goldthorpe *et al.* tested this thesis on some well-paid manual workers in mass production industries in Luton. These workers were prosperous but were not becoming middle class. They did not aspire to become middle class; they did not associate socially with white-collar workers; they were not much involved with their work; they were trade unionists; and they voted solidly for the Labour Party. Therefore, it was concluded, the embourgeoisement thesis was inaccurate. However, these affluent workers were different from earlier generations of manual workers. Their behaviour at work, their social lives, and their reasons for supporting labour organizations were not like those of traditional workers. The new worker was *instrumental* in attitudes to work, unions and politics, and *privatized* in social life. The new worker worked purely for money and was concerned with unions only because collective action was essential for an increased income. That income was, in turn, increasingly devoted to improving the material circumstances of the worker's immediate family. New workers were very family-centred and were not involved in neighbourhood or community life. So, Goldthorpe concluded, a boundary remained between the working and the middle class, but the working class itself was changing from its traditional form.

The case for the emergence of a 'new', privatized and instrumentalist working class itself depended on a model of what the working class used to be like. Indeed, all questions concerning the extent and direction of change depend on some comparison with a previous condition. Goldthorpe et al. used a model of the *traditional proletarian* and many other sociologists have done the same.

The traditional proletarian is attributed with various characteristics. Workers were often impoverished, but not obsessed by money or their lack of it. Poverty was partly compensated for by work, which was more skilled than today and which tended to foster more cohesive work-groups. Poor housing conditions were offset by the existence of close-knit communities where bonds of kinship and neighbourliness prevailed. A distinctive style of life supported a vibrant class culture. This culture included a consciousness of class divisions and a political commitment to the labour movement (unions and the Labour Party, mostly). Workers acted as a fairly homogeneous political force in opposition to capitalist social relations. A contrast between proletarian and new workers is drawn in table 3.8.

Table 3.8 Ideal-typical characteristics of traditional proletarian and instrumental-privatized workers

	Traditional proletarian worker	*Instrumental-privatized worker*
Image of society	'Us' versus 'them': an oppositional and dichotomous view, centring on power inequality	A 'pecuniary' or money model; class differences seen in terms of income and possessions
Involvement in job	High	Low
Social interaction with workmates	High	Low
Community involvement	Extensive; social life often gender segregated, but public	Very limited; spends non-work time in the home with spouse and family
Salience of class	Identifies with class and recognizes class distinctions	Scarcely aware of belonging to a social class
Reason for joining trade union or voting	Class solidarity and communalism	Instrumental; concern with private goal of improving material condition of family

Source: adapted from Lockwood, 1966

A divided class?

This model of the traditional working class was typical of some workers in the past, though probably never of a majority. Using it as a device for comparison tends to exaggerate the differences between the past and the present. Workers have always found themselves in varied circumstances, with different jobs, in different industries and in different regions of the country, which have prevented the working class from ever being a homogeneous 'traditional' proletariat. It is generally assumed, after Marx, that the more homogeneous the class, the more capable it would be of united political action. The traditional proletarian had a propensity for class solidarity. Close cooperation with workmates and neighbours encouraged an awareness of class interests and, thus, industrial and political solidarity in situations of conflict with other classes. The sociological debate concerns whether workers still experience conditions sufficiently similar to sustain such class awareness and solidarity. Some authors claim that the working class is now hopelessly divided, others argue the contrary.

Assessing this argument is difficult because, while there can be no doubt that differences exist among manual workers (the working class is 'internally differentiated'), deciding whether these differences are deep enough to constitute structural divisions is a matter of interpretation.

Examining the evidence

The highly controversial subject of the modern working class can be approached by examining sociological evidence. We look at these issues with respect to various aspects of working-class experience in contemporary Britain: class position (market situation, work situation and status situation), lifestyle and culture (consumption and social participation) and political practices (class consciousness, voting, and membership of political organizations). In each case, we look at changes in circumstances and assess (1) whether these changes make the working class less distinctive, and (2) whether they affect the internal unity of the working class. Throughout the rest of this section we provide evidence and argument to help resolve the two main issues – the distinctiveness of the class and its internal divisions.

Class position

When British sociologists talk of the working class they are usually referring to people currently or formerly employed in manual occupations and to their dependants. Thus, heads of households in manual jobs, retired or unemployed former manual workers, and housewives and children not in employment, are considered members of the working class. This definition is problematic. It is not always easy to decide whether a particular job is 'manual' or 'non-manual'. As the discussion of the proletarianization of office work (section 3.5) indicates, the work and market situations of many non-manual jobs are developing characteristics very like those of traditional manual occupations. Furthermore there are a substantial number of households in which the husband is a manual worker and his wife is in non-manual employment, which makes it difficult to attribute a class position to the household. Nevertheless, despite these difficulties, most sociologists have considered the distinction between manual and non-manual workers important because the work experience and social lives of these two groups have differed significantly in the past.

One important aspect of change has been the declining size of the

Table 3.9   Distribution of manual and non-manual workers, census years 1951–1981

	1951 (%)	1961 (%)	1971 (%)	1981 (%)
Professional	6.63	9.00	11.07	14.66
Employers, managers, proprietors	10.50	10.10	12.43	13.98
Clerical	10.68	12.70	13.90	14.80
Foremen and manual workers	72.19	68.10	62.60	56.55

Source: Routh, 1987, p. 36

manual workforce. Table 3.4 shows that there were 15.6 million manual workers in 1951, but only 13.3 million by 1981. Consequently, as the number of white-collar jobs has increased, the proportion of employees doing manual work has declined, from about 70 per cent in 1951 to about 50 per cent in 1981 (see also table 3.9). The manual working class is no longer a majority of the population.

We examine the class position of the British working class in terms of the three main elements outlined in section 3.1: market, work and status situations.

Market situation

> Market situation . . . the economic position narrowly conceived, consisting of source and size of income, degree of job security, and opportunity for upward occupational mobility. (Lockwood, 1958)

Manual workers are better off than ever before. Real wages have risen over time, which is to say that the actual purchasing power is greater than it used to be. Also, various Acts of Parliament have improved some of the fringe benefits of manual work. Longer statutory holidays are an improvement; so too is the introduction of redundancy payments to remove some financial insecurities. On the other hand, the source of manual workers' incomes and their opportunities for promotion are probably the same as they were 50 years ago. However, the general improvements in market situation alone are insufficient for us to resolve either of our two controversial issues: whether the working class remains distinct from other social classes, and whether the working class is internally divided.

The distinctiveness of the market situation of the working class   Advocates of the convergence thesis point to changes which tend to reduce the differences in the market situation between manual and other workers. During the twentieth century, the average male manual wage, especially of semi- and unskilled workers, has increased relative to that for routine white-collar work. The 1992 *New Earnings Survey* showed that the average full-time male manual wage was £268 per week, whilst the average for clerical and related work was £248 per week. The average non-manual wage was much higher at £400 per week. The convergence of the weekly wage of clerks and manual workers obscures many differences.

First, manual workers work longer hours. The average working week for a male British manual worker in 1992 was 44.5 hours; non-manuals worked 38.6 hours. (Incidentally, working hours are significantly longer in Britain than in other major European countries.) This follows from the fact that high earnings from manual work usually depend upon lots of overtime: on average, overtime was 5.5 hours per week, and 14 per cent of gross weekly earnings derived from overtime.

Second, manual workers have a less attractive profile of earnings over their lifetime. Most non-manual workers have career structures whereby promotion and/or salary increments increase income until fairly late in their working lives. Indeed, as Stewart et al. (1980) showed (see section 3.5), the relatively poor pay of male clerical workers was a statistical artefact, since very few men remained as clerks for their entire working lives. Male clerks are poorly paid, but they either get promoted or change to another occupation. Thus it is that the earnings over an entire lifetime for non-manual workers are considerably greater than those of manual workers.

Third, manual workers suffer from greater insecurity of employment. They are more frequently unemployed (see section 2.9). They may experience short-time working and temporary lay-offs. They are rarely entitled to sickness pay, are unable to take time off with pay to deal with family emergencies, and usually have pay deducted for lateness. Office workers suffer few of these indignities and insecurities: and the higher up the managerial hierarchy one goes, the better are fringe benefits and conditions of employment. It is probably, in the end, the degree of insecurity which most strongly distinguishes manual work. Most manual workers will experience unemployment at some time, making periods of considerable hardship part of the normal life course.

Fourth, some manual workers are very poorly paid indeed. A significant proportion of people in poverty are in work, but are paid an insufficient amount to bring them above the poverty line. Thus, the market situation of manual workers is distinctive and inferior in certain respects even when compared with the most routine white-collar occupations.

Internal differentiation in the market situation of the working class   There is considerable variation in market situation among manual workers. Different jobs in different industries pay different wages. The best-paid manual workers in 1992 were involved in the extraction of mineral oil and natural gas, where the average male wage was £468 per week. By contrast, men in the hotel and catering industry earned only £184 per week on average.

The most systematic difference, perhaps, was the gap between pay for men and women. One in three full-time women manual workers earned less than £140 per week; only one in four women earned more than £200. Although there has been some slight improvement over the last decade, women manual workers earn only 63 per cent of men's even when employed full-time. Many women are part-timers and are even less well paid.

The inferior position of women is often analysed in terms of 'dual labour markets' (see also section 4.2). Women, and to an extent men of ethnic minorities, cluster in the secondary, lower, sector of the labour market, where wages are poorer, jobs less secure, firms smaller and more precarious, and conditions worse. The market situation of women is one source of division among manual workers.

On the other hand, wage differentials between skilled and less skilled manual workers have declined. Both for men and women, unskilled and semi-skilled workers have caught up. Though differentials continue to cause conflict between unions, with skilled workers seeking to maintain their relative privileges, the range of incomes within the class has narrowed. Probably, then, the market situation of the working class is no more differentiated than it used to be. However, differences along the dimensions of gender – or ethnicity – are readily identifiable and might, therefore, create deeper political divisions, especially where the trade unions protecting white males can be seen as contributing to the inferior position of women and black people.

Work situation

> Work situation, the set of social relationships in which the individual is involved at work by virtue of his position in the division of labour. (Lockwood, 1958)

The work situation – or the relationships of authority in the labour process – of manual workers has been discussed at length in section 2.5. It was concluded that many workers had little control over their work, as control had been wrested from them by management. This was the essence of the process of deskilling, one which had had a very considerable impact on manual work and was also spreading to routine clerical work. Most manual workers, other than craftsmen, have little discretion over their own working practices. Equally, manual workers, except for a small percentage of foremen and supervisors, exercise no authority over other workers. Rather, in general, they are in the most subordinate occupational positions. (In section 3.2 and table 3.1 we noted that even fewer women than men held positions of authority.) Consequently, most manual workers have an instrumental or 'economistic' attitude towards work: their principal concerns are with pay and job security rather than with intrinsic features of the work. These attitudes often foster cooperative, or solidaristic, relationships among manual workers themselves.

There is a degree of convergence between manual and non-manual jobs. The work situations of some routine white-collar workers and some lower and middle managers have deteriorated. Nevertheless, even among these jobs, conditions of work are usually more pleasant: they are less dangerous and less noisy, for instance. Indeed, the main contrast in work situations between classes lies in the superior conditions experienced by professionals, senior managers and owners of businesses.

There remains considerable variation within the manual working class in work situation, depending upon the type of industry, the nature of managerial control, and the degree of discretion which the worker has over the work process. This is not, however, a feature of working-class experience which in itself creates serious internal divisions. A man who is a process worker is not likely to feel hostile towards either a worker on an assembly line or a farm labourer just because of the difference in work situation.

Status situation

> Status situation . . . the position of the individual in the hierarchy of prestige in the society at large. (Lockwood, 1958)

The degree of prestige attached to manual jobs, and the social status of the incumbents of those jobs, suggest that manual employment is generally held in low esteem. When people are asked to rank occupations in terms of their desirability, there is a fair degree of consensus. In that hierarchy, manual jobs come at the bottom, though there is some degree of overlap between white- and blue-collar occupations. This suggests a fairly strong separation in most people's minds between manual and non-manual employment.

Another indication of the prestige of manual occupations, which also shows continued separation between manual workers and others, is given by patterns of sociability and friendship. Almost all studies show that the friends and acquaintances of manual workers are themselves predominantly working class. Patterns of sociability continue to be classbound, which contributes to the separation of one class from another.

Again, there is little reason to think that differences of prestige attached to manual jobs cause serious internal divisions. Even supervisory workers in manual occupations, like foremen in the London docks, associate more with manual than non-manual workers.

Working-class culture

Experiences outside work affect class solidarity and political action. For example, the neighbourhood in which a worker lives affects his or her voting behaviour. Two aspects of the changing lifestyle of the working class have attracted special attention recently – consumption patterns and privatization. Consumption patterns emerge from the choices made about how money is spent. Privatization refers to the use of time outside work, particularly the amounts of time spent at home with the family rather than in public and communal activities. Both changed consumption patterns and privatization have been said to reduce working-class identity and solidarity.

Consumption

Although poverty has remained widespread (see section 3.3), most workers in Britain have a better standard of living than 50 years ago. Average real incomes have risen, and manual workers now possess consumer goods which were previously only accessible to a small minority of the population. Working-class households are increasingly likely to own durable goods like cars, fridges and washing machines, and to have a telephone and central heating in their dwellings. Perhaps the most remarked-upon change is, however, the growth of working-class house ownership. In 1988, 72 per cent of skilled manual households, 50 per cent of semi-skilled and 35 per cent of unskilled either owned outright the house in which they were living, or were in the process of purchasing it on a mortgage. This represents a considerable expansion of owner-occupation for, except in a few regions of Britain, manual workers usually used to rent housing from private landlords or the council. It has frequently been assumed that these new consumption patterns would have lasting structural effects on the working class. Indeed, the embourgeoisement thesis was based on observing the spread of the goods associated with a middle-class lifestyle.

Table 3.10 Expenditure of households by occupation of head of household, employees, 1988

	Average weekly household expenditure (£)	Average weekly expenditure per person (£)
Professional	318	113
Employers, managers	339	114
Intermediate non-manual	242	96
Junior non-manual	221	89
Skilled manual	230	71
Semi-skilled manual	195	67
Unskilled manual	164	61

Source: *Family Expenditure Survey, 1988*, HMSO, 1990, table 15. Crown copyright

The consumption patterns of different classes   One weakness of the argument that affluence leads to assimilation of workers to a middle-class lifestyle is the fact that consumption patterns remain markedly unequal between classes. Table 3.10, taken from the *Family Expenditure Survey*, shows that in 1988 household spending varied depending on the occupational class of heads of households. Households of employers and managers spent on average £109 per week more than skilled manual workers and £175 per week more than unskilled manual workers. Routine white-collar households spend about the same as skilled manual workers. However, when expenditure per person is calculated, a different, and more pertinent, impression is obtained. Clerical workers' households are smaller than those of manual workers, so that the level of consumption of each member is considerably higher. Considered in this way, the expenditure of routine non-manual workers is more like that of other non-manual households. That impression is reinforced by examining differences in what exactly is purchased.

Table 3.11 shows expenditure per head of household of different occupational classes, expressed in relation to the pattern of a skilled manual worker. A number of points emerge:

1   Expenditure on food and alcohol varies least across households: expenditure on services and consumer durables varies most.
2   Non-manual household members consume considerably more than their manual counterparts; this applies to routine white-collar workers as well as professionals.

Table 3.11 Expenditure per person on various services and commodities for certain occupational groupings of head of household as proportion of skilled manual households (= 100), 1988

| Commodity or service | Occupation of head of household | | | |
	Professional	Junior non-manual	Skilled manual	Unskilled manual
Housing	170	138	100	91
Food	126	113	100	92
Alcoholic drink	93	95	100	85
Household goods	189	140	100	100
Household services	206	177	100	68
Transport	159	125	100	75
Leisure services	264	132	100	58
Total expenditure per person[a] (£)	113.18	89.00	71.39	60.85
Total household expenditure (£)	318.49	221.04	230.27	163.98

[a] Expenditure per person has been derived by dividing the household expenditure for each commodity or service by the average number of persons per household. These figures have then been expressed as proportions of the equivalent figures for households whose head was a skilled manual worker.

Source: *Family Expenditure Survey*, HMSO, 1990

3   Unskilled workers are relatively deprived compared with other groups, especially with respect to leisure and domestic services.
4   Non-manual workers are most distinctive in the amounts of money they spend on services, consumer durables and housing.

This evidence gives some support to the view that there are quite significant differences between manual and non-manual consumption patterns. Of course, it must be recognized that expenditure varies very much within each group. These are average figures. Levels of household expenditure depend crucially on the number of people in employment in the household, and the number of dependants. Nevertheless, class differences are still significant and are to be expected given the weaker market situation of manual workers.

Internal differences: consumption cleavages?   Although class differences in consumption remain, many writers continue to see the *absolute* improvement in workers' living standards as of wider significance. Some, like Seabrook (1978), consider that the aspirations of the working class towards higher levels of consumption corrode values of solidarity. In a

Table 3.12 Socio-economic group and economic activity status of head of household by tenure, Great Britain, 1983

Socio-economic group and economic activity status of head of household[a]	Owner occupied			Rented				Total (%)
	Owned outright (%)	With mortgage (%)	With job/ business (%)	Local authority/ new town (%)	Housing association/ cooperative (%)	Unfurnished private (%)	Furnished private (%)	
Economically active heads:								
Professional	3	9	10	0	1	1	10	5
Employers and managers	8	27	34	3	3	6	12	15
Intermediate non-manual	4	12	9	2	5	6	13	7
Junior non-manual	3	7	7	3	1	5	11	5
Skilled manual and own account non-professional	12	29	16	17	13	17	14	20
Semi-skilled manual and personal service	4	8	20	11	10	7	9	8
Unskilled manual	1	1	2	5	3	2	1	2
Economically inactive heads	65	7	2	60	65	57	28	38
Base = 100% (no.)	2,393	4,018	166	2,600	222	419	212	10,043

[a] Excluding members of the armed forces, full-time students, and those who have never worked.

Source: General Household Survey, 1988, HMSO, 1990, p. 242

world where 'we are invited to define ourselves by what we can buy rather than what we can create', workers become dehumanized, obsessed with an individualistic urge to consume, and are increasingly money-centred. Such concerns draw workers so heavily into the capitalist order that the values the labour movement embodied – cooperation, mutual support, care for the underprivileged, hope of a more creative way of life – get completely smothered.

Other authors argue that new patterns of consumption, especially of houses, divide the working class internally. Consumption cleavages have arisen between households with predominantly private access to housing and transport and those which depend on public provision (i.e. council housing and public transport). In 1988, 64 per cent of manual workers were owner-occupiers and 68 per cent owned a car. House ownership, in particular, may create differences of status and of material interests within the working class. Most owner-occupiers have benefited financially since the 1960s because house prices have risen faster than inflation and because of tax relief on mortgages. The gains are, relatively, at the expense of tenants in rented housing, who by 1990 were almost entirely working class (see table 3.12). There was also some prestige attached to owner-occupation, and perhaps some sense of greater control over one's life arising from ownership of property. Certainly the sale of council houses to sitting tenants was a very popular policy and many, predominantly working class, people bought their dwellings. Indeed, survey evidence shows that about 90 per cent of the British population prefer owner-occupation to renting. However, it is doubtful whether a change in tenure causes people to alter other aspects of their behaviour.

Privatization

The private ownership of property should be distinguished from privatized social lives. Privatization has been defined as 'a process . . . manifested in a pattern of social life which is centred on and, indeed, largely restricted to, the home and the conjugal family' (Goldthorpe et al., 1969 p. 97). This process was identified in the study of Luton in the 1960s. The social contacts of Luton manual workers were restricted to immediate kin (parents, spouse and children). They rarely met workmates or neighbours. Most of their spare time was spent at home. Similar patterns were observed in other studies: by Young and Willmott (1973) in Greater London, by Pahl (1984) on the Isle of Sheppey and by Hill (1976) in the East End of London among dockers. However, the idea that a process of privatization is progressively affecting the entire working class is much disputed.

Critical appraisal of the privatization thesis again suggests that the ideal type of the traditional working class is misleading because, in this

Plate 3.2 An aerial photograph of Preston in the 1930s. This demonstrates the high density and closely built up nature of the early industrial town. Though open space is lacking, the town is small and open countryside is not far away (though not visible here); and, with factories scattered among houses, the journey to work is short.
Source: Aerofilms

case, it exaggerates conviviality. One aspect of the model of the occupational community was its provision of communal leisure for men. Studies of coal-mining townships (e.g. Dennis et al., 1956) were taken as prototypical, displaying a very pronounced male peer group behaviour; except for a few years while courting, most miners entertained themselves in the company of their male friends and colleagues in public institutions like pubs, clubs, churches and football teams. Such settings provided conditions for working-class solidarity. Solidarities emerging from conflicts with employers were reinforced outside work through overlapping loyalties of kinship, neighbourhood and friendship. Such places exhibited dense social networks and created strong group identities.

Such communities have become less common. Industrial change, urban renewal and geographical mobility have combined together to destroy many of them. Those industries which tended to generate occupational communities (coal-mining, shipbuilding, textiles, the railways) have declined considerably. New industries tend to be located long

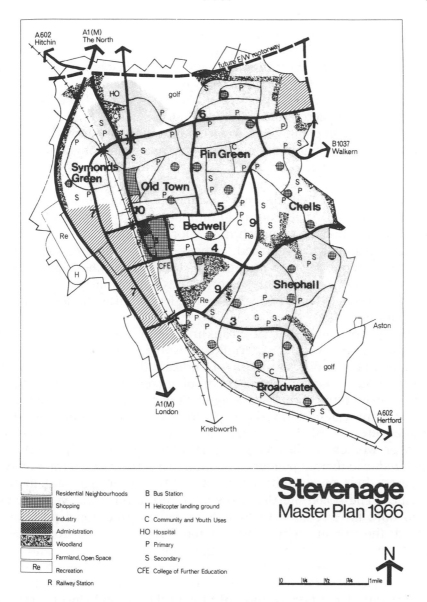

Figure 3.4 Master plan for Stevenage, the first new town to be designated (in 1946): built for London overspill and sited 30 miles north of the metropolis, in Hertfordshire, Stevenage is a good example of the 'mark one' new town of the 1940s, designed on neighbourhood unit principles.

Source. Commission for the New Towns, reproduced with permission

distances away from where their workers live. The geographical separation of workplace from residence is illustrated by comparing the picture of Preston in the 1930s with the ground plan of Stevenage new town (figure 3.4). In Preston, the cotton mills (see the chimneys) are spread evenly across the working-class districts of the town, each surrounded by closely packed terraced houses which would be occupied by the mill workers. Work and non-work were closely knit. The plan of Stevenage shows a sharp separation of industrial areas from commercial and residential areas. Workers in any one factory would be likely to be distributed thinly across the different housing estates (and beyond).

The same urban planning policies have resulted in enforced geographical mobility. Although most manual workers have strongly preferred to stay near their place of birth, because kin and friends are there, when jobs move to new towns and away from the old cities they have little alternative but to follow the work. Even where work remains available in the cities, slum clearance and road building destroy communities. Social bonds of neighbourhood, which take a long time to develop, are broken and cannot quickly be replaced. However, the decline of such settings does not thereby prove the privatization thesis. First, the apparently new 'privatized' behaviour has been shown to exist previously. Second, social contacts remain extensive, even if rather less intense and less masculine than before.

Investigations like that of Franklin (1989), who used oral history techniques to recover the experience of women tobacco factory workers in the Bedminster district of Bristol, indicate that the almost exclusively male communal conviviality of the mining community was not the only form of twentieth-century working-class experience. The expansion of factory employment allowed escape from the narrow and domestically confined lifestyle of the previous generation of working-class women. Younger women at the Wills factory obtained relatively good wages which reduced their dependence on men, drew them out of the home and increased their opportunities for sociability and engagement in public activities. The social life that women from the inter-war years remembered bore little relation to that described as 'traditional proletarian'. Indeed, the privatization argument has largely, and improperly, been based on considerations of changing male behaviour. The major expansion of employment for married women since the 1960s has *reduced* home-centredness for at least the female half of the working class.

Peter Saunders's (1990) study of Slough, Derby and Burnley (see also section 7.4) was concerned to investigate whether privatism developed as a consequence of owner-occupation. He found some evidence for home ownership reducing neighbourhood relations (see table 3.13). Mutual aid and neighbourhood life were, overall, stronger on council estates. However, this was probably due to different rates of geographical mobility: 79 per cent of council tenants, compared with 56 per cent of owner-occupiers, had never lived in any town other than their present one, and thus had had plenty of time to cement their social networks. In addition, tenants had lived in their existing houses longer on average.

Table 3.13   Housing tenure and neighbourhood relations

Neighbourhood relations[a]	Housing tenure Home owners (no.)	(%)	Council tenants (no.)	(%)
At least one close friend living in the neighbourhood	89	35	56	56
At least one close friend living in the town	112	44	57	57
At least one close friend met through the neighbourhood	82	35	44	50
At least one close friend known since childhood	71	31	77	90
Has lived in three or more dwellings since first set up home	182	50	60	46
Always lived in the same town since first set up home	205	56	101	79
Thinks neighbourhood is friendly or very friendly	216	60	77	60
No favours or aid for or from neighbours	100	29	37	30
Regular help by or for neighbours	38	11	23	19

[a] Totals differ for each item due to missing data.

Source: Saunders, 1990, p. 285

Working-class owner-occupiers were, by contrast, more involved than tenants in formal organizations. Nor did Saunders find any relationship between tenure and whether people go out for entertainment: mortgagees were not so heavily burdened by debt that they must stay at home. He found scarcely any examples of people who consciously changed their behaviour and became home-centred as a result of acquiring their own home. He therefore finds the argument that owner-occupation encourages privatism refuted.

Saunders's results are largely corroborated by the national survey of Marshall et al. (1988). This shows little difference between classes in terms of privatism. Working-class leisure is slightly more likely to be undertaken in the home, and those with friends at work are slightly less likely to meet them socially outside work (see table 3.14). But in most respects – for instance, whether leisure is taken with family or friends – class differences are insignificant. The working class is not especially privatized and no more so than the service class. Devine (1992) drew the same conclusion from her in-depth study of Luton manual workers in the 1980s.

Table 3.14 Work-based friendships by Goldthorpe class

(a)   Proportion of his or her friends whom respondent works with at present

| | Class | | | | | | |
	I (%)	II (%)	III (%)	IV (%)	V (%)	VI (%)	VII (%)
None	38	45	49	76	37	34	46
1–10%	38	28	30	14	31	37	30
11–50%	17	15	12	5	19	18	13
51–100%	7	12	9	5	13	11	11
Total (no.)	113	215	234	112	90	145	269

(N = 1178)

(b) Does respondent with friends at work see these people socially outside work?

| | Class | | | | | | |
	I (%)	II (%)	III (%)	IV (%)	V (%)	VI (%)	VII (%)
Yes	91	90	86	89	88	77	67
No	9	10	14	11	12	23	33
Total (no.)	69	117	120	27	57	95	144

(N = 629)

Source: Marshall et al., 1988, p. 217

Affluent workers revisited: a case study

Goldthorpe et al. (1968a; 1968b; 1969) used Luton as a 'critical case study' of the embourgeoisement thesis; there, if anywhere, normative convergence between working and middle classes ought to have been apparent. When the evidence showed not, they felt justified in dismissing the embourgeoisement thesis. However, the study of a single, distinctive town could not convincingly prove their alternative account – that instrumental-privatized workers were, or would become, typical throughout Britain. Subsequent investigations looking for the instrumental-privatized worker claimed that he could not be found. In 1986 Fiona Devine, returning to Luton to interview members of family households containing male manual workers currently employed at the Vauxhall plant, found them neither instrumental nor especially privatized.

Devine (1992) used open-ended interviews with 62 Luton residents, aged between mid 20s and late 60s. She found them not enormously privatized. She argued that Goldthorpe et al. misinterpreted the role of geographical migration. She found that people went to Luton because of threats of unemployment at home, not because they were particularly ambitious and therefore prepared to abandon their kin. Indeed, kin networks were built up in Luton by people from London, the north of England, Ireland and the New Commonwealth, some arriving to join kin already there, others being followed subsequently to Luton by their family members.

Once there, life-course stage and gender were the key determinants of sociability. Young parents were the most home-centred (importantly, Goldthorpe et al.'s original sample included only men between 20 and 45, meaning that most respondents would be at this early stage in family formation, their freedom thereby curtailed). Luton men in the 1980s had more out-of-home leisure than women, but Devine insists that this was not to the exclusion of extensive involvement in family entertainment both in and beyond the home. Her interviewees maintained extensive contact with their own parents and to variable degrees with siblings – as is the case among all social classes throughout the UK. The newly married kept contact with schoolfriends; most people were friendly with the neighbours, with such relationships strong for women home-makers with young children; most had some, though limited, contact with workmates outside work. The interviewees would have liked to see more of their friends (they certainly do not aspire to domestic privatism), but the pressures of maintaining a household, looking after children, being tired after work, having to travel distances to meet friends and being short of money were the predominantly practical reasons for spending considerable amounts of time at home. Devine concluded that they were neither traditional nor privatized.

Indeed the patterns seem to indicate the existence of orderly, routine ways of life, organized around the task of getting-by respectably (i.e. in accordance with standards shared by other members of their social networks) and as comfortably as possible in the face of material insecurity. They hoped for some improvement in material standard of living, though they expected this to happen later in the family cycle. While recognizing that life was somewhat easier than it had been for their parents, they still considered aspects of British society unfair and unjust, but they seemed pragmatically focused on securing the conditions for stable family life.

Recent investigations have concluded that contemporary working-class households consume in a different way to those of the middle class, and

Table 3.15 Attitudes to distributional justice by Goldthorpe class

(a) Is distribution of wealth and income fair?

Class	Yes (%)	No (%)
I	31	69
II	34	66
III	28	72
IV	44	56
V	24	76
VI	25	75
VII	22	78
All	29	71
Total (no.)	368	914

(b) Why not?[a]

	Class I (%)	II (%)	III (%)	IV (%)	V (%)	VI (%)	VII (%)
Distribution favours those at the top							
Gap between haves and have nots is too wide	57	59	63	64	55	63	63
Pay differentials are too wide	21	19	19	19	26	21	19
Too much poverty, wages too low, too many reduced to welfare	13	17	20	16	13	17	18
Some people acquire wealth too easily (unearned income etc.)	31	16	13	13	20	10	9
The higher paid are not taxed severely enough	9	15	11	9	12	20	16
Welfare benefits are too low	6	5	6	2	8	9	6
The lower paid or working class are taxed too severely	2	3	3	5	3	0	2
Inequalities of opportunity (in education, for jobs, etc.)	2	2	2	0	0	1	2
Unequal regional distribution (of jobs, income, etc.)	4	3	3	0	2	1	2

Distribution favours those at the bottom							
There are too many scroungers around	6	5	12	9	15	8	10
Pay differentials are too narrow	5	4	1	3	4	4	4
The higher paid are taxed too severely	4	2	3	8	3	3	3
Other reasons							
Inequality of wealth and income inevitable	1	4	4	2	7	2	2
Key groups of workers can hold the country to ransom	1	1	0	0	0	0	0

ª Percentages in the 'Why not?' columns are based on respondents. Valid cases = 899.

Source: Marshall et al. 1988, p. 186

that there are differences within the working class. Patterns of sociability are, however, not much differentiated by class and manual workers are neither obsessed by consumerism nor excessively privatized. The daily lives of the working class are constrained by their limited resources. Whether the evidence overall justifies the identification of a distinctive working-class culture is a matter of interpretation. Some workers live more privatized lifestyles than others and it remains possible that privatization is a regional phenomenon: all the studies claiming privatism were conducted in the south-east of England. However, no one has yet demonstrated that there is a systematic structural basis for variation in privatism, or that it has been responsible for undermining solidarism.

Working-class politics

In many respects, the debates about the working class are aimed at resolving questions about political consciousness and action. Do workers identify themselves as a class having shared class interests? To what extent does this lead them to support particular political organizations?

Class awareness and identification do not seem to have altered much in recent times. It continues to be the case that the 'subjective' class position of many manual workers (i.e. which class they consider themselves as belonging to) does not entirely correspond with their 'objective' class position. Those manual workers who *do* consider themselves 'middle class' tend to be those with extensive social contacts with non-manual workers and/or those who live in predominantly middle-class areas.

The vast majority of British people (in most surveys more than 90 per cent) recognize the existence of social classes and will see themselves as belonging to one such class. There is a good deal of variation in the way people describe those classes, and little consensus on how many classes there are or precisely what it is that determines which class a person belongs to. Attempts to explain how different 'images of society' (as popular conceptions of class structure are often called) arise and are adopted have mostly failed. However, it is probably the case that the more a manual worker shares the attributes of the traditional proletarian, the more likely it is that she or he will see workers as a class. There is no reliable evidence demonstrating that new images are emerging or spreading.

Distinctiveness: proletarians or citizens

It used to be argued that the working class had a distinctive conception of social and political conflict which sustained their support for the labour movement. Thus, traditional proletarians had a dichotomous image of society, distinguishing sharply between 'them' (the rich, the owners, the bosses) and 'us' (the workers). From this arose both a class identity and a sense of politics as class conflict. It was reported frequently in the 1960s, for instance, that manual workers voted consistently for the Labour Party because it was the party of the workers, of 'people like us'.

Despite many claims to the contrary, recent sociological evidence suggests that this imagery and awareness remains predominant and is the only pattern consistently found among manual workers. Roberts et al.'s (1977) study of class images in Liverpool in the early 1970s suggested that there was only one coherent image of society prevalent among the working class and that was the proletarian image. This was held in different degrees of intensity and consistency: often it was so ill-formed and faint that it seemed unlikely to affect workers' political behaviour. The main exception was a group of manual workers whose attitudes were indistinguishable from those of the lower ranks of the middle class. There was no evidence for the existence of a new privatized-instrumental working class with a distinctive image of society.

The dichotomous image of class is actually widespread. In Marshall et al.'s (1988) study, 63 per cent of the sample 'agreed that the *main* social conflict in Britain today was between those who run industry and those who work for them' (p. 151). Differences of view between classes are mildly apparent on issues of distribution. Table 3.15 shows that the working class (classes VI and VII on the Goldthorpe scale) are most likely to find the distribution of income unfair. However, most of the evidence suggests that manual workers in general are not highly distinctive in their views of social structure.

Respondents to questionnaires show no decline in awareness of class. Class remains something which they can observe and which they experience, and through which they view aspects of both politics and everyday life. Consider, for example, table 3.16. Every so often Gallup Polls, in their regular monthly opinion polls, ask a question about the importance of 'class struggle'. The answers to the same question posed at different times since 1964 show a very substantial increase in the percentage of respondents who consider there to be a class struggle; in July 1991, 79 per cent said there was. Although the validity of the exact figures may be questioned, the trend in answers to the question is remarkable.

Table 3.16 Class struggle: replies to the question, 'There used to be a lot of talk in politics about the "class struggle". Do you think there is a class struggle in this country or not?'

Date	Is (%)	Is not (%)	Don't know (%)
1964 July	48	39	13
1972 June	58	29	13
1973 January	53	33	14
1974 February	62	27	11
1975 April	60	29	11
1981 March	66	25	9
1984 March	74	20	6
1986 February	70	24	6
1991 July	79	16	4

Source: *Gallup Political Index Report*, 371, July 1991; Moorhouse, 1976

The evidence then suggests that working-class people do still feel some sense of class identity and consider that it affects their lives. This is probably the result both of living in a political environment which is structured by class interests, and of the experience of class in everyday life. Table 3.16 implies that members of other classes have of late increased their class awareness. However, class identity only sustains a radical, alternative political value system among a minority of manual workers and is not often translated into class-based political action.

Perhaps the most distinctive feature of the working class is its lack of political participation. Although there are no accurate figures, individual membership of the Labour Party has fallen from about 1 million to 311,000 between 1950 and 1990, and in the process the *proportion* of manual workers (26 per cent in 1990) has probably reduced (Seyd and Whiteley, 1992, pp. 16, 33). Parallel to that is the fall in the proportion of manual workers who are selected as candidates for the Labour Party at elections. The working class has become less involved in Labour Party politics, but has not replaced that by participation in other parties of the left or right. Although many workers in 1991 voted for the Conservative Party and the Alliance, they are not joining them. The indications are that as involvement in Labour politics declines, working-class people cease to participate in party politics, except to vote. Disillusionment with party politics and with governments among the working class is a process widely identified. Marshall et al. (1988) discerned an 'informed fatalism': most people thought that government could, if determined, rectify distributional inequalities and social injustice, but were resigned to the fact that it would not in practice.

Although other social classes express disillusionment with party politics, they have tended to participate through other channels: the campaigns of pressure groups and social movements like the Campaign for Nuclear Disarmament (CND) are mostly run and supported by middle-class personnel. Increasingly, working-class political activity is restricted to voting and to industrial activity, where membership of and support for trade unions remains widespread (see section 2.6).

Voting behaviour is discussed in section 12.2. Briefly, the Labour Party remains dependent on manual workers for votes: of all those who voted Labour in 1987, about two-thirds were manual working class. However, only 48 per cent of manual workers who voted chose Labour. Working-class support was highly concentrated geographically, in the largest cities, in the north, south Wales and Scotland. Only in those areas can it be said that the working class exhibits distinctive, class-like voting behaviour.

In most respects the working class has become integrated into the dominant, national political institutions. This is true of both workers themselves and more so of their principal political organization, the Labour Party.

Most workers accept the political order in Britain. They accept parliamentary institutions (including the House of Lords), the monarchy, the civil service, and law enforcement agencies. It is debatable to what extent this acceptance is based on a belief in the positive desirability of these institutions. Probably acceptance is 'pragmatic': believing that things are difficult if not impossible to change, and because it is unclear what might be better, opposition is negligible. (The people of Northern Ireland are the main exception to this.) Pragmatic acceptance probably fades into a weak endorsement of the legitimacy of those institutions.

The low levels of political class conflict in Britain are partly the result of the Labour Party's success. When in government Labour has pursued egalitarian policies. Having aimed to extend political and social rights to all citizens equally, it has necessarily reduced some of the bases of class resentment. Comprehensive education, the National Health Service and economic planning procedures were justified in terms of their potential for removing class distinctions. When the Labour Party points to its achievements, it legitimizes the mixed economy and the welfare state, encouraging workers to see themselves as *equal citizens* rather than as a deprived social class. In this way the Labour Party, itself an organization deeply involved in the established political system, incorporates the working class into society.

The incorporation process is, however, never likely to be complete, largely because of the experience of work. It is ironic that the popularity of accounts bidding farewell to the working class coincided with the miners' strike of 1984–5, the longest and one of the most bitter conflicts in the history of British industrial relations. The strike, lasting 12 months, was characterized on the one hand by intense solidarity and commitment by men and women in the communities on strike, but on the other hand by divisions within the National Union of Mineworkers which led to the Nottinghamshire miners continuing to work. As the state has become more involved in regulating industrial relations in the last 20 years the boundary between industrial and political conflict has become hard to draw. In this way industrial action by workers increasingly appears as political action.

For these reasons it is unwise to anticipate the end of working-class politics. It is true that worker opposition has moderated in recent years. But this is importantly because the conditions for the mobilization of opposition are unfavourable. First, deep economic recession does not provide fruitful circumstances for industrial conflict: unions are weakened by high levels of unemployment, redundancies and company bankruptcy. Also the party political balance has lain with the Conservative Party for the last decade. The failure of the Labour Party to make much impact either upon the government or upon potential supporters among the working class is also part of the adverse current political climate. A second main reason for the relative political passivity of workers in current conditions probably derives from a lack of unity within the working class. The situation has been described by some authors as the *fragmentation* of the working class.

The politics of a fragmented working class?

As we have seen, the working class *is* internally differentiated. While there never has been a homogeneous working class in Britain, arguably the class is more fragmented now than in the past, and this may account for the declining fortunes of the Labour Party. There are three main accounts of fragmentation:

1   The main body of politically active workers used to be white males. Today, not only is the number of white male manual workers declining, but a larger proportion of all manual workers (close to 50 per cent) are either women or black people. Gender and ethnic differences create some distinctive political interests which have recently been the focus of political action. To the extent that these interests are in competition with those of white men, disunity follows.
2   The existence of many trade unions gives rise to another fragmenting force. Unions are run for their members. Often this results in competition between unions: demarcation disputes are an example, whereby one group of workers tries to exclude other groups from, usually highly paid, tasks. This kind of competition frequently occurs between men and women too. Thus unions become 'sectionalist', that is putting the interests of the section of the class which they represent before the interests of the class as a whole.
3   Differences within the class also occur between those organized in trade unions and those not. The organized tend to be better off because they can exercise some power. However, their gains may be at the expense of the unorganized – which will again include many women and people from ethnic minorities, but also the unemployed and the retired. This is interpreted, by for example Gorz (1982), as a process of polarization whereby the organized perceive their interests to be served by the existing political system and thus become directly opposed to the remainder of workers. The working class is thus fundamentally divided, with the minority of organized workers exercising its power at the expense of the rest.

All three of these accounts contain some truth. Whether any of these divisions justify bidding 'farewell to the working class' is largely a matter of judgment. We deal with some evidence for each account in turn.

First, racist and sexist behaviour, common to all social classes in Britain (see chapters 4 and 5), is sometimes especially apparent in working-class environments. For instance, black people are dispropor-tionately clustered in manual occupations and are likely to live in working-class residential areas. They may thus experience racism directly at the hands of working-class whites, a situation hardly likely to encourage class solidarity. The experiences of women in paid employment are somewhat similar. Some work cultures are aggressively masculine (see section 4.2), exhibiting hostility or contempt towards women. Trade unions often appear as organizations of men and for men, excluding women from participation and defending men's occupational interests. In many workplaces, supervisory workers are men and they use strategies of control which express male power (see section 4.6). Hence, ethnic and gender identities may inhibit class solidarity.

Second, union organizations open up other sectionalist divisions besides those based on ethnicity and gender. A union exists primarily to further the interests of its members (see section 2.6). In the process unions come into conflict with one another: they compete for members and they try to give their own members a better deal than other unions can achieve. As bargaining has become more decentralized recently, with agreements made at plant rather than national level, wage differentials between workers in the same occupation have increased. Unions also fight about rights over particular jobs: one notorious incident of the 1980s was a dispute at Times Newspapers where one union permitted its members to operate new technology which another union had refused to use. So, there are bases for sectionalism among unions. But at the same time it must be recognized that most unions still cooperate at plant, local, national and international levels. There have always been episodes of sectionalism, but allegiance to the trade union movement has not been undermined.

Perhaps the most widely voiced argument is the third, concerning polarization. Organized workers in paid employment are generally better off than the unorganized – not to mention the unemployed and other welfare recipients. Organized workers have benefited from their improved representation in the corridors of power over the last 50 years. The so-called 'corporatism thesis' (see further section 12.4) is one indication of this. Corporatism refers to the presence of institutionalized bargaining between the central organizations of capital and labour (in Britain, the Confederation of British Industry (CBI) and the Trades Union Congress (TUC)), coordinated by the state, with a view to planning the economy and regulating wages. In such a system the interests of the most powerful groups among the working class are represented, but the unorganized are ignored. The weaknesses of the corporatism thesis is that it overestimates the power of the trade unions and fails to recognize the role that the TUC plays in pressing for social reforms which benefit other, weaker, social groups.

In the end, we are inclined to believe that all these divisions are old and persistent and do not imply a qualitatively new type of politics.

Summary

There are no simple and unambiguous solutions to the question of the condition of the contemporary working class. However, the following points may be made:

1 Manual workers are a declining proportion of all workers; and an increasing proportion of manual workers are either female and/or from ethnic minorities.
2 Manual workers in aggregate remain socially distinctive, particularly in respect of their market situation, their status situation, their consumption patterns and their political imagery. However, there is overlap especially with workers in routine non-manual occupations.
3 In some respects, especially of work situation and of privatized lifestyles, manual workers are indistinguishable from routine non-manual workers; but they still remain distinct from professional and managerial workers on these dimensions.
4 There is considerable internal differentiation within the manual working class. This has always been the case, but it may be increasing, creating political divisions within the working class along lines of ethnicity, gender, region and union membership.
5 The effects of these divisions on working-class political movements for social change (socialism) are uncertain, but quite clearly are dependent upon the relations established between manual workers and other non-manual employers.

Related topics

The material dealt with in this section appears in many other places in the book. A few of the more important sections which give greater understanding of the circumstances of the working class are: 2.5 on work; 2.6 on trade unions and industrial relations; 2.9 on unemployment; 3.7 on social mobility; 4.2 on women and employment; 5.3 on ethnic disadvantage; 8.4 on inequalities in education; 10.3 on leisure; 10.4 on working-class youth cultures; and 12.2 on voting.

3.5   The Middle Classes

The growth of the middle class

The starting point of any sociological analysis of the middle class is the

Table 3.17 Occupied population of Great Britain by major occupational groups, 1911–1981

Occupational groups	*Occupational groups as % of total occupied population*							
	1911	*1921*	*1931*	*1951*	*1961*	*1966*	*1971*	*1981*
Employers and pro-prietors	6.7	6.8	6.7	5.0	4.7	3.4	–	–
Non-manual workers	18.7	21.2	23.0	30.9	35.9	38.3	44.3	52.3
Managers	3.4	3.6	3.7	5.5	5.4	6.1	9.8	13.7
Higher professionals	1.0	1.0	1.1	1.9	3.0	3.4	3.8	4.8
Lower professionals and technicians	3.1	3.5	3.5	4.7	6.0	6.5	7.7	10.6
Forepersons and inspectors	1.3	1.4	1.5	2.6	2.9	3.0	3.0	4.1
Clerical and related employees	4.5	6.5	6.7	10.4	12.7	13.2	14.2	14.5
Sales employees	5.4	5.1	6.5	5.7	5.9	6.1	5.7	4.6
Manual workers	74.6	72.0	70.3	64.2	59.3	58.3	55.7	47.7

Source: Price and Bain, 1988, p. 164

growth of certain kinds of occupation in the twentieth century (see table 3.17). The most noticeable shift in the period 1911–81 was the steep decline in manual occupations and the relative growth in non-manual jobs. In that period, manual occupations lost almost 27 per cent of the total employed population. Increases were registered among higher professionals (3.8 per cent), managers (10.3 per cent), clerks (10.0 per cent) and foremen (2.8 per cent). Of the non-manual groups, only those employed as sales assistants showed any decline. The white-collar categories themselves did not all gain equally. The higher-professional group increased in size by five times, managers increased almost fourfold, while those in clerical employment increased between threefold and fourfold. The rate of growth of white-collar occupations has also varied over time. The growth in the clerical grade, for example, was at its highest in the years 1911–21, while the higher-professional category increased most quickly from the 1950s onwards.

There are gender differences in these occupational movements. For both men and women, there has been a shift out of manual work into white-collar occupations. Significantly, disproportionate numbers of women have moved into clerical work. As far as the other categories of non-manual work are concerned, however, the increase in the numbers of male managers, and of higher and lower professionals, is considerably greater than for their female equivalents. During the twentieth century men have tended to go into the higher white-collar jobs and women into the more routine ones.

Some further light on these differences is thrown by table 3.18, which shows the gender composition of major occupational groupings rather than the occupations of men and women. The higher-professional category remains overwhelmingly male. In the lower professions, an initial preponderance of women in 1911 was turned into a position of more or less equality by 1981, largely through the heavy recruitment of male teachers. The sex composition of the clerical grade, on the other hand, was almost reversed. While almost 80 per cent of clerks were men in 1911, the same proportion were women in 1981.

Not only have there been significant movements between classes, there have also been important changes within them. Within the higher professions, for example, the numbers of engineers increased by 17 times from 1911 to 1981, while scientists were 15 times as strongly represented, and accountants 7 times as numerous. The traditional professions – law, medicine, and the military – only doubled their numbers, while the numbers of clergy actually declined. The lower professions are dominated by government service. Teachers and nurses alone accounted for 57 per cent in this category in 1911 and 58 per cent in 1981. Social welfare workers and laboratory technicians increased by some 20 times in the

Table 3.18 Female workers in major occupational groups in Great Britain, 1911–1981

Occupational group	1911 (%)	1921 (%)	1931 (%)	1951 (%)	1961 (%)	1966 (%)	1971 (%)	1981 (%)
Employers and pro- prietors	18.8	20.5	19.8	20.0	20.4	23.7	21.7	24.2
Non-manual workers	29.8	37.6	35.8	42.3	44.5	46.5	46.2	42.8
Managers	19.8	17.0	13.0	15.2	15.5	16.7	18.5	21.4
Higher professionals	6.0	5.1	7.5	8.3	9.7	9.4	10.0	13.0
Lower professionals and technicians	62.9	59.4	58.8	53.5	50.8	52.1	51.9	55.0
Forepersons and inspectors	4.2	6.5	8.7	13.4	10.3	11.4	12.8	23.6
Clerical and related employees	21.4	44.6	46.0	60.2	65.2	69.3	71.9	78.1
Sales employees	35.2	43.6	37.2	51.6	54.9	58.7	59.4	77.8
All manual workers	30.5	27.9	28.8	26.1	26.0	29.0	28.6	28.7
Total occupied population	29.6	29.5	29.8	30.8	32.4	35.6	36.0	38.9

Source: Price and Bain, 1988, p. 166

same 60 years, while the number of teachers and nurses only quadrupled, an increase which included a striking growth in the numbers of male teachers and nurses.

There has, thus, been an impressive growth in the numbers of persons employed in white-collar tasks, a growth concentrated in newer occupations rather than in traditional middle-class occupations such as lawyers, doctors or clergymen. How do we interpret these changes? Does the occupational shift from manual to white-collar employment represent a significant alteration in the class structure towards the creation of a larger and more solid middle class? Three different solutions are offered in the sociological literature to this question:

1   Some argue that there are only two main classes with, perhaps, an intermediate stratum which does not really constitute a middle class. Such a position is usually, though not invariably, informed by Marxist arguments. Critical here is the idea that large sections of the middle class are becoming proletarianized, that is, are becoming more and more like the working class in their conditions of life or 'life chances'.
2   A number of writers suggest that, even if a two-class model might have been appropriate to the nineteenth century, contemporary societies have a three-class structure with a middle class that is prominent if itself subdivided. Giddens (1980) is a well-known exponent of such a position.
3   A third view is that the middle class actually comprises a number of very different elements which make it difficult to see it as a coherent class. Indeed, in this view, the class structure as a whole is so fragmented into different groups that it hardly makes sense to think in terms of discrete social classes.

Routine white-collar workers

One critical issue in deciding between these three theories of the middle class is that of proletarianization. If it can be shown that much white-collar work is, in most respects, similar to manual work, then the idea that there is a large and significant middle class is greatly undermined. However, that is a complex question. First, we cannot necessarily assume that there is one single working class, which parts of the middle class are said to resemble (see section 3.4). Second, the criteria of proletarianization are not entirely clear. Lockwood's (1958) classical study gives us some guidance, in distinguishing market (pay, hours of work, promotion prospects), work (social relationships at work) and status (prestige and political inclinations) aspects of the clerk's position. If, in these three respects, the routine white-collar worker's position is like that of the manual worker, then one might reasonably speak of his or her proletarianization.

Market situation

Earnings There is a well-marked gap between average manual and non-manual earnings which has remained remarkably constant over the last 70 years or so. This apparently persistent difference is reinforced by continuing differences in earnings over the career as a whole, fringe benefits of different kinds, and job security (see, section 3.4). However, comparisons of this kind can be misleading for, if one breaks down the larger categories, there are substantial overlaps between non-manual and manual occupations. In other words, the market situation of *some* non-manual occupations is close to that of manual occupations. Kelly (1980), for example, in his study of civil servants, found that there had been a decline nationally in the manual/non-manual differential which was reflected in civil service salaries. Management grades had, more or less, held their own, but among clerks 'a very definite decline in salaries *vis-à-vis* manual workers has occurred and civil service clerks have done even less well than clerks in other occupations' (p. 131). Nor had clerks actually preserved an advantage in their total career earnings which followed a similar pattern to those of manual workers. In respect of hours of work, fringe benefits, pensions schemes, sick pay schemes and job security, routine white-collar workers are certainly better placed, although the evidence does not allow very precise discriminations within the non-manual sector. There is some evidence, however, that the traditional resistance of clerical grades to unemployment, when compared with manual workers, is being eroded.

Promotion A more subtle way in which the market situation of routine white-collar workers may differ from that of manual workers is in the greater promotion prospects enjoyed by non-manual workers in general. The study by Stewart et al. (1980) offers data which bear on this question, arguing that proletarianization has not occurred. The authors' starting point is a consideration of the age structure of men in the occupation 'clerk' (see figure 3.5). There are two age peaks which seem to represent two distinct elements: those starting as clerks, and former manual workers moving into clerical work with advancing age. The age distribution of clerks is presumptive evidence that clerical work represents a route of promotion mobility for men. Further evidence is provided by examining the promotion propects and histories of clerks (see figure 3.6). If the age 30 is taken as the watershed in a clerical career, only 19 per cent of current clerks over 30 started their careers as clerks. Thus 73 per cent of all those who began as clerks, and are *still* in

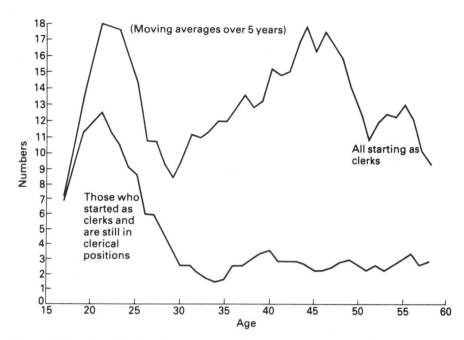

Figure 3.5   Age distribution of those starting their careers as clerks.
Source: Stewart et al., 1980, p. 156, reproduced with permission

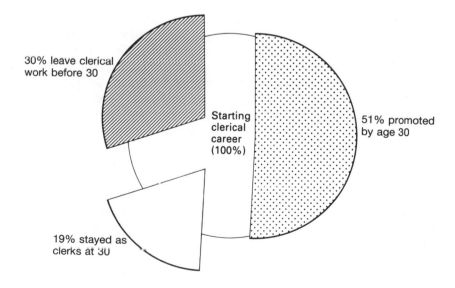

Figure 3.6   The promotion chances of male clerks.
Source: Stewart et al., 1980

white-collar occupations, have been promoted. In fact, 30 per cent of those starting as clerks leave white-collar work altogether. But that still means that half of all those starting as clerks will be promoted. Of course, in considering promotion and mobility one must consider not only the chances of promotion but also the distance travelled. Stewart et al. (1980) believe, for various reasons, that promotion is likely to be long range: once started in the hierarchy, clerks can travel far.

The argument of Stewart et al., that clerical work represents an occupational category through which people pass on their way to management positions, is given some support by the data from the Nuffield Mobility Study (see section 3.7). However, as Crompton and Jones (1984) point out, the relatively good promotion chances of male clerks may depend on a relatively favourable economic situation. First, there has to be a continuing supply of managerial positions for clerks to be promoted to. Second, the high proportion of junior clerks being promoted will only be possible if a substantial minority leave clerical work for other occupations, but other work may be hard to find in a changed economic environment. In addition, Crompton and Jones criticize these recent studies of social mobility because they are based on the experiences of *male* employees. Since these occupations are largely female, a study of male clerical workers can say little about clerical workers as a whole.

Gender differences   As we argued at the beginning of this section, one of the most striking features of the white-collar occupations is the way in which women have moved into the routine jobs, while not greatly improving their position in the higher reaches. In 1911, 21 per cent of clerks were women; in 1921, 45 per cent; in 1951, 60 per cent; and in 1981, the proportion had risen to 78 per cent (table 3.18). In some occupations, the proportion is even higher. Almost 99 per cent of secretaries and 83 per cent of telephone operators, for example, are women. Women formed the bulk of office labour well before office work became noticeably automated. Other white-collar employments, such as that of shop assistant, have been female preserves for some time. This heavy, and increasing, concentration of women in routine white-collar work is reflected in their lower rates of pay.

Promotion prospects for women in routine white-collar jobs are also limited, certainly more limited than those for young men in the same occupations. This is partly because of the way that women's work lives are structured. Generally speaking, in white-collar work, women enter employment directly from school, continue working when they marry, but stop when they start a family. When their children have left home they will go back to work. This break in the career has a number of consequences. First, employers do not believe that younger women will be with them long enough to be promoted. Second, the women themselves do not think it worthwhile undertaking further training which might qualify them for promotion. Women, in other words, have low expectations of their work and employers respond to those expectations. That is, however, only part of the story. Crompton and Jones (1984), in their study of female white-collar workers, concluded that a number of employers (or their managers) actively discriminate against women by, for example, dissuading them from taking examinations which are necessary for promotion. That generates resentment. As one of Crompton and Jones's respondents said: 'Well men get priority, they're looked after first, they move on quicker even when they're not as efficient. The bank say they're not biased but they are. We're not dim, we can see it around us. But when you get passed over you lose interest in your work' (p. 155). Interestingly, Crompton and Jones also found that qualifications did not seem to have much to do with the kinds of skills actually used in work; unqualified women are doing work as skilled as qualified men.

It would be dangerous to assume that the career patterns of women in white-collar work will continue to take this form. The expectations held by women may well be changed, in that they may actively seek promotion and adjust their child-rearing patterns accordingly. Similarly, women may seek the qualifications previously largely reserved by men. There are signs that this is already taking place with increasing numbers of women taking banking and accountancy examinations.

Work situation

A number of features including mechanization, bureaucratization, and changing relations of authority have an impact on the work situation of routine white-collar workers. The computer may represent a particularly dramatic way of reorganizing office work but other machines have also replaced particular traditional skills. Duplicators, photocopiers, dictating and addressing machines and, more recently, word processors have all had a large and growing impact in large offices. Within the period 1956–66 in the civil service, there was a 400 per cent increase in duplicators and photocopiers. Some indication of the extent of office mechanization can also be gauged from the numbers of persons employed in various branches of office work. Routh (1980), for example, shows that the number of typists increased much faster than the rest of the clerical group between 1931 and 1951. In the next 20 years, however, the number of office machine operators rapidly increased, while typists just about kept pace with the group as a whole. There are indications that, since 1971, the proportional rate of decline in the typist category accelerated. In a further index of office mechanization Crompton and Jones (1984) found that 89 per cent of the white-collar workers they interviewed in banking, life insurance and local authorities worked with computers.

Automation can produce conditions of work that appear to be similar
to those enjoyed (or rather not enjoyed) by manual workers. Office work
becomes more routine, involves a smaller sphere of decision and
responsibility, is more subject to managerial control, involves less skill,
and takes place in organizations that are larger, more bureaucratized,
and characterized by a minute division of labour. Downing (1980), for
example, argues 'the move to word processing effectively transfers the
control which the typist has over a conventional typewriter on to the
machine itself. Word processors are designed with supervisory and
monitoring elements built into them. In addition, the word processor can
perform all the elementary functions of typing which take a person years
to perfect' (p. 283). The introduction of the word processor thus takes
away a substantial degree of control over the typist's work, permits a
lower level of skill, fragments the labour process, for example by having
printing done elsewhere, and lessens personal contact between typists,
and between typists and principals. McNally (1979) distinguishes the
secretary from the routine office worker. Her analysis of the latter is
similar to Downing's in that the worker is seen as being machine paced,
performing entirely routine work, and separated from management.

Plate 3.3 Shop assistant at work.
Source: Format

However, in her view, even the personal secretary's position is being undermined by office reorganization, since mechanization has made typing and shorthand obsolete skills.

The recent study of the British class structure by Marshall et al. (1988) comes to rather different conclusions. Most of their interviewees across all social classes did not think that their jobs required any less skill than previously. Those who did note some deskilling were concentrated in the manual working class. Deskilled women appeared equally in the manual working class and in routine white-collar occupations. This might be taken to confirm the idea that routine white-collar women are being proletarianized by being deskilled. However, Marshall et al. point out that the routine white-collar group is actually composed of two parts – clerical workers and personal service workers (including shop assistants, receptionists, supermarket check-out staff). The former group did *not* report deskilling, while a proportion of the latter did.

The same conclusion can be drawn from an examination of the levels of autonomy at work reported by interviewees, measured by such questions as whether the worker can initiate new tasks, decide on day-to-day tasks, work on his or her own initiative or decide the amount and pace of work. Clerical employees – both men and women – had a good deal more autonomy at work than manual workers. Sales and service workers, on the other hand, were very close to manual workers in the low degree of control they had over their work lives. In this sense, this group of routine white-collar workers is proletarianized.

Status situation

The third criterion of proletarianization provided by Lockwood (1958) is that of status or style of life.

If middle-class people see themselves as middle class, or are seen by others as middle class, or behave differently from the working class, then it might be more difficult to speak of middle-class occupations as being proletarianized. There is evidence that, if one takes the middle classes *as a whole*, there are differences between the middle and working classes in their styles of life. Other chapters in this book show some of these differences in education, family life, voting, and residential areas, for example. Evidence on the status and style of life of routine white-collar workers is, however, much more sketchy.

Marshall et al. (1988) again provide evidence concerning the question as to whether this section of the middle class align themselves culturally or politically with the working class. Respondents were asked which social class they placed themselves in. Roughly half of both male and female white-collar workers placed themselves in the working class.

Membership of trade unions and voting Labour are often taken as indices of proletarianization. Taken as a whole, routine white-collar workers are less likely to be union members than the manual working class. The difference between clerical and personal service workers reappears, however. The latter were just as likely to belong to trade unions as skilled manual workers. As far as voting is concerned, routine white-collar workers were significantly more likely to vote Conservative than manual workers.

It is difficult to come to firm conclusions as to the proletarianization of routine white-collar workers. As a whole, the market, work and status situations of clerical workers are different from those of the working class. Personal service workers, on the other hand, are not dissimilar from manual workers.

Managers and professionals: the service class

If there are differences within the routine white-collar worker category, and between occupations within that category and the manual working class, there are even greater differences between routine white-collar workers as a whole and the upper-middle class. This latter group is referred to in recent sociological literature as the service class and is made up of managers, professionals and, in some definitions, small employers.

The market situation of the service class is advantageous. They are

---

Box 3.3   Degrees of control at work

Crompton and Jones (1984) studied white-collar workers in three organizations: a local authority (Cohall), an insurance company (Lifeco) and a bank (Southbank). The data in the table are presented for clerical grades and for administrative grades by the kind of task that each grade performed. The authors distinguished tasks that required the worker:

1   to exercise no control, that is the tasks were governed by simple rules such as data punching;
2   to exercise no control, but where the rules were quite complex, like checking errors; and
3   to exercise discretion and self-control, for example writing non-standard letters.

Clearly, administrative personnel tended to perform the third kind of task and clerical workers the first or second. Only 10 per cent of clerks had self-control in their work, while only 13 per cent of administrators had jobs dominated by simple rules. There were, however, substantial differences between the organizations, differences that reflect the degree of mechanization and division of labour. In the bank, for example, three-quarters of the clerks worked at the lowest level of skill. Supervisors were most self-directed in the bank and the local authority. In general, then, the more mechanized and rationalized the organization, the greater is the difference between clerks and managers.

Organization and grades	No control, simple rules	No control, medium complex rules	Self-control	Total workers
	(%)	(%)	(%)	(no.)
Cohall:				
Clerical	39	41	20	64
Administrative	0	33	67	15
Lifeco:				
Clerical	32	60	8	60
Administrative	23	50	20	20
Soutbank:				
Clerical	79	21	0	58
Administrative	5	26	68	19
All:				
Clerical	50	41	10	182
Administrative	13	37	50	54

Grades have been standardized across the three organizations to allow for comparison. Programmers, systems analysts and certain higher grades have been excluded.

Source: Crompton and Jones, 1984, p. 62, reproduced with permission

paid more and can expect promotion through a career. In addition they have better holiday entitlements, sick pay, and pension arrangements. Even more important, the work situation of the service class gives them considerable freedom from control. Indeed it is more usually they who do the controlling (see section 2.7 on the occupational control exercised by professionals). This provides a sphere of autonomy within which it is possible to organize and pace work as one likes, taking responsibility for the work done. Professional and managerial work is also relatively more skilled, less subdivided and less mechanized. An illustration of the greater skill and control exercised by managerial grades is given in box 3.3. Technical staff also tend to have greater autonomy and skill. Computer programmers and systems analysts, partly because of the technical nature of their work, have considerable freedom from supervision. As Hales (1980) says of his work as a systems analyst: 'At the most basic level of the apparatus of work – time economy – my activity is more or less self-structured. This derives partly from managerial recognition that "problem solving" is an open-ended process and partly from the status of a "responsible" employee who is not expected to need close supervision' (p. 35).

To set against these superior work and market situations, there is some evidence that the processes of mechanization and division of labour affecting routine white-collar work are also having an impact on middle management and, especially, the lower professions. For example, after mechanization and reorganization of offices, the power to make decisions passes up the hierarchy to top management or to the new specialist groups. Computers, for instance, can make many of the more routine decisions previously made by local bank managers. Computer programming, which originally included the whole process of software preparation and demanded the involvement of highly skilled professionals, has become subdivided and rationalized into sets of less skilled tasks. Leggatt (1970) points to the manner in which the work situation of teachers is degraded by employment in bureaucratic institutions which more minutely control what is done in the classroom. In a more general way, Crompton and Jones (1984) present evidence which suggests that the content of some junior managerial work has become more 'proletarian' over time. Many middle- to lower-level managers spend very little of their time exercising what are commonly thought of as managerial functions. Indeed, the content of their job may differ little from that of their alleged subordinates (see also section 2.4).

Even if some elements of the service class are losing skill and autonomy, the class as a whole is becoming increasingly important in British society. Savage et al. (1992), in a recent study of the service class, argue that membership is based on the ownership of *assets* of various kinds – organizational, cultural, and property. *Organizational* assets are those advantages that accrue from being employed, as a manager or professional, in large organizations which offer career opportunities for promotion to posts very well rewarded and very much under the employee's control. *Cultural* assets refer to those elements of lifestyle, taste, and educational qualifications that can function as markers of class membership. These lifestyles are learned, most importantly, from prolonged periods of education. As far as *property* is concerned, this has become more important for the service class than previously. The spread of owner-occupation, combined with a rise in the value of houses, has disproportionately benefited the service class and allowed the transmission of significant amounts of wealth between generations. In addition, the long-term decline in self-employment has been reversed in recent years and the small businesses set up will also generate property assets.

Individual members of the service class may combine these three assets in different ways, although Savage et al. note that there are effectively three divisions within the service class – managers, professionals and the *petit bourgeoisie*, each largely based on one of the assets. These divisions are manifested in a variety of ways. For example, professionals are much less likely to vote Conservative than managers, especially if they have professional parents. Indeed, only working-class people with working-class parents are less likely to vote Conservative.

Savage et al. explore the question of likely changes in the structure of the three types of assets and consequent changes in the internal divisions of the service class. The different types of asset convey different advantages. Property assets can easily be stored and transferred. Cultural assets, similarly, can be stored and transmitted through education. Organizational assets, on the other hand, cannot be passed on because they are dependent on a position in a specific organization. Furthermore, Savage et al. argue, the salience of organizational assets is declining. Most particularly the structure of employing organizations is changing. They are becoming flexible, less hierarchical, and smaller as tasks are subcontracted out (see section 2.5 for further discussion of organizational change). The net effect is that being a manager in an organization is not such a secure asset as it once was. Faced with this, Savage et al. argue, service-class managers will try to convert their organizational assets into other assets. For example, they will make sure that their children are very well educated and hence will acquire cultural assets. The result is that the children of managers become professionals rather than managers. As the authors say: 'Indeed, more children of managers become professionals than managers: 23 per cent of managers' children become professionals compared with 19 per cent who become managers. And this is a crucial issue: managers' children are still advantaged over the children outside the middle classes, but in order to retain a place in the middle classes it would appear that they have to "trade in" their organization assets for educational credentials and entry to professional work' (p. 148).

Conclusion: the divisions in the middle class

We conclude that the occupational category usually referred to as the middle class is divided into two unequal sections, with some intermediate strata in between. The larger part has a market and work situation generally superior to that of the working class but with proletarianization occurring in certain categories. The smaller part has a much more advantageous situation. In between these two sections is a further set of occupations largely composed of lower management, parts of the lower professions, and technicians, who may have better market and work conditions than clerks or shop assistants, but who have neither the control over their work nor the rewards of higher managers and professionals. These groups are particularly vulnerable to the rationalizing and deskilling processes described earlier.

There is one group, not so far mentioned, which also fits in between the service class and routine white-collar workers. These are small businessmen, shopkeepers and traders, or people working on their own account. Many of these people are in a paradoxical position, for their market and work situations diverge. On the one hand, they have some control over their work lives, being able to regulate and pace their tasks and deploy considerable skill. On the other hand, their pay and conditions often approximate to those of clerks or skilled manual workers. For example, many of the small shopkeepers studied by Bechhofer and Elliott (1968) were earning little more than many manual workers. This relatively low income was earned by very long hours of work in poor conditions. The average working day was 10.5 hours, with the two most numerous groups – grocers and newsagents – exceeding this figure.

Summary

1 There has been a substantial growth in the proportion of people employed in middle-class occupations. Women now occupy some three-quarters of the positions in clerical work.
2 The middle class or service class can be divided into two major sections, the upper-middle class and routine white-collar workers, with certain occupational groupings, for example, junior management and some of the lower professions, ranged in between.
3 Routine white-collar workers have very much poorer work and market situations than upper-middle-class workers. Their pay, hours of work, holidays and pension arrangements compare unfavourably. The promotion possibilities for male clerks are, on the other hand, fairly good, although for women, who form the bulk of the occupation, they are not.

4   Service-class occupations, through their ownership of assets of various kinds, have a good market situation and their work situation is such that they have considerable control.

5   Junior management and the lower professions have a better market situation than routine white-collar workers but their work situations are increasingly threatened by mechanization and greater bureaucratic control.

Related topics

Section 2.4 gives detailed consideration to the nature of managerial occupations. Further discussion of professionals is to be found in section 2.7. The position of the middle class is touched on in section 3.2 on occupational change, section 8.4 on credentialism, and section 12.2 on voting.

3.6   The Upper Class

In the previous section on the middle class we distinguished an upper-middle or service class from a routine white-collar middle class. Although the service class *appears* to merge with the upper class, actually the latter is separated by a number of important features which may be summarized as property, networks and power. The upper class is very small, too small to appear in many sample surveys. It is, nonetheless, very important because of its economic, political and social power.

Property and wealth

The most obvious point to make is that the upper class is wealthy. In section 3.3 we have shown how unequal is the distribution of income in Britain and how even more unequal is the distribution of wealth. In this century there has been a long-term trend to greater equality of wealth. Thus the share of personal wealth held by the top 1 per cent of the population fell from three-fifths in the 1920s to one-fifth by 1979, while the proportion owned by the next richest 4 per cent stayed at about one-fifth throughout that period. This trend was halted in the 1980s during the period of the Thatcher government and has remained roughly stable since. Whatever the longer-term equalization of wealth, the absolute amounts of wealth held by the very rich are very large, as table 3.19 indicates.

Income appears to be more equally distributed. Townsend (1979), for

Table 3.19 Britain's rich, 1990

Family	Estimated wealth (£m)	Main source of wealth
1 The royal family	6700	Land and urban property
2 Grosvenor (Duke of Westminster)	4200	Land and urban property
3 Rausing	2040	Food packaging
4 Sainsbury	1777	Food retailing
5 Weston	1674	Food prod. and retailing
6 Moores	1670	Football pools, retailing
7 Vestey	1420	Food production
8 Getty	1350	Oil
9 Maxwell	1100	Publishing
10 Feeney	1020	Retailing
11 Hinduja	1000	Trading
12 Livanos	930	Shipping
13 Goldsmith	750	Retailing and finance
14 Swire	692	Shipping and aviation
15 Ronson	548	Urban property, petrol distribution
16 Barclay[a]	500	Hotels and urban property
17 Branson	488	Music and aviation
18 Cadogan (Earl Cadogan)	450	Land and urban property
19 Jerwood	400	Trading
20 Portman (Viscount Portman)	400	Land and urban property
21 Thompson	400	Food processing, property

[a] Not the family associated with Barclays Bank.

Source: Scott, 1991, p. 83

example, estimates that the top 1 per cent of income earners took only 6.2 per cent of total income. However, since the date of publication of that book, through the Thatcher years there has been a dramatic rise in the income of the higher earners. The absolute levels of earnings of company directors, for example, can be very high indeed, as table 3.20 indicates. (For more detailed treatment of the distribution of income and wealth see section 3.3.)

Since wealth is at least *potential* income, its concentration is the key to the market situation of the upper class. Changes in the way that wealth is taxed in this century may have led wealthy individuals to disperse their wealth more widely in their family during their lifetime. Very importantly, therefore, we are talking not only of wealthy individuals in the

Table 3.20   Britain's highest-paid directors, 1990

	Company	Annual salary (£)
Lord Hanson	Hanson Trust	1,530,000
Tiny Rowland	Lonrho	1,310,000
Dick Giordano	BOC	937,000
Sir Ralph Halpern	Burton Group	899,000
Sir Kit McMahon	Midland Bank	725,844
Sir Peter Walters	BP	708,722
Geoff Mulcahy	Kingfisher	701,000
Cyril Stein	Ladbroke	603,000
Sir Paul Girolami	Glaxo	598,081
Sir Denys Henderson	ICI	514,000
Allen Sheppard	Grand Metropolitan	506,438

Source: Scott, 1991, p. 86; from *The Guardian*, 3 May 1990, p. 9

upper class, but of wealthy *families*. In this context, inheritance is of great significance. In general, individuals or families are wealthy because their fathers were also. As one detailed study concluded, inheritance is the major determinant of wealth inequality. 'The regression analysis attributed some two-thirds of the inequality in the distribution of wealth in 1973 to inheritance. The proportions of top wealth leavers since the mid-fifties who were preceded by rich fathers was shown . . . to be in excess of 60 per cent' (Harbury and Hitchens, 1979, p. 36).

Property confers income and a favourable market situation. It also gives *control*. The upper class, in other words, is not merely passive in the luxurious enjoyment of continuous leisure; it is also actively *uses* property to its advantage.

In section 2.3 we reviewed changes in the pattern of ownership and control in Britain. The most important conclusions were:

1   The ownership of land is more dispersed.
2   Through takeovers and mergers, many businesses have grown larger.
3   Ownership of individual businesses no longer typically lies wholly in the hands of families but is relatively more dispersed via share ownership, particularly to various financial institutions.
4   Wealthy families no longer have their assets concentrated in particular areas such as land or individual businesses but have them dispersed over various fields of activity.

One of the consequences of these changes is, as Scott (1991) points out,
the creation of a unified 'propertied class in the twentieth century, a class
moreover which had to use its capital actively to perpetuate its privileged
position. Class advantages derive from the benefits which accrue from
property and from involvement in the processes through which it is
controlled' (p. 64). In turn, the propertied upper class depends on a core
of those actively involved in the strategic management of business
concerns. Scott argues that this core comprises about 0.1 per cent of the
adult population, about 43,500 people, and it has been estimated that
these people held 7 per cent of the wealth in 1986, worth then about
£740,000 each. The members of this core occupy positions of leadership
in large businesses in Britain, although they will have different ways of
deriving their income and wealth. Members of the core can be involved
either in one or in many business enterprises. At the same time, their
involvement can be either as owner of the enterprise or simply as a
director of it. Figure 3.7 puts together these two dimensions of
involvement.

		Nature of involvement	
		Property ownership	Directorship
Number of involvements	Single	Entrepreneurial capitalist	Executive capitalist
	Multiple	Rentier capitalist	Finance capitalist

Figure 3.7 Capitalist economic locations.
Source: Scott, 1991, p. 66

There are four groups within the active core of the upper class. The
entrepreneurial capitalist has direct and immediate control over all
aspects of business operations. The rentier capitalist is essentially passive
by contrast, but has ownership stakes, though not complete ownership,
in a number of enterprises. The executive capitalist is involved
exclusively in the strategic management of a concern but frequently does
not have a controlling block of shares. The finance capitalist also will not
have significant blocks of shares but will occupy directorships in several
enterprises. By contrast with the executive capitalist, the finance
capitalist does not have an active involvement in any one concern.

In sum, the upper class consists of wealthy families rather than
individuals. Wealth is not passively enjoyed but is actively used. In this

Plate 3.4 The Quorn Hunt. Traditional rural middle and upper class leisure pursuits like hunting still survive.
Source: Martin Dalby

process, a small core of the upper class, involved in the strategic control of large business, perpetuates its privileges. This mention of strategic control, incidentally, shows how the upper class's work situation differs from that of the service class discussed in section 3.5. Members of the service class are essentially managers who carry out day-to-day technical, professional and administrative functions. Although their role in modern business is clearly important, they do not have *strategic* control over the enterprise. That control – decision over investment, new markets, relations with other companies, for instance – lies with the senior executives who belong to the core of the upper class. Of course, many members of the service class are very highly paid – senior lawyers or accountants, for example – and that *might* make the line between the upper class and the service class difficult to draw. However, it is not at all easy to build up substantial wealth from earned income alone without any assistance from inheritance. That fact in itself makes it difficult to cross the class line.

Networks

We have already argued that discussion of the upper class should focus on families rather than individuals and that the relationships between entrepreneurial, rentier, executive and finance capitalists are important in the strategic control of large British business. These points imply that the *networks* of relationships between members of this very small class will be significant.

There are different kinds of networks between members of the upper class. There are marriage or kinship relations, friendship or the 'old boy network', business and financial relationships, and the whole area of common background formed, amongst other things, by school and university. We have already referred to the way that the wealth of upper-class individuals largely derives, by inheritance, from family connections. Members of the upper class also tend to marry other upper-class individuals, giving the class a unity based on kinship and marriage. This has, of course, always been the case. In the nineteenth century, when individual families controlled large businesses, there was extensive intermarriage, as for example between the Quaker families which owned large food firms.

Connections of kinship and marriage are further extended by the ties of friendship and acquaintance which are often summarized in the phrase 'old boy network'. To a large extent, this network is social. It is based on individuals seeing each other regularly, not only in the way of business but also socially.

Social contacts of this kind are possible partly because of common background. Members of the upper class associate together easily because they have the same tastes, attitudes and inclinations formed by being brought up in the same kinds of family and going to the same kinds of school and university. As Scott (1982) argues: 'The integrative role of the public schools concerns their ability to mould the ideas and outlook of their pupils and to ensure frequent and easy interaction among them' (p. 160). Members of the business core of the upper class do, indeed, have a public school background. For example, three-quarters of clearing bank directors in 1970 were from public schools, and one in three were from Eton. In addition, between half and three-quarters of these directors had been to either Oxford or Cambridge Universities. Or, to take a different case, Otley (1973) found that, in 1971, 75 per cent of senior army officers (lieutenant-general and above) had been to major public schools.

A common background in family, school and university gives a common culture to members of the upper class which enables them to interact freely. It also serves as the path of recruitment into the upper class by giving the required qualifications. The result is that the class has a high degree of self-recruitment and social closure. What this means is that current members of the upper class are likely to be the offspring of wealthy individuals and their sons and daughters are also likely to remain in the same social position.

Studies have investigated the social origins of those in elite positions not only of the business core, but in the civil service, the army, the judiciary, and the church. Boyd (1973), for example, found that no fewer than 45 per cent of bank directors and 30 per cent of judges listed in *Who's Who* also had fathers listed (Heath, 1981). We have to conclude

Plate 3.5 Upper class lifestyle.
Source: Network

that entry to the upper class is 'sponsored' in the sense that upper-class individuals have to have the 'right' sort of background; it is not a competitive process. The upper class is relatively closed to outsiders.

One last issue in the formation of the upper class as a network deserves mention. We have referred to the way in which the business core of the upper class can mix its business and social contacts. Business relationships may, however, be cemented in a much more solid way via the networks of interlocking directorships. This is an issue discussed in more detail in section 2.3, but an illustration is provided by Scott (1985) in a study of the directorships of large companies. In 1976, 11 people had a total of 57 directorships in the top 250 companies and had many others in smaller companies. The directorships of 9 of these 11 can be linked together in the chain shown in figure 2.4; a mere 9 people linked together 39 very large companies. Interlocking directorships provide a powerful network linking firms, but they also cement the connections of members of the upper class.

Prestige and power

So far we have argued that the upper class, and especially its business core, forms a relatively closed, coherent and self-recruiting elite. Coherence, combined with great wealth and the effective control of very large business, gives great power. However, that represents only one channel of the upper class's influence. The business core is also connected with other members of the upper class at the top of other fields like politics, the civil service, and the professions.

We have already looked at the recruitment patterns of certain upper-class occupations. There is overwhelming evidence that those in such positions come disproportionately from upper-class families and from public schools and Oxford and Cambridge Universities. They have, in other words, common backgrounds and a common process of education and training. Of the 1987 intake of Conservative MPs, for example, 65 per cent had been to public school, including 6 per cent to Eton, and 42 per cent had received an education at Oxford or Cambridge (Baker et al., 1992). One might have expected the 1990 Cabinet, headed by a woman who had attended a local authority school, to have a more even representation. Of its 23 members, however, 21 went to private schools and 16 had been to either Oxford or Cambridge Universities.

The same pattern of education predominates in the higher reaches of the civil service, two-thirds of whom in 1970 had attended public schools. Senior churchmen and members of the judiciary are also recruited disproportionately from public schools and Oxbridge and, in addition, have a strong tendency to come from families also in high-ranking positions in the church and the law.

The common origins, common education and common experiences of the holders of a variety of elite positions lead many commentators to refer to the 'establishment'. The members of the establishment constitute a coherent and self-recruiting body of men who are able to wield immense power. A similarity of outlook and day-to-day contact between civil servants, politicians, businessmen, churchmen, professionals and the military give the upper class political power to add to the power given by wealth. The argument carries a great deal of conviction. However, common origins and common education do not of themselves necessarily mean common interests or common action, and little is known about how holders of elite positions actually do interact in the use of power.

The coherence, wealth and power of the upper class is reflected in its prestige. Doubtless, in the past, some of the prestige of the upper class derived from a flamboyant and luxurious lifestyle conspicious to all. To some extent, this lifestyle continues to exist; it is, after all, one of the privileges of wealth. The doings of the rich continue to be displayed and even celebrated in the press and television. It could also be argued that an upper-class lifestyle is frequently presented as desirable and as something that everybody should seek. Despite all this, however, upper-class people probably display their lives less conspicuously than they used to do; in this sense the class is becoming more invisible. It may also be that the status and prestige of the upper class are not quite such unitary phenomena as they once were. Instead of there being a single set of status symbols denoting a unified upper-class status system, there are now intersecting and overlapping status circles in the upper class, each with rather different symbols of prestige. It may also be that rank and title command less respect than they once did. New hereditary peerages are not now generally created. Nevertheless, periodically, an honours list is announced which will include knighthoods and life peerages as well as hosts of lesser awards. These higher honours largely go to those who have rendered 'public service', which is defined in such a way that honours will be given to individuals who are, in our sense, upper class. Apart from anything else, the system of nomination for honours ensures that only those who are relatively well connected in public life are likely to be nominated. There are, however, some indications that the honours list is losing its prestige in the wider community and the government has indicated that it will be changed. The appearance of each list is almost routinely greeted by a chorus of disapproval, based largely on the notion that the ideal of public service is being debased.

Summary

1 The upper class is distinguished by its wealth, its coherence, and its power.
2 Members of the upper class are very wealthy. The top 1 per cent of wealth holders own one-third of the nation's wealth.
3 We should see the upper class in terms as much of families as of individuals. Wealth is distributed widely in families, and family origin and influence are important in gaining upper-class positions.
4 The core of the class consists in those actively involved in the control of large businesses.

5 The upper class is very coherent, being bound together in a network
   of kinship, similar education, friendship and business contacts.
6 This coherence gives power which is reinforced by the fact that those
   of upper-class origin occupy powerful positions, not only in the
   business world, but also in politics, the civil service, the military, the
   church and the judiciary.
7 An upper-class style of life still carries a certain prestige, though that
   may be declining.

Related topics

Section 2.3 presents some arguments about ownership and control and
the question of interlocking shareholdings amongst the upper class; the
social position of managers is discussed in section 2.4. Section 3.3,
reviewing income and wealth distributions, gives some account of upper-
class wealth, while section 3.7 analyses social mobility.

3.7 Social Mobility

Social mobility is the process by which people move from one class to
another. *Social* mobility should not be confused with *geographical*
mobility, which refers to people moving their place of residence. In
modern society, nobody is prevented by religious, political or legal
regulations from moving between classes: entry to classes is not closed.
At the same time, though, there are barriers to movement into some
class positions. In practice, entry into the upper class is limited by birth or
access to wealth. There are also effective limits on access to the more
prestigious positions in the professional middle class. To be a doctor
requires a degree in medicine, and only a small proportion of the working
population have that qualification. More interesting, though, is what
kind of people are allowed into medical school to get that qualification.
Most are the children of higher professionals; few are from unskilled,
manual backgrounds. This raises the question of fairness, usually as an
issue of equality of opportunity. Since some groups of occupations
provide better rewards, better conditions and more work satisfaction
than others, it is a matter of concern on what grounds those positions are
filled and whether most citizens have a reasonable chance of obtaining
such posts. Studies of social mobility assess those chances.
    Social mobility bears upon another central social process – that of class
formation and class solidarity. It has usually been thought that high
levels of social mobility would reduce class conflict. There are several

plausible reasons for this. People believing that they have a fair chance of joining the higher social classes may feel little resentment on the ground that privileges are deserved: talent is being rewarded. If there is a lot of movement between classes then solidarity and common identity will be hard to sustain. People may pursue individual rather than collective solutions to their discontents, preferring further education to trade union meetings. Also, the cross-class contacts built up by socially mobile people might reduce the sense of the exclusiveness of social classes and the hostility between them. Indeed, ultimately, if there was perfect fluidity between positions, social background having no influence on occupational success, one key basis for identifying social classes – common life chances – would be removed. The nature and degree of social mobility in Britain are, therefore, interesting from the point of view of class politics.

The concept of social mobility

Social mobility concerns movements between social classes. It is usually estimated by reference to occupational positions. Movement may happen within an individual's lifetime, called *intra-generational* mobility, as for example in the cases of the promotion of a clerk to a manager or of a manual worker obtaining qualifications permitting access to a profession. Or the movement may occur between generations, children coming to fill places in a different occupational class to their parents, which is called *inter-generational* mobility. Examples would be the child of an engine driver who becomes a solicitor or the child of a solicitor who becomes an engine driver. The former would be an example of *upward* social mobility, the latter of *downward* social mobility. It is assumed that occupational classes can be graded in a hierarchy of prestige, and that the criterion of mobility is to shift across a class boundary. It should be noted that people also obtain new jobs without crossing a class boundary, moving sideways so to speak.

Deciding what are *relevant* class boundaries is bound to be contentious. For many people, upward mobility used to be associated with a move from blue-collar to white-collar occupations. However, since many routine white-collar jobs now pay less well and are less satisfying than skilled manual jobs, that boundary may well be thought less meaningful. The most authoritative recent study of mobility in Britain concentrates on movement into and out of the service class (composed largely of professional and managerial occupations), on the grounds that for most people upward mobility is achieved by entering professional and managerial occupations. It is to the finding of this study, the Nuffield Mobility Study, reported by Goldthorpe et al. (1987), that we will turn next. To make sense of the findings of this study, however, it is necessary to be familiar with the class categories being used.

The definitions of the seven occupational classes used by Goldthorpe et al. were listed in figure 3.1. For many purposes, these seven classes are grouped into three – the service class, the intermediate class and the working class. For Goldthorpe et al., the 'service class' includes higher and lower professionals and middle management (a broader definition than we used in section 3.5); the intermediate class comprises routine white-collar workers, small proprietors and supervisory workers; and the working class is defined as manual workers without positions of authority. Their conception of class structure is shown diagrammatically in figure 3.1. Importantly, although Goldthorpe et al. study movement between all seven occupational classes, they consider *only movement into and out of the service class* as socially meaningful mobility.

Contemporary social mobility

Goldthorpe et al. (1987) discovered more inter-generational mass social mobility in Britain since the Second World War than might have been expected. Previous studies had suggested that classes in Britain were largely self-recruiting. Sons would usually end up in the same class as their fathers. (Regrettably, almost all mobility studies, including the Nuffield one, only analyse the movement of men.) It was believed, on the basis of a survey in 1949, that there was a lot of short-distance but little long-distance movement, that the elite was highly self-recruiting, and that the blue-collar/white-collar boundary was a major barrier. Goldthorpe et al. paint a different picture.

Consider table 3.21. This is an 'outflow' table, showing the class *destination* of sons, which indicates the extent to which opportunities are equal. If classes were perfectly self-recruiting, every son would be in the same class as his father and the diagonal boxes would all register 100. What we observe is, rather, much movement between classes. Consider, for example, the row of fathers in class VII – semi-skilled and unskilled manual workers and agricultural labourers. Here 6.5 per cent of sons of such fathers were in class I occupations (higher management and professional) in 1972; another 7.8 per cent were in the lower-professional grade, class II. However, 34.9 per cent of such sons were, like their fathers, in class VII: and a further 23.5 per cent were in the other class of manual workers, that is class VI, skilled manuals. In effect, then, about 6 out of 10 became blue-collar workers.

It is in some degree a matter of judgment whether you will be impressed by the number of sons who were upwardly mobile, or by the number who remained in class VII. But whatever your judgment, the

Table 3.21 Inter-generational occupational mobility of men aged 20–64 in England and Wales, 1972, outflow[a] (percentages, by row)

Father's class when son aged 14 years	Son's class[b] (1972)							Fathers in sample	
	I	II	III	IV	V	VI	VII	(no.)	(%)
I	45.2	18.9	11.5	7.7	4.8	5.4	6.5	688	7.3
II	29.1	23.1	11.9	7.0	9.6	10.6	8.7	554	5.9
III	18.4	15.7	12.8	7.8	12.8	15.6	16.9	694	7.3
IV	12.6	11.4	8.0	24.8	8.7	14.4	20.5	1329	14.1
V	14.2	13.6	10.1	7.7	15.7	21.2	17.6	1082	11.5
VI	7.8	8.8	8.3	6.6	12.3	30.4	25.9	2594	27.5
VII	6.5	7.8	8.2	6.6	12.5	23.5	34.9	2493	24.6

[a] Class distribution of sons by the class of their father when son was aged 14 (a measure of equality of opportunity).
[b] For definitions of classes see figure 3.1.
Total number of respondents = 9434.

Source: Goldthorpe et al., 1987, reproduced with permission

table does show different degrees of self-recruitment. Looking at the diagonal boxes, you can see that only one in eight of sons of routine white-collar workers (class III) were to be found in that class in 1972. The sons of such workers were, in fact, fairly evenly distributed across all occupational classes. By contrast, class I fathers were the most likely to pass on their 'class position' to their sons. Nearly one in two class I sons had class I jobs. It is this capacity for privilege to be transmitted inter-generationally that arouses suspicion about the social significance of the, undeniably large, absolute amounts of mobility. Clearly, the class into which a man was born did not *determine* his class destination; lots of men were upwardly mobile in the period 1928–72. But the chances of ending up in class I were weighted heavily in favour of those with fathers there already.

Issues relating to class formation are best illustrated by considering an 'inflow' table, table 3.22. Based on exactly the same data as the previous table, this shows the *composition of social classes* in 1972, in terms of the class origins of sons. Reading down the columns you can see who has arrived in which classes. Compare class I and class VII. Class I, which comprised about one worker in eight (13.6 per cent) in 1972, had drawn its members from all social classes. Although one in four members also had fathers in class I, the rest came more or less equally from the six

Table 3.22 Inter-generational occupational mobility of men aged 20–64 in England and Wales, 1972, inflow[a] (percentages, by column)

Father's class when son was aged 14	Son's class[b] (1972)						
	I	II	III	IV	V	VI	VII
I	24.2	12.0	9.1	6.0	3.0	1.9	2.0
II	12.5	11.8	7.6	4.4	4.9	3.0	2.2
III	12.0	10.0	10.2	6.1	8.3	5.4	5.3
IV	13.0	13.9	12.2	36.5	10.6	9.6	12.3
V	12.0	13.5	12.5	9.4	15.6	11.4	8.6
VI	15.7	21.0	24.8	19.2	29.2	39.4	30.3
VII	12.6	17.8	23.6	18.5	28.5	29.4	39.3
Sons in sample (no.)	1285	1087	870	887	1091	2000	2214
(%)	13.6	11.5	9.2	9.4	11.6	21.2	23.5

[a] Class composition, by class of father when son was aged 14 (a measure of class formation).
[b] For definitions of classes see figure 3.1.
Total number of respondents = 9434.

Source: Goldthorpe et al., 1987, reproduced with permission

other classes in Goldthorpe et al.'s classification. Class I in 1972 was, then, very heterogeneous (i.e. of very mixed origin); 28.3 per cent of class I were sons of manual workers. Class VII, by contrast, was largely composed of sons of manual workers (69.6 per cent). Only 2 per cent of class VII had fathers in class I. Skilled manual workers had similar origins. Thus Goldthorpe et al. propose that Britain now has a 'mature' working class, alike in its origins, and therefore capable of exhibiting considerable solidarity. If they are correct, and being in the same class for two or more generations does increase solidarity, then their study does suggest the existence of a solidaristic working class and considerable fragmentation among the other occupational classes.

Given the very considerable movement between classes, it might be imagined that Britain had become less dependent on class origins. In an important sense, though, this is a misleading impression. Much of the upward mobility into the service class is merely a consequence of changes in the occupational structure. The number of positions in the service class increased sharply in the period examined by Goldthorpe et al. Men occupied in service-class occupations rose from around 1.2 million in

1931 to 3.5 million in 1971. Compare the proportions of *fathers* in the service class (classes I and II) in Goldthorpe et al.'s sample (13.2 per cent: see table 3.21) and the proportion of *sons* (25.1 per cent: see table 3.22). What Goldthorpe et al. point out is that the service class increased in size to such an extent that, even if every son of a service-class father had obtained a service-class job, there would still have been more men with origins in other classes in the service classes of 1972. This can be seen in table 3.23, which summarizes information on movement across the boundary of the service class. Boxes A and D are percentages of men inter-generationally stable. Box B is the percentage of men downwardly mobile; box C is the percentage upwardly mobile. The upwardly mobile vastly outnumbered the downwardly mobile. Put another way, the service class of the previous generation did not breed fast enough to fill all the new service-class occupations made available in the long boom after the Second World War. A large amount of upward social mobility was inevitable.

This fact led Goldthorpe et al. to try to separate out *absolute* mobility, of which we have seen there is a great deal, from *relative* mobility, which is a measure of whether class differentials have narrowed. In other words, if there had been no change in the occupational structure, would there still have been an expansion of opportunities for the lower classes? Answering such a question is fraught with difficulty, not least because the occupational structure is always changing. However, it is an important

Table 3.23 Inter-generational social mobility into and out of the service class, men aged 20–64, in England and Wales, 1972

Father's social class when son aged 14	*Sons' class (1972)*		*All (%)*
	Service (I–II) (%)	*Other (III–VII) (%)*	
Service (I–II)	7.7 **A**	5.4 **B**	13.1
Other (III–VII)	17.4 **C**	69.5 **D**	86.9
All	25.1	74.9	100.0

Total number of respondents = 9434.

Source: tables 3.21 and 3.22

question because it is unlikely that we will see, during the rest of the twentieth century, further 'upgrading' of the occupational structure which would allow the service class to continue to expand. It will, then, matter to what extent exclusive class privileges can be maintained from generation to generation. Goldthorpe et al. suggest that, relatively speaking, the capacity of service-class fathers to transmit privilege did *not* decline between 1928 and 1972. The simplest indication to this is the low rate of downward mobility from, especially, class I. Look at table 3.21 again: 64.1 per cent of class I sons ended up in the service class; only one in three moved down, and this may be an underestimate given the nature of intra-generational mobility. It seems, then, that a use of material resources accumulated by fathers in lucrative careers and a capacity to secure high educational qualifications for their children have ensured that sons of the service class are heavily protected against downward mobility.

Table 3.24 Inter-generational social mobility into and out of the manual working class, men aged 20–64, in England and Wales, 1972

	Sons' class (1972)		
Father's social class when son aged 14	Other (I–V) (%)	Working (VI–VII) (%)	All (%)
Other (I–V)	34.1	13.8	47.8
Working (VI–VII)	21.2	30.9	52.1
All	55.3	44.7	100.0

Total number of respondents = 9434.

Source: tables 3.21 and 3.22

The importance of the mobility data for understanding class relationships is harder to interpret. Only the working class is inter-generationally stable, being composed of predominantly sons of manual workers, in a ratio of 30.9 per cent with fathers from classes VI and VII to 13.8 per cent with fathers from classes I–V (see table 3.24). Whether that 30 per cent, or 3 men in 10, do constitute a 'mature' working class in the political arena remains to be seen. Voting behaviour until 1979 bore this out to some extent. Heath (1981) showed that working-class men with working-class fathers and working-class fathers-in-law are more likely than any other category to vote Labour. He, indeed, showed that men at every level of the class hierarchy who had working-class connections were more likely to vote Labour than those without. This corresponds to information on the friendship and leisure patterns of the upwardly mobile. Such patterns provide strong evidence that men who are inter-generationally stable, whether in the service class or the working class, have social contact with people of their own class. As might be expected, a man upwardly mobile is more likely to have working-class friends and associates than a man born into the service class. However, there seem to be few problems for the upwardly mobile in becoming assimilated into their new class position. (It used to be thought that such men might be isolated or unwelcome, but such problems have probably been overcome through the sheer volume of the upwardly mobile.) The upwardly mobile have sociable relations across classes.

The third, intermediate, class seems to have relatively little identity, either over time or internally. With the exception of sons of men in class IV, the *petite bourgeoisie*, who because they inherit property are relatively likely to continue in the same line of business as their fathers (see table 3.22), the other intermediate classes spread out across the class structure almost at random. This is, in important part, due to the typical patterns of intra-generational mobility in the period. Men tend to pass through jobs in the intermediate classes. Hardly any men spend their entire working life in occupational classes III–V. Stewart et al. (1980) showed that young men who were routine white-collar workers would, before they reached 35 years of age, either be promoted into managerial occupations or leave to try other jobs, usually manual ones. The other main group of male, routine white-collar workers were older men, over 50, who had been promoted from the shop floor, often because they were no longer physically capable of manual tasks. These are both instances of changes which can be understood in terms of *careers*. (It is important to bear in mind that many people's social and political behaviour may be oriented to their anticipated future rather than to their current situation.) People may be mobile during their lifetime, intra-generationally.

Again, Goldthorpe et al. demonstrate a considerable amount of intra-generational mobility among men. In their survey, they asked for a man's first full-time job and for the job he held after ten years of working life. A very considerable proportion (73 per cent) of those aged 35 and over in the service class in 1972 had had first jobs in other classes. Moreover, there was no evidence that this route into the service class was closing up. (It used to be thought that increased numbers of people getting qualifications in higher education would block channels of upward mobility within firms and organizations.) Another interesting feature of intra-generational mobility is that, while sons of service-class fathers often have first jobs in other social classes, after ten years of working life they have secured service-class posts. Only 27 per cent of service-class sons were direct entrants into service-class occupations, while a further 36 per cent had first jobs elsewhere.

There are two major limitations of existing survey-based studies for social mobility, and the Nuffield study in particular. First, the greatest exclusiveness of social groups is at the very top of the occupational hierarchy, the elite being more highly self-recruiting than any other, but such people are too few to be picked up in a random sample survey. Second, the mobility experiences of women are largely ignored.

The elite and mobility

The Nuffield Mobility Study examined *mass* mobility. It would be false to imagine that the existence of considerable mobility into the service class meant that *all* top positions were equally accessible. While the son of a manual worker may become a solicitor, he is very unlikely indeed to become a High Court judge. The evidence concerning recruitment to the upper class is considered in detail in section 3.6. People at the very top of the hierarchy tend to have impeccable upper-class backgrounds. To take just a single example, of those bank directors listed in *Who's Who* in 1970–1, 45 per cent also had fathers listed in earlier editions of *Who's Who* (see also section 3.6). This is 300 times greater than chance. It does not leave much space for others to be upwardly mobile into top banking jobs! Of course, sample surveys like the Nuffield one could never pick up sufficient of these kinds of people to allow effective analysis. These elites are too small for that. But, at the same time, they are exceptionally powerful, very important persons. No complete understanding of social mobility can afford to ignore this upper class.

Women and mobility

The Nuffield study examined only men, as have most other studies of social mobility. Men move from one occupation to another fairly infrequently during their lifetime; and their 'objective' class position, as measured by their market and work situations, is unaffected by marriage and divorce. Women's experience of social mobility is significantly different from men's. Because occupational sex segregation means that women fill disproportionately few higher-professional, skilled manual or *petit bourgeois* positions, most women experience downward occupational mobility when compared with their family of origin. There is more *absolute* downward occupational mobility for women than men because while fathers have the same number of sons and daughters, the labour market places available strongly favour men. However, what little information there is on *relative* mobility for women suggests that chances are skewed by class of origin in much the same way as for men: daughters of service-class fathers are much more likely than those of lower classes to obtain service-class occupations themselves.

Women's material circumstances are profoundly affected by marriage. They marry men who, on average, have a higher occupational position than their own. Using the conventional measure of class, based on the male head of household's occupational position, women experience what is sometimes called 'marital' mobility. Though partly an artefact of class measurement, it has a real and substantial influence on their personal material situation. When a husband's occupation is used as the measure of his wife's class, then women in the 1980s, on aggregate, experienced neither more nor less downward social mobility than men of their own generation. Marital mobility also appears to influence strongly women's class behaviour and attitudes, to the extent that wives come to share many of the class perceptions and practices of their husbands. Though women's more complex occupational biographies might be expected to reduce the strength of their class identification, marriage encourages a household perception of class position and class interest defined by the husband's occupational circumstances.

There remains a shortage of detailed analysis of women's experiences of social mobility. Existing evidence implies that a married woman's mobility chances are significantly removed from her own control, being dependent on the behaviour of her husband – another instance of the way in which the patriarchal arrangements of labour markets reduce the power of women.

Summary

1   There have been relatively high levels of absolute, inter-generational social mobility in Britain since the Second World War, much of it being upward mobility into an expanded service class. As a result, the service class consists of men of mixed class origins.
2   The high rate of mobility can be attributed to the upgrading of the occupational structure: rapid growth in service-class positions has occurred. This has permitted low levels of downward mobility. Thus, sons of service-class fathers have usually secured service-class positions for themselves. It also follows that most of today's manual workers had working-class fathers.
3   The degree of self-recruitment is highest in the upper class, elite positions being filled by men of exclusive social class background.

Related topics

The Nuffield study included an examination of the relationship between education and mobility, which is examined at length in section 8.4. On elite recruitment, see section 3.6. Further discussion of the careers of clerical workers is to be found in section 3.5.

Further reading

Marshall et al. (1988) is the most recent, comprehensive analysis of the British class structure and it deals with controversies about change in the working class. On long-term occupational change, see Routh (1987). Scott (1991) deals with wealth and the upper class. See Oppenheim (1990) for a recent study of poverty. Heath (1981) is an accessible and interesting analysis of social mobility.

4 Gender

4.1 Introduction

The changing social relations between men and women in contemporary Britain are the focus of this chapter. These are usually called gender relations, gender being the social aspect of the differentiation of the sexes. Sociological discussion in this area recognizes that social rather than biological processes are the key to the understanding of the position of women (and of men) in society. Old-fashioned notions that a woman's anatomy, through her capacity to bear children, determined the shape of her entire life have been replaced by complex debates as to how different social structures have interacted to produce the variety of patterns of gender relations which are to be found across different societies and over time. The nature of sociological discussion on gender has been transformed by the impact of feminism and of women's studies. No longer are issues concerning gender subsumed under 'the family' with its connotations of a happy haven of common agreement. Instead, we find a focus on inequality between women and men and the diversity of forms of gender relations. New concepts have been developed to analyse gender relations which capture the interconnectedness of the different aspects of gender inequality. One such concept is patriarchy – the system of social relationships in which men exploit, dominate and oppress women.

The position of women is often considered to have improved during the last few decades. There is, however, considerable debate as to the extent of change and the reasons for it. Some writers, pointing for instance to the formal legal equality that women have with men, suggest that women are now fully emancipated, and have no need for any further changes. Others, focusing on issues such as the inequality in the wages paid to men and women or the violence that women receive at men's hands, argue that women still have a long way to go before they are fully liberated. Yet others suggest that women have simply added paid employment on to the burden of housework, so that while the form of inequality has changed, the degree has not.

This chapter will examine the different aspects of gender relations in contemporary Britain, to see if the conditions under which women live have improved, as the first set of writers suggests; are unchanged, as the second school of thought has argued; or have changed so as merely to produce new forms of inequality.

Some theories of the position of women in society

The analysis of changing gender relations has drawn on a range of theoretical approaches:

mainstream stratification analysis
radical feminism
liberal feminism
Marxist feminism
dual-systems theory
post-modernism.

The orthodox *stratification analysts*, such as Goldthorpe, have traditionally argued that gender inequality is not particularly important for understanding the unequal distribution of resources in society, or the causes of political change. They assert that this is because women's social and economic position is determined by the position of the family in which they live, and this in turn is determined by that of the male breadwinner. This notion, that gender inequality is thus almost irrelevant for mainstream sociological theorizing, has met with an onslaught of criticism by writers who have argued that it is inappropriate to take the family as the unit of analysis in such a way. These criticisms include the points that: firstly, there is inequality between men and women within the family; secondly, women's earnings are important in the standard of living and position of the household; and thirdly, not all people live in households in which there is a male wage earner, let alone one in which such a man brings in all the family income. That is, the critics assert that there is significant inequality between men and women, and for a woman to be married to a man does not mean that she gains all the privileges he has access to. The outcome of this debate has been a range of detailed empirical studies about the extent to which women's employment and the status of their husbands actually affect women's political views and, vice versa, about the impact of women's employment on their husbands' views. The consensus is now that all these variables have an impact, varying in importance according to context.

In complete contrast to the view that gender inequality is not important, *radical feminists* have argued that it is one of the most, if not the most, significant forms of social inequality. Radical feminist theorists argue that the oppression of women by men is the most important aspect of social inequality in society, and that men's exploitation of women is not a by-product of other forms of inequality. Such forms, for example those based on ethnicity and class, are important but do not alter the fundamental nature of patriarchal power. The basis of the system of patriarchy has been variously accounted for within this perspective. Sometimes it is seen as a seamless web in which all aspects of society are part of a system of male domination. On other occasions it encourages a focus on social institutions which sociologists have tended to neglect, including: men's systematic violence towards women in rape, wife beating, and sexual harassment; the power relations involved in contemporary forms of heterosexuality; the problems for women of men's control over their work, especially in the home as unpaid housewives; and the socialization process through which girls are brought up to be gentle, passive people who will do as they are told, while boys are brought up to be bolder and more aggressive.

Most contemporary writers on gender relations today recognize that there are important aspects of inequality between men and women and that these have a broad social significance. Some appear not to have an overall theoretical perspective, but in fact implicitly draw on a *liberal feminist* approach. There are now many sociological studies of the disadvantages women face in particular situations, from problems in places of employment, to seeking health care, to trying to participate in party politics. Some writers have kept their analyses at the level of specific situations. For instance, one problem not entirely trivial for women pursuing careers is their exclusion from male gatherings in bars, which are important channels for passing on information. Or consider the problem of becoming an MP when the House of Commons starts its sitting in the middle of the afternoon and continues into the evening, which cuts across any conventional domestic commitments. While this small-scale level of analysis has its place, it is severely limited by focusing so much on the detail that it fails to deal adequately with the wider structures which generate these situations. Detailed studies are useful in helping to build up the data necessary for a wider picture, but a full explanation requires a broader view.

A more structural view is that of *Marxist feminist* writers, who have argued that the traditional male-dominated family exists because it is a source of benefit to capitalists since women can be made to labour for free in the reproduction of wage-labourers. In this perspective, the domestic labour which housewives do – housework and child-care – results in the production of children and well-fed, cared-for husbands who go to work for wages. That is, housewives produce or reproduce both the next generation of labourers and the current one. This is much cheaper when done by housewives in nuclear families than any other way, since these women do not get paid for the work, obtaining only their maintenance. Marxist feminists argue that it is capital, or employers, who gain from this exploitative form of labour, since it means that they can pay these women's husbands lower wages than would be the case if male workers had to buy these services, for instance meals in cafés, laundries for clothes washing, and nannies for their children. Women's weak labour-market position, that is their low wages and insecure employment, is seen to result from their position in the family. The familial ideology acts as a further level through which women's oppression is maintained. Women – and men – are persuaded that these particular family forms are natural and good, and the only ones available.

Dual-systems theorists have attempted to combine the best of the radical and Marxist feminist perspectives so as to be able to incorporate both class and gender inequality into the analysis. Here the analysis of gender inequality as a system of patriarchy is combined with an analysis of capitalism. For instance, Hartmann (1979) argues that male workers are able to keep women out of the better jobs because they are organized, and that, as a consequence, women are obliged to marry on unfavourable terms, such that they have to do most of the housework. Hartmann argues that there is a vicious circle in which patriarchy and capitalism tend to maintain each other.

The sweeping nature of some of these grand social theories has been criticized by those working from a *post-modernist* position. Can we really generalize in this way about gender relations? Are not the differences between women too great to warrant such theorizing? Do these generalizations about men and women rest upon a hidden biological reductionism, or essentialism? By speaking of men as a group and women as a group, does this inevitably mean falling back on to biological rather than social categories? The strongest ground for this critique is that around the question of 'race' and ethnicity. The differences in the form of gender relations between ethnic groups, and the impact of racism on gender relations, mean that some of the early theoretical formulations require modification. However, there are gendered social structures which have shown enormous resilience over time, so the post-modernist denial of the possibility of generalization should be rejected.

So, what is the actual position of women in modern Britain? The following sections will examine gender relations in paid employment, the household, sexuality, welfare and politics.

4.2 Women's Employment

Wages

The gap in the earnings of men and women is one of the more obvious indicators of gender inequality. Women working full-time earned only 79 per cent of men's hourly rate in 1992, according to the *New Earnings Survey*, that is an average of £6.40 per hour as compared with £8.07 per hour (table 4.1). When the figures are taken on a weekly basis the gap widens further, so that women earn only 71 per cent of the weekly wages of men, because men are more likely than women to work long hours, to obtain overtime pay, to get premiums for working night shifts, and to be awarded a variety of bonus payments. The gap widens still further when part-time workers are included since they earn significantly less than full-time workers and are largely female.

Table 4.1 Pay and pensions

	Men	*Women*
Pay per hour, 1992	£8.07	£6.40
Proportion of men's pay per hour, 1992	100%	79%
Proportion of men's pay per week, 1992	100%	71%
In company pension scheme, 1989	61%	37%

Source: *New Earnings Survey*, *Employment Gazette*, November 1992

Women are also less likely to benefit from a range of fringe benefits provided by employers. They are much less likely to be enrolled in company pension schemes, with serious consequences for poverty in old age. In 1989, 61 per cent of men and 37 per cent of women employees were in such occupational pension schemes. While there is a gap between full-time male and female workers, the principal cause is the small proportion of part-timers who are covered.

Although there are significant differences between men's and women's earnings within the *same* occupation, the main reason for inequality is that men and women tend to do different jobs. Women are segregated into a narrow range of poorly paid occupations and industries.

The implementation of the Equal Pay Act between 1970 and 1975 reduced the wages gap a little. In 1970 women earned only 63 per cent of men's hourly rate, and only 55 per cent of men's gross weekly pay. The size of the gap has remained nearly constant since 1975: women's full-time hourly rates have fluctuated at around 74 per cent of men's, with a small improvement between 1987 and 1992 (figure 4.1).

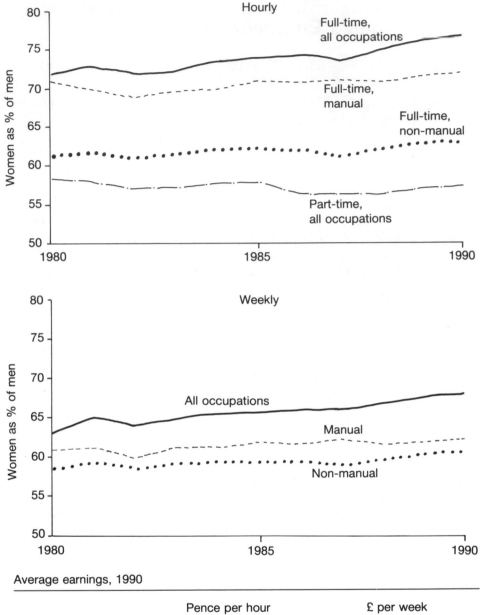

Figure 4.1 The wages gap: earnings differentials in Great Britain.
Source: *New Earnings Survey*. Crown copyright.

The increasing integration of Britain into the EU has affected the legal regulation of labour markets in the UK. Article 119 of the Treaty of Rome, which is the foundation treaty of the EU, lays down that there must be equal treatment of women and men in employment and related issues. The principle of equal treatment is more strongly articulated in the Social Charter and the Social Chapter of the Maastricht Treaty. The implementation of equal treatment has been the subject of prolonged legal and political disputes. Whether or not laws and Directives could close the wages gap depends on whether they tackle the underlying causes of unequal pay. If the cause is direct or indirect discrimination in the labour market, equal opportunities policies are more likely to make an impact than if the causes lie outside, for instance in the form of the family and household.

The question of whether the wages gap is due to discriminatory labour market structures or to the division of labour in the household has been the subject of extensive debate. One view is that men get paid more than women because women cannot work the hours necessary to earn the higher rates, and do not possess the skills to get the better jobs because of the time and effort they expend on the care of home and children. On this view, women's domestic responsibilities get in the way of their paid work, and prevent them from taking the opportunities for higher-paid work. Women are too busy looking after children (and their husbands and elderly parents) to participate as fully as men in the labour market. If we agree with this view, then women's lower wages may be seen either as their just reward or, alternatively, as the result of a most unjust family system.

This argument may be assessed by examining patterns in women's paid work. In a large-scale survey, Martin and Roberts (1984) interviewed 6,000 women about their work histories, current employment and current domestic position. They found that, when women spent time out of paid work bringing up their children, they were placed at a disadvantage in the labour market. However, this survey also found that women spend less time out of the labour market rearing children than is often believed. Women on average spend only five years out of paid work when they are having children, although there are wide variations. They also found that, on their return, many women were unable to utilize the skills that they had acquired before having children. That is, women had felt obliged to take less well-paid and less skilled jobs than those for which they were actually qualified. Not only lack of skills, but lack of opportunity to utilize those skills, depressed women's rate of pay. Since women's break in the labour-market experience constitutes only a small part of their lifespans, other factors must also operate to account for their disadvantaged position.

An alternative view is that women get paid less because of direct or indirect discrimination. Direct discrimination is when men consciously act to prefer men to women, and has been illegal in employment and related areas since 1975. Are women discriminated against simply because they are women? Women are certainly found in a very narrow range of jobs, that is they are segregated from men in the labour market, but conscious exclusion by men is not a commonly held explanation. Indirect discrimination is also illegal but is generally regarded as more persistent. For instance, part-time workers get less pay and benefits than full-time workers. Since most part-timers are women, this may be considered to be indirect discrimination against women. Indirect discrimination is often a consequence of the deep and historic persistence of gendered practices in social institutions. Practices which disadvantage women do not have to be consciously intended for them to have real effects.

Gender composition of employment

Women are less likely than men to be in paid employment (table 4.2). But the gap has closed steadily since the Second World War (table 4.3). In 1992 women constituted 43 per cent of persons in employment in the UK. This is high by international standards: for instance, within the EU the average is 38 per cent and only Denmark has a higher rate at 45 per cent of the workforce. Indeed, when the self-employed are excluded (where women are only 24 per cent), women make up 48 per cent of employees in employment.

Table 4.2 Employees in employment, Great Britain, June 1992, seasonally adjusted

	Males (million)	Females (million)	Total (million)
Full-time	9.865	5.580	
Part-time	1.145	4.638	
Total	11.010	10.218	21.228

Source: constructed from *Employment Gazette*, November 1992, table 1.1. Crown copyright

Life-cycle changes

There is a pattern in which women are likely to leave the labour market at the birth of their first child, and to return a few years later, typically when the last child has entered school. The period that women spend out

Table 4.3 Employment for men and women

	Women employed (000s)	Men employed (000s)
1984	10,933	15,548
1985	11,066	15,642
1986	11,205	15,592
1987	11,457	15,669
1988	11,650	15,811
1989	12,016	15,924
1990	12,094	15,950
1991	12,062	15,841
1992	12,037	15,676

Source: *Labour Force Survey*, *Employment Gazette*, November 1992, table 7.1. Crown copyright

of the labour force for child-care has been steadily reducing over the post-war period. Martin and Roberts (1984) show that, among women whose first child was born between 1970 and 1974, 51 per cent had returned to paid employment with 5 years, and that the median period before return to work for this group was 4.8 years. The median years for return to work for the next cohort, who had their first birth between 1975 and 1979, is estimated to be only 3.7 years. By contrast, the group which had their first babies between 1950 and 1954 had a median of 9.7 years before they returned to paid employment. Before the Second World War the pattern was somewhat different, since in many occupations a marriage bar operated which forced women to resign if they married. In this earlier period, married women found it hard to get employment, except in certain industries such as cotton textiles or as casual employees.

Part-time work

While British women are more likely to be in employment than those in many other countries, they are also more likely to work part-time. In 1992, 45 per cent of women but only 10 per cent of men worked part-time. Most women who work part-time have small children. Among women with children under 5 in Great Britain in 1989, 31 per cent worked less than 15 hours a week. As compared with the EU, the higher proportion of part-time working in Britain is linked to the low level of publicly provided child-care and the greater differentiation of full- and part-time work. The number of part-time women workers has continued to increase in recent years despite the various recessions, growing steadily from 2.8 million in 1971 to 4.2 million in 1984 and 4.8 million in 1989. Since conditions of part-time work are usually poor, this concentration of women in part-time employment represents their segregation into the worst parts of the labour market. Part-time workers who work only a very few hours do not benefit from many of the forms of employment protection introduced by legislation over the last decade or so, although those part-time workers who work at least half the usual hours are covered on some items.

Unemployment

Whether women or men are worse affected by the current high rates of unemployment is a complex issue. Some theorists have suggested that women constitute a reserve army of labour which is pulled into employment when the economy is growing and pushed out when it is contracting. However, while the figures on the changes in women's employment during and after the two world wars fit this theory, those for the numerous other recessions and depressions of the twentieth century do not appear to do so. In recent recessions in Britain, women's employment has not declined more than that of men.

The official unemployment rate is based on those out of work who are claiming benefit in their own right. Using this rather narrow definition, women's unemployment rate in September 1992 was 5.5 per cent as compared with 13.3 per cent among men. However, these figures are often held to underestimate the true amount of unemployment, especially among women. Because the figures are based on the number of people claiming state benefits, they exclude those people who are unemployed and yet *not* claiming social security or unemployment benefit payments. More women than men are excluded on this basis because of the rule that men should normally claim benefit on behalf of the women they are living with (whether they are married or not). Thus many women who are living with or married to a man cannot claim benefits on their own behalf, and do not appear in the unemployment figures. An alternative way of measuring unemployment is by asking a sample of the population whether they are unemployed. The International Labour Office measures unemployment in this way, and the gap between women's and men's unemployment then closes significantly but not totally.

Ethnicity

Racism and cultural difference produce significant differences between ethnic groups in the extent and level of women's participation in paid employment (see also section 5.3). Afro-Caribbean women are most economically active (i.e. in paid employment or looking for it), followed by white women, then women of Pakistani or Bangladeshi origin. Yet Afro-Caribbean women have double the rate of unemployment of white women.

Occupational segregation

Restrictions on women within paid employment are evidenced by the extreme concentration of women within a very narrow range of occupational groups. Over 40 per cent of full-time women workers are to be found in clerical employment, while a very few further occupational groups account for most of the rest of women in paid work. In contrast, men are spread through a much wider range of occupations. This segregation of the sexes in paid employment may be considered to have both a vertical and a horizontal component. Women are confined both to lower-grade jobs (vertical segregation) and to different jobs (horizontal segregation).

Vertical segregation Women are to be found in the lower grades in large numbers but are much less common as the grades go up, until at the highest grade there are almost no women at all.

Horizontal segregation This is the separation of women into different occupations from men. Figure 4.2 illustrates horizontal segregation, showing that in most occupations there is a clear majority either of women or of men: there are very few occupations in which there is an even proportion of men and women. While there have been some minor reductions in horizontal segregation over the last century, the extent of segregation by gender in employment remains a striking feature of the labour market. Further, part of the reduction in horizontal segregation has been a consequence of the entry of men into traditional areas of women's employment, rather than of women moving into those higher-paying sectors traditionally monopolized by men. Segregation is both into occupations (figure 4.2) and into specific industries (figure 4.3).

The segregation becomes more marked, the more detailed the level of investigation. This is because segregation within any given workplace is more severe than that shown by national statistics covering all work-

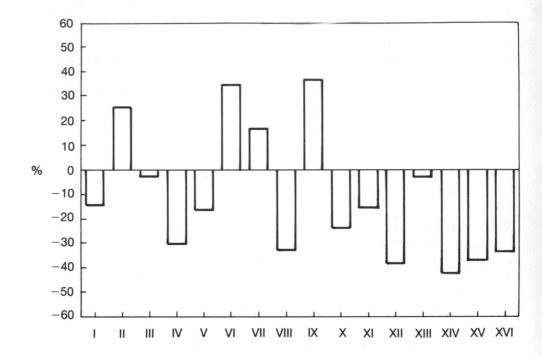

Figure 4.2 Occupational sex segregation, Great Britain, 1989: percentage by which occupations over- or under-represent women.

I	Professional and related support in management and administration
II	Professional and related in education, welfare and health
III	Literary, artistic, sports
IV	Professional and related in science, engineering, technology
V	Managerial
VI	Clerical and related
VII	Selling
VIII	Security and protective services
IX	Catering, cleaning, hairdressing and other personal services
X	Farming, fishing and related
XI	Processing, making, repairing and related (excluding metal and electrical)
XII	Processing, making, repairing and related (metal and electrical)
XIII	Painting, repetitive assembling, product inspecting, packaging and related
XIV	Construction and mining
XV	Transport operating, materials moving and related
XVI	Miscellaneous

I–VIII   are non-manual occupations: IX–XVI are manual occupations.

Source: Equal Opportunities Commission, 1991, figure 7.1; from *Labour Force Survey*, 1989. Crown copyright.

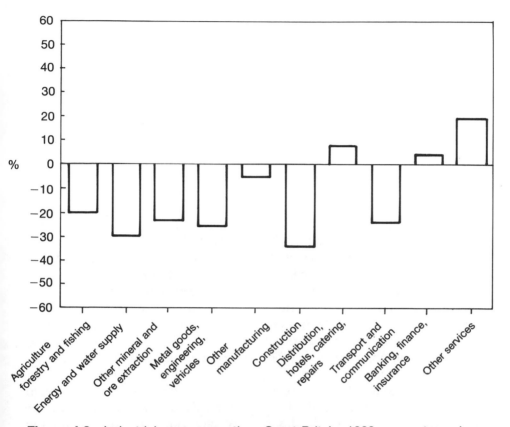

Figure 4.3 Industrial sex segregation, Great Britain, 1989: percentages by which industries over- or under-represent women.
Source: Equal Opportunities Commission, 1991, figure 6.1; from the 1989 Census of Employment, *Employment Gazette*, May 1991. Crown copyright.

places. The study reported by Martin and Roberts (1984) found that over half their female respondents worked only with other women, while of their sample of men (these women's husbands) 81 per cent worked only with men.

It is the segregation of employment by gender which gives the best clues as to why women generally earn less than men. Women are confined to those sectors of the job market which pay the least, whether or not they are skilled. One of the main problems for women's pay is that women are in occupations which are badly paid, rather than that women are poor workers. If women were evenly distributed across the spectrum of employment, their pay levels would be much closer to those of men.

Continuity and change

The number and proportion of women in paid employment have increased significantly since the Second World War, yet there has been only a very small improvement in women's wages compared with those of men, and little growth in the range of occupations in which women are able to gain employment. This contradicts certain of the assumptions and theories which are popular in explaining patterns of inequality in employment. Thus the picture is not one of simple progress, although there is clearly a significant change in the form of gender relations in employment. Increasing labour-market experience does not appear to improve women's position as directly as, for instance, 'human capital' theory would predict. Women's increasing commitment to the labour market has less impact than might be expected.

This overall picture hides significant divergences in the experiences of women. Younger women have obtained levels of educational qualifications not much inferior to those of their male peers and are beginning to enter the professions and better-paying occupations. However, older women returning to the labour market take up work in the expanding, but poorly paid, part-time sector. There is, therefore, an increased polarization among women as labour-market and educational opportunities have changed.

There are a number of explanations for women's disadvantaged position in employment. First, it is a result of their taking greater responsibility than men for the care of children, the house, and the elderly. Women are seen to have fewer skills and less labour-market experience as a consequence, which in turn lead to less skilled jobs and lower wages. However, even women with the same qualifications as men usually earn less.

Second, changes in gender relations in employment have sometimes been attributed to the changing balance between capital and labour, employers and employees. For instance, the growth of 'flexibility' includes the growth of part-time work, which has particularly poor conditions of service and low levels of wages (see section 2.5). This can be seen as a result of employers' needs for flexibility in the utilization of labour and their ability to create this at a time of high unemployment. However, how can the fact that women rather than men take part-time work be explained without an analysis of gender inequality in its own right?

Third, women's disadvantaged position is seen as a result of the restriction of women's access to the best jobs by patriarchal practices in the labour market and the state. These have changed from highly exclusionary in the nineteenth century to merely segregationary in recent years.

Summary

1   Women are disadvantaged in the labour market by comparison with men.
2   A principal cause of inequality is segregation, vertical and horizontal.

4.3   The Household

The traditional approach to the analysis of the family has been in terms of consensual values, norms and roles, and the relationship of family members to their wider kin network (see also chapter 6 on the family). This approach assumed a degree of harmony and stability within the family which was not assumed for other social institutions. Such a romantic view of the family has been rejected by the women's movement and by recent empirical work on domestic relations. For instance, quite high levels of violence have been shown to exist within the family. The romanticized picture of housewives happy over their labour of love has also been challenged by accounts of the higher rates of depression among women with small children who stay at home, of women's eagerness to take paid work even at low rates of pay, and of the hard work and monotony of domestic labour.

Although it is more usual to think of the home as a place of rest, a great deal of *work* is performed within the household. This includes the tasks of cooking, cleaning and child-care, and caring for the emotional needs of others. The alternative ways of looking after children are subject to increasing debate as more women enter paid employment. Employer-provided nurseries are one option, alongside state-run nurseries, child-minders paid for by parents, as well as the traditional model of the mother staying at home. Only 2 per cent of children under three years old have publicly funded child-care places in Britain, the joint lowest level in the EU. For children from three to school age, Britain's position is the second lowest.

While the focus has traditionally been on caring for children and for husbands, the care of the elderly is of growing importance. As people live longer, increasing proportions of the population become not only simply old, but also frail and in need of care. This care can be provided in several different ways: by residential care, by paid care workers, and by relatives. Who cares for the frail elderly – and who pays – are increasingly important and controversial areas of debate.

Sharing housework?

Some writers have suggested that the increase in the number of household gadgets such as washing machines, fridges, freezers, food mixers, vacuum cleaners and non-stick pans must have significantly reduced the amount of housework that women do. These technological innovations might free women from household burdens. Some suggest further that this will lead to women being able to take up paid work instead, further advancing their equality with men. Other writers, more pessimistically, have argued that as one household task is reduced or eliminated by advances in technology, then others are added to the list and standards are raised. Furthermore, some tasks are not affected by the provision of household appliances, in particular the supervision of children and the elderly.

The investigation of this issue is quite problematic since it would obviously be rather awkward for a sociologist to observe families with a stop-watch! When in 1987 respondents to the *British Social Attitudes* survey were asked who was mainly responsible for general domestic duties, 82 per cent said that the woman was responsible and only 12 per cent that it was shared equally (SCPR 1988). However, while 16 per cent of men said that tasks were shared equally, only 9 per cent of women did so. The most egalitarian attitudes were to be found among couples where both were in full-time employment, though even here only one in five said that there was equal sharing.

The most effective method is that of asking all members of a sample of households to keep diaries, noting what they are doing at all times of the day. These time-budget studies, as they are known, reveal that the time that full-time housewives spend on housework and caring, about 50 hours per week on average, has not significantly changed for several decades. However, the proportion of women who are full-time housewives has significantly dropped during the post-war period and, since married women who have paid employment spend less time on housework than those without paid work, this means that overall there has been a significant decline in the amount of time the average woman will spend doing housework. However, Gershuny's (1983) work has shown, like the more recent attitudes survey, that married women typically spend more time on housework than their husbands, even if they also have paid employment. There are complex variations in this: women with young children put in the greatest number of hours of total work, and women with neither young children nor paid jobs the least.

Households are increasingly varied in their form. More people are living outside the traditional model of male breadwinner, full-time housewife and two-children household. The number of lone parents has increased significantly over the last 20 years. Britain now has a higher proportion of one-parent families than any other EU country (see chapter 6).

Today, while class makes little difference to the form of the household, 'race' and ethnicity matter a lot. There are significant divergences between ethnic groups in the sexual division of labour and pattern of household. Half of all mothers of West Indian or Guyanese origin are lone mothers, as compared with 14 per cent of white mothers and less than 10 per cent of Indian, Pakistani and Bangladeshi mothers. West Indian women are the most likely of these three groups to be in paid employment, and the women of Asian origin the least likely.

Equality of consumption in the family?

The household is often treated as a unit of consumption, and it is frequently assumed that all members of a household have equal access to its resources. If this were true, then men and women who are married to each other could be assumed to have the same standard of living. While there are some instances where resources really are shared equally between husbands and wives, men usually have greater access to them than women. For instance, husbands are more likely than wives to have control over the use of the family car, if a car is shared by the household, and are likely to control more of the family income for their leisure pursuits. Jan Pahl, in her study *Money and Marriage* (1989), showed that wives contribute a relatively higher proportion of any income to the household pool. However, except in households on very low incomes (when women are frequently given total responsibility for budgeting), men have more control over the spending of discretionary income.

Summary

1 The structure of the household is undergoing considerable change, with fewer people living in two-parent households with only one wage earner, and a greater diversity of household form.
2 Significant inequalities between men and women in the household remain in both the amount of housework performed and the level of consumption.

4.4   Culture, Sexuality and Welfare

Femininity and masculinity

That boys are supposed to be aggressive and outgoing, strong and demanding, while girls are neat and tidy, gentle and obedient, is central to our stereotypes of masculinity and femininity. Such differences between the genders are encouraged from an early age by a variety of rewards and punishments. These patterns of behaviour are absorbed through the reading materials of children, the toys they play with and the roles they see acted out in television programmes. While the 'Janet and John' type of book, used to teach children to read, portrays slightly less stereotyped roles than 20 years ago, there is still a clear distinction between the activities of males and females in the stories. Some people try to introduce toys that do not reinforce gender stereotypes but, nevertheless, girls are much more likely to get dolls to dress up in the latest fashion, boys more likely to get toys for military-type games. People are thus socialized into the forms of behaviour deemed appropriate for their sex, thereby learning to become 'gendered subjects'.

Although femininity is often a problem for women seeking equal treatment with men – in that it is easier to take advantage of people who are gentle than those who are aggressive and pushy – its positive aspects in terms of openness, emotional expression and human warmth are also important. Indeed, this latter aspect of femininity is emphasized by some recent writers on masculinity, who protest that the social pressures on men to contain rather than express their emotions are oppressive and restrictive, stunting their full emotional development. However, this tends to overlook the extent to which masculinity is bound up with the power and privilege from which men usually benefit.

Much of the early writing on femininity and masculinity adopted a *socialization perspective*, which took as its main topic the processes through which people learned and internalized gender stereotypes. Recent work within a *discourse perspective* has shifted the issue to that of understanding the varied content of femininities and masculinities, not simply how individuals learn to adopt these identities. This latter perspective has developed through an analysis of various kinds of media, especially television, magazines and film.

Women's magazines recognize the experiences of women and, especially, the difficulties of balancing the expectations held by others – in particular husbands and boyfriends – with their own hopes and desires. Stories in the magazines re-create the dilemmas that women face, exploring their various options but with a final resolution in a traditional direction.

Comparisons between different women's magazines show the variety of forms of conduct which can be called feminine. The femininity of *Woman*, with its emphasis on the role of wife and mother, is very different from that of *Cosmopolitan*, where the feminine woman is encouraged to be adventurous in catching the most sexually desirable man, retaining him for as long as he is interesting, and getting a super career at the same time. *Cosmopolitan* is different from *Woman* in its emphasis on the need for a successful career, yet it shares a view of femininity that includes an emphasis on a sleek appearance.

There is no one form of femininity but rather several, and the same applies to masculinities. They vary especially by age, marital status, class and ethnicity. For instance, the forms of masculinity among the working class lay more emphasis on physical prowess than those of the middle classes, where appropriate career is more important because masculine status is defined in terms of success as husband father breadwinner.

Images of femininity and masculinity vary significantly by ethnicity; it would be a mistake to assume that the patterns among British whites are also to be found among black people. At the most obvious level, there are different dress codes to denote masculine and feminine genders. More significantly, the greater participation of Afro-Caribbean than white women in paid employment means that the cultural notion of the dependent domesticated housewife is a white rather than a universal stereotype.

Westwood (1984) vividly captures the ethnic variety of femininity in her ethnography of factory life at Stitch Co. We see the different marriage customs for Indian and white women: the former having arranged marriages with complex, rich ceremonies; the latter having marriages based on short-lived romance with white gowns instead of gold saris. Yet, despite the difference, the attractions of marriage for women in both groups comes through clearly: it both symbolizes and constitutes the movement from adolescence to full adulthood; it means independence from the family of origin; and it is hoped that it will be financially advantageous. Gender identities are ways of life, multi-faceted and sometimes contradictory. Yet they are perceived in terms of a fundamental dichotomy, an insuperable barrier between the lifestyles of women and men.

Sexuality and equality

Sexuality is an area in which women are often supposed to have made great advances towards equality with men. The sexual revolution is supposed to have liberated women from the constraints of Victorian ideology, with its oppressive double standard in which non-marital sex was acceptable for men and not for women. So, do women have equal access to sexual pleasure with men? Is the double standard dead, and are women sexually liberated? Or have the dangers of AIDS introduced new sets of constraints? There have been many changes both in attitudes to women's sexuality and in sexual practices over the last few decades. But how are these to be understood?

Is the double standard dead? While it does seem to be less strong, in that male respondents much less often say that they want to marry only a woman who is a virgin, it is still the case that women are more often criticized than men for engaging in non-marital sexual activity. For instance, analyses of youth culture suggest that young women are still assessed as either 'slags' or 'drags'.

How prevalent and significant are pornography, prostitution and other forms of overtly degrading forms of sexual practice? Pornography appears to be both growing in its availability, and becoming more violent in its content. There are new media through which violent sadistic sexual fantasies are represented, such as video. Not only are these images unpleasant for women in their own right, but there is a further question as to whether such representations encourage men to play out fantasies of power over women through rape, sexual harassment and other forms of sexual molestation of women. The evidence here is complex and mixed, but suggests that such images do have some impact.

The much greater availability of contraception and safe abortion has made the consequences of sexual intercourse for women, in terms of unwanted children, much less likely. Indeed, some writers have suggested that the development of cheap, fairly reliable and fairly safe forms of contraception, together with the liberalization of the laws on abortion, have been among the most important gains to women in recent decades. They have meant that women are no longer quite so much at the mercy of their biology and may engage in sexual intercourse free from the worry of unwanted pregnancy. The 1967 Abortion Act made it possible for women to get abortions if they were in the early stages of pregnancy and could persuade two doctors that they met certain criteria. These criteria were open to interpretation, but meant that a woman could get an abortion if either her physical or her mental health were deemed to be at risk. Some NHS doctors have interpreted this broadly, since an unwanted pregnancy can be catastrophic to the life of a woman, so that abortion is granted to any woman who considers this to be the case. Where the interpretation is more restrictive, non-profit-making abortion clinics have stepped in to fill the gap. However, some writers have been sceptical of the advantages to women of these advances in contraceptive and abortion technology. They have suggested that the changes have simply meant that women are freer to be sexually exploited by men, and that greater sexual activity does not mean better sex.

Acceptance of a wider range of sexual practices, such as gay and lesbian relationships, is sometimes suggested as a sign of progress. However, the extent of this is limited by the reaction against male homosexuals as a result of the AIDS crisis. Further, progress is also qualified by the difficulty some lesbian mothers have in retaining the custody of their children.

The AIDS crisis is changing the context in which decisions about sexual contact are made. The risk of catching AIDS is increased by having more than one sexual partner, and penetrative sex without the use of a condom. However, surveys suggest that, outside the gay community, sexual practices have changed less than the experts have advised.

Traditional analyses of sexuality drew upon a Freudian conception of sexuality as a biological drive. Recent changes in sexual practices have highlighted the malleability of human sexuality in a way which challenges Freudian ideas of a relatively fixed sexuality. Explanations of patterns of sexuality in terms of biological drives have been largely replaced by those which explain changing patterns of sexuality in terms of social and cultural factors.

Contemporary analyses of sexuality draw instead upon concepts of discourse, which emphasize the social construction of sexual practices. Foucault's concept of discourse has been important in these developments. However, Foucault tended to underestimate the significance of gender relations and the unequal power between men and women in shaping sexuality. Sexuality is constructed in the context of gender relations. Power is embedded in these discourses, though not in simple ways.

Summary

1 Discourses of masculinities and femininities are represented in the media and other cultural institutions. These are of complex forms rather than simple dichotomies.
2 Sexual discourses are gendered in ways which more often stigmatize women's conduct and encourage aggressive practices among men, but are nonetheless highly varied.

4.5   Inequality and Welfare

Housing, social security and health

Access to housing, health care and welfare are important components of social citizenship. Full involvement in contemporary society requires a basic floor of income provision and services such as welfare and housing. If women have unequal access here it affects their participation in other areas of society.

Housing

A home is both a material necessity and, if bought, usually a person's most expensive purchase. We might imagine that access to housing would be equal for men and women, since they most often share this in the marital home. However, while many housing units are occupied by both men and women, this is a problem for those women living independently of men.

   Until the late 1970s the ownership of a house in which a married couple lived was usually held by the husband, the woman having little direct legal claim to it. This is now less common since building societies, through which most homes are purchased, will automatically register a property in the names of both spouses. Further, wives' legal access to the marital home has been improved by the recent practices of divorce courts, which have more often allowed the wife to claim possession of a portion of the marital home even if her name did not appear on the title deeds.

   Nevertheless, there remain substantial inequalities in the relative access of women and men to housing because of the fact that men are more likely than women to have an income sufficient to support a mortgage or high rent. This places non-married (divorced, separated, widowed and single) women at a serious disadvantage on the housing market.

Benefits

Welfare benefits form a higher proportion of many individuals' income than was formerly the case, because of the high level of unemployment, the increase in female headed households, and the increase in the number of old people who are dependent upon state pensions and income support. Women are more likely than men to be dependent upon state payments because more women than men head single-parent households and because more women than men live to pensionable age. Changes in the level of welfare benefits thus disproportionately affect women.

Women and men have different levels of access to welfare benefits because of the way that benefits are paid. Some are paid only to people who have made contributions when they have been in paid work. For instance, unemployment benefit is paid on the basis of paying national insurance contributions. Women with a lower level of participation in paid work, as a result of interruptions for child-care or of working only a few hours a week, are less likely than men to be able to claim this benefit. Pensions are also affected by employment record, especially the better occupational pensions to which employers will have made contributions alongside their employees. Those facing old age on only a state pension will be very poor, and this is a disproportionately female group. Those who follow a typical male employment pattern gain the best welfare benefits. The current system is one which routinely disadvantages those who devote their lives to unpaid caring work for others – largely women.

Health

Since women usually live longer than men, health would appear to be one area of life in which women have an advantage. Men are more likely than women to die from occupationally related diseases, such as lung diseases as a result of mining, as well as heart disease. However, some writers have suggested that the diseases commonly found among men are treated with greater concern and more expensive medical treatment than those more commonly found among women. For instance, attention has recently been drawn to the inadequate provision of screening for cervical cancer, despite the fact that this service could provide the means of identifying early forms of the disease before it reaches its incurable and lethal stage.

The development of the new reproductive technologies has also raised questions about the gendered nature of medical research. These are new techniques which enhance women's fertility by a series of intrusive medical interventions. The most famous is that of *in vitro* fertilization (IVF) in which eggs are taken from the woman's ovary and fertilized outside the body with the man's sperm before being replaced in the woman's womb. Its advocates claim that it is a significant enhancer of women's lives in enabling otherwise infertile women to conceive, while its critics counter that it is a disruptive and uncomfortable procedure with such a high failure rate that it benefits experimental medical scientists more than the patient. (More discussion of women and health can be found in section 9.4.)

Education

Education is an area where there has been a transformation of the
position of girls and young women. In schools, not only has the

Table 4.4 Pupils leaving school by highest qualification held, United Kingdom,
1965–1991

	1965–6 (000s)	1975–6 (000s)	1985–6 (000s)	1989–90 (000s)	1990–1 (000s)
Males					
Leavers with GCE A levels, SCE H grade passes:					
2 or more A, 3 or more H	48	61	66	72	72
1 A, 1 or 2 H	12	15	16	16	14
Leavers with GCSE, GCE O level, CSE, SCE O, standard grades alone:					
5 or more A–C awards, CSE grade	26	31	44	41	40
1–4 A–C awards, CSE grade 1	54	101	108	93	85
No higher grades:					
5 or more other grades			86	52	55
1–4 other grades	234	216	65	53	42
No GCSE, GCE, SCE or CSE qualification			59	36	31
Total school leavers	373	423	444	362	338
Females					
Leavers with GCE A levels, SCE H grade passes:					
2 or more A, 3 or more H	32	49	61	74	76
1 A, 1 or 2 H	11	16	18	17	17
Leavers with GCSE, GCE O levels, CSE, SCE O, standard grades alone:					
5 or more A–C awards, CSE grade 1	31	38	51	52	51
1–4 A–C awards, CSE grade 1	56	108	123	97	87
No higher grades:					
5 or more other grades			80	42	41
1–4 other grades	222	190	52	37	30
No GCSE, GCE, SCE or CSE qualification			43	24	21
Total school leavers	352	400	427	344	323

Source: *Education Statistics for the United Kingdom*, 1992 edition, Department for
Education. Crown copyright

Table 4.5 Students[a], United Kingdom, 1990–91

	All students[b]					Males as proportion of all students[b]				
	16–18 (000s)	19–20 (000s)	21–24 (000s)	25+ (000s)	All ages[c] (000s)	16–18 (%)	19–20 (%)	21–24 (%)	25+ (%)	All ages (%)
All students	1401	555	752	2490	5813[d]	51	51	43	33	41[e]
In schools	519	4	–	–	523	49	55	–	–	49
In further education:										
Full-time and sandwich	354	38	24	56	472	46	51	50	38	45
Part-time day	280	102	176	783	1343	69	57	34	25	38
Evening[f]	125	111	300	1252	2397[d]	37	38	36	32	33[e]
All FE	759	250	500	2091	4213[d]	53	48	36	29	36[e]
In higher education:										
Full-time and sandwich	112	265	182	107	667	51	52	55	47	52
Part-time[g]	11	36	71	291	410	69	72	61	53	56
All HE	123	302	253	398	1077	52	54	57	51	54

a Excludes students enrolled on nursing and paramedical courses at Department of Health establishments. 81,700 (provisional) in 1990–1. Excludes students attending private sector colleges.
b Age at 31 August.
c Includes sex and ages unknown for Scotland: ages unknown for Wales.
d Includes students on some courses of adult education for whom age is not known: 605,700 in 1990–1.
e Based on the total excluding some in adult education (note d).
f Includes estimated age for students aged 16 years or more in adult education centres: 1,580,600 in 1990–1.
g Includes the Open University.

Source: Education Statistics for the United Kingdom, 1992 edition. Crown copyright

Table 4.6 Higher education qualifications[a], United Kingdom, 1980–1990

	Below degree level[b,c]			First degrees[d]			Postgraduate[e]			All		
	Males	Females	Persons	Males	Females	Persons	Males	Females	Persons	Males	Females	Persons
All HE graduates[f] (000s)												
1980–1	45	17	62	76	48	124	24	13	37	144	78	222
1981–2	46	18	64	76	51	127	24	13	37	146	82	228
1982–3	47	19	66	76	53	129	24	13	36	146	85	231
1983–4	51	22	72	77	56	133	24	13	37	152	91	243
1984–5	54	25	79	80	60	139	26	15	41	160	99	260
1985–6	54	26	80	78	61	139	27	16	42	158	103	262
1986–7	53	32	85	79	64	143	29	17	46	161	113	274
1987–8	50	33	83	80	66	146	30	19	50	160	118	279
1988–9	54	35	89	81	68	149	32	22	54	167	125	292
1989–90	62	45	107	82	70	152	33	24	57	177	140	316
Subject group 1989–90 (%)												
Arts[g]	10	17	13	14	30	21	25	48	35	15	29	21
Science[h]	43	31	38	48	24	37	44	22	35	46	26	37
Social Studies[i]	44	47	45	24	27	25	29	28	28	32	34	33
Other[j]	3	5	4	14	19	17	2	3	3	8	12	10

[a] The following refer to calendar years for the second year shown: university diplomas and certificates, CNAA qualifications prior to 1985–6.

[b] Includes higher TEC/SCOTEC, BEC/SCOTBEC, BTEC/SCOTVEC, HND/HNC, first university diplomas and certificates, CNAA diplomas and certificates below degree level and estimates of successful completions of public sector professional courses.

[c] Trends in qualification numbers and enrolments may not be directly comparable because, *inter alia*, qualifications may not be assigned to the year in which they are achieved.

[d] Includes university degrees and estimates of university validated degrees (GB), CNAA degrees (and equivalent) and successful completions of public sector professional courses. Also includes certain CNAA diplomas in management studies.

[e] Includes universities, CNAA and estimates of successful completions of public sector professional courses. Postgraduate certificates in education are included.

[f] Excludes successful completions of nursing and paramedical courses at Department of Health establishments, 31,000 in 1989–90. Excludes private sector.

[g] Education; language, literature and area studies; arts other than languages; music, drama, art and design.

[h] Medicine, dentistry and health; engineering and technology; agriculture, forestry and veterinary science; science; architecture and other professional subjects.

[i] Administrative, business and social studies.

[j] Combined and general; Open University.

Source: Education Statistics for the United Kingdom, 1992 edition.

traditional gender gap been closed but girls have overtaken boys; while in higher education the gender gap is closing steadily. (See also section 8.4.)

Girls do better than boys in the exams taken by schoolchildren at 16. In 1990–1, 70 per cent of girls but only 61 per cent of boys left school with A-levels, Highers, GCSE, GCE O level or SCE grades A–C, or CSE grade 1 (calculated from table 4.4). At 18 the gender difference is also in favour of girls, with 76,000 leaving school with either two or more GCE A levels or three or more SCE H passes, as compared with 72,000 boys in 1990–1. These are very significant and recent changes. As recently as 1985–6 more boys obtained GCE A levels and Scottish Highers than girls: 66,000 boys but only 61,000 girls obtained two or more.

Women are now more likely to be found in further education than men, making up 64 per cent of the students (see Table 4.5). When the definition of education is broadened there are nearly equal numbers of young men and women: of those 16–18 years old, 60.3 per cent of young men and 60.5 per cent of young women are participating.

In higher education, however, there are fewer women than men, especially doing postgraduate degrees, although this gap has also been declining in recent years. Men took 54 per cent of the places in higher education in 1990–1. (Table 4.6 shows the increase which has taken place over the decade 1980 to 1990.) While higher education has expanded and the numbers of men have increased, most of the increase has been found among women. In universities there has been an increase between 1980–1 and 1990–1 of 16 per cent in the number of men and 50 per cent in the number of women. In the old polytechnic and college sector (which was reorganized in 1992) in the same period, the figures are even more striking: a 29 per cent increase in men and a 103 per cent increase in women.

In the higher levels of higher education, in postgraduate study, there is a smaller proportion of women than at the first degree level. Among postgraduates there were 33,000 men and only 24,000 women in 1989–90 in the UK (table 4.6). Nonetheless this is a significant increase in the proportion of women over 1980–1 when there were only 13,000 women gaining postgraduate qualifications as compared with 24,000 men.

This picture of increasing equality in the number and level of educational qualifications gained by women and men should, however, be qualified by a consideration of the degree of segregation of women into certain fields of educational endeavour. Women are more likely to gain arts and domestic science qualifications, while men are more likely to gain scientific and technical ones. However, even this appears to be subject to change and should not be overstated. In 1990–1, GCSE mathematics was attempted by 84 per cent of girls and 82 per cent of boys, and GCSE science by 82 per cent of girls and 81 per cent of boys (table 4.7). The traditional divisions are to be found in technology,

Table 4.7 GCSE subjects attempted, Great Britain, 1990–1991

	Persons (%)	Males (%)	Females (%)	Persons (000s)
English	88.6	86.7	90.5	564.5
Mathematics	83.1	82.1	84.2	529.7
Science	81.0	80.5	81.6	516.5
Technology	35.6	52.4	18.1	227.0
Modern languages	54.1	46.4	62.3	345.0
History and/or geography	62.0	63.4	60.5	394.9
Creative arts	41.9	37.0	47.1	266.9
English and mathematics	81.5	80.0	83.0	519.0
English, maths and science	77.2	76.1	78.5	492.1
English, maths, science and modern languages	50.1	43.3	57.1	319.0
All leavers (000s)	637.2	326.1	311.1	637.2

Source: *Education Statistics for the United Kingdom*, 1992 edition. Crown copyright

attempted by 52 per cent of boys but only 18 per cent of girls, and in modern languages, attempted by 62 per cent of girls but only 46 per cent of boys.

The figures on segregation at university level are more marked than those in schools. Among men studying for first degrees in 1989–90, 48 per cent were doing so in science as compared with 24 per cent of women, and 14 per cent in arts subjects as compared with 30 per cent of women (table 4.6).

These changes in education mean that there is less inequity in qualifications among young people than among old people. Among people aged 16–24, slightly more men than women have no qualifications (23 per cent of men compared with 20 per cent of women); while among those aged 50–59, 37 per cent of men and 57 per cent of women have none (table 4.8).

Increasing success in the formal educational system is one of the most dramatic improvements in the position of women in society. These changes contradict some the earlier explanations of women's lack of success in education. It was variously held that early socialization into femininity was incompatible with educational success; that early upbringing and/or the structure of the brain meant that women could not think mathematically as well as men; that orientation to a domestic role would lead to women dropping behind in school at puberty since they 'wanted' a boyfriend/husband more than a job. These theories are contradicted by

Table 4.8   Highest qualification by age, United Kingdom, 1991

	16–59 (%)	16–24 (%)	25–29 (%)	30–39 (%)	40–49 (%)	50–59 (%)
			Age			
Males						
Degree or equivalent	11	4	13	15	14	9
Higher education below						
degree level	5	3	6	6	6	5
GCE A-level or equivalent	35	32	36	38	35	33
O-level or equivalent	15	29	16	11	9	6
Other qualification[a]	9	9	11	8	8	9
No qualification	25	23	18	21	28	37
Other[b]	1	1	1	1	1	1
Males base = 100% (000s)	16,366	3618	2302	3866	3708	2872
Females						
Degree or equivalent	6	3	9	10	6	3
Higher education below						
degree level	7	3	8	8	8	8
GCE A-level or equivalent	16	25	20	16	13	9
O-level or equivalent	24	37	31	24	17	11
Other qualification[a]	12	11	13	11	12	12
No qualification	34	20	19	30	43	57
Other[b]	1	1	–	–	1	1
Females base = 100%						
(000s)	16,242	3500	2265	3844	3709	2924

[a] Includes CSE below grade 1, YTS certificate, other qualifications.
[b] Includes unknowns and non-respondents.

Source: *Education Statistics for the United Kingdom*, 1992 edition. Crown copyright

the evidence of women's superior educational achievements up to 18 years old, and the greater proportion of girls than boys taking GCSE mathematics.

The explanation of these changes should draw on several related factors. One part of the change was a legal one, but its significance should not be overestimated. Discrimination against women in education was made illegal in the 1975 Sex Discrimination Act, helping to lead to the removal of the quotas against women in some university subjects, such as medicine, and to the removal of compulsory streaming of girls out of technical subjects in schools. More important was the increase in the opportunities for women in the world after education as the labour market gradually opened up. A further contributory factor might be the changing orientation to marriage, which is less likely to lead to a financially secure lifelong future, given the rise in the divorce rate. The context of cultural changes and the increasing diversity of acceptable forms of femininity under the impact of the feminist movement may also have played a part.

The implication of these changes for other aspects of gender relations is a further question. For instance, the issue of whether the closing of the education gender gap will lead to a closing of the wages gap depends on the extent to which qualifications determine relative levels of pay. Nonetheless, despite such caveats, they are likely to have some impact on women's increasing participation in the public sphere of employment and politics.

Summary

1   There are inequalities between men and women in housing, welfare benefits and health which affect women's access to a full social citizenship.
2   Girls up to 18 years old now achieve better formal educational qualifications than boys, reversing a previous gender gap in the opposite direction. The gender gap in students in universities is also closing.

4.6   Politics, Power and Violence

Power takes many different forms. This section looks at overt struggles over power. It will encompass issues of the force men use against women, gender relations in the formal political arena, and the variety of women's resistance to their subordination.

Male violence

Male violence takes many different forms including rape, wife beating, sexual harassment, and child sex abuse. The official statistics reveal only a relatively small amount of such violence, yet most women are sufficiently convinced of its prevalence to organize their lives quite carefully in order to protect themselves from being exposed to such violence. For instance, most women are reluctant to walk by themselves at night.

Sociologists have varied quite considerably in their assessment of the situation. Some have taken official statistics at face value and assumed that such violence is the infrequent action of a few psychologically disturbed men. Others have argued that the official statistics are inadequate and seriously underestimate the extent of such violence, and hence its significance for women.

The official crime statistics show that, in 1987, 2471 cases of rape were recorded by the police, of which 18 per cent ended in a conviction. This is an increase of 143 per cent in recorded cases since 1977. However, the statistics seriously underestimate the incidence of rape, since the majority of women do not report cases to the police, probably considering that they have faced enough distress without taking such a case through the courts. (See section 11.3 for discussion of official statistics and other ways of estimating such crimes.)

A community study of violence by Hanmer and Saunders (1984) shows that male violence against women is widespread and that the official figures are a gross underestimate. In their study, they interviewed women in one neighbourhood in depth about the violent experiences they had suffered. Rather than only recording those instances of violence that the women had reported to official agencies such as the police, they explored a wide range of violent incidents from the women's points of view. They concluded that the level of violence was high and reported that, in a period of one year, 59 per cent of women had experiences of violence. These researchers divided this violence up into three categories: violence, threats and sexual harassment. They found that over the course of the year, two-thirds of the women interviewed reported experiences of sexual harassment, one-quarter had experienced threats, and one-fifth violence.

Conventional accounts of violence against women suggest that most men who are violent to women are mentally unstable in some way. They argue that these men have suffered bad childhood experiences which have prevented their normal development. These accounts imply that incidents of violence against women are few and far between, that they are products of a few sick individuals. However, these explanations of violence against women are not consistent with the evidence of the extent of the violence, or of its continuity with other forms of male conduct towards women.

Rape and battering are one end of a continuum of aggressive forms of behaviour by men towards women. This continuum includes flashing, sexual harassment and wolf whistles. It also has links with exploitative forms of sexuality such as prostitution and pornography. These forms of behaviour by men towards women, while by no means universal, are regularly repeated features of social life. The limited response of the law enforcement agencies is taken by some writers as evidence that the state should be considered a patriarchal institution rather than a neutral body. The harsh treatment of women who complain of rape by the courts, and the sometimes lenient sentences handed down by judges, add to this view. For instance, it tends to be easier for men to plead the mitigating circumstances of 'provocation' if they have killed their spouse than it is for women. For while men may strike women immediately after an incident, women are more likely to strike only after having sought out a weapon, and thus may be unable to argue that they acted in the heat of the moment, as has been necessary for the defence of provocation. The neglect by the police force of women's complaints of rape, domestic violence and other forms of physical abuse by men is notorious, although there are now attempts at reform, such as trained officers and specialized departments at police stations.

Hanmer and Saunders (1984) suggest that women's low expectations of police assistance led them to become ever more dependent upon other men who were also untrustworthy. They suggest that this causes a vicious circle for women: the fear of violence leads women to greater dependency upon a known male; dependency makes the woman particularly vulnerable to attack from this male, because he has no fear of retaliation; when women go to the police about such attacks, nothing is done; consequently many women consider that the police are unhelpful, and this reinforces women's fear of violence and dependence upon individual male protectors. This vicious circle is shown in figure 4.4.

Formal politics

While women now have many of the formal political and legal rights that men have, there is still a striking absence of women from positions of public power and authority. This raises questions about women's effective participation in political decisions.

Over the last 150 years, women have won most of the same legal and political rights as men, thus obtaining formal political citizenship. Women won the vote in two stages. Firstly in 1918 women over 30 who possessed some property won the right to vote, followed in 1928 by all women over 21. Having won the vote, women were able to make good their claims to the right to sit on juries and to take up seats in Parliament and local government.

Though formally equal, women do not have effective equality with men in access to public positions, and this is significant for the representation of women's interests. Women MPs make up only a very small proportion of the total number of MPs. In the 1992 general election, women won only 9 per cent of the seats in the House of Commons, so that the UK has only 60 women MPs. The proportion has

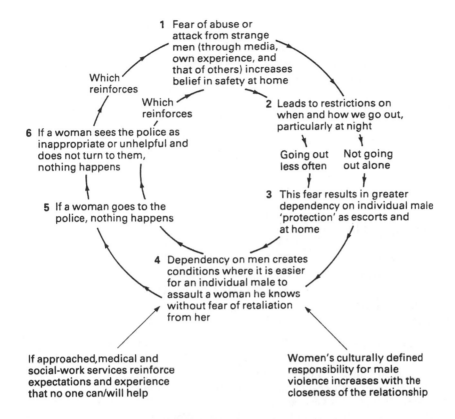

Figure 4.4 Perpetuation of the division between the public and private spheres of women's lives.
Source: Hanmer and Saunders, 1984, p. 66

improved only a little in recent years and Britain has one of the lowest proportions of women in its national elected legislature in Western Europe. The average in the EU is 13 per cent. There are some differences between the parties, with the Conservatives having a lower proportion of women MPs than the Labour Party – 6 per cent as compared with 14 per cent. The Conservative Cabinets have been particularly striking in their absence of women. There is a slightly higher proportion of elected women representatives in local government than in central government.

Women hold a very small proportion of other public offices. In 1984 the government appointed 31,172 men to public bodies, compared with only 7233 women, that is 19 per cent. Government departments varied in their appointment of women, from only 3.5 per cent of employees in Agriculture, to 32 per cent in the Home Office. There are very few women judges, and very few women on the boards of nationalized industries. There have never been any women chief constables, and women generally hold low-ranking positions in the armed forces. The

Equal Opportunities Commission (EOC) noted in 1991 that despite the fact that 79 per cent of the NHS workforce is female, only 17 per cent of its unit general managers and 4 per cent of district and regional general managers are women.

Table 4.9   Women in trade unions, 1990

Women's representation	NUPE (%)	NALGO (%)	GMB (%)	USDAW (%)	TGWU (%)
As members	71.3	53.1[a]	30.8	61.7	16.9
On national executive committee	46.1	42.0	29.4	31.3	7.7
Among delegates to annual conference	33.3	–	17.4	27.1	–
On TUC delegation	36.1	41.7	19.8	26.9	20.6
As full-time national officers	38.5	31.6	11.8	20.0	3.4
As full-time regional officers	11.0	13.4	3.6	18.6	–
Women members (no.)	430,000	398,660[a]	267,371	251,371	210,758

NUPE: National Union of Public Employees.
NALGO: National and Local Government Officers' Association.
GMB: GMB (general workers' union).
USDAW: Union of Shop, Distributive and Allied Workers.
TGWU: Transport and General Workers' Union.
[a] 1989.

Source: Snyder, *European Women's Almanac, 1992, p. 370; data from Women in Trade Unions – Action for Equality*, Labour Research Department

Among trade unions, the picture is little different. Table 4.9 shows that women in trade unions occupy a much smaller percentage of the leadership positions than their proportion of the membership, even in unions where women are the majority of the members. However, some trade unions now have special women's committees to assist the representation of the views of their women members in an effort to ameliorate the problem.

Women form only a slightly higher percentage of British Euro-MPs, at 15 per cent. The European Parliament has been an important source of pressure on the British government to improve its sex equality legislation. The EC declared that the 1975 Sex Discrimination Act (which incorporated the 1970 Equal Pay Act) did not come up to its standards, and that the British government had to make it stronger. This is the reason that the 'equal value amendment' was passed, which means that a woman seeking equal pay can compare herself with a man doing work of similar value, rather than the more stringent condition of a man who is actually doing exactly the same work. This has led, in 1985, to a series of significant equal pay decisions to women's advantage.

Instances such as this raise the question whether a higher number of women in public positions would significantly improve the position of women in society. Indeed, there is a pressure group to get more women MPs, called the 300 Group, which seeks 300 out of the 651 seats in Parliament for women. However, others are more sceptical of the significance of simply having more women in positions of influence in the state. This is partly because they fear women in such positions simply get incorporated into the structures as they exist, and merely reproduce the same decisions as the dominant male group. Some suggest that it is more important to be able to bring political pressure to bear, so that the elected representatives of whatever sex will pass legislation of benefit to women. Still others argue that Parliament is not the most important site of political struggle for women, and that they would be better spending their political energies at the level of local politics or in everyday struggle.

In short, women are relatively absent from the formal positions of power in contemporary British society. This is a problem both in its own right, and because it reflects the relative lack of power that women have in contemporary Britain.

Feminism

Feminist responses to these forms of gender inequality have taken a variety of forms and have mobilized women to different degrees. The strong feminist wave of the 1970s is the second such wave this century, the early one being instrumental in winning political citizenship for women. Feminism is not a new social movement but one with a long history.

The contemporary period is characterized by the widespread acceptance of many of the feminist ideas of the 1970s, which were considered outrageously radical at that time. For instance, male violence is now recognized as a significant problem for women and the subject of serious discussion by the police as well as feminists. Equal pay for equal work is likewise an early feminist demand now accepted into mainstream policy initiatives such as Opportunity 2000, rather than being seen as a fringe concern. Indeed some of these issues are now so mainstream that they are barely recognized as feminist.

It has been argued that women are to be found less often in public life because of their domestic responsibilities, which take so much of women's time, together with a socialization into gentle rather than assertive behaviour. However, the extent to which women have been politically active renders these accounts problematic.

Gender politics is not exclusively represented by feminism. Some women have represented the interests of women as needing to be protected within the home. This underlies some of the concerns which have been raised by the new right, but these have not met with a popular response in contemporary Britain.

Today the dominant perspective in gender politics is that represented by 'equal opportunities', to which politicians and activists of otherwise divergent views subscribe.

Summary

1   Male violence against women is a serious problem which is under-recorded in the official statistics. There is increasing attention being paid to this in public policy.
2   Women have achieved parity in formal legal and political rights, but this has not led to equality overall.
3   There are comparatively few women in public positions, in Parliament or public bodies.
4   Feminist concerns are taking new forms, and increasingly influencing mainstream politics, while the radical autonomous parts of the women's movement are losing their previously high public profile.

4.7   Conclusion

This overview of the relations of the genders in contemporary British society has demonstrated extensive inequality between men and women today. While the situation has improved to some extent in recent years, especially in the field of education, the basic pattern of inequality remains in all aspects of the social structure, from paid work to the household division of labour, from sexuality to violence.

The inequality between men and women, and the extent to which the different aspects of this are interconnected, mean that it is appropriate to use the concept 'patriarchy' to describe this set of social relations. Patriarchy is a social system through which men dominate, exploit and oppress women. It is the interconnectedness of the different aspects of this which makes the concept of patriarchy particularly appropriate. However, this inequality takes many different forms, especially in different ethnic groups, and among people of different ages and classes. The diversity of gender relations is a crucial part of its pattern in contemporary Britain.

One way in which gender, ethnicity and class have been seen to fit together is as a consequence of capitalist social relations: women are exploited in the workplace because of the direct benefit that employers derive from this, and in the home because employers need to have a new generation of workers produced as cheaply as possible. Some of the evidence of the earlier part of this chapter supports this view. Women are paid less than men, and employers do benefit from this. Women do a lot of unpaid work in the home – significantly more than men. However, other data presented here suggest that this is not an adequate explanation.

Within paid employment, male workers benefit from their ability to keep the best and most skilled jobs for themselves; they are beneficiaries of occupational segregation by gender. Men also gain from the unequal division of labour within the home, in which women do disproportionate amounts of housework. Further, the physical and sexual abuse of women, which the evidence shows is much more widespread than is popularly believed, cannot be understood in terms of anything other than patriarchal relations.

This suggests an analysis in terms of both capitalist and patriarchal relations. However, this is insufficient because by itself it does not enable us to understand the diverse experience of women of different ethnicities. Women of colour who face racist practices cannot be simply incorporated into models which assume white women as the norm. Hence, any adequate analysis must take into account the intersection of capitalist, patriarchal and racist structures in order to understand gender relations in contemporary British society.

Related topics

Discussions of gender relations will be found in all of the other chapters of this book. Accounts of various aspects of women's work are to be found in sections 3.2, 3.4 and 3.5. Chapter 6 is concerned with analysis of the household and women's place in it. The relationships of women to the health-care system and to the criminal law are dealt with in sections 9.4 and 11.4, respectively. Section 8.4 treats the educational disadvantages of women, amongst other topics. Femininity, masculinity and youth cultures are also discussed in sections 10.2 and 10.4.

Further reading

A useful textbook collection of readings on women's position in society is

Humm (1992). A more complex account of changes in gender relations can be found in Walby (1990). A useful source of data on the inequalities between women and men in employment and related arenas is *Women and Men in Britain*, an annual publication from the Equal Opportunities Commission.

5 Ethnicity and Racism

5.1 Introduction

A good deal of this book is about the inequality that exists in British society. Sociologists have often talked about this inequality in terms of differences in social class. However, recently there has also been emphasis on inequalities that arise out of gender or ethnic differences. This is not simply a question of looking at the differences in income, wealth, or educational opportunity between men and women or between different ethnic groups. It also involves a consideration of the interrelationships of class, gender, and ethnic inequalities, of the way in which, for example, black people may tend to have working-class jobs.

Inequalities between the British white population and ethnic minorities of various kinds have not always been the focus of sociological interest. In the period 1955–70, a good deal of sociological work in ethnic relations was centred around a different but related problem – that of the integration of black immigrants into British society. Of course, in a sense Britain is wholly an immigrant society, subject to successive waves of incomers of diverse origins in earlier centuries. More recently, it has been estimated that there were some 20,000 black people in Britain in the eighteenth century; and, in the nineteenth century, substantial numbers of Irish entered the country, expecially following the potato famines of the 1840s. Immigration is not a new phenomenon.

More recent attention, public and sociological, has focused on immigration since the Second World War from the so-called New Commonwealth, chiefly from the Caribbean and the Indian subcontinent. Sociologists used to operate with a model which conceived of the problem as being one of integration. How would numbers of black, culturally different, people be integrated into British society? The leading assumptions of this model are as follows (Richardson and Lambert, 1985):

1 The immigrants are strangers by virtue of their colour and culture.
2 The host society is confused and insecure and, as a result, reacts with both hostility and intolerance.
3 The host society is stable and does not have any fundamental conflicts within it.
4 This stability is temporarily disturbed by immigrants. Order is restored, however, when the immigrants adapt to British society and the white population accepts immigrants.
5 This process of adaptation and acceptance may be broken into several phases which can proceed at varying speeds and may be complete only after several generations have passed.

Such a scheme, the *immigration-integration model*, directs attention to certain research problems. In particular, commentators record the persistent racism of British society, which impedes integration and may function to perpetuate the inequalities suffered by black people. Again, wider cultural differences, including those involving religion, education, and family life, will have an effect on the speed with which ethnic minorities become adapted to British society.

However, the immigration-integration model is also misleading in a number of important respects. First, immigration, at least from members of the New Commonwealth, has been greatly slowed by various immigration Acts. Second, a concentration on racism as a set of discriminatory attitudes and practices towards *black* people ignores the relationship between racism and wider xenophobic attitudes. Thus racism towards blacks is related to the nationalistic beliefs widespread in British society that emerge at particular times, as in the debate over membership of the European Community in the early 1990s. Similar attitudes are also revealed in the relationship of the English to the Irish, Welsh, and Scots. All these racist and ethnic attitudes and beliefs have in common a fearful, and often hostile, view of some social group defined as different. Third, a stress on integration and immigration tends to ignore the degree to which ethnic minorities are heterogeneous. Within the black community there are differences – of language, social class, religion, age – which can make them more different from each other than from the white community. Fourth, the immigration – integration model assumes the possibility, and desirability, of *integration*. The alternative is to recognize and celebrate cultural difference. Fifth, and last, one cannot consider the position of ethnic minorities without taking into account the fundamental inequalities of British society. This last issue will be the main focus of this chapter.

5.2 The Structure of the Black Community

There are now some 2.6 million non-whites living in the United Kingdom compared with perhaps 100,000 before 1950 (Coleman and Salt, 1992). This represents a profound change in the constitution of British society – a change largely dependent on the British economy's demand for labour.

After the Second World War, migration into Britain was regulated partly by a work permit scheme which did not, however, apply to British Commonwealth citizens. The British economy was growing, providing an increased demand for labour. Both government agencies and large employers encouraged immigration from the Commonwealth to meet labour shortages throughout the 1950s. At this time, the largest numbers were coming from Caribbean countries, secondarily from the Indian subcontinent, with fairly small numbers from Africa and the Far East. By the early 1960s, however, there was increasing pressure for control over immigration. Acts of 1962, 1968 and 1971 restricted immigration from Commonwealth countries but, because the entry of dependent relatives of earlier immigrants was not restricted, the total numbers of migrants continued to grow throughout the 1960s. Since the 1971 Act most immigrants have needed work permits, and these have been granted mostly for work in those industries, like the health service and hotels, where there is a shortage of domestic workers. The numbers of work permits issued have fallen as the British unemployment rate has risen. Furthermore, the proportion of work permits issued to inhabitants of Commonwealth countries has also fallen. It seems likely that permits are increasingly being given for non-manual occupations, which has tended to favour the white inhabitants of developed countries such as the USA and South Africa. The 1971 Act also effectively discriminated against black workers by the introduction of the concept of 'patrials' which was intended to give the right to residence to persons with close ties to Britain but not others. In practice, the majority of overseas patrials have been found in the 'white' Commonwealth of Canada and Australasia.

Table 5.1 demonstrates the changing pattern of immigration. Over the period since 1975, the proportion of immigrants coming from the New Commonwealth has steadily declined from 35.4 per cent to 23.8 per cent. The European Community and other foreign sources have, on the other hand, contributed a rising proportion, being responsible in 1989 for rather more than half of the total number of immigrants. These figures

Table 5.1 The origins of immigrants into Britain by country of last residence, 1975–1989 (annual averages)

	Old Commonwealth[a] (%)	Indian subcontinent[b] (%)	Other New Commonwealth[c] (%)	European Community (%)	Other foreign[d] (%)	All countries (000s)
1975–9	19.7	15.2	20.2	15.2	29.6	186.6
1980–4	13.2	14.1	17.8	20.2	34.6	186.3
1985–9	15.1	10.1	13.7	25.0	36.1	232.1

[a] Canada, Australia, New Zealand.
[b] India, Pakistan, Bangladesh, Sri Lanka.
[c] New Commonwealth except Indian subcontinent.
[d] Including USA, Middle East, South Africa and others.

Source: calculated and adapted from *Social Trends*, 1992, table 1.17. Crown copyright

should be treated with a certain amount of caution. They represent *inflows* and there are, of course, also considerable outflows of population. Furthermore, they conceal the often substantial proportions of people coming from New Commonwealth countries who are white. For example, in the 30 years following 1955, one-fifth of those coming from the New Commonwealth were white. By contrast, only 2 per cent of those coming from the Old Commonwealth (Australia, New Zealand, and Canada) were black (Coleman and Salt, 1992).

Data on simple numbers of people entering the country also conceal changing age and gender ratios of immigration, particularly for the Indian subcontinent in recent years. The proportion of married women and young people is much higher, as dependants follow the male head of household. In the 1950s, the bulk of immigration was from the Caribbean, the men coming first, followed by their families. Immigration from this area is now very small: in 1981, only 2 per cent of all immigrants were from the Caribbean. The same pattern is now being repeated for immigration from the Indian subcontinent. The number of men being admitted has declined as work permits become restricted, but there is a catching-up process as families come to join their menfolk. This point is

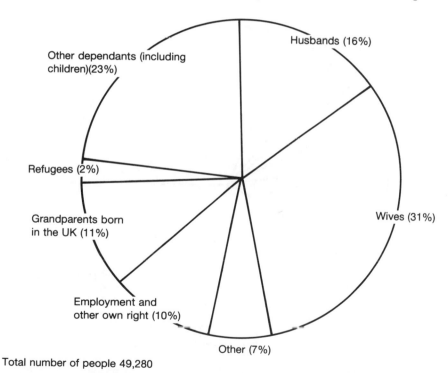

Total number of people 49,280

Figure 5.1 Acceptances for settlement by category, 1988.
Source: Coleman and Salt, 1992, p. 453; from Home Office statistics

illustrated in figure 5.1, which shows that wives and children account for half of the acceptances for settlement in 1988.

As we have already said, a concentration on immigration can be misleading for it implies, amongst other things, that the bulk of black people are new to the United Kingdom. This is far from being the case. Between 1984 and 1986 the size of the ethnic population was around 2.4 million, about 4.5 per cent of the population (figure 5.2). Of these, 40 per cent were born in Britain, with some variation between different groups (see figure 5.3). All non-white ethnic groups have populations younger than whites, less so among the West Indian, Chinese, and African and more so in the Bangladeshi and Pakistani groups. The proportion of men is generally higher: 57 per cent in the African and 56 per cent in the Bangadeshi conpared with 49 per cent in the white groups.

If one simply takes age and sex distributions, there are, therefore, substantial differences between various ethnic minorities. There are also differences of religion and of family structure, and quite different expectations about the possibility, or desirability, of returning 'home'. West Indians, for example, came to Britain with the intention of settling, Pakistanis with the conviction that they would eventually return.

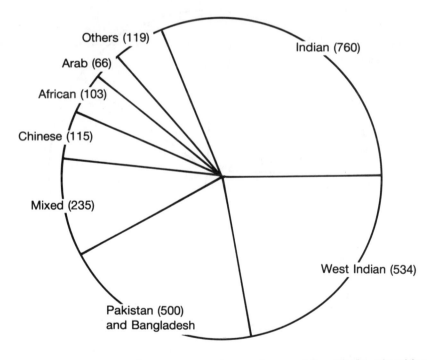

Figure 5.2 Estimates of average numbers of non-white ethnic minorities, 1984–1986 (thousands).
Source: Joshi, 1989, p. 183; from *Labour Force Surveys*

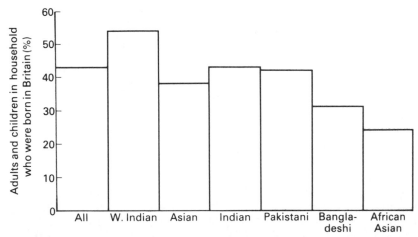

Figure 5.3 Birthplace of Asians and West Indians in Britain, 1982.
Source: adapted from Brown, 1984, p. 25, with permission

Summary

1 Immigration into Britain has been slowed down. There is also a decreasing proportion of men, as wives and children come to join men already in the country.
2 Over 40 per cent of people labelled as of Asian or West Indian origin were born in this country.
3 The balance of the sexes among the West Indian population is very similar to that in the white population. Among Asians there is a relatively high ratio of men to women.

5.3 Ethnic Disadvantage

The male black population is heavily concentrated in certain industries. As can be seen from table 5.2, male ethnic minorities are over-represented in distribution and catering, transport, and other manufacturing industries, including textiles. Ethnic minority women have a distribution nearer that of the white population except that they are over-represented in the health services and in other manufacturing industries. There are also differences *within* the black population. For example, Asians, particularly Pakistanis, are more concentrated in manufacturing than West Indians, the ethnic balance being reversed for transport and for services more generally.

Another way of considering the position of black workers is to consider

Table 5.2 Persons aged 16+, in paid employment or on government scheme, by ethnic origin, industry division and sex, UK, spring 1985

Industry division	Males		Females	
	White (%)	Ethnic minority (%)	White (%)	Ethnic minority (%)
Agriculture, forestry and fishing	3.1	0.2	1.3	0.1
Energy and water supply	4.4	0.9	1.0	0.8
Other mineral and ore extraction etc.	4.4	2.5	1.8	1.4
Metal goods, engineering and vehicles	14.7	15.7	5.0	6.5
Other manufacturing industries	10.6	14.7	9.9	15.4
Construction	11.7	5.2	1.6	1.0
Distribution, hotels, catering, repairs	15.8	25.1	25.5	23.0
Transportation and communication	8.0	12.4	2.9	4.5
Banking, finance, insurance etc.	8.6	6.3	10.3	6.3
Other services of which:	18.2	15.1	40.2	39.5
Education	4.2	3.0	11.4	6.0
Health services	2.1	5.3	10.5	16.8

Source: Bhat et al., 1988, p. 65; from *Employment Gazette*, January 1987

their socio-economic group (see section 3.2 for discussion of this measure), for this will show what *level* of job black workers hold. *Generally* speaking, black people hold jobs lower down the socio-economic scale, being under-represented in comparison with whites in non-manual occupations, and over-represented in the less skilled manual occupations, as table 5.3 shows. This distribution in socio-economic group is reflected in the level of qualifications attained in various sections of the population. In 1990, for example, while 72 per cent of the white population had some form of qualification, only 48 per cent of the Pakistani or Bangladeshi community did. Again, there are marked differences within the black population.

For example, a higher proportion of Asians than West Indians is found in the professional occupations. Indeed, the proportion of African Asians who are professional is higher than that of the white population. A high proportion of West Indians are skilled manual workers. Interestingly, for women workers, there is rather less difference between the white population and ethnic minorities, the latter being relatively over-represented in semi-skilled occupations and under-represented in non-manual jobs as a whole. As before, these differences within the black community are reflected in differences in levels of qualification. Higher education qualifications are held by 19 per cent of Indian male

Table 5.3 Socio-economic category by ethnic group, 1982

Job level	White (%)	West Indian (%)	Asian (%)	Indian (%)	Pakistani (%)	Bangladeshi (%)	African Asian (%)	Muslim (%)	Hindu (%)	Sikh (%)
Professional, employer, management	19	5	13	11	10	10	22	11	20	4
Other non-manual	23	10	13	13	8	7	21	8	26	8
Skilled manual and foreman	42	48	33	34	39	13	31	33	20	48
Semi-skilled manual	13	26	34	36	35	57	22	39	28	33
Unskilled manual	3	9	6	5	8	12	3	8	3	6

Source: Brown, 1984, p. 197, reproduced with permission from Gower Press.

workers, compared with 6 per cent of West Indian (and 15 per cent of white). One striking feature of table 5.3 is the relatively high proportion of African Asian and Hindu minorities who have non-manual occupations. One aspect of this finding is the tendency among these minorities to self-employment. In 1982, for example, 18 per cent of Indians and 23 per cent of African Asians were self-employed (Hamnett et al., 1989). To some extent, this self-employment may be as home-workers or as small shopkeepers who may struggle to survive. Equally, though, some of it represents an 'Asian enterprise' of some significance.

As one might expect, the socio-economic position of black workers affects their earnings. White men on average earn a good deal more than black men, although the earning differential between groups of women is much less. A study conducted in the early 1970s found that non-manual ethnic minority workers earned 77 per cent of the earnings of their white colleagues; skilled manual earned 89 per cent; while for semi-skilled and unskilled manual workers the earnings were the same. However in this last case, in order to achieve this equality of earnings, ethnic minority workers have to do more shift work because their jobs are intrinsically worse paid. These differences derive from a number of factors. For example, black workers are concentrated in certain industries which traditionally pay low wages. Again, it is the case that in certain occupations, older people are paid more than younger ones. We have already seen earlier in this chapter that the black population is younger than the white, and this will in itself depress wages. Further, within any broad socio-economic category, white workers tend to occupy more promoted positions. But lastly, having eliminated these factors, black workers seem to be paid less than white ones simply because they are black.

So far, we have discussed the position of black people who are in employment. Particularly in times of high unemployment as in the 1980s and early 1990s, it is obviously also important to consider those who are unemployed. Rates of unemployment in the black community are higher than in the white. In 1990, for example, 7 per cent of whites were unemployed, compared with 11 per cent of West Indians and 17 per cent of Pakistanis (*Social Trends*, 1992). Downturns in the economy hit black people first. Over the last two decades, differences in rates of unemployment between ethnic minorities and the white population are greatest as unemployment rises. A whole range of explanations is available for differences in proneness to unemployment. Black workers may work in industries particularly hard-hit in the recession, or there may be a high proportion in given age groups particularly prone to unemployment. One way of looking at the effects of the kind of industry they work in is to see whether black people and whites living in the same area – inner cities for example – have similar rates of unemployment. In fact, although the differences between black and white unemployment are much reduced in these areas, they do not disappear entirely. Similarly, if one compares blacks and whites *within* any age group, there are still differences in vulnerability to unemployment. In 1985, for instance, 30 per cent of West Indian, 28 per cent of Indian, and 37 per cent of Pakistani or Bangladeshi men aged between 16 and 24 were unemployed, compared with 20 per cent of whites.

In sum, as far as employment is concerned, ethnic minorities are disadvantaged even if there are differences between minorities. They are heavily concentrated in particular industries, often those in relative decline; occupy lower socio-economic positions; have lower earnings; work longer, and often unsocial, hours; and are more prone to unemployment. Further, this disadvantage extends to other areas of social life. For example, the quality of housing occupied by ethnic minorities is much lower than that occupied by whites. Properties are older and more likely to be terraced houses or flats; they have fewer rooms but more people per room; and they are less likely to have a garden. As with other areas, global comparisons between black and white populations hide differences within the black population. Asians and West Indians, for example, favour very different types of accommodation. The proportion of the former who are owner-occupiers is higher than that amongst whites. West Indians, on the other hand, have a low rate of owner-occupancy and a high rate of tenancy of council accommodation compared with the white population. These different tenures mean that Asians and West Indians have different housing problems. It still remains true, however, that when compared with the white population, black people have worse housing conditions.

The black population is similarly disadvantaged in health and health care. As we show in chapter 9, there are strong differences in health and illness between social classes. Because of their employment – or unemployment – prospects, one would expect the black population to suffer the ill-health of the white working class. Indeed they do so, but even more extremely. For example, even allowing for social class, the stillbirth and infant mortality rates are three times as high, and complications during pregnancy and low birthweights are much more common in the black community (Bhat et al., 1988).

Summary

1   Ethnic minorities, in general, are concentrated in certain industries, have jobs lower down the socio-economic scale, and tend to have lower earnings than the white majority population.

2 In other respects ethnic minorities are disadvantaged. For example, they tend to have poorer housing and health.
3 It is important to note that there are differences within the ethnic minority population.

5.4 Class and Racism

Explaining ethnic inequalities

In the previous section, we sought to show that the black population suffers from a set of multiple disadvantages. The question remains, however, how to interpret these data of ethnically based inequality. What are the factors involved in producing this situation? The essential problem is whether the explanation of racial disadvantage lies in the nature of the British class structure or in the racism, and its associated practices of racial discrimination, which pervade British culture. We will first roughly contrast these explanations.

Class explanations of racial disadvantage

In terms of this approach, ethnic disadvantage is essentially a function of the British class structure. British society is unequal, with those at the bottom of the hierarchy having many overlapping disadvantages. Black immigrants form part of this class structure, having jobs which tend to place them at the bottom. They, therefore, share class disadvantage with many white people. Although the culture of immigrants may separate them out from the white community, the children of immigrants will gradually become assimilated into white society, into the wider working class and some, by upward mobility, into the middle classes. To the extent that black people are not assimilated into white society, the obstacle will be the way that they preserve a separate cultural identity. For example, if they refuse to allow their children to attend British schools, do not learn English, or insist on forming ethnically based work-groups, their assimilation will be impeded. The sociological question here, then, is the way that black people are integrated into white society and the effect that their separate cultural identity has on the rate of integration. Clearly there are policy implications of this view. The suggestion seems to be that integration is desirable and possible if the obstacles posed by black culture are removed. The problem, in other words, is caused by the ethnic minorities themselves. This is the view implicit in much newspaper and television coverage.

White racism as an explanation of racial disadvantage

The other view essentially starts from the proposition that the problem is caused by whites, and the disadvantages suffered by black people are the result of white racism and the discriminatory practices that flow from it. It is white racism that keeps ethnic minorities at the bottom of the hierarchy and separated from white society as a whole. In no meaningful sense are black people part of the British working class. Such racism is very profound, going to the roots of British society. It is highly visible in racial attacks or the activities of the British National Party, but it also exists in subtler forms at all levels of society in Britain. It is even there in much sociology which, so proponents of this view would claim, is implicitly racist in treating ethnic minorities as the deviants from the British norm. Indeed part of the prevalent culture is the belief that black people have no culture of their own or that what there is will impede their attempts to 'get on' in white society. The sociological implications of this view, that racism produces ethnic disadvantage, are that attention should focus on the history and mode of operation of racism rather than the ways in which ethnic minorities do or do not adapt to British society. The political implication is that blacks should be self-assertive and proud of their black identity and not rely on well-meaning attempts to assimilate them into white society.

Explaining disadvantage in education

The differences between these two ways of approaching ethnic disadvantage show most clearly in the case of education. The former view would see education as one of the most important means by which black people become integrated into the mainstream of white British life. As black children go through the education system, they not only learn to speak English but also gain qualifications, which help them with jobs, and acquire British cultural values, which enable them to assimilate. It is, therefore, a question of black children *fitting into* the educational system, and the sociological problem might be to explain why they fail to integrate. Thus, failure could be due to reluctance to speak English, to the way that black children are suspended between two worlds, or to the manner in which black, particularly West Indian, families do not encourage educational success. From the second point of view, the central issue would be not 'What is it about black children that causes them to fail?' but 'What is wrong with an educational system that produces failure and does not recognize the cultural distinctiveness of black people, whether West Indian or Asian?' In this view, the fault lies not with black children or their families but with white teachers who label black children as educational failures. This debate over the education of black children is reminiscent of an earlier one over the failure of white working-class children in British schools (see section 8.4). This failure was attributed to defects of language or of home background rather than to an educational system that only valued one kind of language and actively discriminated against working-class culture. To take the analysis further, we need to look in more detail at racist beliefs and discriminatory practices.

Racism and discrimination

Plate 5.1 Nationalist sentiments expressed by marchers.
Source: Press Association

British culture can often be fiercely nationalistic. The British way of life may be thought best and the ways of foreigners inexplicable. Furthermore, the nationalism is anxious. We mean by this that alien or foreign ways of life not only are treated as odd, but also are very threatening. Nationalistic feelings of this kind are often kindled by war but they also emerge easily in other circumstances, as in dealings with the European Community for instance.

Nationalism is also closely related to racism (Gilroy, 1987). So, ideas of what it is to be British are used against people who are defined as foreign and can be identified as belonging to a particular racial or ethnic group. In fact, the British Isles contain representatives of a large number of different cultures; there is no such thing as a single *British* way of life.

Now, it is, of course, true that many countries exhibit fearful nationalistic reactions of this kind which appear as violent hostility to minority groups. An example from recent times is the treatment of Jews in Germany in the 1930s. However, British people probably have reasons for reacting to *black* immigrants in this way. Britain, after all, was an imperial nation. Until relatively recently, the British benefited greatly from lordship over large numbers of people in many different countries, most of whom were black. For the past 300 years, first as travellers to places deemed exotic, and later as imperial masters, the British have learnt to identify blackness of skin with inferiority, strangeness, and allegedly repellent religious and cultural practices. The decline of empire has only made these deep-seated attitudes more pronounced. The loss of the colonies and the consequent lessening of Britain's position in the world goes hand in hand with the independence of black nations. Immigrants from the New Commonwealth arrived at just the time that Britain lost an empire and with it her position in the world.

Surveys of attitudes tend to confirm this general racism. One study (Jowell and Airey, 1984), for example, found that rather more than one-third of the sample described themselves as racially prejudiced. In a recent survey, almost half of the white population sampled disagreed with the statement 'Immigration has enriched the quality of life in Britain' (*Independent on Sunday*, 7 July 1993). Racism of this kind is constantly experienced by black people at all levels of society even if it takes the more subtle form of simply being treated differently. Here is a black middle-class man speaking:

> Professional blacks are treated as rare specimens by most of their white colleagues. I am no exception. Generally speaking, racist humour is used to make simple conversation and reactions to these jokes generally leaves us, the black individuals, feeling guilty that we have challenged them. It is a continuous process that those blacks like myself, who have moved up (in a manner of speaking) in society, have very often to contend with the labels that not only do we carry 'chips on our shoulders', but we are over-sensitive to racial issues . . . Making it in Britain is simply a dream for many whites let alone blacks. My colour, my cultural norms and me – a person – will always be viewed through white coloured lenses with all their distortions. (Husband, 1982, p. 181)

Racism and discriminatory attitudes can be reflected in – perhaps fostered by – media treatments of issues like immigration or racial attacks. For example, a conception of the black community as a peculiarly crime-prone group took hold in the 1970s in press treatments of attacks on, and thefts from, innocent people in the street; these attacks subsequently became known as 'muggings'. It became widely accepted that the attackers were predominantly black and the victims white, although there was little evidence for this belief. This effectively defined black people in the street, especially young people, as potential criminals. Not surprisingly, in view of the public pressure relayed through the media, the police responded by adopting routine tactics of stopping and searching black people in the street, especially in areas where muggings were thought to be commonplace.

Actually, ethnic minorities are much more likely to be the *victims* of crime than white people, as table 5.4 shows. Furthermore, many of these crimes against black people are racist. A Home Office report of 1981 on racial attacks estimated the rates of racially motivated incidents per 100,000 of the population at 1.4 for whites, 51.2 for West Indians and Africans, and 69.7 for Asians in a three-month period. This refers to all incidents, not just those involving offences against the person. These

Table 5.4 Victims of one or more crimes[a]: by ethnic origin and type of offence, England and Wales 1987

| Offence | Ethnic origin of victim | | |
	White (%)	Afro-Caribbean (%)	Asian (%)
Household vandalism	5	4	8
Burglary	6	10	6
Vehicles (owners):			
Vandalism	9	9	14
All thefts[b]	18	26	20
Bicycle theft (owners)	4	8	2
Other household theft	6	6	8
Assault	3	7	4
Threats	2	4	5
Robbery/theft from person	1	3	3
Other personal thefts	4	6	3
Sample size (no.)	9874	733	996

[a] Based on incidents occurring over the full recall period
[b] Includes theft of and from vehicles and attempted theft

Source: Social Trends, 1992, p. 207; from *British Crime Survey*, Home Office. Crown copyright

figures, however, certainly underestimate the true rates of racially motivated attacks, for they are based on reports to the police and, as is well-known, large numbers of incidents are not reported. Indeed one study (Brown, 1984) calculated that a more accurate estimate would be at least ten times the Home Office figure. The case study that follows illustrates these points in more detail.

Racial harassment: a case study

Hesse et al.'s (1992) book, *Beneath the Surface: Racial Harassment*, is a study of racially motivated harassment in the London borough of Waltham Forest from 1981 to 1989. It is clear from their work that harassment of many different kinds is a fact of life for most black people throughout the country. Table 5.5 shows an increasing number of incidents in the Metropolitan Police area.

Table 5.5 Recorded racial incidents in the Metropolitan Police area, 1982–1989

Year	1982	1983	1984	1985	1986	1987	1988	1989
Total	1516	1277	1515	1945	1733	2179	2214	2697

Source: Hesse et al., 1992, p. 55; from Metropolitan Police Commissioner's reports

In the Waltham Forest area, racial harassment involved constant verbal abuse or physical assault in the street, the daubing of graffiti on homes and schools, missiles thrown through windows at night, and, most important of all, the fire-bombing of houses. Although there were several incidents of arson of this kind, the most notorious involved the Khan family in July 1981. Mrs Khan and her three children were burned to death after petrol was sprayed into the hall of their house and ignited while they slept. Mr Khan jumped from a window and was saved but died of a heart attack some time afterwards.

In reporting incidents of racial harassment, black people in Waltham Forest faced the problem that the police had difficulty in interpreting attacks as racially motivated and preferred other explanations or no explanation at all. Furthermore, complainants not infrequently found themselves suspected. The authors illustrate this point:

In April 1982 a Black youth, Emile Foulkes and his mother, Esme Baker were assaulted by police officers from Leyton division. Emile was sitting on a wall near his home on Priory Court estate, Walthamstow, when police officers from an Instant Response Unit arrived, accused him of taunting

white youths and called him a 'black nigger'. When Emile's mother tried to
intervene she was grabbed and both of them were forced into the police
van. They were charged with threatening behaviour and assaulting the
police, but were subsequently acquitted. In August 1982 the Sadiq family
eventually left their home in Lawrence Road, Walthamstow, after several
arson attempts. The police, however, did not accept these were racial
attacks. Three months later in November Mr Hussein's home in Walthamstow was burgled. He called the police, but when they arrived ninety
minutes later, they took no interest in the crime, preferring instead to
search his brief case and examine his family's passports. In the same
month, a Black youth, Phillip King (15) was on his way home when a white
youth racially abused him. He chased the white youth. Plain clothes
officers in the vicinity however, confronted Phillip in Hoe Street,
Walthamstow and assaulted him. He was taken to Chingford police
station, his parents were not informed, no doctor was called and he was
subsequently charged with burglary. He was later acquitted. (Hesse et al.,
1992, p. 20).

The local council, particularly the housing, education and social services
departments, was also drawn into the debate about racial harassment.
Like the police, the council was slow to recognize these as cases of *racial*
harassment and did not make a solution a very high priority.

It is possible to see in the responses of the police force and the local
council a kind of institutionalized racism, in which the problem is not
recognized as a racial one, responses are greatly delayed, and there is a
tendency to blame the victim.

Employment, housing and the police

Racism permeates practices which discriminate against ethnic minorities
and contribute to their unequal position in British society. There are
many spheres of life where ethnic groups are faced by discriminatory
practices, including recruitment to jobs, access to housing and contact
with the police. We deal with each of these in turn.

We have already seen in section 5.3 that the employment situation of
black people is not nearly as good as that of whites. Black people are
concentrated in declining and low-wage industries, work unsocial hours
for low wages, have poor promotion prospects and are at greater risk of
unemployment. A good deal of this position can be attributed to
discrimination on the part of employers.

One standard way of establishing the degree of discrimination in
employment is to arrange for equally qualified black and white workers
to apply for the same job. The method is for, say, a West Indian to

pretend to apply for an advertised job and then to be followed a little later by a white person applying for the same job. These experiments generally show that there is discrimination against black people in the sense that the black actor is not given the job, or is told that it is filled, while the similarly qualified white actor *is* given the job.

One study (Smith, 1977) found that the white actor was preferred ten times more often than the black one. Similar tests were devised for white-collar jobs by applying for advertised posts by letter in the name of fictitious black and white applicants, again with similar qualifications, but making clear what the applicants' ethnic origins were. In this case, the test of discrimination was whether the applicant was invited to interview. This is a weak test because an invitation to interview is only the first stage of selection. Discrimination is even more likely actually at interview. In the event, nearly one-third of black applicants failed to get to interview because of discrimination. Discrimination was highest for male junior clerical jobs, management trainees and accountants, and lowest for female clerical jobs.

There is, therefore, active discrimination against black workers in both manual and non-manual occupations, being probably more pronounced in the latter. The net effect will be to push ethnic minorities into jobs that are low paid and dirty, involve shift work, and are vulnerable in an economic recession. It is very difficult to say how much of this discrimination is the result of policy decisions by employers. Many large firms will have official anti-discrimination policies, although the personnel management at local level may practise discrimination, perhaps avoiding hiring black workers or laying them off first in time of recession. Further, firms' employment policies may be discriminatory even when they appear not to be. Thus some northern textile firms set out to hire black workers because white workers will not work shifts at low wage levels.

Similar tests, using black and white actors, have been utilized in studies of the private housing market. These experiments show that at least one-third of landlords discriminate against ethnic minorities on grounds of skin colour. However, as we show in section 7.3, the private renting of housing is no longer nearly as important as it once was; owner-occupancy and council renting are now the most significant forms of housing available. Evidence of discrimination in these sectors is less easy to obtain. However, it seems likely that there is little direct discrimination by building societies and banks in the provision of finance for owner-occupation. There may be some degree of indirect discrimination, in that building societies are sometimes reluctant to lend for houses in certain run-down areas of the city. These may be precisely the areas in which ethnic minorities may have to buy houses because they are cheap. In any event, as we have already seen, owner-occupancy among ethnic minorities, especially those of Asian origin, is higher even than that among whites and, on these grounds, discrimination in this sector is unlikely to be severe. However, a number of studies have shown that the allocation of council housing is likely to be discriminatory. Black people can be denied eligibility by rules which were originally drawn up for completely different purposes; property let to ethnic minorities tends to be of lower quality than that allocated to the white population; and black families, which tend to be larger, may not find council accommodation which is large enough for their needs (Brown, 1984).

A question that has, from time to time, preoccupied newspapers and television is the relationship between the police and black people, especially young black people. There is a good deal of evidence of such discrimination. Thus, a recent survey of the Metropolitan Police suggested that the culture of the police was pervaded by racially abusive talk. A lecturer at a police training college published essays written by officers in training which showed them to be openly racist. Of course, studies of police attitudes or talk, however racist, do not necessarily show the police to be discriminatory in practice. However, there is also evidence of active discrimination of this kind. A privileged account of racial prejudice in the police is provided by an interview with the first black policeman to join the Metropolitan Police, Sergeant Roberts, who is still a serving officer 19 years later:

> While still a recruit at the Hendon police training centre, he began receiving notes that said 'Nigger go home' – on the kind of paper that only his fellow recruits were using . . . 'If anyone tells you that there isn't prejudice they have got to be lying' . . . 'If you were brought up in Brixton or Hackney, and have been stopped regularly for no reason by the police, you are bound to view them with a bit of hatred' . . . But Roberts discovered that it did not matter much where he grew up when he was driving through Southwark late one night on his way home from work. He was pulled over by a policeman who verbally abused him after he had challenged the officer's authority.
>
> 'He said to me, "Look, you black bastard, I can do what I bloody well like" ', Roberts says. 'I thought, bloody hell, it does really happen.' (*The Guardian*, 13 May 1986, with permission)

In discussing the prevalence of racism and discriminatory practices in British society, we have often drawn a distinction between the racism of lower levels of an organization and the official anti-discrimination policies of the organization itself. We can, therefore, distinguish the employment policies of the head office of a large firm from the activities of local personnel managers, the stand taken by unions from the racism of union branches, or the declaration of senior police officers from the practices of the individual junior officer. It is, similarly, often argued that the racism manifested by the central institutions of British society is actually due to the activities of a few individuals – the rotten apples. However, too much is made of the distinction between official policies and the lower levels of an organization, and the rotten-apple argument largely misses the point. The central issue is that racism is so widespread that it is institutionalized. As we have shown in employment, housing allocation and the police force, discriminatory attitudes and practices are so pervasive as to be part of the everyday, routine culture of the organizations concerned. To some extent, also, the very operating procedures of an organization may be discriminatory in practice even though not overtly intended to be.

The underclass

At the beginning of this section, we distinguished two kinds of explanation of ethnic disadvantage; one concentrates on racism and discrimination and the other on the economic mechanisms of the British class structure. As we have said, these explanations are not inconsistent and both contain elements of the truth. The economic and social requirements of British society create disadvantaged positions in the class structure, and it is the racism of British society that ensures that black people continue to fill them. A number of European countries are dependent on migrants from poorer European or Third World nations to make up a labour shortage in certain industries. Britain is one of them. Effectively, racist policies not only fill these jobs with black workers but then discriminate against them in a number of ways including, in the case of certain countries, the possibility of expulsion. One of the consequences of this is an ambivalent attitude to black immigrants. On the one hand the white population needs them to work, while on the other their presence is resented.

To show the unity of the two types of explanation, one using the analysis of class and the other the concept of racism, we turn to a study which proposes the concept of the underclass. Rex and Tomlinson's (1979) study of Handsworth in Birmingham was undertaken with the intention of discovering something of the relationship of Asian and West Indian immigrants and their children to the class structure of contemporary British society. Their conclusion is that the black population is not absorbed into the white working class and is unlikely to become so within the foreseeable future. Quite the reverse: ethnic minorities form an underclass, a class beneath the white working class, disadvantaged by jobs, housing, and education. Blacks and whites work in different labour markets. West Indian and Asian populations are more concentrated in labouring jobs in hot and dirty industries and are poorly represented in professional, scientific and administrative jobs. Of course there is some overlap between the two; there are some black people in professional and management work, just as there are whites in unskilled labouring jobs, as we showed earlier in the chapter. Nonetheless the situation is almost one of a 'dual labour market'; one set of jobs is reserved for one category of the population (blacks) and another for the other (whites). In housing, as the authors say, 'The white authorities are torn between two discriminatory policies. One of these is the segregation of the black immigrant population in the least desirable housing, and here they are positively helped to find homes. The other is to disperse them so that their unwanted presence may be put more or less out of sight' (p. 280). Education provides a final measure of inequality. The inequality built into the education system simply reinforces the position of black children.

The black population thus effectively constitutes an underclass, placed in a structurally different location from the white working class. Their position is made the more disadvantaged because of the hostility directed at them by white society. Rex and Tomlinson (1979) are clear that the position of ethnic minorities and the conflicts that surround race and ethnicity in Britain can only be understood in the light of Britain's imperial past and the recent collapse of empire; 'a serious sociological analysis of race relations problems must rest upon a concept of the social structure of empire and of the class formations which occur within it' (p. 286). The point is that the fact of empire affects both white and black communities. Much of Britain's prosperity was founded on exploitation of colonial territories, an exploitation based on the assumption that black people were inferior. That perception of inferiority in turn means that some sort of caste barrier is erected between black and white. For black people, similarly, colonialism has left its imprint. West Indians, for example, less than 200 years ago were sold into slavery and separated from their African culture. They have, therefore, fewer cultural resources with which to resist the forces that place them in the underclass. For Rex and Tomlinson, the only way in which black people are likely to change their own situation is to develop forms of self-defence and self-help which are, in a sense, anti-colonialist, in that they are based on Third World models, 'looking to a change in the balance of power and resources between rich and poor nations as a means to their own liberation' (p. 293).

We have argued that one cannot counterpose the class and racism models of ethnic disadvantage. A proper explanation has to employ both, even if there is room for argument about the weight to be placed on each factor. The mechanisms of the class structure create positions – jobs – which are filled by ethnic minorities, originally entering the country as migrant workers. Racism, and its associated discriminatory practices, are part of the explanation of the way in which black workers fill the worst-paid jobs. Any correction of ethnic disadvantage, therefore, has to focus both on racism and on the mechanisms of class disadvantage.

Summary

1 Ethnic minorities are disadvantaged both by white racism and by their position in the class structure.
2 The racism of British society is manifested in a number of ways including employment and housing practices, treatment by the police, trade union activity and physical assault.

Related topics

For some account of the way that newspaper and television discuss immigration issues, see section 10.2. Material on ethnic youth culture can be found in section 10.4. More discussion of the interrelationship between gender, ethnicity and class is given in section 4.7. Issues of health care are dealt with in section 9.4.

Further reading

A survey of race relations in Britain is provided by Skellington and Morris (1992). A 'cultural' view of ethnicity in Britain appears in Gilroy (1987) and a good survey of theories of race and racism is to be found in Miles (1989).

6 Families and Households

6.1 Introduction

The family is a central institution of modern British society, at least in the sense that almost everybody has had experience of living in a family at some time in their lives. Most people also assume that their family experiences are normal and that all families resemble their own. This assumption is false, as this chapter will show. There is, in fact, an enormous diversity of family forms in modern Britain.

The fact that everybody has had experience of family life also means that families appear as natural and inevitable ways of organizing human social life. They seem built into human nature and it is often impossible to imagine a society without them. Thus, it seems natural to love one's children, to respect parents, and to share a house with blood relations. These feelings are misplaced. Even if some form of family is natural or inevitable, that does not imply that any *particular* form is. Furthermore, people often associate the feeling that families are part of human nature with the further assumption that families are good for you. If we appear to be unable to do without families, then they must be beneficial for us. We cannot assume that. For many people their family life is positively harmful and, probably for the majority of people, their experiences with families bring a good deal of pain as well as pleasure.

All of us, then, tend to make a number of assumptions about the family based on our common-sense, everyday experiences, and these assumptions find their way into sociological research. This is particularly true of what has been called the functionalist theory of the family. This theory proposes that the family performs certain functions for society. A sophisticated variant of this view is offered by Parsons (1956). He argues that societies change by a process of structural differentiation. This means that, in simple societies, each institution performs several functions. As the society develops, these functions become separated out into different institutions. Thus, the pre-industrial family in Britain will have not only cared for its members but also educated them and been the focus of their work activities. As the society becomes industrialized, the family loses its education and work functions to other institutions which develop to cater for them; schools educate and factories provide a workplace. In Parsons's view, the modern family deals with the socialization of children and gives stability to adult personalities.

In sum, as societies become industrialized, so the family loses its range of functions and comes to concentrate on only a few. The most significant implication of this idea of Parsons concerns family size and the connections the family has with the rest of society. Parsons's view is that the modern industrial family is relatively isolated from society, certainly more so than its pre-industrial predecessor. Concretely, modern families are nuclear, consisting only of parents and children, and conjugal, emphasizing the relationship between husband and wife rather than either of their relationships with their own families of origin. When a man and a woman marry they, typically, set up a new household independently of their relatives and their responsibilities are towards one another, not towards the wider family. Pre-industrial families tended, on the other hand, to be extended, that is to involve relatives more widely. Marriage partners will feel obligations to their wider kin which may even transcend those they feel towards each other. Parents and children will live near to other relatives or even share a house with them.

The idea that industrialization created the relatively isolated nuclear family has been very influential in the sociology of the family and has stimulated a wide range of studies, many of which have been critical. First, a number of historical studies have shown that the nuclear family was common before the industrial revolution, if only because people did not live long enough for older relatives to be living nearby or with their younger kin. Furthermore, it seems doubtful if the pre-industrial family had the resources to serve the functions of education, medical care or support of the elderly. Perhaps even more striking is the finding that the upheaval of the industrial revolution actually promoted the formation of extended family groups. In this period of rapid social change, involving families moving from the countryside to the town, the support given by the wider network of relatives was of great importance for individual families. For a short time at least, families became relatively less isolated. Last, a good deal of research effort has been put into the study of families in contemporary society. One of the conclusions of this research is that nuclear families are not isolated but are actually placed in a network of relationships with kin and others. We will be looking at this issue later in the chapter.

So far, we have argued that much sociological research into the family has been influenced by functionalist theory which is, in turn, apparently dependent on some common-sense, everyday beliefs about family life. We now look in more detail at these everyday images of families in Britain.

6.2 Of Cereal Packets and Nuclear Families

The family is the fundamental unit of contemporary British society. Judging by the critical reaction to certain passages in the third of my recent Reith Lectures, this dogma is very widely held to be a self-evident truth. But what is it supposed to mean? We use the word 'family' in so many different ways . . . but the standard stereotype seems to be provided by the jolly scenes on the back of a packet of breakfast cereal – a young married couple in their middle thirties with two or three pre-adolescent children. (Leach, 1986)

Most societies have a prevailing image of what desirable family life would be like; modern Britain is no exception. In our everyday lives, we are constantly subjected to such images. The process of socialization involves forming ideas of family life in children by a variety of devices including the stories that children read. In the old card game 'Happy Families', every family involved is made up of a father, a mother and two children. Mr Dose the doctor, for example, not only has a Mrs Dose but also a Master and a Miss Dose. In adult life, similar images are formed. The medium of advertising is one obvious example of this image-making, as illustrated in the advertisement involving a 'typical' family.

What does the image of the typical, normal or conventional family consist of? There are two parents aged between 20 and 45, legally married to each other, and not having been married to anyone else previously. Two children, born of these parents (and not others), live with them. The husband's work is a priority and, even if the wife has work, it is part-time or interrupted by child-rearing and does not form part of a career. The wife takes on the bulk of the household tasks even if the husband may help occasionally. The family itself is a self-contained, almost private, institution – a world to itself. Lastly, its members are happy.

This manner of thinking about the family is not just an image that can be presented in advertisements or children's stories. It is very widespread and can have real social consequences. For example, many of our social security, welfare, and taxation policies 'embody assumptions about the

Plate 6.1 Advertising the nuclear family. Adverts often are more effective in reinforcing people's image of dominant institutions than in selling particular products.
Source: The Advertising Archives

nature of families and thereby influence what families are expected to be' (Parker 1982).

There is evidence that everyday images of family life are changing and, in any case, it is doubtful if such images ever accurately described the majority of families in Britain. In this chapter, we will review a whole range of factors which affect family life and which produce a diversity of family forms often very different from the cereal-packet norm that we have described. For example, the changing age structure, with people living longer, is producing an increasingly large proportion of elderly households often containing only one person. Earlier marriages with fewer children mean that couples are together for a long time after their children have left home. Changing social values have increased the numbers of homosexual, unmarried, or single-person households. The fact that a large proportion of women now work has potential implications for the balance of power and dependency within families and the way that domestic tasks are performed. Families are not necessarily self-contained or happy, as the rising rate of divorce partly indicates.

The diversity of family forms produced by these changes is indicated in table 6.1. Since the 1960s, there has been a significant rise in the proportion of households containing people living alone, from 11 per cent to 26 per cent. It is notable that this rise is not attributable simply to the ageing of the population. It also reflects an increasing tendency for single people under pensionable age to set up households by themselves. There is also an increase in the proportion of households containing single parents with dependent children. The proportion of households consisting of a married couple with dependent children is gradually

Table 6.1 Households by type, Great Britain, 1961–1991

	1961 (%)	1971 (%)	1981 (%)	1990–1 (%)
One-person households:				
Under pensionable age	4	6	8	11
Over pensionable age	7	12	14	15
Two or more unrelated adults	5	4	5	3
One-family households:				
Married couple[a] with:				
No children	26	27	26	28
1–2 dependent children[b]	30	26	25	20
3 or more dependent children	8	9	6	4
Non-dependent children only	10	8	8	8
Lone parent[a] with				
Dependent children[b]	2	3	5	6
Non-dependent children only	4	4	4	4
Two or more families	3	1	1	1
Number of households (000s)	16,189	18,317	19,492	9604[c]

[a] Other individuals who were not family members may also have been included.
[b] These family types may also include non-dependent children.
[c] Sample size (number).

Source: *Social Trends*, 1992, p. 41; from Office of Population Censuses and Surveys data. Crown copyright

declining; in 30 years it has gone from 38 per cent of the population to 24 per cent. However, the category 'married couples with dependent children' is not the same as the cereal-packet image. Some of these married couples will include partners who have been divorced, working wives, unemployed men, and children from previous marriages. The cereal-packet image represents very much a minority phenomenon. In the rest of this chapter, we will look in more detail at the diversity of family life in Britain and at some of the factors that affect it.

Summary

1   A particular image of 'normal' family life prevails.
2   In many respects this image no longer reflects the actual structure of families in Britain, which are becoming more and more diverse.

6.3   The Family Life Cycle

In the previous section we argued that the cereal-packet image of family life in modern Britain was seriously misleading in that, at any one time, relatively few families conform to the image and many households never do. It not only neglects the diversity of family forms at any one time, but also obscures the changes that all families go through. There is a family 'life cycle', only part of which is represented on the back of cereal packets, which is illustrated in figure 6.1. Again, we must stress that this is the life cycle of a 'typical' family. Many families will not have life cycles of this type. Many people choose not to marry, for instance, or not to have children.

What appears as typical will change greatly over time. A whole variety of factors will affect the cycle, changing lengths of each stage or the relationship between stages. For example, people are living longer than they used to. The expectation of life at birth for women born between 1985 and 1987 was 77.8 years, while for those born 60 years earlier it was 59.3 years. For men, the comparable expectations were 72.1 and 55.4 years. One of the implications of this is that married couples will be together for longer. It may also mean that there may be a sharper 'problem' of old age as people live longer after their retirement from work.

The centrality of the family as a social institution means that its structure and the family life cycle are affected by an enormous range of other changes. Demographic processes, concerning not only the expectation of life but also changes in the birth rate, for instance; economic

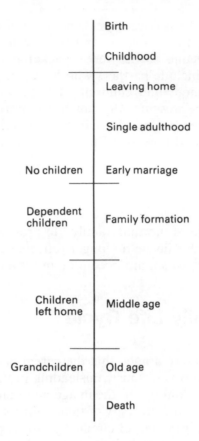

Figure 6.1 Life cycle of typical person.

change, including the increase in the numbers of married women working; and even government policy, all affect the family. To illustrate these points we are going to consider three of the life-cycle stages identified in figure 6.1 – marriage, family formation, and old age.

Marriage

Despite the fact that conceptions of marriage are changing, as box 6.1 indicates, the institution of marriage is still central to contemporary British society. The vast majority of people will be married at some time in their lives (over 90 per cent in 1988) and marriage still represents the usual manner in which adults of the opposite sex live together. It is still the norm for children to be brought up by parents who are married (or, at least, who *have* been) and hence marriage is the basis for the formation of households. Furthermore, attitudes to marriage still remain positive.

Box 6.1   Changing images of marriage

Three old images of marriage have become obsolete in the twentieth century. The first is that marriage confers on a woman a secure, settled income and a status and a role based on children and housekeeping around which most of the rest of her life revolves. The second is that marriage lasts for the rest of an increasingly long life. The third is that marriage is the setting for almost all child-bearing and sexual cohabitation. New ideas, new economic roles for women, new laws, and especially family planning have changed all that. Small family size has given decades of adult life back to women. Many have used it to go back to work. As a result they are more independent of men inside the home, and can compete with them on more even terms outside it. Now that contraception has taken the waiting out of wanting for sex, some of the other advantages of married life also seem less clear. Births outside marriage are more common than at any time in recent history. The welfare state has narrowed the gap between single and married states by assuming some of the financial role of the husband.

With or without child-bearing, cohabitation is a common preliminary to marriage, especially to remarriage, and is to some extent a replacement for it. Divorce is now threatening to end one marriage in three. It is a potent force behind the increase in the number of new households and homelessness. And although remarriage is retarded by cohabitation, younger divorced people have higher marriage rates than single people; indeed, many divorce in order to remarry. Remarriage, now one wedding in three, is creating new patterns of family life and relationships between step-siblings and step-parents, now made complicated, unlike those of the past, by the presence of former partners. So our conventional picture of marriage and family life needs to be redrawn.

Source: Coleman and Salt, 1992, p. 175

Nonetheless, despite an apparent continuity in the institution of marriage, there have been considerable variations in the form that it takes in the present century. For example, as figure 6.2 shows, for much of the century the average age at which men and women were first married has been falling, particularly quickly in the 1950s and 1960s. This

Figure 6.2 Mean age at first marriage, bachelors and spinsters, 1911–1989.
Source: Coleman and Salt, 1992, p. 181; from Registrar – General and OPCS statistics

was associated with an increase in the proportions ever marrying. In 1921, for example, only 83 per cent of women aged 45–9 had married at some time in their lives. In 1951 the proportion was almost the same, but by 1970 it had risen to 92 per cent.

However, more recently, in the 1970s and 1980s, the age of first marriage has been rising again. These average figures conceal considerable variations in different age groups. For example, in the period 1971 to 1988 there was a dramatic fall in teenage marriages, from 2.6 per cent of the age group in 1971 to 0.6 per cent in 1988. The rate of teenage marriages was therefore less than one-quarter of the 1971 rate and had returned to the levels of 1921. Less dramatically, the proportions ever married in their early twenties in 1987 are now only 60 per cent of what they were ten years earlier (Coleman and Salt, 1992). There are also differences between social classes. People from social class 1 are about three years older at marriage than class 5, a difference that has remained remarkably constant during much of the twentieth century. Also, a higher proportion of men in the higher classes ultimately get married (93

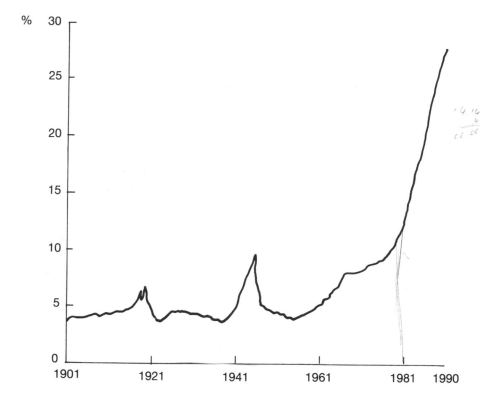

Figure 6.3   Live births outside marriage as a percentage of all births, United Kingdom, 1901–1990.
Source: *Social Trends*, 1992, p. 47. Crown copyright.

per cent compared with 74 per cent). For women the position is reversed. Women in class 5 are more likely to get married (98 per cent) than those in class 1 (86 per cent).

A falling rate of marriage within the last two decades could be due either to a simple postponement of marriage, or to a decision not to marry ever, or to some combination of the two. It is still too early to tell, but some light can be thrown on the question by considering two other social trends related to marriage: cohabitation and births outside marriage.

There is evidence that the practice of cohabitation (a man and woman who are not kin living together without being married) is on the increase. Only 5 per cent of women married in the 1950s reported having cohabited with their husbands before marriage. By the late 1980s, half of all couples marrying for the first time, and three-quarters of those marrying for the second time, had previously lived together. What is more, the length of time that couples have cohabited is increasing. Cohabitation is related to rising age of first marriage; much of it simply takes the form of a kind of trial marriage. However, it seems that cohabitation cannot account for all of the postponement of marriage; people are also deciding to marry later without living together first.

It seems likely that the increase in cohabitation is part of a new pattern of marriage, including the postponement of the formal ceremony, rather than any fundamental change in social values. Other trends, however, do seem to indicate a shift in the values concerning the relationship between sex, parenthood, and marriage. The evidence suggests that sex before marriage has become the norm (Joshi, 1989). During the 1950s, less than one-third of women had had pre-marital intercourse. In the late 1960s the proportion was increasing but was still less than 50 per cent, while at the end of the 1970s it had risen to 80 to 90 per cent. If marriage and sex are no longer linked, then neither are marriage and pregnancy. As figure 6.3 indicates, the number of babies born outside marriage as a proportion of all births remained roughly constant from 1901 to 1961 at about 5 per cent, rose to almost 10 per cent by 1981 and then, very rapidly indeed, to about 28 per cent in 1990. Interestingly, the great bulk of this increase in extra-marital births during the 1980s was registered by both parents at the same address. Couples, in other words, are increasingly choosing not to marry before having children, even if they may marry later.

Family size

Probably the most important factor in the twentieth century affecting family formation is that people are choosing to have fewer children, although nine out of ten first marriages do have children.

There are various different ways of measuring fertility. The most satisfactory involve consideration of the fertility experience of a cohort of women – measuring the average number of births per woman over the reproductive span for a group born or married in the same year. Clearly, for later cohorts a certain amount of projection will be needed since their reproductive span is not yet completely over.

Figure 6.4 shows the trend in fertility in the twentieth century for cohorts of mothers born in various years. The average number of babies born has fallen from 3.4 for mothers born in 1872, to a low of 1.8 for cohorts born in 1906 and reaching maximum child-bearing age in 1930. There was then a rise to about 2.4 for mothers born in 1934. The rate has fallen again for just over 2.0 for the 1955 cohort.

During the twentieth century, married couples have not only reduced the size of their families, but also completed their families much earlier in the marriage. In general, at the present time, married couples complete their families within ten years even though the intervals between the births of children are longer now than earlier in the century. However, it

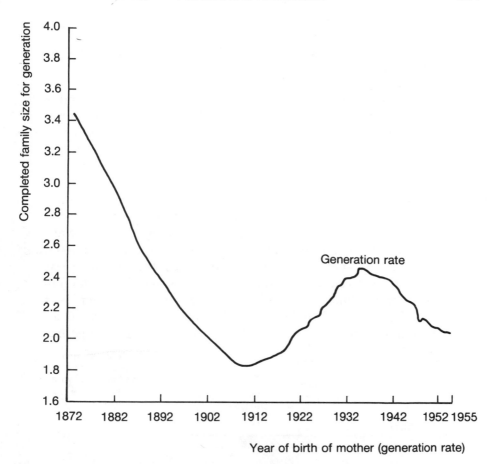

Figure 6.4   Trends in generation fertility rates, England and Wales.
Source: adapted from Coleman and Salt, 1992, p. 114; from OPCS statistics

should also be noted that the interval between marriage and the birth of the first child has lengthened since the early 1970s. Couples seem to be delaying the start of a family even though they then go on to complete it within the same time. Some of the historical trends are summarized and commented upon in box 6.2.

The net effect of these changes is, of course, that women are relatively free of child-rearing for a much longer period of their active lives and are therefore more likely to seek paid employment. One of the most significant changes in the labour market in the twentieth century is the rising proportion of the labour force made up of married women returning to work after completing their families. As one might expect, women's paid work is very closely related to the *ages* of their children. Table 6.2 shows how women enter the labour force as their children grow older. Greater participation by women in paid work and changes in

Box 6.2 Length of stages in the family cycle for successive marriage cohorts, 1860–1950.

The figure shows changes in the length of the family cycle and is based on the assumption that all the brides involved (in all of the periods) were aged 22.5 years at marriage. For a couple marrying in 1860 the wife was 40 before she had had her last child, while in 1930 the corresponding stage would have been reached before the wife was 30. This difference reflects changes in family size. The Victorian family would have had young children around until the parents were in their late middle age. If we take into account the fact that women are now marrying at a younger age as well, twentieth-century families will be completed even earlier than the chart indicates. One final point completes the picture. For families in the twentieth century, not only is middle age largely free of care for children, but old age is lengthened by an increased expectation of life. Married couples in the 1980s can expect to spend a much greater part of the later part of their lives together without their children.

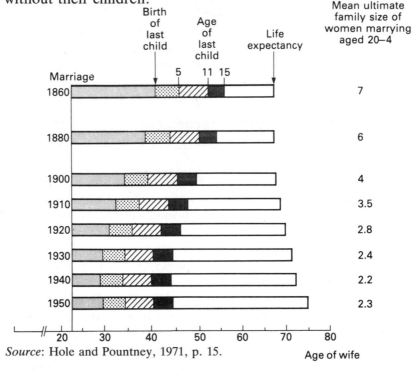

Source: Hole and Pountney, 1971, p. 15.

Table 6.2 Mothers in paid employment by age of children, 1978

Mother's employment	Age of children				
	0–2 (%)	3–4 (%)	5–9 (%)	10–15 (%)	All ages 0–15 (%)
None	79	69	52	36	51
Part-time	16	25	37	42	35
Full-time	5	6	11	22	14

Source: Rapoport et al., 1982, p. 101

family structure thus seem to be closely related, although what the mechanisms are that connect the two changes is less clear.

A final note of caution should be sounded. Much of the evidence we have presented in this section is based on averages which do, of course, conceal great variations between groups within the population. In particular, there are significant social class differences in family structure. We have already noted differences in the age of marriage. Even birth intervals are strongly class related. For example, the interval between marriage and the birth of the first child for professional and managerial families is twice as long as that for the families of unskilled workers.

Parenting: a case study

The capacity to be a parent is not something that people are born with. It has to be learned and, more than this, it has to be negotiated continuously in interaction, chiefly with spouses but also with the growing children. This is the subject of a study by Backett (1982).

Backett studied a group of middle-class parents and their everyday experiences of parenthood. All the couples operated against a background of assumptions. Most particularly, these assumptions concerned the images that parents had of their children. Backett distinguishes abstract images from the grounded images that are developed in the course of everyday parental experience. Parents have abstract images of the child's wants and needs and idealized pictures of the course of childhood. But actual parenthood also makes them develop images of a 'comparative' kind in which the parents make sense of the child by placing him or her in the context of overlapping sets of social situations.

Most of the couples in Backett's sample claimed that their parenting was a joint effort with some equality of parental behaviour. In fact motherhood was, perhaps not surprisingly, different from fatherhood. First, mothers are in the front line in looking after the children, having much greater direct involvement. Second, mothers developed a much greater knowledge of home and family which gave them a more important role in the negotiation process. Lastly, the main characteristics of motherhood were responsibility and constant availability. Fathers were, in practice, regarded merely as helpers.

Although motherhood had several entirely accepted and taken-for-granted characteristics, fatherhood was altogether more problematic. It was more difficult to define a satisfactory role for fathers because they did not have a direct involvement.

The elderly

Britain has an ageing population produced by two factors. First, as pointed out in the previous section, there has been a falling birth rate which has relatively reduced the numbers of young people. Second, the expectation of life has been rising in the twentieth century. For men born in 1901, the expectation of life at birth was 45. For those born in 1941 it had risen to 61 and for those born in 1981 it is 71. The rise in numbers of the elderly is dramatic, as is illustrated in figure 6.5, which shows a steep rise in this age group in the first half of the twentieth century and a levelling out at about 15 per cent from the 1980s well into the next century.

Figure 6.6 presents data for the age structure of the population in more

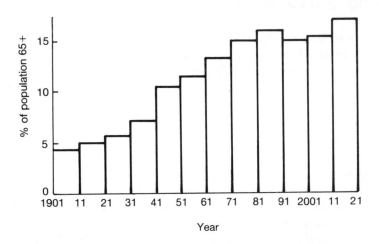

Figure 6.5 Percentage of the population over 65, 1901–2021.
Source: Family Policy Studies Centre, 1984, p. 1, reproduced with permission; from OPCS and Government Actuary data

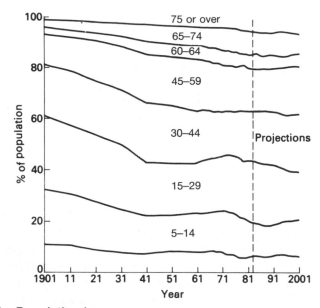

Figure 6.6 Population by age group.
Source: *Social Trends*, 1985, p. 21. Crown copyright.

detail. In 1983, the 65 and over age group represented 15 per cent of the population, compared with 5 per cent in 1901. The proportion will not increase greatly towards the end of the century because of low birth rates in the 1930s. However, *within* this age group there is a rising proportion of those over 75 and even more so of those over 85, who are projected to make up 12 per cent of the elderly in 2001, compared with less than 8 per cent in 1983.

At present, only some 5 per cent of the elderly population live in institutions. The remainder live in private households. Because they live longer, women over 65 are much less likely to be living with their spouse than men of a similar age. For example, 83 per cent of men aged between 65 and 70 live with their spouses, while the corresponding proportion for women is only 55 per cent. Again, as one would expect, the numbers of old people living alone increases with age. Although only 32 per cent of women between 65 and 70 live alone, the proportion rises to 60 per cent for those over 80. Only 25 per cent of women over 80 who have no surviving spouse live with other members of their family.

The fact that the proportion of elderly people in our society has increased rapidly, together with an even greater increase in those aged 75 or over, creates a number of social problems. This is partly a question of the so-called 'burden of dependency'. Old people take up a disproportionate share of health and social security resources and they are also a non-earning sector of the population, thus partly dependent on those at work. The most obvious factor here is health. Older people are prone to ill-health, which often confines them to their homes. Naturally enough, they make demands on the National Health Service (NHS). For example, those aged 65 and over accounted for one-third of all NHS prescriptions and about 40 per cent of acute hospital bed occupation. The health problems of the elderly are compounded by their declining income. It has been estimated that three-quarters of the elderly, compared with one-fifth of the non-elderly, live on or below the poverty line. Part of this, clearly, is due to the loss of earned income. In fact, the proportion of men over 60 who are still working has declined from over half in 1931 to some 15 per cent in 1979. The result is that a large proportion of the elderly are solely dependent on the state pension.

There are, however, a number of writers who believe that the burden of dependency argument may be exaggerated (see Thane, 1989). First, as figure 6.5 shows, the proportion of elderly people in the population will remain fairly constant for the next two decades. Second, the anticipated rise in the numbers of elderly is to some extent offset by a projected fall in the numbers of very young children who are equally dependent. Third, older people may be becoming healthier than in the past, and hence less dependent, particularly as interest in fitness and diet spreads through the population. Fourth, and last, although income drops with retirement, there are some indications that the situation may improve in coming years. For example, an increasing proportion of the population are in occupational pension schemes, and are becoming house owners, both of which effectively confer assets on retirement.

We have already noted that a substantial proportion of old people live alone; one-third of those over 65 do so and the proportion increases with age. Many of these people will feel lonely and socially isolated, especially if they are very old and, hence, relatively inactive. It is, perhaps, difficult to find a universally acceptable index of loneliness. One study (Hunt, 1978), however, found that one-quarter of the 65–75 age group 'would like a relative to visit more often'. This response was given by 36 per cent of those over 85. One cannot, however, jump to the conclusion that, because many old people live alone, they have little support from their families. A government survey found that, of those elderly people who were having some difficulty in coping with the tasks of everyday life, about half were helped by members of their family, who provided help with shopping, cleaning, the preparation of meals and laundry. In practice, family care of this kind is usually provided by women.

Although social isolation is undoubtedly a problem for many old people, many more do have an active family life. Furthermore, the lines of support do not always run in one direction. Elderly people are a source of child-care for the offspring of their own children. Men, for example, can be expected to live an average of 14 years after the birth of their first grandchild, and women 23 years. The elderly are, therefore, still involved in extended family relationships, a point taken up again in section 6.6.

Summary

1   The great majority of people will marry at some time in their lives. The age of first marriage rose in the 1970s and 1980s.
2   The pattern of marriage is changing. A greater proportion of people are cohabiting before marriage, and more than one-quarter of all babies are born outside marriage.
3   Families are much smaller than they were at the beginning of the century, a trend related to the greater participation by women in paid work.
4   The proportion of elderly in the population is rising. There is a debate as to what extent this will create a serious 'burden of dependency'.

6.4   The Division of Labour within Families

Part of the image of the family in our society depends on assumptions

Plate 6.2   Housework: an element of the gendered division of labour.
Source: Network

about the relationships of men and women *inside* the home. The cereal-packet image assumes that the man is the breadwinner and the woman is responsible for domestic tasks including child-care, cleaning and cooking. Men make the large-scale decisions affecting the family, while women only control those areas that are strictly 'domestic'. There is, in other words, a *division of labour* within the home.

This image may well have borne some relation to reality between 1850 and 1950 following the process of industrialization which took men out of the home to work in factories. But is it still the case?

The symmetrical family?

Young and Willmott (1973) argue that, in modern Britain, this is *not* the case; a new family form – the symmetrical family – which does not require a domestic division of labour, is slowly emerging, in which the roles of men and women are less differentiated. A whole series of factors have combined to produce the change from families with a high division of labour to those in which domestic tasks are more equally shared. These include the rise in the proportion of married women in paid work, the trend towards smaller families (see section 6.2), the 'privatization' of the family (see section 6.6), and changing social attitudes about the proper role of men and women. It has also been argued that changes in patterns of employment may alter the balance of domestic work. For example, if the wife is employed full-time, one might expect that the husband would carry out more of the domestic tasks.

For Young and Willmott, the symmetrical family has three main features. First, the married couple and their children are very much centred on the home, especially when the children are young. Second, the extended family counts for relatively less and the immediate nuclear family for relatively more. The third and 'most vital' characteristic is that the roles of men and women have become less segregated and more balanced. Young and Willmott's detailed empirical study found that in poorer and older families there was still a considerable domestic division of labour but that, nonetheless, the great majority of married people in their sample formed the newer symmetrical family (p. 94).

A study by Gershuny (1992) offers support for this proposition. Gershuny's objective is to measure *changes* in the domestic division of labour by re-analysing a set of studies, done at different times, all of which look at the use of *time* in the household. He investigates the 'dual-burden' hypothesis which states that, even as wives enter the labour market and take on full-time jobs, they continue to carry the burden of domestic work; 'women remain housewives even when they become breadwinners' (p. 73). Gershuny concludes that this hypothesis is only

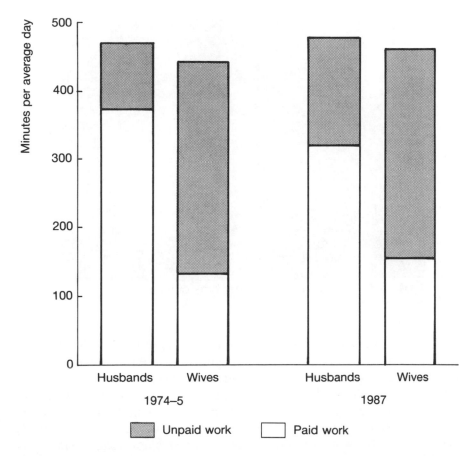

Figure 6.7 Changes in couples' work patterns between 1974–5 and 1987.
Source: Gershuny, 1992, p. 78

partially correct. Figure 6.7 shows the amount of work, paid and unpaid (domestic), carried out by husbands and wives. The critical point for Gershuny is that over the period 1974–5 to 1987 the proportion of domestic work carried out by husbands has risen in a context of increased paid work by wives and increased total work by both spouses.

It could be argued that the growth in men's domestic work is actually not in the core tasks of cleaning and cooking but rather in odd jobs, repairs, and decorating. Again, Gershuny argues that his evidence does not bear this out. Over the period from 1974–5 to 1987, husbands of full-time employed wives doubled the amount of time they spent in cooking and cleaning. Gershuny concludes that, although women still carry the principal burden of domestic work, there is a lagged adaptation to their increasing paid work as men take on more household tasks.

In Gershuny's account, as in many others, a crucial feature in the domestic division of labour is the way that the husband and wife are

Plate 6.3   Do it yourself: another type of work.
Source: Cefn Newsham

involved in paid work. A study by R. Pahl (1984) of the Isle of Sheppey also contributed to this debate (see section 2.8). Pahl constructed an index of the division of domestic labour composed not only of 'female' tasks such as cooking, clothes washing or child-care but also of 'male' jobs such as house repairs, car maintenance or beer-making. One of his most striking findings was that the more hours a woman was employed, the more domestic work was shared. However, it is not quite as simple as that. Although households in which both partners are employed do manifest a more equal division of domestic labour, women still do the bulk of the domestic work; more equal certainly does not mean absolutely equal. Furthermore, the balance of the domestic division of labour does not seem to be related to the work done by *men*. It does not matter if the man is full-time employed or unemployed; the balance of domestic work is still determined by the woman's employment status.

Morris (1990) carried out a study of the relationship between male unemployment and domestic work. She argues that women do not take over from their unemployed men as the main breadwinners, and unemployed men do not take over the housewife role. Traditional gender roles are relatively unaffected. For good measure she adds, as against Gershuny, that 'married women's employment does not prompt a significant rise in domestic involvement on the part of husbands' (p. 189). It is worth adding that, in another study of the relationship between men's unemployment and the domestic division of labour, Wheelock (1990) comes to the opposite conclusion: 'Amongst the thirty couples interviewed there was a marked shift towards a less traditional division of household work, with men undertaking more domestic work and child-care when they became unemployed' (p. 3).

Domestic work

There is therefore still considerable debate about the trends in the division of labour as women enter the labour market. What all the commentators agree upon, however, is that women, on average, whatever their employment status, take on the majority of household tasks.

In our society, a woman's identity is still organized around the home, domestic work and child-rearing. These features of her life provide her identity, whereas a man's identity is given at least partly by his work. This has the further consequence that a woman's life is largely confined to *private* spaces – the home – while men dominate the public spaces outside the home. The result is that the majority of women are engaged at least for part of their lives in *full-time* domestic work, especially while their children are young. Such a position is very unusual for men.

What are the characteristics of the full-time housewife role? The most important point to stress here is that, as Oakley (1974) points out, housework is *work* and should be compared with paid jobs outside the home. A good deal of work is involved: the average working week in Oakley's sample was 77 hours, with a range from 40 to 105. It is demanding and monotonous work. Oakley compared housewives' feelings about the various domestic tasks with workers' feeling about their jobs as revealed in Goldthorpe et al.'s (1968a) study. Oakley found that they experience more monotony, fragmentation and speed in their work than do workers in a factory. The gap is narrowed considerably when the comparison is with assembly-line workers, a comparison which reveals a great deal about the nature of housework.

However, domestic work is also *not* like paid work, especially factory employment, in other respects. Two of the most obvious differences are the degree of social isolation and the possibilities of autonomy. These cut in different directions. Many of Oakley's respondents complained about the loneliness of housework. On the other hand, housework offers the housewife considerable autonomy. She has a fair amount of control over her work; 'being one's own boss' was a phrase used by over half the sample. In this respect housework contrasts favourably with many kinds of paid work.

A good deal of women's identity as wives and mothers is organized around the provision of food. A study by Charles and Kerr (1988) illustrates this point. In almost all the households they studied, women were responsible for the provision of food for their families: they

Table 6.3 The importance, frequency and pattern of decision-making in different areas of family life

Decision area	Perceived importance	Frequency	Decision-maker (majority pattern)
Moving	Very important	Infrequent	Husband
Finance	Very important	Infrequent	Husband
Car	Important	Infrequent	Husband
House	Very important	Infrequent	Husband and wife
Children's education	Very important	Infrequent	Husband and wife
Holidays	Important	Infrequent	Husband and wife
Weekends	Not important	Frequent	Husband and wife
Other leisure activities	Not important	Frequent	Husband and wife
Furniture	Not important	Infrequent	Husband and wife
Interior decorations	Not important	Infrequent	Wife
Food and other domestic spending	Not important	Frequent	Wife
Children's clothes	Not important	Frequent	Wife

Source: Edgell, 1980, p. 58, reproduced with permission

shopped for it, cooked it, and cleared it away. Food was a way in which the women showed their love and affection for their families. Furthermore, it had to be *proper* food – meat and two veg preferably – and properly cooked. Any failure to give proper food, for reasons of low income perhaps, was felt as a serious personal deficiency. In preparing food, the women in Charles and Kerr's sample tended to neglect their own tastes and inclinations. It was the men who effectively determined what was eaten and, furthermore, they tended to get the best food. 'However, although women felt *responsible* for their family's health and felt that the food eaten was important to the maintenance of health, the *control* over the food eaten by the family often lay with the men. If men disliked wholemeal bread, for instance, it was not bought even if women felt it was important for nutritional and health reasons' (p. 230).

Another area in which traditional gender roles are still fairly well established is decision-making and the mangement of money. This is an area investigated by Edgell (1980). At first sight, table 6.3 seems to indicate that decision-making is roughly balanced. Some decisions are shared equally and the remainder are split between husband and wife. However, this does not take account of the *importance* of decisions, and amongst the research families there was widespread agreement about which decisions were important and which were not. Generally, the more important though less frequent decisions tend to be husband dominated, whereas the less important though more frequent decisions are made by the wife. There is some evidence from studies of families in which both wife and husband have careers that even in these situations the husband dominates decision-making, partly because his job is granted more importance.

The decisions associated with the management of money are obviously crucial in most families. J. Pahl (1989) found that in the majority of the households she studied, men were dominant in financial decision-making. She also found that this was related to earning power. Husbands were more likely to dominate decisions where the wife did not have a job. Conversely, the minority of wives who were dominant were usually in paid employment. For very poor couples, where neither partner was in employment, husbands were often dominant in decision-making, although the wife might actually directly control the money.

We can conclude that there is still a substantial and unequal division of labour between men and women in British families; the symmetrical family is not here yet. It should be noted that this is not an outright refutation of Young and Willmott's position as outlined at the beginning of this section, for they were arguing only that there is a *tendency* towards a less gender segregated division of labour, a tendency demonstrated by Gershuny. However, they also suggest that the symmetrical family form 'trickles down' from the middle classes to the working class. As we have said, there is little evidence for this, as professional families manifest considerable segregation of domestic tasks. Indeed, there is little differentiation by class at all in domestic divisions of labour. R. Pahl (1984) found that only women's employment and stage in the life cycle affected the extent to which domestic tasks were shared. When children are young and the wife is not employed, an asymmetrical division of labour is especially likely. As she grows older, and perhaps re-enters the labour market, domestic tasks are shared more equitably.

Summary

1 It has been argued by some that families are becoming more symmetrical, with domestic work being more balanced between men and women. Recent evidence indicates that, although there may be such a tendency, it is still not very pronounced.
2 Even when women take paid employment, they still do the bulk of the domestic work and men take the important decisions.
3 The degree of sharing of domestic work depends on the amount of paid work taken on by the wife and the stage reached in the family life cycle. Social class seems to make little difference.

Related topics

Further discussion on the domestic division of labour can be found in section 4.3, especially as it affects the inequality between men and women. The background to R. Pahl's (1984) study can be found in the case study in section 2.8.

6.5   Divorce, Single People and Alternative Households

In this section we look at another, and perhaps more obvious, way in which the idealized image of family life is misleading, namely family dissolution through divorce. Although, as we shall see, a large proportion of divorced people remarry, there are at any one time a good number of single-person households or single-parent households created by divorce. In addition, there are people who choose to live not in 'conventional families' but by themselves or with others in what we might call 'alternative households'. This section will also briefly consider these alternatives to the family.

Divorce and marriage breakdown

The rate of divorce

As newspapers and television are always telling us, divorce is more common than it was a generation ago. The *numbers* of divorces granted have risen dramatically. The number granted in Britain jumped from 27,000 in 1961 to 191,000 in 1985; this should be compared with under 3000 in 1921 and a mere 700 in 1911. These figures do indicate that divorce is more popular. However, the numbers of divorces could be misleading in that not only has the general population risen in numbers, but marriage itself is more popular. A larger number of people are getting married, so a larger number of people will get divorced even if the divorce rate stays the same. The method of allowing for this is to show how many divorces there are per 1000 of the married population. This gives a more accurate idea of the *rate* of divorce. Even expressed in this way, however, the rise in the divorce rate has been striking. In 1961, just over 2 persons divorced per 1000 married people in England and Wales, while in 1981 it was almost 12. In 1931, it was under 0.5. A yet more revealing way to consider the change in the popularity of divorce is to look at the proportion of each marriage cohort that divorces after a particular period of time. For example, one could compare the divorce rate of those married in 1971 with those married in 1981, both after a period of, say, ten years. Detailed studies of this kind do show that divorce is more frequent for later marriage cohorts. Recent estimates are that one-third of current marriages are likely to end in divorce.

Causes of a rising divorce rate

Why has the divorce rate increased? The most obvious initial explanation is that changes in legislation have made divorce easier. As marriage is a legal contract, divorce requires legal approval; if this approval becomes easier to obtain, then there will be more divorces. The assumption behind this explanation is that there used to be many couples who wanted a divorce but could not have one because their case was not covered by any legislation. All that legislation does is to *permit* these marriages to end. It is true that there have been spurts in the divorce rate as legislation becomes more and more permissive. However, changes in the law cannot really be the only *cause* of increases in the rate of divorce. The law, rather, reflects social changes, in that it permits marriages that have in practice effectively ended to be legally dissolved. We have, therefore, to consider why marriages effectively end, as well as why couples will go as far as the courts to legally separate, and what social factors underlie the responses to changes in legislation.

One such factor is *the changing role of women in society*. The position of women has changed in a number of ways, such that a wife does not have to put up with an unsatisfactory marriage in the way that her mother might well have done. Women are not expected to be socially subservient to their husband as was often the case even 50 years ago. The financial constraints on wives are also not so serious, as an increasing proportion of married women are in full-time work. One cannot press this argument too far. There are still inequalities within marriage, as are documented both in this chapter and in chapter 4. Women's work does not generally pay as well as that of men, which clearly gives wives less potential for financial independence than their husbands. Nevertheless, women have more independence than they had and that will influence their decision to leave a marriage. Very relevant to the changing social role of women is the finding that women are, in general, less satisfied by their marriages than men. In their study of a sample of divorcees, Thornes and Collard (1979) found that wives tended to believe that there were marital problems much earlier on in the marriage. By the third wedding anniversary, 69 per cent of wives had concluded that there were problems, compared with 46 per cent of husbands. Women are more likely to find marriages unsatisfactory and they account for 72 per cent of the *petitions* for divorce.

In sum, any relaxation of marital constraints on women is likely to lead to a rise in the divorce rate, whether these constraints are ones of tradition, custom, or finance. Indeed, a further factor in the rise in divorce rate is, precisely, *the relaxation of traditional attitudes to divorce*. Divorce is no longer so shameful and is popularly seen as a permissible solution to marital difficulties. The more common it is, the more people will know of others who have been divorced, and they are correspondingly less likely to condemn this action. As Allan (1985) points out, contemporary attitudes to divorce are illustrated by the prevailing opinions as to the effect of divorce on children. While in former years parents were encouraged to stay together for the sake of their children, more recently emphasis has been put on the damage done to children by parents who *do* stay married but are in constant conflict. In these circumstances, divorce is often popularly thought to be the preferable alternative.

It is not only a question of social attitudes to divorce. The frequency with which marriages dissolve will also be related to the way married couples – and the family – are integrated socially. As Allan (1985) argues, within the last century, *the family has become increasingly defined as a private institution* in which people find a haven in a heartless world. The wider family, and society at large, do not have the right to interfere in family life. But, since the family unit is then not supported by its integration into a wider social network, family problems cannot be so easily shared. As a result modern marriages are under considerable stress. On the one hand, a great deal is expected of them, particularly in the capacity to provide emotional and physical support for husband and wife. On the other hand, the marriage does not itself have support from wider society: 'There is less pressure for a couple to stay together because their break-up has little impact outside the domestic sphere and causes fewer ripples than it would in a society where kinship is more central to the wider social organization' (Allan, 1985, p. 104).

Who divorces?

These three factors – the position of women, moral attitudes to divorce and the involvement of the family in wider society – are important in explaining the rise in overall divorce rates. For a fuller understanding of the factors affecting divorce, we have to consider not only changes in rates over time but also differences between social groups. For example, the age at marriage is strongly associated with the likelihood of divorce. Generally speaking, the older people are when they marry, the less chance they have of divorcing. Couples who marry in their teens are almost twice as likely to divorce as those who marry between the ages of 20 and 24. The divorce rate also varies by the amount of time the marriage has lasted. For example, in 1979, nearly half of all divorces occurred within the first ten years. This may, however, underestimate the volume of marital breakdown in the earlier years of marriage, for several studies have shown that couples may split up, on average, five years before they actually divorce. One investigation (Thornes and Collard, 1979) found that of all marital separations (rather than legal divorces), 60 per cent occurred before the tenth year of marriage. The divorce rate also rises with early child-bearing, pre-marital pregnancy, and childlessness. Young spouses, young parents, and young marriages are most at risk.

Table 6.4   Divorce rates by social class of husband, 1979, England and Wales

Social class of husband	Divorces per thousand husbands (aged 16 to 59)
Professional	7
Intermediate	12
Skilled non-manual	16
Skilled manual	14
Semi-skilled manual	15
Unskilled manual	30
Unemployed	34

Based on a sample of 2164 divorces in 1979.

Source: Haskey, 1984, reproduced with permission

Social class is also closely related to the incidence of divorce. As can be seen from table 6.4 the divorce rate for unskilled husbands is more than four times that for professionals. For the unemployed the rate is almost five times that for the professionals. These social class differences are even more marked for younger husbands, where the unskilled manual rate is 5.5 times as great as the incidence in the professional category.

Divorce, remarriage and single parents

So far, we have shown that divorce is increasingly popular and more common in some social groups than in others. This does not mean, however, that marriage as an institution is less popular, for substantial numbers of divorced people remarry. Present estimates are that some two-thirds of divorcees will eventually remarry. The chances of remarriage reduce with age: 70 per cent of women aged 25–34 remarry, 50 per cent within six years; 50 per cent of women aged 35 or older at divorce remarry (Ermisch, 1989). The chances of remarriage for women are also, not surprisingly, increased by their level of education and their work experience. More surprisingly, children are not, generally, an impediment to remarriage. Further, the fact that there has been such a steep rise in the number of divorces, combined with a fairly high rate of remarriage, means that a rising proportion of all marriages are of people marrying for at least the second time. In 1961, for example, 14 per cent of all marriages involved remarriage, but by 1982 the proportion had risen to 34 per cent.

Remarriages are also more prone to divorce and are twice as likely to fail as first marriages. In 1961 about 7 per cent of men divorcing were previously married. By 1986 this had risen to 17 per cent.

Reconstituted families

The frequency of remarriage after divorce must mean that so-called *reconstituted* families have become an increasingly significant social phenomenon. These are families, often with children, in which one or both of the parents have been married previously. The involvement of children is of particular importance. As we have seen, the younger the marriage and the younger the partners, the higher the rate of divorce. These marriages, of course, are also more likely to be childless since the couples will not have had time to have children. Nevertheless, the number of children who experience the divorce of their parents is considerable. Currently, the total number of children involved in divorce is about 160,000 per year in England and Wales. These children tend to be young. In 1982, two-thirds of the children in separated families were aged less than 11 and one-quarter were under 5. Not a great deal is known about the numbers of these children who end up in remarriages, but Burgoyne and Clarke (1982) estimate that 7 per cent of all children under 17 live with a step-parent.

Reconstituted families are clearly different from the cereal-packet norm. Most particularly, such families have, or are likely to have, close ties outside the family, through children, with the previous partners. Children will be pulled in two directions between their natural parents and may well have tense relationships with their step-parents. These features make the life of reconstituted families very complex; they cannot be seen as enclosed entities. This position is complicated by the fact that society has no established customs surrounding either the step-parent role or, perhaps even more acutely, the role of the divorced parent no longer living with his or her children but visiting them from time to time.

Reconstituted families are, therefore, of a different type. As Burgoyne and Clarke (1982, p. 290) say:

> It is clear that the warp and woof of everyday life in step-families differs from that of unbroken families not merely because of external constraints which frustrate the efforts of those who may seek, as some do, to recast their family lives in the mould of the nuclear family, but because family norms themselves may also be markedly altered, tempered to fit the limits of the new situation and fabricated anew from the post-marital residue of family beliefs and sentiments.

Reconstituted families will become increasingly common but do not yet have a clear identity in British social life.

Single-parent families

In considering the impact of divorce on family life, popular attention to the mass media focuses more on the situation of single-parent families than on reconstituted ones. As one might expect from the rise in the divorce rate, the proportion of single-parent families has been increasing. Divorce is, of course, not the only cause. Death of a spouse will also contribute to the numbers of one-parent families, as will the rising numbers of unmarried mothers. As can be seen from table 6.5, the proportion of all families with dependent children which are headed by a single parent increased from 8 per cent in 1972 to 15 per cent in 1989–90. The bulk of this increase comes from families headed by a lone *woman* and, most often, a divorced woman. Although single-parent families have, on average, fewer children than married couples, clearly a considerable number of children will be living in a one-parent family at any one time. The National Council for One-Parent Families estimated that, in 1982, there were about 1 million one-parent families containing 1.6 million children. Many more children will, at some time in their lives, experience living in such a situation.

The social and economic situation of one-parent families is very disadvantageous. This is partly a consequence of the fact that the great majority of single parents are women and partly because such families are disproportionately working class. The Finer Report (1974) on one-parent families found that only 1 child in 18 in social classes I and II lived in a single-parent family, while in class V the proportion was almost 1 in 7. The combination of these two factors – social class and gender – means that many one-parent families live in poverty. As we have seen in chapter 4, women's work is generally less well-paid than men's. In addition, married women may well have had their careers interrupted by child-rearing. Single-parent women earn relatively little money, out of which they will have to pay the expenses of child-minding. Hence many lone women parents do not work. Indeed, it is estimated that one-half of them have to depend on state benefits. Single-parent men are generally much better-off financially. Not only do they have better-paid jobs, but society expects that they should work and, for this reason, they may receive more help with looking after children.

The social situation of single parents is often one of stress. They are poor and have to cope with young and demanding children on their own. They are also often isolated. The network of friends people built up when married depends on their being part of a couple. Divorced and separated women often complain of the speed with which they lose contact with their married friends. New friendships tend to be formed with people who are also on their own, and this tends to reinforce the feeling of having lost the desirable married status. There is little special social provision for single-parent families and, indeed, government policy is much more favourable to the widowed parent than to the divorced parent, even if their situations are very similar. There is, in sum, no socially recognized place for single-parent families in Britain.

Indeed, social attitudes to divorce in general, and single parenthood in particular, are still disapproving despite the changes noted earlier in this chapter. As the Finer Report (1974, p. 6) said:

> To fail in marriage nowadays is to go bankrupt in a business of life in which everyone engages and in which the large majority at least appear to be successful. So it is likely that a family in which a mother or father has to bring up children single-handed will think of itself, and be treated by others, as a little cluster of deviates from the marital norm. (quoted in Popay) et al., 1983, p. 18)

Single mothers can often be the target of unfavourable press attention in which single parenthood is associated with 'welfare scrounging'.

In these circumstances of deprivation, stress and social disapproval, it is not surprising that the first priority of single parents is to get married and re-enter the 'secure' state. As we noted before, some two-thirds of divorcees can be expected to remarry. This has been used as evidence of the continuing popularity of marriage. More likely, however, divorcees and single parents do not remarry out of dedication to the institution. It is just that they have no other choice.

Table 6.5 shows one way in which the cereal-packet norm is becoming dented; single-parent families are becoming more common. It would be difficult, nonetheless, to argue that single parents are rebelling against the conventional family form in principle. However, some people do strive after alternative ways of organizing 'family' life.

Table 6.5 Dependent children[a] by type of family, Great Britain, 1972–1990

	1972 (%)	1975 (%)	1981 (%)	1989–90 (%)
Married couple with:				
1 dependent child	16	17	18	18
2 or more dependent children	76	74	70	67
Lone mother with:				
1 dependent child	2	3	3	4
2 or more dependent children	5	6	7	9
Lone father with:				
1 dependent child	–	–	1	1
2 or more dependent children	1	1	1	1
All dependent children (= 100%) (sample size)	9474	9293	8216	5827

[a] Persons under 16, or aged 16–18 and in full-time education, in the family unit and living in the household.
Source: *Social Trends*, 1992, p. 42: from *General Household Survey* data. Crown copyright

Alternative household forms

There have always been objections to the family structure of Western industrial societies. Families have been felt to be rigid, narrow, and highly constraining institutions which repress the individual and stop the development of his or her individuality. In contemporary Britain, a whole series of alternatives are offered. The way in which the conventional family depends on heterosexual relationships, for example, has inspired the open proclamation of the desirability of homosexual households. Some theorists, on the other hand, feel that the orthodox household confines heterosexual sexuality too much and that more 'open marriage' is required in which the partners are free to experiment sexually. Feminists often argue that marriage merely reproduces and reinforces the inequality between the sexes prevalent in wider society. Many of them, therefore, set up households composed solely of women – heterosexual or homosexual. A not uncommon solution to the feeling that the conventional family stunts the individuality of its members is for people to elect to live on their own. A contrary solution, to the same perceived problem, is to live in large households or communes.

Communal living received publicity partly as the result of the experiments with alternative lifestyles widely advocated by members of the middle classes in the 1960s. As McCulloch (1982, p. 324) writes:

The struggle systematically to open up the domestic and intimate relations of the normal kin-based nuclear household is premised on the belief that what is chiefly at fault with the conventional family household is that it is excessively closed and rigid. Furthermore, this isolation (of the nuclear family) is a threat to the very integrity and expression of the self.

It is very difficult to estimate the numbers of people living in communes as this is not an area recorded by government statistical surveys. A number of publications in the area suggest, however, that there are probably no more than 100 communes in Britain at any one time. Clearly, communes differ considerably from one another. They can be differentiated along a continuum, one end of which consists of a community of individuals, sharing everything, while the other end is characterized by a number of family groups which share a house, and perhaps other things as well, but whose degree of involvement as individuals in the collective is limited. The first type could be called communal and the second collective (Lee, 1979). Many proponents of commune life would probably not regard the collective solution as a real commune but, in reality, most British communes are collections of couples living together. Communal arrangements tend to be very short-lived and are, ironically, often beset by the same problems that plague the cereal-packet family. For example, communes have difficulty in coping with adolescent children. Indeed, children only very rarely stay in communal arrangements as they grow up.

Summary

1 When parents get divorced they, and their children, enter into new kinds of family arrangements which are becoming increasingly frequent in Britain.

2 Reconstituted families, formed by the remarriage of divorcees with children, are fairly common and may generate difficult and non-institutionalized relationships between (a) step-parents and resident children, and (b) the previous spouse and children.

3 Around 15 per cent of households with children contain only one parent. Single parents are more frequently women and they suffer from considerable social and economic stress.

4 Some people seek to avoid nuclear-family living and make alternative household arrangements.

6.6   Families and Others

Social attitudes and images of the relationship between the nuclear
family and the wider kinship grouping of uncles, aunts, grandparents,
cousins and in-laws are various and sometimes confusing. On the one
hand, 'family life', by which is meant the life of the nuclear family, is
much praised in government statements. On the other hand, the nuclear
family is sometimes said to be selfish and inward-looking, failing in its
wider duty, especially towards the elderly.

Extended families

One early sociological argument, now rejected, ran as follows. Before
the industrial revolution in Europe, the predominant family form was
extended; people had regular and extensive contact with their wider kin.
Industrialization, however, changed that. With the requirement for
greater geographical mobility, people lost contact with their extended
family and families shrunk to the minimal, nuclear size. Emotional and
personal needs are met within this smaller unit. So, the nuclear family
'fits' into industrial society while the extended family is more characteristic of pre-industrial society.

A number of studies, both sociological and historical, carried out in the
late 1950s and 1960s provided the basis for a critique of this position.
First, it was argued by historians (for example Laslett, 1965) that the
family in pre-industrial England was not extended. A low expectation of
life, high infant mortality, relatively low fertility, and late marriage
combined to produce small households which were not multi-
generational. Grandparents were rare, compared with the situation
today, and the population as a whole was relatively youthful. On
Laslett's estimate, only 1 household in 20 contained more than two
generations. Family structure, in other words, conformed closely to the
nuclear form.

A second line of argument maintained that the industrial revolution
did not produce a nuclear family form through the disruption of rural
communities. Rather, the reverse was true. Anderson (1971), for
example, suggests that there was actually an increase in extended
households in urban areas in this period. Parents lived with their
working, married children and provided child-care while receiving
support in their old age.

Third, a number of sociological studies suggested that the isolated
nuclear family is not the predominant family form in contemporary

Britain. Nuclear families are deeply involved in many ways with their wider kinship groupings. The classical study is that by Young and Willmott (1957). They found that families in the heart of London, in Bethnal Green, lived near their kin and had frequent contact with them. Of particular strength was the tie between mother and daughter. Bethnal Green was, at that time at least, an area of residential stability; a lot of the people interviewed by Young and Willmott had lived there all their lives. However, not all regions of the city have this kind of stability. Young and Willmott also investigated a new housing estate to which some East-Enders had moved. They found that the people living on the estate did not have such intimate contact with their extended kin. The nuclear families were instead relatively enclosed and inward-looking. Successive studies of family and community life in different areas of the country found, as one might expect, different relationships between nuclear and extended family. Most of them suggest, however, that most members of families in Britain have *some* contact with their wider kin.

We cannot, therefore, draw too sharp a distinction between nuclear and extended family types. However, the image of modern families as isolated and inward-looking does not only extend to relationships with kin. It is also often supposed that there is less contact these days with neighbours and friends; in Young and Willmott's (1957) telling phrase, modern life on council estates is not face-to-face but window-to-window. Family members become more interested in the home and more inclined to follow their leisure pursuits in the home rather than in the wider community. Modern families are, in other words, 'privatized' in a whole range of respects.

Privatization of the family

The argument that certain kinds of family are becoming privatized has been put by Goldthorpe et al. (1969) in their study of affluent workers in Luton in the early 1960s. They define privatization as a process 'manifested in a pattern of social life which is centred on, and indeed largely restricted to, the home and the conjugal family' (p. 97). The primary reason for the adoption of this lifestyle is the attitude to the economic rewards of work. The Luton workers valued the high incomes that they could earn; they were involved in a 'quest for affluence'. This meant that they had often moved to their present jobs away from their previous connections of kin and friends. Furthermore, the jobs themselves left little time and energy for sociability outside the home because they involved both overtime and shift-work. The Luton families studied had relatively little free time left after work given the multifarious activities required to keep a house, garden and car even minimally organized. What time there was free was devoted to leisure pursuits such as watching television. For example, of all the spare-time activities reported by affluent workers and their wives in the few days before being interviewed, 62 per cent were in or about the home itself. Three-quarters of all activities were ones carried out by the husband or wife alone or together with other members of the household. Almost a quarter of the couples had engaged in *no* activity together with people from outside the household.

Although the main reason for this privatization of family life is the instrumental orientation to work, it is not the only one. Apart from the constraints of work life, many of the affluent workers studied actually appeared to prefer their home-centred lives. For example, even those who did live near their kin did not see them especially often. In interviews, respondents would emphasize the central place that their immediate family had in their lives. These 'familistic' values were demonstrated in other ways. For example, there was relatively little leisure-time involvement by husbands with their mates, but considerable participation in what traditionally has been regarded as women's work, especially child-rearing.

Devine (1989) went back to Luton 20 years later and interviewed families similar to those studied by Goldthorpe et al. She concluded that men and women do lead family-centred lives. Work, both paid and unpaid, fills a substantial proportion of any day and people do not have the time to pursue active leisure outside the home. However, Devine concludes that, *contra* the affluent worker study, people did not positively want to live a confined existence excluding others; they enjoyed the company of family, neighbours, workmates, and friends.

Privatization can, of course, mean many things, not all of which necessarily run together. It can, for example, refer to an increased interest in the home; or to a conviction that families should be the main focus of interest; or to a greater sharing of domestic and child-rearing tasks between husband and wife; or to a generalized tendency to treat the home as the focus of leisure and consumption activity. There is some evidence, besides that offered by Goldthorpe et al., that many British families do exhibit these features. One obvious indicator is the extent of home ownership. In 1988, 64 per cent of households owned their own homes, the proportion in 1971 being only 49 per cent. Homes have become a centre for creative endeavour via a greater interest in furnishing and DIY. The proportion of households owning domestic equipment of various kinds has also increased.

In 1989–90, 99 per cent of all households owned a television set, 60 per cent a video cassette recorder, and 19 per cent a home computer, which all may contribute to keeping householders at home for their leisure pursuits. There may well be a greater stress on nuclear family commitments and we reviewed some of the evidence on sharing tasks in section 6.4. However, three points of qualification should be made:

1 Comparative data are difficult to obtain. This should make one wary of talking about *changes* in family life as the evidence about the privatization of families even in the recent past is not available. There is a tendency to see the past as a golden age, a time of mutual aid and neighbourliness. In fact, what evidence there is suggests that privatization has a long history, back into the nineteenth century. There is nothing new about wanting to spend time at home with one's family (Devine, 1989; Saunders, 1990).

2 An interest in home and family does not *necessarily* imply that modern British families are inward-looking. Home-centredness can still go with a measure of sociability with family and friends. It can also go with collective participation. In his study of home owners, Saunders (1990) illustrates this point. As table 6.6 shows, he argues that home owners are more likely to join organizations for the collective good than are council tenants, even after controlling for class.

Table 6.6 Organizational activity by housing tenure

| | Housing tenure | | | |
| | Home owners | | Council tenants | |
Organizational activity: belongs to	*(no.)*	*(%)*	*(no.)*	*(%)*
At least one local organization	209	56	45	34
Residents' organization (all)	39	11	5	4
Residents' organization (where available)	39	50	5	10
Trade union or other work-based association	117	33	23	18

Source: Saunders, 1990, p. 287

3 It is also important to note that the degree of privatization will vary with stage in the life cycle. For example, couples are naturally more home-centred when they have young children. The experience of privatization will also vary between social classes and even more significantly between men and women. We are now going to explore some of these variations, first in the context of contacts with family and friends, and second in leisure pursuits.

Gender, class and the privatized family

So far, we have argued that people in modern Britain give great importance to their immediate family, that is their husband or wife and children living with them in the same house. Despite the image of the introverted family, however, wider kinship connections continue to be important, especially the relationship between parents and older children who no longer live with them. A range of studies have demonstrated the vitality of the parent–child tie, sustained not only by visiting but also by flow of assistance of various kinds in both directions.

Kin as companions

Obligations felt towards kin, and the patterns of visiting and assistance that flow from them, are characteristic of all social classes. In a review of the available evidence, Finch (1989) suggests that assistance of various kinds, accompanied by a sense of obligation, is still of considerable

Table 6.7 Average number of relatives and friends seen in previous week

	Professional and managerial	Clerical	Skilled	Semi-skilled and unskilled	All
Married men working full-time					
Local friends[a]	2.8	1.8	2.8	3.8	2.9
Work friends[b]	3.0	0.3	0.8	1.1	1.4
Other friends	5.2	2.1	2.7	2.2	3.3
Total friends	11.0	4.2	6.3	7.1	7.6
Total relatives	2.6	3.2	3.9	3.7	3.4
Total friends and relatives	13.6	7.4	10.2	10.8	11.0
Sample (no.)	168	69	238	107	582
Married women aged 64 or under					
Local friends[a]	2.6	1.6	2.5	2.1	2.4
Work friends	0.3	0.3	0.3	0.1	0.3
Other friends	3.4	1.1	1.3	1.3	1.9
Total friends	6.3	3.0	4.1	3.5	4.6
Total relatives	2.9	3.8	3.8	3.3	3.5
Total friends and relatives	9.2	6.8	7.9	6.8	8.2
Sample (no.)	156	70	258	104	388

[a] Living within ten minutes' walk.
[b] If work friends lived within ten minutes' walk they were counted in the category of local friends. There were in fact very few such people in any class.

Source: Young and Willmott, 1973, p. 229

importance. Assistance can take a very large number of forms from outright gifts of money, the exchange of services such as baby-sitting, the care of the elderly, even to help in finding a job. There are patterns in who gives what to whom; for example it is observed that 'older generations give support to younger more than the other way round; that people of Asian descent living in Britain are more likely than white people to give help to their in-laws; that giving financial assistance is more common in better-off families than in poorer ones; that most women are involved more extensively than most men in exchanges of assistance between relatives' (p. 239). Further, assistance is more likely to pass between certain kin than others. Finch speaks of inner and outer circles in this respect. Assistance is more probable in the inner circle, comprising close relatives like parents or children, than in the outer which might include aunts or cousins.

There are some class differences, however. Young and Willmott (1973) found that those lower down the occupational scale were more family-centred than the professional and managerial classes. Table 6.7 shows the average number of friends and relatives seen in the week before the interview. The professional class saw fewer relatives but greatly more friends. Some care should be exercised, however, in interpreting these contact rates. A lower contact rate may say nothing about the quality or duration of the contact, but may be due to the physical separation from kin caused by the relatively greater mobility of the middle class. It should also be noted that Young and Willmott's data do not record the number of contacts with each relative, only the number of relatives contacted. This may well understate the extent of contact by the working class who may well see their relatives living nearby several times in one week.

Class and friendship

The working class has more frequent contact with kin than does the professional and managerial class. The reverse is true for patterns of friendship, as table 6.7 shows. Professional men, for example, see half as many friends again as unskilled workers. Clerical workers are least sociable in this respect.

A number of studies indicate differences between middle – and working-class people in their friendships. An investigation by Allan (1979), for instance, found that not only did the middle class have more friends, but they were also drawn from a greater variety of social settings and covered a wider geographical area. Allan argues that these class differences are due to very different ways of organizing friendship: 'Briefly, whereas the working-class respondents tended to restrict interaction with their friends (and with their other sociable companions) to particular social contexts, the middle-class respondents developed their friendships by explicitly removing them from the constraints imposed by specific settings' (p. 49). Middle-class friendships start in particular settings, such as work or a sports club. However, people only truly become friends when the interaction is continued outside that setting. So, for example, someone met initially at work may be brought home to a meal, or arrangements may be made to go out to the theatre, perhaps. The point is the transfer of friendship outside the original setting. The meaning of middle-class friendship is not given by the original place of meeting but by the individuality of the people concerned who can now interact in *any* situation. The same is not true of working-class people, whose social contacts tend to be confined within particular settings. In this case, people met at work or in the pub will not be asked home or invited to go dancing. Sociability is confined to the original setting. Allan's working-class respondents, therefore, experienced their social contacts in terms of their setting: there were workmates, people in the pub, or neighbours, but *not* friends whose relationship transcended the original setting. Part of the consequence of this was that working-class respondents were often unwilling to use the term 'friend', being unsure if they were using it appropriately. They preferred instead to use the designation related to the setting – neighbour, for example. They also tended to see their social contacts as unplanned. For example, although they might see the same people every night in the pub, that was not a planned attempt to see *those* people but an unplanned consequence of being there. In sum, Allan suggests that middle-class sociability involves a 'flowering out' of friendship while, for the working class, there is a confinement of social contact to *particular* settings.

Gender and companionship

So far, we have dealt with class differences in patterns of contact with family and friends. Gender differences are equally as important, as table 6.7 shows. In all social classes, women have less social contact with friends than men do, the disparity being most marked in the case of professionals and managers. In all classes, however, women see more relatives than men, although the differences, interestingly, are not very great. *Comparatively* speaking, therefore, women tend to be involved with relatives, men with friends. In a sense women do not inhabit the public world where they might meet and develop friendships; men are less privatized than women. This social position is the outcome of women's confinement to the home by domestic and child-care responsibilities. This is made worse for working-class women by the convention that working-class families do not, in general, see their friends in their homes. In these circumstances, women turn to their close relatives. Working-class women, particularly, may see few relatives but they see them more often, a fact not revealed by the data in table 6.7. A young working-class woman's mother, and perhaps sister, constitute her trade union – an essential circle of support and advice.

The relative isolation of women from the public world of their husbands has an impact not just on their access to relatives and friends but also on their use of leisure facilities outside the home (see also section 10.3). Part of the reason for this is, again, the way in which women are effectively confined to the home at least for some part of their lives. Also relevant, however, is the manner in which leisure in our society is defined in opposition to work. Because work is still considered a male role, leisure, similarly, is thought to be a male preserve. For women, social customs do not permit such a clear distinction between work and leisure. The result is that men and women inhabit different leisure worlds; in access to leisure activities, class is very much less important a variable than gender.

Summary

1   Families in modern Britain are in certain respects more privatized than they used to be, with a greater interest in the home and the immediate family of wife or husband and children. However, this is not inconsistent with engagement in activities outside the home.
2   Wider kinship relations are still of great importance, particularly the ties between adult children and their parents, which are actively sustained by visiting and the exchange of support and help.
3   The relationships between members of the nuclear family and other people are differentiated by class and gender. This is true for relations with wider kin, but also for friendships. Middle-class and working-class people, and men and women, have quite different patterns of friendship.

Related topics

Section 3.4 deals with some other aspects of privatization. The question of leisure and the family is discussed in section 10.3.

Further reading

An excellent introductory book on the family is Allan (1985). Coleman and Salt (1992) and Joshi (1989) are good accounts of demographic aspects. Allan and Crow (1989) provide a good recent collection of essays on aspects of the family and household.

7 Towns, Cities and the Countryside

7.1 Introduction

In this chapter we will consider how social inequalities occur not just between social groups in Britain but also between different areas. For example, particular regions, towns, and areas of the countryside are wealthier and more desirable to live in than others. We will analyse what some of these differences are and what causes such variations. We will be interested not only in economic differences but also why the perceived quality of life may differ. It will be seen that these perceptions of place will vary for different social groupings. In some situations such groupings will have the power to change the character of the town, the city or the rural area, which may then come to reflect their interests.

We will begin by briefly describing the history of places in Britain. Up to the sixteenth century, most people lived in the countryside. The English countryside looked very different from today, with a lot more woodland and hedgerows, smaller fields, no agricultural machinery, very many more people working in the fields, and with occasional fairs as the hub of social life and leisure. In Scotland, by contrast, sheep farming was dominant in rural areas.

Towns were relatively small and of little importance. By the end of the fifteenth century the largest town, London, accounted for just 2 per cent of the population. The second largest town, York, had a population of only 11,000. Such towns were mainly market centres for local areas. They contained few public buildings except perhaps a corn exchange and some churches, and they were dominated by the countryside where wealth and power were concentrated.

This situation changed after 1500 or so. By the end of the sixteenth century London's population had grown to 200,000, out of a total population of 3.5 million. King James I declared that 'soon London will be all England'. By 1700, its population was over half a million, while by the beginning of the nineteenth century contemporaries described it as 'the metropolis of England, at once the Seat of Government, and the Greatest Emporium in the known World'. There had been an extraordinary growth of world trade controlled by merchants and financiers who lived and worked in London. Others parts of England and later Scotland were dominated by London's monopoly of trade and commerce. These same London merchants also came to control the rapidly expanding agricultural production, particularly of wool which was the main material for the production of clothing. London, though, was not just an economic and political centre. From the time of the Tudors and Stuarts onwards (the sixteenth and seventeenth centuries), London was the centre of culture and commerce in England, with elegant houses and multiple entertainments, including the theatres where Shakespeare's plays were first staged. By 1724 the novelist Daniel Defoe wrote of the 'general dependence of the whole country upon the city of London . . . for the consumption of its produce'.

However, it was outside and well away from London that the most significant change for the whole development of modern societies took place: the industrial revolution from the late eighteenth century onwards. This involved not just new kinds of work but whole new sorts of town and city, organized around mining and manufacturing industry. Many of these were very small at first, located close to where coal was mined. They were generally settlements that either were entirely new or had been small towns relatively free of control by medieval guilds. They grew at a tremendous rate in the nineteenth century. In 1801 only one-fifth of the population of England and Wales lived in towns and cities; by 1901 it was four-fifths. In such industrial towns and cities there were dreadful levels of ill-health, overcrowding and social deprivation. Engels (1969) provided a well-known description (box 7.1).

London too was characterized by exceptional levels of social inequality. It grew extremely rapidly, having a population of 6 million by the end of the nineteenth century. It was easily the largest city in the world. However, its wealth was based not on industry but rather on finance, government, the professions, transport and trade. Very many workers were employed on a casual basis, some working in small sweatshops. The effect was that the world's largest and richest city contained the world's most extensive slums at the time.

For the first half of the twentieth century there was an accelerating physical expansion of large towns, which had an increasing influence over the surrounding countryside. Four million houses were built between the

Box 7.1   Life in a nineteenth-century northern city

Every great city has one or more slums, where the working-class
is crowded together. True, poverty often dwells in hidden alleys
close to the palaces of the rich; but, in general, a separate
territory has been assigned to it, where, removed from the sight
of the happier classes, it may struggle along as it can. The slums
are pretty equally arranged in all the great towns of England, the
worst houses in the worst quarters of the towns; usually one- or
two-storied cottages in long rows, perhaps with cellars used as
dwellings, almost always irregularly built. These houses of three
or four rooms and a kitchen form, throughout England, some
parts of London excepted, the general dwellings of the working-
class. The streets are generally unpaved, rough, dirty, filled with
vegetable and animal refuse, without sewers or gutters, but
supplied with foul stagnant pools instead. Moreover, ventilation
is impeded by the bad, confused method of building of the whole
quarter, and since many human beings here live crowded into a
small space, the atmosphere that prevails in these working-men's
quarters may readily be imagined. Further, the streets serve as
drying grounds in fine weather; lines are stretched across from
house to house, and hung with wet clothing.

Source: Engels, 1969, p. 60

two world wars. By 1939, one-third of all British houses were less than 20
years old. However, the rate of increase was uneven across the country.
There was a slowdown in the rate of population growth in the industrial
areas in the north of England, and in the industrial parts of Scotland and
Wales. Towns and cities in the southern half of Britain increased in
population, while those in the north, which suffered very high rates of
unemployment, lost population. Over 1 million people migrated to the
south east from the rest of Britain between 1921 and 1951.

The area around London grew rapidly in population, and it also
acquired higher proportions of people (mainly men) with professional
and managerial jobs. The suburbs rapidly expanded, although most work
remained concentrated in town and city centres. There was an increased
separation between the place of work and the home. This led to the
development of widespread commuting, to the need for improved public
transport, and to increased isolation for the housewife unable to escape
from her suburban home.

Plate 7.1 An inter-war suburb.
Source: Cefn Newsham

Up to the Second World War, different industries in Britain were concentrated in different regions. Cotton textiles and textile machinery were produced in the north-west of England, coal-mining and steel-making in south Wales and central Scotland, woollens and worsteds in Yorkshire, arable farming in East Anglia, vehicle-making in the Midlands and so on. The type of industry concentrated in a particular region affected the development of towns and cities in that region. The politics of a town often reflected the social relations found in the dominant industry.

In the period since the Second World War this regional concentration of mining and manufacturing industries became less marked. Particular industries are no longer overwhelmingly concentrated in particular regions. There is a decline in regions as distinct units of economic and political organization. One consequence is that there are instead marked variations *within* regions, for example, in the north-west between economically depressed Liverpool and relatively prosperous Cheshire.

More generally over the past two decades, the largest urban centres have tended to suffer economically and to lose population, while smaller towns and rural areas have tended to prosper and to attract industry, services and population. In the 1960s and 1970s there was extensive growth in manufacturing employment in the more rural parts of Britain: East Anglia, central Wales, the south-west and so on. This was in turn related to the general process of *counter-urbanization* from the early 1960s onwards. By this is meant the tendency for large cities to lose population and for smaller settlements to acquire population. For example, between 1961 and 1981 the population of the six largest conurbations in Britain fell by 2 million. This decentralization of the British population has been caused by a number of processes:

1   The policy of 'urban containment' as found, for example, in the 1947 Town and Country Planning Act. Because it was thought that towns and cities had grown too fast in the 1930s, it was decided to restrict the growth of cities and to disperse populations into new towns, such as Stevenage and Milton Keynes.

2   The population living in council housing in Britain increased from 18 per cent in 1950 to 32 per cent in 1980. This growth in public housing was particularly marked in Scotland. Such rehousing programmes in the 1950s and 1960s had the effect of moving large numbers of people out of slum properties in inner-city areas, causing a general depopulation of the central areas of large cities.

3   Successive Conservative governments have encouraged owner-occupation (normally through a long-term loan or mortgage). Since few properties had been available for purchase in central areas this also encouraged suburbanization and movement to smaller towns.

4   Car ownership became widespread. Over two-thirds of households now own a car and this has meant that men especially are able to commute considerable distances, often from rural homes.

5   Strong attitudes have developed in Britain which emphasized the desirability of living in suburbs or in semi-rural areas. People have come to believe that such environments provide a cleaner and quieter context, especially for bringing up young children. There is a long-standing antipathy to cities and urban living within British culture.

There was some reversal of this decentralization of population in the 1980s. Two processes were involved. First, a number of inner-city areas were increasingly thought to contain attractive Georgian and Victorian terraced houses that could be 'gentrified' and made suitable for middle-class occupation, especially by those who were relatively young and childless. Islington in north London is the most striking example of where the middle class has moved in and almost taken over what had been extensive working-class areas. Second, the collapse of employment in British ports and docks made a large amount of land and property available. Some of this has resulted in relatively high-cost housing in various docklands, in London, Liverpool, Cardiff and so on. This rediscovery of some inner-city areas by middle-class professionals has

Plate 7.2 Images of town and country.
Source: Maggie Murray/ Format and Janet and Colin Bord

resulted from a changing valuation placed on cities as opposed to suburban and rural areas (Savage and Warde, 1993, chapter 3).

Different social groups in Britain tend to have strong feelings about what it is like to live in rural or in urban areas. These feelings tend to change over time. Sociologists have themselves tried to develop concepts that capture the nature of both 'rural' and 'urban' life. These will be discussed in the following sections.

7.2   The Countryside

There has been a long-standing debate about whether urban life is different from rural life. In the inter-war period it was argued that there were indeed some marked differences, that there is an urban way of life distinct from a rural way. Urban life is thought to be characterized by large size, a high density of population, a marked heterogeneity of social

---

Box 7.2   Patterns of rural life: ideal-typical features

1   It is organized as a *community* with people frequently meeting together and being connected to each other in lots of different ways. People keep meeting each other as they take on different roles in relationship to each other.
2   People have close-knit social networks; in other words, one's friends know each other as well as oneself.
3   Most inhabitants work on the *land* or in related industries. There is a high proportion of jobs that overlap and there is a relatively simple division of labour. Most workers are relatively unspecialized farm labourers.
4   Most people possess an *ascribed* status fixed by their family origin. It is difficult to change the status through achievement. People are strongly constrained to behave in ways appropriate to their status. This status spreads from one situation to another, irrespective of the different activities in which people engage.
5   Economic class divisions are only one basis of social *conflict*. Various strategies are developed to handle potential conflicts that cannot be overcome because people keep meeting each other. Generally, social inequalities are presumed to be justified, often in terms of tradition.

groups, anonymity, distance and formality between people, and the need for people's actions to be formally regulated by law rather than through community and custom. The rural way of life is set out in box 7.2.

One problem in assessing whether or not these ideal types are correct is that they overlap with more general images that people themselves hold. Indeed throughout British history people have fought for or against powerful images of rural or urban life. Much literature and art stems from or relates to attempts to represent what the countryside or town is really like. Moreover, these conceptions invariably imply a contrast with its opposite. To form an image of the town is to imagine the countryside, and vice versa.

These are however deceptive contrasts. The 'countryside' has in fact changed enormously. It is not something that is unchanging. Moreover, it is a concept that is generally blind to the very people who have done most work in such areas, namely agricultural labourers. In fact the 'olde English village' (Scotland, Wales and Ireland have always been different anyway) is a relatively recent creation, resulting from the eighteenth-century enclosure movement and improvements in agriculture. It had only just come into importance when the 'unnatural' towns and cities of the industrial revolution conjured up some of the most dramatic and 'romanticized' of contrasts.

Continuity is a particularly powerful part of the rural image. Since the countryside involves working the land, and that land has in a sense been here forever, so there appears to be something eternal about rural life, its rhythms and patterns, that city life can never reproduce. Indeed because of its aesthetic claims – the lie of the land, the thatched cottages, the grazing livestock – there is a belief that life in the countryside must be

Plate 7.3 'What on earth do you mean – no stuffed olives?'
Source: Reproduced by kind permission of Methuen London © Norman Thelwell

meaningful, worthwhile and able to support a socially desirable pattern of life for everyone, whether rich or poor.

Life in the East Anglian countryside: a case study

The model of life in rural society represented in box 7.2 was more or less true of parts of rural England in the early years of this century. It would never have fitted highland Scotland which had already experienced huge rates of depopulation as those living on the land were cleared off it during the past two or three centuries.

In the last decade or two there has been a marked increase of research into the changing patterns of rural life, particularly in England. Newby was responsible for initiating this interest in a series of studies of rural life in East Anglia (1985). He argues that it is the ownership of land that shapes the rural social structure. The crucial consideration determining someone's place in rural society is whether a person owns land, rents land, or works for someone who owns or rents land.

In the nineteenth century most land in Britain was owned by a few landowners. This was leased by tenant farmers, who in turn employed large numbers of agricultural labourers. In the twentieth century, three main changes have occurred in this ownership pattern in England and Wales. First, there has been a large increase in owner-occupation so that about three-quarters of farmland is now farmed by its owners. Second, there has been a substantial increase in the ownership of agricultural land by large institutions, especially those based in the City of London. Third, there has been an irreversible rationalization of agriculture. It is much less a way of life and more a business. There has been the striking development of agri-business, where large food-processing companies control and direct the output and product quality of individual farmers. Agriculture has been 'industrialized' and this is seen most clearly in the development of 'factory farming'.

One aspect of these developments has been the increased mechanization of farm work. This has dramatically reduced the workforce employed on farms. About one-half of all farms employ only one worker and many employ none, labour being provided by family members. As a consequence of this reduction in the size of the labour force, the one or two workers still employed have to be skilled at most tasks undertaken. In other words, mechanization has increased the variety of skills needed; it has reduced, not heightened, the division of labour (see section 2.5 on the contrasting patterns in other industries).

The reduction in the numbers of farm-workers has weakened the basis of agricultural trade unionism, the peak membership of the National Union of Agricultural and Allied Workers being in 1948. The reduction has also helped to reduce the bureaucratization of farms and to lessen the social distance between farmers and their workers. This though helps to sustain the deferential relationship between the farmer and farm-workers since there is no longer a clear oppositional rural working-class subculture.

However, Newby also shows that the connections between farmers and their workers have been strengthened by the large influx of people from towns and cities, urban newcomers who live permanently in the countryside or buy cottages for the weekend. To some extent the rural community is organized around the farm and farming in opposition to these urban newcomers. Farmers and their workers come to form a community within a community. This has reinforced a 'nostalgia' for the past when rural societies were thought to be relatively undivided communities. The influx of urban newcomers has generated the feeling that the quality of rural life is being threatened by their arrival. It is believed that the newcomers do not appreciate or recognize the value and nature of agricultural work. And at the same time it is thought that such newcomers also seek to preserve quaint and inappropriate aspects of rural charm, what has been called 'the village in their mind'. This has given rise to considerable social tensions, since newcomers will often oppose new shopping developments or council houses which would be of particular benefit to farm-workers. Sometimes alliances develop between farmers and their workers against the conservation efforts of newcomers who want to preserve the village that they have recently moved into. Newby says:

> The newcomers often possess a set of stereotyped expectations of village life which place a heavy emphasis on the quality of the rural environment . . . many newcomers hold strong views on the desired social and aesthetic qualities of the English village. It must conform as closely as possible to the prevailing urban view – picturesque, ancient and unchanging . . . [this has led] many newcomers to be bitterly critical of the changes wrought by modern farming methods. (p. 167)

Considerable conflicts also arise over leisure activities. Again, local farmers and their workers may engage in and support various 'field sports' including hunting, while the urban newcomers will seek to prevent such 'uncivilized' activities. Farmers are also increasingly having to develop leisure-related sources of income as farmland is being taken out of agricultural production under European Community policies. Again, the newcomers may often campaign against some of these developments since it is held that too many 'tourists', as opposed to those who have bought property, will destroy the 'true' character of the village.

Thus rural areas are full of social conflicts and tensions which are not easy to resolve. Part of what fuels such conflicts are various images of town and countryside.

Summary

1 The terms 'town' and 'country', 'urban' and 'rural', are often contrasted with each other, both in everyday life and in sociological formulations.
2 Such contrasts are overdrawn since there is no fixed and unchanging countryside. In the twentieth century there has been a growth in owner-occupancy of farms, the increasing ownership of agricultural land by financial institutions, the mechanization and industrialization of farming, the appearance of urban newcomers in rural communities, and the increasing transformation of the countryside as a resource for leisure. It should be noted that most research has been conducted on English lowland rural areas and that other parts may well be very different.

7.3   Towns and Cities

Urban villages

Rural life is often seen in terms of the existence of a community: close relationships between inhabitants, often reinforced by family ties. We will now consider whether it is in fact possible for 'communities' to exist in urban areas something which would again undermine a simple contrast between the countryside and the town.

Research conducted in the 1950s did indeed suggest that 'urban villages' can develop in certain enclaves within large cities. The best-known study was that conducted in Bethnal Green (see Young and Willmott, 1957). At the time Bethnal Green was a relatively compact borough of about 50,000 people concentrated within a small area of about 2 square miles. No major roads ran through it. Almost three-quarters of the male labour force were manual workers and most of those who were not ran shops or pubs. Although there was no single dominant industry in the area, it was an overwhelmingly working-class locality. There was a distinctive pattern of social life (box 7.3).

Other towns and cities in Britain have been organized along similar lines. In the strike of coal-miners in 1984–85 the working-class community within which each mine was located strongly reinforced the

---

Box 7.3 Life in an urban village

One consequence of . . . immobility is that everyone is surrounded by people very like himself, most of whom he has always
known. Bethnal Green has many points of similarity with a
village, or rather with a whole series of overlapping and
interlocking villages. The opportunities for close, long-term
relationships are greater than is usually the case in a large,
metropolitan, residential area. The likelihood of an inhabitant
having neighbours who are strangers, or whose way of life is very
different from his own has, until recently, been very slight. This
immobility also makes it essential for him to be on good terms
with his neighbours, as they are likely to be there, for better or
worse, for most of his life.

Source: Frankenberg, 1966, pp. 185–6

---

militancy of the strikers. In most mining areas the strong sense of
'community' stems from the overwhelming importance of the coal-
mining industry and from the shared experiences this produces for male
miners. In particular, a strong sense of community has been reinforced
by the highly localized nature of mining knowledge and experience. The
colliers' skill, seniority and even knowledge of technical terms was not
transferable from pit to pit, village to village, or coalfield to coalfield.
This local knowledge has bound miners to their home towns and their
local collieries and this is one reason why they are generally unwilling to
move elsewhere to work. Such a community spirit has also been
reinforced through the shared misfortune of mining disasters.

Inner cities

There are however large parts of cities which are nothing like either of
these communities. People living in many inner-city areas do not stay
there because they are attracted by feelings of 'community'. On the
contrary, they cannot escape. they are unable to rent or buy a house or
flat elsewhere, and often they do not possess the qualifications or
appropriate skills to move. In certain areas, a large proportion of the
local population is in this position, and this reinforces the sense of decay
and despair found in many city areas. There are various measures which

---

Box 7.4   Indicators of inner city deprivation

- Population loss
- High levels of unemployment
- High proportion of long-term unemployed
- Large number of lone-parent households
- High proportion of people over pensionable age
- Significant number of houses without an inside toilet
- Large proportion of people without higher degrees or diplomas
- High ratio of people with unskilled or semi-skilled jobs

---

can be used to assess which inner-city areas are suffering particularly high levels of deprivation (box 7.4).

One inner-city area, Hackney in east London, has been well described by Harrison (1985). He points out that this was once a fashionable and wealthy area. In the eighteenth and early nineteenth centuries it was an area of country houses, pleasure gardens and farms. It was during the latter part of the nineteenth century that the landowners sold their land to developers in very small lots. At the same time population was rapidly expanding, so housebuilders constructed many small houses as cheaply and as quickly as possible (many did not have proper foundations). This led to Hackney's problem of substandard housing. Charles Booth, who undertook a famous study of London's poor in 1900, commented:

> Hackney is becoming poorer. The larger houses are turned into factories. The better-to-do residents are leaving or have left . . . Their places are taken by a lower or middle grade. Each class as it moves away is replaced by one slightly poorer and lower. (quoted in Harrison, 1985, p. 41)

These processes have continued to the present day. Those who can leave generally do so. Those who cannot remain trapped by poor housing, declining job opportunities, inadequate public services, high rates of vandalism and crime, deteriorating educational provision with severe teacher shortages, declining likelihood of new employment opportunities, increasing probability of disturbance and riot, and so on. What happens is that a kind of vicious circle develops in certain areas within Britain's larger cities.

Three processes have particularly contributed to the worsening of the condition of such inner cities during the 1980s and 1990s. First, there has been the reduced availability of affordable housing. Few houses were built for the poor, and one-quarter of council houses have had to be sold off by local authorities. And yet semi-skilled and unskilled workers mostly do not buy their own houses but have to rent them. The 1980s have seen a remarkable growth in homelessness as a consequence.

Second, there have been major changes in the location of industry and employment. Many plants in central urban areas have closed. Less than 15 per cent of employment in most large cities is now to be found in manufacturing. One factor contributing to this has been the process of acquisition by which firms get taken over and merged into larger companies (see section 2.3). These larger companies often own plants in different regions of Britain as well as in other countries. They are able to pursue a global strategy often involving the closure of older plants in inner-city areas. Astonishingly this occurred in the 1980s even in the west Midlands, which had been a very powerful and wealthy manufacturing region within the UK space economy as a whole.

Third, many inner-city area are centres for various kinds of crime, mostly against property but not entirely.

It should be noted that some of these characteristics of inner cities are also now found on various outer estates of major cities. This is because some areas of council housing and new industrial estates on the edge of major cities have also suffered catastrophic economic and social collapse.

The outer estates of Liverpool: a case study

Research conducted by Meegan (1989) showed the changing fortunes of Kirkby and Speke, which are located on the edge of Liverpool. These were boom areas in the 1950s and 1960s. There was an influx of new companies, including such household names as Birds Eye, Kodak, Ford, Distillers and Kraft, and the rehousing of large numbers of people in new council estates away from the centre of Liverpool. These newly established communities were overwhelmingly working class and young. Most people worked in manufacturing companies which were part of UK or foreign-owned multinationals.

The rapid growth of these outer estates was followed by spectacular collapse in the 1970s and 1980s. The loss of jobs in Kirkby was far higher than the national rate. Between 1971 and 1984 there was a 57 per cent decline in the number of jobs in manufacturing industry. Table 7.1 lists the main redundancies and plant closures in Kirkby, Speke and Halewood between 1978 and 1987.

A number of factors produced this extraordinary collapse. First, there was a lack of investment in new capacity so that some of the plants were technologically obsolete. Second, 90 per cent of the redundancies were

Table 7.1 Major redundancies (150+) and plant closures in Kirkby, Speke and Halewood, 1978–1987

Year	Company (ownership)	*=MNC[a]	Location[b]	No.	Comments
Food, drink and tobacco					
1978	Birds Eye (UK, Unilever)	*	Kirkby	450	
1981	Cousins Baker (UK)		Speke	260	Closure
1981	Kraft (US)	*	Kirkby	370	
1982	Kraft (US)	*	Kirkby	930	
1983	Seagram (Canada)	*	Speke	220	
Chemicals and allied industries					
1979	Evans Medical (UK, Glaxo)	*	Speke	230	
1980	AKZO Chemie (Holland)	*	Kirkby	115	
1984	Synthetic Resins (UK, Scott Bader Commonwealth)		Speke	125	Closure
1986–7	Glaxo	*	Speke	450	
Metal manufacture					
1981	Yorkshire Imperial (UK, IMI)	*	Kirkby	200	
1981	Yorkshire Imperial (UK, IMI)	*	Kirkby	317	
Mechanical engineering					
1979	KME (UK, Silverines Ltd; ex-Fisher Bendix and KME Workers' Cooperative)		Kirkby	700	Closure
1980	Ward and Goldstone (UK)		Kirkby	160	Closure
1981	Otis Elevators (US, United Technologies)	*	Kirkby	125	
1982–3	Cross International (US)	*	Kirkby	355	
Electrical engineering					
1978	Plessey (1) (UK)	*	Kirkby	380	Closure
1978	Plessey (2) (UK)	*	Speke	330	Closure
1979	BICC Connolly (UK)	*	Kirkby	500	Closure
Vehicles					
1978	Triumph (UK, British Leyland)	*	Speke	4,600	Closure
1980	AC Delco (US, General Motors)	*	Kirkby	370	
1980	Ford (US)	*	Halewood	400	
1980	Massey Ferguson (Canada)	*	Kirkby	550	Closure
1981	AC Delco (US, General Motors)	*	Kirkby	159	
1980	Ford (US)	*	Halewood	260	
1981	Pressed Steel Fisher (UK, BL)	*	Speke	900	Closure
1983	Ford (US)	*	Halewood	1,300	
1983	Ford (US)	*	Halewood	600	
Clothing and footwear					
1978	F.D. Centre (Switzerland, Starlux)		Kirkby	200	Closure
1981	Commonwealth Curtains (Canada)		Kirkby	131	Closure

Timber and furniture				
1978	Hygena (UK)		Kirkby	200	
1980	Hygena (UK)		Kirkby	300	
1982	Hygena (UK)		Kirkby	700	Closure
Paper, printing and publishing				
1980	Metal Box (UK)	*	Speke	300	
1981	John Dickinson (UK, DRG)	*	Kirkby	214	
1983–4	Metal Box (UK)	*	Speke	218	
Other manufacturing				
1979	H. Hunt and Co. (UK)		Speke	150	
1979	Dunlop/1 (UK)	*	Speke	2,300	Closure
1980	Dunlop/2 (UK)	*	Speke	233	Closure
1981	United Reclaim (UK, Dunlop)	*	Speke	153	Closure
Total all manufacturing				20,455	

[a] MNC = multinational corporation.

[b] The list is restricted to job losses and plant closures in the three study estates. It therefore excludes those occurring in other outlying areas (most notably Aintree, Huyton and Prescot) and, of course, any in the inner city.

Source: Cooke, 1989, p. 208

declared in multinational corporations, which are generally much more able to expand and contract in pursuing a global strategy. Third, some companies had in fact invested in the area but in a way that substantially reduced employment levels. Fourth, the area was wholly unable to attract service industries of the sort that were rapidly expanding elsewhere in the 1980s. Finally, the area proved a poor location for the establishment of new small firms in either manufacturing or services.

The effects have been devastating: social polarization between those in work and those without jobs; large numbers of long-term unemployed, with many young people never having worked (in 1987 only 7 per cent of school-leavers had a job); huge reductions in household income: increasing reliance upon the state; and increasing numbers of households with rent arrears. Interestingly, though, Meegan suggests that this has not resulted in fatalism about the future. Apart from the famous Liverpool humour, which involves a lively scepticism towards authority, the unemployed people on these estates do not seem to have formed themselves into a separate underclass. He notes the 'confidence of local unemployed people in their own abilities to organize a collective response to their situation' (p. 229). People living in these outer estates seem to demonstrate a great attachment to their locality. Meegan identifies 'strong attachments to the area by local residents, the family-based support networks and the refusal of some of the unemployed to be marginalized in the social life of the locality' (p. 230).

The suburbs

We will turn now to consider not so much the outer estates of council flats and houses but the areas of suburbs where most if not all the houses are privately owned. Box 7.5 sets out the main features of suburban life.

Box 7.5   Suburban life

1   Life is centred not on the neighbourhood or the street but on the home.
2   This 'home-centredness' is reflected in a strong emphasis placed on obtaining consumer durables, on an orientation to consumption.
3   There is relatively less emphasis on contact with relatives and relatively more on choosing, making, and keeping friends, often from a fairly wide geographical area and not just from the neighbourhood or street.
4   Where households are made up of husbands and wives there is more emphasis (compared with say Bethnal Green) on sharing tasks *and* sharing friends.
5   There is fairly high participation in a variety of informal and formal organizations and the development of friendships out of this voluntary participation.

Clearly these characteristics are not found to the same degree in all suburban areas. There is variation depending upon social class, household composition, ethnic group, and stage in the life cycle. Households with one or more members holding manual jobs are likely to place less emphasis upon making and sustaining extensive friendship patterns and more upon contact with relatives (see section 6.6). Some working-class households will not necessarily have the resources (car, train travel) to make and keep wide friendship networks. Households where there are young children will be less likely to entertain friends in a relatively formal way, compared with when their children get older or have left home.

It is conventional to think of suburbs as 'middle class'. In section 3.5 we noted that there are important differences within the middle class, in particular between routine white-collar workers and the service class, the latter comprising professional and managerial occupations. In the following case study we will consider how the service class is geographically mobile, moving between suburbs in different regions.

The service class and spatial mobility: a case study

Savage and his collaborators (1992) investigate the general connections between the formation of social class and mobility between regions. They argue that the south-east region functions as an 'escalator region', one in which young people destined for the service class are often trained and where they initially work, but from which they then tend to move away as their careers develop. So although the south-east appears to be over-represented in the service class, quite a significant proportion will in fact leave to pursue their careers elsewhere. Thus to understand what different regions are like it is necessary to research not just those who currently live and work in them but also the patterns of spatial mobility within and between them.

In the 1970s and 1980s the south-east of England came to play a particularly important role within the overall British economy (see McCrone, 1992 on related developments in Scotland). There was an exceptional growth of companies producing services, both for consumers (such as hotels, restaurants, bars, and leisure centres) and for producers (such as lawyers, accountants, advertisers and bankers) (see section 2.7). Many of these firms contained very significant numbers of service-class personnel. Savage et al. examine how these were recruited, especially between 1971 and 1981, using a particular sample from the censuses conducted in those two years. They show that the south-east attracted a large number of potential recruits to the service class from those attending higher education institutions in the region. It seems that there was a great deal of mobility between firms and occupations for those young service-class recruits in the south-east. Further, many of these people were rapidly promoted into positions of authority within these south-east firms. But then as their careers matured quite a proportion of them left that region. Hence the service class outside the south-east contained a surprisingly high proportion of people who were 'south-erners' or had been 'southerners'. Savage et al. summarize:

> Many of the children of middle class parents throughout Britain will spend time in London and the South East. Rather than there being a permanent split between Londoners and provincials, the circulation of the southern middle class to the regions – and of their children to the South East – may allow the social and cultural practices associated with the London middle classes to be more widely disseminated. (1992, pp. 184–5)

They thus suggest that there may be a process of national homogeniza-tion of the service class as a result of these mobility patterns. Interestingly, though, many such people become particularly keen on conservation, either of rural or of urban areas. Bagguley et al. (1990) show this in the case of Lancaster. It is the service class that provided much of the input behind various campaigns to stop the large-scale redevelopment of the city centre. They suggest that because there has been a recent reduction in the mobility of the service class, especially of those over their mid 30s, they become particularly interested in what happens to their locality and, in many cases, very keen to prevent new developments (as we saw in the case of urban newcomers in the countryside). So the service class is 'nationalized' but also increasingly involved in local issues. Processes of social class formation are thus importantly spatial and not simply social (see section 3.5 for further discussion of this study).

Summary

1 Urban villages have survived in some urban areas.
2 There are extensive areas of urban decline, in inner cities and in some outer estates. This is brought about by both firms and better-qualified people 'emptying out' of such places. However, it should not be assumed that these are places where everyone has given up trying to organize improvements.

7.4 Services and the City

In this section we will consider a rather different series of issues, namely: the kinds of services that are provided within towns and cities; their allocation to different individuals and groups; and the effects of that allocation on the patterns of urban life.

Research in Britain in the early 1970s focused upon the issue of 'urban managerialism'. It was argued that there are some centrally significant resources in towns, such as transport, housing, leisure, schools and so on, to which access is controlled by various 'gatekeepers' or 'urban managers' (see Pahl, 1975). These resources are increasingly public or state provided. Various studies showed how different social groups were losers or gainers from the ways in which these resources were allocated.

The urban managerialist position was strongly criticized by Castells (1978), who argued more theoretically that it is necessary to connect the character of towns and cities to the broader character of capitalism as a distinct form of society. Castells argued that the modern city is 'capitalist', that it has a particular spatial form resulting from its functions of developing and maintaining 'collective consumption'. By this he meant the provision of education, transport, parks, leisure facilities and the like that are normally provided within the orbit of the city and are necessary for maintaining the workforce in a capitalist society. He thus saw the city as a vast state-run agency for producing and refreshing the labour force which mainly works in privately run factories and offices. Castells saw that collective consumption is highly political and that major forms of social conflict would develop around the level of provision and its financing. He expected that collective consumption processes would give rise to a new sort of urban politics and to a widespread radicalization of people within the city.

Certainly some of the conflicts he predicted did occur in Britain in the late 1970s and early 1980s. Examples include rent strikes, campaigns for cheaper bus fares, the forming of tenants organizations, disputes over types of schooling and so on. However, a number of writers argued that much of the British urban experience was rather different from what Castells had predicted.

First, Saunders (1979) showed, in a study based on Croydon (in south London), that urban politics could well be conservative rather than radical in its effects. In the 'deep south' of Croydon there was an extremely effective organization of the suburban middle class. This was successful in keeping down the level of rates (the property-based form of local taxation that existed until the late 1980s), in maintaining the very low densities of housing in the area (by pushing new developments into other areas of the borough), and in preserving large tracts of green-belt land in the south of the borough. Saunders summarizes: 'middle class amenity groups are nearly always willing to impose what they regard as disastrous proposals for their own districts on "soft" working class districts elsewhere' (p. 272).

Second, it is now clear that not all services do in fact have to be provided within increasingly centralized cities. We have already noted the strong trend towards counter-urbanization, based on the belief that the city is often rather poor at providing the desired range of facilities and services. However, it is true that some services are becoming provided almost exclusively within towns, for example hospitals and buses. Many people find that services in rural areas are rather poor, especially if their households do not have access to a car.

Third, Castells underestimated the degree to which services could be privatized. Across much of Europe and North America, governments have been attempting to introduce commercial practices into the provision of many services which seemed in the 1970s to be 'essentially' collective and public. Examples in Britain include water, council housing, electricity, gas, telephones, buses and coaches, leisure centres and so on. The Conservative governments since 1979 have sought to

Plate 7.4 Different densities of housing: two parts of Croydon.
Source: Malcolm Pendrill

remove almost all services from local government control (see section 12.5).

Finally, Castells did not sufficiently investigate the notion of consumption, as in 'collective consumption'. What is now clear is that what people consume, and how they consume it, is of great importance for social life and for the forming of political beliefs and practices. This argument about the effects of consumption has been most clean-cut in relationship to housing.

A nation of home owners: a case study

Saunders (1990) argues that privatized consumption is of increasing social importance. There is a new division of interest between those who are able to purchase products and services individually on the market, and those who are forced to rely on state welfare. This new division or 'cleavage' leads to the decline of social class and its replacement by consumption differences as the main axis of social conflict (compare section 3.4).

Increasing standards of living have enabled people to meet most of their consumption needs through individual purchase (even if subsidized) rather than through standardized state provision. This results in further decline in the state-provided services, as has been found on many council estates in England (but less so in Scotland). This results in social polarization, in which most people consume privately and only those who have no choice resort to the state.

For Saunders the private ownership of housing is not merely one alternative amongst several but superior to both private and public renting. This is because, first, it enables considerable capital gains to be achieved as house prices, until the early 1990s, kept well ahead of the rate of inflation. Second, it gives much greater control to the owners who are able to change and develop their properties, so deriving considerable satisfaction. And third, owner-occupation provides people with a sense of identity and security. He argues that since people's identities are increasingly formed not at work but from what they consume, the shift to the private purchase of housing is profoundly important. It gives people a really significant stake in 'Britain'.

There are a number of criticisms that can be made of this. First, his arguments are more true of England and especially the south-east. Scotland and Wales have higher rates of council house renting. Second, many of the capital gains made in the 1980s were lost in the collapse of house prices in the 1990s. Those people with 'negative equity' – a mortgage higher than the current value of the house – can experience

Plate 7.5 Different types of council housing.
Source: Mike Abrahams/Network (bottom)

neither capital gains nor security. Indeed much of his argument ignores the often very high cost of borrowing (through a mortgage if one is lucky) that can be involved in house purchase. Third, Saunders attempts to generalize from the case of housing to other spheres of consumption, such as health or transport, where he also argues that private provision through the market is desirable. However, this is a dubious argument since housing is a peculiar commodity. One can buy (if one is lucky) a whole house but not a whole hospital or bus. In the latter cases all one can purchase is a service, which cannot be resold to make a capital gain. Furthermore, the housing market in Britain is not a 'pure market' but has been structured by specific policies, especially that of maintaining tax relief on mortgages and encouraging council tenants to purchase their homes through 'right to buy' legislation. So it may be that the increasing desire for home ownership in Britain in the 1980s was not so much the expression of a deep-seated preference for obtaining all sorts of products and services through the market but much more a contingent effect.

Summary

1   There has been a lively debate as to the relationship between cities and services. Some have argued that cities essentially are locations for collective consumption and for radical politics.
2   Others have argued that much urban politics is in fact conservative. In particular, private consumption – especially of housing – both is intrinsically preferable and reduces the likely effects of class.

7.5   Changing Cities

Saunders (1990) concentrates too much on housing and ignores a wide range of other ways in which towns and cities are affected by, and in turn affect, consumption. We consider here a number of important points.

First, people increasingly buy a wider and more varied range of goods and services. It is sometimes said that there is now no fashion, only fashions. Part of what is used to sell goods is the images which get attached to particular commodities. One very important set of images is those of place. Some British examples include the 'English countryside', 'historic Edinburgh', the 'green valleys of Wales', the 'mysterious highlands' and so on.

Second, central to the character of different places are the services which are available within them, such as financial services in London, entertainment services at Blackpool, cultural services within Glasgow,

Plate 7.6 Wigan Pier Heritage Centre.
Source: John Urry

educational services within Cambridge, sports facilities in Sheffield, and heritage services in the north-west of England.

Third, these services are increasingly important in attracting new firms, new residents and visitors. There is a process of competition between places, and in part British towns and cities are having to compete with places abroad, especially in Europe. The designation of Glasgow as the 1990 European City of Culture is a good example of an effort by a British city to refashion itself in this competition. Likewise the bid by Manchester to host the Olympic Games in the year 2000 was a further example of this competition between what have been called 'European city-states'.

Fourth, many towns and cities have sought to develop their range of leisure, cultural, entertainment and sporting services so as to be increasingly attractive to tourists. This has been one of the fastest growing areas of investment and employment in the 1980s and many local authorities have seen it as one of the few sources of jobs and income. Some places have established successful tourist sites, such as Wigan's Pier Heritage Centre and the Beamish Industrial Museum in the north-east, and have found that the developments often produce more general positive images for the area.

Finally, many of these towns and cities have sought to present themselves as 'historical' or as 'heritage cities'. This has involved the conservation of many old buildings constructed in the local vernacular style, including factories, mills, workmen's cottages, alleyways, docks, warehouses and inns. Often this preservation first occurred because of campaigns by members of the service class, as we noted earlier in the case

Plate 7.7   Beamish Museum, County Durham.
Source: John Urry

of Lancaster (see Bagguley et al., 1990). But this conserved environment
can then be turned by a mixture of public and private interests into a set
of townscapes suitable for what one may term 'visual consumption'. This
is achieved by cleaning up the environment to produce a 'heritage effect',
decorating it with suitable street furniture, and then encouraging the
private sector to establish appropriate shops, restaurants, bars, leisure
clubs and so on (see Corner and Harvey, 1991 on the interconnections of
heritage with ideas of enterprise).

So far we have discussed mainly what has been happening in small and
medium towns and cities. There is though one huge city in Britain,
London, which as we saw earlier has long dominated the rest of the urban
system in Britain. Finally then in this chapter we will return to London
and consider certain facets of its extraordinary development in the last
decade or so.

London and the Docklands: a case study

London is one of three global cities, the others being New York and
Tokyo (see the various chapters in Budd and Whimster, 1992). In some
ways the relations between these three cities are more important than
their relations with their national economies and societies. They form a
system, and contemporary Britain has to be understood in terms of the
connections that London has with other cities, especially the two others
also dominant in world financial markets.

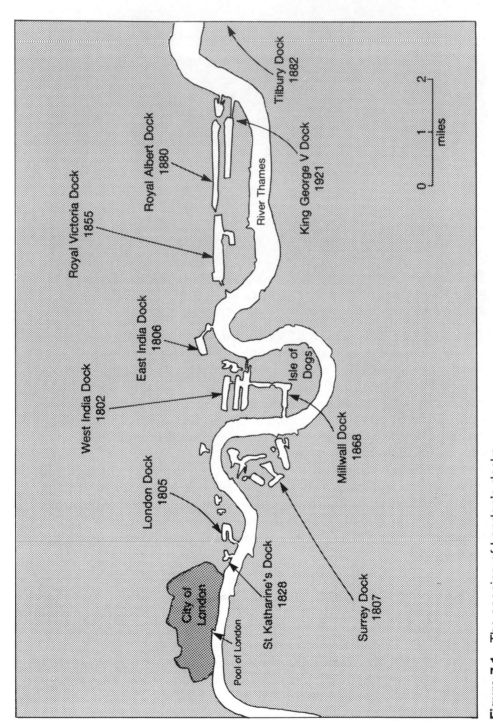

Figure 7.1 The opening of London's docks.
Source: Budd and Whimster, 1992

There are very important effects which follow from being a world city. The most obvious is that London is dependent upon the extraordinary turbulence of world financial and property markets. The expansion of those markets helped to generate the plan to establish the largest new office complex in Europe, at Canary Wharf. The subsequent collapse of those same markets caused the developers Olympia and York to have serious financial difficulties.

The origins of the Canary Wharf development go back to the closure of all London's docks, except Tilbury, between 1967 and 1981. A huge area to the east of the City of London became derelict. Figure 7.1 sets out when each of the docks had been originally established. At the same time as these closures there was an acute shortage of office space in the City of London which was subject to very strict planning controls. In 1979 the election of the neo-liberal Conservative government, in the context of the development of new electronic technologies in financial trading, led to the establishment of the London Docklands Development Corporation in 1981. It was given wide powers to acquire land in the Docklands

Plate 7.8 Canary Wharf.
Source: John Urry

and to provide a basic infrastructure (such as the light railway). Its approach to planning was 'liberal', endeavouring to generate a market-led regeneration of the area. The Isle of Dogs was designated an 'enterprise zone', whereby a variety of financial and infrastructural inducements were provided to developers. The Conservatives attempted to establish a developer-led regeneration of the Docklands.

New technologies in financial trading meant that the face-to-face contact characteristic of the 'square mile' of the City of London was no longer necessary. Huge new dealing rooms were demanded by the overseas banks and other financial service companies that flooded into London in the mid to late 1980s. There was a very substantial physical expansion of the City, south of the river to Hays Galleria more or less opposite the Port of London, west to Covent Garden in the West End, and east most dramatically to the Docklands and especially to the extraordinary development of Canary Wharf in what had been the West India Dock.

An enormous project was planned at Canary Wharf, covering 71 acres and intended to provide 10 million square feet of space and 50,000 jobs. Local councils in the area opposed the development, particularly because of its scale and the lack of an adequate transport infrastructure. However, in the atmosphere of the late 1980s developer interests were dominant. At first it seemed that there would be sufficient demand for office space, partly because similar developments had been restricted in the City itself. However, the latter policy was relaxed and so, as the Canary Wharf project got seriously under way in 1987 under the direction of Olympia and York, a burst of office construction simultaneously began in the City itself; the amount planned over a ten-year period was greater than that available in Canary Wharf. Nevertheless Paul Reichmann, chairman of the developers Olympia and York, declared in 1989:

> London will be in the absolute forefront of Europe. International companies will want facilities they cannot find in the City, and that is another reason why the success of Canary Wharf is an inevitability . . . A model working environment for the next century, unparalleled in Europe. (quoted in Budd and Whimster, 1992, p. 239).

By late 1992 the dream had turned sour. Only about one-third of it was built and there were huge uncompleted buildings right next to some of the highest-quality offices in Britain. The project is now run by administrators. Occupancy rates are low, and rents and property prices are tumbling all over London and the south-east. There is still no decent transport to and from Canary Wharf. And the biggest irony of all is that the 50th floor of the tower, Canada House, is now given over to tourists at weekends who are able to enjoy one of the great views of London, to Windsor, the North Downs and the mouth of the Thames. The developer-led regeneration of the Docklands, and especially the focus upon office building for the City outside the central area, has produced a high-quality development seemingly most attractive not to financial service companies but to tourists.

Summary

1   It is clear that towns and cities are importantly bound up with the delivery of various kinds of services, both public and, increasingly, private.
2   There is an increasing competition between cities in terms of the services provided and of the images that these enable a place to present to its own residents and to potential investors and visitors.

Further reading

Useful general books in urban sociology are Dickens (1990) and Savage and Warde (1993). See Jacobs (1992) on urban policy, especially for comparisons with the US where many of the 1980s policies originated. For a study of changes in a number of English towns and cities, see Cooke (1989).

8 Education

8.1 Introduction

Educational institutions have two basic functions. On the one hand, they act as agencies of *socialization*, transmitting social rules, norms and values; on the other hand, they are mechanisms of *allocation*, channels for selecting and training people to fill the many occupations of industrial economies. This dual function of socialization and allocation *is* fulfilled to some degree by all educational systems. However, in a society with a complex division of labour there is often a contradiction between the two functions of socialization and allocation.

The contradiction arises because one objective, preparation for work, requires enormous differentiation between individuals. Different skills and capacities must be transmitted. Some, however, will subsequently be highly rewarded, others not. To have gained access to the most valuable skills, which are opened up by different routes through the education system, confers privilege. Unequal outcomes ensue.

The second objective, preparation for citizenship and membership of a shared national culture, is an ideological foundation of liberal-democratic societies. Citizenship of democratic nation-states presupposes a certain level of equality and certain shared rights and obligations among all its members. Educational systems are expected to transmit and reinforce a sense of belonging and mutual responsibility. These commitments may, however, be jeopardized by unacceptable inequalities which cause resentment. They are also rendered difficult because different groups of students are being prepared for objectively different occupational positions. The norms and values transmitted to any group of children have to be somehow related to the kinds of skills they are being taught. To take an extreme example, it would be highly anomalous if schools taught the kinds of social behaviour appropriate to the aristocracy to children destined to become unskilled manual labourers. The culture of the aristocracy is not the same as that of the working class.

In practice, the pursuit of the two objectives cannot easily be separated, for they occur at the same time within educational establishments. The sociology of education has explored in detail how this contradiction has affected behaviour in school and its consequences for the subsequent careers of children. This contradiction creates practical dilemmas within schools and provides a principal axis of political debate about the fairness of education policy.

8.2 Education and the State

Education is financed and regulated by the state. Legislation has *compelled* children to attend school for ever greater lengths of time. In the middle of the nineteenth century most children attended primary schools for only two or three years. By the early 1990s, the majority of children were spending 14 years or more in full-time education. In all there were about 9.5 million full-time students in schools and colleges in Britain in 1992. State expenditure on education – on schools, colleges, universities and their administration – amounted to £24 billion in 1989–90 and comprised 4.6 per cent of GDP. The state also oversees the complex system of qualifications and accreditation. In addition it maintains responsibility for inspection and monitoring – of schools, pupil performance and examination boards.

Provided largely from public funds, the character of the education system is, in important part, the direct result of political decision-making. Consequently there has always been considerable dispute over its purposes and its organization. Social groups and political parties have persistently tried to change the nature of the education system to suit their various material interests and political convictions. Some educational reformers have sought to reorganize schools and improve access to them so as to promote social equality between classes. Others, by contrast, have sought to segregate children in different kinds of schools on the basis of ability, or according to the capacity of parents to pay for education. Much consideration has also been given to what the schools should teach and in what ways they should try to influence their pupils.

Ideology and policy since 1944

Recent years have been characterized by a vast array of new policies designed to reform education and training. The policies of the 1980s are

Plate 8.1 Different types of schooling.
Source: Raissa Page/Format and John Shurrock/
Network

best seen in historical context, for they represent a radical departure from previous arrangements which were established after the Second World War.

Educational policies after the Second World War were primarily concerned to facilitate greater, and more equal, *access* to educational qualifications. This was attempted in the 1944 Education Act which sought to make entry to selective secondary schools and universities *meritocratic*, that is dependent on ability rather than social status or wealth. This was not achieved, as sociological research in the 1950s and 1960s demonstrated. One explanation was that the organization of the schooling system was at fault. The system of competitive selection for secondary schools (the 11-plus examination), the continued existence of elite private schools, and the streaming of school classes, were subjected to particular criticism. It was argued that it was the schools themselves, and not just their selection procedures, which needed to be altered to prevent working-class children both leaving education at an earlier age and acquiring disproportionately fewer educational certificates. It was hoped that the expansion in the 1960s of *comprehensive* secondary schools, with more flexible internal arrangements for teaching and to which entry was non-competitive, might solve the problem.

Dale (1989) interprets the period between 1944 and 1976 as one of relative political consensus about education. Three powerful agencies were involved: central government, local authorities and the teaching profession. They established an equilibrium. Central government was represented by officials at the Department for Education, who were not politically partisan and who outlined the rules and limits of acceptable policy which was exercised in the name of the public interest. Local education authorities (LEAs) had practical day-to-day administrative control of schools and colleges, distributing funds allocated by central government in accordance with *local* political priorities. The expertise of the organized teaching profession was acknowledged through representation on central and local education committees. Also, in general, despite public examinations and the existence of school inspectors, teachers had considerable discretion regarding the content and style of classroom activities.

In 1976 a Labour government initiated what became known as 'the great education debate'. The debate was partly about educational standards and styles of teaching, but was primarily motivated by concern about the inadequate skill level of the labour force, which was thought to explain the declining competitiveness of British industry. The result was a shift towards much greater emphasis on the role of the educational system in preparation for employment. Subsequent policy included the establishment of the Manpower Services Commission with a remit to stimulate vocational training (see section 8.3).

The Conservative governments after 1979 put the improvement of training in the forefront of their policies, although by the middle of the 1980s their principal efforts were redirected towards implementing a national curriculum. Their endeavours altered fundamentally the ways in which the education system operates. The objectives were several and partly contradictory: to re-emphasize basic skills like reading; to improve standards and to monitor them through systematic testing of pupils; to discourage progressive teaching methods and restore a more traditional and standardized content to the curriculum; to reduce the cost of the system; to expand access, particularly to further and higher education; and to extend 'consumer' choice and control. The pursuit of these goals produced a wide range of initiatives, culminating in the 1988 Education Reform Act. Their attainment, however, required the alteration of the powers of the different agencies involved. A key part of government strategy was to reduce the power of the professional educators at all levels – at the Department for Education, in the LEAs and in classrooms.

Organizational reform

A general goal of the governments of Margaret Thatcher was to reduce public expenditure and to subject public organizations, including educational ones, to market competition as a means of increasing their efficiency (see also section 12.5). It was intended that schools should become more like private business organizations, responding to the preferences of their customers. This corresponded to the central ideological tenet of the Conservative governments of the 1980s: that the market is the optimum mechanism for distributing goods and services. Political opponents objected, arguing that while this was true for some commodities, the market was not appropriate for determining the form and content of education. Schooling, it was argued, should be considered a matter of public rather than private interest, and should be subject to criteria of effectiveness not efficiency. Nevertheless, strategies with similar logics were used by the government in other areas too – in higher education, in the health service – as part of the programme to make public sector service industries cheaper and more accountable.

This necessitated extensive organizational change, producing much controversy and entailing the redistribution of power within the education system. It was intended that LEAs should lose most of their powers, some to central government, others to individual schools. Probably the main instrument for achieving this has been the use of financial incentives to reward approved innovations and acceptable performance. Local management of schools (LMS) entailed giving control of the school budget to the headteacher, in consultation with governors, who can decide on most matters regarding the use of that income. The level of income is determined largely by the number of pupils taught. In addition, schools have been strongly encouraged to 'opt out' of local authority control by becoming grant maintained, in which case their funds are allocated directly by central government.

At the same time, promising parents more choice in deciding between schools, 'open enrolment' was introduced; schools no longer had a quota of pupils fixed by the LEA. Since there are now more school places than children to fill them, schools must compete for pupils and market themselves to parents even to maintain existing levels of activity. State schools have also been instructed that they must publish their examination results, and beginning in 1992 'league tables' of schools' performance have been made available. It seems likely that this will then lead to more emphasis being placed on passing exams, to the detriment of other educational objectives. In such fashion, central regulation of finance will result in some schools introducing 'voluntarily' educational practices preferred by the party in government but of which they disapprove. Thus, for instance, teachers expressed great scepticism about the prescribed content of the national curriculum and the regular, standardized, compulsory testing of pupils at ages 7, 11, 14 and 16. Yet their own and their schools' survival will depend on their students' performance in those tests.

One calculated effect of government policy towards public sector services has been to reduce the power of professional practitioners. Teachers in schools lost some of their autonomy through the introduction of the national curriculum, for they could no longer decide what to teach. Changes in the composition of school governing bodies, which increased parent and local business representation, reduced another channel of professional influence. As schools came to be more like business organizations, financial management, in which teachers are not trained, came to be more important than educational philosophies, where teachers could claim expertise. Given that teachers were also deprived of national union bargaining rights in 1987, subjected to a personal appraisal scheme and faced with increased workloads, many have become demoralized and dissatisfied.

Legislation, however, is neither simply nor easily translated into practice. Bowe and Ball (1992) studied the implementation of recent policies in four schools in the south of England. This indicated that financial imperatives had had a considerable impact on activities and organizational cultures: senior staff became engrossed in intensified managerial roles and more hierarchical and bureaucratic arrangements emerged; competition to attract pupils was stimulated; and much attention was paid to indicators of performance. However, there was still a great deal of room for manoeuvre, and schools implemented the policies flexibly and conditionally. For instance, the schools planned to teach the national curriculum in very different ways, adapting it to existing practice. The specific manner of implementation of any policy depends on context – the history and development of particular schools, the variable commitment of teachers, and political manoeuvres within the school and in its local area.

Education policy became subject to more partisan political direction during the 1980s. The Conservative government aimed to reform all state provision and thereby to reduce public expenditure. There were few extra resources for new initiatives, merely financial penalties for failing to comply. Not only schools, but further and higher education institutions have been much changed as financial restrictions have coincided with expansion of student numbers and institutional reform.

Summary

1 Recent, extensive education reforms represent a breaking down of the political consensus that lasted from the end of the Second World War until the late 1970s.
2 Conservative governments since 1979 have sought to alter the structure of power within the educational system, in particular by introducing market pressures. Key policy innovations included local management of schools and the national curriculum.

8.3   Education and Economic Production

Economic production in contemporary Britain is characterized by a complex division of labour, a high degree of organization, advanced technology and a disciplined workforce. Sociologists argue about the precise contribution of educational institutions to economic production. However, broadly speaking, the education system has two, related, important *economic* effects – training and selection. Schools and colleges can *train* students in two ways: by giving instruction in useful skills, and by teaching the personal characteristics and social orientations required in work. From an employer's point of view, skills – like literacy, numeracy, carpentry and cookery – are beneficial only if workers turn up regularly, on time and will do the tasks allotted to them when at work. The habits and motivations of *work discipline* have to be instilled into each new generation of workers.

Educational institutions also perform a *selection* function: the very many positions produced by a highly specialized division of labour require some means of allocating people to those positions. Schools are closely involved in allocating young people to occupational positions. This occurs most obviously because schools prepare pupils for the examinations which confer qualifications. But it also occurs because there are differences in prestige between schools, and having attended one with a good reputation may also subsequently benefit its pupils. Selection procedures present pupils with different job opportunities and ensure that the economy gets the differentiated workforce which it requires.

The positive economic contribution of the educational system stretches beyond training and selection. Universities in particular play an important part in scientific and technological innovation, and educational institutions themselves provide a lot of jobs.

In this section we will consider various aspects of training. In the next (section 8.4) we will consider selection. Remember, however, that training and selection are interrelated: schools select pupils for different kinds of training, and the kinds of training offered limit occupational choice. Remember also that training and selection are often in a relationship of tension with the 'socialization function' of the school (considered in section 8.5).

Policies for vocational training

Britain has a poorly qualified workforce in comparison with its major industrial competitors (see table 8.1). In the past neither the content of schooling nor the system of formal qualifications was explicitly motivated by labour-market considerations. Indeed, it is only in this century that educational policy-makers have thought it especially important to train young people in technical skills; in the nineteenth century it was thought far more important that a moral and religious education for 'citizenship' should be provided to the mass of the population. Britain's poor economic performance has increasingly been blamed on the defects of its educational system. Protagonists in recent debates on educational policy have recommended both that education should be more practically relevant to work and that new attitudes towards work and industry should be transmitted to students.

The 1980s witnessed some fresh experiments designed to extend training within schools with a view to improving Britain's economic performance. The Training and Vocational Education Initiative (TVEI) experiment was the most prominent example. Introduced in 1984, TVEI invited schools to put forward schemes for new courses of instruction for students of all abilities in the 14–18 age range. Courses designed for approval had to meet certain criteria which are overwhelmingly related

Table 8.1 International comparison of 16–18 year olds in education and training[a], by age and type of study, 1987[b]

	Minimum leaving age (years)	16 years			16 to 18 years		
		Full-time (%)	Part-time (%)	All (%)	Full-time (%)	Part-time (%)	All[c] (%)
United Kingdom[d] 1987	16	50	41	91	35	34	69
1989	16	53	40	93	37	33	70
Belgium	14	92	4	96	82	4	87
Denmark	16	89	3	91	73	6	79
France	16	80	8	88	69	8	77
Germany (Fed. Rep.)[e]	15	71	29	100	49	43	92
Italy[b]	14	54	15	69	47	18	65
Netherlands[b,e]	16	92	6	98	77	9	86
Spain[f]	15[k]	65	–	65	50	–	50
Australia[b]	15[l]	71	11	82	50	16	66
Canada[g]	16–17	92	–	92	75	–	75
Japan[h,i]	15	92	3	96	77	3	79
Sweden[j]	16	91	1	92	76	2	78
USA[h]	16–18[m]	95	–	95	80	1	81

[a] Includes apprenticeships, YTS and similar schemes.

[b] 1985 for Sweden, 1982 for Italy, 1986 for Netherlands and Australia.

[c] Includes higher education for some 18 years olds.

[d] Includes estimates for those studying only in the evening, also includes estimates of private sector further and higher education.

[e] Includes compulsory part-time education for 16 and 17 year olds.

[f] Excludes 18 year olds in universities.

[h] Includes private sector higher education.

[i] Estimated for special training and miscellaneous schools providing vocational training.

[j] Includes estimates for part-time.

[k] By 1988–9; formerly 14.

[l] 16 in Tasmania.

[m] Varies between states.

Source: Social Trends, 1992, p. 60; from Department of Education and Science data. Crown copyright

to future employment. Courses had to: (1) tie in to other training and job opportunities; (2) include a 'work experience' component; (3) be constructed in the light of local and national changes in employment opportunities; and (4) include technical education. Successful schools were provided by the Manpower Services Commission (MSC) with additional resources to mount appropriate courses. Significantly TVEI involved moving control and provision of training away from the Department for Education to the MSC, a branch of the Department of Employment which was also responsible for the Youth Training Scheme (YTS) (see section 2.9).

TVEI symbolized a change in priorities: one intention was to overcome the resistance of defenders of liberal educational values in order to introduce more practical and relevant training. As Shilling (1989) described its operation, the covert rationale of the scheme was to prepare students for employment in capitalist organizations – to accept and adapt to the routines, the hierarchical social relations and some of the indignities associated with mundane jobs. He evaluated the operation of TVEI in one local area. For the students, work placements were often experienced as exploitative, boring and demeaning. Knowing in addition that many of their adult relatives experienced work in such a way, the effect was not necessarily to create positive orientations to employment. Overall, Shilling concluded that while the scheme had some virtues – particularly where a conducive placement confirmed the trainee's preference for such a job – it did not do a great deal to prepare pupils better for work. TVEI will survive until 1997, but it is attracting less funding, the MSC itself having been dismembered.

Ultimately, schools are not well placed to pass on technical competence relevant to employers. Apart from the inclusion of information technology in the national curriculum, job-related training in schools is very limited. Extended experience in real workplace situations is probably the only effective way of giving relevant technical training. Employer-provided, workplace-based apprenticeships, and later schemes under the auspices of industrial training boards, have traditionally been the main sources. These, however, both contracted sharply during the 1980s. Throughout the twentieth century, these channels have been supplemented by technical and vocational training in further and higher education institutions. Policies have been introduced to try to improve these. The government has made plans to rationalize the system of vocational qualifications for students in the 16+ age group, through the National Council for Vocational Qualifications (NCVQ). This organization aims to standardise all vocational qualifications, including those obtained from the pre-vocational courses offered by the Business and Technician Education Council (BTEC), the Royal Society of Arts (RSA) and the City and Guilds of London Institute. The number of places in higher education on vocational degree courses also sharply increased during the 1980s. Otherwise, government training schemes, now mostly run by local training and enterprise councils (TECs), have been the main vehicles for skills training.

Discipline and the hidden curriculum

While job skill training in schools is necessarily quite limited, schools are in a better position to teach attitudes and motivations towards work. Such teaching is part of what has become known as the *hidden curriculum*. The concept of the hidden curriculum implies that the social knowledge which is imparted as a by-product of schooling is more important than the content of the visible, 'formal' curriculum – i.e. geography, maths, technical drawing. The hidden curriculum teaches many things – from obedience and punctuality to gender identity and political awareness – which contribute to producing and reproducing a labour force.

One influential and controversial account of this process was given by Bowles and Gintis (1976). They argued that schools are vital in the teaching of regularity, conscientiousness and obedience. The personal characteristics, attitudes and social behaviour of the ideal labourer are taught *indirectly* in schools: the school timetable does not have slots called 'obedience' or 'conformity'! According to Bowles and Gintis, the personal qualities desired at work develop because of the *form* of schooling rather than its overt content. They assert that there exists a correspondence between the organizational environment of the school and the workplace. Merely attending school, following its rules and routines, experiencing its hierarchical organization, instils into pupils the attitudes and outlooks required later in the workplace. Successful pupils exhibited traits of perseverance, consistency, dependability, loyalty to the school, obedience and punctuality. These characteristics are almost identical with the ones sought by supervisory staff in industry when hiring new workers. In short, the principal contribution of schooling is that it prepares *obedient* workers. It does this by getting children accustomed to the behaviour demanded by hierarchical organizations. This has come to be known as the 'correspondence principle' and has been subject to critical evaluation by other authors.

Resistance, compliance and differentiation

Though the controllers of the education system want schools to create

Plate 8.2   The 'hidden curriculum' prepares children for working life.
Source: R. Taylor/Camera Press and Jenny Matthews/Format

disciplined workers, there is much evidence that this is not straight-forwardly achieved. Complex processes of resistance and adjustment intercede. First, some pupils are indisciplined during their school careers, playing truant regularly, disobeying school rules or refusing to do school work. Other pupils offer only qualified cooperation, a compromise that might disintegrate now that transitions from school to work have become protracted and uncertain. Given the absence of jobs for young people (about 870,000 people under 25 were unemployed at the end of 1992), schooling and training, unless leading to high-level qualifications, may seem to lose its relevance.

Resistance

In schools of all types, pupil subcultures, hostile to schooling, develop. Contesting the authority of teachers, disobeying rules, rejecting the values of the school, are characteristics of 'anti-school cultures' which flourish among groups of, usually, academically unsuccessful male pupils. Such subcultures have been shown to exist in grammar, comprehensive and secondary modern schools.

A celebrated, graphic account was given by Paul Willis in *Learning to Labour* (1977). He studied a group of working-class boys in a secondary modern school in the midlands. The behaviour in and out of school of a group of friends, 'the lads', was documented by recording conversations and participating in their activities. The priorities of the lads were almost wholly opposed to those of the school, the teachers, and the conformist pupils (whom they charmingly called 'ear 'oles'). The lads openly broke school rules about dress, smoking and the like. They played truant sometimes but, more imaginatively, they systematically avoided working whenever in school. Willis records one group discussion in which he asked, halfway through one term, 'when was the last time you've done some writing?' One of the lads replies:

Fuzz: Oh are, last time was in careers, 'cos I writ 'yes' on a piece of paper, that broke my heart.
Willis: Why did it break your heart?
Fuzz: I mean to write, 'cos I was going to try and go through the term without writing anything. 'Cos since we've cum back, I ain't dun nothing.

Lack of involvement and commitment in the formal aspects of school life gave the lads time to 'have a laff'. The laff, Willis explains, is 'irreverent, marauding misbehaviour', ranging from joking to vandalism, which counters authority and relieves boredom.

The lads' resistance to authority and rejection of some dominant values are typical of elements of working-class culture, especially of the factory shop floor. Willis suggests that messing about in school and resisting the teachers' authority actually prepared 'the lads', *culturally*, for life on the shop floor. Toughness, masculinity, being able to stick up for yourself and enjoying a laff are central to the way labouring men in non-skilled manual work come to terms with repetitive, but often hard, work. Officially denied any control over work, labourers fight back through attempts to recover some control from supervisors, by time-wasting, by insubordination, and by pilfering. Paradoxically, these were things which the lads' behaviour at school had prepared them for. Their independent, oppositional culture was actively created. It led to failure in academic terms. But in the end it turned out to be 'vocationally relevant', in the sense that insubordination at school prepared them for subordination in unskilled manual work. However, during the 1980s, the number of unskilled manual labouring jobs reduced markedly. The lads were increasingly likely to face long bouts of unemployment.

Most observers consider that girls, while overall no less discontented with schooling, are less likely to form anti-school subcultures. Opposition is expressed in ways more consistent with feminine identities. Their responses are more individualized and private, which often serves to draw them towards traditional female domestic roles.

Compliance

Anti-school subcultures, while highly visible sources for colourful ethnography, affect a relatively small proportion of school students. Brown (1987) identified two other types of response by working-class pupils. One is to accept the teachers' definitions of schooling as directed towards educational credentials which will lead them, via higher education, into middle-class occupations. This too is a minority response. The most common response among working-class pupils is instrumental compliance.

Brown described the majority of working-class pupils as 'ordinary kids' who are unenthusiastic about school but nevertheless participate. They 'neither simply accept nor reject school, but comply with it . . . the ordinary kids made an effort in school because they believed that modest levels of endeavour and attainment, usually leading to CSEs, would help them to get on in working-class terms. In the working-class neighbour-hoods of Middleport [south Wales] 'getting on' usually meant boys being able to find apprenticeships and girls entering clerical and personal service jobs' (p. 31). Brown argued that compliance was ensured in the past because modest qualifications and a good reference did secure the kind of jobs that ordinary kids wanted. However, occupational change and high levels of unemployment mean that many young people currently are seriously disappointed when they obtain poorer jobs than they anticipate.

For Brown this constitutes the basis of a crisis in schools, since the rationale for the compliance of most working-class students is being eroded. The transition from school to work has become a protracted and very ragged process. Very few young people go straight into work at the end of compulsory schooling. The survey by Banks et al. (1992: see later) showed that in the years 1985–7, no more than 15 per cent of their sample left at 16 to take up employment. This was only one of five major routes (see figure 8.1). Some entail a long interval between leaving school and steady employment. Which route a youth takes is usually determined in earlier years of secondary education, with educational attainment the main conditioning factor. But in key respects schooling is becoming less immediately relevant to job prospects.

Instrumental compliance with school authority can also occasionally be detected among the academically successful. Mac an Ghaill (1988) describes the Black Sisters, a group of young women of Afro-Caribbean and Asian parentage, at an inner-city sixth-form college in the midlands, who were deeply dismissive of school and teachers, but who calculated that achieving qualifications was in their best interests. They complained that teachers held racist stereotypes and underestimated their abilities; streaming discriminated against them; they were subjected to a curriculum that ignored the history and experience of black people in Britain. Nevertheless, they pursued their studies through to higher education, mostly by dint of peer-group support and their collective determination to succeed. The womens' response was one of acting mostly as they were expected to, but without any commitment or investment of self-identity in the content of their activity: their strategy was 'anti-school but pro-education'. A white male teacher's observation that the four of them in his class behaved unusually betrays, incidentally, his expectation of conformity among the academically successful:

> They are very strange. I didn't, I mean at first I didn't think that they were as clever as they undoubtedly are. Their written work is very good, at times excellent, especially Judith. But they have a strange attitude, I mean not the usual attitude for clever kids. They sit there huddled together in the class, chatting away, never directly interrupting but not fully cooperating either, if ye know what I mean. If it was the normal case of being directly cheeky or whatever, you could handle it in the usual way but what do you do with the likes of them. I don't know what makes them tick. Give me a cheeky lad any day. (pp. 27–8)

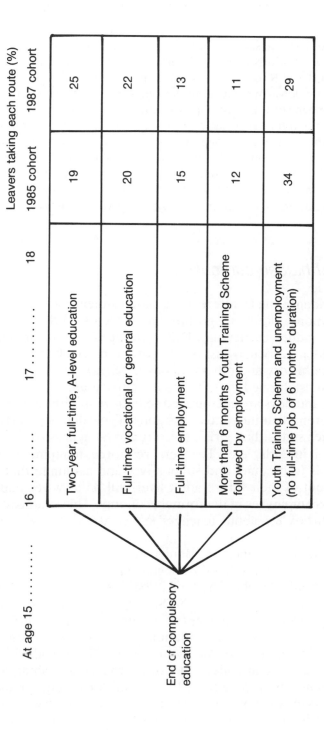

Figure 8.1 Early career routes after completion of compulsory schooling, 1985 and 1987.
Source: compiled from Banks et al., 1992

The rationale for the women's practice is summed up by 'Judith':

> With me like I go into school and I listen to the teacher and I put down just
> what they want. Christopher Columbus discovered America, I'll put it
> down, right. Cecil Rhodes, ye know that great imperialist, he was a great
> man, I'll put it down. We did about the Elizabethans, how great they were.
> More European stuff; France, equality, liberty, and fraternity, we'll put it
> all down. At that time they had colonies, enslaving people. I'll put it down
> that it was the mark of a new age, the Age of Enlightenment. It wasn't, but
> I'll put it down for them, so that we can tell them that black people are not
> stupid. In their terms we can tell them that we can get on. In their terms I
> come from one of the worst backgrounds but I am just saying to them, I
> can do it right, and shove your stereotypes up your anus. (p. 28)

Varieties of hidden curriculum

There is evidence that different accomplishments are systematically
rewarded among different groups of students. Schools present a
differentiated hidden curriculum. Different types of pupil are exposed to
different hidden curricula, just as the formal curriculum requires some
pupils to take history and others domestic science.

It has been established that the hidden curriculum is differentiated by
gender: girls and boys are encouraged to behave in different ways and to
develop different identities and aspirations. Typically, boys' activities are
granted higher status than girls', boisterous and aggressive behaviour is
less tolerated in girls, etc. Teachers reinforce feminine stereotypes,
expecting girls to be quiet and submissive, and assuming that the most
central element of their future adult lives will be as wives and mothers
rather than as employees in the formal economy. This is suggested by the
quotations in box 8.1 about teachers' expectations of the prospects of
their female students.

There is some evidence in Banks et al. (1992) that the hidden
curriculum is also differentiated by social class. The paths followed after
the end of compulsory schooling tend to be class confirming. Observation
of the behaviour of groups on YTS, BTEC and A-level courses in
Sheffield suggested that courses were recruited from different class
backgrounds and that the social relations between teachers and students
varied accordingly. The young men on a YTS bricklaying scheme
behaved on their day in college in exactly the same fashion as Willis's
lads. The women on a parallel YTS scheme for caring for the elderly
were equally dismissive of the value of their day in college, doing almost
no work, refusing to cooperate and devoting their attention primarily to

Box 8.1   Teachers' expectations

The typical expectations held by teachers were documented by
Stanworth (1983, pp. 30–1) when she asked staff teaching A-
levels to predict what their female students would be doing five
years on. Some of the responses were as follows:

Of a girl believed capable of getting a university degree:
Female teacher: Well, I can see her having a family, and
                    having them jolly well organized. They'll get
                    up at the right time and go to school at the
                    right time, wearing the right clothes. Meals
                    will be ready when her husband gets home.
                    She'll handle it jolly well.

Of a girl intending to qualify as a psychologist:
Female teacher: Obviously married. She's the sort of girl who
                    could very easily be married in five years'
                    time.
Interviewer: Would she be working then, do you think?
Teacher: She might. But she's that sort of girl, I think,
                    to stay at home with the children. She's a
                    caring person, as I said.

Of a girl with outstanding academic capacity:
Male teacher: Well, I'd be surprised if she wasn't married.
Interviewer: Is she the sort of person you would expect to
                    marry young?
Teacher: Well, not necessarily marry young, but let's
                    see . . . 16, 17, 18, 19 years old . . . some-
                    where along the line certainly. I can't see
                    what she'd be doing apart from that.

Of a girl of average ability:
Male teacher: Definitely married.

Stanworth notes that marriage was mentioned only once with
respect to boys' futures and that on only one occasion did a
teacher view early marriage for a girl as a potentially harmful
interruption to her development.

Source: Stanworth, 1983

the rather quarrelsome relationships within the group. Drawn from unskilled working-class backgrounds, their placements habituated them to tough and unattractive personal service work in retirement homes. Two BTEC groups – girls learning fashion design and a mixed group on a hotel and catering course – were less overtly antagonistic to college teachers, but found the academic assignments onerous and often irrelevant. They grudgingly tolerated college, spurred partly by exaggerated expectations of the careers that might become available if they were successful on the course. Students, while unimpressed by tutors, were deferential – the kind of response that might be seen as appropriate in particular to those whose future employment was dealing with customers in hotels. The BTEC students tended to come from skilled working-class and lower white-collar backgrounds. Only among the A-level group did Banks et al. find the children from professional and managerial households, and only there did they find informal and personal relationships of mutual respect between teachers and students.

The varied relationships between teachers and students with diverse class origins on different post-compulsory courses suggest that different 'hidden' curricula operate. This suggests a more complex interpretation of the 'correspondence principle' which may be assessed further by considering the extent to which the children of manual workers do get manual jobs. How consistently does the education system transmit class privilege from one generation to the next? This raises the question of *selection*.

Summary

1 Schools and colleges train students by teaching both some useful work skills and work discipline. Also by distributing qualifications they perform a central allocative function for the economy.
2 Schools have a hidden curriculum, inexplicitly teaching social attitudes which prepare children to become employees. This hidden curriculum is differentiated by gender and class: different types of student are encouraged to develop orientations specific to their likely future work roles, paid and unpaid.

8.4   Inequality and Selection in Education

Educational qualifications are a principal determinant of job opportunities. Employers use examination results as a way of screening applicants, usually prescribing a minimum level of qualification for any position.

Schools are thus a vital link in the allocation of individuals to places in the workforce. Achievement is a continuous process, but is symbolized by decisions made at key stages in a child's educational career. The type of school attended, the stream within the school to which a pupil is allocated, and the age of leaving full-time education, all affect the acquisition of the certificates important in determining long-term life chances.

Table 8.2 Highest qualification level of the population[a], by ethnic origin and sex, Great Britain, 1988–1990

Highest qualification held[d]	White (%)	West Indian/ Guyanese (%)	Indian (%)	Pakistani/ Bangladeshi (%)	Other[b] (%)	All[c]
Males:						
Higher	15	–	19	8	22	15
Other	57	58	51	40	56	57
None	29	36	30	52	21	29
Females:						
Higher	13	16	13	–	20	13
Other	51	52	46	28	52	51
None	36	32	41	68	28	36
All persons:						
Higher	14	11	16	6	21	14
Other	54	55	49	34	54	54
None	32	34	36	60	25	32

[a] Aged 16 to retirement age (64 for males and 59 for females).
[b] Includes African, Arab, Chinese, other stated and mixed origin.
[c] Includes those who did not know or did not state their ethnic origin.
[d] Excludes those who did not know or did not state their qualifications.

Source: *Social Trends*, 1992, p. 65; from *Labour Force Survey* data. Crown copyright

Levels of achievement are systematically related to the social characteristics of pupils. Thus table 8.2 shows differences in qualifications by ethnic origin and gender at the end of the 1980s. White men and Indian men are better qualified than female counterparts, though the gender difference is reversed among people of West Indian and Guyanese origin. Inter-ethnic differences indicate that men of West Indian and women of Pakistani and Bangladeshi origin are much more disadvantaged. Indians are, on average, better qualified than whites, though this is partly a consequence of their being younger: younger generations have higher levels of qualification because educational provision has expanded rapidly in the recent past.

Class origins are also important, as table 8.3 indicates. The children of white-collar workers are very much better qualified than their peers from manual backgrounds. Ethnicity and gender interact with class in the determination of educational attainment. To understand the causes of unequal attainment requires attention to all three factors.

Class inequalities in education

Origins and Destinations: a case study

One major landmark in the development of education during the twentieth century in England and Wales was the 1944 Education Act which required that all children be provided, free of charge, with a place at secondary school. Previously most children had remained in elementary education (until age 14) throughout their schooldays, as selective secondary schools, which charged fees, were available only to a minority. The 1944 Act reorganized schooling on a tripartite system: with the exception of those in private education, children were to be transferred at age 11 to either a grammar, a technical or a (secondary) modern school, on the basis of their individual abilities and aptitudes. The expressed wish was that all three types of school should be accorded 'parity of esteem'; each should cater for different kinds of children by offering different training. It was imagined that this system would provide better, and more equal, educational opportunities, eradicating the waste of talent among working-class children. Halsey et al. (1980) studied the workings of the tripartite system, inquiring into the extent to which inequalities in education had been reduced for boys born between 1913 and 1952. This study remains the most authoritative regarding the nature and change in the relationship between social class and educational attainment in England and Wales.

Halsey et al. examined the educational biographies of 8526 men aged between 20 and 60 in 1972, a part of the national sample taken in the Nuffield Mobility Project. These men were assigned to groups by their *social class of origin* and by *age cohort*. The class categories used were the same as in Goldthorpe et al. (1987: see figure 3.1), based upon the father's occupation when the respondent was 14 years old. An age cohort is a group of people born between two given dates. Halsey et al. considered four separate cohorts, of those born in the years 1913–22, 1923–32, 1933–42 and 1943–52. Thereafter, the educational experiences of each cohort were compared, to test whether equality of access and attainment had *changed over time*. This comparison was made in order to assess the argument, advanced by Jencks (1972) and Bowles and Gintis (1976), that the organization of schooling made little difference to the

Table 8.3 Highest qualification level attained[a], by socio-economic group of father, Great Britain, 1989

Highest qualification level attained	Professional (%)	Employers and managers (%)	Intermediate and junior non-manual (%)	Skilled manual and own account non-professional (%)	Semi-skilled manual and personal service (%)	Unskilled manual (%)	All persons (%)
Degree	38	17	18	5	4	3	11
Higher education	18	16	16	12	7	6	13
A-level	10	14	13	9	8	6	10
O-level	20	24	27	22	20	14	22
CSE	4	8	9	13	13	13	11
Foreign	5	5	3	3	2	3	3
No qualifications	6	17	14	37	47	54	31
Sample size (= 100%) (no.)	440	1656	835	3383	1059	438	7811

[a] Persons aged 25–49 not in full time education.

Source: Social Trends, 1992, p. 66; from *General Household Survey* data. Crown copyright

chances of success of working-class pupils. The cohorts were chosen so that all men in the last two cohorts (born between 1933 and 1952) would have experienced the tripartite system, since the men born earliest, in 1933, would have passed into the secondary system, at age 11, in the year of the introduction of the new Education Act. If the organization of the education system did affect social structure and social inequalities, Halsey et al. reasoned, then comparison between the first two and the last two cohorts should show this to be the case.

The findings of Halsey et al. suggested that the 1944 Act made very little difference to inequality between classes. Of course, the total number of places in educational establishments increased, which allowed more children of all classes to attend selective schools and universities, with corresponding increases in the qualifications achieved. But the differentials between classes hardly changed. In general the proportions of children from each class remained more or less the same. Among the 1913–22 cohort, 7.2 per cent of sons of the service class (classes I and II) attended university but only 0.9 per cent of the working class (classes VI and VII). Of the 1943–52 cohort, who would have gone to university between 1961 and 1970, 26.4 per cent of the sons of the service class reached university but only 3.1 per cent of working-class boys. The *rate* of increase is thus more or less the same for each class: the proportion of sons going to university grew 3.5 times for both classes. As with some of the other reforms associated with the growth of the welfare state after the Second World War, the dominant rather than the subordinate classes benefited most. Not *all* trends confirm the hypothesis of constant class differentials: the chances of working-class boys, relative to their service-class peers, staying at school a year beyond the minimum leaving age did improve substantially over time, for example. Nonetheless, in most respects the service class maintained its educational advantages, relative to both intermediate and working classes, over the 40-year period examined.

Halsey et al. sought to show how, and to a lesser extent why, such unequal educational selection takes place. Dealing successively with the key 'decisions' which define an educational career (private or state primary school; selective or modern, private or state secondary school; when to leave school; whether to enter higher or further education), they evaluated explanations of educational inequality.

Despite much debate, it has never been established conclusively whether the cause of working-class under-achievement is material poverty or the cultural attributes of typical working-class families. Halsey et al. approached this question by attempting to separate out the effects of material circumstances and cultural background. They measured the former by family income, the latter by the cultural characteristics of parents (particularly their educational experiences). They found that cultural background, and specifically parental values, were of principal importance in determining the child's progress up to age 11. Whether a child went to a private primary school, and whether he subsequently entered a selective secondary school, were most clearly related to cultural background. After age 11, however, material circumstances became much more important in determining at what age, and with what qualifications, a boy was likely to leave school. This reflects the financial expense of keeping a child at school, a cost more difficult for working-class parents to bear. This discovery undermines arguments that working-class children have inadequate cultural preparation for engaging in the intellectual pursuits required of academically successful children.

Success in secondary schooling was, according to Halsey et al., most importantly determined by the school which a pupil attended. Jencks (1972) and Bowles and Gintis (1976) had argued that the type of school attended made no difference to achievement because all schools were merely 'class confirming' institutions. Halsey et al. disagreed. They found that it did not matter whether a child went to a private or a state *primary* school. However, the kind of *secondary* school a boy attended was considerably more important than any other factor, including the material circumstances of the family. The chance of a boy in a secondary modern school surviving past the minimum school-leaving age, or of obtaining any certificates, of course, was much lower than for a boy at grammar school. What Halsey's analysis showed, however, was that this fact is accounted for directly by neither social class composition nor IQ. Rather, it is an effect of the type of school. Under the tripartite system, survival past the minimum school-leaving age was usual if a child attended a selective secondary school. It was thus the case that the 'decision' made at age 11, by the 11-plus examination, was the critical point in determining whether children 'succeeded' or not.

Incidentally, this does not imply that social class and IQ are irrelevant. What Halsey et al. did was to *standardize* for these variables, showing that if class and IQ were held constant for any two children there would still be a very significant difference in educational outcome depending upon which schools were attended. Thus, for example, *holding social class constant*, the success of boys in gaining O-levels was the same in state-maintained grammar schools as in the leading public schools; but the *actual* proportion of boys gaining O-levels at these two types of school was quite different, since the public schools took in boys from higher class backgrounds. Hence, Halsey affirms that type of school *does* matter. Box 8.2 illustrates the main determinants of educational success according to Halsey et al.

Critics of Halsey et al. have tended to concentrate on whether the limited biographical information collected in the study was sufficient to test the theoretical positions which they evaluated. In particular, it is

Box 8.2   Main determinants of the educational careers of men born 1933–52

This model shows the *main* causal determinants only. It indicates that a child's cultural background is mainly relevant to explaining the nature of primary schooling and entry into secondary school. When considering qualifications, the material circumstances of the child's home become important, along with the type of secondary school attended. The qualifications obtained are the primary determinant of entry into the various forms of further and higher education.

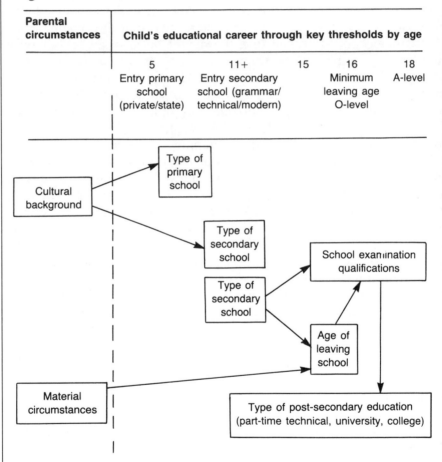

Parental circumstances	Child's educational career through key thresholds by age

5	11+	15	16	18
Entry primary school (private/state)	Entry secondary school (grammar/ technical/modern)		Minimum leaving age O-level	A-level

Source: constructed from Halsey et al., 1980

argued that their measures of cultural background were too crude for the purpose. Two other limitations are apparent: Halsey et al. have almost nothing to say about either comprehensive schools or girls. The first limitation was unavoidable: of their sample only 121 boys attended comprehensives because such schools, having developed only recently, were unavailable to most men born between 1931 and 1952. To have neglected girls was very disappointing.

Social class and comprehensive schooling

Since the later 1960s significant numbers of pupils have been educated at comprehensive secondary schools. The reasons for their introduction were partly that, as Halsey et al. conclusively demonstrated 15 years later, the tripartite system did not seem to ensure equal educational opportunity: the segregation of 11-year-olds into the three different types of school did not produce a meritocracy. But also, the movement for comprehensive education had social objectives, particularly that class divisions and prejudices might be dissolved if there were greater mixing between those social classes at school.

Whether a fully comprehensive system of secondary education was ever likely to achieve its meritocratic and social goals will remain a matter of speculation, for recent policies have changed direction. Incentives for schools to opt out of local authority control, city technology colleges and encouragement of independent fee-paying schools have entailed greater selectivity. The percentage of pupils in private schools increased from 5 per cent in 1976 to 7 per cent in 1990 (although there are signs of a fall in the recession of the early 1990s).

Informed opinion was fairly pessimistic about the likely success of comprehensivization. The survival of selective schools, and private schools, itself was detrimental to the comprehensive project. It was also frequently observed that streaming and banding within comprehensive schools segregated pupils within those schools, thereby replicating the old tripartite divisions. Most comprehensive schools were internally organized in a way that facilitated differentiated treatment of pupils, permitting teachers to transmit different hidden curricula. Beachside Comprehensive, a school studied by Ball (1981), had a policy of putting children into 'bands' on the basis of their performance at primary school. This resulted in the top band initially containing a disproportionate number of middle-class children. Because the bands were taught different subjects (i.e. the formal curriculum was different) there was very little movement between bands. Thus, the bands tended to coincide with social class differences and to generate different patterns of interaction between pupils and teachers as an oppositional culture emerged within the lower band. During the time that Ball was examining Beachside, the school's policy changed to mixed-ability grouping. For the first three years in the school, pupils were put into classes without reference to their academic abilities. This system seemed to prevent the emergence of an oppositional, anti-school culture and to increase social interaction between pupils with different class backgrounds. However, at the time of entry into their fourth year, the pupils' friendship networks were sharply delimited by social class and academic attainment.

The transitions from compulsory schooling of young people aged 16–19, in the years between 1985 and 1988, were investigated by Banks et al. (1992). Most respondents had attended comprehensive schools. Results in exams at 15 or 16 indicated that class differences in performance persist. Besides the fact that girls were more successful than boys, household social class and the educational levels of both mother and father were the principal social determinants of attainment. However, household class characteristics explained only a small proportion of the variance in pupil performance.

Gender inequalities in education

For many years, girls have had better pre-adolescence educational records than boys, scoring higher on IQ tests; they have also obtained more and better GCSE passes. By 1990, they were embarking on more A-level courses than boys and being marginally more successful in obtaining passes. They still, however, have slightly less chance of attending university. In the past women obtained fewer of the advanced qualifications necessary to obtain the most prestigious, professional jobs. However, differences at these levels have decreased sharply since the 1970s. The rate at which girls embark on A-level courses has become more like that for boys: in 1969, 43 per cent of A-level registrations were for girls, whilst in 1990 the proportion was 51 per cent. In the same period, as table 8.4 indicates, the proportion of women university undergraduates has increased, from a mere 31 per cent in 1970–1 to 45 per cent in 1989–90. By then, the sex ratio on degree courses at polytechnics (which mostly became new universities in 1992) was more or less even.

There is no agreement on the reasons for these improvements. It may be that changes in the schooling system have benefited girls, though some authors contend, on the contrary, that coeducational schooling hampers girls. More likely, it is a consequence of the general impact of feminism which publicized the extent and injustices of inequality between boys and girls. In addition, it probably reflects more intense involvement in paid employment in the recent period, in preparation for which young women

Table 8.4 Full-time students in higher education, by sex, origin and age, United Kingdom, 1970–1990

	Males					Females				
	1970–1	1975–6	1980–1	1985–6	1989–90	1970–1	1975–6	1980–1	1985–6	1989–90
Full-time students by origin (thousands)										
From the United Kingdom:										
Universities[a]: postgraduate	23.9	23.2	20.7	21.0	21.2	8.0	10.2	11.3	12.6	15.0
first degree	128.3	130.1	145.1	134.3	143.1	57.0	73.6	96.2	99.9	115.3
other[b]				1.5	1.4				1.2	1.4
Polytechnics and colleges	102.0	109.3	111.9	143.5	157.4	113.1	120.1	96.4	132.2	161.4
Total full-time UK students	254.2	262.6	277.7	300.4	323.1	178.2	203.8	203.9	245.9	293.2
From abroad	20.0	38.6	40.7	38.4	46.1	4.4	9.9	12.6	15.3	26.6
Total full-time students	274.2	301.2	318.4	338	369.2	182.6	213.7	216.5	261.3	319.8
Full-time students by age (percentages)										
18 years and under	10	11	[c] 16	15	15	17	14	[c] 19	17	17
19–20 years	36	35	37	38	36	45	42	41	42	38
21–24 years	38	36	30	29	30	24	28	25	26	27
25 years and over	15	19	17	18	18	14	16	15	15	19

[a] From 1984 origin is based on students' usual places of domicile. Prior to 1984 origin is on fee-paying status except for EC students domiciled outside the United Kingdom, who from 1980–1 are charged home rates but are included with students from abroad.
[b] University first diplomas and certificates.
[c] In 1980 measurement by age changed from 31 December to 31 August.

Source: Social Trends, 1992, p. 61; from Education Statistics for the United Kingdom. Crown copyright

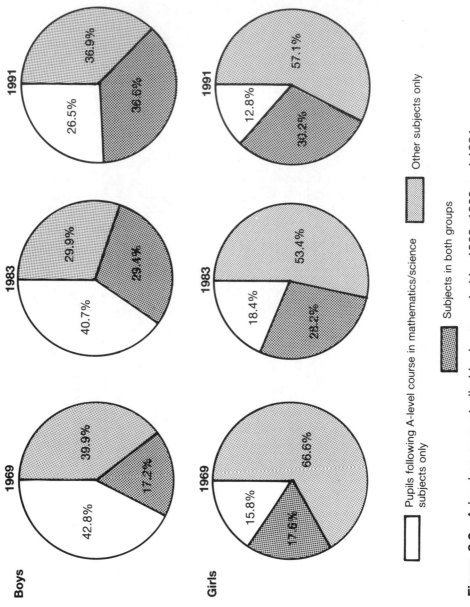

Figure 8.2 A-level courses studied by boys and girls, 1969, 1983 and 1991.
Source: Department of Education and Science, *Statistics of Schools*, 1985, pp. 41–2 and 1991, p. 175. Crown copyright.

have become more concerned to gain relevant, formal qualifications. Nevertheless, as they approach entry into the labour market, discriminatory processes become more powerful. Vocational training, for instance, whether apprenticeships or government schemes, is renowned for the way that men in predominantly male trades are hostile to female recruits (see for example Cockburn, 1987). Professional qualifications, except in nursing and teaching, have also been monopolized by men, though the situation improved considerably during the 1980s as young women entered medicine, law and accountancy in increasing numbers (see for example Crompton, 1992).

Improvements have certainly not made educational opportunities identical for men and women. A major differentiating process is choice between subjects in the formal curriculum (see figure 8.2). Only seven girls for every ten boys embarked on at least one A-level in a mathematical or science subject. There is thus a shortfall of women undergraduates reading natural science and engineering degrees. Girls are dissuaded from taking certain subjects – like technical drawing, physics and chemistry – and are, instead, directed towards studies considered more fitting for females. Young women provide most recruits to courses leading to qualifications in home economics, teaching and the caring occupations. Such courses re-emphasize familial values which, when internalized, may detract from concentrated pursuit of an occupational career.

Subject choice suggests that inequalities within schools are related to other aspects of gender inequality, though the precise nature of such a relationship is disputed. The sex segregation of the labour market (see section 4.2) is perhaps the most important factor, since many girls will orientate themselves towards occupations known to offer reasonable access for women. Restricted job opportunities are compounded by conventional perceptions of appropriate gender identities. The pressure not to transgress the boundaries of femininity is one of the hardest obstacles to overcome. This is not just a matter of sexist attitudes, but is embedded in routine, everyday practice. Both Griffin (1985) and Banks et al. (1992) show that in their teenage years women are more closely pulled into the domestic arena than men: they make substantially greater contributions to housework; they are more constrained in their leisure activities, being less mobile and highly dependent on the availability of a female 'best friend'; and the predominant form of peer-group culture revolves around the anticipation of heterosexual partnerships. This emphasizes the extent to which a gender-specific hidden curriculum interacts with the formal content of education. Levels of formal achievement of girls continue to improve. However, gender identities associated with other spheres of activity are reinforced within schools, which cannot compensate for the wider patriarchal culture (see section 8.5).

Racial inequalities in education

Table 8.2 documented some striking inequalities of attainment between and within different ethnic groups. The aggregate statistics document sharp gender divisions within different minority groups, indicating that gender and race interact with each other. Class differences likewise also exist within ethnic groups. Those Asian groups with high levels of educational attainment often contain an extensive middle class.

Ethnic minorities face some of the same obstacles to high levels of educational attainment as do white people. Inferior class position, low parental levels of education, and social and religious restrictions on female social participation, present barriers. These affect some ethnic groups more than others. Language difficulties may occur, but they apply largely to first-generation immigrants. Probably the most potent distinctive hindrance is British racism. The testimonies of students frequently record racist assumptions and treatment in school. These include recalling racist harassment from fellow pupils, observing that teachers deploy racial cultural stereotypes, and expressing antipathy to parts of the curriculum that glorify British imperialism.

Schooling, inequality and the economy

In this section and section 8.3, we have seen how complex is the relationship between schooling and economic life. The many objectives of schools are difficult, if not impossible, to achieve simultaneously. The conditions that promote equal opportunities are hard to reconcile with the school's role in social control and allocation. From the process of schooling, certain unintended effects emerge which produce conflict both within the school and in the wider society. Figure 8.3 illustrates how the legitimate, economically relevant objectives of schools generate social divisions and conflicts.

Summary

1 The study of education and social mobility suggests that although, in absolute terms, more working-class boys are taking A-levels and going on to college, their chances *relative to other classes* have not improved much since the Second World War.
2 Sociological research showed that under the tripartite system the type of school a pupil attended was the main factor determining educational achievement. The introduction of comprehensive schooling was designed to remedy class inequalities, but the statistical relationship between class and attainment is still evident.

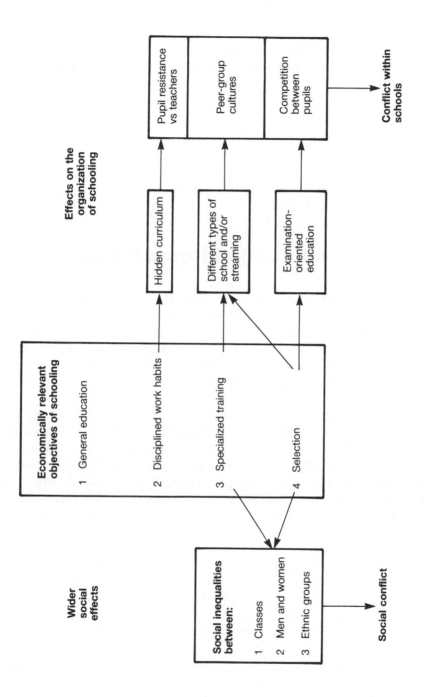

Figure 8.3 Some economically related effects of schooling: a simplified summary

3 Gender inequalities in educational achievement had been almost
   entirely eliminated by 1990, with females performing as well or better
   than males until aged 18+. Inequality becomes very apparent,
   however, on entry into the labour market.
4 Ethnicity affects educational attainment, though it is mediated by
   class and gender.

Related topics

A detailed consideration of the other major part of the Nuffield Mobility
Study can be found in section 3.7. Gender inequalities in education are
discussed further in section 4.5.

8.5   Social and Cultural Reproduction

Schools do not merely prepare children for work. They also help
reproduce social norms and cultural preferences. Intentionally or
unintentionally, schools play a part in the creation of adults socialized to
be consumers, Britons, decent citizens, spouses and the like. That people
should accept such identities, and adopt corresponding patterns of
behaviour, is just as important to the maintenance of society as is
economic production.

Schools encourage their pupils to absorb social rules, manners and
values – like those which mark out gender divisions in society. Boys and
girls are treated differently by their teachers, who expect and encourage
different behaviour from the two sexes. For instance, as box 8.1 showed,
a group of teachers at A-level, when asked what their students would be
doing in five years' time, replied almost exclusively with reference to
work in the case of boys, but marriage in the case of girls. Girls may
'learn to lose' through schools. When asked to rank fellow students in
terms of academic performance there is a strong tendency for girls to
underestimate their own attainment when making comparison with boys.
Boys overestimate their own attainment in comparison with girls. Images
of superiority and inferiority abound. Teachers at all levels frequently
highlight gender differences, whether by having competitions between
the boys and the girls, or by comparing the behaviour of one sex with the
other for the purpose of maintaining discipline. Social norms regarding
gender, exhibited in the mass media and other cultural institutions, are
rehearsed and performed in the classroom.

A similar point, concerning a different aspect of social reproduction,
was made by Rutter et al. (1979). They argue that 'to an appreciable

extent children's behaviour and attitudes are shaped and influenced by their experiences at school and, in particular, by the qualities of the school as an institution' (p. 179). They advanced evidence for believing that the organization of the school was itself partly responsible for levels of delinquency. Delinquency (the measure of which was having been 'officially cautioned or found guilty of an offence in a Juvenile Court on at least one occasion') varied considerably among pupils at 12 non-selective secondary schools in inner London. For example, the rate for boys varied between 44 and 16 per cent, that for girls between 11 and 1 per cent. Other factors are important in predicting whether an individual is likely to be delinquent (academic attainment, parental background, etc.) but the secondary school itself has an independent influence. In this sense, schools make a difference to social reproduction.

Schools also familiarize students with a distinct British cultural tradition. Dickens and Shakespeare, Handel and hymns, and the history of the British Empire and British parliamentary democracy, find prominent places in the school curriculum. Tolstoy, reggae and international communism are less common. One objective of government advocacy of the national curriculum was to reinforce the former, traditional elements. Thus, for example, the English curriculum emphasizes the canon of classical British literary texts and excludes authors who are not themselved British born. What is worth knowing, which books are worth reading, and the like, are defined selectively, though before the national curriculum not very systematically, by schools for their pupils. To some degree a British culture is reproduced over time as generations of pupils are exposed to similar cultural themes. This generates some overt conflict, especially among students from ethnic groups who see themselves and their predecessors as victims of dominant and racist elements of British culture. The West Indian and Asian groups whom Mac an Ghaill (1988) talked with all held that some elements of their school curriculum were either culturally irrelevant or offensive.

While the educational experience certainly does include exposure to the values and beliefs which legitimate the social, economic and political arrangements of British society, the importance of the school in social and cultural reproduction is easily overestimated. Many writers on education have described this exposure as a process of the transmission of a 'dominant ideology'. Loosely, the 'dominant ideology' refers to a set of beliefs, attitudes and dispositions which presuppose that Britain is the best of all *possible* worlds. It is argued that the dominant ideology has the effect of persuading subordinate groups and classes that they owe allegiance to existing laws, institutions and practices. Put another way, schooling legitimates the existing social order and each individual's location within that social order. In this way individuals come to 'fit in' with the social system, performing willingly the social roles into which they become inserted. Under such conditions there would be a high degree of *social integration* based upon *consent*. Some authors see this as an ideal situation, consensus being the basis of an orderly society. Others see the dominant ideology as disguising or excusing unacceptable inequalities which benefit privileged groups and classes. But there are a number of problems with either of these versions of 'the dominant ideology thesis'. It is doubtful whether it adequately describes the condition of modern Britain. And it is doubtful whether schooling has this kind of effect.

First, it may never be possible to estimate to what extent a dominant ideology is transmitted through schools because it is almost impossible to isolate their effects from those of other institutions that also contribute to social and cultural reproduction. For instance, it would be difficult to tell whether girls learn the characteristics of the wife-mother role more from the school than from within her own family, or from reading newspapers and magazines, or from her peer group. Social norms are reinforced by countless experiences and episodes, only some of which occur within the school. McRobbie's research on a group of schoolgirls reminds us how complex are the processes of social reproduction. The subculture of the group of working-class girls studied by McRobbie (1978) was contrary to the values of the school. The resistance of these girls, however, revolved around an *exaggerated* model of femininity: 'marriage, family life, fashion and beauty all contribute massively to the feminine anti-school culture.' McRobbie points out that by paying attention to these interests, to an obsessive extent, the girls are 'doing exactly what is required of them'. Paradoxically, their own culture, created in resistance, becomes the most effective agent of social control over their adult roles. What McRobbie also shows, though, is that at least for these girls the peer group is much more influential than the school in the process of social reproduction. The girls resisted the cultural and social models of behaviour preferred by the school, but the identity adopted instead was even more likely to reproduce working-class wives, with all the attendant disadvantages of that position.

A second and more substantial objection to the dominant ideology thesis is the proposition that there is no one set of beliefs identifiable as a dominant ideology. There is little agreement as to the content of the dominant ideology in Britain. Evidence from attitude surveys regarding social and moral beliefs and political opinions shows widespread disagreement. One ambitious attempt to see if there was social consensus in Britain found that no value was shared by more than 75 per cent of the population, except for a vague nationalism. If there is a dominant ideology, a large proportion of the population has failed to 'internalize' it. The ideological role of the school thus can be little more than a negative one, excluding or dismissing unacceptable beliefs and values, preventing pupils being exposed to the unthinkable and the unspeakable.

Third, the variety and inconsistency of most people's beliefs, the widely charted existence of subcultures, even the existence of different kinds of schools for different kinds of pupils, should make us sceptical of accepting any simple view of the process of the transmission of a dominant ideology. Indeed, it would be surprising if the educational system transmitted the same kind of knowledge and norms to all students when their future lives are likely to be widely different. It might, then, be argued that the most important ideological effect of the schooling system is to persuade people to accept their own place in the division of labour in an unequal society. Schools and colleges sort people by giving them different qualifications or 'credentials'. Credentials are widely considered to justify why some people get better jobs than others. Somehow, possessors of credentials are thought to *deserve* their privileges. Credentials, obtained during formal education, are usually justified in terms of *merit*. Students are said to succeed because of hard work and aptitude. Those who obtain well-paid jobs or positions of power claim to deserve their privilege. This disguises the existence of social distinctions of class, gender and ethnicity, which lie behind examination performance.

Summary

1 Schools make a contribution, difficult to measure, towards social and cultural reproduction. This occurs in a more complex way than is suggested by the dominant ideology thesis.
2 Perhaps the most important 'ideological effect' of schooling is that the distribution of qualifications is considered adequate justification of the allocation of people to positions, unequally rewarded, in the division of labour. The experience of compulsory educational competition serves to legitimate general social inequality.

Related topics

Issues of dominant and subordinate cultures are dealt with in sections 10.1, 10.2 and 10.4. More material on femininity and cultural stereotypes of women is to be found in section 4.4.

Further reading

The textbook by Burgess (1986) is a useful survey of evidence about Britain. A brief introduction to the study of education and mobility is Heath (1980). There are a number of ethnographic studies which quote extensively pupils' own accounts of their, predominantly negative, experiences of secondary schooling, including Griffin (1985) on girls and Mac an Ghaill (1988) on ethnic groups. The survey-based research reported by Banks et al. (1992) examines the transitions of young people on reaching the minimum school-leaving age.

9 Health

9.1 Introduction

> What does illness mean? Our level of 'being well' is wrong. Most people
> are half not well most of the time. The thing is that so many people are not
> actually aware of it. It is the way that expectancies of what constitutes a
> healthy person are being lowered that I find so distressing. If we have a
> good year, or a good day, we think 'Wow!', but it should not be like that.
> What makes us sick is the environment we live in. ('Vera' in Mitchell,
> 1984)

The topic of health is an emotive and political one. During the 1980s the
Conservative government's first concern was to reassure the public that
health provision was being maintained and to argue that with greater
efficiency the service could be improved, even without additional
resources. However, despite the language of reform, the public has
consistently shown that it is less than convinced about progress, being
concerned by the apparent decline of the National Health Service
(NHS).

At the same time, there has been a growing awareness of new hazards.
Questions such as the dangers of radiation, which seemed rather
academic just a few years ago, or issues such as the debilitating
consequences of long-term unemployment, which used to affect only a
small proportion of the population, are now – more and more –
occupying the centre of the political stage. Although many politicians
may regret or even try to ignore the fact, there is no doubt that questions
of health which came firmly back on the political agenda in the 1980s are
here to stay.

Two legislative Acts – the National Health Insurance Act of 1911 and the National Health Service Act of 1946 – are landmarks in the evolution of British health-care policy. The National Health Insurance Act of 1911 represented an incomplete revolution in British health-care policy. This scheme of Lloyd George's Liberal government applied to only a small portion of the British people and, even by the 1940s, a mere 40 per cent of the population was covered by national health insurance. By 1946, there was overwhelming popular, professional, and political enthusiasm for the notion that health care should be a right for all people and an obligation of the state. Aneurin Bevan, the Labour government minister responsible, later described the NHS as 'the most civilized achievement of modern government'. Well over four decades after its birth, many people remain more than willing to echo those sentiments. It is largely for this kind of reason, of course, that the Conservative government under Mrs Thatcher first of all tried to keep a fairly low profile in the area of health and to make fundamental shifts in health-care provision without any fanfare.

Now, as before, there is popular and professional dissatisfaction with the existing medical-care system; complaints arise from both the providers (doctors, nurses and ancillary workers) and the consumers (patients). Also, the change in party control in 1979, with the election of a Conservative government, was equal in significance to the Liberals coming to power in 1906 and the Labour Party in 1945. Undoubtedly, the Conservatives also have demonstrated a mission to change the nature of health-care provision. There, perhaps, the similarities end. In the earlier periods, the inadequacies of the health-care system were highlighted by Britain's involvement in war – the Boer War at the turn of the century and then the Second World War. The low standards of health in Britain were vividly revealed as the population was mobilized into the war efforts. The Conservative's policy shift, in contrast, has been more concerned to limit state involvement in health-care provision and argue for financial restraint. In fact, the 1980 government report *Inequalities in Health* (known as the Black Report after the chairman of the working group, Sir Douglas Black), which did reveal the shortcomings of the health care of the nation, was released quietly in the hope that the contents and recommendations would go unnoticed. So, in contrast to the administrations that received much heralded reports in earlier eras – the report of the Commission on the Poor Law (1909) and the Beveridge Report (1942), which set the tone for the health reforms that followed – Mrs Thatcher's government tried to muffle the most significant report on health to emerge in the present era. By the mid 1980s, however, the question of the future of the NHS was developing as a major public issue, and by the beginning of the 1990s the Conservative government had made an important contribution in setting into place a series of significant reforms. The NHS reforms, first unveiled in the 1989 White Paper

Working for Patients, heralded some remarkable activity. The aim of the government proposals was to make the NHS more sensitive both to patients' needs and to market forces. Much attention focused on the effect of the reforms on the hospitals, particularly following the Tomlinson Report (1992) on changes recommended for London. However, the reforms under way in community care services were equally radical, although at first they received less prominence in the media. Nevertheless, the 1990 NHS and Community Care Act provided the considerable potential to reshape community care services in Britain. In many respects the situation remains volatile and it will take the rest of the 1990s to appreciate fully the impact. Indeed, it remains unclear whether these reforms are simply a staging post to further changes or whether a period of consolidation lies ahead. While any increasing privatization and commercialization of medicine and the accompanying demise of the NHS are likely to continue to arouse deep emotions within many sections of the electorate, the issues of health go way beyond the question of the funding of the NHS. Indeed, we need to ask whether any of the political parties have really grasped the problems in the current provision of health care.

9.2 Sociological Interest in Medicine

Among sociologists, concern with health and illness is comparatively recent. Even after the Second World War, the sociology of medicine was very slow to develop. The important point to grasp is the tremendous feeling of satisfaction and accompanying complacency that followed the launching of the NHS in 1948. It raised all sorts of hopes that the benefits of health would be available to all, irrespective of wealth or position in society. In short, unlike the early developments in the sociology of education, there was not the feeling that the health-care system was a major determinant of social stratification. The question of whether health determines your place in society, the kind of issue posed in other fields decades earlier, only began to be addressed in the early 1980s. Against this background, the importance of (and the potential political dynamite contained within) the Black Report can be appreciated (see later).

The past decade has been an important period in the examination of health problems. Probably the most important contributions of sociologists in this field have been to provide fresh insights that implicitly challenge traditional medical assumptions. The crucial shift, which occurred towards the end of the 1970s, was the recognition that sociologists should be concerned with issues of health and illness rather than of medicine. Stacey (1978) emphasized that we should have a sociology surrounding the problems of health and illness and of suffering. Stacey suggested that the shift should be towards being more patient-oriented than doctor-oriented. In other words, we should not readily assume that what is in the interests of the doctor is equally in the interests of the patient. The wider implications of this message are that the medical profession may have a somewhat narrow or limited vision in terms of improving health (see also Stacey, 1988).

Sociological analyses of medical-care systems provided some relevant, but mostly unheeded, messages for policy-makers. Most importantly, feminists have come to identify the health-care system as one of the major arenas of the subordination of women. Increasingly, the work of feminists has been crucial in one major respect – challenging the male-dominated professionalism of medicine, while re-creating or reasserting female self-confidence by 'demedicalizing' (that is, taking out of the direct medical sphere) such natural female functions as menstruation, conception, pregnancy and child-bearing. The most fundamental challenge revolves around the definition of health and the treatment of illness.

Health and illness: medical or social conditions?

As Kelman (1975) has pointed out, 'perhaps the most perplexing and ambiguous issue in the study of health since its inception centuries or millenia ago, is its definition' (p. 625). Kelman argues that the definitional problem is crucial to the determination of health-care policy. Usually the problem is dodged by assuming, implicitly or explicitly, that 'health' is the absence of illness. However, this simply evades the issue.

The first scientific approach to health originated with the development of the machine model of the human body. With this conception, 'health' came to be regarded as the perfect working order of the human organism. Kelman argues that the methodologies that developed from this view (and continue to dominate in the practice of medicine today) consider illness to be both *natural* (biological) and occurring on an *individual* basis. It then follows that treatment is pursued essentially on an individual basis, using surgical or chemical means of treatment. This approach relegates the recognition and implications of social causes of illness to secondary importance.

While an appreciation of the social basis of many diseases and ill-health has a long history, the great thrust in this direction came with the publication of the Chadwick Report in the mid nineteenth century. The report showed that the gross inadequacy of water supplies, drainage and facilities for the disposal of refuse in big towns were the biggest sources of disease. The study of epidemics – or *epidemiology* – had begun in earnest. Since that time there has been a great deal of writing and research on social epidemiology, and the development of an *environmentalist* approach to health. However, this approach is clearly in conflict with the biological and individual orientation of the classical school which underpins most of modern medicine.

Some theorists take the argument one stage further by suggesting that health is primarily socially, rather than strictly biologically, determined. In short, we cannot view 'health' as independent of the form of society in which it is studied. This insight lays the foundation of a materialist or radical epidemiology, which has gained support among some sociologists. They argue that, since the advent of capitalist industrialization, the primary determinants of death and illness in the West have shifted gradually from infectious and communicable disease – spread by unhealthy conditions such as malnutrition, overcrowding or inadequate sanitation – to a rather different set of problems, such as cancer, heart disease, hypertension, stroke, mental illness and drug addiction.

The total number of deaths in Britain in 1990 was just under 642,000. The largest cause of death was from circulatory disorders and the next largest was from cancer. As figure 9.1 illustrates, there have been identifiable shifts since the Second World War. The data, standardized for age, show that rates (expressed as numbers per 1000 population) for all causes have fallen for both males and females with the exception of cancer. Rates for circulatory diseases, including all types of heart disease, fell by almost a quarter for males and a third for females.

The death rates for cancer can be divided into rates for different types of cancer (figure 9.2). While female death rates from cancer of the cervix uteri have remained relatively unchanged over time, those from lung cancer increased rapidly over the 20 year period since 1971 and by 1990 had almost doubled. Nevertheless, despite this large increase, lung cancer remained only the second largest cancer killer of women behind cancer of the breast. While female mortality rates from lung cancer have increased dramatically since 1971, the rates for males have dropped by 16 per cent after remaining fairly static until the early 1980s. This is thought to be the outcome of the beneficial effects of anti-smoking campaigns targeted at young and middle-aged males. Similarly, stomach cancers have shown significant reductions – for both males and females – and this in turn is thought to be due to improved eating habits. Cancer, of course, is not necessarily a fatal disease and about half of all people with cancer have a good chance of survival.

The most striking feature of figure 9.1 is the virtual disappearance of deaths due to infectious diseases (notably the disappearance of tuberculosis). Relatively, very few young people die, particularly those aged between 5 and 35, and a high proportion of the deaths in this age group

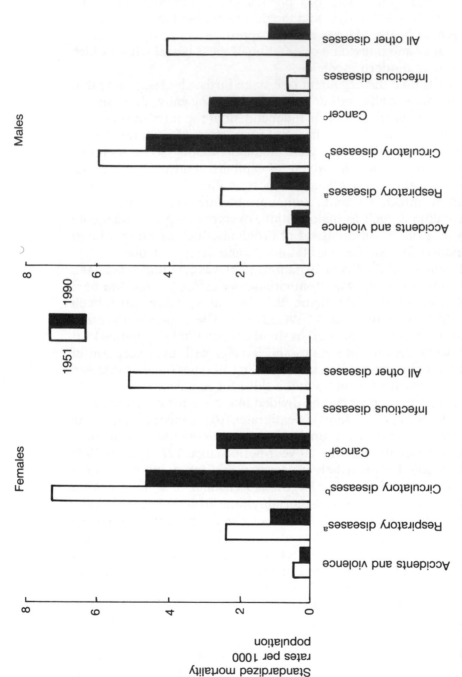

Figure 9.1 Selected causes of death, males and females, United Kingdom, 1951 and 1990

a In 1984 the coding procedure was changed, reducing the number of deaths assigned to respiratory causes.
b Includes heart attacks and strokes.
c The figures for neoplasms include both malignant and benign cancers.
Source: Social Trends, 1992; from OPCS and Register Office data

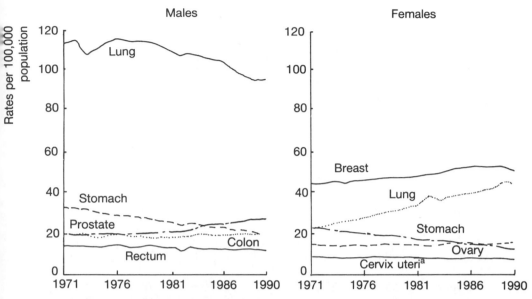

Figure 9.2 Standardized mortality rates from cancers, by sex and selected sites, United Kingdom, 1971–1990

[a] Includes fallopian tubes and broad ligaments.

Source: *Social Trends*, 1992; from OPCS data

are caused by accidents and violence rather than disease. Today victims do not die in physical proximity to one another, or in a socially concentrated space at a particular moment in time. Yet the 'new' diseases are as much the epidemics of our century as tuberculosis was in the nineteenth century. In contrast to traditional medicine, which looks to disease or illness as an individual problem, the environmentalist approach therefore emphasizes the fact that the victims of poor health share a common social history.

Sociologists differ in their emphasis, but all probably recognize the dangers of being too complacent about the success of conventional medicine. We should recognize two features of Western society that are easily overlooked. First, whereas death rates have declined owing to the reduction of childhood illnesses and other infectious diseases, premature death has increased, particularly among males, owing to conditions arising from self-destructive behaviour, such as industrial cancers, diet-related disorders and routinized stress. As table 9.1 shows, the main shift in life expectancy relates to a much greater expectation of childhood survival. The dramatic decline of infant mortality, for example, is shown in figure 9.3.

Second, and equally disturbing, is the fact that medicine is almost wholly ineffective against some of these new epidemics. There is thus a

Table 9.1 Expectation of life[a], by sex and age, United Kingdom, 1901–2001

	1901	1931	1961	1981	1991	2001
Males						
At birth	45.5	58.4	67.9	70.8	73.2	74.5
At age:						
1 year	53.6	62.1	68.6	70.7	72.8	74.0
10 years	50.4	55.6	60.0	62.0	64.0	65.2
20 years	41.7	46.7	50.4	52.3	54.2	55.4
40 years	26.1	29.5	31.5	33.2	35.1	36.2
60 years	13.3	14.4	15.0	16.3	17.6	18.7
80 years	4.9	4.9	5.2	5.7	6.3	7.0
Females						
At birth	49.0	62.4	73.8	76.8	78.8	79.9
At age:						
1 year	55.8	65.1	74.2	76.6	78.3	79.3
10 years	52.7	58.6	65.6	67.8	69.5	70.5
20 years	44.1	49.6	55.7	57.9	59.6	60.6
40 years	28.3	32.4	36.5	38.5	40.0	41.0
60 years	14.6	16.4	19.0	20.8	21.9	22.7
80 years	5.3	5.4	6.3	7.5	8.3	8.8

[a] Further number of years which a person might expect to live.

Source: *Social Trends*, 1992; from Government Actuary data. Crown copyright

Rate per 1000 live births

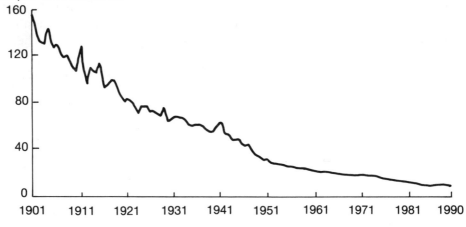

Figure 9.3 Infant mortality: Great Britain, 1901–1921; United Kingdom, 1922–1990.
Source: *Social Trends*, 1992; from OPCS and Register Officer data

danger of focusing entirely upon what doctors manage to accomplish. In fact, Stark (1977) argues that 'death is now socially constructed and distributed with barely any reference to nature or to disease in the traditional sense. It is endopolic, not endemic, the outcome of politics, not biology' (p. 686).

Summary

1   Sociological interest in this area was late to develop. Recently, it has moved its focus from studying doctors and medicine to consideration of the conditions for health and illness.
2   There is an argument over whether medical or environmental models of health are most appropriate. Among environmentalists, radical epidemiologists have pointed to new sorts of illness characteristic of the twentieth century which may be attributable to social pressures and forces.

9.3   The National Health Service

Public opinion and the NHS

One of the remarkable features of the NHS is the speed with which it became 'a national institution as British as the Battle of Britain or Wimbledon. Like the Monarchy, it is at once beyond fundamental criticism and the subject of interminable complaint' (Widgery, 1988, p. 28). However, the early 1990s have featured discontent with both the monarchy and the NHS. The *British Social Attitudes* survey aims to monitor underlying changes over time. Since 1983 the surveys have asked people about their levels of satisfaction with the National Health Service in general and with specific services in particular. Between 1983 and 1990, the proportions reporting dissatisfaction with the running of the NHS nearly doubled. Table 9.2 shows that by 1990 the proportion had

Table 9.2   Levels of satisfaction with the way the NHS is run, 1983–1990

	1983 (%)	1984 (%)	1986 (%)	1987 (%)	1989 (%)	1990 (%)
Satisfied (very or quite)	55	51	40	41	36	37
Neither	20	19	19	20	18	15
Dissatisfied (very or quite)	25	30	39	39	46	47

Source: Harrison, 1992; from *British Social Attitudes* surveys

dropped to just over one-third expressing satisfaction, with nearly one-half expressing dissatisfaction.

In most years the respondents were asked specific questions concerning satisfaction with particular aspects of the health service. As table 9.3 demonstrates, most dissatisfaction is expressed in relation to hospitals. Dissatisfaction with being an in-patient doubled between 1983 and 1990, while the level of dissatisfaction with hospital out-patient work has remained consistently high since 1986. In contrast, dissatisfaction with other areas of the health service has remained remarkably low throughout the past decade.

Table 9.3   Dissatisfaction with parts of the NHS, 1983–1990

| | *Quite or very dissatisfied* | | | | |
	1983 *(%)*	*1986* *(%)*	*1987* *(%)*	*1989* *(%)*	*1990* *(%)*
Local doctors/GPs	13	14	13	12	11
NHS dentists	10	10	9	11	11
Health visitors	6	8	8	8	8
District nurses	2	3	3	4	4
Being in hospital as an in-patient	7	13	13	15	15
Attending hospital as an out-patient	21	29	29	30	28

Source: Harrison, 1992; from *British Social Attitudes* surveys

Solomon (1992) has considered the apparent anomaly between the comparatively high level of dissatisfaction with the NHS as a whole and the low levels of dissatisfaction for specific services. He suggests that respondents reply to questions about specific services primarily on the basis of their own experience. In contrast, it may well be that the general question about the National Health Service elicits views based more on political opinion than on personal experience. Solomon concludes from the *British Social Attitudes* surveys that there appears to be a lot more dissatisfaction with the political institution known as the National Health Service than with the specific health services offered within it. However, Solomon reports results from two other surveys which 'indicate that the same questions asked in a different context . . . elicit a slightly different picture of the attitudes of the public towards the NHS,' suggesting more satisfaction. Nevertheless, the shift in attitudes over time remains and, whatever the 'true' figure, there are substantial levels of dissatisfaction reported in all the recent surveys of public opinion regarding the NHS. Solomon points to the consistent evidence in surveys of widespread perceptions of the need for improvement in a range of specific services. There are certainly differences according to the service (table 9.4). So,

Table 9.4 Aspects of the NHS in need of improvement, 1987–1991

	Saying in need of some or a lot of improvement			
	1987 (%)	1989 (%)	1990 (%)	1991 (%)
GP services				
GPs' appointment systems	47	45	41	45
Amount of time GP gives to each patient	33	34	31	35
Being able to choose which GP to see	29	30	27	29
Quality of medical treatment by GPs	26	27	24	31
Hospital services				
Hospital waiting lists for non-emergency operations	87	85	83	76
Waiting time before getting appointments with hospital consultants	83	86	82	71
Hospital casualty departments	54	59	52	50
Condition of hospital buildings	53	61	54	58
Quality of medical treatment in hospitals	30	36	31	36
Quality of nursing care in hospitals	21	27	24	27

Source: Harrison, 1992; from *British Social Attitudes* surveys and OPCS *Omnibus Survey*, August and November 1991. Crown copyright

for example, around 80 per cent identify waiting lists for non-emergency operations, and waiting time before getting appointments with hospital consultants, as areas where improvement is needed. In contrast, people seem relatively happy with the quality of care which they receive once they are in hospital. Similarly, there seem to be fewer worries about the GP services, although again it is in the area of appointment systems where most think that improvements need to be made.

The success of the NHS

Spending on health care in Britain, as in other industrialized countries, has grown steadily since 1960, both in total and as a share of the gross national product (GNP). However, even though more resources than ever before are being used in the health sector, the system shows increasing signs of strains. Those who established the NHS believed that demand would fall once a high standard of care was freely available to all. This clearly has not happened. In fact, the trends in use of the NHS are upwards. Does this mean that, as a nation, we are getting less healthy and so the NHS needs to cope with the increasing number of health problems? Or does it mean that people are getting more healthy but are wanting treatment for less serious complaints which in previous times they may not have bothered about? Certainly, the apparently simple question 'Has the NHS been a success?' needs a rather complex answer.

Leichter (1980) raised this question before the start of the Conservative programme of health reforms. He contrasted the health-care policy of four countries – West Germany, Britain, the Soviet Union and Japan – and stressed that 'the most obvious difficulty lies in the definition and measurement of the term success.' Leichter went on to illustrate this difficulty. For him, one measure of the relative achievement of the NHS would be to compare the intention and purposes of the original Act with its actual accomplishments. The purpose of the National Health Service Act was 'the establishment in England and Wales of a comprehensive health service, designed to secure improvement in the physical and mental health of the people in England and Wales, and the prevention, diagnosis, and treatment of illness'. Furthermore, it was the intention of the Act 'to divorce the care of health from questions of personal means or other factors irrelevant to it'.

Essentially – but we say this with increasing reservations – medical care is available to all the residents of Britain, regardless of their ability to pay. In broad terms, therefore, the original objectives of the NHS have been achieved. But there are other questions that need to be asked. Are the British healthier under the NHS than before? Leichter noted that, compared with the period at the start of the NHS, people today are much less likely to die in infancy, and are less likely to die from diseases such as tuberculosis, influenza and pneumonia, appendicitis, or whooping cough. In contrast, they are more likely to die from heart disease and cancer (see figure 9.1). However, Leichter stressed caution, for he noted that the general trends that appear in Britain are similar to those appearing in other economically developed countries such as the USA, France, West Germany, the Soviet Union and Japan over roughly the same period of time. The crucial point is that the explanation for the similarity of these trends lies less in the nature of their health-care delivery systems (that is, the way their health-care systems are organized) – which vary enormously in the countries mentioned – than in their general socio-economic conditions. So, while the overall health of the British people is better today than it was before the NHS was introduced, it would be unsafe simply to attribute these improvements to the NHS.

Problems of interpreting health statistics

There are immense problems in defining and measuring health outcomes, even within individual countries where definitions and reporting conventions are relatively uniform. Studies of patterns of ill-health are handicapped by the difficulty of obtaining information on sickness and disease rates. As a consequence, mortality rates continue to be the main focus of attention, but they may be of more limited value than is sometimes realized. The historical decline of infectious diseases and tuberculosis, and the increased incidence of chronic and degenerative diseases (like multiple sclerosis, cancers, strokes etc.), suggest that the relationship between mortality (i.e. death rates) and morbidity (i.e. sickness rates) has changed and may now be fairly weak. Therefore, the study of mortality rates may not provide an adequate or accurate picture of patterns of ill-health: inequalities in death may not be similar to inequalities in health. This, essentially methodological, problem may be particularly serious in the case of mental illnesses, which rarely result in death but yet account at any one time for around one in four NHS patients.

Schieber and Poullier (1989) conclude that 'measuring outcomes – beyond aggregate measures such as life expectancy, infant mortality, and cause-specific mortality – is not generally feasible.' Whether this is true or not, the difficulty in measuring outcome or performance explains why most comparative studies are focused on *inputs*, such as the number of doctors and hospital beds, or what some term *intermediate outputs*, such as the number of physician visits, the lengths of stay in hospital, the number of procedures and so on. A particularly important intermediate outcome is the question of access to care. A concern is whether there is an 'inverse care law' operating – that is, whether those with the greatest medical need have the least access to care.

Health-care expenditure: international comparisons

Comparing health-care expenditures across countries is hazardous. International comparisons are only as good as the basic underlying data upon which they are based. In fact, countries produce data for their own administrative reporting systems, not for international comparisons. Nevertheless, strenuous efforts have been made to produce meaningful figures, and Schieber et al. (1992) have analysed health-care expenditure and utilization trends in the 24 member countries of the Organization for Economic Cooperation and Development (OECD), a Paris-based international organization whose members are the Western industrialized countries (table 9.5). The most striking finding is that the United States spends considerably more on health than other countries, both in

Table 9.5 Total and public health expenditures for 24 OECD countries, 1980–1990

Country	Total expenditure (% GDP)			Public expenditure (% total exp.)		
	1980	1985	1990	1980	1985	1990
Australia	7.3	7.7	8.2	63	72	68
Austria	7.9	8.1	8.4	69	67	67
Belgium	6.7	7.4	7.5	83	82	83
Canada	7.4	8.5	9.3	75	75	73
Denmark	6.8	6.3	6.3	85	84	83
Finland	6.5	7.2	7.8	79	79	81
France	7.6	8.5	8.8	79	77	74
Germany	8.4	8.7	8.1	75	74	73
Greece	4.3	4.9	5.5	82	81	76
Iceland	6.5	7.1	8.6	88	91	87
Ireland	9.2	8.2	7.0	82	77	75
Italy	6.9	7.0	7.7	81	77	76
Japan	6.4	6.5	6.5	71	73	72
Luxembourg	6.8	6.8	7.2	93	89	91
Netherlands	8.0	8.0	8.2	75	75	71
New Zealand	7.2	6.6	7.4	84	85	82
Norway	6.6	6.4	7.4	98	96	95
Portugal	5.9	7.0	6.7	72	56	62
Spain	5.6	5.7	6.6	80	81	78
Sweden	9.4	8.8	8.6	93	90	90
Switzerland	7.3	7.6	7.7	68	69	68
Turkey	4.0	2.8	4.0	27	50	36
United Kingdom	5.8	6.0	6.2	90	87	84
United States	9.2	10.5	12.1	42	41	42
OECD average	7.0	7.2	7.6	76	76	74

Source: Schieber et al., 1992, p. 4; from OECD data

absolute dollar terms and relative to gross domestic product (GDP). It is the only country to be spending over 10 per cent of its GDP on health.

Table 9.5 contains the estimated shares of *total health expenditure* as a percentage of GDP for the OECD countries for 1980, 1985 and 1990. In 1980, the share of total health spending in GDP ranged from 4.0 per cent in Turkey to 9.4 per cent in Sweden, with 9.2 per cent in the United States and with an OECD average of 7.0 per cent. The United Kingdom was below this average with an expenditure of 5.8 per cent and, although its health expenditure has risen, it has remained significantly below the average for OECD countries throughout the period. Prior to the 1980s, the OECD average had increased steadily, but it has risen at a slower rate ever since, reaching a mean or average of 7.6 per cent in 1990. In 1990, the shares ranged from 4.0 per cent in Turkey to 12.1 per cent in the United States, with the United Kingdom at 6.2 per cent.

Table 9.5 also indicates *public* health expenditure as a percentage of total health expenditure for OECD countries. In fact, the trends for the public share of health spending relative to GDP largely mirror those for total expenditure. Health spending in the public sector accounts for about three-quarters of health spending, on average, in the OECD countries, and for more than 60 per cent of spending in all countries except the United States and Turkey, where it is 42 per cent and 36 per cent respectively. That 84 per cent of health expenditure in the UK is within the public sector suggests a high commitment to the National Health Service. However, with only 5.2 per cent of GDP devoted to public health the total amount spent is, comparatively, very low. The figure is below the average of expenditure among the 24 OECD countries. Less surprisingly, the United States is well below the OECD average in this respect. What is evident from table 9.5 is how health spending in the public sector has been relatively stable since 1980 among the Western industrialized countries.

Certainly the evidence suggests that – despite claims to the contrary – the National Health Service has not been profligate with resources compared with most other industrialized countries.

Summary

1 Between 1983 and 1990, the proportions reporting dissatisfaction with the running of the NHS nearly doubled. Dissatisfaction with the NHS as a whole appears to be much higher than that with the specific services it offers.

2 Spending on health care in Britain, as in other industrialized countries, has grown steadily since 1960, both in total and as a share of gross national product.

3 The similarity in trends in health care among industralized countries lies less in the nature of the health-care delivery systems (that is, the way health-care systems are organized) than in general socio-economic conditions.

4 Compared with other industrialized countries, health expenditure in Britain is low.

9.4 Unequal Access to Health Care

Distribution of, and access to, the health-care system remains important.
Is there equal access, by all people, to the nation's health services? Is
there reasonable uniformity in the quality and quantity of services
available to all people? This is related to the question of whether an
'inverse care law' operates: do those with the greatest medical need have
the least access to care?

Traditionally there has been concern over three major problems of
inequality from which the health service suffers: a geographical maldistribution of medical resources; a related social class maldistribution of
resources; and irrational priorities within the medical community. On all
three counts, the NHS fails to provide all sections of the British
population with equal health services. The regional and social class
variations inherited by the service in 1948, and which were part of the
rationale for developing a National Health Service, have not really been
remedied in the last four decades or so. Also the priorities of medical
care continue to cause concern and dispute as resources become more
restricted. In the past decade, gender and race inequalities in health care
have been much more widely recognized. We will now consider regional,
class, gender and ethnic inequalities and then focus on the problem of
relative priorities in the NHS.

Regional variation

In the 1970s, there was considerable regional variation in the availability
of medical personnel and services. Although there were exceptions, the
general picture showed that the industrial areas of northern England and
Wales had fewer and older hospitals, fewer hospital beds per head of
population, higher patient/doctor ratios, and inadequate specialized
medical personnel and facilities. One result of these regional differences
is that there tend to be higher mortality rates in the northern regions of
the country than in the southern regions. Townsend et al. (1988) have
recently focused particularly on the link between poor health and
material deprivation within 678 wards in the north of England. Their
principal findings were that differences in health between local populations are very considerable and 'perhaps more consistently wide than
presumed in recent scientific discussion' (p. 153). There have been
attempts to remedy this situation, for instance by prohibiting general
practitioners from starting new practices or taking over existing practices
in over-doctored districts. However, there has always been a general

tendency for the NHS, through its system of funding health facilities, to perpetuate these geographical inequalities. Those regions which were well off in terms of hospital beds and doctors in 1948 have been given relatively more money, while those with fewer resources have been given less. The recent attempts to move somewhat closer to a policy of reallocating resources to needy areas is not new, but, when resources are limited, trying to make such shifts inevitably results in some levelling down rather than a general levelling up of services.

A useful advance in the past decade was the attempt to produce figures by which one can assess variations in service – in terms of both input and output. In the annual report of the NHS ordered by the Social Services Secretary (DHSS, 1984), there was a breakdown of finance for each of the 14 English health regions, showing whether their level of spending was within targets to meet the Conservative government's estimate of patients' needs in those areas. The figures showed that the government had succeeded in cutting back finance to three of the 'over-provided' regions: the North-West Thames, North-East Thames and South-East Thames regional health authorities. They provided extra resources for another three: the North-Western, Trent and Northern regional authorities. Continuing to try to correct regional imbalances, while restraining spending in the public sector, helps to explain the outcry from areas where medical facilities have been traditionally well resourced.

Most spectacularly, there were varying responses to Sir Bernard Tomlinson's Report (1992) on health provision in London in which plans to cut London's hospital services by almost a quarter caused particular consternation. In one respect the report was no surprise for everyone knew that London had too many hospital beds. Apart from the expected outcry from directly interested parties, the underlying concern of others was whether enough resources would be put into alternative provision by family doctors and community health teams. Health care should not be seen in isolation from other services. For example, London has a very poor provision of residential care for the elderly. An equitable allocation of resources needs to take account of a wider range of factors.

Variation by social class

There is, of course, a relationship between the health status of people from different social classes and the regional differences we have just discussed. Some of the geographical areas traditionally starved of resources also contain a higher proportion of people from the lower social classes. While the social class aspect has generally been less talked about, the evidence suggests that the differences in health care provision for different social classes have *not* diminished since the introduction of the NHS. In some instances, the sad fact is that these differences have actually increased. The persistent efforts of Peter Townsend in particular, together with the work of pressure groups such as the Child Poverty Action Group, have meant that this point was never entirely lost. In 1977, David Ennals, the Secretary of State for Social Services of the then Labour government, set up a working group on inequalities in health, under the chairmanship of Sir Douglas Black, to review information about differences in health status between the social classes, to consider possible causes of such differences and the implications for policy, and to suggest further research. The report of the working group (Black Report, 1980) was submitted to the Secretary of State of the new Conservative government in April 1980. It received a chilly reception. Instead of the report being properly printed and published by the DHSS or HMSO, it was arranged that only 260 duplicated copies of the typescript be publicly made available, in the week of the August bank holiday. Major organizations within the NHS, including health authorities, did not receive copies. There was, in other words, an attempt by the government to bury the report. In most respects this plan backfired, for the media, their curiosity aroused, became much more interested in the contents of the report than they might have been otherwise. With its subsequent publication (Townsend and Davidson, 1982), the Black Report has been brought to the attention of an even wider audience. Why was this report regarded as so alarming that the government tried to disown it?

Its overall message was that the health problems of the British working class are probably more a function of their overall standard of living than of the health system itself. This had immense political implications for the Conservative government, whose economic policy – whether deliberate or not – involved lowering the living standards of certain vulnerable sections of British society. The last thing the government wished to be told was that, while a better distribution of health facilities and personnel would have some impact on the health status of the poor, an improvement in their general standard of living would have a much greater impact.

What was particularly important about the Black Report was that it provided evidence, previously only available in academic journals, that the lower down the social scale you are, the less healthy you are likely to be and the sooner you can expect to die. Furthermore, it also pointed out that if you are working class, then your *children* will also be at greater risk of injury, sickness and death. Using later statistics than those contained in the Black Report, figure 9.4 shows that this is still the case. Despite improvements in infant mortality, differences between the social classes remain. Rates are higher for those whose fathers are in the unskilled or semi-skilled groups. Infant mortality rates were over three-quarters higher among babies whose fathers were unskilled than those

Figure 9.4   Infant mortality, by social class of father, England and Wales, 1989 (deaths under 1 year of age per 1000 live births within marriage).
Source: *Crown copyright*, 1992; from OPCS data

whose fathers had a professional occupation. No other statistic more clearly illustrates the unequal level of health enjoyed by different sectors of the population.

Inequalities are often hard to measure and difficult to interpret. For example, although the figures clearly show that working-class children are much more vulnerable to fatal injury and illness, their parents are less likely than those in the middle classes to take them to the doctor. This may be because they perceive the quality of care to be poor and costly rather than because they are unconcerned about illness. Health services in predominantly working-class areas are often less accessible and of poorer quality. In fact, working-class adults may typically be more sick than middle-class adults before they seek help. Middle-class patients tend to get better care from their GPs, not only because they live in areas which are better served, but also because they are more skilled at demanding and obtaining the care they need.

It is impossible to do justice to the contents of the Black Report by quoting a couple of examples. However, taking mortality rates as an indicator of health, the report showed (see table 9.6) that, since the Second World War, men in occupational classes IV and V had made no

Table 9.6 Mortality rates per 100,000, men and married women, England and Wales, 1949–1972

Occupational class	Age	Men 1949–53	1959–63	1970–2	Married women 1949–53	1959–63	1970–2
I and II	25–34	124	81	72	85	51	42
III		148	100	90	114	64	51
IV and V		180	143	141	141	77	68
I and II	35–44	226	175	169	170	123	118
III		276	234	256	201	160	154
IV and V		331	300	305	226	186	193
I and II	45–54	712	544	554	427	323	337
III		812	708	733	480	402	431
IV and V		895	842	894	513	455	510
I and II	55–64	2,097	1,804	1,710	1,098	818	837
III		2,396	2,218	2,213	1,202	1,001	1,059
IV and V		2,339	2,433	2,409	1,226	1,129	1,131

Source: Townsend and Davidson, 1982, p. 68. Black Report © DHSS 1980. Introduction © Peter Townsend and Nick Davidson. Reproduced by permission of Penguin Books Ltd

improvements in their health, even in absolute terms. Between 1949 and 1972, the number of deaths per 100,000 working-class men in the 45–54 age group dropped by only 1 from 895 to 894, while in the 55–64 age group the death rate actually *increased* from 2339 to 2409.

In contrast, women fared better than men in these comparisons: their health had shown an improvement in all occupational and age groups. But, again, there were differences between social classes. Upper-class women were getting healthier a lot more quickly than their lower-class contemporaries: also, their chances of surviving childbirth and producing healthy babies were greater. In 1972, the maternal mortality rate for class V women was nearly double that for women in classes I and II.

Beyond showing class differences, the Black Report made bold assertions regarding the implications of the evidence. The poorer health of the lower social classes, it said, was a result not just of failings in the NHS, but of glaring inequalities in income, education, nutrition, housing and working conditions, as well as cultural differences. The crucial conclusion was that quite drastic shifts in social policy were needed to establish equal health standards. However, Whitehead in *The Health Divide* (1988) noted in a report, which confirmed and updated the evidence of the Black Report, that 'a co-ordinated policy to reduce inequalities in health in the UK has not been adopted,' (p. 341). The government had explicitly rejected the implications of the Black Report.

Health care and the subordination of women

Since the mid 1970s, the health-care system has become more and more an area of concern for feminists. There has been the spread of direct, collective action by women, reflecting and influenced by the women's health movement in the USA. An increasing number of local women's health groups meet regularly in Britain. Indirectly stemming from this activity, there has been growing recognition of the significance of medical care in women's everyday lives. Medicine affects women to a much greater degree than it does men. The gender role system, which relegates caring and nurturing duties to women, results in them being involved in the health-care system not only as workers but also from within the family, in a way in which most men are not.

While the vast majority of workers in the health-care system are women, they are concentrated at the bottom end of the medical hierarchy. Nearly 90 per cent of nurses, but only just over one-fifth of practising doctors, are women. Few of those at the top of the profession are women: only 1 per cent of surgeons and 12 per cent of gynaecologists. In brief, males dominate the highly technical and the most responsible roles in the medical hierarchy – those, incidentally, which also provide the greatest status and salary. In contrast, those jobs involving the greatest contact with the patient and the most practical, day-to-day, caring functions are occupied by women.

The ambivalent relationship between women and medical care has a long history. Before the rise of the modern medical profession, lay healers were traditionally female; midwives in local communities, for instance, were also skilled herbalists or 'wise women'. Gradually, during the Middle Ages, women began to be forced out of medical care by men. Eventually, women were left only midwifery, and even this came to be taken over in the seventeenth century by male barber-surgeons after the invention of forceps which women were not allowed to use. Certainly, by the eighteenth century, the medical profession had become completely male-dominated.

However, the outlawing of the traditional female healer that was associated with the rise of the medical profession did not bring an end to women's traditional caring role. Women were simply relegated to the subordinate role of helpers in the increasingly technological, expanding, male medical profession.

Women are, however, the biggest users of health-care facilities, which is largely due to their twin roles of child-bearers and child-rearers. The enormous variations in access to NHS abortion services across different regions illustrates one kind of problem; it is difficult to believe that such discrepancies would be tolerated in services that affected men more directly. More generally, many women are dissatisfied with the attitudes of the health service to their health problems and needs, particularly on consultations with doctors and in the tendency to treat pregnancy and childbirth as illnesses. Indeed, the appropriateness of the intervention of the medical profession in women's lives is a fact of health care challenged by the women's health movement. Much of the feminist literature and practical action in the women's movement has focused, in a critical manner, on the medical control of reproduction through control of contraception, abortion and childbirth facilities, as well as the management of the supposed female 'disorders' such as the menopause. Giving birth, preventing birth, or even having an abortion, are not intrinsically the concern of the medical profession. Women are not necessarily, or even normally, ill in connection with these matters, although of course they may be so. There is tremendous resistance towards attempts to 'demedicalize' reproduction, because of the threat to medical specialities dealing specifically with women, for example gynaecology and obstetrics.

Feminists argue that male control over women's reproduction is central to the question of male domination and female subordination. Feminists want women to control their own health and fertility. Recent action towards this goal has taken the form of women's health groups, where women learn about their own bodies, and 'well woman clinics', where women are able to consult other women about their health. There are calls for a woman's right to choose whether or not she gives birth at home with the help of a midwife, or in hospital. At present, something like 99 per cent of births in Britain take place in hospital and home births are definitely discouraged. Furthermore, labour is often induced for the convenience of the hospital and women are forced to assume the delivery position which affords most ease to the doctor.

Ethnicity and health

In considering the ethnic dimension of inequality in health, the Black Report (1980) noted the sparseness of evidence. One curious feature of the Black Report was that in the poorer occupational classes, it seemed that men born in India, Pakistan or the West Indies tended to live longer than their British-born counterparts. There is a whole set of reasons to explain this apparent anomaly. Certainly, as the authors of the Black Report point out, men and women prepared to cross oceans and continents in order to seek new occupational opportunities in Britain do not represent a random cross-section of people, any more than did the

Pilgrim Fathers who crossed from Britain to America in 1620. Neverthe-less, this finding is in stark contrast to the stereotype of the black immigrant, which was widely circulated in the 1960s and early 1970s, as someone who brought disease into the country and who, once here, created a risk of epidemics because of origin and living conditions.

McNaught (1984) suggests that health authorities in areas where ethnic minorities live have not developed adequate strategies to meet the needs of these groups. The pattern of mortality and morbidity that emerges from a variety of studies is that, apart from those haemoglobinopathies such as sickle cell anaemia and thalassaemia that have a clear race/genetic link, the health conditions that affect ethnic minority groups in Britain are the same as for the population as a whole. However, he notes that the incidence of certain conditions is much higher among ethnic minority groups, and this can be linked to their socio-economic conditions in Britain, including changing patterns of diet, increased smoking and urbanization. In short, McNaught stresses that the social consequences of racial inequality are much more powerful determinants of the health status of ethnic minority groups than genetic or racial susceptibilities.

Not only do ethnic minorities suffer the general problems that reflect their class position, but they experience additional difficulties because of language and cultural differences, or because of racial discrimination. Many people from the ethnic minorities, particularly women, either speak no English or speak it poorly as a second language. Consequently, they have difficulty in obtaining treatment, advice and guidance from health workers. Health authorities have tried to surmount this, but their initiatives have been very patchy. Cultural barriers have also created problems for the NHS. Perhaps most well-known in this regard is the insistence of some Asian women on seeing only female doctors. McNaught (1984) reports that some health authorities have responded to this need, but many have not. More recently, McNaught (1988) has argued that 'it is possible for the NHS to develop a strategy which encourages both more ethnically sensitive services and equal opportuni-ties in NHS employment' (p. 123) and he sets out proposals for policy development in this area. As with women's concerns, there is the view in ethnic minority communities that effective change in the NHS will only occur if they are more active in identifying and lobbying for their interests. McNaught acknowledges that this may be true, but also points out that consumer pressure can be ignored or subverted by managers. He stresses that 'in developing a strategy to engage with the NHS, *ethnic minorities* will need to be familiar with the character of decision-making on policy issues in the NHS' (p. 123, italics added). While much more attention is being paid to ethnicity and health care, not everyone is confident about the appropriateness of the outcome.

Sheldon and Parker (1992) have suggested that the importance of ethnicity or race as a variable is perhaps being overstated. Their point is that 'ethnic groups, in so far as they exist, are not socially homogeneous and may span different class locations. Therefore, analysing studies by ethnic groups may hide wide differences in important characteristics. In brief, the concentration on ethnicity tends to displace the importance of class.' Their argument raises the spectre of the process of 'racialization' in the collection and use of official statistics. Discussion has largely centred around the collection of 'race' data and ethnic monitoring, particularly crystallizing around the issue of an 'ethnic question' in the decennial census. A new form of routine ethnic data collection is the minimum data sets which all provider units in the National Health Service have to generate for each patient. In addition to personal details and health-related information, ethnicity is to be recorded using the same categories as in the census, though no individual socio-economic group information will be recorded. Sheldon and Parker suggest that we can expect a flood of papers in the mid 1990s looking at ethnicity and medical outcomes such as hospitalization, diagnosis and length of stay. The political consequence may be that we will be increasingly encouraged to conceptualize the population along ethnic lines (racialization).

Focusing on ethnic groups usually leads to concentrating on so-called cultural differences rather than on socio-economic structure and racism. The centrality of racism in structuring black people's experience is implicitly denied. Sheldon and Parker stress how there may be elements of victim blaming, or of portraying ethnic cultures as alien, deviant, deficient and in need of change. In epidemiological studies, differences in outcome are often wrongly ascribed to racial differences. A telling example from an earlier time usefully makes the point. At the turn of the century, high mortality rates in Glasgow were attributed to the racial stock of the Irish immigrants even though mortality rates in Ireland were a lot lower. In reality, the excess was much more the outcome of the poor social conditions in which migrant labour lived (Williams, 1990).

The pathologizing of groups or cultures is perhaps most marked in psychiatry, where all black minority groups have a greater chance of being diagnosed as schizophrenic or as suffering from the more serious forms of mental illness (Grimsley and Bhat, 1990). These figures are deeply contentious. Socio-biologists would perhaps suggest that these figures represent very real differences between ethnic or racial group-ings. The figures may be partially explained by the severity of prejudice, but may also reflect the racist bias in the diagnostic categories and methods used by psychiatrists.

The extent to which racial discrimination actually occurs in the NHS is difficult to determine. A significant number of black people are convinced that it does occur and, as McNaught (1984) argues, this may be more important than attempting to demonstrate its actual incidence or volume. He goes on to suggest:

> What this issue does demonstrate is that interaction of poor professional standards and racial discrimination reduces access to services, causes unnecessary suffering, discomfort and probably deaths. This has a corrosive effect on the relationship of individual black and ethnic minority patients and health workers. Further it weakens these groups' support for the National Health Service. (p. 26)

Priorities in health care

In broad terms, there has always been a tendency for the less glamorous medical-care problems and medical specialities to receive a disproportionately small share of the available resources. Although the 1984 NHS Report (DHSS, 1984) showed some improvement, the elderly, the mentally ill and the mentally retarded in long-stay institutions still tend to be neglected. In contrast, the medically more prestigious, acute, health-care problems attract both the more able physicians and more government resources than the areas of chronic illness. In particular, the recent concern has been whether the shift to community care and away from the use of long-stay institutions has been adequately resourced. Furthermore, as private medicine increases and there is an increased stress on the commercialization of public medicine, an extra ingredient will be that the more financially rewarding medical work will get increasing attention. Sadly, Leichter's (1980, p. 194) macabre comment, 'that those who are neither quick to die nor quick to recover tend to be short-changed under the NHS', still obtains.

Summary

1 The demand for health care continues to rise, though it is unclear whether this means that people are less healthy than before.
2 The new kinds of illness from which Britons suffer are equally prevalent in other advanced industrial societies.
3 Access to health care in Britain is unequal. There are differences by region, by social class, by gender, by ethnicity, and as a result of decisions about priorities in allocating resources between medical specialisms.
4 Women, especially because of their conventional role in the family, are likely to have more contact with the health services than men.
5 Women are poorly represented among the higher ranks of the

medical profession, and many feel that male medical control over women's health is unacceptable.

6 Ethnic minorities tend to suffer from the same illnesses as the rest of the population but, owing to their class position and restrictions on access to health care, they are prone to relatively high levels of ill-health.

7 The pathologizing of groups or cultures is most marked in psychiatry, where all black minority groups have a greater chance of being diagnosed as schizophrenic. The reasons for this are highly contentious.

9.5   The Controversies of the 1980s

The chief causes of unequal health identified in the Black Report were poverty and the relatively poor access of low-income groups to the knowledge and facilities that help to maintain physical fitness. The main recommendation which followed was that a determined shift of resources should be regarded as a top priority – a shift towards community care and greater provision for mothers, young children and the disabled. The report proposed a whole set of measures, for example: free milk for infants without their parents undergoing means tests; an enlarged programme of health education; better facilities for recreation in the inner cities; the establishment of national health goals; and strong anti-smoking measures. It recommended that child benefit allowance be increased to 5.5 per cent of average gross male industrial earnings.

In a somewhat curt foreword to the report, Patrick Jenkin, the then Social Services Secretary, claimed that the report's 37 recommendations, if implemented in full, would cost upwards of £2 billion a year, and added that this was 'quite unrealistic in present or any foreseeable economic circumstances . . . I cannot, therefore, endorse the group's recommendations.'

The report was as 'unrealistic' for some radical critics as it was for the Social Services Secretary of the Conservative government. Gray (1982) points to its implicit contradictions. In brief, the report notes the important role of economic and associated socio-structural factors, the persistent and deep-rooted nature of unequal income and wealth distribution, and the possibility that the present economic system may actually promote inequality. Yet, at the same time, the report assumes that a number of major changes are capable of being enacted to substantially reduce or eliminate inequality, whilst still leaving the framework of these economic and social-structural factors unchanged.

Gray is not denying that there is scope for making changes that might help to reduce the severity of inequalities and their origins, but rather suggesting – quite rightly as it turned out – that such changes would be resisted. Perhaps the authors of the report were the ones who were being 'unrealistic' in their assumption that a favourably inclined government would really go very far along this road.

The Black Report is too radical for some, not radical enough for others. Nevertheless, whatever view one takes, one must recognize that one of the original contributions of the report is the willingness to see medical care as only one (and perhaps not even a very efficient) way in which health can be influenced. It revives the possibility of focusing health programmes on other areas of social policy such as housing or income maintenance.

The epidemiological debate is between those who emphasize the importance of the lifestyle or behaviour of individuals, and those who stress the importance of the socio-economic environment. The former 'the individualists', are essentially conservative in seeing the problem being solved within the existing class structure – by members of the working class changing their lifestyle so that it more closely matches that of the healthier social classes. In contrast the latter, who can be termed 'the environmentalists', form a more radical group in terms of health, seeing the need to change the way that society is structured, to enable the health status of the working class to be improved.

Each group emphasizes different aspects of the economic system. The conservative group stresses the process of consumption: for example, social differences between social groups in smoking, diet and exercise. The radical group stresses the process of production: for example, social differences in exposure to dangerous work systems and industrial chemicals. There are many ways of summarizing the arguments, but roughly the distinction can be posed as – does smoking kill workers or does working kill smokers?

One issue concerns the dangerous substances to which members of the working class are particularly exposed. It has long been recognized that there is a close association between certain occupations and diseases. For example, in 1755 Sir Percival Pott noted that chimney sweeps' intimate contact with soot led to a high incidence of scrotal cancer (Graham and Reeder, 1972), while the expression 'mad as a hatter' came into the English language long before we knew the effects of mercury, which was used in felting, on the central nervous system. Nowadays the notion of occupational diseases is familiar territory, but the attack has been widened. For example, Robinson (1984) suggests that the high level of cervical cancer among the wives of men working in dusty jobs, such as underground miners, or with leather, chemicals, metals or machine oils, can be explained by their exposure to the industrial chemicals inadvertently carried home on their husbands' clothes and bodies.

Further, it is argued that a much wider public is being exposed to the hazards of industrial chemicals through air and water pollution. Again, it is the members of the working class who are most at risk. As Thunhurst (1982) stresses, 'the geography of the modern industrial city testifies to two centuries of uneven social distribution of the noxious discharges from the production process.' So the more expensive, uphill and upwind middle-class areas traditionally contrast with the cheaper, downhill and downwind working-class areas – many of which are also now subject to high lead levels from car exhausts.

While working produces its hazards, so too does unemployment. Within the existing economic system, unemployment is an increasing source of stress, and thus of ill-health. As the working class is especially vulnerable to the stresses of unemployment during a recession – and consequently to the stresses associated with reintegration into the economy in the subsequent period of economic growth – the cyclic nature of the economic system causes, as Brenner (1979) noted, 'a widening of the socio-economic differentials in mortality'. Of course, radical commentators have made less of the possibility that removing workers from the hazardous environment of the workplace may actually produce better health. For some, unemployment may have actually saved their lives!

A report by Leonard Fagin on unemployment and family health came out in 1981. As with the Black Report, only a few expensive copies of the report were released, without proper publicity, though it was later published commercially (Fagin, 1984). Fagin's report illustrates that the use of unemployment as a tool to control inflation has far greater costs than simply the loss of production and tax revenues, the additional payments of supplementary benefits, and so on. He catalogues the severe consequences of long-term unemployment, echoing previous research that goes back to the recession of the 1930s. Significantly, Fagin concentrated on the family as a whole rather than simply the male 'breadwinner', and found that there was financial worry and family tension and that husband, wives and children all displayed signs of distress – depression headaches, asthmatic attacks, loss of appetite.

Government policy has been highly resistant to recognizing such structural causes of ill-health. According to its view, eliminating health inequalities primarily requires those individuals currently at risk adopting a more healthy lifestyle. Emphasis is placed on the consumption process within which individual choice is regarded as of paramount importance. The approach is often termed 'the lifestyle theory of health' because of its emphasis on individuals' behaviour patterns, or lifestyle. An early exponent expressed it forcefully: 'we are today altogether too willing to forget . . . that we are in an important way responsible for our own state of health, that carelessness, gluttony, drunkenness, and sloth take some of their wages in illness' (Kass, 1975). Thus, diet, smoking and other behaviour patterns are seen to be major determinants of health. Health differences between social classes are therefore largely regarded as a reflection of the different lifestyles of each group; members of social class I live longer than members of social class V primarily because of their more healthy lifestyle. According to the conservative model of health, social class differences are to a large extent explained by different class *attitudes* towards health and medical care. It is said that lower-class individuals do not place a high value on health, implying that working-class people are their own worst enemy.

Critics describe the lifestyle model of health as expressing an ideology of 'victim blaming' and suggest that the emphasis on the behaviour of the individual, rather than on the economic system, is welcomed and even exploited by the forces that benefit from the lack of fundamental change within the system. For example, the food and cigarette industries, sometimes with the assistance of government, maintain existing, profitable consumption patterns, using the pressures of various kinds of advertising and marketing techniques.

In an important study, *Health and Lifestyles*, based on a national survey of 9000 individuals, Blaxter (1990) focused on issues such as measured fitness, declared health, psychological status, life circumstances, health-related behaviour, attitudes and beliefs, but especially on the question: 'Which is the more significant for health: the social circumstances in which people live, or lifestyle habits such as exercise and smoking?' The results were very revealing and, in particular, help us to understand the complex relationships between the various factors. After all, one would expect that *both* lifestyle and environment would have some effect. In fact, her broad conclusion was that ' "circumstance" – not only socio-economic circumstances and the external environment, but also the individual's psycho-social environment – carry rather more weight, as determinants of health, than healthy or unhealthy behaviours' (p. 233). Moreover, Blaxter identifies that some behaviours, particularly not smoking, *are* relevant to health. However, her important finding is that 'they have most effect when the social environment is good: rather less, if it is already unhealthy.' Or, put another way, 'unhealthy behaviour does not reinforce disadvantage to the same extent as healthy behaviour increases advantage.' The corollary to the finding that social circumstances are more important than lifestyle habits is that lifestyle may have greater effect among the more privileged than the disadvantaged.

Summary

1   The Black Report demonstrated severe and persistent class inequali-

ties in health and attributed this more to *social* causes than to restricted access to health-care facilities.

2   The report recommended a shift in resources. It declared that improvements in social conditions were essential to reduce the degree to which lower social classes suffered more illness. Nothing has changed since the publication of the report.

3   Unemployment leads to additional ill-health for both the unemployed person and other members of the household.

4   An epidemiological debate continues between those who emphasize the lifestyle or behaviour of individuals, and those who stress the importance of the socio-economic environment.

5   Blaxter (1990) indicates that social circumstances are more important than lifestyle habits; also, that changing lifestyle habits may have greater effect among the more privileged than among the disadvantaged.

9.6   NHS Reforms

The government's concern in espousing the importance of healthy lifestyles has recently been overshadowed by the 'revolution' in the organization and management of the NHS. Both the size and the symbolism of the NHS have made it such a daunting target for reform. It became the largest employer in the country and, probably also in the whole of Europe. While the Labour Party, as the main opposition, focused on what it regarded as incremental privatization and increasing commercialization, the nature of the 'revolution' in the NHS has perhaps been missed. The crucial feature is the centre – periphery relationship, the fact that the NHS delivers *local services* but is a *nationally funded* organization. This has produced a basic tension within the NHS throughout its history. The contradiction between moving towards the localization of priority-setting and decision-making on the one hand, and the tendency towards centralization on the other, has been one aspect of developments in many areas of the public sector, such as education and law and order. In brief, stress on local accountability can be seen as a mechanism by which local management were to be made much more accountable to the centre.

Increasingly, the Thatcher admininistrations (1979–90) focused more directly on good management as the major solution to the problems of the NHS. The linchpin of the approach emerged with the Griffiths Report in 1983, *NHS Management Inquiry*, and is concerned with the link between local accountability and central control. It successfully challenged the principle of consensus management by a team, and

instead strongly advocated the appointment of chief executives or
general managers at all levels in the NHS. The government required all
health authorities to implement such change by the end of 1985. The
changing inter-professional relationships in health care were quickly
noted by the health-care professions but only much later came into public
consciousness. At this stage, as far as public perceptions were concerned,

Source: *The Guardian*, 10 October 1991

the emphasis appeared to be upon achieving 'efficiency savings' which
simply meant the attempt to obtain more by way of service from the same
level of spending. While these so-called efficiency savings quickly
produced adverse public reaction, the process was not different in kind
from the practice of cash limitation which had been started under the
Labour governments of the 1970s.

The Conservative manifesto for the 1987 election did not promise – or
indeed threaten – much radical change for the NHS. However, as a result
of increasing concern about funding, the government announced a
review of the NHS. Discussions surrounding the review were wide-
ranging. The only option which everyone soon recognized as being
disallowed from the outset was significantly *increased* funding, for this
would be in conflict with the primary fiscal objective of holding down
public expenditure to facilitate reductions in income tax.

The majority of proposals which emerged for the future of the NHS in
Britain can be split into two main groups: those which sought to change

the funding base of the NHS and those which sought to introduce greater internal competition and a more efficient delivery system. There was much discussion surrounding the three basic models of funding: national taxation, social insurance, and private insurance. The most fundamental ideas to survive into the final draft of the review were the opt-out plan for hospitals, and the highly controversial American-inspired scheme to fund GPs to go out and buy health care for their patients. The White Paper *Working for Patients* published in January 1989, was perhaps the most

Table 9.7   Comparison of old and new NHS

Old system	*New system*
Role of district health authorities DHAs have confused responsibilities covering both the overall planning of services and the running of hospitals and other units.	DHAs' main responsibility becomes the health of local people. They will assess health needs and decide how best they can be met.
Funding of health services DHAs funded for the services which happen to lie within their boundaries, largely on the basis of historic patient flow.	DHAs will be funded to purchase services on behalf of their residents. Funding will, over time, reflect the size, age and relative health of DHA populations.
Hospitals and other units receive a budget from their DHA, often bearing little relation to the number of patients they are expected to treat in the coming year (inadequate funding arrangements for patients from other DHAs).	Hospitals and other units receive funding from those DHAs with which they agree NHS contracts (or service agreements). These contracts set out the quantity, quality and cost of services to be provided through the year. (Smaller patient flows not covered by contracts in advance dealt with by on-off 'cost per case' contracts.) This links funding and the activity required to meet identified health needs.
Management of health services Too many tiers of bureaucracy controlling the activities of hospitals and other units.	All hospitals and other units take on greater responsibility for their own affairs, so the people providing services are the ones taking decisions. Some become self-governing NHS trusts, independent of DHAs but still firmly within the NHS.

Role of GPs

Few incentives for hospitals to respond to the needs and preferences of GPs and local people.

DHAs consult extensively with local GPs on preferred referral patterns and conduct surveys of local opinion as part of the process of agreeing contracts with hospitals on the services to be provided.

Some GPs become GP fundholders, giving them the financial backing to purchase certain hospital services directly for their patients.

Integrating health services

Very little integration between primary and secondary care, and little attention focused on achieving the right balance of prevention and treatment. FPCs not under management of regional health authorities.

DHAs (responsible for hospital and community health services) and FHSAs (responsible for primary health care services) both under the management of RHAs, ensuring effective joint working to improve the health of local residents. DHAs' new role in focusing on health puts them in a better position, jointly with FHSAs, to achieve a balance of prevention and treatment.

Community care

Progress in community care had been slower and less even than hoped for, with some areas making great strides while others were less well advanced.

The NHS will play a key role, alongside local authorities and the voluntary and private sector, in the new arrangements.

Arms-length inspection units and new complaints procedures will contribute to improvements in quality of care in residential homes. New specific grants will benefit people who suffer from mental illness or abuse alcohol and drugs. Preparations have been made for the publication of local authority community care plans and the introduction of new funding structures to support people in residential and nursing homes.

Source: Harrison, 1992, p. 8.

important document to emerge in the 40 years since the inception of the NHS.

The implementation of the National Health Service and Community Care Act 1990, which incorporated proposals for reforming the way that health and social services are provided throughout the UK, has the underlying concept of the creation of a competitive market. As there was no precedent for such a system within the UK and experience abroad was also limited, the scale of the experiment is quite remarkable. Indeed, in an editorial feature *Health Care UK 1991* suggests 'it represents a very bold venture in public sector reform, the boldest of all the many measures that the Government have taken in their 12 years of office' (Harrison, 1992, p. 7). How the Department of Health sees the differences between the old and the new NHS in shown in table 9.7.

Purchasers and providers

The most crucial shift in setting up the internal health market is the requirement that all district health authorities should divide themselves into a purchasing arm and a providing arm. The task of districts is now to concentrate on their purchasing and commissioning functions, which involves assessing the health needs of their population, identifying the services to meet those needs and setting priorities when resources are insufficient to meet all identified needs. As figure 9.5 shows, contracts are the centrepiece of the new system. Purchasers define by contracts what the providers are to do and the prices at which they will be paid for their services.

What figure 9.5 shows is that district health authorities are only one kind of purchaser, and the Act also provided for groups of GPs to

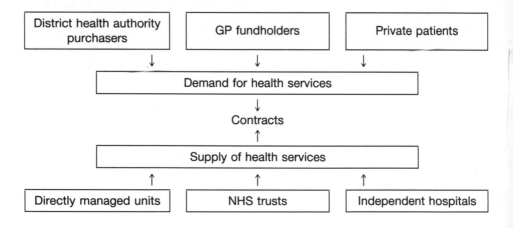

Figure 9.5 The central role of contracts.
Source: Harrison, 1992

become fundholders and to establish contracts with providers in rather similar ways. The GPs involved are allocated budgets out of the funding that would previously have gone to health authorities. While the GP fundholding scheme only began on a small scale, there were early signs that it may be proving effective in improving care standards as GPs 'shop around' in order to get better services for their patients (Harrison, 1992, p. 12). However, it could eventually prove to be the case that the extra administration involved may offset these possible benefits and some unintended consequences may follow.

The other shift which has attracted considerable attention is the development of NHS trusts as provider units. The central presupposition behind introducing trusts is that greater independence from district management will result in better performance. While the notion of competition between different providers is rapidly gaining acceptance as appropriate, already it is becoming clear that the government is not willing to allow the trusts to be quite so genuinely independent, particularly in the key area of capital finance, as some enthusiasts for the idea had hoped. It will take a long time and some ingenuity to assess the effects of the trusts scheme.

While much of the media coverage has concerned the desperate plight of some hospital acute units, there are other shifts taking place which have been less noticed. Described as 'the best known piece of external auditing in the 1980s' (Harrison, 1992, p. 19), the Audit Commission's report *Making a Reality of Community Care* in 1986 identified a number of serious problems in the existing arrangements for financing and providing care for the so-called priority groups – frail elderly, mentally ill and handicapped people. The government reacted by asking Sir Roy Griffiths to consider the issues. His report *Community Care: Agenda for Action* (1988) 'accepted most of the criticisms [of the Audit Commission's report] but did not fully absorb their logic. In particular, he attempted to keep a clear line between social and health care and, by emphasising the need for joint planning rather than changes to the existing pattern of responsibilities, made no proposals relating to changes in the boundaries of health or local authorities' (Harrison, 1992, p. 19). The government's own proposals were even further watered down (especially rejecting the proposal that funds for community care should be ring-fenced – that is, funds could be earmarked and only used for that purpose). However, there are still important measures for community care in the 1990 National Health Service and Community Care Act which represent radical change, opening the way for innovation, in both market and administrative behaviour. Whether it is all likely to work is a moot point. Certainly Hudson (1992), focusing on the central role of care management in the new community care strategy, is very sceptical.

There are two other areas of government initiatives in health which bear the hallmark of the 1990s. The first is in public health strategy, and the second is the health component in the Citizen's Charter, designed to make public service providers more attentive to the needs of users. The Patient's Charter lists seven existing rights (see box 9.1) and adds three new ones: a maximum waiting time for elective surgery, access to information on services, and full and prompt treatment. It is tempting to see the charter movement as a series of presentational gimmicks and, for the Patient's Charter to mean anything, 'it needs to be more precise and hence enforceable' (Harrison, 1992, p. 26).

A shift from a preoccupation with health care to more concern for the better health of the population is clearly a move to be welcomed. The consultative document *Health of the Nation* (Department of Health, 1992) was heralded as the first time in England (a similar framework had already been prepared for Scotland and Wales) that a range of

---

Box 9.1 The Patient's Charter rights

Every citizen has the following established National Health Service rights:

- to receive health care on the basis of clinical need, regardless of ability to pay;
- to be registered with a GP;
- to receive emergency medical care at any time, through your GP or the emergency ambulance service and hospital accident and emergency departments;
- to be referred to a consultant, acceptable to you, when your GP thinks it necessary, and to be referred for a second opinion if you and your GP agree this is desirable;
- to be given a clear explanation of any treatment proposed, including any risks and any alternatives, before you decide whether you will agree to the treatment;
- to have access to your health records and to know that those working for the NHS are under a legal duty to keep their contents confidential;
- to choose whether or not you wish to take part in medical research or medical student training.

Source: Harrison, 1992

performance targets had been suggested, the achievement of which would require action across most parts of government. However, some commentators already suggest that 'the omens for the success of the *Health of the Nation* are not good', pointing to, for example, the leisurely timetable set out. Quite simply, however, Harrison states the fundamental weakness: 'the document fails to address the central issue of poverty' (Harrison, 1992, p. 23).

The organizational and financial reforms contained in the National Health Service and Community Care Act 1990 and the introduction of policies for achieving better health based on prevention rather than treatment are fundamental realignments. It will take a long time for all the benefits and the costs of the transformation to emerge. It is hard to predict how the 'revolution' in the public provision of health care will eventually be viewed.

Summary

1 The fact that the NHS delivers *local services* but is a *nationally funded* organization has produced a basic tension within the NHS throughout its entire history.
2 The Griffiths Report (1983) successfully challenged the principle of consensus management by a multidisciplinary team by advocating the principle of chief executives or general managers at all levels in the NHS.
3 The White Paper *Working for Patients* in 1989 marked an important watershed in presenting the thinking of the Conservative government.
4 The National Health Service and Community Care Act 1990 had the important underlying concept of the creation of a competitive market.
5 The most crucial move in setting up the internal health market is the requirement that all district health authorities should separate out their purchasing and provisioning functions.

Related topics

The medical profession is discussed in section 2.7. On the physical and psychological effects of unemployment see section 2.9. On racism and ethnic inequalities in health see chapter 5. On more general aspects of change in welfare provision, see section 12.5.

Further reading

A useful sociological text is that by Margaret Stacey (1988), while some sociological insights on specific topics are contained in Gabe et al. (1991). Recent developments in health policy are covered by Harrison et al. (1990) and by Audrey Leathard (1990). However, anyone wishing to keep abreast of developments in the rapidly changing provision of health care needs to read the newspapers and professional journals.

10 Culture and Media

10.1 Introduction

The term 'culture' is defined very broadly in sociology. It is most commonly used to delineate the *symbolic* aspects of human society so as to include beliefs, rituals, customs, conventions, ideals or artistic endeavours. In this usage, culture contrasts with the biological aspects of human behaviour on the one hand, and society or social institutions on the other.

Culture does, therefore, cover a very wide range of social phenomena and that is why so many varied topics are included in this chapter, each of which is a branch of sociology in its own right. We begin with a section on the media. Here the central sociological questions are: what sort of view of the world is presented by radio, television and the press? Why are some views excluded or included, and what effect, if any, does the presentation of a particular view of the world have on the audience?

A somewhat different set of questions is raised by the study of leisure and popular culture. In this section, we look at the way social groups use their leisure time in different ways; women's leisure, for example, is much more home-based than that of men. Some of these issues arise again in a rather different form in the study of youth cultures. We show the way in which youth groups, whether based on class, gender or ethnic differences, have quite distinct cultures. We also discuss the way in which youth cultures acquiesce in, or are resistant to, parent cultures or the dominant culture in a society. In our discussion of religion in modern Britain, we pose a different set of questions, contrasting the decline of orthodox Christianity with the vitality of newer sects often inspired by Eastern faiths.

As we have said, each of these areas of culture raises its own questions.

There is also, however, an important sociological problem common to them all, namely the relation of culture to power. Is there an overarching dominant culture which subordinates all other cultures and thereby helps to preserve existing social arrangements? Or are there numerous different cultures appropriate to different social groups which are not assimilated to a dominant culture, even if that exists?

A way to illustrate this problem is to consider two alternative models of the relationship between culture and power. One model sees a culture common to most members of a society which effectively holds that society together. This culture is *dominant* in three senses. First, it is the culture that pervades all institutions in society and is transmitted by those institutions, like the family, the school and the mass media. Second, the dominant culture is the culture of the dominant social groups in society. More accurately, we should say that the dominant culture helps to keep dominant groups in power. It is not the case, of course, that the upper class deliberately formulates such a culture as a kind of propaganda. It is, however, an unintended effect of the dominant culture that challenges to the dominant groups are not heard more often. Third, the very pervasiveness of a dominant culture suppresses alternative cultures, different ways of looking at the world. For all members of a society the dominant culture is so much part of everyday life that alternatives almost literally cannot be thought of. This is not to say that alternatives do not exist at all; the dominant culture is not that powerful. However, it does mean that the alternatives are subordinate to the dominant culture and do not have the capacity to be actively resistant.

The other model denies that there is a dominant culture linked to the powerful. Indeed, it may deny that there is any connection between power and culture at all. Rather, societies are seen as composed of a very large number of cultures which compete with one another. Each culture is an expression of the way of life of a particular social group. Some writers see this 'pluralization' as a special feature of modern societies. Older societies, of the last century or earlier, were organic wholes with a relatively static social structure, unified around some common system of beliefs and values, usually a religious one. Social changes since then have tended to produce a more fragmented social order. The class structure of modern Britain, for example, is more complex than that of Victorian Britain. Each class fraction, so the argument runs, will form its own culture, perhaps further complicated by ethnic or gender divisions.

These are, of course, extreme models of the relationship of culture and power. We do not claim that any sociologist holds either of them in a pure form. The more likely position, and the one illustrated in this chapter, lies somewhere between these extremes. The diverse social groups in modern Britain do, indeed, formulate cultures expressing their own way of life – cultures which are often very different from each other.

We show, for example, how male and female youth cultures differ from one another, and how different religious movements appeal to different sections of the population. At the same time, there is a rudimentary dominant culture centred on certain values and beliefs which is transmitted via the mass media and the education system. As we show, particularly in the next section on the mass media, however, the dominant culture is rather fragmentary and not very coherent. The important sociological question raised in this chapter is the relationship between the dominant culture and diverse other cultures. In what ways does the dominant culture organize or subordinate other cultures? As we will argue, there is no simple or straightforward answer to this question. There are conforming cultures (e.g. middle-class youth cultures) but there are also resistant cultures (e.g. working-class youth cultures). However, there are also cultures that effectively involve a withdrawal from society (e.g. some new religious movements) or in which there is a form of accommodation or negotiation with the dominant culture. In modern Britain, much working-class culture takes this form, involving a capacity to live with dominant values while not embracing them fully.

10.2   The Mass Media: Radio, Television and the Press

Media content

> *What the BBC and ITN present as news is not news at all, it is pure, unadulterated bias. News presents a 'digest' of what's going on. In order to achieve 'balance' it* must *reflect all the elements comprising that phenomenon called truth. Yet the truth about the miners' strike is absent from most television news broadcasts. The truth about the Plan for Coal. The truth about Britain's energy needs. The truth about the Coal Board and government plans to butcher our industry. We won't find them reported by the BBC or ITN.*
> Arthur Scargill, New Socialist, *1984*

> *This, in our view, is the most serious charge we have to bring against the men who are now in control of the BBC – that they abandon its principles in the face of the onslaught of anti-God . . . At present the BBC seems to many people to be trying to lead the country in a very definite direction, and it is not towards a God-centred, but a man-centred society.*
> *Mary Whitehouse,* Cleaning Up TV

One often hears accusations of bias directed against the media, accusations that can come from widely different political perspectives as

these two quotations show. Yet social surveys also show that a large proportion of the population believes that radio and television objectively
report the news, even if they also show that this proportion is declining.

What is the truth of the matter? This is a complicated question. There
is a large variety of different communications media – newspapers,
magazines, radio, film, television, books and advertisements, for
example – and it might seem unlikely that all of these will be biased in the
same direction and to the same extent. Furthermore, although news
broadcasts must involve the *selection* of newsworthy items from the
events of the day, and hence give a partial view, that selection may not
always be made according to the same principles. Similarly, 'Coronation
Street' will not be a perfect mirror of everyday life in Salford, but neither
will it *necessarily* be a mirror that always distorts in the same way.

The mass media, therefore, *cannot* give a flawlessly objective
presentation of the world around us because they must select from the
flow of events and they have to create dramas that will involve an
audience. Media personnel, in other words, have to make choices, and
the choices that they make are partly determined by social factors. To see
whether or not this amounts to bias we have to investigate the principles
on which choices are made. We have to try to find out what picture of the
world is presented by the media if, indeed, any coherent picture is
presented at all.

News and current affairs

The presentation of news and current affairs is a good place to start this
investigation. If news presentation was biased, there might well be
serious consequences because television broadcasts and newspapers are,
for most people, the only source of information about events in the wider
world. Newspapers, of course, often do not even claim to be unbiased
and their proprietors sometimes freely admit that they use their
newspapers or magazines for the purposes of propaganda. The broadcasting media – television and radio – claim greater objectivity, a
characteristic actually demanded by the charter of the BBC. The study of
television thus provides a good test case of principles of selection. An
additional reason for concentrating on television is its power and
pervasiveness. Of households in Britain in 1990, 99 per cent own at least
one television set; of the UK population, 94 per cent spend some time
each week watching television. As can be seen from table 10.1, on
average each person in Britain took in almost 24 hours of television per
week, to which could be added the use of the television screen for video
recordings and satellite transmissions.

It is not only the amount of time that people spend watching television

Table 10.1   Television viewing[a], by social class, United Kingdom, 1986–1990

	1986	1987	1988	1989	1990
Social class (hours:mins per week)					
ABC1	20:47	20:54	20:14	19:48	19:31
C2	25:18	24:40	25:25	25:00	24:13
DE	33:11	31:47	31:44	30:57	30:13
All persons	25:54	25:25	25:21	24:44	23:51
Reach (per cent)[b]					
Daily	78	76	77	78	77
Weekly	94	93	94	94	94

[a] Viewing of live television broadcasts from the BBC, ITV and Channel 4
[b] Percentage of UK population aged 4 and over who viewed TV for at least three consecutive minutes.

Source: *Social Trends*, 1992, p. 177; data from Broadcasters' Audience Research Board, British Broadcasting Corporation, AGB Limited. Crown copyright

that is important but the credibility that they attach to it. One survey showed that 58 per cent of the population rely on television as their principal source of news. Even more significantly, 68 per cent believed that television news reporting was the most objective available, while only 6 per cent believed this of the press.

Television and radio do not attempt to be unbiased about everything. It is, for example, official policy not to be impartial in the conflict between terrorism and ordered government. For some parts of the audience, this may make the broadcasting institutions suspect, as 'terrorism' may itself be difficult to define. Supporters of the republican cause in Northern Ireland, for example, may well believe that the BBC is being improperly biased in its treatment of the Irish Republican Army (IRA), particularly as its freedom to report is now officially restricted by government policy. Of greater significance is the question of whether, in general, the presentation of views on the television is dictated simply by the flow of events, as many broadcasters claim, or whether some set of factors intervenes to select certain events for particular treatment in particular ways.

Selectivity

The evidence overwhelmingly favours the second of these possibilities. A number of closely linked factors are involved. First, news, and even current-affairs programmes, have a marked tendency to report events as

Box 10.1 Setting the agenda

The diagrams below show the results of a survey of the treatment by television news and current-affairs programmes of the 1992 General Election campaign. Particular topics dominate, mainly those to do with opinion poll findings, and other major policy items are largely ignored. Besides constructing an agenda in this sense, the media also structure the debate by allocating time differently to politicians of the three parties. Most important of all, agendas are set by the way that commentators are used: they are apparently neutral, but are actually supporters of one party or another, usually the Conservative Party. As Peter Golding, one of the authors of the survey, said:

Among the most important commentators are the city analysts, the hard-headed realists from the Square Mile who adjudicate in Olympian majesty from computer laden offices. A MORI poll last month showed that 90 per cent of top financial executives would be voting Conservative. Yet this particular group of analysts . . . are called upon with increasing regularity as neutral analysts in election news.

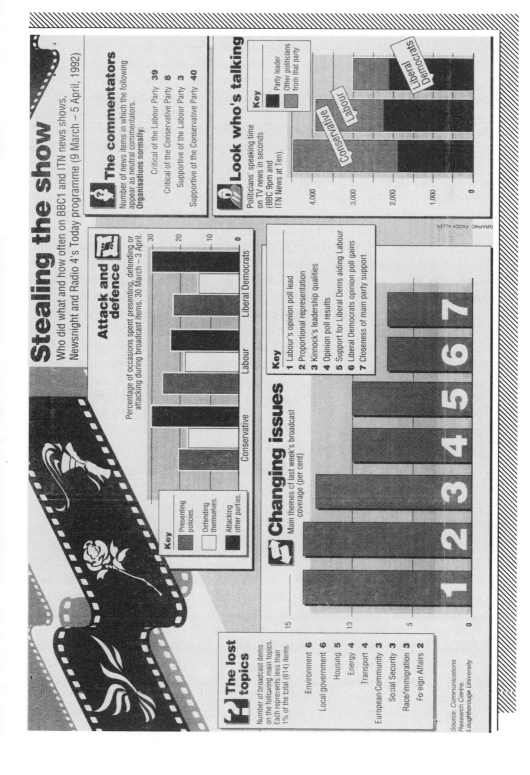

Source: The Guardian, 6 April 1992

they occur and not to discuss the background to these events; the opening of a new building may be news, but its construction is not. The result of this tendency is that people's actions, strike action for instance, will appear irrational and immoral because they have no *explanation*. Second, journalists operate by a set of values about what is newsworthy, what events they think the audience will find interesting. Broadcasters have to imagine their audience, and that constrains their presentation of news in much the same way as the producer of a drama series has to imagine the way in which dramas will appeal to viewers.

The most important factor, however, is what has become known as *agenda-setting*. This means that the broadcasting media effectively decide what are important issues, promoting some and leaving others out altogether (see box 10.1). For example, in the treatment of race relations in Britain, discussions in the media have tended to establish racial *conflict* as the central, newsworthy issue, leaving out factors that may explain such conflicts – the multiple disadvantages that black people experience in Britain, for example. Black people, therefore, become defined as a threat, an implicit assumption which structures news reports. Agenda are constructed using a variety of methods. Particular issues are taken up while others are ignored; one viewpoint is stressed while others receive less extensive treatment; some sources are seen as authoritative and neutral while others are seen as biased; participants in a story will be treated in different ways, some being subjected to hostile interviewing; particular words will come to be associated with particular issues (conflict with race for instance), while language used in other issues will be more neutral; and visual material is used as evidence for a spoken commentary when it does not provide relevant illustration.

Fictional programmes and social values

Many studies confirm the way in which television sets the agenda for public debate in its news and current affairs programming. An even more difficult question concerns the output of television as a whole. Is a particular view of the world also presented in drama, soap operas or documentaries? Does television, as a whole, present a coherent world-view? It is, in fact, very difficult to assess the output of television as a whole, because of the enormous diversity of programmes on offer. It is impossible, at first glance, to see what quiz shows, 'Inspector Morse', current-affairs programmes, 'Coronation Street' and 'Blind Date' have in common. The range of interest is so wide that it makes no sense to talk of television programmes as presenting a coherent view of the world. It might, however, be the case that certain kinds of programme have common themes. Take, for example, the representation of gender relations in James Bond films (frequently shown on television) and 'Dr Who'. Although the former are adventure films, and the latter is a science fiction series largely aimed at children, they have some things in common. The central point is that men are active and women passive. Men make things happen and women stand and stare or, worse, positively get in the man's way. Both Bond and 'Dr Who' have female helpers who are portrayed as essentially 'feminine'. They tend to be silly, irrational, prone to bouts of hysteria or panic, to make mistakes, or to get into situations from which they have to rescued. At the same time, they are warm, loving and trusting and, in the case of James Bond films, desirable sexual objects as well. To emphasize the 'feminine' role of women, both 'Dr Who' and James Bond films contrast the silly, if faithful, helper with evil women who are opponents. These women exemplify undesirable qualities, being cold, calculating, unsympathetic and, occasionally, sexually ambiguous. This contrast between 'good' and 'bad' femininity is further emphasized by styles of dress. The helpers adopt feminine styles, wearing dresses and skirts with lots of frills and colour. Opponents, on the other hand, affect a masculine appearance, wearing trousers, drab colours and harsh fabrics like leather.

Programmes of this kind may, therefore, convey a certain view of femininity and masculinity. Even in this area of drama, however, it would be difficult to find uniformity, let alone in other areas of television work such as news or current affairs. Women may be portrayed who break the stereotype and who do not conform to either helper or opponent model. Several recent series have tried to show women not as passive and dependent adjuncts to men but as active and forceful, as in 'Prime Suspect' for example. To conclude, although there will be some coherence in some areas of television presentation, there is no sense in which television output as a whole is organized around one view of the world.

These conclusions raise two crucial further questions: *why* do the media produce a particular view or views in some areas of their output, especially news? Do these views influence the way in which people think about their world? We consider these questions in the following two sections.

Media productions: external and internal constraints

No one argues that the particular way in which television news is structured is the result of a conspiracy by television journalists. We have to look for other factors that account for the view (or views) of the world presented by the media. It is convenient to divide these into factors external and internal to the institutions in which media personnel work.

External factors

The state and the government We have already implied that the institutions of the state can be something of a constraint on the media by saying that the BBC does not regard itself as impartial towards terrorism or any other force that might obviously threaten the stability of the state. Of course, governments of the day will seek to extend the definition of what threatens the state. In 1926, for instance, the government succeeded in making the BBC take its side in the General Strike against the labour movement. Furthermore, governments ultimately have financial control over the BBC, in that they can decide on the level of the licence fee. Ministers and government departments have access to broadcasting institutions through their public relations agencies and the expression of ministerial displeasure and, hence, some measure of control can be very effectively conveyed. More subtly and, therefore, probably more efficiently, governments can make their influence felt by the way in which the media portray the institutions of state as neutral and as above political controversy. Government statistics and even some government spokesmen are treated as objective, impartial observers on a particular news item when, say, trade union or management representatives are not. Government *policy* can, therefore, seem beyond media comment. However, although governments do exercise some control, this is not very great. There are several instances of the BBC resisting ministerial interference. More importantly, we have to look elsewhere for an explanation of the way in which the media assume that the institutions of the state and of parliamentary democracy are neutral.

Ownership In looking at newspapers one might easily think that their ownership had something to do with control of their content. Proprietors do interfere with editorial policy and it would be surprising if they did not. Lord Beaverbrook, for example, said that he only kept his newspapers (the *Daily Express*, for example) for the purposes of propaganda. Independent television and radio, since they are privately owned, are also *potentially* subject to influence from their owners. Even the BBC, though dependent on the state for its revenues, may be indirectly influenced by commercial interests since it has to compete with privately owned broadcasting institutions for a share of the audience. The ownership of broadcasting organizations, then, is another possible source of external control of the media.

   As you will see from section 2.3, British industry has, especially since the Second World War, been characterized by a wave of mergers and takeovers which have resulted in the agglomeration of firms into much larger units. At the same time, the tendency for individual or family ownership of firms to be replaced by joint-stock or share ownership has not in practice resulted in widening of ownership. Ownership of large firms tends to be relatively concentrated in the hands of individuals or institutions that hold large blocks of shares. All this is equally true of the communications industry. Firms have become larger, there are fewer of them, and most sectors of the industry are dominated by a handful of firms:

> In central sectors such as daily and Sunday newspapers, paperback books, records, and commercial television programming, two - thirds or more of the total audience are reading, hearing, or looking at material produced by the top five firms in that sector. Other markets, notably cinema exhibition and women's and children's magazines, are even more concentrated, with the lion's share of sales going to the top two companies in each. (Murdock, 1982, p. 118).

Furthermore, communications companies have become more diverse. Some have become part of holding companies with interests in several sectors of industry, while others have diversified inside the industry and have stakes in different media of communication. At the same time, ownership remains concentrated in fairly few hands, not only those of the investing institutions, but also, if unusually, families, particularly in the case of newspapers.

Figure 10.1 illustrates some of these points. Most of the major newspaper groups have shareholdings in other areas of the communications industry, including television, radio and book publishing. News International Corporation, for example, owns a string of newspapers – *The Sun, News of the World, The Sunday Times, The Times, The Times Educational Supplement, The Times Literary Supplement, Times Higher Educational Supplement* and *Today*. However, it also has interests in a number of magazines, in television via Sky Television, and in a major book publisher, Collins. It also has shareholdings in Reuters and in two other large media groups, Reed and Pearson. Other companies in the communications industry are equally diverse. Furthermore, as the case of News International illustrates, media companies, while they may appear to compete with one another, are also joined together. This is achieved partly by overlapping ownership and partly by interlocking directorships (a concept discussed in more detail in section 2.3)

External control over media content Firms in the communications industry are, therefore, bigger, more diverse, fewer, and relatively concentrated in ownership. What consequences does this have for the control of the output of the media? There is little evidence of widespread direct proprietorial interference, where an owner will insist on having a

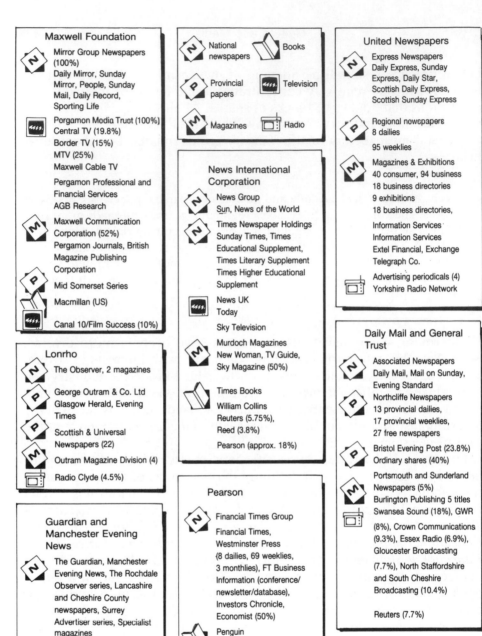

Maxwell Foundation

Mirror Group Newspapers (100%)
Daily Mirror, Sunday Mirror, People, Sunday Mail, Daily Record, Sporting Life

Pergamon Media Trust (100%)
Central TV (19.8%)
Border TV (15%)
MTV (25%)
Maxwell Cable TV

Pergamon Professional and Financial Services
AGB Research

Maxwell Communication Corporation (52%)
Pergamon Journals, British Magazine Publishing Corporation

Mid Somerset Series

Macmillan (US)

Canal 10/Film Success (10%)

Lonrho

The Observer, 2 magazines

George Outram & Co. Ltd
Glasgow Herald, Evening Times

Scottish & Universal Newspapers (22)

Outram Magazine Division (4)

Radio Clyde (4.5%)

Guardian and Manchester Evening News

The Guardian, Manchester Evening News, The Rochdale Observer series, Lancashire and Cheshire County newspapers, Surrey Advertiser series, Specialist magazines

17% of Picadilly Radio, Red Rose, Red Dragon, Radio Aire

Anglia TV (5%), Broadcast Communications (14%)

National newspapers   Books

Provincial papers   Television

Magazines   Radio

News International Corporation

News Group
Sun, News of the World

Times Newspaper Holdings
Sunday Times, Times Educational Supplement, Times Literary Supplement Times Higher Educational Supplement

News UK
Today

Sky Television

Murdoch Magazines
New Woman, TV Guide, Sky Magazine (50%)

Times Books
William Collins
Reuters (5.75%), Reed (3.8%)
Pearson (approx. 18%)

Pearson

Financial Times Group
Financial Times, Westminster Press (8 dailies, 69 weeklies, 3 monthlies), FT Business Information (conference/ newsletter/database), Investors Chronicle, Economist (50%)

Penguin
Viking, Michael Joseph, Hamish Hamilton, Puffin, Frederick Warne

Yorkshire Television (20%), British Satellite Broadcasting (13%), Pickwick Group (21%)

Longman
Ladybird, Pitman

United Newspapers

Express Newspapers
Daily Express, Sunday Express, Daily Star, Scottish Daily Express, Scottish Sunday Express

Regional newspapers
8 dailies

95 weeklies

Magazines & Exhibitions
40 consumer, 94 business
18 business directories
9 exhibitions
18 business directories,

Information Services
Information Services
Extel Financial, Exchange Telegraph Co.

Advertising periodicals (4)
Yorkshire Radio Network

Daily Mail and General Trust

Associated Newspapers
Daily Mail, Mail on Sunday, Evening Standard

Northcliffe Newspapers
13 provincial dailies,
17 provincial weeklies,
27 free newspapers

Bristol Evening Post (23.8%)
Ordinary shares (40%)

Portsmouth and Sunderland Newspapers (5%)
Burlington Publishing 5 titles
Swansea Sound (18%), GWR (8%), Crown Communications (9.3%), Essex Radio (6.9%), Gloucester Broadcasting (7.7%), North Staffordshire and South Cheshire Broadcasting (10.4%)

Reuters (7.7%)

Hollinger

Daily Telegraph (83%)
Daily Telegraph, Sunday Telegraph

Spectator

United Newspapers (3.36%)

Figure 10.1 Ownership of the media.
Source: Wagg, 1989, p. 19

story written a particular way. There are, however, a number of well-known instances of commercial considerations overriding editorial ones, because a newspaper or television station is losing money. But this does not really represent continuous intervention by owners in the social or political policy of television, radio or newspapers. One other source of commercial intervention comes from advertising. Advertisers may well want to advertise their products together with programmes that offer a view of the world that favours those products. For example, after the second world war, US television drama was dominated by plays with working-class settings. Advertisers became worried by the emphasis, since it did not give the required glamour. As a result, they moved their advertising to adventure series slots that implied a fast-moving, affluent and glamorous world in which their products might have a place (Murdock, 1982).

The values, themes and topics promoted by the media may well fit in with those espoused by owners. One might guess that, other things being equal, owners would like to see the media take a central position, leaning neither to the left nor to the right, emphasize consensus on common values, and set the agenda on items of public debate, all features described in the first section of this chapter. Apart from the fact that this is assuming rather a lot about owners, and it ignores the diversity of the media, it does not, however, explain *why* there might be a coincidence between owners' interests and the content of media output. We know, especially in the case of radio and television, that this is not because owners *directly* control the media. The point may be that owners do not *need* to intervene because they already *share* social values with the people who produce newspapers and television and radio programmes; owners, producers and audiences are bound together in a set of social values that are continually reinforced in media content.

Internal factors

This last point draws attention to factors that may constrain media output that are internal to media institutions. These will, chiefly, be factors to do with the social characteristics of people working in these organizations or with the structure of media institutions. We have concluded earlier that media output is diverse, sometimes contradictory, and that it is difficult to describe the output of television as representing a *coherent* view of the world. Despite these qualifications, what appears on our television screens is not random or arbitrary. It is socially constructed, by which we mean that certain topics are excluded and certain themes, social myths or ways of life receive undue and unrepresentative emphasis.

Organizations   The way in which media institutions are organized has an effect on their output. The BBC, for example, is organized as a bureaucracy in which the upper levels to some extent control the lower ones. Not unnaturally, media personnel feel some pressure to conform when their careers, or even their continued employment, may be at stake. Sensitivity to outside criticism can make the BBC exercise internal control. Burns (1977) points out, in a study of the BBC, that if producers feel in any way uncertain about a programme they are expected to refer the problem to their superior.

Media professionalism   In all occupations there is pressure to conform to the particular occupational culture. Where these occupations are professionalized, these pressures can take a distinct form. While there is no recognized profession of broadcasting in the sense that medicine is a recognized profession, several studies note the way in which people who work in the media stress the 'professionalism' of their work. This has become so pronounced that professional values appear to take precedence over all others. This attitude implies a view of the purpose of broadcasting very different from that of the early days of the BBC, when the role of broadcasting institutions in raising the British nation to new moral heights was stressed. As Kumar (1975, p. 232) says, 'To make professional presentation the goal of broadcasting, to elevate, so to speak, the means to the ends, is to indicate a very different reading both of the possibilities of broadcasting and of the social environment in which it operates.' In practice, an adherence to professional values means an emphasis on *methods of presentation* rather than content, on skill in devising programmes, in being efficient and craftsmanlike, in imagining the audience and producing programmes to satisfy it, in achieving balance and impartiality. Television and radio are, then, seen as the means by which the various voices or interests in a society may be heard and balanced. These voices, however, are not equally skilled, resourceful or even obvious, and the professional's role in merely representing them will be to include some while leaving others out. In other words, the very professionalism of broadcasting and journalism, the dedication to methods rather than content, will have the agenda-setting consequences that we have already noted.

Professionalism, however, also has another consequence which might, under certain circumstances, run counter to this. The emphasis on skill, experience, and efficiency enables broadcasters to defend themselves from interference, either from management or from the outside world. They can present themselves as impartial professionals who do a good job and have no axe to grind. Here lies one of the sources of resistance to control by governments. Nonetheless, although professionalism might well act against *direct* control, it might still allow the indirect distortion associated with agenda-setting.

Class origins of personnel   One final, familiar, factor of constraint on the media should be noted. Journalists and broadcasters are recruited from a relatively narrow segment of the population. Their social origins will inevitably influence the way they look at the world. Some viewpoints will seem more important than others and some topics will be altogether lost to their sight. All social groups have some ways of looking at the world that differ from those held by other groups. The generally middle-class origins of most broadcasters and journalists will predispose them to respect expert opinion and to treat it as unbiased, to find it easier to talk to fellow members of the middle class than to the working-class population, and to seek out other middle-class opinion – that of management for instance. The middle-class experience of life often excludes the recognition of other experiences. It may, therefore, be quite natural for a broadcaster or journalist to be unaware of whole areas of working-class life, to believe that ranges of problems and difficulties do not exist and, therefore, not to represent certain voices or topics on programmes. Clearly, the professional training of media personnel must be partly designed to overcome this partiality of vision. It cannot, however, entirely succeed.

The impact on the audience

As McQuail (1977, p. 81) says: 'A long list of studies can be cited showing the media to have certain inbuilt tendencies to present a limited and recurring range of images and ideas which form rather special versions of reality.' The media *project* socially constructed images of the world, even if these can be confused and incoherent. The question remains as to *how the audience interprets* these 'media messages'. Does it, for example, uncritically accept them? Or does it evaluate and assess them in the light of its own experience?

One popular answer is that the media do, indeed, have a powerful effect on the audience, particularly when the medium is television and when the audience concerned is made up of children. Thus, there have been several public debates about the exposure of children to violent scenes on television and 'video nasties'. These debates are often founded on the assumption that children are profoundly affected by what they see on television, even to the extent of being moved to commit acts of violence themselves. Similar feelings have been expressed about advertisements, which are thought to persuade people to buy things that they neither need nor really want. Again, there is the assumption that people cannot or do not react critically to the media of communication; the audience is seen as empty vessels into which media messages are poured. At the other extreme is the view that the media have no effect on the audience at all. People resort to radio and television as entertainment and any message merely washes over them. This view is also dubious, particularly when radio, television and newspapers may be the only source of information about those aspects of social life of which the audience has no direct experience.

Problems of method

It is notoriously difficult to say how audiences interpret the output of the media, and many studies avoid it altogether simply by *assuming* that audiences are affected. There are substantial methodological problems in the way of any empirical investigation of the audience. Even if it is clear that people react to, and are influenced by, television programmes in the very short term, it is very difficult to measure long-term changes. Any long-term study will find it awkward to isolate changes in the audience due to the media from those stemming from other social influences. It is not even obvious what is to be measured. For example, is one interested in the influence of the media on the attitudes that people have or on their knowledge of events?

For some time, research into these questions was dominated by laboratory and experimental methods, which took selected audiences, exposed them to some media experience, and then measured the changes in attitude that might result. This method is unsatisfactory as a means of sociological analysis. It is too artificial, extracting audiences from their regular social settings; it concentrates exclusively on the concept of attitude; it focuses on short-term changes rather than more fundamental long-term influences; and it tends to treat audiences as unrelated individuals rather than collectivities involving relationships *between* individuals. In addition, laboratory studies cannot agree about the limited effects they measure. Some researchers believe that television violence encourages violent acts by children, others that violent programmes act as a safety-valve for children who would otherwise be violent in everyday situations.

Given all these difficulties, it is not surprising that we do not have any clear answer to questions about the way in which audiences interpret media messages. There is, however, a little evidence in certain areas. One investigation of the impact of the media on race relations showed, for example, that the media did not have any noticeable effect on the creation of attitudes in schoolchildren but did contribute to the definition of black people as creating problems for society, particularly in areas with *small* black populations.

Uninvited guests: a case study

'Passivity' is an odd term to describe the manner in which so many of these people watched their screens. In the early days of television, it may have been true that the flickering box in the darkened room could actually 'entrance' its audience: nowadays this hardly fits any description of its use. But neither should we go to the opposite extreme and declare that people hardly watch it at all; that it flickers away unattended in the corner while they go on with making tea, hoovering the carpet and completing their aerobic workouts. Sometimes it is watched with great intensity and emotional involvement (quite enough to produce tears of sorrow or joy): at other moments, with an irreverent concern (in which actors and plot readily become mere laughing matters). In both cases it is likely to be a subject for conversation and comment among those present either during or after the specific programme. And whatever may have been the case in the past, nowadays, with at least four channels available and a prerecorded film for hire a few hundred yards down the road, choice is likely to be continually exercised. (Taylor and Mullan, 1986)

Taylor and Mullan's (1986) book, from which this quotation is taken, is a report of a study of audience responses to television programmes of various kinds. It is based largely, though not completely, on tape-recorded transcripts of group discussions involving people who watched television. The groups were chosen from those sections of the population that tended to watch the shows in question. So, for example, discussions of game and quiz shows were held principally by people over 40 in skilled and semi-skilled occupations.

The fundamental conclusion of the study is that television audiences can be deeply involved in what they watch, though they are not passive spectators but are active, critical and creative. There is, therefore, a sense in which the audience is simultaneously involved and detached. Involvement is shown in the detailed conversations that people have about television programmes. For example, participants in the study talked about characters in soap operas as if they were real. 'Coronation Street' and 'Brookside' strike a chord because they are so realistic and the audience can respond to the problems or joys experienced by the characters. It is not, however, just that members of the audience acknowledge the reality of such soap operas by talking about the characters as real people. Is is also that their involvement in the drama moves them deeply. As one of the (male) participants said of 'Coronation Street': 'I must be perfectly honest, I watched it when Stan died, I watched it and I cried. I sat down and watched it when Stan died

because it was so real and I could relate to it. I just sat there and cried'
(Taylor and Mullan, 1986, p. 45). The audience's involvement through
the realism of television goes well beyond the presentation of drama.
Even in chat shows, for example, audiences in this study greatly
preferred hosts who were 'real', not apparently putting on an act. Thus,
Terry Wogan was the most popular presenter because his television self
was seen to be most like people thought he would be at home.

Despite these symptoms of involvement, audiences are also detached
and critical. In general, people watching television are aware that,
however 'real' the presentation, it is not *actually* real. They know, for
example, that 'Coronation Street' is a fiction. The groups in Taylor and
Mullan's study were very quick to analyse programmes in terms of their
realism. American soap operas were felt to be less realistic than British
ones, at least partly because the range of human emotions is not
realistically portrayed. Audiences analyse the performances and skills of
the actors, well aware that these *are* actors playing a role, not real
people. The tricks and techniques utilized by television are also noted
and commented on. Viewers noticed stock film used over and over again,
mistakes in the setting out of rooms in soap operas, and unconvincing car
crashes. Audiences, in other words, are quite clear that television events
are not real and this very lack of reality is itself a topic of conversation.
The offices in 'Dallas' and 'Dynasty' are not real offices because nobody
seems to do real work. Even 'Coronation Street' lacks realism in this
respect. As one viewer said of Mike Baldwin's factory: 'There aren't
enough machinists, to start off with. There are only four of them and
they're making jeans for half the population of England' (p. 16).

People are, therefore, involved in television but simultaneously aware
of their involvement and able to criticize and analyse all kinds of
programmes. This combination of involvement and detachment is
intimately connected with the relationship of television to everyday life.
For Taylor and Mullan, television is *used* by audiences to make sense of
their everyday lives. The function of conversation about television is to
interpret events on television so that they relate to everyday lives. People
will, therefore, talk about characters in 'Coronation Street' as if they
were real because that is how the link with their everyday lives is forged.
Audiences do not respond to television programmes passively; they
actively use them for their own ends.

Audience differentiation

One of the implications of these studies is that, if the media do have an
influence, the effect is different for different sections of the audience.
Just as it is risky to see the output of media organizations as

homogeneous, so it is even more dangerous to assume that the audience is monolithic. Even in such an apparently straightforward medium as advertising, particular advertisements may be interpreted in different ways by different groups of people, a factor which may, or may not, work to the advertiser's advantage. One study (Morley, 1980) shows up the differentiation of audience response particularly well.

In Morley's study, various different groups (28 in all), including black students in further education, shop stewards and bank managers, were asked about their responses to the current-affairs programme 'Nation-wide', by getting them together for group discussions of the programme. Different groups had very different reactions. Morley classifies these reactions into three types: dominated, negotiated and oppositional. If a section of the audience responds in the dominant mode, they are using the values, attitudes and beliefs that are dominant in society. If they use oppositional modes, they are, as the term implies, employing a way of thinking that contradicts the dominant mode. Other groups within the audience using the negotiated mode are neither oppositional nor dominant but have a meaning system that can live with dominant values without believing or accepting them. However, as box 10.2 indicates, the division of audience into these three blocks still oversimplifies the social structure of the audience. For example, both black students and shop stewards had oppositional ways of thinking and saw 'Nationwide' as biased against the working class. However, they were also very different from each other. The black students essentially withdrew, considering the programme as irrelevant to them. The shop stewards, on the other hand, tended to be actively critical, seeing 'Nationwide' from a radical working-class perspective. Similarly, among those adopting the dominant mode there are great differences. Bank managers were traditionally conservative. Apprentices, on the other hand, tended to be much more cynical about people appearing on the programme, whoever they were, but at the same time held 'dominant' attitudes on the evils of trade unionism or of the social security system. Audiences for television programmes cannot therefore be seen as a solid block all reacting in the same way. They comprise different groups, all with different responses, partly based on their position in society.

One other feature of audience differentiation deserves mention. The media may work on sectors of the audience that are potentially powerful and, thus, have strong effects *through* them. There is considerable evidence that politicians, police and judges, for example, are sensitive to media comment that affects them and may act accordingly, even if the comment is ill-informed. The media, by concentrating on an issue, can create a 'moral panic' defining certain people or events as social problems. A recent example of this process is the treatment of 'raves' (see section 10.4).

Box 10.2   Audience responses to 'Nationwide', 19 May 1976

The figure shows three basic modes of audience response to a
'Nationwide' programme. Dominant responses were those that
adopted the prevailing or dominant values of society. People
taking up oppositional responses, on the other hand, had
opinions and beliefs opposed to the dominant values of society.
Negotiated interpretations of 'Nationwide' occupy an intermediate position, because people with this response have a system of
values that partly reflects dominant conceptions but also incorporates values, perhaps based on their everyday experiences, that
run counter to dominant conceptions.

   The three sorts of response are presented as circles because
there are differences *within* each response; they cannot be ranked
along a single dimension of opposition or conformity.

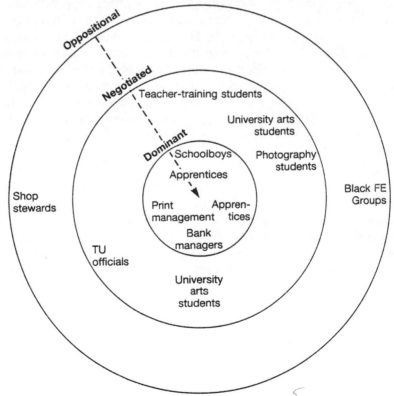

Source: Morley, 1980, p. 136, reproduced with permission

Summary

1   The mass media are inevitably selective and partial. They have some tendency to reflect central political positions and certain social values, like those concerning gender. They do not, however, present anything like a coherent message and, for that reason alone, it is difficult to see the media as expressing the culture of a dominant class.

2   The kinds of television programme or newspaper story that appear are determined by a variety of factors, internal and external to media organization. Internal factors include bureaucratic organization, a sense of 'professionalism' and the class origins of media personnel. Among external factors are pressures from the state and from the private owners of the mass media.

3   The audience for the mass media cannot be treated as a solid, coherent block, passively accepting all media output. Although the assessment of audience response is difficult, different sections of the audience react in very different ways.

10.3   Leisure

Since the Second World War, there has been a great deal of public discussion about the 'leisure society'. People have spent less time working and, consequently, have had more time to themselves and more time for leisure. Even more recently, the very rapid rise in unemployment in Western Europe and other parts of the world, combined with all sorts of new technologies which replace human labour, seems to mean that people's lives will in future be much less organized around work.

These statements imply that leisure is defined in terms of work. That is, indeed, how our society sees it. Leisure is the opposite of work. We will accept this definition of leisure time as that which is left over after work. Perhaps partly because of the way that our society perceives work as a constraint and a limitation, the definition of leisure as non-work also includes the idea that leisure represents free time and activities that people have *chosen*. However, this definition is clearly problematic for those people who do not have work with which they can contrast leisure. The groups most notably affected are women at home, the retired, the unemployed and young people. For these sections of the population, leisure is still defined as comprising that time over which they have control. For women at home, for example, their leisure occupations are

contrasted with domestic work. The same is true for large numbers of
elderly and unemployed, although they will have more time for leisure
and, to some extent, their lives are organized not around work but
around what other groups of people would regard as leisure. As we shall
see in the next section on youth culture, this is even more true of young
people, who will see their lives in terms not of work but of leisure – even
if this perception only lasts a few years. More radically still, it could be
argued that for everybody, not just those without work, it is wrong to see
leisure as representing free time and activities that have been freely
chosen (see Rojek, 1985). On this account, what passes as leisure in
modern Britain is just as highly organized and constraining as work.
There is frequently not enough time for leisure; people often engage in
leisure pursuits, especially sport, out of a feeling of compulsion; much
leisure involves keeping up appearances in front of others.

Our discussion so far suggests that, if we have a 'leisure society', it
must have been created at least partly by a reorganization of *time*. Most
obviously, the amount of time that people spend in paid work has been
falling steadily. At the beginning of the century male manual workers
actually worked an average of some 54 hours per week. By 1950 this had
fallen to about 46 hours and by 1992 to under 44.5 hours. It seems,
however, that any more extensive lessening of the time spent at work will
come, not from a shortening of the working day or week, but from longer
holidays. The custom of giving manual workers paid holiday entitlement

Table 10.2 Time use in a typical week, by employment status and sex, Great
Britain, 1990–1991

| | Full-time employees | | Part-time employees, | | |
	Males (hours)	Females (hours)	females (hours)	Housewives (hours)	Retired (hours)
Weekly time spent on:					
Employment and travel[a]	48.3	42.6	20.9	0.3	0.7
Essential activities[b]	24.1	39.6	52.1	58.4	33.0
Sleep[c]	49.0	49.0	49.0	49.0	49.0
Free time	46.6	36.8	46.0	60.3	85.3
Free time per weekday	4.5	3.3	5.4	8.4	11.6
Free time per weekend day	12.1	10.3	9.5	9.3	13.6

[a] Travel to and from place of work
[b] Essential domestic work and personal care, including essential shopping, child-care,
cooking, personal hygiene and appearance.
[c] An average of 7 hours sleep per night is assumed.

Source: *Social Trends*, 1992, p. 176: from Henley Centre for Forecasting data. Crown
copyright

is comparatively recent but, by 1972, most such workers had been given three weeks' holiday a year. Much more recently, the practice of closing factories and offices for longer periods at Christmas and Easter has been growing.

Opportunities for leisure may have been created by the greater availability of free time – at least to those groups of people who can actually work. Table 10.2 shows how free time varies between people employed full-time, part-time women employees, housewives, and retired people. Fully employed men have almost as much free time as time they expend working or travelling to work. Anybody in paid work has less free time than those without, even after allowing for domestic

Table 10.3 Average weekly household expenditure on selected leisure items, United Kingdom, 1981–1989

	1981 (£)	1986 (£)	1989 (£)
Alcoholic drink consumed away from home	5.39[b]	5.93	6.92
Meals consumed out[a]		4.38	5.51
Books, newspapers, magazines, etc.	2.00	2.73	3.31
Television, radio and musical instruments	3.26	4.85	5.65
Purchase of materials for home repairs, etc.	1.57	3.06	2.89
Holidays	3.08	5.39	7.76
Hobbies	0.08	0.06	0.09
Cinema admissions	0.14	0.10	0.16
Dance admissions	0.12	0.12	–[d]
Theatre, concert, etc. admissions	0.17	0.29	0.35
Subscription and admission charges to participant sports	0.43	0.71	0.85
Football match admissions	0.06	0.08 ⎫	0.20
Admissions to other spectator sports	0.02	0.04 ⎬	
Sports goods (excluding clothes)	0.26	0.37	0.62
Other entertainment	0.24	0.41	0.70[d]
Total weekly expenditure on above	16.82[c]	28.52	35.01
Expenditure on above items as a percentage of total household expenditure	13.4	16.0	15.6

[a] Eaten on the premises, excluding state school meals and workplace meals.
[b] Including home consumption.
[c] The total for 1981 is not comparable with later years since the figure for the category 'Meals consumed out' is not available.
[d] For 1989, 'Dance admissions' have been included with 'Other entertainment'.

Source: *Social Trends*, 1992, p. 187; from Central Statistical Office data. Crown copyright

work. The manner in which people can avail themselves of leisure time,
however, clearly depends on the money that they can spend. Since the
Second World War, as people have become more affluent, their
expenditure on leisure has increased. Between 1966 and 1976, for
example, consumer expenditure of all kinds rose 21 per cent in real terms
after allowing for inflation. There have also been small rises in the
proportion of household expenditure that goes on leisure items. Table
10.3 shows that in the 1980s the proportion of leisure expenditure rose
from 13.4 to 15.6 per cent.

Households and leisure

The *pattern* of expenditure is also changing. Compared with 30 years ago,
people are spending a higher proportion of their budget on alcohol
consumed at home, and less on tobacco and cinema visits. These changes
in expenditure are related to an increasing tendency to take leisure within
the home. Some two-thirds of all leisure time is spent within the home
(Gershuny and Jones, 1987).

   Many sociologists have seen this as a relatively new phenomenon,
dating perhaps from the Second World War, as part of a growing
tendency to *privatization*, to the increasing involvement of people with
their immediate family and their homes. (For further discussion of this
issue see section 3.4 and section 6.6.) While the process of privatization
probably has a longer history than this, there is some reason to think that
leisure activities are more private than they used to be. There is, in other
words, less involvement in 'public' spheres of recreation. It is not only
that people participate less in public events such as carnivals, religious
festivals, processions, and fairs (or 'public' holidays). It is also that there
is relatively less involvement in leisure activities outside the home. So
there are fewer visits to the pub or cinema in favour of more drinking at
home and a greater dedication to watching television. This process of
privatization of leisure is described more fully in box 10.3.

Gender, class and lifecycle in leisure

Gershuny and Jones's (1987) analysis of the time spent in various leisure
activities shows up a number of gender differences which have also
changed over time. For men, travel, playing sport, going to the pub and
visiting friends are the most popular activities outside the home (table
10.4), and the first three of these have taken up more time over the
period 1961 to 1983–4. These are, with the notable exception of playing
sport (still very much a masculine preserve), also the most time-

Box 10.3   The privatization of leisure

The privatization of leisure is a long-term trend in Britain. It is a product of a more mobile population, the decline of local neighbourhood communities, and the rise of the relatively independent nuclear family. The spread of car ownership has accentuated privatization: families with cars can even go out in private. Radio and television have strengthened the home's position as most people's main leisure centre. In recent decades home-centred lifestyles have been further strengthened by the spread of home ownership. Two-thirds of Britain's dwellings are now owner-occupied. This has helped to promote the various forms of do-it-yourself. Home repairs, decorating, car maintenance and gardening are now the nation's main hobbies.

In the 1980s more time than ever is being spent at home, partly as a result of the declining proportion of lifetime claimed by employment. In addition, however, more money is being spent on in-home recreation, and this spending is mainly by the employed sections of the population. Britain's main growth areas in leisure spending in the 1980s have been on sound and vision reproducing equipment, telecommunications, and computer technology.

The proportion of employment in service sectors has increased, but much of this employment is in producer services such as banking and insurance. The proportion of consumer spending on services has actually declined. There has been a trend towards purchasing goods which are then used for self-servicing. Transport is a prime example. We are buying more motor cars to transport ourselves instead of purchasing bus and train journeys. For entertainment we are purchasing televisions, videos and music centres instead of attending live performances.

Participation has declined in most forms of out-of-home recreation that can be replicated or closely substituted by in-home entertainment. Cinema and theatre audiences, and paid admissions at spectator sports events, are in long-term and continuing decline. In Britain they have now been joined by out-of-home drinking. We are consuming more alcohol per capita than during any previous period in twentieth-century history, but there is less drinking in public houses and more off-sales for home consumption. Drink, film and sports producers have survived by gearing to increasingly home-centred markets. Most films are now made for television and video distribution rather than cinema performances. Live sport is played to tele-viewing audiences. Commercially successful sports promotion now depends on television coverage. The presence of the media attracts sponsors, and attracting the media requires top-level performers. Hence the changing structure of professional sports occupations. Stars command astronomical fees while the rank and file must be motivated primarily by the slender prospect of joining the elite.

Lifestyles are generally home-centred in all social strata, but homes vary tremendously in their comforts. Individuals in employment, who spend least time at home, can best afford large and well-equipped dwellings. Home has different connotations for most of the unemployed and retired, many of whom have become trapped in home-based lifestyles by poverty, and as a result of local community facilities – cinemas, sports teams and pubs – either declining or disappearing completely.

Source: Roberts, 1989, pp. 52–4

consuming activities for women. Interestingly, going to pubs used to be a very gender differentiated activity in 1961; in 1983–4 it is much less so.

Table 10.4 Leisure outside the home (minutes per average day)

Activity	Men, full-time employed			Women, full-time employed		
	1961	1974–5	1983–4	1961	1974–5	1983–4
Travel	5	12	24	5	12	21
Excursions	10	5	1	9	5	0
Playing sport	4	7	10	2	1	2
Watching sport	3	3	2	1	1	1
Walks	4	5	9	4	2	4
Church	3	2	2	4	2	6
Civic duties	6	4	3	2	3	7
Cinema, theatre	4	2	1	6	2	2
Discos, dances, parties, bingo	2	17	5	3	17	7
Social clubs	4	8	5	1	6	2
Pubs	4	14	13	0	3	10
Visiting friends	19	21	18	24	27	21

Source: adapted from Gershuny and Jones, 1987, pp. 38–9

As far as leisure activities within the home are concerned (table 10.5), the most obvious feature is the importance of television watching, which takes up much more time than all other activities put together for both men and women. Hobbies and conversations show some increase between 1961 and 1983–4, while listening to the radio shows a marked decrease. There is no great gender difference in privatized leisure pursuits. Men and women may indeed share leisure in the home, while outside, where men are dominant, there are greater differences.

Table 10.5 Leisure inside the home (minutes per average day)

Activity	Men, full-time employed			Women, full-time employed		
	1961	1974–5	1983–4	1961	1974–5	1983–4
Radio	23	5	3	16	3	2
Watching TV	121	126	129	93	103	102
Listening to music	1	3	1	1	1	1
Study	0	1	3	0	0	2
Reading book/ papers	28	19	24	13	13	20
Relaxing	20	31	16	27	31	14
Conversations	2	7	14	1	7	21
Entertaining	5	6	6	5	10	7
Knitting, sewing	0	0	0	14	8	7
Hobbies, etc.	8	7	12	3	7	11

Source: adapted from Gershuny and Jones, 1987, p. 42

In some ways, gender differences in leisure activities are more obvious than those of class. A study by Young and Willmott (1973) showed few class differences between married men, except in certain areas like active sports, reading or gardening. The sharpest class differences are between unskilled or semi-skilled men and other classes taken together. In almost all areas of leisure, whether at home or as active or spectating participants in sports, the professional and managerial classes do more than any other class. This is a finding very much in line with other evidence about non-work activity patterns (which are further discussed in section 6.6), and it must reflect, amongst other factors, the greater financial resources available to the professional and managerial classes. We should also note that, although Young and Willmott do not show great class differences in most leisure activities, this may in some respects be misleading. For example, the 'quality' of leisure activities will vary across classes. So, even if people of all classes go out occasionally for a meal, professionals may well eat better than the unskilled.

A person's age, or more accurately his or her stage in the life cycle, also affects participation in leisure activities. The young and the elderly have more free time than other age groups and, in a sense, the lives of both these groups are organized around leisure, although these are also times when income is at its lowest. This is especially true of young people whose leisure culture is discussed in the next section. Married couples with young children experience most constraints. They have less money and less time. As children grow up, household income is rising to its peak and husband and wife are beginning to have more free time, even if they are still involved with their children on a day-to-day basis. When children have left home, couples have more time available even if their income is no longer rising. For middle-class couples at least, this is a period when they return to a pattern of shared leisure pursuits that they may have followed when they were much younger.

A consumer society?

The privatization of leisure is connected with the growth of a commercial leisure industry. There is a flourishing industry providing goods and services for people's leisure. Very large firms like the Rank Organization, the Grand Metropolitan Group or the big brewing groups provide for leisure activities across the social spectrum. Furthermore, this commercialization of leisure provision does not extend only to activities outside the home. Many home-based forms of leisure are obviously commercialized – from video recorders to home improvements.

These dual processes of privatization and commercialization have persuaded some sociologists that the appearance of a distinctive set of leisure activities can have some undesirable effects. The consumer, it is suggested, is fed with ready-made leisure – at a price and making a profit for someone – which serves to divert attention away from real problems by giving spurious pleasure. This cultural influence is all the more pervasive because it is brought right into the home. The result is that consuming things, including leisure goods, becomes a central life interest, and shopping a major national preoccupation. Consumption becomes a question of *identification*:

> People have increasingly turned to commodities to differentiate themselves as individuals, to imbue themselves with a distinctive style and create for themselves an identity perceived as lacking elsewhere. Products of all kinds – particularly clothes, but also electrical appliances, cars, beverages and food – have come to signify *who* their wearers are. Consumption has ceased to be purely material or narrowly functional – the satisfaction of basic bodily needs. Today, consumption is both *symbolic* and *material*. It expresses, in a real sense, a person's place in the world – his or her core identity. (Gardner and Sheppard, 1989, p. 45)

Such a view of a passive, hedonistic and manipulated consumer is an exaggeration and oversimplifies the social process involved. Some light is thrown on these questions by a study of 'enthusiasms' by Bishop and Hoggett (1986).

Organizing around enthusiasms: a case study

The authors are interested in describing the organization of enthusiasms in British society – those leisure pursuits undertaken, collectively with others, in clubs or societies. Bishop and Hoggett point to the huge variety of such enthusiasms, from soccer to tropical fish, from model railways to dress-making, and from stamp collecting to fancy rats. Indeed the only activities that the authors did not find represented in an organized form were cookery and DIY.

The study was conducted in two areas of Bristol and Leicester. Having identified the groups existing in these two areas, the authors isolated a sample and conducted some interviews. They were surprised at the sheer scale of activity. In Kingswood, the area of Bristol, for instance, there were at least 300 groups (with an average membership of 90) for a population of 85,000 people. These groups were often well established and long-lived; one-half had been running for over 15 years. The activities can run very deep. For example, in the area of Leicester with a population of 68,000, the authors estimate that some 3000 men are involved in playing football on Saturdays alone. As to the gender and class composition, although some activities, particularly sports, were dominated by men, others were dominated by women and the majority were mixed. There were class differences in the types of activity supported; tennis, for example, tends to be a middle-class pursuit, while boxing is generally the preserve of the working class. However, these class differences were much less sharp than expected. Poverty and unemployment, on the other hand, do make a significant difference to participation in enthusiasms.

'The concern of this book is with activity which is freely given yet typically assumes the form of highly skilled and imaginative work, whilst remaining leisure and not employment. We wish to look at the self-confessed amateurs who go about their activity in a highly professional manner and yet for whom the "social aspects" of their pursuit are indispensable' (Bishop and Hoggett, 1986, p. 1). So enthusiasms involve skills that are practised in the enthusiasm itself – being knowledgeable about tropical fish or being dextrous in the modelling of railway locomotives, for example. They also involve the development of standards of judgment of the contributions made by the participants – standards which almost inevitably involve competition. At the same time, enthusiasms are *social*, involving mutual aid and reciprocity, even when the activity, as in the case of gardening, is not an intrinsically collective activity.

Enthusiasts, in other words, are not passive, manipulated consumers. What, then, are the relationships of enthusiasms to the commercial provision of leisure? On the whole, enthusiasms are not greatly commercialized; they tend to produce what they consume. However, they also vary in the degree to which they are open to commercial influences. Bishop and Hoggett distinguish closed from open enthusiasms. Closed enthusiasms are so called because they express a much higher degree of independence from the wider society. They tend to generate change from within and from the bottom up. Open systems, on the other hand, are more likely to be influenced from outside and to be open to pressures from commercial organizations.

Railway modelling is an example of a relatively closed system. There is a long-established pattern whereby enthusiasts begin to develop a talent for a particular aspect of the activity, start to develop workshop facilities within their own home, move into mail order and perhaps eventually become small manufacturers. They remain small scale, however. Change and initiative is generated from the bottom up, which enables the railway modelling enthusiasts to maintain a fairly closed system, apparently impervious to commercial influence.

Enthusiasms organized around sport, by contrast, tend to be more open and more subject to commercial and wider professional influences. Tennis is a case in point. Not only is equipment commercially provided, but the conduct of tennis clubs is clearly influenced by professional tennis. Bishop and Hoggett suggest that the introduction of the tie-break into club tennis is an example of this tendency. In professional tournaments, the tie-break was introduced because of the difficulties of time management. Many clubs have taken up the practice although they do not, as a rule, have any such problem. For many tennis clubs, therefore, the idea of what is 'proper' authentic tennis is taken from outside the enthusiasm, not generated from within.

Summary

1 People nowadays have more time, and rather more money, for leisure, which is defined in terms of non-work.
2 There are gender, life-cycle and class differences in leisure patterns.
3 The great bulk of leisure time is spent in the home, especially in watching television.
4 Involvement in leisure is not necessarily a passive pursuit.

Related topics

For further discussion of the way that different members of the family are sociable inside and outside the home, see section 6.6. The way in which youth culture is organized around leisure is discussed in section 10.4.

10.4 Youth Culture
Spectacular youth cultures

In modern Britain, young people have become a focus of attention; they have become a *problem*. It is assumed that being young is somehow special; it is a state that requires public notice from the middle-aged and the old. Obviously, a wide variety of attitudes are mixed up in this, including envy, fear, dislike and even sympathy. Whatever the attitude, however, the young are seen as *different*.

To some extent, sociological analysis of youth culture (or cultures) has adopted the common-sense view of young people as a problematic category in that it has focused on *spectacular* youth cultures. These are cultures that construct themselves as spectacles; it is as if they are meant to be seen, looked at. Consequently, participants dress flamboyantly and distinctively, are noisy and demonstrative in public places, and appear to behave defiantly in such a way as to attract condemnation. Critical to this spectacularity is the adoption of a particular *style*. Each youth culture has its own particular style, a blend of special tastes in music, clothes, hairstyle or even body language. Furthermore, young people are creative in putting together elements of style drawn from quite different sources; punk style is a case in point. Despite these disparate sources, the elements of youth culture styles do fit together. Different styles separate one culture from another, give members an identity, and enable them to recognize themselves and others.

The post-war period in Britain has seen many examples of spectacular youth cultures differentiated by style: Teddy boys, mods, rockers, skinheads, punks, hippies, and ravers. The majority of these youth cultures are working class, which finding raises the question as to why working-class youth cultures are more spectacular than middle-class ones. Answers to this question are heavily influenced by studies from the Birmingham School of Contemporary Cultural Studies, and in particular a book by Hall and Jefferson entitled *Resistance Through Rituals* (1976). They argue that there are certain problems faced by working-class youth because of their class position that are intensified by their age. They lack power and authority, have few material resources, and cannot expect rewarding employment. Their adult life does not hold out much hope for

Plates 10.1, 10.2, and 10.3   Youth cultures.
Source: Format

them. In these circumstances, the adoption of a subcultural style gives other rewards of status and approval, an identity and a place in a world circumscribed by fellow participants, and a sense of being in control of at least some part of life. The adoption of a youth culture of this kind is, therefore, a *symbolic* resistance to society's definition of working-class life. It is symbolic because it takes over conventional images and gives them new, unusual and perhaps surprising meanings. Skinheads, for example, in wearing jeans, braces and boots, transform the meaning of working-class work clothes. These clothes are aggressively worn rather than shamefully carried as the badge of a manual worker.

This view, that working-class youth cultures represent a form of resistance to the conditions of working-class life, has to cope with the objection that there are large differences between youth cultures. Mods, for example, cultivate a neat and sometimes sharply dressed image, while skinheads aggressively assert what are assumed to be the masculine qualities of working-class life. There may, furthermore, be equally large differences between any of the more obvious youth cultures and 'conforming' youth. To some extent, these diversities may be 'merely' a question of the choice of one style rather than another. However, as we show in section 3.4, the working class is not homogeneous but is internally differentiated. Mods and skinheads may, therefore, be drawn from separate sections of the working class (or lower-middle class) and have dissimilar experiences that are reflected in the adoption of their distinctive styles.

The argument is, then, that working-class youth cultures are a form of symbolic resistance against a dominant culture which assigns working-class life a subordinate place. On this view, it is impossible to see these youth cultures independently of that dominant culture, or, for that matter, of the culture of parents that provides many of the experiences on which youth cultures are based. However, resistance of this kind is not necessarily effective, although it is obviously true that the behaviour and style of young people can excite considerable adult fury. This lack of effectiveness derives partly from the fact that any individual's participation in a youth culture is short-lived, and partly from the very fact that resistance is symbolic and not 'real'.

There are also certain paradoxes in the resistance offered by working-class youth cultures. One of these is nicely illustrated by skinhead culture. On the one hand, skinheads are defiant of society and perhaps of their parents' generation. On the other hand, their activities seem to celebrate some traditional working-class values. Skinhead behaviour, chiefly their attacks on other people, frequently get them into trouble with authority. They are aggressive and violent with people they think of as outsiders – black people, students, and anybody who looks 'odd'. At the same time, as Clarke (1976) suggests, skinhead culture also represents the parent, working-class, culture; it is a 'magical recovery of community', a reassertion of the virtues of collective solidarity that once held working-class communities together but no longer do so. For Clarke, the skinhead insistence on territory, the dislike of anybody different, and the antipathy to authority are all elements of working-class life. The simultaneity of resistance and a firm embeddedness in working-class culture may have further paradoxical consequences. For example, a study by Willis (1977), described in more detail in section 8.3, gives an account of a group of working-class boys who defy the authority of their school but, in doing so, condemn themselves to dead-end jobs because they do not aim at gaining qualifications. Resistance, in this case, leads to eventual subordination.

There have been many criticisms of the approach taken by *Resistance Through Rituals*. Cohen (1980), for example, points out that the adoption of some styles may be conservative rather than resistant. He also notes the difficulty of interpreting symbols, the lack of evidence about how the young people themselves actually use them, and the importance attached by the sociologists to symbols which can be relatively meaningless. But the approach also raises a series of other questions. First, most young people do not belong to spectacular youth cultures but are 'ordinary' young people; this, in turn, raises the question as to why some working-class young people belong to spectacular youth cultures while others do not. Second, there are spectacular, and defiant, youth cultures that contain middle-class young people, or are even largely middle class. Third, most members of spectacular youth cultures are male and white and there is a need to consider how female and black young people are involved in youth cultures. Fourth, it is clear that detailed consideration needs to be given to the reactions to young people from 'adult' society.

'Ordinary' youth

According to a recent study by Willis (1990), only 13 per cent of young people questioned claimed to belong to a spectacular youth culture. There is indeed considerable evidence which suggests that most young people are not greatly different from their elders (see Davis, 1990). In general, inter-generational relationships within the family are harmonious. In one study, for example, almost 90 per cent of 16-year-olds said that they get on well with their mothers, while three-quarters say the same about their fathers. Perhaps even more surprising, only a small minority of young people feel that school is a waste of time. Another study (Furnham, 1989) found that two-thirds of adolescents favoured capital punishment for murderers and the same proportion agreed that crime does not pay. The same study also argued that 'young people seem to be involved with both youth culture and adult culture, seeking neither to subvert the latter nor to replace it with the former. This is not to say that they are against change, but rather that the change they appear to favour is moderate and limited' (p. 192). In sum, the majority of adolescents are conforming and conventional. As another study concluded: 'The participants in this inquiry did not show much resemblance to the adolescent of popular stereotype: they were not mindless consumers, practioners of violence and sensuality, rebels against all authority, degenerate, feckless or lazy' (Kitwood, 1980). Indeed, in many studies it is not so much the hostility of young people towards society that is in evidence but the reverse; adults manifest considerable fear of young people, a topic we return to later. But nonetheless there is still a sense that every young person is a participant in youth culture, even if not a spectacular participant. Young people were not always treated as a problem or a special category; there have not always been well-marked characteristics of appearance or tastes in music, films, or books special to the young; there has not always, in other words, been a distinctive youth culture. This suggests that youth cultures are not biologically determined by the facts of ageing but are, rather, social constructions. Different societies treat ageing in different ways and have different favourite ages. It would, after all, be possible for British society to become especially aware of some other age group and for a culture appropriate to that group to develop. There are signs that that may be happening for the middle-aged and, perhaps, also for the elderly.

What social factors, then, account for the creation of youth cultures and the identification of youth as a separate social category and a distinctive phase of life? The most general reason for this change is that the transitional period from dependent childhood to independent adulthood has been greatly lengthened in modern industrial societies. This change has been promoted by attitudes and policies towards education and work. With the separation of home and work, children no longer slip imperceptibly from childhood into the world of work. The gradual rise in the school-leaving age, and the apparent insistence on educational qualifications for many jobs, lengthen the period before young people go out to work. Lastly, young people in the post-war period are better-off than those before the war, whether they are in full-time education or at work. The young have, therefore, become a market for records, clothes and books that can be commercially exploited. For example, in a relatively early study of the teenage consumer, Abrams (1959) calculated that, compared with 1938, the real earnings of teenagers in 1958 had increased by 50 per cent (twice as much as their parents' increase) and their real discretionary spending power (that is, the money left over after necessities have been paid for) had almost doubled in the same period.

Box 10.4   Symbolic creativity

Clothes shopping has been a central part of post-war youth
cultural consumerism. As a cultural practice, however, shopping
has tended to be marginalized in much of the writing about youth,
style and fashion. Shopping has been considered a private and
feminine activity and part of the process of incorporation into the
social machinery.

But young people don't just buy passively or uncritically. They
always transform the meaning of bought goods, appropriating
and recontextualizing mass-market styles. That appropriation
entails a form of symbolic work and creativity as young
consumers break the ordered categories of clothes, the suggested
matches and ideas promoted by shops. They bring their own
specific and differentiated grounded aesthetics to bear on
consumption, choosing their own colours and matches and
personalizing their purchases. Most young people combine
elements of clothing to create new meanings. They adopt and
adapt clothing items drawn from government surplus stores, for
example, or training shoes, track suits, rugby shirts, Fred Perry
tops from sportswear shops. They make their own sense of what
is commercially available, make their own aesthetic judgments,
and sometimes reject the normative definitions and categories of
'fashion' promoted by the clothing industry.

While many of the young people we spoke to obtain their ideas
about clothes from friends or from simply observing how clothes
looked worn on other people, many also use the media to
understand and keep up with the latest fashions. They get ideas
about clothes from sources such as television programmes, like
'The Clothes Show', fashion and music magazines, or from the
personal dress styles of particular pop artists. Aspects of the
clothes and outfits worn by pop groups like Bananarama and
Amazulu, for example, were taken up *en masse* by young women
in the early and mid 1980s, particularly items such as haystack
hairstyles, dungarees and children's plimsolls.

Since the early 1980s, media and marketing attention has
shifted towards the employed with high salaries such as the 25–40
age group and the 'empty-nesters'. Changing economic circumstances, particularly the growth in youth unemployment and the
start of what will be a long-term decline in the youth population,
have made the 16-to-24-year-old market far less attractive and
lucrative. This has meant that there now exists a substantial block

of young people for whom the retail boom has provided few benefits. With many working-class youth now denied the sources of income which financed the spectacular subcultures of the 1960s and 1970s, the right to 'good clothes' can no longer be automatically assumed.

The young unemployed especially find it difficult to develop their own image and lifestyle through purchased items. For these young people, using clothes to express their identities, stylistically, is something of a luxury. With social identities increasingly defined in terms of the capacity for private, individualized consumption, those who are excluded from that consumption feel frustrated and alienated.

For many working-class young people, impotent window shopping is a source of immense frustration. One young woman said that she would not go window shopping for this reason:

> I don't like window shopping very much. Especially if I don't have the money . . . 'cause if you see something and you want it, you can't afford it. So I don't go window shopping unless I have money.

Remarkably, however, even young people with limited spending power still often find ways to dress stylishly and to express their identities through the clothes they wear. Young women and men still manage to dress smartly and make the most out of slender resources, buying secondhand clothes or saving up to buy particular items of clothing. For some the emphasis on presenting a smart or fashionable image is a priority above everything else and results in quite disproportionate amounts being spent on clothes. One young woman said that she bought a clothing item every week, but sacrificed by going 'skint' for the rest of the week. Her rationale was that quality was better than quantity:

> I'd rather buy things that'll last me than cheap things what won't, and you don't get the quality in them, do you? . . . I feel better in myself if I know I've got summat on like expensive, instead of cheap.

Source: Willis, 1990, pp. 85–7

The generalized youth culture that is created by these forces has three important features. First, it is a culture of *leisure* rather than work; the primary focus of attention is on non-work life, and that provides the best means of self-expression. Second, the social relationships of youth cultures are organized around the *peer group*; they are as much collective as individual. Lastly, as we have already pointed out, youth groups are characterized by a strong interest in *style*. It is this interest in style that enables us to talk simultaneously about youth culture and youth *cultures*. There are many youth cultures; each is differentiated from the others by its own distinctive style, even if they blend into one another at the boundaries. However, it is also possible to speak of a youth culture that is differentiated from other age cultures in our society by the three features just mentioned. It is obvious that youth cultural styles are related to commercial provision, especially clothes and music. It is an exaggeration, however, to see style simply as manufactured by consumer sociey. A number of studies have pointed to the ways in which young people are creative of their style. For example, in a study of the way that young people *use* television, cinema, music, or clothes, Willis (1990) stresses 'the dynamic and living qualities of everyday culture and especially their necessary work and symbolic creativity' (p. 18) (see box 10.4).

Youth cultures are, then, characterized by leisure interests, peer groups, and style. Adult groups of various kinds also have these characteristics but they are not so marked. The *culture* of any social group represents a way of defining and coping with the world and making some coherent sense of everyday experiences; cultures are 'maps of meaning'. Youth cultures represent ways of dealing with, and giving meaning to, the particular experiences of youth in modern industrial society. Young people have to manage the period of transition that we referred to earlier and they have to acquire a sense of identity and control over their lives. However, in whatever ways youth cultures succeed in performing these functions, they are not isolated from the rest of society. Youth cultures relate to parent cultures on the one hand, and to the wider, dominant cultures of society on the other. These relationships provide part of the reason for referring to youth cultures as *subcultures*.

If young people relate to the culture of their parents, and if parent cultures differ from one another, then so too will youth cultures. Growing up is not a similar experience for everyone, and young people from different social groups will have different problems to face and will construct different maps of meaning. To a very large extent, these differences will depend on the parent culture. For example, generally speaking, middle-class parents have different experiences and cultures from working-class parents. The children of these parents will, similarly, have different experiences from each other and different youth cultures will result. However tempting it is to talk of youth culture as a single undifferentiated block, therefore, it is important to remember that it is internally fragmented as well, not only by style, but also by class, gender, and ethnicity. Youth cultures reflect other social divisions.

Middle-class youth cultures

The middle classes do, of course, participate to a limited extent in the more spectacular youth cultures that we have described. There are also spectacular, and apparently resistant, youth cultures which are *largely* middle class. These are not so easy to understand from the perspective of *Resistance Through Rituals* (Hall and Jefferson, 1976), since they would appear to have no need of resistance; they are not in as subordinated a position as the working class. Nonetheless, such cultures have been fairly well established in the post-war period, from the beats to the hippies to the political movements of the 1960s and to the new religious movements. What unifies these cultures is a counter-cultural tendency, a system of explicit values that opposes the currently dominant one. One important element in this value system is a belief in the importance of the self – self-development, individualism, the significance of expressing feelings. These middle-class youth cultures represent a way of life which can involve active political opposition or a withdrawal from society.

In their stress on these values, the middle-class youth cultures of the 1960s have a striking resemblance to the new religious movements discussed in section 10.5. There is a line of descent from hippies to the religious cults, both also spectacular cultures. Some of the same themes occur in Aggleton's (1987) study of a middle-class group of educational misfits, teenagers who did not do especially well educationally despite having parents who valued education. He argues that this group did have a powerful and resistant culture and did adopt a recognizable style. The boys' clothes, for example, were a mixture of working-class and upper-class styles – braces, boots, collarless shirts, straw hats and cream coloured summer jackets. Most distinctive, however, was their commitment to values of individual creativity and personal autonomy. Indeed, they came close to the belief that their own individual talents would, of themselves, help them to succeed educationally without any work. The parents of this group were not only middle class but were from a particular section of the middle class, namely those employed in the 'expressive' occupations – the arts, social work, teaching. Interestingly, both new religious movements and the hippies recruit disproportionately from this section of the middle class. At this point we have to repeat the warning that we have already given in the analysis of spectacular working-class youth cultures. Political or spectacular middle-class youth cultures will also only represent a small proportion of middle-class youth.

The culture of the 'ordinary' majority may be altogether less one of resistance.

Gender and ethnicity

There are two important questions to ask when investigating the relationship between gender and youth cultures. Do girls participate in the spectacular youth cultures that we have described? Or do girls have youth cultures of their own, that are distinctively feminine (McRobbie, 1991)?

Girls do join in youth cultures. There are female skinheads or mods, for instance. However, the rate of participation by girls is very much lower; skinhead and mod cultures are predominantly male and, what is more, they are organized around masculinity; style and spectacularity are largely male. There are several reasons for this. Girls are much more tightly controlled by parents and local community. There is the ever-present fear of getting into trouble, especially sexual trouble. For boys, taking risks is exciting, while for girls it is dangerous. The result is that girls have less of a public street life and are more confined to home. They are furthermore expected to carry out more domestic tasks, which gives them less spare time. They are not at the centre of a group but become supporters of or helpers to the boys; the boys talk to, and interact with, each other. There are exceptions to this marginal participation in predominantly male youth cultures, with punk and traveller cultures containing significant numbers of girls.

McRobbie answers the second question – about the existence of distinctively female youth cultures – by again pointing to the marginality and subordination of women in modern Britain. It is true that young girls do create a 'teenybopper' culture of their own, based in their homes and organized around records, rock stars and fan magazines which allow an imagined relationship with the idols. This culture can, to some extent, allow girls to 'negotiate a space of their own'. It can also act to create groupings of girls that exclude boys. However, at the same time, the teenybopper culture also *subordinates* girls, for it is essentially oriented to boys, marriage and the family as the only desirable goals, and it prepares girls for the role of girlfriend as a 'hanger-on' to a boy.

To a considerable extent, black and Asian young people are even more marginalized in spectacular youth cultures than women. Some such cultures, Teddy boys and skinheads for example, are indeed positively hostile to ethnic minorities. Possibly partly as a result, young blacks form their own subcultures as defiant as punks or skins. One of the most significant black subcultures is Rastafarianism, which can be seen as reaction to the dominance of white society, for Rastafarians rejoice in being black, believing that they are the lost tribe of Israel, while they see white society as corrupt and immoral. Rastafarianism is an essentially cultural and religious response that effectively means a withdrawal from society rather than a confrontation with it. It does have the same subcultural emphasis on style that we have noted in youth cultures, although it may also involve larger numbers of older people in a way that punks, for example, do not.

Young blacks do, then, form spectacular youth cultures. It has also been argued that white youth cultures are affected by black culture indirectly (Hebdige, 1979). An obvious example here is black music which, in various forms, has been influential in youth cultures since the war. Jones (1988) goes further than this, arguing that there is at least the basis for an alliance between white and black young people. A changing social and economic context gives common experiences of schooling, the transition from school to work, unemployment and employment, and relations with the police.

Reaction

As we noted at the begining of this section, the media often see youth as a problem, concentrating on drugs, appearance, and violence. Indeed, all the youth culture styles of the post-war years in Britain – rockers, teds, mods, skinheads and punks – have been regularly reviled in the press. What is, perhaps, striking about the response of adult Britain (or older opinion-leaders at any rate) is the way that it repeats history. The same things are said about each style: chiefly that young people form gangs which are threatening and aggressive, they are immoral, workshy, and unable to engage in what their elders regard as constructive pursuits. A 'family doctor' writing in a newspaper in the 1950s could speak for many of his successors who comment on youth cultures:

> Teddy boys . . . are all of unsound mind in the sense that they are all suffering from a form of psychosis. Apart from the birch or the rope, depending on the gravity of their crimes, what they need is rehabilitation in a psychiatric institution . . . Because they have not the mental stamina to be individualists they had to huddle together in gangs. (quoted in Brake, 1980)

We have also noted that this is a very misleading picture. Actually, the mass of young people conform. What seems to be happening is that adult society is *projecting* its fears about the state of society on to young people; young people are made to stand for the ills of society. This projection can have very real social consequences; as Cohen (1980) points out, they can develop into what he calls a 'moral panic'. He argues that, at certain times of social stress, societies get into moral panics when a great deal of attention is focused on the behaviour of certain social groups. These panics are amplified in the media and, because of this attention, the agencies of social control – the police and the courts – crack down on the groups concerned. This gives a further turn to the screw. Arrests, prosecutions, and convictions give further credibility to the panic – and so it goes on.

Summary

1 The post-war period in Britain has seen an emphasis on young people as a specific social category. There is a general culture of youth which is distinct from that of other age groups.
2 There are many varieties of youth culture, often based in class, gender or ethnicity. Each adopts particular styles that differentiate it from other youth cultures.
3 Many surveys indicate that the majority of young people are conforming in attitude and behaviour.
4 Besides focusing on the characteristics of young people and youth cultures, sociological attention should also be given to the reactions of adult society to young people.

10.5 Religion

In many ways, religion is a very powerful force in Britain. Chuchmen are listened to and their pronouncements can stir up a good deal of controversy. They are often asked to comment on social issues of the day – inner-city poverty, for instance. Religious worship is compulsory in schools. There is a strong religious component to many of our public ceremonies – coronations, for example. The same goes for private ceremonies; weddings in church and baptisms are still much favoured. In these senses, then, Britain is a religious, even Christian, society.

At the same time, two trends seem to point in a different direction. First, there has been something of a decline in individual adherence to Christian religious belief, as measured, for example, by the numbers of people who regularly go to church. Second, there is growth in newer religious movements which are often not Christian. These are frequently 'sectarian' and 'communitarian' in their social organization. This means that worshippers are organized into small groups in which everybody knows each other and is very committed to their religion. These new religious movements are often seen as alternatives to the dominant religious bodies (the Church of England or the Roman Catholic Church) and, occasionally, as dangerous and threatening. In the remaining part of this section we consider these two issues in more detail.

The Christian churches and secularization

Table 10.6 gives some idea of the changes in the *membership* of the Christian churches in the period 1970 to 1987 and shows that there has been a steady decline in most of the churches. In 1987, only one in seven of the adult population of Britain was a member of a Christian church. There are, however, significant differences between different parts of the country. In England, for example, only 11 per cent of the adult population were church members, while in Northern Ireland the corresponding figure was 70 per cent.

Table 10.6 Membership of the Christian churches, 1970–1987

	1970 (000s)	1975 (000s)	1980 (000s)	1983 (000s)	1985 (000s)	1987 (000s)
Anglican	2548	2270	2154	2083	1985	1928
Methodist	694	615	558	529	526	517
Baptist	295	270	240	235	239	241
Presbyterian	1807	1646	1509	1430	1383	1346
Other Protestant	530	526	533	545	573	605
Total Protestant	5874	5327	4993	4821	4707	4637
Roman Catholic	2715	2534	2342	2215	2128	2059
Orthodox	193	202	209	214	220	231
Total Christian	8782	8063	7544	7251	7055	6927
% of adult pop.	20.7	18.6	16.9	16.0	15.3	15.0

Source: adapted from Davie, 1990, p. 398

Membership may, however, be an unreliable guide to the numbers of people who take their religion seriously. Membership figures may be inflated because they do not adequately reflect turnover, that is, they include people who have lapsed from membership. Much more important, people who are members of churches may not attend acts of worship particularly frequently. Thus, although one in seven of adults in Britain is a member of a Christian church, only one in ten goes to church at all regularly. The relationship between religious belief, church attendance, and church membership is illustrated in figure 10.2.

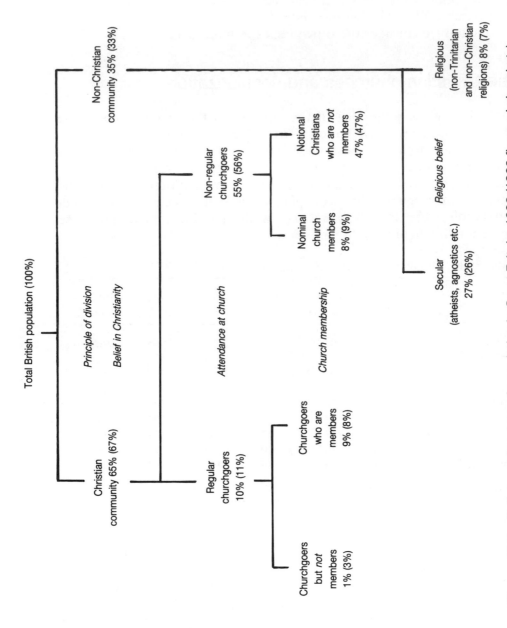

Figure 10.2 Religious structure of population in Great Britain, 1990 (1980 figures in brackets).
Source: Brierley, 1991, p. 203

There has been a gradual decline in participation in Christian churches – a process of secularization. There are many ways in which secularization can be measured. It is convenient to distinguish active participation in religious activities from attendance at one or two rituals that happen to be religiously solemnized. An example of the first would be regular attendance at church, and of the second would be marriage in church. The point is that secularization is more marked for the first than the second. Thus, in the mid nineteenth century, probably some 40 per cent of the population attended church on Sunday. The corresponding figure in 1989 is around 10 per cent. Other activities that indicate a degree of commitment have also declined significantly. Both church membership and participation in Sunday schools, for example, have declined sharply. Involvement in the major rituals that mark out an individual's life – baptism, marriage, and burial – have also declined over the past century but not by so much. For example, some 70 per cent of the population are married in some form of religious ceremony while at the turn of the century it was about 75 per cent.

So far, we have argued that there has been a decline in the rate at which the population of Britain participates in formal religious institutions; fewer people are members of churches, and acts of worship and other religious ceremonies are less frequently attended. There are a number of reasons for this decline in what we can call *institutional adherence*. The state has grown in power and the Church of England is less involved in the political process. Science and the institutions of scientific work have grown in importance and claim to solve problems, like those of health for example, which previously were the province of religious institutions. Many of the welfare and charitable functions of the churches are now also performed by other agencies.

The decline in institutional adherence does not, however, necessarily mean that Christianity – or religion in general – is a spent force in Britain. There are two further issues that have to be considered: civic rituals and privatized religion.

Civic rituals

We have already referred to the way in which the Church of England is integrated into the national culture. A whole series of national events – or civic rituals – have a religious component. The Archbishop of Canterbury, for example, presides at coronations, royal weddings and services of thanksgiving. Children are brought up in a religious culture at school, and there are many schools administered and controlled by religious bodies in which religious instruction is taken seriously. The Christian churches, in short, still have a considerable amount of power and influence, even political influence.

Church influence does not only operate at the national level, however. Major events in the lives of ordinary people are often commemorated in religious settings. As we have pointed out, the majority of people still prefer to have their births, marriages, and deaths solemnized in church or chapel. One can, of course, argue that civic rituals or the religious sanctification of births, marriages and deaths do not have any particular *meaning* for the majority of the population. However, these forms of participation do indicate that the church still carries considerable *institutional* weight.

Archbishop angers MPs with attack on Government

Carey says riots linked to poverty

Maev Kennedy

THE new Archbishop of Canterbury, Dr George Carey, last night dismissed the Government's explanation for the Newcastle riots and laid the blame squarely on social deprivation. He also attacked many aspects of Conservative education policies, and said church schools were suffering "financial strangulation".

Figure 10.3   The Archbishop Speaks.
Source: *The Guardian*, 9 September 1992

Meaning

The second issue concerns the question of meaning. It may well be that institutional adherence to the church has declined, but that does not imply that people are not *privately* religious. Berger (1968), for example, argues that religion in modern societies is pushed increasingly into the sphere of the family or even the individual. Religion becomes a question of private feeling rather than of public worship or even public morality. There is some evidence that, in Britain, religion does flourish in the private sphere, even when its public significance is in decline. According to a survey of personal values in Britain (Abrams et al., 1985), three-quarters of the sample believed in the existence of God, three-fifths saw themselves as 'religious persons', half regularly felt the need for prayer, meditation, or contemplation, and one in five reported having had a profound spiritual experience. The degree of religious commitment is higher the greater the age of the respondent, and women as a group tend to be more religious than men of any age. Religiosity does not, however, seem to vary at all with social class membership. An earlier study (Abercrombie et al., 1970) found a large reservoir of beliefs which, if not precisely religious, are at least non-scientific or spiritual. A considerable proportion of respondents engaged in superstitious or luck-bringing practices, like touching wood or throwing salt over the shoulder. As the authors say: 'It seems that for many people, probably the great majority, religious beliefs and practices merge almost indistinguishably with superstitions of all sorts, to be summoned only in special situations of crisis and anxiety' (p. 113).

Religious growth

The continuing, if muted, significance of civic ritual, and the apparent importance of private as distinct from institutional religion, are reasons for moderating *extreme* theories of secularization that might be based solely on the decline of institutional adherence. On balance, though, the case for the existence of a process of secularization in the major Christian churches is very strong. However, this does not mean that there is no religious growth at all. First, although churchgoing in the Anglican communion as a whole is in decline, *individual* congregations are increasing in size. This is particularly so in rural areas. Thus 40 per cent of rural churches grew in the period 1985 to 1989. Second, some movements within Christianity have shown great vigour. Table 10.7 shows that the category of 'other' Protestant increased in membership while others were falling. Within this category the more evangelical churches are even more active. The number of persons attending services of the House Church movement between 1979 and 1989, for example, increased by 144 per cent (although the actual numbers remain small at 108,000 in 1989). Third, as table 10.7 shows, membership of all non-Christian religions except Judaism grew in the period 1975–90.

Table 10.7 Estimated church membership, United Kingdom, 1975 and 1990

	Adult members (millions)	
	1975	1990
Trinitarian churches		
Anglican	2.27	1.84
Presbyterian	1.65	1.29
Methodist	0.61	0.48
Baptist	0.27	0.24
Other Protestant	0.53	0.70
Roman Catholic	2.53	1.95
Orthodox	0.20	0.27
Total	8.06	6.77
Non-Trinitarian churches		
Mormons	0.10	0.15
Jehovah's Witnesses	0.08	0.12
Spiritualists	0.06	0.06
Other non-Trinitarian	0.09	0.13
Total	0.33	0.46
Other religions		
Muslims	0.40	0.99
Sikhs	0.12	0.39
Hindus	0.10	0.14
Jews	0.11	0.11
Others	0.08	0.23
Total	0.81	1.86

Source: *Social Trends*, 1992, p. 191; from *UK Christian Handbook*, 1992–3. Crown copyright

New religious movements

The Moonies we had met at the camp were robots, glassy eyed and mindless, programmed as soldiers in this vast fund-raising army with no goals or ideals, except as followers of the half-baked ravings of Moon who lived in splendour while his followers lived in forced penury. (*Daily Mail*, quoted in Barker, 1984)

The religious growth described in the previous section does involve a fairly large number of people. However, it is often the smaller and more exotic religious movements that seem to attract most attention and unfavourable comment, as the quotation at the beginning of this section shows. Such movements (often called 'cults') are of considerable sociological interest in themselves; almost all of them involve a conversion experience (in contrast to the 'orthodox' faiths) and give some insight into how that process works; they all involve conviction and hence illustrate how values are formed and transformed; and most of them excite controversy and demonstrate how society defines deviant groups.

There are a very large number of what have been called new religious movements (NRMs); Barker (1989) estimates that there are 500 in the UK. Among those that have appeared regularly in the press are the Unification Church (the Moonies), the Hare Krishna movement, Transcendental Meditation, and Scientology. There is a temptation to believe that these movements are all the same; they are undoubtedly new and religious and, above all, seem to inspire their believers with a degree of commitment and dedication missing in many churchgoers, let alone the bulk of the population. However, new religious movements are diverse. Wallis (1984) proposes a typology of new religious movements. He suggests that there are two polar types – world rejecting and world affirming – which, as their names suggest, have opposite characteristics. Both of these can, in turn, be contrasted with a third type which he calls world accommodating. These relationships are shown in figure 10.3.

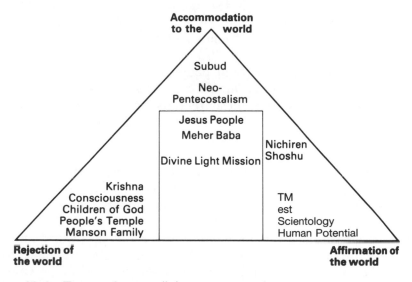

Figure 10.4 Types of new religious movement.
Source: Wallis, 1984, p. 6, reproduced with permission

Figure 10.3 is an ideal-type description and many types of NRM actually fall at various points between the extremes. *World-rejecting* movements can be characterized as follows. They tend to be exclusive, being based on the importance of the community as against the individual. Converts are expected to renounce their past lives and emotional ties, including those of their family, and the outside world is seen as threatening. The virtues of sharing money, clothes and affection are emphasized in contrast to the individual possession of these things. The submerging of personal identity is sometimes reflected in the similarity of appearance or dress or in the way in which converts may take new names.

World-affirming movements, on the other hand, may see the prevailing social order as having certain virtues. Mankind is seen not as essentially evil but, rather, as perfectible and having powers that can be released by participation in the given NRM. These may well be part-time movements without acts of collective worship or precise theologies. In contrast to the collective orientations of world-rejecting movements, world-affirming NRMs are individualistic, aiming to unlock the hidden powers latent in each person. The sources of unhappiness, in other words, lie not in the society outside but rather within oneself. There is no rejection of the world involved but rather an attempt to relate to the world more effectively.

The method and pattern of recruitment of the two types of movement differ substantially. Conversion to the world-rejecting movements tends to be more sudden, involving a sharp break with the convert's previous life. Because world-affirming NRMs do not cut themselves off from the outer world so much, recruitment can be a more gradual process and one that uses existing networks of friends and relatives. Similarly, different types of people are attracted to the different NRMs. World-rejecting movements recruit relatively young people in their early or mid twenties, who are disproportionately of middle-class origins and highly educated. Wallis (1984) suggests that these recruits are, in addition, socially *marginal* in some way, perhaps in having dropped out of higher education. By contrast, world-affirming movements recruit from socially *integrated* people, not necessarily middle class, with an average age of about 35 and who may be successful in life. On this account, therefore, world-rejecting NRMs appeal to those who have found no satisfaction in the conventional world; world-affirming movements recruit from those who are successful but who could be more so.

We have already mentioned that world-rejecting and world-affirming movements are pure types, and many if not most NRMs are in fact found between the extremes. A third type – *world-accommodating* – contrasts with both the other two. For world-accommodating movements, religious experience is not social or collective but is, instead, personal and individual. It is the importance of individual religious *experience* which is at the heart of these movements, like the charismatic, evangelical, renewal movements within Christianity which we have seen are a growth point. Acts of worship are enthusiastic and vital, giving participants a spiritual element to their lives which they feel is lacking in the more orthodox Christian churches.

The making of a Moonie: a case study

Further light is thrown on the recruitment to world-rejecting movements by Barker's (1984) study of the Unification Church, members of which are usually called Moonies after the leader of the church, the Reverend Moon. Two main problems are addressed in this study. First, there is the problem of how people are recruited into the movement. Second, there is the need to explain who is recruited, and why.

The Moonies have often been accused of brainwashing their converts. The assumption in much public discussion is that nobody could join a movement like that *unless* they were brainwashed. Barker describes the steps in the process of becoming a Moonie as follows. There is, first, an initial contact which may be through the personal networks of existing members, but is more likely to involve casual meetings in the street or in the course of everyday life. What follows is an invitation to a Unification Church centre where the potential convert may be offered a meal. A friendly and welcoming atmosphere prevails. Those who visit a centre will be invited to go to Unification Church workshops of varying lengths, from a weekend to three weeks (figure 10.4). These workshops consist mainly of courses of lectures. Having been to advanced workshops and 'graduated', the recruit becomes a member of the Unification Church.

This process of recruitment is clearly rigorous and it has also been claimed that it deprives the potential recruits of the power of choice by subjecting them to a barrage of propaganda, by depriving them of proper sleep and nourishment while at the workshops or by giving them too much love and attention. However, Barker's research shows that the process of recruitment is actually very *inefficient*. Nothing is known about how many people initially contacted actually get to a centre but, since many of these contacts are in the street, it seems unlikely that it is a particularly large proportion. However, Barker estimates that of those who go to a centre only one in ten go on to any kind of workshop. Thereafter, as figure 10.4 illustrates, recruits drop out at every stage of the process. Only 5 per cent of those who start on the workshop stage of recruitment are still in the movement after two years. If one takes as the starting point a visit to a Unification centre, only 0.005 per cent of recruits are still members of the Unification Church after two years.

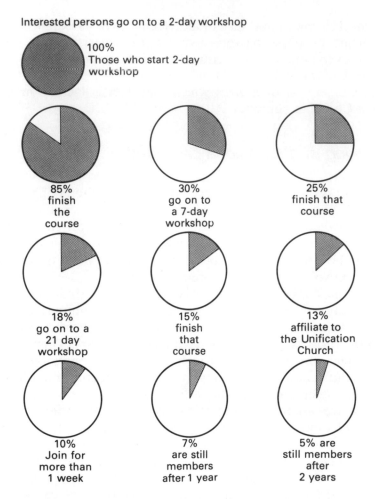

Interested persons go on to a 2-day workshop

100%
Those who start 2-day
workshop

85%
finish
the
course

30%
go on to
a 7-day
workshop

25%
finish that
course

18%
go on to a
21 day
workshop

15%
finish
that
course

13%
affiliate to
the Unification
Church

10%
Join for
more than
1 week

7%
are still
members
after 1 year

5% are
still members
after
2 years

Figure 10.5   The Moonie recruitment process, after initial visit to a Unification Church centre.
Source: Barker, 1984, p. 146

This very low rate of recruitment does strongly suggest that *particular* kinds of people become Moonies; it is not the case that all people are equally likely to become members of the Unification Church. Barker hypothesizes that it is not the recruitment methods that make a convert but, rather, the prior experiences that potential converts bring with them to the first meeting. The first step in testing this hypothesis was to compare Moonies with the population as whole. The conclusions were that Moonies are younger (with an average age of 26), from more middle-class family backgrounds, better educated and disproportionately male. More precise conclusions were made possible by a comparison with a control group matched for age, gender, social class, education and religious characteristics. Barker concludes from this comparison that Moonies are not inadequate or drifting personalities. They come from families as happy and secure as those of the control group. But she did find some other important differences.

Moonies tend to come from more conventional and 'respectable' homes, in which traditional values of family life, morality and decency are prized. Perhaps related to this kind of family background, Barker also found that many Moonie recruits had encountered the problems of life relatively late on and were ill-prepared to meet them. Before meeting members of the Unification Church, they may well have experienced an 'emotional dip' which the warm family atmosphere of the Moonies helped them to cope with.

More important still, although the Moonie group and the control group were both drawn from the middle class, the parents of Moonies were less likely to be in jobs concerned with making money and more likely to have occupations 'usually associated with values of duty or service, either to individuals (e.g. doctors, nurses, teachers) or to their country (e.g. the police, the armed service, the colonial service)' (p. 211). This parental background may well have given the Moonie recruits a particular set of values and attitudes that has been described as 'seekership'. Many of the Moonies were seeking something, some spiritual not material experience, but they were unclear what it was precisely. The Unification Church met that need.

Many of the new religious movements are very small in membership. Barker (1989) estimates that the largest movements have only a few

Plate 10.4 Moonie mass wedding.
Source: Camera Press

hundred members working anything like full-time for the movement. Many more will have a looser association. The Transcendental Meditation movement, for example, says that about 150,000 people have learned to meditate at a four-day course. Some authorities (Robbins, 1988) believe that there has been a slowing down in growth of NRMs. This may well indicate that there are intermittent bouts of religious ferment in modern societies.

The small size of these cults makes it very difficult to understand the ferocity of public reaction to them. Of course, societies do sometimes react violently to the presence of strange and unfamiliar groups in their midst. This reaction is likely to vary with what Beckford (1985) has called the 'mode of insertion' of cults into society. Those cults that are world-affirming and are more integrated with wider society will attract less controversy than the world-rejecting NRMs. One possible explanation for societal reaction to world-rejecting movements such as the Moonies lies in the centrality of family life in modern societies. The accusations of brainwashing stem from the sudden and apparently inexplicable way that people are converted and move away from their families. This sudden cessation of 'normal' family ties seems unnatural and, not surprisingly, the relatives of Moonie converts often become extremely upset about it. Ultimately, societal reaction is determined by the definition of a certain pattern of family relations as natural, right and proper; deviations from this norm are considered abnormal or even downright wicked (see chapter 6).

In conclusion, we return to the question raised at the beginning of this section on new religious movements, concerning the relationship of these movements to the process of secularization. The new religions have recruited people who are not satisfied by the religious experience offered by the declining main Christian churches. Where traditional religion remains a powerful force, as in Ireland, the new religions do not make much headway. Elsewhere, however, they appeal only to certain very small sections of the population, disproportionately young and middle class, who are only likely to spend a small part of their lives in the movement. In no sense, therefore, do the new religious movements in Britain compensate for the decline of the traditional religions or counteract the process of secularization.

Summary

1　There has been a process of secularization over the last century in Britain, at least as far as active participation in the Christian churches is concerned.

2　Nevertheless, a number of national events are organized around the church and significant numbers of people participate in religious, life-cycle rituals and hold beliefs privately that might be characterized as religious.

3 Although the main Christian churches are in decline, there has been a growth in a number of non-Christian sects and in newer branches of Christianity. However, these groupings still only command the allegiance of a very small proportion of the population.

4 New religious movements are very different from one another in their outlooks, constituencies and methods of recruitment.

Further reading

A good general introduction to the study of the mass media is Curran and Gurevitch (1991). Television, as the most important form of mass medium, is the subject of Fiske (1987). Leisure studies is a growing area but there is a shortage of basic textbooks; a deliberately argumentative book is Rojek (1985). Sport is dealt with in the readings collected by Horne et al. (1987). Brake (1980) and Frith (1984) are good surveys of the whole field of youth culture, while Willis (1990) is a recent study. Wallis (1984) is a good introduction to the topic of religious secularization, and Davie (1990) gives recent data on the UK. Robbins (1988) is an introduction to new religious movements.

11   Deviance, Crime and Control

Today, institutions fundamental to the British system of government are under attack: the public schools, the House of Lords, the Church of England, the holy institution of marriage, and even our magnificent police force are no longer safe from those who would undermine our society. And it's about time we said 'enough is enough' and saw a return to the traditional British values of discipline, obedience, morality, and freedom – freedom from the reds and the blacks and the criminals, prostitutes, pansies and punks, football hooligans, juvenile delinquents, lesbians and left-wing scum; freedom from the niggers, and the pakis and the unions, freedom from the gypsies and the Jews, freedom from the long-haired layabouts and students – freedom from the likes of you.

Tom Robinson Band, 'Power in the Darkness'

11.1   Introduction

Social problems are inherently political phenomena. Social problems in general, and deviant behaviour in particular, are not objective 'givens' of social life, but are identified and shaped in an ongoing political process. We do not all agree on what is deviant behaviour. What is regarded as a problem by one group may not be seen in this way by another group in society. We are, therefore, engaged in a controversial political process in which the values and interests of various groups are frequently in direct or indirect opposition to each other. The task – or perhaps the trick – of one group is to try to convince others that conditions which challenge *their* values or threaten *their* interests are *objectively* harmful and need to be corrected. In this sense, deviancy is created or socially constructed, it is a case of somebody defining some person or behaviour as deviant.

Police action against the travelling convoy of people wanting to hold a summer solstice festival at Stonehenge has received considerable media coverage in recent years. This is just one example of conflicting interests of landowners and travellers. In 1986 Tim Greene, a London solicitor acting for many travellers charged after a police crackdown at Stonehenge, complained of the contrasting attitude of the Dorset police towards farmers and travellers: 'There is a one-sided view. Whatever the farmers do, whether it be carrying offensive weapons or threatening breaches of the peace, the police don't take action against them. . . But the minute members of the convoy – who have been very peaceful here today – take one step out of line they are arrested' (*The Guardian*, 2 June 1986). Those groups who command relatively greater power resources stand a much greater chance of seeing their particular definitions of deviance accepted widely and of having their favoured solutions or strategies put into practice. In 1992 the government announced an urgent enquiry into the laws governing New Age travellers after a weekend where property allegedly worth £2 million was damaged. Lord Ferrers, the Home Office minister, 'accused the travellers of "military-style" tactics and using high-tech fax machines and portable telephones to plan their operations' (*The Guardian*, 11 August 1992). A week later it was announced that gypsies as well as travellers would face curbs on illegal camping, as part of the government proposals to give greater protection to landowners. The proposals were denounced by local authorities and by gypsy groups, representing the country's 13,500 gypsy caravans. Hughie Smith, president of the National Gypsy Council, called the government consultation paper 'a modern-day charter for the persecution of gypsies' (*The Times*, 19 August 1992). He went on to say that it 'was particularly unfair to tar gypsies with the brush of New Age travellers'.

Approaching the study of deviance, crime and control means that one needs to avoid gross and potentially damaging stereotypes and to consider more closely and dispassionately the social interaction involved. In fact, a 'revolution' has taken place in the sociology of deviance since the 1960s. This has involved the rejection of absolutist definitions of deviant behaviour (which assume that everyone agrees about what is deviant) in favour of an approach that sees such behaviour as that which is defined or labelled in a particular way. This approach does not endear sociologists to those in power, for the latter are in the business of trying to make their own definitions of deviance hold. It is not in their interests for the idea to get around that deviance is a relative concept and that there may be alternative versions of reality.

The two major insights regarding deviance that sociologists have recognized since the 1960s are, first, that the explanation of crime and deviance is logically bound up with the explanation of social control, and, second, that we need to re-establish the links between crime and the political, which orthodox criminology has totally neglected. So, instead of focusing exclusively on the controlled (the criminal, the delinquent, the mentally ill, the mentally retarded and so on), sociologists are now as much concerned – if not more so – with the controllers (the police, the judiciary, the medical profession, etc.).

However, it was recognized by sociologists that this was still too narrow an area of analysis. In short, the links between crime and the political became more explicitly drawn into sociological analysis with the advent of the 'new criminology' that emerged in the 1970s. The appreciation of the theoretical and empirical links between deviance and control, which was certainly the hallmark of the work of the American sociologists Becker (1963), Matza (1964) and Lemert (1967), was challenged in the 1970s by a group of radical young British sociologists. This was the first time that theoretical ideas about deviance had been exported from Britain to the USA instead of the other way round. The emergence of radical or critical criminology, associated most closely with Taylor et al. (1973; 1975), called for an even greater theoretical and empirical widening of scope and, by implication, for a more radical politics. To use an analogy, traditional criminology tends to look at the animals in the zoo; the 1970s saw the development of an interest in those who controlled the animals (the police, the judiciary and so on); while more recently there has been a resurgence of interest in who exactly owns the zoo! Box 11.1 illustrates the links between the deviant, the social control agencies and the victim; recent work has stressed that we cannot afford to overlook the political context in which these interactions take place.

In the last decade, issues of gender and race have more clearly come on to the agenda. In particular, there is now a vast range of work which encompasses feminist approaches. It would be dangerously misleading to think that there is one feminist perspective for, as Gelsthorpe and Morris (1990) remind, there are disparate and sometimes conflicting perspectives among feminist writers. However, all have exposed in various ways traditional criminology as the criminology of men. Of course, as Downes and Rock (1988) stress, women are not the only group who have been ignored. White-collar criminals certainly continue to attract less attention than they deserve when one considers the financial devastation for some small investors that their actions sometimes cause. In contrast, there is now a considerable amount of research on the experiences of black men in the criminal justice system. However, Rice (1990) has stressed how writing has focused either on the sexism of criminology or on the experience of black men and so usually ignored the extent to which sexist and racist ideologies interact. Nevertheless, despite some differences in

Box 11.1 The relationship between deviant, victim and social control

It is important to note that the links between deviant and victim are not always clear (hence the dotted line in the diagram). Who is the victim when someone smokes cannabis? Who is the deviant when someone is the victim of environmental pollution?

1 *Prior to the mid 1960s*, traditional criminologists focused almost exclusively on the deviant.
2 *Since the early 1970s*, sociologists have increasingly stressed how the explanation of crime and deviance is logically bound up with the explanation of social control.
3 *In the 1980s*, the importance of the victim has been increasingly recognized, both in real terms (e.g. the problems of the rape victim) and in estimating the extent of crime. The victim does not always report crime to social control agencies.
4 *Current interests* increasingly focus on the links between deviance and the political.

The political context

Social control
(Police, judiciary, medical profession, etc.)

Deviant — — — — — — — — — — — — — — — Victim

approach among sociologists, there is a growing tendency to stress the political nature of deviance and to structure empirical investigations around this emphasis. However, while all deviance may be *essentially* political, some deviance may *appear* to be more or less so in the eyes of observers, whether they be sociologists or lay persons: there is a variation in the degree of *overt* political emphasis that may be observed in particular cases. At any given point in time, some issues excite considerable disagreement, while others seem to command a basic consensus.

11.2   Varieties of Deviance

A Canadian criminologist, Hagan (1984), has developed a framework that identifies the varieties of deviance. From the starting point of defining deviance as a variation from a social norm, he argues that we should think of deviance as a continuous variable. Quite simply, there is an obvious difference between multiple murder and adolescent marijuana use. He suggests that most deviant acts can be located empirically on a continuum of seriousness between these two extremes. Hagan identifies three measures of seriousness:

Degree of agreement about the wrongfulness of the act   This assessment can vary from confusion and apathy, through high levels of disagreement, to conditions of general agreement.
Severity of the social response elicited by the act   Social penalties can, of course, vary from life imprisonment to polite avoidance.
Societal evaluation of the harm inflicted by the act   Here the concern is with the degree of victimization and the personal and social harm a set of acts may involve.

Hagan argues that, in most modern societies, these three measures of seriousness are closely connected. So, what he is saying is that the more serious acts of deviance are those likely to evoke broad agreement about their wrongfulness, a severe social response, and an evaluation of the act as being harmful. This approach provides insights but is also contentious. Hagan portrays the situation in visual terms as a pyramid, with the less serious forms of deviance at the base and the more serious forms of deviance at the peak (see figure 11.1). This is an interesting notion, for the form of a pyramid suggests that the most serious acts of deviance in a society tend also to be less frequent, while less serious acts may be quite common. Hagan's framework provides a useful basis from which to consider the current British situation.

Hagan's major division is between criminal and non-criminal forms of deviance. In fact, he argues that 'the most serious forms of deviance are defined by law as criminal'. This can certainly be challenged, for one of the arguments of the radical criminologists is that the powerful manage either to prevent some of *their* more dangerous activities being

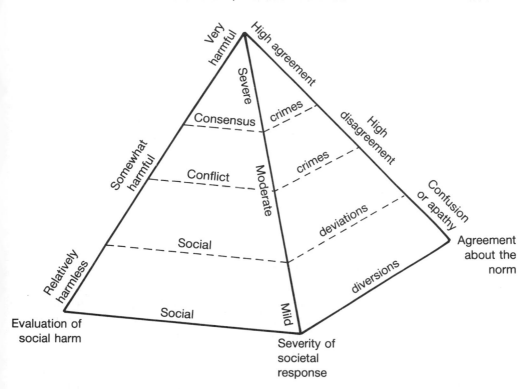

Figure 11.1 Varieties of deviance.
Source: Hagan, 1984, p. 111

proscribed (that is forbidden) by criminal law, or to ensure that any sanctions are ludicrously light (such as small fines). For example, environmental pollution, health and safety in factories and unethical business practices can adversely affect vast numbers in the population. However, the criminal law is either not operative in these areas or is not enforced to any significant degree.

Hagan's *consensus crimes* – murder, rape, robbery, etc. – are those that outrage and scare the public. One of the effects of the women's movement has been to make us all much more aware of the seriousness of the offence of rape. Many people now – not just women – think the problem of rape should be tackled much more seriously and, where appropriate, offenders should be punished much more severely than at present.

The next category, *conflict crimes*, are activities about which public opinion is more divided. Social class and various interest groups may well be the source of such conflict. With these offences, there are examples of how the criminal law can be used by one class or interest group to the disadvantage of another. There are a whole range of conflict crimes. Hagan includes public disorder offences (e.g. vagrancy, creating a public disturbance), chemical offences (e.g. alcohol and drug offences), political crimes (e.g. espionage, terrorism and conspiracy), minor property offences (e.g. petty theft, vandalism) and the 'right-to-life' offences (e.g. abortion, euthanasia). In many ways these contain the most interesting varieties of deviance, for, as Hagan stresses, the feature that unites these offences is the public debate that surrounds them. In short, 'we lack societal consensus on the dimensions of public disorder, the use of comforting chemicals, permissible politics, the protection of private property and the limits of life' (p. 16). While Hagan applies his framework to Canada, it is equally, if not more, true of contemporary British society. In the past decade we have been in the midst of debates at varying levels about all these areas. The miners' strike, the Campaign for Nuclear Disarmament, Greenham Common women, the Irish question, poll tax non-payments, drug addiction, abortion, and so on, have all raised issues about the use and appropriateness of the criminal law as a weapon in social conflict.

One important point that should be recognized is that persons involved in conflict crimes are less likely than those who commit consensus crimes to differ in significant ways from the general population. In brief, there is probably nothing distinctive about political criminals apart from the fact that they happen to have been identified as current or potential political threats. While those in power often try to give pejorative labels to those who oppose their policies – 'troublemakers', 'mad', 'wicked', 'evil', and so on – this is simply part of the political game of defining deviance. In contrast, a person who kills his or her mother – a consensus but, fortunately, rare crime – is much more likely to suffer from some form of psychiatric disorder that makes him or her differ in significant ways from the general population. In short, a psychological explanation is much more likely to be useful for this type of crime, while the political context is likely to be much more important than personality in considering political crime.

Criminal forms of deviance depend for their definition on the *formal* process of control – police, courts, prisons, etc. – while non-criminal forms of deviance depend for their definition on the *informal* processes of social control, such as the family, peer groups and other community groups. Hagan considers two types of non-criminal forms of deviance, which he terms social deviations and social diversions. The distinction is not precise, but examples of *social deviations* would be psycho-social disturbances, the violation of trust and various adolescent pranks. The crucial point is that these activities and experiences are not considered criminal but are, nonetheless, disreputable. In contrast, *social diversions* tend to be frequent and faddish activities but which are not always looked upon favourably. Certain symbolic diversions (styles of dress, speech and mannerisms) are sometimes used in the development of stereotypes as indicators of more serious forms of deviance but, in themselves, are usually harmless.

Changes in definitions of deviant behaviour

Before leaving Hagan's pyramid, it is important to underline one point. As it stands, the pyramid, like the pyramids of Egypt, looks rather static. In studying deviance, however, it is crucial to recognize that there are significant shifts in what holds the centre of the stage of political debate. As Hagan stresses, probably the most important change that can occur in the societal evaluation of an act involves the movement of that act from criminal to non-criminal status. In the 1960s and early 1970s, there was much debate about and some action in decriminalizing certain activities. The so-called 'victimless' crimes were the main focus of this change, in particular abortion, homosexuality and soft-drug use. Changes in the law have undoubtedly made some difference here. Abortion is now available in a much wider range of situations than prior to the 1967 Abortion Act; homosexuality – while still more restricted by law than heterosexual activity – is no longer outlawed in the way prior to the passing of the 1967 Sexual Offences Act; while the penalties for the possession of soft drugs have been considerably reduced since the mid 1960s. Nevertheless, a cursory glance at newspapers or even a brief listen to neighbourhood gossip hardly suggests that such activities are totally acceptable. Having an abortion, declaring yourself homosexual or even smoking pot can still be personally hazardous.

The focus on mugging and football hooliganism in the past couple of decades illustrates how interest seems to shift. One needs to ask whether the nature of deviance or the focus of attention has changed. Like all such questions, there is no easy answer to this. Patterns of deviance can change *and* shifts of focus can take place, but neither happens as drastically as we are sometimes led to believe. The developing interest in historical criminology is important in this respect. Historical research can indicate that a supposedly 'new' moral panic such as football hooliganism is not unprecedented. A study by Pearson (1983) exploded the myth that street crime and hooliganism are the product of a permissive society or evidence of rapid moral decline from the stable traditions of the past. Pearson stresses the violent realities of street life in the past. He shows that successive generations have voiced identical fears of social breakdown and moral degeneration. In his lively and fascinating study, we can begin to identify the parallels between the 'garotters' and the original 'hooligan' gangs of late Victorian London with the 'muggers' of contemporary urban streets. Pearson discovered that the word 'hooligan' made an abrupt entrance into common English usage, as a term to

Plate 11.1 'A Briton in time of peace'.
Source: Punch Publications 1856

describe gangs of rowdy youths, during the hot summer of 1898. However, there was clearly considerable unease about what was happening in earlier periods.

More recently, 'new' kinds of deviance have been identified. For example, baby-battering, wife-battering, even granny-bashing, have had their media coverage, but one suspects that the 'newness' of these activities is more a feature of their becoming noticed. Nonetheless, there is no doubt that a focus on a specific activity, particularly by the media, can have the outcome of changing the phenomenon. More importantly, there has been much more concern about the increasing criminalization of activities that were previously considered to be legitimate forms of dissent.

Finally, the considerable focus on child sexual abuse vividly highlights the delicate relationship between deviant, victim and social control. Everybody wants 'something done' about the problem, and social workers, as social control agents, often find that they are at the centre of irreconcilable demands about protecting the interests of both the alleged parental abusers and their victims. Whether a problem should more appropriately be regarded as a criminal, a medical or a social issue tends to underpin many debates about the nature of deviance.

Drug-taking and crime

Different types of deviance come into focus at different times, but the question of drug-taking seems to be of continuous interest. In fact, there are many perceptions of drug use. Indeed, much drug-taking is condoned or even encouraged when directed by a medical doctor, while other drug-taking is harshly condemned. The approach to the use of drugs such as marijuana continues to be in contention; such use generally attracts social disapproval but less severe sanctions than a few decades ago, perhaps establishing a compromise situation which pleases few but seriously aggravates even fewer. More recently, concern has developed regarding the possible connection between drug-taking and crime, in particular violent crime. So, for example, a 14-year-old killed by a gunman in a Manchester takeaway quickly raised the spectre of young children being involved in a vicious spiral of criminal activity with drugs as the backcloth: 'The Right Rev. Colin Scott, Bishop of Hulme and acting Bishop of Manchester, said that the violence and drug-trafficking in Moss Side were the result of unemployment, dilapidated housing and the lack of job opportunities, particularly for school-leavers. He feared that the rising violence could drive traders and businesses away: "That will do even greater harm to the community"' (*The Guardian*, 5 January 1993). How accurate is the bishop's analysis?

The possible link between drug-taking and crime has attracted interest for a long time. Bean and Wilkinson (1988) have noted how the links can be examined in terms of three main questions: to what extent does drug use lead to crime, to what extent does crime lead to drug use, and to what extent do crime and drug use emerge from a common set of circumstances? Bean and Wilkinson draw upon the results of a major study in Nottingham and note how the rather static and deterministic approach implied in the first two propositions offers little by way of explanation of a relationship between drug-taking and crime. They argue that, following the third approach, one can usefully consider to what extent crime is part of the drug user's world. They focus on the users' link to the illicit supply system, suggesting that the system is central to the users' world whether for crime or for drugs. Indeed, they conclude that 'our evidence, in Nottingham at least, suggests that the presence and structure of an illicit drug supply system provide the best evidence for the link between drug-taking and crime. The crimes committed, and the nature and extent of those crimes, all point to contact with the illicit supply system which not only involves illegal drug transactions but crimes related to those transactions. These in turn are related to the users' position on the illicit supply network.' While the bishop's comments do not quite echo the Bean and Wilkinson conclusions, they agree that focusing on the subtle interactive effects of various factors should be the very stuff of sophisticated analysis. Sadly, the simple relationships so often posited between, say, drug-taking and crime are not so straightforward; they are certainly misleading and often wrong.

Summary

1   There are varieties of deviance. The major division is between criminal and non-criminal forms of deviance.
2   Crimes divide into consensus crimes (which outrage and scare the public) and conflict crimes (where public opinion is much more divided about the appropriate status). Non-criminal forms of deviance can be divided into social deviations and social diversions.
3   There are significant shifts in definitions of deviance over time. The most important shifts involve the movement between criminal and non-criminal status. Historical research often indicates that a supposedly 'new' moral panic, such as football hooliganism or child abuse, is not necessarily a startlingly new phenomenon.
4   Links between different types of deviance, such as drug-taking and crime, are often complex. However, varieties of deviance may sometimes emerge from a common set of circumstances.

11.3   Crime Statistics

There is a whole set of problems in studying official rates of deviance. Crime figures may well tell you more about the organizations that produce the figures than the actual occurrence of crime and deviance. Sociologists have warned (and to some extent the message has got through) of the dangers of reading too much into the official crime figures. Even a cursory glance at the newspapers today suggests that the media will continue to make allegedly rising crime rates a major issue. Politicians, however, are perhaps becoming less willing to highlight the crime figures, and it has been reported that ministers have been considering less frequent publication of the crime statistics.

Sociologists have somewhat diverse views on the value of official statistics in resolving debates about the extent of deviance and the social origins of deviants. Some continue to stress that official crime statistics are seriously misleading, owing to the vast numbers of crimes that are not reported to the police (known as the 'dark figure'). Other criminologists think that some of the criticisms of the official statistics have been exaggerated, arguing that crime statistics do reflect a reality. So, for example, radical sociologists tend to believe that the law is essentially a 'class law' (that is, operating against the interests of the working class), and hence, they argue, what is so surprising about a disproportionate number of working-class people appearing in the crime statistics?

The intricacies of the construction of official crime statistics are dealt with quite adequately in several texts (e.g. Box, 1981), but we still need to face basic questions such as the extent of crime, who is at risk and how we should handle the fear of crime. A major development in the 1980s which enables us to probe more accurately some of these issues was the rise in interest in victimization surveys. Surveys of victimization involve asking samples of the general population about crimes (whether or not reported to the police) that may have been committed against them in some preceding period (usually a year). Certainly they provide a measure of crime much closer to reality than the statistics of offences recorded by the police and court statistics which are published annually under the title *Criminal Statistics*. In truth, the latter provide a useful index of the workload of the police and a record of the working of the court system, but are not a reliable indicator of crime levels.

The decision by the Conservative government in mid 1981 to carry out the first national survey of crime victimization not only heralded a series of these government studies but also spawned some fascinating local studies, e.g. in Merseyside (Kinsey, 1985), in Islington (Jones et al., 1986) and in Hammersmith (Painter et al., 1989), which both complemented and challenged some of the findings from the national studies. The importance of such local surveys cannot be overestimated, and there is no doubt that the British Crime Surveys do have their limitations. For example, the surveys have had considerable difficulty in probing the number of offences against women – 'wife-battering', indecent assault, attempted rape and actual rape. In the first national survey, the number of sexual offences was clearly an underestimate for at least two kinds of reasons. Respondents may be reluctant to relive a painful or embarrassing experience for the benefit of a survey interviewer. Furthermore, with domestic violence, their assailant may be in the same room at the time of the interview. The questions about sexual attack were changed for the subsequent British Crime Surveys, but it still seems unlikely that they have probed this area very accurately. Indeed, in the most recent report the authors admit that '*there is little doubt that BCS counts of sexual offences and domestic or non-stranger violence are understimates*' (p. 5: emphasis in the original) and 'in all, only some 15 sexual offences were uncovered by the survey among nearly 5500 women' (p. 8).

In contrast, studies conducted by the women's movement have consistently shown more disturbing figures. A pioneering survey directed by Hall (1985) indicated that more than one in six women questioned in the survey claimed to have been the victim of a rape. In fact, this survey claims that nearly one in three women had been sexually assaulted, one in five had survived an attempted rape, and nearly one in every 100 had been raped by a gang or by more than one man. Importantly, the reporting rates to the police were disturbingly low. Only 8 per cent of those surveyed had reported rape to the police and 18 per cent had reported sexual assault.

In fact, Hall's figures refer to sexual assaults on women *at any point in their lives*, while the British Crime Survey figures refer to *one particular year*, so, of course, one can expect what seem to be widespread discrepancies. Certainly, in comparing figures there are considerable dangers which need to be considered. What is classed as 'rape'? Does it include 'marital rape', for example? What is the response rate? In Hall's survey 62 per cent of the women responded, and one needs to ask whether particular kinds of persons tend to respond to questionnaires. If women are interviewed, to whom would they tell such intimate details of their lives which may have remained secret but are never forgotten?

Despite the dangers and the shortcomings, there is considerable value in the information collected by the ongoing British Crime Surveys. There have now been three surveys (Hough and Mayhew, 1983; 1985; Mayhew et al., 1989) and they continue to improve methodologically. Perhaps as important as improvements is the fact that we can measure change as the studies accumulate.

The British crime surveys

In the early part of 1982, 1984 and 1988, one person aged 16 and over was interviewed in each of over 10,000 households in England and Wales (in 1982 and 1988, an additional 5000 households in Scotland were also interviewed). In 1988 an ethnic minority 'booster' sample of some 1349 Afro-Caribbeans and Asians was taken to examine victimization risks among ethnic minorities, and their attitudes to and experiences of the police. Everyone in the main sample was asked whether they had been victims of various offences during the previous year (1981, 1983 and 1987).

The value of the British Crime Surveys is that they yield estimates of the extent of various crimes that include incidents unreported to the police. They cover violence against the person, and theft of and damage to private property. Figure 11.2 shows British Crime Survey estimates of the number of criminal incidents in 1987 by crime type. What becomes quite evident from figure 11.2 is that the vast majority of crimes do not involve violence against the person but are offences against property. Together, crimes of violence and common assault comprised 17 per cent of the total. Thus, while serious crimes of violence certainly occurred, in numerical terms they were overshadowed by the large number of comparatively trivial offences, particularly involving motor vehicles. Losses in most thefts were relatively low, under £50 in 70 per cent of incidents. All the British Crime Surveys show an inverse relationship between the seriousness and the frequency of incidents. This last finding,

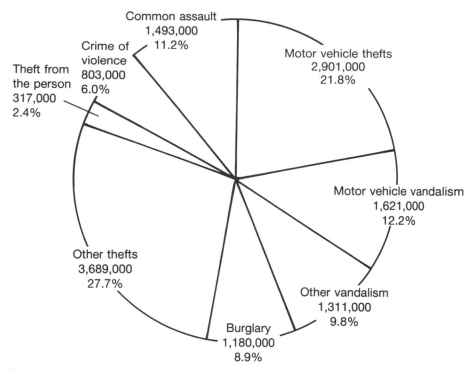

Figure 11.2 British Crime Survey estimates of certain offences in England and Wales, 1987.
Source: Mayhew et al., 1989. Crown copyright.

of course, gives some support for Hagan's use of the pyramid structure in considering varieties of deviance (figure 11.1).

In a fascinating manner, the material from the British Crime Surveys enables us to probe the dark figure of unreported and unrecorded crime. Figure 11.3 shows unreported incidents, those that were reported but not recorded, and those that found their way into police records. The interesting feature is the varying ratio of recorded and unrecorded crime. Except for thefts of motor vehicles, a large proportion of incidents went unreported for all types of crime. The overall reporting rate for crimes shown in figure 11.3 was 37 per cent. Further, many of the offences reported to the police do not get recorded as crimes. Overall, for example, the police would appear to record about two-thirds of the property crimes known to them. Of the remainder, perhaps the police do not accept the victims' accounts of incidents or there is simply insufficient evidence to say that a crime has been committed.

The gap between survey estimates of total crime committed and the figures of offences recorded by the police is an important one. Indeed, the value of the British Crime Surveys in covering both recorded and

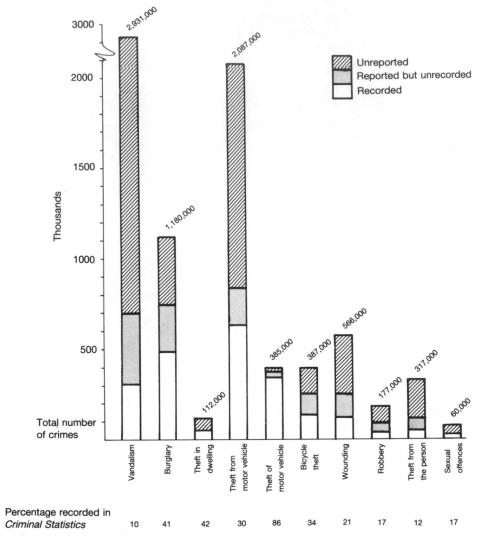

Figure 11.3   British Crime Survey estimates of levels of recorded and unrecorded crime, England and Wales, 1987.
Source: Mayhew et al., 1989; recorded crime from *Criminal Statistics*, 1987. Crown Copyright.

unrecorded crime is that one can have some idea of what an apparent rise in crime rates actually means. The third survey shows that, overall, crime in 1987 as measured by the BCS had risen significantly less since 1981 (in fact, by 30 per cent) than offences recorded by the police (who identified a rise of 41 per cent). This suggests that at least some of the increase in recorded crime since 1981 has been the result of people reporting more of the crimes they experience, and the police may be recording more of the reports they receive. Interestingly, the most comprehensive BCS

Table 11.1 Offences in England and Wales, 1981, 1983 and 1987: British Crime Survey estimates[a]

	1981 (000s)	1983 (000s)	1987 (000s)	Change 1983–7[b] (%)	Change 1981–7[b] (%)
Household offences					
Vandalism	2695	2774	2931	6	9
Burglary[c]	744	907	1180	30**	59**
Attempts and no loss	373	457	665	46**	78*
With loss	371	450	515	14	39**
Theft in a dwelling	147	129	112	−13	−24
Theft from motor vehicle	1277	1525	2087	37**	63**
Theft of motor vehicle	284	282	385	37**	36**
Bicycle theft	215	286	387	35	80**
Other household theft[c]	1537	1693	1823	8	19
Personal offences					
Sexual offences[c]	30	65	60	[−8	100][d]
Common assault[c]	1402	1429	1493	4	6
Wounding	507	423	566	34	12
Robbery[c]	163	145	177	22	9
Theft from the person[c]	434	505	317	[−37	−27][e]
Other personal thefts[c]	1588	1730	1794	4	13
All household offences	6898	7599	8885	17**	29**
All personal offences	4123	4297	4407	3	7

[a] BCS estimates of the number of crimes has been derived by applying rates to the household and adult (aged 16 or more) population of England and in Wales in each of the years. The numbers are 'best estimates' only. Best estimates for 1981 and 1983 are slightly different from those published before, mainly on account of updated household and adult population figures. Because of rounding, subtotals do not always add to totals.
[b] The statistical significance of the changes between years is calculated on the basis of rates to take population changes into account. Double-starred differences are significant at the 5 per cent level (two-tail test, taking complex standard error into account). This means that the chances are less than 1 in 20 that the change has occurred simply through sampling error. Single-starred differences are significant at the 10 per cent level.
[c] Includes attempts.
[d] The increase in sexual offences after 1981 is due to questionnaire changes.
[e] The drop in theft from the person in 1987 is due to classification changes.

Source: Mayhew et al., 1989. Crown copyright

estimate of violent crime (including wounding, robbery and common assault) showed a relatively modest increase of 8 per cent since 1981. Table 11.1 shows how between 1981 and 1987 there was a 29 per cent increase in 'household offences' compared with the much lower rise in 'personal offences' of 7 per cent.

Identifying these recent trends tends to support the theory that links criminal patterns with the economic cycle. The suggestion is that property crimes increase more rapidly in a recession, while violence tends to abate because perpetrators have less to spend on drink and potential victims stay at home more.

Appreciating the difference as well as the links between unrecorded and recorded crime should help to disentangle the importance or otherwise of some apparently disturbing crime figures. Recorded crime increased by 79 per cent during Mrs Thatcher's premiership, in spite of consistent real growth in the law and order budget and the recruitment of 15 per cent more police officers. Indeed, an analysis showed that recorded crime has more than doubled in 27 of the 43 police force areas of England and Wales since the Conservatives took office in 1979 (*The Guardian*, 12 December 1991). In fact, the number of offences registered by police in England and Wales rose from 2,536,700 in 1979 to 4,542,800 in 1990. Furthermore, in the year to the end of September 1991, the number of notifiable offences exceeded 5 million for the first time over a 12 month period. Certainly such figures, particularly when they fit in well with attacks on the government from opposition parties prior to an election, are frequently used with vigour by newspapers to stress a massively rising crime rate, but hopefully our earlier analysis on *unrecorded* crime suggests we should proceed with caution before fully accepting all the implications of such claims.

Interestingly, a paradoxical point which is often overlooked relates to the overall crime levels in Northern Ireland, which has suffered from the 'troubles' over the past two decades: crime levels there are far lower than in England and Wales. A 1988 international victimization survey found Northern Ireland had the lowest fear of street crime of any country. It found 29 per cent of the population in the United States became victims of crime in any one year; in England, Scotland and Wales the rate was 19 per cent; but in Northern Ireland it was 15 per cent (*The Guardian*, 28 March 1991). This rather surprising result should clearly illustrate the complexity of the crime phenomenon and perhaps the need to understand the relationship between crime and other forms of dissent.

Fears of crime

One aspect which has been of particular interest in the last decade or so is the question of the fear of crime. In pointing to the interrelationship of various factors, Hough and Mayhew (1983) tend to question the appropriateness of the fear of crime, suggesting that this in turn can lead to a downward spiral:

> Increasingly it is being said that fear of crime in Britain is becoming as great a problem as crime itself. Criminologists suggest that preoccupation with crime is out of all proportion to the risks; that fear is needlessly reducing the quality of people's lives; and that fear of crime can itself lead to crime – by turning cities at night into empty, forbidding, places. (p. 22)

While the British Crime Surveys tell us nothing about the psychological effects of being a victim, they do locate various fears about crime (box 11.2). For example, previous surveys have suggested that one in nine women under 30 thought it very or fairly likely that they would be raped in the next year. Nearly one out of six people felt themselves likely to be a victim of mugging. In general, the surveys have found that fear of crime

---

Box 11.2   Some findings from the British Crime Survey on the extent and sources of fear of crime

- Women, the elderly and those in inner cities registered most anxiety about walking alone in their neighbourhood after dark. Fear of falling victim to robbery or 'mugging' plays a large part here, though more diffuse and unfocused anxieties appear to be implicated too.
- Asked how worried they were about different crimes, women expressed most fear of rape. Four out of ten women under 30 said they were 'very worried'. Aside from the alarming nature of the offence, exaggerated estimates of its likelihood may underpin some of this worry.
- Burglary causes widespread anxiety, in particular among women. The degree of worry in different areas tracks actual burglary risks, suggesting that most people have some grasp of the *relative* likelihood of break-ins. On the poorest council estates, where risks were highest – 19 attempted and actual break-ins per 100 homes in 1983 – four out of ten residents said they were 'very worried' about burglary.
- Even so, people in all areas tended to exaggerate the risks of burglary. Over half of respondents saw it as the most common crime in their area. Overestimation of actual risks is highest in areas where burglary is relatively infrequent, and those who overestimate most express most anxiety.

- Worry about becoming the victim of 'mugging' is as wide-spread among women as worry about burglary, though relative to other age groups neither elderly men nor elderly women appeared disproportionately worried. Again, people overestimated the risks of mugging: nearly one in six people thought they were very or fairly likely to be a victim in the next year.
- Fear of crime restricts people's behaviour. Half the women in the sample, for instance, said they avoided going out unaccompanied after dark; in high-crime areas one person in 25 said they *never* went out after dark wholly or in part because of fear of crime. The figure for the elderly in these localities was 18 per cent.
- Across the country as a whole, crime and vandalism are outranked as the worst problems of local areas by other social and environmental factors. However, crime and vandalism take the lead in multi-racial areas and in the poorest council estates. Crime levels and fear of crime were also highest in these areas.

Source: Hough and Mayhew, 1985, p. 41, Crown copyright

was widespread and intruded into people's routine behaviour. Fear of crime may make people alter their lives. They may also stay away from certain streets or areas after dark. Among additional topics included in the 1988 survey, there was some focus on participation in neighbourhood watch schemes which have been the most visible outcome of community crime prevention efforts in Britain. By 1988, 90 per cent had heard of neighbourhood watch and 14 per cent of households were actually members of schemes. While patterns may, of course, be changing, members of these schemes tend to be the better-off owner-occupiers rather than those living on the poorer council estates or in racially mixed city areas. It was evident that members of the schemes had appreciated a greater sense of security from having their homes watched and certainly felt that neighbourhood watch schemes deter crime. However, whether the approach actually does reduce crime is still not clear. In making people more alert to the risks of crime, they also become more worried about burglary: hence, paradoxically, those who are the most fearful may be the least victimized. However, an important part of the explanation for this apparent anomaly may, of course, be that fear leads many people to avoid risky situations and thereby to minimize their chances of being a victim.

Embracing a 'new realist' approach, Young and his colleagues at the Middlesex Centre for Criminology (Jones et al., 1986; Painter et al., 1989) have argued that local surveys enable us to move beyond the abstraction of aggregate national statistics. They have identified that for people living in certain areas, the fear of crime is not an empty one. As Young (1991) points out, 'crime is extremely geographically focused and policing varies widely between the suburbs and inner city'. In combining these very different geographical areas to produce national figures, he suggests we distort what life is really like for those living in some parts of an inner city. In other words, Young's work begins to challenge the notion of irrational fears of crime. He notes that the first British Crime Survey suggested that 'the "average" citizen would suffer a robbery once every five centuries; burglary once every 40 years; and assault resulting in injury (even slight) once every century' (Young, 1991, p. 103). Hence, for the 'average' citizen it may be an irrational fear to get seriously worried about most crime. But Young's point is that fears become highly rational for certain groups, particularly those living in certain city areas. So, for example, he suggests it may be unwise to ascribe irrationality to women regarding their fears of violence. Not only are crimes such as domestic violence often masked in official figures, but women also experience harassment on a level which is unknown to most men. Women simply do not know which of the minor incivilities, as Young terms the wide range of abuse, could escalate to more serious violence. Even burglary is feared, not only as a property crime, but as a possible precursor to sexual assault. As Young (1991) notes, 'if crime deteriorates the quality of life for men, it has a much more dramatic impact on the lives of women in the inner city'.

So Young argues powerfully that we should take seriously the public's fear of crime. In reality, for most adults, the biggest single area of risk of crime is with motor vehicles. In 1987 more than one in five owners experienced some form of vehicle crime. However, fear is not simply about frequency. For example, being the victim of one vehicle crime a year is for many little more than a nuisance, while being raped once in a lifetime is a traumatic event that will never be forgotten. Young's point (1991) is that social surveys help us to differentiate the safety needs of different sectors of the community. In the estate in Islington, north London, chosen for his crime survey in 1986, Young has maintained that the outcome of a series of anti-crime initiatives involving tenants, police and the council together has resulted in a significant fall in the crime rate.

Hidden crime

It is crucial to remember that what criminologists and politicians pay attention to is not necessarily the most serious kinds of deviance. In the 1950s and 1960s, criminologists paid enormous attention to youth gangs, but this interest cannot be explained completely by the actual seriousness of gang delinquency and its extent relative to other kinds of criminal activity. In the 1970s, mugging and football hooliganism occupied a disproportionate amount of media attention. While it would be foolish to deny that these problems exist, they may not be so widespread or even so important as the media and the politicians tend to suggest. Indeed, there are other hazards for the community that do not figure in the criminal statistics but are potentially much more serious and widespread in their effects.

Indeed, environmental pollution, health and safety in factories, and even unethical business practices, may be much more crucial to the survival and well-being of the community than many of the issues highlighted by the media and the politicians. However, it is difficult to find such activities recorded in *Criminal Statistics*, and those who design victimization surveys usually fail to consider these kinds of problems. More importantly, though – and this illustrates the most serious drawback of victimization surveys – what happens if people are not even aware that they are victims? For example, environmental pollution may be affecting everyone, but if no one notices, then there can be no record. To do something about deviance, one must know that it exists.

There are increasing challenges to the commonly accepted notion that the job of the criminal law is to protect *all* the members of society. Questions about who makes the law and who really benefits from it have led to the view that, in fact, the criminal law does not serve the interests of the majority in society, but only appears to do so. It is suggested that the criminal law is virtually dictated by small and powerful groups in society and, as a result, serves the interests of these groups and works against the interests of larger but much less powerful ones. Certainly, much of the activity of large, powerful organizations, such as companies and corporations, is potentially very dangerous, but it is often not covered by the harsh rigours of the criminal law. We need to recognize the ability of transnational corporations to shape new legislation relating to their corporate activities. This clearly enables corporations to prevent some of the avoidable deaths, injuries and economic deprivation they sometimes cause from being included in the criminal law and, as a consequence, in crime statistics. In this sense, then, crime statistics and victimization surveys provide evidence of the extent of only a *particular* kind of deviance and not necessarily the most dangerous and destructive behaviour.

Summary

1 Official crime statistics may indicate more about the work of the organizations producing the figures than the actual occurrence of crime and deviance.
2 Surveys of crime victimization show an inverse relationship between the severity and the frequency of incidents of crime. The vast majority of crimes do *not* involve violence against the person but are offences against property.
3 There is a varying ratio of recorded and unrecorded crime (the 'dark figure'). The British Crime Surveys indicate that less than half the number of burglaries, only one in five of woundings and one in ten of incidents of vandalism appear in the *Criminal Statistics*.
4 The occurrence of offences against women – 'wife-battering', indecent assault and rape – is very difficult to estimate accurately.
5 Those who are most fearful of crime are the least victimized. Part of the explanation is that fear leads many people to avoid risky situations and, thereby, to minimize their chances of becoming victims. However, for those living in certain areas, fear of crime reflects its likely incidence.
6 Official statistics and victimization surveys only provide evidence of particular kinds of deviance. Other, particularly corporate, activity that is potentially dangerous may not be covered by the harsh rigours of the criminal law.

11.4 Social Control

Since the 1970s, there has been a new interest in the societal response to acts and persons labelled deviant. There is a wide range of agencies involved in formal social control, from the police, judiciary and prison service to other agencies less obviously part of the control framework, namely social workers and the medical profession. The focus has largely been on the decision-making activities of agencies of social control. There has been increasing concern about structurally generated injustices, reflected in class prejudice, racism and sexism. Questions have been raised about the assumed prejudice of decision-makers, and there has been an increasing recognition – though not always by government – of the limited access of socially disadvantaged persons to resources for their protection.

It is important, first of all, to identify a typical sequence of agency responses to deviance, starting with initial detection and going through to the final outcome. An important contribution of sociologists has been to

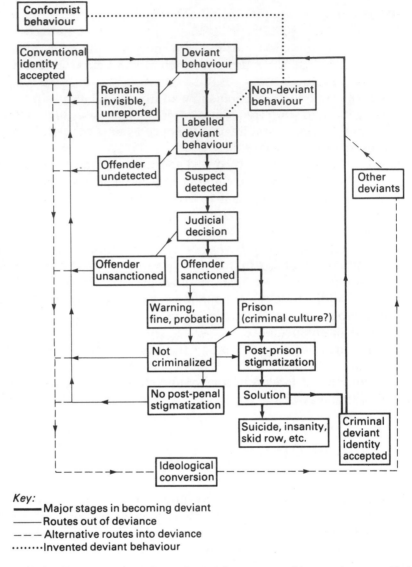

Figure 11.4 The bureaucratic and social process of becoming an official deviant.

Source: Box, 1981, p. 21, reproduced with permission

indicate the processes by which social control itself can play a considerable part in transforming a 'normal' person into a 'deviant'. Box (1981) usefully summarizes much of the work that identifies the bureaucratic and social processes through which an individual becomes officially registered as deviant.

Figure 11.4 identifies the major stages in becoming deviant as well as – and most importantly – routes *out* of deviance. Sociologists have become known for suggesting that social control may well lead to further deviance, although it would be foolish to think this was an inevitable process. Nevertheless, the crucial point remains that, as each cycle of offence/detection/punishment/stigmatization is completed (follow the thick black line in figure 11.4), the chances of the next cycle are increased.

In terms of criminal deviance the two most important 'gatekeepers' are the police and the judiciary. In the Western world, there has been much work on the police as guardians of 'public morality', particularly on what happens during the 'on-the-street' encounters with suspects or suspicious persons. Box (1981) points out that it is when the policeman is in the community that *his* discretion is widest. Backing up the police as guardians of moral boundaries are 'judges and magistrates who have considerable discretionary space to display enough of their personal, social and political sympathies when arriving at verdicts and dispensing sentences for us to glimpse a disturbing truth beyond our proud myths about fair justice' (p. 178). In general terms, Box's concern is that '*when processing individuals who have behaved similarly*, the judicial system will discriminate against some, particularly the poor, the unemployed, and the ethnically oppressed' (p. 180).

More recently, there has been concern that the legal system behaves differently towards women. So, for example, Eaton (1986) focuses on women and magistrates' courts but her work has relevance for the criminal justice system as a whole. Her basic question concerned the equality of men and women before the court. She concludes 'by recognising that *within its own terms* Hillbury Court treats men and women equally, i.e. they receive similar sentences when they appear in similar circumstances' (p. 97). However, her main point is that men and women rarely appear in similar circumstances, and so 'formal equality within the strictly defined area of the court does not affect the substantial inequality of women and men who appear before the court' (p. 97). She argues that men and women are socialized, educated and employed to act and react in different ways, stressing that these differences are most forcefully expressed within the family. Eaton makes a strong case that by upholding the dominant model of the family 'the court is contributing to the cultural reproduction of society and, thereby, to the continued subordination of women.' Hence, pointing to the familial ideology which underpins summary justice, she maintains that women are not equal to men in court, since the court is operating from a perspective which defines women as different and subordinate.

Similarly, there is now much more information about the experience of ethnic minorities in the criminal justice system. The special focus on ethnic minority risks in the most recent British Crime Survey (Mayhew et al., 1989) considers whether Afro-Caribbeans and Asians are disproportionately victims of crime. It also enquires whether there is a racial element in the offences they experience. Certainly the evidence is that both Afro-Caribbeans and Asians tend to be more at risk than whites for many types of crime. Most importantly, Mayhew et al. (1989) stress that this finding is largely explained by social and demographic factors, particularly the areas in which they live. Nevertheless, even after taking account of these factors, ethnic minorities are probably more vulnerable to crime than whites. Asians in particular are at greater risk from vandalism and robbery/theft from the person. Furthermore, ethnic minorities, particularly Asians, see many offences against them as being racially motivated. In fact, Asians seem rather more vulnerable to victimization by groups of strangers, and to rather more serious offences (see further discussion in section 5.4).

Moving on to the reaction of social control agents, studies (e.g. Smith and Gray, 1983) show that young black men are roughly ten times more likely to be apprehended by the police than their white counterparts. Other evidence also suggests somewhat different treatment, in so far as black male offenders reach the courts at an earlier stage in their criminal careers (McConville and Baldwin, 1982; Crow, 1987) and are more likely to receive longer custodial sentences than their white counterparts (NACRO, 1989; Crow, 1987). While black people are over-represented in the criminal statistics, they continue to be under-represented in the criminal justice system: 'although they make up 5.2 per cent of the population they represent only 1 per cent of police officers and less than 1 per cent of prison officers' (*The Guardian*, 16 November 1992).

While pointing to the contribution of 'black criminology', Rice (1990) powerfully reminds of the neglect of black women in these studies. She stresses that 'concern about the high rates of arrest of black people on the streets does not extend to black women who are harassed by the police on suspicion of soliciting' (p. 58). She notes that black women make up over 20 per cent of the female prison population, but only 5 per cent of all women. (Overall the proportion of black prisoners rose from 12.6 per cent in 1985 to 16 per cent in 1992.) There is nothing new in this phenomenon of discrimination in the bureaucratic procedures in the processing of crime. In short, the poor, the unemployed and ethnic minorities always get a bad deal, whether one is focusing on the last decade of the twentieth century or indeed any other time or place.

Summary

1 Social control can play a considerable part in transforming a normal person into a deviant.

2   In terms of criminal deviance, the two most important 'gatekeepers'
    are the police and the judiciary.

11.5   The Police

In the sense that deviance can only be understood as a political process,
then, of course, any form of policing becomes political. The notion that
the police may be serving a political function rather than occupying an
independent role between conflicting groups has been the focus of
considerable public debate over the past decade. No longer can the
government of the day expect us to accept without question the idea that
the police are necessarily acting for the general welfare of the
community. There has been much controversy over the role of the police
in recent riot situations and, even more problematic, in some industrial
disputes. Certainly, the police have been, quite literally, in the middle of
disputes between various sections of the community in ways not
previously experienced in post-war Britain. Furthermore, because of the
presence of television in virtually every home, these encounters between
police and protesters have been witnessed by a much wider audience than
ever before. In some situations, the police have been accused of simply
being the agents of the government, helping to impose a particular
industrial and economic strategy upon the nation. Such accusations have
deeply concerned some members of the police force, who do not regard
their task as helping to carry out the political will of the government in
this way. There is quite widespread concern that the police have
increasingly been drawn into the political arena.

The police have shifted dramatically since the 1970s from having a
comparatively low profile in society to being a high-profile occupation.
The riots of 1981, followed by the Scarman Report (1981) and the
controversial policing of the 1984 miners' strike, produced examples of
police action that indicate that the police role in contemporary society is
in need of reappraisal. More recent but sporadic clashes in various parts
of the country, some of which seem loosely organized while others
appear to be almost spontaneous, continue to raise concerns about the
nature and success of policing. The police themselves have increasingly
proclaimed their own particular views in public debates about social
control in ways which would previously have been unthought of.

Two major issues underpin debates on changing police behaviour: the
growth of professionalism within the police; and whether there has been
a shift from consensus policing (that is, policing by consent) to something
much more akin to military policing. Even more dramatically, some
commentators have been asking whether Britain is turning into a police

state. A contemporary development in the police which raises the spectre of 'Big Brother' is the use of computerized information systems. A recent study (Ackroyd et al., 1992) has shown how this area of technology has difficulties, limitations, dangers and, before the cynic entirely takes over, some important gains. There seems little doubt that policing is an increasingly difficult job both to define and to do.

The development of professional policing

Much of the discussion about increased professionalization of the police stems from the appointment of Sir Robert Mark as Commissioner of the Metropolitan Police in the early 1970s. Mark claimed the support of a 'long tradition of constitutional freedom from political interference in our operational role . . . the police are not servants of government at any level. We do not act at the behest of a minister or any political party, not even the party in government. We act on behalf of the people as a whole' (quoted in Reiner, 1985, p. 1).

One of the crucial, indeed defining, characteristics of a profession is that it is a body that can claim significant autonomy in the ordering of its own affairs. The claiming of status and discretion under the banner of professionalism has helped to free chief constables from the constraints of their local police authority. This has allowed the formulation and implementation of policing policies with virtually no public consultation. Some chief constables have handled controversial situations, such as riots and the policing of certain industrial disputes, particularly the miners' strike of 1984, in such a way that they have been challenged by local police authorities concerned about the lack of control over the actions of their chief constables. However, as Holdaway (1983) has pointed out, public control of the police has always been less than generally assumed.

Inside the British police: two case studies

In recent years there have been quite dramatic changes in the nature of policing and Holdaway's (1983) work captures many of these developments. This is essentially an ethnography of an urban police subdivision at work. It is an attempt to map out police organization, laying bare the assumptions that police officers make about their routine work.

The police, like the prison service, is a disciplined force similar in structure to the military. Holdaway has argued that the traditional militaristic style of command in the police has changed to one of 'management'. More specifically, he identifies the emergence of 'managerial professionalism'. While discipline in the force has remained paramount, it is now maintained more by persuasion, consultation and encouragement than by enforcing blind obedience to authoritative commands.

There has been greater specialization in the police force, and the importance of the growth of technology should not be underestimated. However, what Holdaway highlights as perhaps the most striking feature of his participant observation study was the continuing dominance of the occupational values of the lower ranks. Curiously, the occupational culture of policing maintained by the lower ranks – the 'cop culture' – has survived the various changes associated with the introduction of professional policing.

'Cop culture' is crucial. Holdaway relates a whole series of police anecdotes, stories and jokes that feed and sustain this occupational culture. They may be true, they may sometimes be false: accuracy is not the point of the humour and the numerous tales that are told. The task is to ensure that the perspective of the lower ranks survives despite various onslaughts. Holdaway regards the questioning of prisoners as one of the areas of police work where there is a clear separation between the 'working practices' of certain officers and the requirements of formal policy and law, and this provides fodder for humour and narrative (pp. 148–9):

> After his annual appraisal interview with the Chief Superintendent, a constable returns to duty in the station. A colleague asks: 'How did you get on?'
> *PC*: Fine, fine. 'Enthusiastic' I am, you know.
> Both officers laugh.
> *Colleague*: Yes, really enthusiastic.
> *Officer interviewed*: Professional ability, nil. Appearance, nil, grotesque.
> Yes, but he can't half hit prisoners.
> Both laugh.

Holdaway charts both continuities and changes in the police service. Specifically, he maintains that the development of professional policing has resulted in a greater freedom for all ranks of the force. Senior officers articulate and implement policies appropriate to managerial professionalism and this, in turn, frees them from significant public constraint. More perniciously, however, the old views and practices of the rank-and-file police officers – though often in opposition to the publicly stated intentions of managerial policy – persist in greater comfort by hiding under the powerful symbolic cloak of professionalism. The lower ranks are still able to undermine any new systems that are introduced by modifying them so that their own interpretations of police work remain dominant.

More recently, Ackroyd et al. (1992) have studied the new computer and information systems, including the Police National Computer, and argued that 'whether intentionally or not [they] enhance the discretion and autonomy of the "on the ground" officers' (p. 120). Not that technical innovation in police work is a particularly recent phenomenon. A former chief constable, John Alderson, has described the move to the 'technological cop':

> The impact of science and technology on the police over the thirteen years from 1966 to 1979 was very considerable . . . it had a profound effect on police methods, public image and reputation, to say nothing of police psychology. The police have been helped considerably, even crucially, by technology . . . Stemming from the universal introduction of personal pocket radio . . . together with the availability of cheap motor vehicles and later on expensive computerized command and control systems, what was basically a preventive foot-patrolling force has become a basically reactive patrolling force. (Lea and Young, 1984, p. 181)

Information technology has become more pervasive. Ackroyd et al. (1992) suggest that new technology was introduced into policing in a context of clashes and contradictions between different types and philosophies of management. One of the clearest 'threads' to emerge from this web was a concerted effort to use technology to 'direct' policing to enhance its *effectiveness* in the 'fight against crime', and its *efficiency* in the deployment of resources. 'The assessments about IT innovation become caught in a cycle of over-enthusiasm and hype, cynicism and doubt' (Ackroyd et al., 1992, p. 147). Success was variable: 'Put as its crudest, some systems (usually the most modest) succeed in their intended purpose; some are successfully put to use for purposes never anticipated in their design; some fail altogether and some are modified to make them workable' (p. 149).

Interestingly, the surge of development in information technology has come at a time when there has been quite unprecedented interest in the police. Furthermore, issues about accountability relating to the police are now in the public domain as never before. While the police were previously protected from the ravages of the early Thatcher administrations on spending within the public sector, financial stringencies have now become the focus, and the relevance of information technology will come increasingly under scrutiny. So, for example, the 1991 Audit Commission report, *Reviewing the Organisation of Provincial Police Forces*, urged that some police forces should cut staff at headquarters

with a general prescription that they should decentralize their management. The report went on to suggest that the existing 'pyramid' structure
of management is archaic and inappropriate to modern policing, and
argued that 'rigid rank structures are inherited from an era when junior
officers were regarded as relatively unskilled. In the modern service,
officers are increasingly professional, and are selected, trained, and paid
to act on their initiative. Management structures above them need to
recognise that' (*The Guardian*, 25 February 1991). So, while the
potential use of computer technology by the police will always remain of
concern to those interested in the preservation of civil liberties, there are
other more immediate issues relating to the deployment of police in our
society.

Consensus policing versus military policing

At the time Holdaway was completing his fieldwork in the late 1970s, it
was unlikely that he could have envisaged some of the conditions under
which police officers would be called to work in the next decade or so.
Reiner (1985), to whom we will return later, has argued that, since the
1981 riots, there has been a significant redirection of police thinking and
strategy. There is evidence of attempts by some sections of the police to
be seen as less political. However, with the effects of Conservative
government policy becoming more apparent, particularly following the
1983 and 1987 elections, the chances of any redirection of police thinking
being recognized as a shift towards a lower profile have been slim.
Several commentators, far from recognizing any shift of emphasis from
the strident tones of the 1970s, have come close to suggesting that the
police were actively encouraging and welcoming the tougher approach of
the Conservative government and, in certain respects, this seemed to
resemble the growth of a police state.

Paradoxically, while Holdaway has argued for the emergence of
'managerial professionalism', others have noted what Lea and Young
(1984) describe as a drift to military policing. However, it is important to
distinguish between the nature of the police command structure, which
may well be less militaristic than formerly, and the military style of
policing practice.

Lea and Young stress that the harassment of the public, or at least
sections of it (particularly the black community), is a major political issue
in Britain today. The enquiry carried out by Lord Scarman characterized
the Brixton riots of 1981 as 'a spontaneous act of defiant aggression by
young men who felt themselves hunted by a hostile police force'. It went
on to note that 'the weight of criticism and complaint against the police is

so considerable that it alone must give grave cause for concern' (quoted in Lea and Young, 1984, p. 65).

In an attempt to identify what has been happening to policing, particularly in the inner-city areas and in areas with a high concentration of ethnic minorities, Lea and Young contrast two general types or styles – consensus and military policing. They identify three major differences between these contrasting styles in terms of the support of the community, the flow of information, and the role of stereotypes. These contrasts are set out in box 11.3. Consensus and military policing in their pure forms are polar extremes: policing in most situations falls between these two extremes. It is fair to say that, in certain inner-city areas, consensus policing may never have existed in anything like its pure form. Nevertheless, Lea and Young are suggesting that policing practices in the inner city are moving away from the consensus type. There have always been areas the police have regarded as being more crime-prone than others. But recent practices in these areas have moved closer to the model of military policing. The kinds of actions that encourage the view that such a shift is taking place include random stopping and searching, raids on youth clubs and houses, and operations that involve the use of the more explicitly 'military' sections of the force, such as the Special Patrol Groups.

Causes of changes in policing

Lea and Young (1984) enquire why these kinds of changes have been taking place. They note that the obvious explanation would be to point to the generalized recession of the capitalist economy, the emergence of long-term structural unemployment among youth in general and black youth in particular. It could be argued that there is no longer a willingness to acquiesce to poverty, discrimination and lives of despair, and that young people today have been conditioned through the mass media and the education system to expect something better from life. From this point of view, the move towards military policing in inner cities is part of a general move in state policy towards the 'pole of coercion' in the control of a new generation of unemployed and disillusioned, and so the drift towards military policing is a development to keep down new forms of struggle against the capitalist crisis.

Lea and Young find difficulty with this explanation on at least two grounds. First, they feel that it leads to an exaggerated concentration upon the initiatives of the centralized state apparatus, as if they were consciously formulated. Second, they suggest that this leads to the other simplistic view that military policing is keeping the lid on a progressive struggle for emancipation by those suffering the consequences of

Box 11.3 Consensus and military policing

Consensus policing

1 Policing with the *support* of the community. The community supports the police because it sees them as doing a socially useful job. They are protecting the community against crime, and crime is something that the community recognizes as harmful to its well-being.

2 Because of the support, there is a reasonably *high flow of information* concerning crime. People do come forward with information.

3 All policing involves the use of *stereotypes* to some degree. The more information is provided, however, the more the police can begin their investigations following actual leads and the *less* recourse there is to stereotypes as the basis for starting investigations.

Military policing

1 Policing *without* consent. Here the community does not support the police because it sees them as a socially or politically oppressive force in no way fulfilling any protective functions.

2 The flow of information to the police concerning 'crime' can be expected to *approach zero*. Hence, instead of 'certainty of detection', much police activity will consist of random harassment. The community may develop a type of surrogate policing, such as vigilante squads, which may operate clandestinely.

3 *Maximal use of stereotypes*. For example, beliefs develop that 'all blacks are criminal'.

economic crisis. In truth, however, much of crime is the poor robbing the poor and is not part of a struggle for emancipation.

Lea and Young, instead, attribute the shift towards military policing in certain areas to three closely related factors:

1 A combination of rising rates of street crime with a lessened public

disapproval of *petty* crime. Both of these result from unemployment and deprivation. Large numbers of young people hanging around on the streets begin to take on a lifestyle associated, in the eyes of the police, with petty crime. This encourages the police to stereotype a whole community as 'crime people'.

2 Racial prejudice within the police force enables a smooth transition in the mind of the police officer from the proposition that certain areas with a high black population also have a high crime rate, to the proposition that all blacks are potential criminals. Lea and Young argue that such thinking, in turn, smooths the path for the transition to military policing.

3 The changes in methods following the introduction of modern technology and communications have aggravated the situation by making normal, day-to-day, peaceful contact with the public a low priority.

Lea and Young argue that once the move in the direction of military policing is established, then a vicious circle is set in motion so that this drift becomes self-reinforcing (see figure 11.5). They describe this vicious circle, talking in particular about relations between the black community and the police, as follows (p. 193):

> Initial moves in the direction of military policing result in antagonizing the older generation of blacks, and in a further reduction of the flow of information; the weakening of effectiveness of other institutions of social integration result in more youngsters spending more time on the streets and in contact with the police, which reinforces the processes of stereotyping the community as a whole as crime-prone; and the propensity to collective resistance to arrest, when unchecked, threatens to make any attempt at policing a major military operation in the literal sense of the term.

Lea and Young's analysis is concerned largely with inner cities but, even so, military policing would only be one aspect of the development of a 'police state' – a spectre that already concerns many civil libertarians.

Towards a police state?

In Reiner's (1985) view, a 'police state' results from five associated trends in policing, which he identifies as centralization, increasing police powers, militarization, pervasiveness and de-democratization. We have

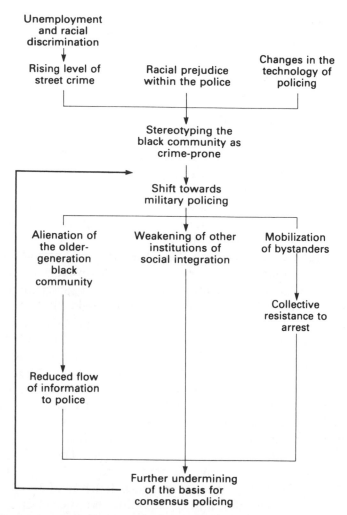

Figure 11.5 The self-reinforcement of military policing.
Source: Lea and Young, 1984, p. 194

already dealt with militarization and de-democratization (that is, the lack of accountability developed under the guise of professionalism).

Centralization

The increase in the centralization of policing cannot be disputed. Amalgamations have reduced the number of police forces in England and Wales from the pre-war total of 183 to the present 43. Furthermore, police increasingly perceive themselves as a national force, rather than as a local force serving a particular town or locality, as was shown spectacularly in the policing of the 1984–5 miners' strike. In contrast, the Audit Commission (1991) is encouraging decentralization and in effect challenging the traditional military structure. But what of the other markers of a police state?

Growth of police powers

In considering the growth of police powers, Reiner distinguishes between an increase in police resources on the one hand, and a strengthening of their legal powers on the other. There has been a substantial increase of police manpower. Indeed, 'law and order' has been one of the few areas in the public sector where expenditure increased quite significantly from the Conservatives taking office in 1979. So while in 1961, as Reiner notes, there was only one police officer for every 602 people in Britain, by 1982 this had increased to one per 394. However, as mentioned earlier, by the 1990s the honeymoon period with the government seemed to be over and financial stringencies are increasingly the focus.

Whether the legal powers of the police have been extended is a much more contentious issue. One of the main planks of the Conservative government's law-and-order policy was the 1984 Police and Criminal Evidence Act. As a result of this Act, sweeping reforms of police powers and practices, coupled with a new code of rights for citizens, have come into force. The changes have provoked criticism from all sides. Civil libertarians have seen the legislation essentially as a strengthening of police powers (such as those to stop and search, arrest, enter, search and seize), with only 'illusory' safeguards for suspects. The police, for their part, fear that their investigations are being increasingly hampered by the need to adhere to detailed codes of practice (such as the first statutory scheme of rules for detention and questioning in police stations). So, in theory at least, the extension of police powers is hemmed in by wide-ranging safeguards.

Reiner (1985) has pointed out that many critics of the 1984 Act have overstated the extension of police powers by understating their previous powers. In fact, while its safeguards regarding the abuse of power may be inadequate, in some respects the Act still represents a move away from a certain arbitrariness and absence of legal limits. While the Act has now been in place for a while, it is still not clear whether it has improved police practice, or whether breaches of the codes are the exception rather than the norm. Since its introduction, the police have suffered some serious and severe challenges to both their competence and their probity. There have been widely publicized accounts of quashed convictions and triumphant appeals – the Darvell brothers, Judith Ward, Stefan Kiszko, the Guildford Four, the Birmingham Six and the McGuire Seven. The tactics of the now disbanded West Midlands Serious Crime Squad produced widespread concern. Curiously, most of these now infamous cases occurred years before PACE (Police and Criminal Evidence Act) set out the rules of procedure, so these important cases are no test of present safeguards.

In the 1990s there has been a noticeable shift in the public presentation of the police and in the recognition of possible causes of crime. So, for example, Sir Peter Imbert, retiring commissioner of the Metropolitan Police, signalled a volteface in the willingness to identify some link in crime growth to inner-city deprivation, saying 'society ignores at its peril the importance of the deprived and disadvantaged underclass in the growth of crime', and going on to say that 'in the years to come, the idea of better service delivery would have more impact on policing than rigid enforcement' (*The Times*, 30 July 1992). Further, the chief inspector of police for England and Wales, Sir John Woodcock, was reported as acknowledging that officers were 'economical with the truth' as a matter of course and that the service was 'shot through with corner cutting and expediency' but that 'the police showed a willingness to admit fault and to change' (*The Guardian*, 14 October 1992). While it would be unwise to suggest that a few well-chosen public words by senior policemen represent a fundamental change of direction, they do perhaps indicate that the dangers of some of the excesses of the past couple of decades have been recognized and that the challenge to the credibility of the police service is a serious one.

Pervasiveness

Finally, Reiner's notion of pervasiveness refers to the process whereby the police begin to penetrate and take over other social agencies. In this way, the police become the dominant state apparatus and there is a subtle redefinition of social and political issues as mere policing problems. The concern about the general extension of social control is a theme which will occupy us in the next section.

Summary

1   Over the past decade, the police have shifted quite dramatically from having a low profile in society to being a high-profile occupation.
2   The two major issues concerning the police are the growth of professionalism within the force and the shift from consensus policing (that is, policing by consent) to something more akin to military policing.

3   Lea and Young (1985) identify three major differences between the contrasting styles of consensus and military policing, in terms of the support of the community, the flow of information, and the role of stereotypes.
4   Lea and Young identify a shift towards military policing in certain areas as the consequence of unemployment and deprivation, racial prejudice within the police force, and changes in policing methods following the introduction of modern technology and communications.
5   Reiner (1985) suggests that a 'police state' results from five associated trends in policing – centralization, increasing police powers, militarization, pervasiveness, and de-democratization.

11.6   Prisons and Punishment

There are many, varied relationships between forms of punishment and the society within which they are exercised. Methods of punishment are historically specific, different ones being employed under different economic, social and indeed religious conditions. Changes in these conditions make it possible, desirable and in some cases even necessary to abandon certain methods of punishment in favour of others.

Since the 1970s, there has been much discussion about decarceration and deinstitutionalization. Thorpe et al. (1980) note that the term 'decarceration' is really shorthand for a state-sponsored policy of closing down asylums, prisons and reformatories and replacing them with 'a range of facilities which will enable [delinquents] to be supported in the community'. Thorpe et al. focus on delinquents, but discussion about decarceration also encompasses areas of mental health (questioning the use of psychiatric hospitals), gerontology (old-people's homes), and so on.

In general, the various community control schemes for criminals are presented as enlightened reforms. Of course, few would deny that schemes that enable criminals to be dealt with in the community rather than being sent into custody should be applauded. However, the situation is rather more complex than it at first appears. In fact, most of the discussion about decarceration programmes stems from the United States of America which still has one of the highest rates of imprisonment in the world. Similarly, in Britain there has also been much talk of deinstitutionalization programmes which are more enthusiastically embraced by governments as they recognize that they may be a cheaper as well as a more effective alternative. So, for example, the average cost of holding someone in custody for a month is £2,000, compared with £89 for a probation order and £76 for a community service order (*The Times*, 2 November 1992). Nevertheless, the United Kingdom still imprisons – with 93.3 prisoners per 100,000 population – a higher proportion of its citizens than any other country in Western Europe (NACRO, 1993).

Prison conditions in Britain are being increasingly criticized. A devastating indictment was recently made in the report of the Council of Europe Committee for the Prevention of Torture and Inhuman or Degrading Treatment, in what was probably the most embarrassing critique so far of the deficiencies of some of our largest Victorian jails. Its inspectors said that conditions at Leeds, Brixton and Wandsworth prisons violated basic human rights by subjecting inmates to a pernicious combination of overcrowding, bad hygiene and inactivity. At the same time, we are experiencing the biggest prison building programme since the turn of the century, but few of the old prisons are being closed down. The contradictions continue, for the Criminal Justice Act which came into force in 1992 is based on the principle that prison is of highly dubious value, both to the particular offender and the interests of wider society. However, while several sections of the Act restrict courts, the main structure still leaves them with wide discretion. The government, though, has made the Act's policies clear: long sentences for serious offenders and for the 'dangerous'; more community sentences and less prison for the less serious offenders, particularly those who commit several minor offences.

Community controls are also being set up. However, some fear that there is no liberalization in the new method but, rather, a deepening and increasing repression of dissent. As imprisonment is no less used, perhaps it is simply that a wider framework of formal social control is being developed. Of course, one explanation of the massive increase in the numbers of people controlled by the criminal justice system is that this is simply a response to increased crime. Let us consider these developments in a more systematic way.

Community control

Cohen (1985) has been influential in exposing some of the illusions of the community control movement. He notes that decarceration has not been taking place particularly rapidly. However, he is unsurprised that the establishment of various supposed alternatives to incarceration does not necessarily decrease imprisonment rates, or necessarily have beneficial effects on the rest of the system. He argues that there is so much investment in the 'delinquency business' that some see crime and delinquency as having a definite function: delinquents keep the courts busy and provide legal-aid work for lawyers; the crime problem helps to justify the employment of more policemen; and delinquency management generates an expanding range of penal and social responses, drawing in more and more agencies and providing a range of services and intervention right across the delinquent and criminal career spectrum. In short, there is an enormous vested interest in the continuation of the crime and delinquency business.

Cohen (1985) and others have argued that when new and extensive forms of intervention do result, they may actually be quite hard to distinguish from the old institutions and may produce *in* the community the very practices they were designed to replace. Cohen expands on the various problems of community control, and we will mention two aspects as examples here – what he calls blurring and widening.

Blurring

This refers to the increasing invisibility of the boundaries of the social control apparatus. Prisons – segregated and insulated from the community – made the boundaries of control obvious enough. In today's world of community control, such boundaries are no longer as clear. As half-way houses, rehabilitation centres and cheap lodgings are usually only available in the more run-down areas of town, certain inner-city areas, patrolled more visibly by police and controlled less visibly by other agents of social control, will increasingly have the characteristics of an open prison. There is, we are sometimes told, a 'correctional continuum' or a 'correctional spectrum'. The danger from the civil liberties standpoint is that the same treatment is sometimes used for those who have actually committed an offence and those who are thought to be 'at risk' of committing one. Certain legal niceties about the difference between guilt and innocence are, therefore, sometimes blurred.

Widening

On the surface, one of the ideological thrusts behind the new movements towards 'community' and 'alternatives' was that the state should do less, rather than more. It is ironic that among the major results of the new network of social control has been an increase, rather than a decrease, both in the *amount* of intervention directed at many groups of offenders and in the total *number* of offenders who get into the system in the first place.

In other words the 'alternatives' are not alternatives at all, but *new* programmes that supplement the existing system or expand that system by attracting new populations. The net of social control is thus widened. Hence, there is concern that recent legislation (e.g. from trade union laws to laws restricting the owners of dangerous dogs) increases the numbers and kinds of criminal deviants in our midst.

While Cohen (1985) points to some of the dangers in the new movement, he also stresses that to be aware of these dangers is not to defend the old system. Undoubtedly, some programmes of community treatment or diversion are genuine alternatives; they are more humane and less intrusive. However, this should not allow us to obscure what social control is all about. For Cohen, what is more striking are the continuities with the system that established state control of crime in Britain two centuries ago. Certainly, the move to community entails more subtle calibrations of care, control, welfare, punishment and treatment. New categories and subcategories of deviants are being created before our very eyes. Cohen concludes that 'community' only exists for middle-class, white, healthy, middle-aged, socially powerful males. The rest have all been classified by them as various kinds of deviants who are only fit to live in ghettos which are patrolled as open prisons in the community. Sadly, the lyrics from the Tom Robinson Band's song 'Power in the Darkness', which headed this chapter, begin to have an authentic ring about them.

Summary

1   With the increase in community controls and the continued high use of imprisonment, a wider framework of formal social control is being developed.
2   Two problems of community control are identified by Cohen (1985) as the blurring and the widening of boundaries.

Related topics

Crimes against women are discussed in section 4.6. Section 5.4 deals with the relationship between ethnic minorities and the police.

Further reading

There are many books in this area but the work of the late Steven Box remains impressive. His *Deviance, Reality and Society* (1981) provides an excellent overview of the theoretical issues on deviance and is particularly helpful in discussing the social construction of official statistics. His two later books, *Power, Crime and Mystification* (1983) and *Recession,*

Crime and Punishment (1987), focus on important contemporary issues. Another good background book is Heidensohn (1989), while Bottomley and Pease (1986) provide a useful account of the criminal justice system.

12 Politics

12.1 Introduction

There is a sense in which all of this book could be seen as being about
'politics'. When we consider the relationship between one social class and
another, or the character of gender relations, we are in a way dealing
with matters that are 'political'. In order, then, to be clearer about what
we shall be discussing in this chapter, it is necessary to distinguish
between two senses of the word 'political'. On the one hand, 'politics' can
be taken to refer to all aspects of social life where there is some inequality
of power between two or more people and there are attempts to sustain
or to change that unequal relationship. In that sense, politics is
everywhere: all social life is political. As the contemporary women's
movement argues, the 'personal is political', which means that even
people's closest personal relationships, with mothers and fathers,
brothers and sisters, wives and husbands, friends and colleagues, are all
in some sense political because they involve inequalities of power and
attempts to sustain or to change those inequalities.

On the other hand, 'politics' can be taken to refer to the main social
institutions that are concerned with organizing and regulating society.
This is 'the state'. The relevant social institutions in Britain here consist
of Parliament, which makes laws; the civil service and local government,
which implement laws and organize a wide range of legally regulated
public services; the legal institutions including the police, which ensure
obedience to the law; and the army which protects the citizens of Britain
against attack.

There is another distinction worth making. If we were to accept that
the second sense of politics is of great importance, what is the connection
between the state and the political organizations that operate within it

(political parties, political movements such as Greenpeace, and pressure groups such as the National Farmers Union), and the rest of society? Is politics here independent, a set of institutions separate from the rest of society? Can politics be studied on its own? Or, when we consider Parliament, the civil service, political parties, political movements and pressure groups, do these in fact reflect the social divisions, such as those of social class, that are found within the wider society? If the state and politics are part of society, exactly how does society affect them?

These questions involve complex issues, which we will consider shortly. There are two further points to note. First, that we can talk of the 'state' on the one hand, and 'society' on the other, is the result of a revolution in people's thinking, which particularly occurred in the eighteenth and nineteenth centuries. Before then, the state and society were viewed as one; the state was society, and it was impossible to think that there was something called society which might significantly 'cause' the state to have a particular form.

Second, the present arrangements between the 'state' and 'society' in Britain are the result of a long process of historical development, particularly involving the reduction in powers of the monarchy. In the nineteenth century, power came to reside much more with the House of Commons. There were substantial extensions of the franchise (those entitled to vote in elections), and the boundaries of different constituencies were changed so that they became more similar in size. Political parties also began to develop in the House of Commons, and pressure groups, such as the Anti-Corn Law League, first emerged to try to put pressure on Parliament to initiate or to amend legislation. It also became normal for the person chosen to be Prime Minister to have a majority of supporters in the House of Commons.

Elections, therefore, greatly increased in importance and so did a need to contact voters through well-organized political parties based on mass membership, particularly as voting was made secret and people could not be openly coerced in their voting patterns. People increasingly voted for such political parties and the parties developed 'programmes' of competing policies. Oncc elected, a party was expected to implement its programme and this, in turn, centralized power in the hands of the party leaders, especially the Cabinet, which had become the key element in the state by 1900. This was also reinforced by further extensions to the franchise, especially to women, so that by 1928 all adults over 21 had the vote. Twentieth-century British politics has thus come to centre on the mobilization, organization, and control of mass public opinion, particularly as this is expressed in support for different national political parties and their leaders. Modern British politics appears in part to be a competition between two or three indivduals, between the Prime Minister of the time and the leaders of the main opposition party or parties.

At the same time, there have been enormous developments in the size, range and power of the modern state. First, the modern state has at its disposal greatly enhanced powers of observing, recording, and repressing the population. Second, the British state provides a huge range of social services administered by large bureaucracies (both the civil service and local authorities). It has gradually become accepted that the state should plan and act on behalf of society as a whole and that, if matters were left to each individual, many people would suffer inequality and deprivation. During the twentieth century, there have been a number of major expansions in the expenditure and activities of the state, as it has intervened in pursuit of 'collective' goals and against purely individual interests. This was best seen in the development of an extensive welfare state in the period 1945–50, after a Labour government was elected at the end of the Second World War. Much contemporary politics is based upon divisions caused by this development. For example, while the contemporary Conservative Party has attempted to reduce the size of the welfare state and to lower the taxation needed to pay for it, the Labour Party has been committed to maintaining aspects of a welfare-state system.

In the following section, we consider the question of elections, by analysing the factors that appear to influence the way people in Britain vote in general elections. In section 12.3, we try to determine how power is organized in modern Britain: is it widely distributed or concentrated? If it is concentrated, which groups have power? In section 12.4, we consider the state directly, particularly its source of power, internal organization and recent changes in its relations with other social forces in society. The chapter will be concluded with an assessment of current changes in British politics, particularly in the area of social policy.

12.2 Voting Behaviour

Elections are important because they usually determine which party shall form a government and because they offer a periodic opportunity for mass participation in political affairs. Far more people vote than take part in other forms of political activity, like writing to MPs or joining demonstrations. Elections are generally seen as the most legitimate form of popular political action, equated with the valued concepts of democracy and representation. People's behaviour at elections gives an indication of their preferences regarding policies and governments, and their more abiding underlying political values and commitments.

There is no simple sociological explanation of why people vote the way they do. There has always been a quite strong statistical relationship between a voter's social characteristics and his or her choice between parties at elections. The social characteristics most closely associated with voting choice include occupation and class, ethnic group, union membership, housing tenure, religion, education and generation. Such 'correlations' have never been overwhelmingly strong and they have fluctuated from election to election. However, 30 years ago, in the 1960s, if a voter came from a manual household the odds were 2:1 that he or she would vote Labour; if the voter was from a non-manual household the odds were about 4:1 in favour of voting for the Conservatives. Class was thus a powerful predictor of party choice. Then, sociologists tended to be most concerned to explain exceptional behaviour, and especially why a substantial proportion of working-class people voted Tory.

The 1960s saw the height of *class alignment* in British elections. The possibility of predicting a person's vote on the basis of occupational class (or any other social variable) has fallen since then. The explanatory problems for psephology (the study of voting behaviour) are now quite different. The key question concerns whether or not there has been a fundamental transformation in voting behaviour since 1970. The spur for such speculation has been the poor electoral performance of the Labour Party, particularly since 1979, raising the question of whether 'the two-party system' has become exhausted.

Sociological inquiry has focused on re-examining the findings of the British Election Studies. At each election since 1964 a national sample survey of voters has been asked questions about political attitudes and behaviour (party affiliation, which issues concern people most, which party they actually voted for, etc.) and about socio-demographic characteristics (occupation, age, ethnic group, etc.). This unique series of surveys, where broadly similar questions have been asked intermittently over a 30-year period, gives enormous scope for rigorous exploration of trends and for heated disagreement about their interpretation. The principal current dispute concerns the adequacy of the argument advanced by Ivor Crewe and coworkers who identified a process of *dealignment*, occurring after 1970, which signified a change of direction for British politics. The main alternative position, that of Anthony Heath and his associates, sees greater continuity throughout the post-war period, one characterized by 'trendless fluctuation' rather than by any fundamental shift. (Crewe was responsible for the British Election Studies of 1974 and 1979, Heath for those of 1983, 1987 and 1992.)

Dealignment

Dealignment refers to the breaking down of the patterns of voters' choice characteristic of the period 1945–66. Dealignment has two aspects, which are not necessarily directly related to one another. First, voters have become unwilling to vote regularly for either of the two major parties. Second, a person's occupational class gives an increasingly poorer guide to his or her party choice. These aspects are called partisan dealignment and class dealignment, respectively. Since dealignment is a *process* we must look at change over time and hence, at a number of consecutive elections, making a comparison with the patterns of the 1950s.

It is generally agreed that between 1950 and 1966 voting preferences had two stable elements. First, individual voters identified with, and regularly voted for, one of the two major parties, that is either the Conservative Party or the Labour Party. This partisanship, a sustained preference for a particular political party, derived from the political socialization process whereby voters were strongly influenced by the political persuasions of their parents. Second, they tended to vote Conservative if they lived in a white-collar household, and Labour if the head of the household was a manual worker. Such regularities were explained in terms of class interest: the Labour Party, with its partly socialist tradition, was thought of as being more likely to promote the interests of the working class, and the Conservative Party was likely to favour the middle classes. These were, however, by no means *laws* of voting behaviour. Disapproval of party performance led to abstention from voting. People changed party between elections. And other social factors besides social class were related to party choice: age, region and religious affiliation affected voting and cut across class divisions.

Partisan dealignment

A partisan is someone who feels a sense of identity with, or loyalty to, a political party. Partisanship is usually measured by asking people whether they consider themselves to be a supporter of a particular party, and how strong is their attachment to that party. The assumption is that partisans will usually vote for the party with which they identify, though they will not always do so. All things being equal, the higher the extent and intensity of partisanship among the electorate the more will voters regularly vote for the same party at each general election. Three different kinds of evidence suggest that partisanship has declined since 1970.

First, election results over the last 30 years show that after 1970 the British voter began to desert the two major parties. In the elections between 1950 and 1970, on average 92 per cent of the poll (i.e. of votes actually cast) was shared between the two major parties, Conservative and Labour. In the five elections following, those between February 1974 and 1987, this two-party share of the poll had fallen to 75 per cent. This is presented graphically in figure 12.1, which shows the rising support for other parties. These 'others' are primarily nationalist and liberal parties.

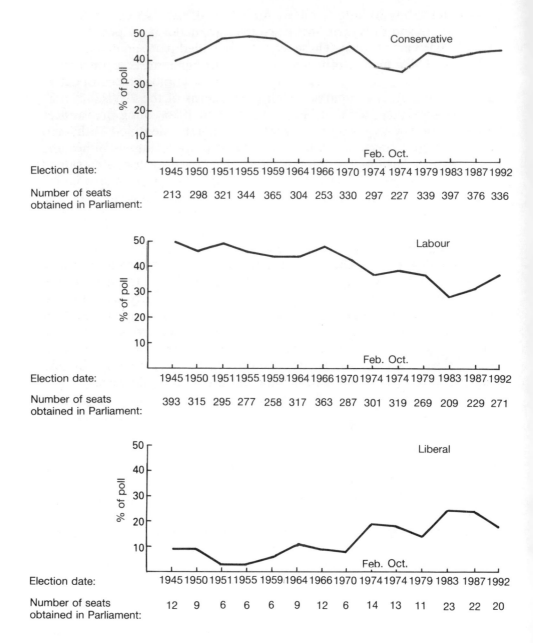

Figure 12.1 Share of the poll in general elections for the Conservative, Labour and Liberal Parties, 1945–1992 (Liberal votes in 1983 and 1987 include those for Social Democratic Party).
Source: Butler and Sloman, 1980, pp. 208–10; Heath et al., 1985, pp. 2–3; Denver, 1989, p. 136

The former group includes the Scottish National Party, Plaid Cymru and the parties of Northern Ireland. In Northern Ireland neither of the two major UK parties were represented at all in elections from 1970 to 1987; votes there were cast for one of several Unionist parties, for the Social Democratic Labour Party, or for Sinn Fein. In the 1992 election, the Liberal Democrats, formed after the 1987 election from the amalgamation of most members of the old Liberal Party and the Social Democratic Party (which had itself split off from the Labour Party in 1980), were the most successful third party in the UK. Figure 12.1 shows that the Liberal Party and its allies made substantial gains in 1964, 1974 and 1983, with a tendency for its share to subside in the intervening elections.

Second, while some of the increased support for 'other' parties may have come from people who would otherwise have abstained, most is taken from the two major parties. This has reduced the likelihood of electors *regularly* voting Labour or Conservative, but only slightly. It might not have reduced partisanship overall if people had become attached to the nationalist parties or the Liberals instead. As a matter of fact, however, there is little sign of people becoming Liberal Democrat partisans. Liberal supporters appear to be fickle voters, rarely supporting the party at two consecutive elections. Thus one study (Sarlvik and Crewe, 1983) showed that, in both the 1960s and the 1970s, only 30 per cent of people who shifted their votes from a major party to the Liberals at one election voted Liberal again at the next. A significantly larger proportion, 45 per cent, returned to the party they had voted for previously. The generally increased support for Liberals has meant that a lot of people are shifting votes between elections. However, the degree of movement, often called 'volatility', does not seem to have increased substantially since 1964. When there were basically only two parties to choose between, many voters would abstain, and others would swap from Conservative to Labour and vice versa from one election to the next.

A third body of evidence concerning partisan dealignment has been obtained by asking people whether they identify with a particular party and, if so, how strongly they are attached to that party. The number of electors who feel some attachment to a party seems to have remained fairly constant: in 1987, 86 per cent of voters volunteered that they considered themselves supporters of a party compared with 90 per cent in 1966. The intensity of their attachment has declined, though. Table 12.1 shows that in the 1964 election survey 48 per cent of voters who identified with a party said their sense of identification was very strong, but by 1987 the proportion was only 23 per cent. (Unsurprisingly, the stronger the party identification the more likely is an individual to vote for that party.)

The reason for declining intensity of identification is disputed, but several factors may be relevant. First, there is some disillusionment with

Table 12.1 Trends in strength of party identification

| | Identifiers who felt . . . | | | |
	very strongly (%)	fairly strongly (%)	not very strongly (%)	Respondents (no.)
1964	48	40	12	1623
1966	48	42	11	1688
1970	47	41	13	1651
Feb. 1974	33	48	19	2162
Oct. 1974	29	52	19	2063
1979	25	53	23	1621
1983	25	47	28	3231
1987	23	48	29	3134

Source: Heath et al., 1991, p. 13

the major parties because of their failures when in government. This may have reduced commitment to them. This might also account for a slight tendency for abstentions (non-voting) to have increased recently. Second, voters may be becoming more instrumental, choosing between parties on the basis of which party they think will best satisfy their personal interests. Identification and loyalty to a party would thus become less relevant. Third, voters may now be more concerned with political issues. Before, stability of identification was the result of political socialization, party identity being passed on from parents to children and rarely being abandoned thereafter. In such circumstances it would make no difference to voters what their favourite party intended to do if it won power. If voters became concerned with particular issues and discriminated between parties in terms of proposed policies – e.g. on law and order, defence, trade unions, economic regulation, or whatever – then old regularities would cease. The erosion of Labour Party support has been explained in these terms by Crewe (1981). He argued that the Labour Party has increasingly offered policies to the electorate which its own supporters and identifiers dislike. However, in the 1987 and 1992 elections Labour's policies were generally the more popular ones, yet they still suffered substantial defeats, rather discrediting such an explanation.

Class dealignment

Class dealignment refers to the declining probability that any individual will vote for the party associated with his or her social class.

Table 12.2 Class and vote: the political distinctiveness of white-collar and blue-collar workers, 1964–1987

Party voted for	1964 (%)	1966 (%)	1970 (%)	Feb. 1974 (%)	Oct. 1974 (%)	1979 (%)	1983 (%)	1987 (%)
White-collar workers								
Conservative	60.7	58.2	59.3	48.9	47.0	58.0	54.6	53.4
Labour	23.9	28.5	29.3	26.9	28.3	24.6	15.7	19.4
Liberal	14.3	12.8	8.9	22.6	21.4	15.7	28.7	25.6
Other	0.9	0.8	2.5	1.6	3.3	1.7	1.1	1.5
Respondents (no.)	669	643	641	1035	980	753	1490	1643
Manual working class								
Conservative	26.3	24.9	34.4	24.6	23.5	35.5	34.5	34.0
Labour	65.6	69.5	57.1	57.0	58.2	50.7	42.6	43.7
Liberal	7.7	5.2	6.1	15.1	14.2	12.2	21.3	21.2
Other	0.4	0.5	2.4	3.3	4.1	1.6	1.7	1.1
Respondents (no.)	861	900	763	921	873	744	1486	1418

Source: calculated from Crewe et al., 1991, p. 19

Whereas we would have been moderately successful in predicting how a person would vote in the 1964 election merely by knowing whether the head of the household was a white-collar or a blue-collar worker, this is no longer the case. Using conventional measures the correlation between occupational class position and voting has fallen. Table 12.2 shows that in 1987, compared with 1964, fewer white-collar respondents were voting Conservative, and fewer manual workers voting Labour. This shift occurred in two stages. Between 1964 and 1974 it was due to an increase in white-collar support for the Labour Party. This support seems to have come from people working in the public sector, and particularly from those in welfare services. In that period there was no perceptible trend for manual workers to vote more frequently for the Conservative Party. However, in 1979 about 10 per cent more manual workers voted Conservative and the proportion remained constant during the 1980s at around 35 per cent. In addition, since 1966, there has been a fairly steady decline in the proportion of manual workers, especially skilled workers, voting for the Labour Party.

One simple way in which the decline of class voting has been measured is using the so-called Alford index. It is calculated by subtracting the Labour Party's percentage share of the vote among non-manual workers

Table 12.3 Alford index of class support for Labour Party, 1964–1987

	1964	1966	1970	Feb. 1974	Oct. 1974	1979	1983	1987
Index	42	41	38	40	40	36	27	25

Source: calculated from table 12.2

from its share among manual workers. Thus for 1987 the value is (44 − 19) = 25. The index, which is one measure of relative class voting, is computed for all elections since 1964 in table 12.3. This appears to show a fall, particularly sharply after 1979, in class differentiated support for Labour, for the size of the index declines. Apparently the old class–party alignment is weakening.

However, it is disputed whether this means that class behaviour has altered decisively or whether there has just been a temporary deviation due to the fluctuating popularity of the parties. There are serious interpretative and technical problems involved in establishing either that class dealignment *causes* partisan dealignment or that class is now less important in electoral behaviour than before.

Trends constructed from the available data significantly depend on the way in which class is defined and class dealignment is measured. Table 12.3 uses a hybrid version of the categories of the Market Research Society and the Registrar-General's social class schema. However, as we have seen in chapter 3, these have often been thought unsatisfactory as a basis for sociological analysis. Measured in other ways, class dealignment seems much less pronounced. Heath et al. (1985; 1991), in their British Election Studies of the 1983 and 1987 elections, suggest that the class dealignment thesis grossly exaggerates the degree of change in voting behaviour. They argue that what is important is change in the class structure and the political climate. Thus, Labour's poor performances were the result of a cross-class decline in political appeal, combined with the reduced size of the working class, rather than any process of class dealignment.

Heath and his colleagues maintain that advocates of the class dealignment thesis have used inappropriate class categories and measurement techniques. They contest the validity of grouping all manual workers together, for they show that self-employed manual workers and manual workers in supervisory positions vote in a different fashion from the mass of manual workers. The behaviour of the last group has not altered systematically between 1964 and 1987; manual workers who are not in positions of authority vote Labour in the same proportions as before. Two others things have changed, however. First, this group is considerably smaller in size than it used to be (see box 12.1). Second, the Labour Party was unpopular politically in the 1980s. Thus they conclude their investigation of the 1983 election by arguing that, once changes in the class structure and the political climate are taken into account, there is no sustained trend towards class dealignment:

> The impact of these changes upon the electoral fortunes of the parties has probably been far greater than that of any class dealignment which may or may not have occurred. There is little evidence that class differences have withered away or that the classes have changed their character, but there can be no question that the *shape* of the class structure has been gradually changing throughout the post-war period. (Heath et al., 1985, p. 36)

In the view of Heath et al., class position remains the major influence on an individual's voting behaviour. Table 12.4 shows the political distinctiveness of the voting behaviour of different classes in the 1987 election. The continued existence of class differentiated voting is apparent. Almost half, 48 per cent, of working-class voters chose the Labour Party, while only 15 per cent of the salariat (professionals and managers) did. The petite bourgeoisie (the self-employed) were the staunchest of Conservative supporters. The Alliance was favoured a little more by the salariat than by other classes, but the differences between classes were not great. Table 12.4 shows how people in particular classes cast their votes.

Table 12.4 Class and vote in 1987: the political distinctiveness of the classes (percentages, by row)

	Conservative (%)	Labour (%)	Alliance (%)	Respondents (no.)
Salariat	56	15	29	839
Routine non-manual	52	26	23	576
Petite bourgeoisie	65	16	20	101
Foremen and technicians	39	36	24	176
Working class	31	48	21	1024

Source: Heath et al., 1991, p. 69

Another interesting way of examining class difference is by looking at the class support of each party separately. Table 12.5 shows the extent to which parties relied on particular classes for support. It shows that the Labour Party in 1987 drew most of its support from the working class, while the Alliance was heavily dependent on the salariat. It is worth

Box 12.1   Party support in 1964

The following tables offer a simple comparison, on identical
definitions, between the years 1964 and 1987. The first shows that
class differences were somewhat more pronounced in 1964,
though it is significant that the Liberal share of the vote was lower
in 1964, that the class support for the Tories was not very
different, but that working-class Labour support was much
stronger (compare table 12.4). However, Labour won that
election and it might be expected that their 'natural' supporters
would be voting heavily in their favour in such circumstances.

Class and vote in 1964: the political distinctiveness of the classes
(percentages by row)

	Conservative (%)	Labour (%)	Liberals (%)	Respondents (no.)
Salariat	62	19	18	268
Routine non-manual	58	26	16	197
Petite bourgeoisie	75	14	12	102
Foreman and technicians	38	46	15	117
Working class	25	68	7	691

A comparison of the next table with table 12.5 shows that the
Labour Party obtained rather more of its support from white-
collar workers in 1987 and rather less, therefore, from the
working class. But this has to be interpreted in the context of
change in the class composition of the electorate as a whole.

Class and vote in 1964: the class distinctiveness of the parties
(percentages, by column)

	Conservative (%)	Labour (%)	Alliance (%)
Salariat	29	8	30
Routine non-manual	20	8	20
Petite bourgeoisie	13	2	8
Foreman and technicians	8	8	11

| Working class | 30 | 73 | 30 |
| respondents (no.) | 574 | 640 | 158 |

The final table shows the class composition of the electorate in 1987 and compares it with 1964. Given the decline in size of the working class and the increase in the salariat, it is almost inevitable that the class distinctiveness of the parties would alter.

Class composition of the electorate,[a] 1964 and 1987

	1964 (%)	1987 (%)
Salariat	18	25
Routine non-manual	18	24
Petite bourgeoisie	7	7
Foreman and technicians	10	6
Working class	47	38
Respondents (no.)	1475	3826

[a] Electors classified by own current or previous occupation if economically active or retired, by partner's current or previous occupation if described as involved in solely in housework.

Source: Heath et al., 1991, p. 68; 1985, p.36; and unpublished data. Thanks to Anthony Heath for providing these unpublished data from the 1987 British Election Survey.

noting the great similarities in the profiles of the Conservative Party and the Alliance. This shows that the Labour Party is still predominantly a working-class party in terms of its support.

Social transformation or political turbulence?

British political parties thus still reflect class differences. Undoubtedly the degree to which that was the case in the elections of 1983 and 1987 was less than in the mid 1960s. (See box 12.1 for data from the 1964 election on political distinctiveness of classes and the class distinctiveness of parties.) It is, however, unclear whether the changes apparent indicate

Table 12.5 Class and vote in 1987: the class distinctiveness of the parties (percentages, by column)

	Conservative (%)	Labour (%)	Alliance (%)
Salariat	38	15	37
Routine non-manual	25	18	20
Petite bourgeoisie	5	2	3
Foremen and technicians	6	7	6
Working class	26	58	33
Respondents (no.)	1221	847	652

Source: calculated from Heath et al., 1991, p. 69

that voters have changed, or whether it is just the political environment that has altered. Incontestably, fewer manual workers voted Labour in the 1980s. But, as Heath et al. (1991) insist, fewer white-collar workers did too. This might be interpreted to mean that the Labour Party was simply unpopular in that decade, without any real implication for class preferences in the long term.

Heath et al. generally maintain that there has been limited change except for the short-run events in the political sphere, with no change in voter psychology; rather, changes are due to changing political context and social structural change. Thus they argue: that there has been no real change in voter volatility since 1964; that attitudes are fairly stable, though the parties' ways of tapping those opinions are not; that the levels of political knowledge and sophistication in the electorate, as measured by relationship between attitudes and votes, has altered very little since the 1960s; that people in the same classes behave in much the same way as before, though of course the relative sizes of the classes have altered; that Labour's poor electoral performance since 1979 is just that – inept political management – which, in association with increased Liberal Party competition, has reduced their overall support; that both salariat and working class are internally divided and sectional, but this is neither new nor different from 1964; and that there has been limited change in popular attitudes, despite the campaigns of the Thatcher governments. In effect, they argue both that recent commentators have exaggerated systemic change and that the orthodox account of voting behaviour in the 1950s and 1960s itself was overdrawn and stereotyped. Of course they do recognize some changes, particularly those due to the parties themselves having shifted in terms of ideology and programme, the emergence of wider support for parties other than Labour and Conservatives, and the emergence of some significant regional differences.

Table 12.6 The hypothetical effects of social change, 1964–1987

| | Share of the vote | | |
Source of change	Conservative (%)	Liberal/ Alliance (%)	Labour (%)
Class	+3.8	+0.7	−4.5
Housing	+4.6	+0.6	−5.0
Region	−0.1	+0.1	−0.1
TU membership	+0.5	−0.1	−0.4
Higher education	−0.4	+0.8	−0.5
Ethnicity	−0.7	−0.3	+1.0
Religion	−4.0	+0.1	+4.1
Combined effects of class, housing, religion, ethnicity and education	+2.7	+1.8	−4.0

Source: Heath et al., 1991, p. 209

One way in which they express this is by estimating the size of the effects on the parties of different components of social and political change over the period 1964–87. The methods for doing this are complex and the results are speculative estimates based on the premise that: '*associations* between [social and demographic] characteristics and voting behaviour have (with a few notable exceptions like region) remained fairly stable throughout the period, but the *proportions* with the different characteristics have changed quite substantially' (Heath et al., 1991, p. 202). The effects of social changes are summarized in table 12.6. Thus,

Table 12.7 The effects of social and political change, 1964–1987

| | Share of the vote | | |
	Conservative (%)	Liberal/Alliance (%)	Labour (%)
Social change	+2.7	+1.8	−4.0
Extension of the franchise	−0.3	+0.4	−0.1
Liberal candidates	−2.4	+6.7	−4.3
Tactical voting	+0.4	−0.4	−0.6
Formation of the SDP	−0.7	+1.3	−0.6
Ideological polarization	−2.0	+4.0	−2.0
Total predicted	2.3	+13.8	−11.6
Actual change	+1.7	+12.8	−15.3

Source: Heath et al., 1991, p. 220

the changing shape of the class structure is estimated to have decreased the Labour vote by 4.5 per cent and increased the Conservative vote by 3.8 per cent. Increased owner-occupation likewise helps the Conservatives at the expense of Labour, but decline in religious affiliation works in the opposite direction. The overall effect of these social changes is much less than the actual shift in vote between 1964 and 1987. Much more of the variation is accounted for, according to Heath et al., by political changes, the strength of which is estimated in table 12.7. This suggests that it is the fact of Liberals contesting all parliamentary seats, compared with only about 55 per cent in the 1960s, that makes most difference. The ideological polarization of the two main parties (though much less pronounced in the early 1990s) is also important.

Alternative interpretations

Most other psephologists accept that class dealignment has occurred, but disagree about its significance. If class is no longer the basis of electoral choice, what, if anything, disposes people to choose between parties? Has some other social factor emerged to take its place? It seems not. There are other social characteristics correlated with voting. Members of trade unions still tend to vote disproportionately for the Labour Party, as do council house tenants and people from ethnic minorities. People who own houses, who do not have trade union members in the family, and who are in the highest income brackets tend to vote Conservative. But none of these factors, alone or together, seems to account regularly for the pattern of voting. Nor are patterns much affected by gender or age.

Issues, attitudes and opinions

The failure to obtain strong correlations with social variables has led some psephologists to turn their attention to electors' political opinions and attitudes. Asking people questions like 'Which party do you think will govern best?' gives some fair indication of how they will vote. The electorate's judgment of which is the best party is influenced by both its evaluation of the policies of the parties and its assessment of how well they have been performing in the recent past. This might seem unsurprising, since people may be expected to use their political knowledge and judgment when deciding how to vote. But many studies from the 1960s suggested that people had very limited political knowledge; voters were unable to distinguish the policies of one party from another, for example. Wider knowledge may have made issues and policies more important. If this is so it becomes necessary to understand how people develop opinions and arrive at judgments. Workmates, friends and neighbours are important in this process. So too is the mass media, though it is very hard to isolate the effects of media exposure on voting.

One problem with analysis in terms of issue voting is that it is hard to see how voters aggregate their policy preferences by issue, since they might quite easily like both Labour's policy on unemployment and the Conservative policy on defence. Unless they see one particular issue as overwhelmingly important it would be hard to select a party. It is also hard to determine whether people adopt their preferred party's policy stances rather than decide for themselves issue by issue. In this respect some commentators argue that electors maintain fairly stable ideological convictions, aligning with the party closest to their principles rather than deciding by issue. But perhaps the strongest objection to explanations in terms of issue voting is the power of instrumental calculation. In 1987 Labour offered the more popular policies, but probably lost the election because many voters did not think that they would successfully implement them. In other words, they doubted Labour's competence, particularly in the economic field, and feared that they would be materially worse off if a Labour government were elected. This may also have been significant in the 1992 general election (see box 12.2). Other voters, of course, made a different calculation, and this might perhaps explain one of the most striking electoral trends of the last 30 years – increased regional differences.

Geographical change

One of the strongest recent trends in voting behaviour has been increasing regional differences. This was very marked during the 1980s. For example, in the 1983 election, excluding the two big metropolitan counties of London and the west midlands conurbation, Labour won only three seats in England south of Derbyshire. The Liberal Alliance won another four. The Conservatives won all the rest. The Labour Party won almost all its seats in inner-city metropolitan areas (e.g. central London, Glasgow, Liverpool) and in the mining and manufacturing areas of central Scotland, south Wales and the north of England. Labour support was concentrated in particular types of constituency in distinctive geographical areas. Indeed, support for both the Labour Party and the Conservative Party has steadily become more concentrated geographically since 1955. The Labour Party has increasingly obtained its support from urban and northern constituencies whilst the Conservatives gained support from rural and southern constituencies. Each party has consolidated its support in different types of constituency. This has several consequences for British elections. First of all it reduces the number of

Box 12.2   The 1992 general election

It will be several years before we have as thorough an analysis of
the 1992 election results as has been possible for the period 1964–
87. However some, relatively superficial, observations are possible which give an indication of how electoral behaviour is
developing.

	Total votes (no.)	MPs elected (no.)	Share of UK vote (%)	Share of GB vote (%)
Conservative[a]	14,049,508	336	41.8	42.8
Change from 1987	+313,171	−39	−0.4	−0.4
Labour	11,557,134	271	34.4	35.2
Change from 1987	+1,527,190	+42	+3.6	+3.7
Liberal Democrat[b]	5,998,446	20	17.8	18.3
Change from 1987	−1,342,706	−2	−4.8	−4.8
Welsh/Scottish Nationalists[c]	786,348	7	2.3	2.4
Change from 1987	+245,886	+1	+0.6	+0.7
Others[d]	433,870	0	1.3	1.3
Change from 1987	+282,353	0	+0.8	+0.8
Northern Ireland parties[e]	785,093	17	2.3	–
Change from 1987	+54,941	0	+0.1	–
Total	33,610,399	651	United Kingdom turnout	77.7
Change from 1987	+1,080,835	+1	Change from 1987	+2.3

[a] The figures for the Conservative Party exclude 11 candidates in Northern
Ireland who polled a total of 44,608 votes.
[b] The Liberal Democrats exclude 73 candidates standing for the Liberal Party
who polled 64,744 votes: they are compared with the Liberal/SDP Alliance in
1987.
[c] The figures for the nationalists include 3 joint Plaid Cymru/Green candidates.
[d] The figures for 'others' exclude all candidates and votes in Northern Ireland:
they include 253 Green candidates (170,047 votes), 73 Liberal Party candidates
(64,744 votes), 300 candidates for the Natural Law Party (60,617 votes), and 220
'other' candidates who polled a total of 138,462 votes.
[e] The figures for Northern Ireland include all candidates and votes including
Conservative (11 candidates), Natural Law (9), Workers (8) and 'others' (8), as
well as the Ulster Unionists, the Democratic Unionists, the Popular Unionists,
the SDLP, Sinn Fein and the Alliance.

The result is shown in the table. The Conservtives, under a new
leader, John Major, won a fourth consecutive parliamentary

majority. The overall majority was 21 seats, compared with 99 in 1987. Despite the Labour Party having been marginally ahead in most opinion polls just before the election, the Conservative Party obtained 42 per cent of the votes cast, the Labour Party only 34 per cent. The Liberal Democrat share of the vote fell from 23 to 18 per cent.

Exit polls show that the Conservative lead over Labour was strong among women and among people aged over 45. Geographically the regional differences persisted, though the Conservatives lost some seats in the south of England. Labour recovered some of its support among manual workers and there was something of a swing among professional and managerial workers from the Liberal Democrats to the Labour Party. Although many of Labour's policies were popular, concern was expressed that Labour would not manage the economy very effectively. Also Neil Kinnock, the party leader, was not popular. It seems probable too that erroneous estimates of support in the opinion polls might have persuaded wavering supporters to vote Tory.

Overall, the 1992 general election appears structurally little different from those of 1983 and 1987, suggesting that the Conservative Party has a rather bigger core of support than do either of the other large parties. Patterns of voting seem relatively stable.

Source: Crewe, 1992, p. 2; data from House of Commons Public Information Office

marginal constituencies, as each major party has cumulatively increased its support in those constituencies which each habitually wins. A second important consequence of the widening gap between socio-geographically defined parts of Britain concerns the electoral success of third parties. The nationalist parties have benefited from regional variation because their potential support is inevitably geographically concentrated. Liberal Democratic votes, by comparison, are very evenly dispersed across the country. Thus it was that in 1992 the Liberal Democrats got over 18 per cent of all votes while winning only 3 per cent of seats. To their supporters this was unfair, proving the case for proportional representation. The same scenario is, however, consistent with the observation that class and region are important determinants of the vote. Without either a regional or a class base it is difficult to win seats under the British first-past-the-post electoral system.

Table 12.8   Region and vote in the working class, 1987

	Conservative (%)	Alliance (%)	Labour (%)	Other (%)	Respondents (no.)
Wales	14	13	69	4	(71)
Scotland	10	21	62	8	(92)
North	24	16	59	0	(345)
Midlands	38	23	40	0	(245)
South	44	26	30	0	(281)

Source: Heath et al., 1991, p. 108

There has always been some regional variation, but it has clearly increased, especially among working-class voters. Table 12.8 shows the size of regional differences in 1987: 69 per cent of working-class voters in Wales, but only 30 per cent in the south of England, voted for the Labour Party. Some accounts attribute such regional variation to rational calculation about likely local and regional economic prospects, with people thinking not so much about their own individual livelihood as that of the majority of other people living in the same place. Others see it as the outcome of sustained regional cultures. Whichever it is, it remains an interesting paradox that while an individual's occupational grade is not much guide to voting behaviour, the class composition of a constituency as a whole is a sound predictor of the success of the major parties.

Summary

1   The evidence regarding changes in voting behaviour is complex. Different measures give different results and the available statistical techniques, thought increasingly sophisticated, are often insufficient to discriminate between explanations. Disagreement is intense over how to interpret changes in the relationship between class and vote.
2   Accounts that suggest radical secular change in voter behaviour are probably exaggerated; there are some strong continuities throughout the post-war period.
3   The Conservative Party has obtained a parliamentary majority at four consecutive elections after 1979, though always with less than 50 per cent of the total votes cast.
4   Party choice remains importantly based on anticipated material outcomes, and the past and estimated future economic performances of the competing parties are critical to the voting decision.

12.3   Power and Politics in Britain

In this section, we step back somewhat from elections and voting patterns and consider the underlying distribution of power in Britain. There are three models of how power is distributed: the pluralist, elite and ruling-class analyses (see Dunleavy and O'Leary, 1987). We show that each model highlights certain aspects of contemporary politics but that none of them fully explains how politics is organized in modern Britain.

The pluralist approach

Pluralists argue that political power in Britain is dispersed and fragmented, that there are a very large number of different groups and

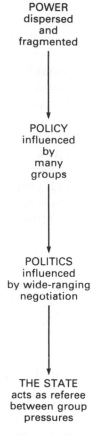

Figure 12.2   The distribution and exercise of pluralist power.

interests that seek to influence policy, and that no particular group is able to control the state or influence policy on a large number of different issues (figure 12.2). In other words, different groups influence policy on different issues and, in many cases, the outcomes result from pressure from a large number of separate groups. Individuals are seen as free to join groups and attempt to influence policy. Any particular individual will be likely to have more than one interest, such that the individual's concerns will pull in different directions at different times on different issues: he or she will be 'cross-pressured'.

Pluralists, further, maintain both that all interests may be represented and influence policy and that no particular interest, such as trade unions or the employers, is dominant within the state. The resources available to different groups are widely dispersed and are not cumulative. New issues come on to the political agenda and new groups can develop. Politics is always a matter of negotiation and competition for ideas and votes. The state is open to influence and it is not systematically biased towards any particular interest or another, although in the last decade it has been thought to be 'overloaded' and 'ungovernable'. The role of the state is twofold: first, to maintain the rules of the game by which this competition between different groups takes place, that is to be a referee; and second, to implement appropriate policies through responding to the balance of political forces on each relatively separate and distinct issue.

The main evidence supporting a pluralist view of Britain is as follows.

1 *Many different groups attempt to influence policy.* There are groups that support a sectional interest, such as the National Union of Teachers, and groups that promite particular causes, such as the Campaign for Nuclear Disarmament. In general, such pressure-group activity is *not* as extensive as in the USA but it is both widespread and growing. In the 1970s there were over 4000 groups attempting to influence political decisions in Birmingham alone. Furthermore, of the groups listed in the *Guardian Directory of Pressure Groups and Representative Associations*, over half had been formed in the 1960s and 1970s. Many of the most effective groups are those that are relatively hidden from view, and the very well-known ones are often those that do not have ready access to the organs of power. Also very many people are members of interest groups – for example, about 9 million people in Britain are members of trade unions, while nearly 7 million are members of Christian churches – and many will be members of, or at least sympathetic to, more than one interest group.

2 *Groups are generally involved in only one major political issue or at most two.* Very few are involved in a large number of issues. There are some conflicts where the sides change from issue to issue. Moreover, groups involved in policy-making enjoy both victories and defeats. No

one group appears to be generally successful in getting its way. This pattern varies between different issues. So although few groups are consistently involved in foreign policy decisions, in other areas there is a plurality of groups involved. The influence of government bodies themselves varies. In foreign policy they are very powerful, while on other issues, such as social policy, transport and environment, they are less effective. Conflicts also occur between different parts of the state, between those ministries concerned to expand expenditure (on new schools, roads etc.) and the economic ministries (especially the Treasury) that seek to reduce public expenditure. Specifically in the 1980s there has been a marked widening of the individuals and groups able to influence policy. For example, all the recent Conservative leaders (Heath, Thatcher, Major) come from relatively unprivileged backgrounds, many prominent business people did not come from elite families (Richard Branson of Virgin, Alan Sugar of Amstrad), and the City of London has been transformed by the influx of overseas banks and the recruitment of many men and women with modest educational qualifications.

The elite approach

The elite view of British politics is based on challenging much of the pluralist account. In particular, it emphasizes how some topics are prevented from becoming issues for political resolution at all, how it is only *some* interests that are organized, and how there is a systematic bias in the political system, which favours certain groups rather than others over the long term (figure 12.3). Although quite a lot of people are members of organized groups in Britain, many others are not. For example, fewer than half the working population are members of trade unions. Moreover, many groups themselves are generally undemocratically organized and lack participation by their membership. They are often run by 'self-perpetuating oligarchies'. Many interests are not represented by organizations (for example, young people or some groups of consumers), or are represented poorly (for example, women members of trade unions). Some other interests by contrast, such as the City of London, are very well represented (through the Treasury, the Bank of England and the financial institutions themselves). These powerful elites tend to be relatively invisible, working behind the scenes in many spheres of social life. The main evidence put forward to substantiate the claim that there are powerful elites in modern Britain is as follows (see section 2.3 and section 3.6).

1 *There are certain key institutions in British life* (Parliament, civil service, judiciary, church, the armed forces, business, finance, press,

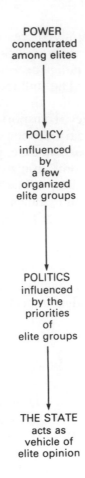

Figure 12.3 The distribution and exercise of elite power.

universities, etc); *each of these is run by an elite; and each of these elites is recruited in approximately similar fashion*. In other words, it is argued that most elite members are white males who received private rather than state school education, went to Oxford or Cambridge Universities (Oxbridge), frequent similar London clubs, and are connected to each other through kinship, friendship and overlapping elite membership. Thus, for example, a study in the early 1970s showed that 80 per cent of the directors of large banks, insurance companies, pension funds, etc. had been to fee-paying schools, 87 per cent had been to Oxbridge, and 46 per cent were members of London's prestigious clubs. Nearly all these major institutions were linked to each other through 'interlocking directorships'. Likewise, two-thirds of the directors of industrial companies and of judges had been to fee-paying schools and Oxbridge; 85 per cent of Anglican bishops had a similar background (Coates, 1984). Until very recently, not a single senior army officer, Anglican bishop, or High

Court judge, had a manual worker as their father; none were black and almost none were female. There is also considerable interchange between these various elite groups. It is common for former MPs to become directors of private companies. Conservative MPs hold, on average, two chairmanships and four directorships of companies. One study suggested that three-quarters of elite members in government, the civil service, private companies, the armed forces, the judiciary, the media, and the aristocracy, all belonged to a small number of exclusive London clubs.

2 *Elite groups structure the form of political debate.* They prevent some issues coming on to the political agenda (such as proposals to abolish private property, or to produce equality of opportunity for blacks and Asians or genuinely equal pay for men and women). Issues which are 'on the agenda' are relatively safe and do not challenge the general distribution of power and privilege.

3 *Decisions made favour the interests of these elite groups.* Thus, fee-paying schools are still thriving and providing an educational route straight into many elite occupations. Likewise Oxford and Cambridge are the two most financially favoured universities in Britain. Also, there has been relatively little change in the distributions of income and wealth. And when tax rates on high incomes are reasonably high (as in the late 1970s), then ways are found to minimize tax liabilities and, in time, these tax rates get reduced (as they have been throughout the 1980s). So over time the elite groups appear to benefit from the range of political decisions made (see Scott, 1991, chapter 5).

The ruling-class approach

The ruling-class analysis of British politics maintains that there is a centrally significant class structure in Britain, of capitalist employers and propertyless workers, and that politics and the state reflect this structure (figure 12.4). It argues that elite theorists, although correct in criticizing pluralism, inadequately analyse this most fundamental feature of British society. It is not, the ruling-class model asserts, merely a question of there being a number of elites in a variety of social institutions. Rather, it is the class structure that lies at the very heart of British society, and the state is, to a considerable extent, the 'instrument' of the capitalist employing class. Much of contemporary politics, including voting patterns, is viewed as relatively unimportant compared with this more fundamental set of relationships. It is the civil service rather than Parliament that is significant. It has the ability to implement decisions that sustain the economy, based on the private ownership of the means of production. Parliamentary politics is 'ideologically' important, in giving

POWER
concentrated
in
capitalist
classes

POLICY
influenced
by
capitalist
business

POLITICS
influenced
by class
conflict,
exercised by
state officials

THE STATE
acts as
instrument
of the
ruling class

Figure 12.4   The distribution and exercise of power by the ruling classes.

the partly false impression that people *can* significantly affect political outcomes. Ruling-class theorists assert that all the major political parties are 'capitalist', since they are concerned to run the capitalist economy as efficiently as possible and hence to maximize the rewards accruing to the capitalist class. The evidence to support this thesis is as follows.

1   *No elected government in Britain in the twentieth century has sought to abolish the capitalist economy based on private ownership.* The most radical Labour government was in power from 1945 to 1950. There was considerable nationalization of economic resources but this mainly involved industries that were at the time unprofitable in private ownership (for example, railways, coal). Nor has any government seriously tried to reorganize industry so that it is run by the workers themselves or even in conjunction with employers. Nor has any

government in Britain extended the welfare services so that they provide adequate provision for *all* the population 'from the cradle to the grave'. The Conservative Party obviously represents the interests of capitalist employers; the Liberal Democrats and the Labour Party, at the most, seek merely some modest reforms of the system of capitalist production.

2 *Business interests are not merely one group amongst a number, but are the most significant and the best organized.* Business interests are the wealthiest of all groups and were able, as in the early 1970s, to mount extensive newspaper campaigns against the nationalization of the banks in Britain. They are also able to derive support from most MPs, very many of whom are actually employed by private companies. Many Cabinet ministers have previously been company directors. The state is, moreover, dependent upon private industry to provide both employment and taxation revenue. Any radical government would not be able to finance large increases in public expenditure unless private industry continued to employ most of the working population, to pay them reasonable taxable salaries, and to provide some taxation themselves.

3 *The most well-organized group in Britain is the City of London*, that is, the commercial banks (such as NatWest), merchant banks (Hill Samuel), insurance companies (Guardian Royal Exchange), pension funds, finance houses, the Stock Exchange, foreign currency dealers, and the Bank of England. These institutions have been exceptionally important in the British economy, providing high levels of what are known as invisible exports. Much British economic policy has been devoted to protecting these particular institutions through, for example, maintaining a strong value of the pound sterling, through enabling these institutions to invest abroad on a massive scale, and through ensuring that foreign confidence in the City of London is maintained by the pursuit of safe policies which are more deflationary than expansionary.

Summary

1 There are three well-known models of the distribution of political power in Britain.
2 *Pluralists* argue that political power is fragmented and dispersed among many different groups, which all influence policy on different issues. No one group or interest is dominant.
3 *Elite theorists* argue that power tends to be concentrated in the hands of the few – the leaderships of organized groups and people at the top of a variety of key institutions. These elites control political processes, and political decisions tend to favour their interests.
4 *Ruling-class* theorists believe that politics reflects the class structure, which consists fundamentally of the relationship between capitalist

employers and propertyless workers. The state is the *instrument* of the capitalist class.

5 None of these models are wholly accurate: they do not provide much analysis of the nature of the state itself and especially of increasing state intervention; they ignore international processes which affect political outcomes; and they have little to say about the politics of gender, race and place.

6 None of them predicted the growth of the new right Thatcherite state.

12.4 The British State

In this section we will turn to consider the state directly, in terms both of its internal organization and of some of the policies it attempts to carry out.

The state and its powers

The state consists of that set of centralized social institutions concerned with passing laws, implementing and administering those laws, and providing the legal machinery to enforce compliance with them. All these institutions rest upon the fact that the state enjoys a monopoly of legitimate force within a given territory and, as a result, it can ensure that most of the time the laws are upheld. All those activities we take to be part of the state ultimately rest upon the threat of legitimate force by the state. In Britain, the state comprises an extraordinary diversity of social institutions: Prime Minister, Cabinet, Parliament, political parties, civil service, judiciary, police, army, local government, schools, colleges, universities, National Health Service, Post Office, British Coal, BBC, and so on.

By contrast with most countries, the powers of many of these different social institutions are not formally specified in a written constitution. Rather, in Britain, the constitution of the country is substantially unwritten but, nevertheless, binding. The partly unwritten character of the constitution means that changes can more easily occur in many of the institutions that make up the state. For example, the power of the civil service had increased in recent years and that of Parliament had declined. In other words, there had been a *restructuring* of the state made possible by the substantially unwritten constitution. This, further, means that the powers of the government in Britain are extremely far-reaching, since they are not circumscribed by a written constitution that might serve to protect individual rights. Provided the government has appropriate authority to make and enforce certain laws, the judiciary will generally uphold them and ensure compliance. For example, in 1972 the Home Secretary introduced a bill in the House of Commons that retrospectively legalized various actions of the British Army in Northern Ireland, actions which the Northern Ireland High Court had determined were illegal. That bill was approved by both the Houses of Commons and Lords on the day that it was first introduced.

Thus, the first power of the state is the almost unlimited ability to make and enforce laws. Some of these laws delegate authority to ministers to make what are, in effect, further laws (statutory instruments) without the necessity of bringing a whole new Act to Parliament. No other social institution possesses such powers. No private company, however powerful, is able to compel all British citizens to act in particular ways that are justified as being in accordance with the 'rule of law'. People in Britain generally obey the directives of the state, not because these directives are particularly popular, or just, or even necessarily sensible, but because they are the *law*. About 60 per cent of people questioned in 1989 would not break a law even if they were very strongly opposed to it. The levels of sanction necessary to enforce compliance are less marked in Britain than in other countries. There are proportionately fewer policemen and women in Britain. And apart from Northern Ireland, the police do not normally carry weapons, there is no large paramilitary force to maintain public order, and the army generally keeps out of policing work.

The second major power of the state is its ability to raise very large sums of money. In 1989, taxation and contributions to social security accounted for just over one-third of national income (GDP) in Britain. However, this ability to raise taxes is not unlimited. If the government tries to raise taxes to very high levels then this may reduce the size of the national income because it will lessen the amount of business activity in the country. As a result, the actual take from taxes would be lower than if there had not been an attempt to increase taxes in the first place. There is, thus, some restriction on the ability of governments to raise revenue through taxation, although there is much dispute as to where this limit actually lies. The Conservatives believe that taxes on income have been too high in Britain and that this stifles initiative and entrepreneurship. By contrast, both Labour and the Liberal Democrats think that there are considerable opportunities for increasing taxes further in order to provide improved transport, communications, hospitals or schools, that this will itself enlarge the national income, and hence that future tax rates will not have to be so high. In their view, tax increases largely pay for themselves.

The third power of the state is the ability to employ large numbers of people. In wartime, for example, most of the male population were conscripted into the armed forces or organized into war-related civilian employment. In peacetime, about one-third of the labour force was employed by the state, particularly in providing services in education and the health service, distributing benefits through DHSS offices, and producing goods and services in the nationalized industries (railways, coal and formerly gas, electricity etc.). Under the Conservatives between 1979 and 1992 the proportion was reduced to less than one-quarter.

The fourth power of the state consists of its control over land. It is a major landowner in its own right; it can acquire land through compulsory purchase on favourable terms; it regulates the use of land through planning legislation; it can alter the relative value of privately owned land (through building a new motorway, for example); and it can establish new uses for existing land (by establishing new towns like Milton Keynes).

Finally, the state controls various instruments of economic policy. The state has been a major investor in, and producer of, many commodities; it exercises some control over the exchange rate between sterling and other major currencies and, hence, affects the relative price of exports and imports; it has a certain degree of control over interest rates and the supply of money; and, through taxation and public borrowing, it affects the general level of economic activity in Britain – the national income, level of output, pattern of price increases, and rate of unemployment.

So far, then, we have seen that the state is a particularly powerful set of interdependent social institutions. The British state has the power to pass and implement laws, to raise taxes, to employ people, to control land, and to regulate the economy (figure 12.5). No set of private institutions possesses such a range of powers. Before considering some of these in more detail, we will briefly consider the internal and external organization of the British state.

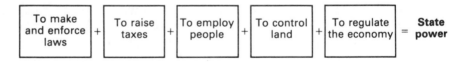

Figure 12.5   The powers of the state.

The organization of the British state

The first point to note is that the British state is part of various international state organizations. It plays a subordinate role in the American military defence system, as evidenced by the former siting of American-owned and -controlled cruise missiles on British territory. Britain is part of the International Monetary Fund which, especially in the 1960s and 1970s, dictated deflationary economic policy to a succession of British governments. But most importantly Britain is part of the European Community, which enjoys legal authority over the British state. European laws take precedence over British laws where they conflict and it is possible for the actions of the British government to be declared illegal. In some cases, British laws such as those on immigration, or very weak British laws such as on sex discrimination at work, have been declared illegal by the European Court.

The British state is also divided internally into different levels – national, regional and local. There has been a steady reduction in the powers of the local level of government, both in the range of services provided through local authorities and in the degree of financial autonomy that they enjoy. This is of importance because this is one level of government that is relatively open to popular representation and accountability. Local authorities still spend differing amounts on different services (e.g. on education per child), which suggests that they possess *some* ability to decide matters on a local basis. However, three processes have reduced the powers of local authorities.

First, the Conservatives have endeavoured to restrict the power of local government to raise local taxes, initially in the 1980s by limiting by *law* any rate increase proposed by a local council; then, by introducing the ill-fated poll tax; and finally, by replacing that with the new council tax. Local taxes on business are now set centrally and local authorities cannot increase the returns from them.

Second, as some services have since the 1930s been taken out of local government, they have been administered instead by *regional* state institutions, such as gas and electricity boards (before privatization). These were run by regional bodies, non-elected, directed by technical experts who were not accountable to anyone, and generally did not resist central government. The development of these bodies represented a reorganization of the state towards non-elected, undemocratic bodies and away from elected local authorities. And in the recent period most of these regional state organizations have been, or are going to be, privatized, so they are even less under the control of locally elected bodies.

Third, other services have been transformed, either by removing them from local government control, such as the 'opting out' of grant maintained schools or colleges of further education, or by setting up central government institutions which operate at the local level, such as urban development corporations like that for the London Docklands. Local authorities are thus squeezed between ever-greater centralization of the state and what has been called 'central government localism'.

We will now consider three further issues concerning the British state. Is it a capitalist state; or a corporate state; or a secret state?

Is Britain a capitalist state?

Does the British state basically work in the interests of private capitalist employers? Does it act as the ruling-class model, described in section 12.3, would suggest?

The first point to note here has been the way in which, from the 1930s until the later 1970s, there was an increasing involvement of the state in the management of the British economy. This took a number of different forms:

1   growth of extensive welfare provision;
2   attempts to regulate demand in the economy to ensure fairly low levels of unemployment and a reasonably healthy balance of trade with the rest of the world;
3   some experiments with planning the output levels of different industrial sectors;
4   various policies designed to regulate income and price increases; and
5   the nationalization of, and support for, various companies and industries that were economically unprofitable in the private sector.

Since 1979, there has been a concerted effort by the Conservatives to reverse these policies (see Jessop et al., 1988). This has been partly successful in that many nationalized industries have been 'privatized', there is no policy to control incomes in the private sector, and the inflation of wages and prices has been intermittently checked by monetary policies rather than by planning. However, the *attempt* to reduce state intervention has not brought about the revitalization of the British economy that was expected. Also, it has been more difficult to reduce government expenditure than was anticipated. Indeed, the total government expenditure as a proportion of national income increased in the first year of Conservative government, although it is now lower. There has, however, been some change in the distribution of state expenditure under the Conservatives. Expenditures on defence, law and order, and social security payments increased, while those on education, housing and overseas aid have remained constant or been reduced.

Although some changes have occurred in the past few years, the British state continues to be heavily involved in economic policy. However, much British economic policy has been relatively unsuccessful and the long-term decline of the economy has not been halted. There are a number of reasons for this. First, the British economy has always been heavily dependent on the state of the world economy; it is an especially 'open' economy. Crises occurring within the world economy, such as the quadrupling of oil prices in 1973 or the Third World debt crisis in the 1980s, particularly affect the British economy and cause it to be unstable. Second, although the British state appears highly centralized with strong political parties, an effective civil service, and widespread popular support, it is in fact rather weak. It has not developed strong ties with industrial companies or developed the capacity for detailed support, planning and subsidy of industry that has occurred in other countries, such as Japan. The British state has not developed a close and effective working relationship with industry. Third, and in contrast, financial interests (the City of London) have been highly integrated into the British state. The Treasury and the Bank of England are both part of the state and, at the same time, are institutions of financial capital. The following are some of the effects of this domination of the British state by finance: home-based industry has been sacrificed in the interests of the City of London; free trade has allowed foreign imports to undercut domestic producion; an overvalued pound has priced British exports out of foreign markets; the flood of capital overseas has starved home industry of new investment; and support of the balance of payments has necessitated deflationary measures which have reduced the growth of demand for industry's products.

So far, a ruling-class account of the distribution of power in modern Britain would seen convincing, given that this dominant class is seen to consist of essentially financial interests (sometimes termed 'finance capital'). However, although this is an extremely influential class, there is no justification for seeing the British state as the simple 'instrument' of such finance capital. This is for three reasons.

First, economic policy in Britain has never been fully able to overcome major contradictions between different objectives, such as full employment, stable prices, a healthy, balance of trade, rising productivity and output. All economic policy has been, in a way, unsuccessful and has failed to meet the interests of the major social classes and groups. However, this is also because the state operates partly separately from individual groups of employers. It makes a more general attempt to secured at least some of the conditions required for continued capitalist production and investment, conditions that would and could not be provided by individual employers. Examples of such conditions include a national motorway network, a comprehensive educational system, a system of unemployment benefit, and so on. A crucial reason why the state seeks to ensure some of the conditions necessary for continued production is because the state is, itself, dependent upon the success of the economy to provide a base for raising sufficient taxation revenue to pay for its disparate activities.

Second, the state carries out a wide range of different policies and, although some of these reflect the interests of finance capital, others will relate to other dominant interests, especially those of men and of whites. The British state is not only 'capitalist' but also 'patriarchal' and 'racist'. Examples of how the British state is patriarchal include the failure of the police and courts to protect women from sexual harassment, rape and, especially, 'domestic violence' within the family; the ways in which the social security system works to treat women as necessarily dependent upon a male 'breadwinner'; and the overwhelmingly male composition of the upper levels of the state institutions. That the British state is racist can be seen most clearly in the Immigration Acts of 1962, 1968, 1971 and 1982. After the 1971 Act, the status of Commonwealth immigrants was dramatically changed to being that of black migrant workers who might or might not be granted citizenship after a four-year period of probation. As Hall et al. (1978, p. 299) argue, it is from the time of this Act that we find 'the really tough "hassling" of the immigrant communities – the police "fishing expeditions" for illegal immigrants, the inspection of passports and documents, the routine "moving on" of groups of black youths, the heavy surveillance of ghetto areas, the raids on black social centres'.

Third, the peculiar character of every advanced capitalist economy is that it is based on the generalization of market relationships. This means that there are countless individuals, groups and classes who are differently located within these complex market relationships. They make up a highly fragmented structure as they seek to maintain or improve their market position by various sorts of actions. Examples of such actions include organizing against other workers, forming trade unions, organizing with those of the same gender or ethnic group, taking industrial action and forming a professional group. In particular, the capitalist economy creates a mass of propertyless wage-labourers – the working class – which is forced to attempt to preserve itself by struggling against the employing class. One feature of the British state's recent development has been the expansion of its size and range of activities in the post-war period, partly brought about by pressure from this working class, expressed through the Labour Party. This, in turn, reflected a significant change in working-class politics that occurred in the inter-war period. This was the way in which working-class leaders, especially in the trade unions, began to see the key to establishing a gradual advance to socialism as lying in the substantial expansion of state-provided and centralized social-welfare facilities. This expansion was particularly prevalent during the 1945–50 and 1964–70 Labour governments, although up to the 1970s many Conservatives also supported the expansion of state expenditure (see Edgell and Duke, 1991 on the social effects of 'Thatcherism').

Is Britain a corporatist state?

Thus, the ruling-class theory does not altogether fit (although see Scott, 1991 for further supporting evidence). What though about the pluralist and elite theories? In the 1970s, there was considerable debate about the plausibility of an approach that combined pluralist and elite approaches, namely corporatism. It was argued that in the early days of British capitalism the role of the state was minimal, concerned with enforcing a legal structure necessary for trade to flourish. But this changed after the First World War with heightened international competition, increased size of firms, the growth of monopolies, the development of well-organized trade unions, rapid technological change and mass unemployment. As a result, social conflicts became heightened and new ways were sought to reorder British society. Large and powerful interest groups came together to coordinate entire economic sectors. In exchange for controlling their members, groups of employers on the one hand, and trade unionists on the other, increasingly began to participate in government, especially after the Second World War. The pluralist pattern became less significant as two powerful interest groups – employers and unions – almost became part of the state itself. They provided the social order which markets could not deliver. As long as they controlled their members, they could continue to share in the fruits of government: the employers received state expenditure on social infrastructure and some level of subsidy; and trade unions received extensions of social welfare provision in exchange for engaging in only modest levels of industrial action and disruption.

This corporatist model certainly provides a reasonable account of some trends in Britain which became particularly noticeable in the 1960s and 1970s as a 'bargained corporatism' was established (Scott, 1991, p. 148). However, as a more general theory of the state it has some marked deficiencies. First, trade unions have in fact not been able to control their members and prevent strikes. Trade union leaders have only infrequently been taken 'into' the British state and indeed have been excluded from it since 1979 with the election of Thatcher. Second, employers' associations have not been part of the state for periods. The most important organization representing industrial employers – the CBI – was only formed in the 1960s. Before then, industrial capital had no fully representative association. Third, corporatist arrangements are unlikely during times of high unemployment and recession, since there is less need to buy off workers with promises of a 'social contract'. Differences of interest between groups of workers can make policies to control incomes almost impossible to sustain over a lengthy period. Fourth, the development of the 'new right', especially with Margaret Thatcher becoming leader of the Conservative Party in 1975, meant that a sustained attack was launched on all aspects of 'corporate bias' in the British state (see also section 12.5). Finally, establishing corporatist arrangements (as in the mid 1970s) has the further effect of encouraging the politicization of other social groups which lie outside the corporatist bargain: women, blacks, pensioners, consumers, environmental groups, community action groups, anti-nuclear protestors, etc. To some degree, these newer political forces have supplanted the working class as the major sources of opposition in modern Britain. They are strong in certain cities in Britain and have influenced the politics of some local Labour Parties, as in parts of London, Sheffield, the west Midlands etc. Such councils have subsidized feminist groups, declared their areas nuclear-free zones, tried to protect the environment by encouraging the use of public rather than private transport, supported local community and arts groups, and tried to develop policies of anti-racism. These have not been entirely successful, and the Conservative government has used criticisms of these policies to justify its reduction of the powers of local government.

Some of these groups have become known as 'new social movements'. These include feminism, green and anti-war movements. They challenge the politics of social class in three important ways:

1 They assert that there are a wide range of groups discriminated against in society and not just the 'working class'.
2 They argue for new political forms that are democratic, anti-hierarchical, small scale, and relatively decentralized. CND, for example, consisted of well over 1000 different local groups through-out the 1970s and early 1980s, each with a considerable degree of autonomy from the central organization.
3 They maintain that the state is by no means a benevolent body that can simply redress injustices in the wider society. Rather, the state is itself to be fought against. It is the problem rather than the solution. The new social movements are thus often 'anti-statist' and have some similarity with aspects of the new right critique of the so-called 'nanny-state'. New social movements are especially opposed to the secrecy of the British state.

The secret state in Britain

Parts of the British state are democratic and open but there is also an extremely powerful secret state. This consists of those state institutions that are non-elected, that enjoy considerable autonomy from Parliament and from the government of the day, and that tend to be closed and secretive in the manner in which they exercise their extensive powers. The nationalized industries (coal, railways, Bank of England, for instance), the legal system, the police, the security services and the armed forces, make up the secret state in Britain (see Dearlove and Saunders, 1991 chapter 5).

There are two points to note about this aspect of the state. First, there is the fact of secrecy itself. Civil servants rarely appear in public to explain or justify their actions and to be subjected to questioning or investigation. Judges maintain that their deliberations are secret and they never have to explain why particular judgments are made. The police are not really accountable to anyone apart from the Home Secretary. This is particularly true of the most powerful force, the Metropolitan Police, which does not even have a local police authority or committee to whom it is minimally responsible, for it answers directly to the Home Secretary. The security services are the most secretive of all. The three most important are MI5, which is not established by statute or recognized in law; MI6, which does not officially exist; and the Government Communications Headquarters (GCHQ) at Cheltenham, which is at the centre of a world-wide network of spying, eavesdropping and communications. These bodies operate almost entirely outside the law, since there are few, if any, laws that relate to their work. All are protected by section 2 of the 1911 Official Secrets Act, which makes it a crime for anyone employed by any of these bodies to disclose any significant information learnt in the course of his or her job. It is also an offence to receive such information. Likewise the Defence, Press and Broadcasting Committee 'advises' the press not to publish what are meant to be sensitive matters of information relating to state actions and policies.

The second point is that the secret state is extremely powerful. For example, although in theory ministers control their departments of state, in fact the permanent civil servants exercise a great deal of control *over* ministers. This was well shown in the BBC television programme 'Yes, Minister', which illustrates how permanent civil servants can undermine the reforming intentions of new ministers. Among the nationalized industries in Britain, the most powerful is the Bank of England, which is in some cases more or less able to determine government economic policy. The 'advice' given by its Governor carries great weight in questions of government policy determination. This is because only those in the Bank, the Treasury and the Cabinet know what that advice happens to be and no one outside can, therefore, put forward counter-arguments. Leading judges, who in theory are bound by the laws made by Parliament, are in fact actively engaged in making the law. This is because they are continuously involved in interpreting the existing law; and this process of interpretation, particularly through the establishment of 'precedents', itself creates the law. As Dearlove and Saunders (1991)

Plate 12.1 Special Branch officers load material removed from BBC offices in Glasgow, in a move to prevent the broadcasting of the controversial Secret Society series (February 1987).

Source: Stephen Gibson

note, 'judicial rule-making is inherently undemocratic.' Likewise, although the social background of the police is very different from the other groups considered here (being a working-class, non-public-school and non-university background), it similarly attempts to limit its accountability, particularly to local authority representatives. The police are powerful because they have the scope to exercise discretion. Amongst the millions of law-breakers, the police decide who to stop on suspicion, and they do so in terms of a number of crude stereotypes of who looks like a criminal. The security services also enjoy a very high degree of autonomy in their operations and operate largely outside the law. The elected parts of the state have little idea of what the security services do, or of the scale of their operations. Even on occasions the Prime Minister has not been aware of the scale of operation of the security forces.

Summary

A number of conclusions can be drawn from the discussion in sections 12.3 and 12.4:

1 The *pluralist* account is by and large incorrect, except in pointing out the wide and increasing variety of interest and promotional groups attempting to influence the state, especially at the local level.
2 As the *elite* view maintains, the central and regional levels of the state, and many pressure groups, are undemocratically organized, often maintaining exceptional levels of secrecy.
3 As the *ruling-class* analysis maintains, British financial interests have been extremely powerful in sustaining central aspects of British economic policy. But, since this has not obviously been in the wider interests of producing a growing and prospering economy, a ruling-class analysis is not altogether correct.
4 The state is patriarchal, racist and secretive in aspects of its composition and in its policies.
5 Both the new right and new social movements have launched savage critiques of the state, of both its powers and its bureaucratic and secretive procedures. Much recent political debate has focused around the very existence, role and function of the British state.

Related topics

Much of the discussion in chapter 3 on class is relevant to theories of the state, especially section 3.6 on the upper class. Questions of sexism and racism in politics and state policy are discussed in chapters 4 and 5.

12.5 Political Change and Social Welfare

Other than to discuss changes in voting behaviour, we have said little in this chapter about party politics. This serves to emphasize that politics is not just a matter of party leaders, parliamentary debates and Cabinet meetings. Nevertheless, parties are important in understanding social and political change. The 1980s saw certain new directions in political affairs in Britain. The 30 years following the end of the Second World War witnessed a period usually described as *consensus politics*: the two major parties, which attracted almost everybody's vote, pursued similar objectives and policies. This epoch drew to a close as the major parties diverged in the 1980s and new political actors emerged.

The dynamics of consensus politics

After 1945, economic policy revolved around obtaining high levels of economic growth in a mixed economy. (A mixed economy is one in which the state owns a significant proportion of industrial enterprise, though the majority of production occurs in the private, capitalist sector.) The pursuit of economic growth entailed considerable direct state intervention and planning. The state tried to regulate the behaviour of the multitude of economic agents – firms, unions, individuals – by setting policies for prices and incomes, providing selective incentives to firms, changing the value of the currency, imposing foreign exchange controls, establishing training schemes for workers, and developing long-term strategic economic plans. The state also exercised control through the nationalized industries (coal, electricity, rail, telecommunications, etc.), to which direct instructions could be given. In addition the state had control over enormous spending power and, in allocating public expenditure, it could also influence the general economic climate and levels of consumer demand.

One principal area of public expenditure is in the sphere of social welfare. Expenditure on welfare has increased greatly during the twentieth century, indicating an expansion of the public provision of services, the quality and quantity of which are determined by political decision and implemented by state officials. The social functions of welfare are many. Among other things, welfare policies permit some control over the behaviour of recipients; they encourage loyalty to a state that guarantees material security; they provide a way of regulating the distribution of resources between social classes, between men and women, between the employed and those without work; and they recycle income to maintain levels of consumer demand (in accordance with Keynesian economic theory).

A commitment to expanding and improving welfare services (housing, health care, education, personal social services) was a plank of consensus politics and, indeed, between 1960 and 1975 the annual rate of growth of public expenditure on social services was a rapid 8 per cent. During these years the level of most services, and hence the levels of employment in welfare, increased significantly.

To summarize, the bases of consensus politics were: economic growth; the coexistence of capitalist and state economic enterprises in a mixed economy; economic planning; institutionalized conflict between employers and workers; and expanded welfare services that sought to promote both material security and greater equality of treatment and opportunity to all citizens. In many respects, the consensus represented a political compromise between two parties acting as representatives of the interests of social classes.

This political compromise collapsed in the middle of the 1970s when, with the onset of recession, the rate of economic growth became insufficient to subsidize both industrial recovery and the provision of expanding welfare services. As Pierson (1991, p. 160) points out, welfare states always face a major problem 'under circumstances of recession, as national product and taxation revenue *fall*, while demands for welfare compensation *rise*'. In the late 1970s this situation was often diagnosed as a crisis. Political strategists, of both left-wing and right-wing persuasions, concluded that because popular demand for welfare spending was inexhaustible, pressures for more public expenditure necessarily compounded national economic problems. Governments, at first Labour, then Conservative, sought ways to alleviate the situation. The two major parties diverged, suggesting different solutions to the social and economic problems. Consensus dissolved, challenged most fundamentally by the Conservative governments to whose policies the Prime Minister gave her name – 'Thatcherism'. (See box 12.3 for an ideal – typical contrast between consensus politics and Thatcherism.) In the same moment, mass political activities shifted towards involvement in unconventional protest through what have come to be called 'the new social movements'.

Conservative governments, 1979–1992

The distinctiveness of the post-1979 Thatcher administrations is that their

Box 12.3 Two ideal types of political strategy: consensus politics and Thatcherism

	Post-war settlement: *consensus politics*	*Thatcherism:* *conviction politics*
Economic strategy		
Policy	Interventionist	Non-interventionist
	Mixed economy	Private ownership of industries
	Keynesian demand-side central planning	Monetarist supply-side free market deregulation
Economic objectives	Growth	Competitiveness
	Generate resources for public use	Contain inflation
Employment	Full employment	Market determination of unemployment level
	Monistic	Dualistic
	Secure, full-time	Secure, full-time *and* flexible, part time
Wages	Male breadwinner norm	Dual-earner norm
	Union negotiated	Performance related
	Centralized collective bargaining	Local or personal negotiation
Welfare Policies		
Fiscal orientation	High taxation	Minimize public expenditure
Projection	Expansion	Retrenchment
Objective	Social justice	Social minimum
Entitlement	Universal citizenship (mostly)	Selective by desert (mostly)
Benefits	Mildly redistributive	Reflect market position
Provider	Primarily the state	Private sector where possible
	Decommodification	Recommodification
Quality	State optimal	State minimal, market optimal

Political management		
Party system	Two-party consensus	Party competition
Class relations	Capital–labour compromise	Capital predominance
Union involvement in politics	Consultation	Exclusion
Ideology	Pragmatic consensus	Ideological conviction

policies on public spending, public/private sector employment, public/private sector consumption and trade unions add up to a major qualitative and quantitative break with the post-1945 Keynesian-based political consensus regarding the character and management of the British economy. (Edgell and Duke, 1991, p. 16)

The Conservative governments developed a fairly coherent set of objectives, revolving around reducing the role of the state in the management of economic activity and welfare provision, and increasing the sphere of private, market competition. Similar emphases characterized many other Western governments of the period, all of whom were faced by the consequences of world-wide recession. The key areas of innovation were economic regulation through monetary policy rather than intervention, sharp contraction of public ownership and public sector employment, reduction of public expenditure by restructuring of the welfare services thereby permitting cuts in direct taxes, acceptance of high levels of unemployment, and the reduction of the powers of trade unions.

Jessop (1992, p. 30) identified six key elements in the neo-liberal economic strategy of the Conservative governments of the 1980s:

liberalization, promoting the free market (as opposed to monopolistic or even state-subsidized) forms of competition as the most efficient basis for market forces;
deregulation, giving economic agents greater freedom from state control;
privatization, reducing the public sector's share in direct and indirect provision of goods and services to business and community alike;
recommodification (or commercialization) of the residual public sector, to promote the role of market forces, whether directly or through market proxies;
internationalization, encouraging the mobility of capital and labour,

stimulating global market forces, and importing more advanced processes and products into Britain;
tax cuts, to provide incentives and demand for the private sector.

Objectives of economic policy included a contraction of the role of state-operated industry, influencing economic development through monetary policy rather than by direct intervention, and restraining wages, by allowing unemployment to rise and by passing legislation to reduce the power of trade unions. State-owned enterprises were subject to various types of reorganization. Many nationalized industries, including British Airways, British Aerospace, British Gas, British Shipbuilders, British Telecom, were transferred to private ownership. Other state-owned industrial enterprises were made to reduce costs and staffing levels, and parts of their activities were privatized or subjected to quasi-market mechanisms in order to simulate competition over the price of services, as with subcontracting in the NHS. One result has been to reduce state employment substantially: Edgell and Duke (1991, p. 10) note that in the ten years from mid 1979 the proportion of the UK employed workforce in the public sector fell from 30 to 23 per cent. This had calculated political benefits for the Conservative Party since both trade union density and Labour voting are high among public sector workers. Trade union reform (see section 2.6) was one element, acceptance of high unemployment another, in a sustained attempt to impose lower wage settlements. Whether the economic strategy had positive economic consequences is less clear. In terms of comparative international performance, Britain's economic position deteriorated during the decade, comparing unfavourably with other major industrial societies. Of the 24 OECD countries, by 1990 the UK was 18th in the league table as measured by growth in GDP per head, being poorer than all except New Zealand, Spain, Ireland, Greece, Portugal and Turkey (see table 12.9; see also chapter 2 for information on trends in occupational change, trade union membership and unemployment). Despite radical surgery for the public sector, encouragement of private enterprise and financial inducements to capital, the problems of the British economy remained as significant as ever.

One objective of both the economic and social policies of Thatcherism was to alter the values of the British population. Individualism, independence, competitiveness and self-reliance were encouraged. In economic life these values were thought to reside in self-employment, exposure to market forces, performance bargaining over pay and reductions in taxes on incomes and profits. The same values were also invoked in respect of the reform of welfare provision where, guided by an overriding priority to reduce public expenditure, legislative and adminis-

Table 12.9 Ratings in the GDP growth league, OECD, 1970–1990

	1970	1979	1985	1990
Switzerland	1	2	2	2
United States	2	1	1	1
Sweden	3	7	6	9
Luxembourg	4	6	5	3
Germany	5	4	4	6
Canada	6	3	3	4
Netherlands	7	8	14	17
France	8	5	8	8
Denmark	9	9	7	10
Australia	10	11	10	15
New Zealand	11	19	18	19
UK	12	14	19	18
Belgium	13	13	15	13
Austria	14	12	12	11
Italy	15	15	17	14
Finland	16	18	16	12
Japan	17	17	13	7
Norway	18	16	9	16
Iceland	19	10	11	5
Spain	20	20	20	20
Ireland	21	21	21	21
Portugal	22	23	23	22
Greece	23	22	22	23
Turkey	24	24	24	24

Source: *The Guardian*, 12 March 1992; data from *OECD National Accounts*

trative intervention was extensive. Smaller revenues from taxation entailed trying to reduce the cost of welfare services. Among the means to achieve that are efficiency gains, lowering the quality of services, rationing or decommodification (persuading people to buy privately what the state had previously delivered). Opinion polls have always indicated that state welfare provision, and in particular the National Health Service, is held in high public esteem – very much more so than, for instance, nationalized industries. Thus government plans for reform were politically controversial.

Despite its intentions, government found it very hard to reduce real public expenditure on welfare. Although the state's share of all spending is lower than it was at the beginning of the 1970s, when it reached the highest proportion outside wartime, it remains around 40 per cent. Table 12.10 shows spending on various welfare services expressed as a proportion of gross domestic product. Spending on housing dropped

Table 12.10 Public expenditure on various services as proportion of government

	1979–80 (%GE) (%GDP)	1980–1 (%GE) (%GDP)	1981–2 (%GE) (%GDP)	1982–3 (%GE) (%GDP)	1983–4 (%GE) (%GDP)	1984–5 (%GE) (%GDP)	1985–6 (%GE) (%GDP)
Housing	7.3 / 2.7	6.2 / 2.4	4.1 / 1.7	3.4 / 1.4	3.7 / 1.5	3.5 / 1.4	3.0 / 1.2
Defence	11.9 / 4.7	12.2 / 4.8	12.2 / 5.0	12.4 / 5.0	12.6 / 5.2	13.0 / 4.9	12.9 / 4.7
Social security	25.9 / 9.6	26.3 / 10.2	28.5 / 11.3	28.8 / 11.7	29.9 / 11.9	30.2 / 12.0	31.3 / 11.9
Education and science	14.5 / 5.4	14.9 / 5.8	14.4 / 5.7	13.8 / 5.6	13.7 / 5.5	13.3 / 5.3	13.1 / 5.0
Health	12.1 / 4.5	13.0 / 5.0	13.1 / 5.2	12.7 / 5.1	12.7 / 5.0	12.7 / 5.0	12.7 / 4.9
Law and order	4.1 / 1.5	4.3 / 1.6	4.4 / 1.8	4.4 / 1.8	4.5 / 1.8	4.7 / 1.9	4.7 / 1.8

[a] Estimate.

Source: *The Guardian*, 12 March 1992, p. 26; derived and calculated from *Public Expenditu*

dramatically, from 2.7 per cent of GDP to 1 per cent, the result of the decision more or less to cease building council houses. The proportion spent on education fell slightly. However, health spending showed a gradual rise because of the changing demographic profile of the population, the labour-intensive nature of care and the extra cost of increasingly sophisticated treatments. Social security rose more, a result of consistently high unemployment and a larger number of people receiving pensions. Expenditure on law and order increased.

Overall, more people required services which it was not politically prudent to discontinue. An ageing population increases the pool of people needing health care and pensions (see section 6.3). Higher levels of unemployment meant more people eligible for social security payments. Concern about the education and training needs of the British economy entailed expanded numbers of students. Inducements to people to take out private insurance (in health care) or to pay for private schooling had relatively limited impact: private health insurance increased, but private schooling scarcely did. Nor did 'efficiency gains', meaning less labour-intensive service delivery (a decrease in staff – student ratios in higher education, for example), though achieved, manage to reduce total expenditure. Nor, yet, has the introduction of quasi-market mechanisms (for instance, in subcontracting in the health service) had a financial impact.

The lack of a significant quantitative shift in spending should not be

expenditure (GE) and GDP, 1979–1992

	1986–7 (%GE) (%GDP)	1987–8 (%GE) (%GDP)	1988–9 (%GE) (%GDP)	1989–90 (%GE) (%GDP)	1990–1 (%GE) (%GDP)	1991–2 (%GE) (%GDP)
Housing	2.8	2.7	2.1	2.9	2.5	2.7[a]
	1.1	1.0	0.7	0.9	1.0	1.0
Defence	12.4	12.2	11.8	11.7	11.2[a]	
	4.4	4.0	4.0	4.0	3.9	
Social security	31.8	31.5	30.8	29.7	30.1	31.7[a]
	11.9	11.3	10.4	10.2	10.7	11.8
Education and science	13.5	14.0	14.5	14.6	14.5	14.2[a]
	5.1	5.0	4.9	5.0	5.1	5.3
Health	12.9	13.4	14.1	13.8	14.2	14.4[a]
	4.8	4.8	4.7	4.7	5.0	5.3
Law and order	4.8	5.1	5.4	5.6	5.8	5.9[a]
	1.8	1.8	1.8	1.9	2.0	2.2

Analyses to 1994–5, HM Treasury

taken to imply that the quality of services had remained constant. Although measuring 'quality' objectively is difficult, the quality of provision almost certainly declined for groups towards whom the government was unsympathetic: social security claimants became relatively poorer, unemployed young people between 16 and 18 became ineligible for benefit, and the terms on which compensation for unemployment was offered deteriorated. Groups who might previously have expected to occupy rented public housing (increasingly, again, poor members of society) were disappointed and homelessness has risen significantly.

We are not, then, witnessing the end of the welfare state. Rather, as Pierson (1991) observes, the welfare state is being *reconstructed*, undergoing consolidation and some retrenchment rather than replacement. What kind of welfare regime will result (i.e. the terms on which welfare services are made available) remains to be seen. For Western societies differ markedly in the normative basis upon which welfare is provided, with consequences for the quality of state provision and the attitudes towards recipients. Under consensus politics, welfare was presented as a universal right of citizens and some efforts were made to redistribute resources to the poorer sections of the population in order to improve the quality of life. Recent policies in areas such as social security seem to be inclining towards provision for minimum subsistence only, increasing the role of selective and means-tested benefits, which have the

Plate 12.2   Homelessness in the 1990s.
Source: Network

tendency to stigmatize the recipients as unworthy because unable to fend for themselves in market competition. Those services which are used more heavily by the middle than the working classes – education and the health services, for instance – seem least prone to reduction in quality.

It is very difficult to estimate the effects of any single policy, both because intervention often has unintended consequences and because other forces besides official policy have an impact on any outcome under consideration. Thus, for instance, the increased expenditure on social security during the 1980s was the result not of generous provision but of high levels of unemployment. There are, however, changes in levels of welfare for sections of the population that might reasonably be considered as the outcome of the whole package of Thatcherite policies. Inequalities of wealth and income increased. Using EC definitions, some 10.5 million people were beneath the poverty line in 1987 compared with 4.9 million in 1979 (section 3.3). This is one sense in which sociologists talk of a polarization in UK society. Unemployment, and the low wages which increasingly accrue to jobs at the lower end of the labour market, have depressed the incomes of poor households, and it is precisely they who are unlikely to benefit from the reconstruction of welfare; for tax cuts, inducements to take out private health insurance, mortgage tax relief and the expansion of higher education benefit precisely those people in secure, well-paid and generally middle-class jobs.

As regards altering popular attitudes towards welfare, the government's objectives included the desire to absolve the state of responsibility for many sorts of personal social problem and to reduce popular expectations of state benevolence. 'A revival of family values' was sought, implemented as policies for community care, youth training schemes, etc. One paradoxical aspect of this, explicable in terms of patriarchal structures, was that while more women were encouraged to enter the labour market, no substitute provision was devised to reduce their domestic caring activities. The potential benefits to women of wider labour market participation were thus compromised, as they were now expected to be economically active and to take on more domestic responsibilities than before. Many households have had great difficulty in managing the consequences, which in part may explain recent increases in divorce and separation.

The government pronounced it virtuous for people to provide for their own welfare, and that therefore the state should deliver nothing more than a minimal 'safety net' of last resort. However, there is little evidence that government propaganda campaigns have proved convincing. While there has been a slight shift in public opinion on general political issues towards the right, and a generally positive reception for the programme of council house sales, opinion surveys suggest that popular attitudes were hardening in defence of established public welfare services and against government policies by the late 1980s. Thus, the report about welfare from the *British Social Attitudes* survey of 1989 concluded that:

> large majorities want more state welfare spending on 'core' services and benefits and say they are prepared to pay the taxes required to finance them; the expansion of private medicine within the NHS is viewed with much disquiet; equality through redistribution as a policy aim is endorsed (again by a substantial proportion of the population) and there is little support for restricting the role of the state to the provision of highly selective benefits for the poor; the claim that state provision in itself has a debilitating effect on work and civic responsibility is not widely endorsed. On the other hand, substantial majorities of the population also suspect that there is widespread welfare scrounging and a core of workshy unemployed people: government measures to tackle these abuses are therefore likely to receive considerable approval. What must be most worrying for the present government, however, is not merely that the tide of public opinion continues on the whole to move against its core welfare policies, but that even its own supporters appear increasingly to have moved with that tide. (Jowell et al., 1990, p. 11)

New social movements

Overwhelmingly, media attention focuses on parliamentary party politics, yet citizens become involved in politics in other ways too. People write letters to MPs and local councillors, sign petitions, boycott goods, form pressure groups, mount demonstrations and sometimes even plant bombs. One particular form of *political mobilization* attracted sociological attention during the 1980s, the so-called *new social movements*. These comprise loosely linked groups of people seeking social and political change. The most important in Britain are the women's, peace and environmental movements. Their fortunes have fluctuated in recent years: the anti-nuclear movement was especially prominent in the early 1980s (crowned by enormous demonstrations including the one in Hyde Park), and most recently the 'green' movement has steadily gained publicity. The *British Social Attitudes* survey indicates increasing an aversion in the late 1980s to industrial pollution, destruction of the countryside, nuclear waste, and so forth (Jowell et al., 1990, pp. 80–1).

Explaining new social movements has been controversial. Dispute has arisen as to whether they really are 'new'; whether they are effective politically; whether they have replaced class movements; and whether they present alternative ways of organizing society or are just single-issue campaigns.

Plate 12.3 A demonstration of the movement for peace: the CND rally, Hyde Park, 1983.
Source: Jenny Matthews/Format

There are two contrasting ways in which these movements have been interpreted by sociologists. The first sees them as primarily *political*, each addressing a set of ethical issues, operating with decentralized and participatory organization, whose success is to be measured ultimately by the extent to which they persuade governments and other organizations to change course. For instance, the goals of the women's movement include equality with men in paid work and eliminating women's exposure to male violence. In this view, new social movements are using unconventional means to achieve political ends. The second view considers them more as *cultural*, social collectivities expressing commitment to a shared way (or style) of life that challenges dominant norms. The point is not so much to affect state legislation as to inspire collective, ethical practice: people may live in and through their ecological or feminist convictions. Explicitly suspicious of state intervention, the project is to establish alternative cultures. We look at both interpretations in greater detail.

The *political* view is summarized in table 12.11. The new social movements are considered to signify the emergence of a new kind of politics, to be contrasted with the consensus politics of the post-war settlement. Each is concerned with a particular set of *issues* with respect to which they *protest* about government policies. Each stands for greater *control* for the mass of people over the conditions of everyday life. Control is more important than money or material wealth; they are sometimes said to convey *post-materialist values*.

The new social movements organize for action in novel ways. Internally, they consist of supporters of campaigns around particular issues. Becoming a member is not considered especially important; rather, people are supporters or sympathizers who act together for the duration of a particular campaign, often at the local level. The absence of high levels of central organization corresponds to the valuing of self-management and democratic control. The women's liberation movement is the clearest example; it refuses to set up a substantial, national, central organization and rejects hierarchy (there are no leaders), because these structures are both undemocratic and typical of the masculine forms of behaviour to which the movement is opposed. Instead it works on the basis of small, egalitarian groups without formal membership. The movement acts together by engaging in particular campaigns around gender issues, on abortion legislation, reclaiming the night, equal opportunities and pay, for example. Sporadic involvement in temporary campaigns causes some difficulties in coordinating action, as there are no channels for regular negotiation and consultation as is the case with pressure groups and trade unions, but this is consistent with its anti-centralist values. *Looseness of internal organization* influences the tactics of these movements. The march, public demonstration, petition, civil

Table 12.11 Summary of distinctiveness of new social movements

'Old' politics	'New' politics
Issues and values	
Economic growth and management; social security; material distribution	Preservation of peace and the environment; establishment of equal human rights
Security; equal opportunity; personal consumption and material improvement	Opposition to centralized, bureaucratic or state control; in search of personal autonomy and democratic self-management
Organization of action	
Internal organization: formal organization and large representative associations (e.g. parties, pressure groups)	Internal organization: informal, spontaneous, egalitarian, impermanent groups of campaigners
Channels of interest: interest-group bargaining; competitive party politics	Channels of interest: protest based on demands, formulated in negative terms about single issues, using unconventional tactics
Social bases of participants	
Classes and occupational groups acting in their own group interests, especially with respect to material rewards	Certain socio-economic groups (especially the 'new middle class') acting not in own interests but on behalf of other ascriptive collectivities (e.g. women, youth, humankind)
Axis of politics	
Class interest	Moral concern

Source: adapted from Offe, 1985, p. 832

disobedience (intentional, non-violent, law-breaking) are among the main means by which the movements express protest and try to influence the public and the politicians. Such tactics are relatively unconventional, designed to alter public opinion and mobilize widespread popular concern about the issues. The formal channels of representative party politics are generally avoided, the aim being to place issues on the political agenda rather than to create state policy. Direct action – as with the women's camp at Greenham Common or animal rights protests – serves to alert the public to an issue and challenge the legitimacy of current practice.

The people involved in these movements are far from a cross-section of British society. The most prominent group involved are the so-called 'new middle class' – professional and technical-scientific workers, highly educated, relatively young and often in state employment. However, they do not act *as* a class. Rather they act on behalf of other kinds of collectivities; youth, ethnic groups, women and humanity are collectivities defined without reference to achievement, mobility, property ownership or occupation (which are the defining attributes of class). Hence it is said that the axis of politics has shifted from class interest to ethical concern.

The second, *cultural*, understanding of the movements developed partly because participants felt that their behaviour was systematically misunderstood if described merely as forms of unconventional politics. The preference for high levels of local and democratic participation, the dislike of bureaucratic and hierarchical organizations (parties as much as the state), the building of networks without leaders, the refusal to compromise themselves through incorporation into orthodox politics, the challenge to the boundary between the public and private realms, a search for self-reliance and cooperative autonomy, all expressed disenchantment with established political structures and a determination to create alternative sets of social solidarities in everyday situations. Being part of a network of like-minded people and taking sporadic direct action were to be faithful to the movement's objectives and valuable for their own sake. To take a trivial example, the green slogan 'think global, act local' can be honoured by restricting unnecessary personal consumption and by using the most environmentally acceptable of available goods and services. As Melucci put it, the movements

> do not fight merely for material goals, or to increase their participation in the system. They fight for symbolic and cultural stakes, for a different meaning and orientation of social action. They try to change people's lives, they believe you can change your life today while fighting for more general changes in society. (1985, p. 797)

As Melucci also observed, the movements signal the existence of social problems, rather than propose national solutions, so that their success is not to be evaluated primarily in terms of implementation of preferred policies. Channelling information and changing people's everyday lives are the principal objectives – politics with a small 'p'.

New social movements represent mass mobilization in protest about issues taken insufficiently seriously by governments. The main quandary for the movements is how their proposals might be implemented politically, for they are not themselves organized to achieve state power.

To do so would probably entail that they take on undesirable character-istics of existing political parties – with leaders, permanent memberships and comprehensive programmes. However, if they remain outside the parliamentary arena, they risk achieving nothing more than that existing parties adopt some of their proposed measures, inevitably diluted, to placate the public concern expressed through the movements.

Summary

1 Consensus politics, which entailed a stable two-party system, broad agreement over policies for running a mixed economy and a welfare state, and a politically passive population, largely disappeared in the 1980s.
2 The political ideas underpinning the economic policies and welfare service provision by the Conservative governments since 1979 have altered the ideological climate of British politics.
3 The new social movements have encouraged unconventional political action around issues that have little to do with class politics.

Related Topics

Aspects of the social and welfare policies of the Conservative govern-ments between 1979 and 1992 are dealt with in section 2.9, section 8.2, and chapter 11.

Further reading

On voting behaviour, Heath et al.'s (1991) study of the 1987 general election is the most recent thorough sociological study of trends since the 1960s. A good introductory book, espousing Crewe's position, is Denver (1989). The most useful single book on the British state is Dearlove and Saunders (1991). Other useful sources are Dunleavy and O'Leary (1987) and J. Scott (1991). On Thatcherism see Edgell and Duke (1991) and Jessop et al. (1988). On new social movements, a sound text describing different sociological approaches is A. Scott (1990).

References

Abercrombie, N., Baker, J., Brett, S. and Foster, J. (1970) Superstition and religion: the God of the gaps *Sociological Yearbook of Religion in Britain* 3: 93–129.

Abrams, M. (1959) *The Teenage Consumer* London Press Exchange Papers, no. 5.

Abrams, M., Gerard, D. and Timms, N. (eds) (1985) *Values and Social Change in Britain* Basingstoke, Macmillan.

Ackroyd, S., Harper, R., Hughes, J. A., Shapiro, D. and Soothill, K. (1992) *New Technology and Practical Police Work* Milton Keynes, Open University Press.

Aggleton, P. (1987) *Rebels without a Cause: middle class youth and the transition from school to work* Brighton, Falmer.

Allan, G. (1979) *A Sociology of Friendship and Kinship* London, George Allen and Unwin.

Allan, G. (1985) *Family Life* Oxford, Basil Blackwell.

Allan, G. and Crow, G. (eds) (1989) *Home and Family: creating the domestic sphere* London, Macmillan.

Allatt, P. and Yeandle, S. (1992) *Youth Unemployment and the Family: voices of disordered times* London, Routledge.

Allen, J. and Massey, D. (eds) (1988) *The Economy in Question* London, Sage

Anderson, M. (1971) *Family Structure in Nineteenth Century Lancashire* Cambridge, Cambridge University Press.

Atkinson, A. B. and Harrison, A. J. (1978) *Distribution of Personal Wealth in Britain* Cambridge, Cambridge University Press.

Atkinson, J. (1985) The changing corporation, in D. Clutterbuck (ed.) *New Patterns of Work* Aldershot, Gower.

Audit Commission (1986) *Making a Reality of Community Care*.

Audit Commission (1991) *Reviewing the Organization of Provincial Police Forces* Police papers no. 9, London, IIMSO.

Backett, K. C. (1982) *Mothers and Fathers* London, Macmillan.

Bagguley, P., Mark-Lawson, J., Shapiro, D., Urry, J., Walby, S. and Warde, A. (1990) *Restructuring: Place, Class and Gender* London, Sage.

Bailey, R. and Kelly, J. (1990) An index measure of British trade union density *British Journal of Industrial Relations* 23(1): 71–92.

Ball, S. J. (1981) *Beachside Comprehensive: a case study of secondary schooling* Cambridge, Cambridge University Press.

Banks, M., Bates, I., Breakwell, G. Bynner, J., Emler, N., Jamieson, L. and Roberts, K. (1992) *Careers and Identities* Milton Keynes, Open University Press.

Baker, D., Gamble, A. and Ludlam, S. (1992) Response: the social background of British MPs *Sociology* 26(4).

Barker, E. (1984) *The Making of a Moonie* Oxford, Basil Blackwell.

Barker, E. (1989) *New Religious Movements* London, HMSO.

Bean, P. T. and Wilkinson, C. K. (1988) Drug taking, crime and the illicit supply system *British Journal of Addiction* 83: 533–539.

Bechhofer, F. and Elliott, B. (1968) An approach to a study of small shop-keepers and the class structure *European Journal of Sociology* 9: 2.

Becker, H. (1963) *Outsiders: studies in the sociology of deviance* New York, Free Press.

Beckford, J. (1985) *Cult Controversies* London, Tavistock.

Bell, D. (1973) *The Coming of Post-Industrial Society* New York, Basic Books.

Berger, P. (1968) *The Social Reality of Religion* London, Faber and Faber.

Berle, A. A. and Means, G. C. (1932) *The Modern Corporation and Private Property* New York, Macmillan.

Berman, M. (1983) *All that is Solid Melts into Air: the experience of modernity* London, Verso.

Beveridge Report (1942) *Social Insurance and Allied Services* London, HMSO.

Beynon, H. (1973) *Working for Ford* London, Allen Lane.

Beynon, H., Hudson, R. and Sadler, D. (1986) *The Growth and International-isation of Teesside's Chemical Industry* Durham, Working Paper no. 3. Middlesborough Locality Study.

Bhat, A. Carr-Hire, R. and Ohni, S. (1988) *Britain's Black Population* Aldershot, Gower.

Bird, D. (1990) Industrial stoppages in 1989 *Employment Gazette* July: 336–46.

Bishop, J. and Hoggett, P. (1986) *Organizing around Enthusiasms* London, Comedia.

Black Report (1980) *Inequalities in Health: report on a research working group* London, DHSS.

Blackburn, R. and Mann, M. (1979) *The Working Class in the Labour Market* London, Macmillan.

Blau, P. and Duncan, O. (1967) *The American Occupational Structure* New York, Wiley.

Blaxter, M. (1990) *Health and Lifestyles* London, Routledge.

Bottomley, S. K. and Pease, K. (1986) *Crime and Punishment: interpreting the data* Milton Keynes, Open University Press.

Bowe, R. and Ball, S. with Gold, A. (1992) *Reforming Education and Changing Schools: case studies in policy sociology* London, Routledge.

Bowles, S. and Gintis, H. (1976) *Schooling in Capitalist America* London, Routledge and Kegan Paul.

Box, S. (1981) *Deviance, Reality and Society* 2nd edn, London, Holt, Rinehart and Winston.

Box, S. (1983) *Power, Crime and Mystification* London, Tavistock.

Box, S. (1987) *Recession, Crime and Punishment* London, Macmillan.

Boyd, D. (1973) *Elites and their Education* Slough, NFER.

Brake, M. (1980) *The Sociology of Youth Culture and Youth Subcultures* London, Routledge and Kegan Paul.

Braverman, H. (1974) *Labor and Monopoly Capital: the degradation of work in the twentieth century* New York, Monthly Review Press.

Brenner, M. H. (1979) Health costs and benefits of economic policy *International Journals of Health Services* 7(4): 581–623.

Brierley, P. (1991) *'Christian' England* London, MARC Europe.

Brown, C. (1984) *Black and White Britain* London, Heinemann.

Brown, P. (1987) *Schooling Ordinary Kids: inequality, unemployment and the new vocationalism* London, Tavistock.

Buck, N. (1985) Service industries and local labour markets: towards an anatomy of service employment. Presented at the Regional Science Association Annual Conference, September.

Budd, L. and Whimster, S. (eds) (1992) *Global Finance and Urban Living* London, Routledge.

Burgess, R. (1986) *Sociology, Education and Schools: an introduction to the sociology of education* London, Batsford.

Burgoyne, J. and Clarke, D. (1982) Reconstituted families, in R. N. Rapoport, M. P. Fogarty and R. Rapoport (eds) *Families in Britain* London, Routledge and Kegan Paul.

Burns, T. (1977) *The BBC: public institution and private world* London, Macmillan.

Burns, T. and Stalker, J. (1961) *The Management of Innovation* London, Tavistock.

Butler, D. and Sloman, A. (1980) *British Political Facts 1900–79* 5th edn, London, Macmillan.

Campbell, M. (1981) *Capitalism in the UK* London, Croom Helm.

Castells, M. (1978) *City and Power* London, Macmillan.

Chadwick, E. (1842) *Report on the Sanitary Conditions of the Labouring Population of Great Britain* London, Clowes.

Charles, N. and Kerr, M. (1988) *Women, Food and Families* Manchester, Manchester University Press.

Child, J. (1972) Organizational structure, environment and performance: the role of strategic choice *Sociology* 6(1).

Clarke, I. M. (1982) The changing international division of labour within ICI, in M. Taylor and N. Thrift (eds) *The Geography of Multinationals: studies in the spatial development and economic consequences of multinational corporations* London, Croom Helm.

Clarke, J. (1976) Style, in S. Hall and T. Jefferson (eds) *Resistance through Rituals* London, Hutchinson.

Coates, D. (1984) *The Context of British Politics* London, Hutchinson.

Cockburn, C. (1987) *Two-Track Training: sex inequalities and the YTS* London, Macmillan.

Cohen, R. et al. (1992) *Hardship Britain* London, Child Poverty Action Group.

Cohen, S. (1980) *Folk Devils and Moral Panics* 2nd edn, Oxford, Martin Robertson.

Cohen, S. (1985) *Visions of Social Control* Cambridge, Polity.

Coleman, D. and Salt, J. (1992) *The British Population* Oxford, Oxford University Press.

Cooke, P. (1989) *Localities: the changing face of urban Britain* London, Unwin Hyman.

Corner, J. and Harvey, S. (eds) (1991) *Enterprise and Heritage* London, Routledge.

Crewe, I. (1981) The Labour Party and the electorate, in D. Kavanagh (ed.) *The Politics of the Labour Party* London, George Allen and Unwin.

Crewe, I. (1992) Why did Labour lose (yet again)? *Politics Review* September: 2–11.

Crewe, I., Day, N. and Fox, A. (1991) *The British Electorate, 1963–1987: a compendium of data from the British Election Studies* Cambridge, Cambridge University Press.

Crompton, R. (1992) Where did all the bright girls go? Women's higher education and employment since 1964, in N. Abercrombie and A. Warde (eds) *Social Change in Contemporary Britain* Cambridge, Polity, 54–69.

Crompton, R. and Jones, G. (1984) *White-Collar Proletariat: deskilling and gender in clerical work* London, Macmillan and Philadelphia, Temple University Press.

Crow, I. (1987) Black people and criminal justice in the UK *The Howard Journal of Criminal Justice* 26(4): 303–14.

Curran, J. and Gurevitch, M. (eds) (1991) *Mass Media and Society* London, Edward Arnold.

Dale, P. (1989) *The State and Education Policy* Milton Keynes, Open University Press.

Daniel, W. (1990) *The Unemployed Flow* London, Policy Studies Institute.

Daniel, W. and Millward, N. (1983) *Workplace Industrial Relations in Britain: the DE/PSI/SSRC survey* London, Heinemann.

Davie, G. (1990) An ordinary God: the paradox of religion in contemporary Britain *British Journal of Sociology* 41(3).

Davis, J. (1990) *Youth and the Condition of Britain* London, Athlone Press.

Deane, P. and Cole, W. A. (1967) *British Economic Growth 1688–1959: trends and structure* 2nd edn. Cambridge, Cambridge University Press.

Dearlove, J. and Saunders, P. (1991) *Introduction to British Politics: analysing a capitalist democracy* 2nd edn, Cambridge, Polity.

Dennis, R., Henriques, F. and Slaughter, C. (1956) *Coal is our Life* London, Eyre and Spottiswoode

Denver, D. (1989) *Elections and Voting Behaviour in Britain* London, Philip Allan.

Department of Health (1989) *Working for Patients* Cmnd 555, London, HMSO.

Department of Health (1992) *The Health of the Nation: a strategy for health in England* London, HMSO.

Devine, F. (1989), Privatised families and their homes, in G. Allan and G. Crow (eds) *Home and Family: creating the domestic sphere* London, Macmillan.

Devine, F. (1992) *Affluent Workers Revisited: privatism and the working class* Edinburgh. Edinburgh University Press.

DHSS (1984) *The Health Service in England: annual report* London, HMSO.

Dickens, P. (1990) *Urban Sociology* Hemel Hempstead, Harvester Wheatsheaf.

Downes, D. and Rock, P. (1988) *Understanding Deviance* Oxford, Clarendon Press.

Downing, H. (1980) Word processors and the oppression of women, in T. Forrester (ed.) *The Microelectronics Revolution* Oxford, Blackwell.

Dunleavy, P. and O'Leary, B. (1987) *Theories of the State: the politics of liberal democracy* London, Macmillan.

Eaton, M. (1986) *Justice for Women? Family, court and social control* Milton Keynes, Open University Press.

Edgell, S. (1980) *Middle-Class Couples* London, George Allen and Unwin.

Edgell, S. and Duke, V. (1991) *A Measure of Thatcherism: a sociology of Britain* London, Harper Collins.

Engels, F. (1969) *The Condition of the Working Class in England* London, Panther.

Equal Opportunities Commission (1991, 1992) *Women and Men in Britain: a statistical profile* London, EOC.

Ermisch, J. (1989) Divorce: economic antecedents and aftermath, in H. Joshi (ed.) *The Changing Population of Britain* Oxford, Blackwell.

Fagin, L. (1984) *The Foresaken Families: the effects of unemployment on family life* Harmondsworth, Penguin.

Family Policy Studies Centre (1984) *An Ageing Population* London, Family Policy Studies Centre.

Finch, J. (1989) *Family Obligations and Social Change* Cambridge, Polity.

Finer Report (1974) *Report of Committee on One-Parent Families* London, HMSO.

Fiske, J. (1987) *Television Culture* London, Metheun.

Frankenberg, R. (1966) *Communities in Britain* Harmondsworth, Penguin.

Franklin, A. (1989) Working class privatism: a historical case study of Bedminster, Bristol *Environment and Planning D: Society and Space* 7(1): 93–114.

Frith, S. (1984) *The Sociology of Youth* Ormskirk, Causeway.

Furnham, A. (1989) *The Anatomy of Adolescence* London, Routledge.

Gabe, J., Calnan, M. and Bury, M. (1991) *The Sociology of the Health Service* London, Routledge.

Gabriel, Y. (1988) *Working Lives in Catering* London, Routledge.

Gallie, D. (1978) *In Search of the New Working Class: automation and social integration within the capitalist enterprise* Cambridge, Cambridge University Press.

Gallie, D. (1983) *Social Inequality and Class Radicalism in France and Britain* Cambridge, Cambridge University Press.

Gardner, C. and Sheppard, J. (1989) *Consuming Passion* London, Unwin Hyman.

Gelsthorpe, L. and Morris, A. (eds) (1990) *Feminist Perspectives in Criminology* Milton Keynes, Open University Press.

Gershuny, J. (1978) *After Industrial Society* London, Macmillan.

Gershuny, J. (1983) *Social Innovation and the Division of Labour* Oxford, Oxford University Press.

Gershuny, J. (1992) Change in the domestic division of labour in the UK, 1975–1987: dependent labour versus adaptive partnership, in N. Abercrombie and A. Warde (eds) *Social Change in Contemporary Britain* Cambridge, Polity.

Gershuny, J. and Jones, S. (1987) The changing work/leisure balance in Britain, 1961–1984, in J. Horne, D. Jary and A. Tomlinson (eds) *Sport, Leisure and Social Relations* London, Routledge.

Giddens, A. (1980) *The Class Structure of the Advanced Societies* 2nd edn, London, Hutchinson.

Gilroy, P. (1987) *There Ain't No Black in the Union Jack* London, Hutchinson.

Goldthorpe, J. (with Llewellyn, C. and Payne, C.) (1987) *Social Mobility and Class Structure in Modern Britain* 2nd edn, Oxford, Clarendon Press.

Goldthorpe, J. H., Lockwood, D., Bechhofer, F. and Platt, J. (1968a) *The Affluent Worker: industrial attitudes and behaviour* Cambridge, Cambridge University Press.

Goldthorpe, J. H., Lockwood, D., Bechhofer, F. and Platt, J. (1968b) *The Affluent Worker: political attitudes and behaviour* Cambridge, Cambridge University Press.

Goldthorpe, J. H., Lockwood, D., Bechhofer, F. and Platt, J. (1969) *The Affluent Worker in the Class Structure* Cambridge, Cambridge University Press.

Gorz, A. (1982) *Farewell to the Working Class: an essay in post-industrial socialism* London, Pluto.

Graham, S. and Reeder, L. G. (1972) Social factors in the chronic illnesses, in H. E. Freeman, S. Levine, and L. G. Reeder, (eds) *Handbook of Medical Sociology* Englewood Cliffs, NJ, Prentice-Hall.

Gray, A. (1982) *Inequalities in Health*. The Black Report: a summary and comment *International Journal of Health Services* 12: 3.

Griffin, C. (1985) *Typical Girls? Young women from school to the job market* London, Routledge.

Griffiths, R. (1988) *Community Care: Agenda for Action* London, HMSO.

Griffiths Report (1983) *NHS Management Inquiry* London, DHSS.

Grimsley, M. and Bhat, A. (1990) Health, in A. Bhat, R. Carr-Hill and S. Ohri (eds) *Britain's Black Population* 2nd edn, Aldershot, Gower.

Hagan, J. (1984) *The Disreputable Pleasures* Toronto, McGraw-Hill.

Hales, C. P. (1986) What do managers do? A critical review of the evidence *Journal of Management Studies* 23(1): 88–115.

Hales, M. (1980) *Living Thinkwork* London, CSE Books.

Hall, R. (1985) *Ask any Woman* London, Falling Wall Press.

Hall, S., Critcher, C., Jefferson, T., Clarke, J. and Roberts, B. (1978) *Policing the Crisis* London, Macmillan.

Hall, S. and Jefferson, T. (eds) (1976) *Resistance through Rituals* London, Hutchinson.

Halsey, A. H., Heath, A. F. and Ridge, J. M. (1980) *Origins and Destinations: family, class and education in modern Britain* Oxford, Clarendon Press.

Hamnett, C., McDowell, L. and Sarre, P. (eds) (1989) *The Changing Social Structure* London, Sage.

Hanmer, J. and Saunders, S. (1984) *Well Founded Fear* London, Hutchinson.

Hannah, L. (1976) *The Rise of the Corporate Economy* London, Methuen.

Hannah, L. (1983) *The Rise of the Corporate Economy* 2nd edn, London, Methuen.

Harbury, C. D. and Hitchens, D. M. W. N. (1979) *Inheritance and Wealth Inequality in Britain* London, George Allen and Unwin.

Harrison, A. (ed.) (1992) *Health Care UK 1991* King's Fund Institute.

Harrison, P. (1985) *Inside the Inner City* Harmondsworth, Penguin.

Harrison, S., Hunter, D.J. and Pollitt, C. (1990) *The Dynamics of British Health Policy* London, Unwin Hyman.

Hartmann, H. (1979) Capitalism, patriarchy and job segregation by sex, in Z. Eisenstein (ed.) *Capitalist Patriarchy* New York, Monthly Review Press.

Haskey, J. (1984) Social class and socio-economic differentials in divorce in England and Wales *Population Studies* no. 38.

Heath, A. (1980) Class and meritocracy in British education, in A. Finch and P. Scrimshaw (eds) *Standards, Schooling and Education* London, Hodder and Stoughton.

Heath, A. (1981) *Social Mobility* London, Collins.

Heath, A., Jowell, R. and Curtice, J. (1985) *How Britain Votes* Oxford, Pergamon.

Heath, A., Jowell, R., Curtice, J., Evans, G., Field, J. and Witherspoon, S. (1991) *Understanding Political Change: the British voter 1964–1987* Oxford, Pergamon.

Hebdige, D. (1979) *Subculture: the meaning of style* London, Metheun.

Heidensohn, F. (1989) *Crime and Society* London, Macmillan.

Hesse, B., Rai, D.K., Bennett, C. and McGilchrist, P. (1992) *Beneath the Surface: racial harassment* Aldershot, Avebury.

Hill, S. (1976) *The Dockers: class and tradition in London* London, Heinemann.

Holdaway, S. (1983) *Inside the British Police* Oxford, Basil Blackwell.

Hole, W. V. and Pountney, M. T. (1971) *Trends in Population, Housing and Occupancy Rates 1861–1961* Department of the Environment Building Research Station, HMSO.

Horne, J., Jary, D. and Tomlinson, A. (1987) *Sport, Leisure and Social Relations* London, Routledge.

Hough, M. and Mayhew, P. (1983) *The British Crime Survey: first report* London, HMSO.

Hough, M. and Mayhew, P. (1985) *Taking Account of Crime: key findings from the second British Crime Survey* London, HMSO.

Hudson, B. (1992) Inter-agency collaboration: can care management fix it?, in A. Harrison (ed.) *Health Care UK 1991* King's Fund Institute.

Humm, M. (ed.) (1992) *Feminisms: a reader* Hemel Hempstead, Harvester Wheatsheaf.

Hunt, A. (1978) *The Elderly at Home* London, HMSO.

Husband, C. (ed.) (1982) *'Race' in Britain* London, Hutchinson.

Jacobs, B. (1992) *Fractured Cities: capitalism, community and empowerment in Britain and America* London, Routledge.

Jencks, C. (1972) *Inequality: a reassessment of the effect of family and schooling in America* New York, Basic Books.

Jessop, B. (1992) From social democracy to Thatcherism: twenty-five years of British politics, in N. Abercrombie and A. Warde (eds) *Social Change in Contemporary Britain* Cambridge, Polity, 14–39.

Jessop, B., Bonnett, K., Bromley, S. and Ling, T. (1988) *Thatcherism: a tale of two nations* Cambridge, Polity.

Johnson, J.H. (1972) *Urban Geography* Oxford, Pergamon.

Jones, B. (1982) Destruction or redistribution of engineering skills? The case of numerical control, in S. Wood (ed.) *The Degradation of Work? Skill, deskilling and the labour process* London, Hutchinson, 179–200.

Jones, B. (1988) Work and flexible automation in Britain: review of developments and possibilities *Work Employment and Society* 2 (4): 451–86.

Jones, S. (1988) *Black Culture, White Youth* London, Macmillan.

Jones, T., Maclean, B. and Young, J. (1986) *The Islington Crime Survey* London, Gower.

Joshi, H. (ed.) (1989) *The Changing Population of Britain* Oxford, Blackwell.

Jowell, R. and Airey, C. (1984) *British Social Attitudes* London, Gower.

Jowell, R., Witherspoon, S. and Brook, L. (1990) *British Social Attitudes: the 7th report* Aldershot, Gower.

Kass, L. R. (1975) Regarding the end of medicine and the pursuit of health *Public Interest* 40 (summer): 11–42.

Kelly, J. (1990) British trade unionism 1979–89: change, continuity and contradictions *Work, Employment and Society* special issue: 29–65.

Kelly, M. P. (1980) *White Collar Proletariat* London, Routledge and Kegan Paul.

Kelman, S. (1975) The social nature of the definition problem in health *International Journal of Health Services* 5(4): 625–42.

Kinsey, R. (1985) *Merseyside Crime and Police Surveys: final report* Edinburgh, Centre for Criminology, University of Edinburgh.

Kitwood, T. (1980) *Disclosures to a Stranger* London, Routledge and Kegan Paul.

Kumar, K. (1975) Holding the middle ground: the BBC, the public and the professional broadcaster *Sociology* 9(3).

Kumar, K. (1978) *Prophecy and Progress: the sociology of industrial and post-industrial societies* Harmondsworth, Penguin.

Laslett, P. (1965) *The World We Have Lost* London, Methuen.

Lea, J. and Young, J. (eds.) (1984) *What is to be Done about Law and Order? Crisis in the eighties* Harmondsworth, Penguin.

Leach, E. (1986) The cereal packet norm *The Guardian* 29 January 1986.

Leathard, A. (1990) *Health Care Provision: past, present and future* London, Chapman and Hall.

Lee, C. H. (1984) The service sector, regional specialisation, and economic growth in the Victorian economy *Journal of Historical Geography* 10(2): 139–55.

Lee, R. M. (1979) *Communes as Alternative Families* MPhil thesis, North East London Polytechnic.

Leggatt. T. (1970) Teaching as a profession, in J. A. Jackson (ed.) *Professions and Professionalization* Cambridge, Cambridge University Press.

Leichter, H. (1980) *A Comparative Approach to Policy Analysis: health care policy in four nations* Cambridge, Cambridge University Press.

Lemert, E. (1967) *Human Deviance, Social Problems, and Social Control* Englewood Cliffs, Prentice-Hall.

Lockwood, D. (1958) *The Blackcoated Worker* London, George Allen and Unwin.

Lockwood, D. (1966) Sources of variation in working class images of society *Sociological Review* 14(3): 249–67.

Mac an Ghaill, M. (1988) *Young, Gifted and Black: student–teacher relations in the schooling of black youth* Milton Keynes, Open University Press.

McConville, M. and Baldwin, J. (1982) The influence of race on sentencing in England *Criminal Law Review* October: 652–8.

McCrone, D. (1992) *Understanding Scotland: the sociology of a stateless nation* London, Routledge.

McCulloch, A. (1982) Alternative households, in R. N. Rapoport, M. P. Fogarty and R. Rapoport (eds.) *Families in Britain* London, Routledge and Kegan Paul.

McNally, J. (1979) *Women for Hire: a study of the female office worker* London, Macmillan.

McNaught, A. (1984) *Race and Health Care in the United Kingdom* London, Centre for Health Service Management Studies, Polytechnic of South Bank.

McNaught, A. (1988) *Race and Health Policy* New York, Croom Helm.

McQuail, D. (1977) The influence and effects of mass media, in J. Curran, M. Gurevitch and J. Woollacott (eds.) *Mass Communications and Society* London, Edward Arnold.

McRobbie, A. (1978) Working class girls and the culture of feminity, in Birmingham University Centre for Contemporary Cultural Studies, Women's Studies Group *Women Take Issue: aspects of women's subordination* London, Hatchinson.

McRobbie, A. (1991) *Feminism and Youth Culture* London, Macmillan.

Marshall, G., Rose, D., Newby, H. and Vogler, C. (1988) *Social Class in Modern Britain* London, Unwin Hyman.

Martin, J. and Roberts, C. (1984) *Women and Employment: a lifetime perspective. The report of the 1980 DE/OPCS women and employment survey* London HMSO.

Matza, D. (1964) *Delinquency and Drift* Chichester, Wiley.

Mathew, P., Elliott, D. and Dowds, L. (1989) *The 1988 British Crime Survey* London, HMSO.

Meegan, R. (1989) Paradise postponed: the growth and decline of Merseyside's outer estates, in P. Cooke (ed.) *Localities* London, Unwin Hyman, 198–234.

Melucci, A. (1985) The symbolic challenge of contemporary movements *Social Research* 52(4): 789–816.

Michels, R. (1915) *Political Parties: a sociological study of the oligarchical tendencies of modern democracy* Illinois. Free Press of Glencoe.

Miles, R. (1989) *Race and Racism* London, Routledge.

Millward, N., Stevens, M., Smart, D. and Hawes, W. (1992) *Workplace Industrial Relations in Transition: the ED/ESRC/PSI/ACAS surveys* Aldershot, Dartford.

Mitchell, J. (1984) *What is to be Done about Illness and Health?* Harmondsworth, Penguin

Moorhouse, H. F. (1976) Attitudes to class and class relations in Britain *Sociology* 10(3): 469–96.

Morley, D. (1980) *The 'Nationwide Audience'* London, BFI.

Morris, L. (1990) *The Workings of the Household* Cambridge, Polity.

Murdock, G. (1982) Large corporations and the control of the communications industries, in J. Curran, M. Gurevitch and J. Woollacott (eds) *Mass Communications and Society* London, Edward Arnold.

NACRO (1989) *Some Facts and Figures about Black People in the Criminal Justice*
System London, National Association for the Care and Resettlement of Offenders, Briefing Paper.

NACRO (1993) *Imprisonment in Western Europe: some facts and figures* Briefing
paper, National Association for the Care and Resettlement of Offenders.

Newby, H. (1979) *The Deferential Worker: a study of farm workers in East Anglia* Harmondsworth, Penguin.

Newby, H. (1985) *Green and Pleasant Land? Social change in rural England* London, Wildwood House.

Oakley, A. (1974) *The Sociology of Housework* Oxford, Martin Robertson.

Offe, C. (1985) New social movements: challenging the boundaries of institutional politics *Social Research* 52(4): 817–68.

Oppenheim, C. (1990) *Poverty: the facts* London, Child Poverty Action Group.

Otley, C. B. (1973) The educational background of British army officers *Sociology* 7.

Pahl, J. (1989) *Money and Marriage* London, Macmillan.

Pahl, R. (1975) *Whose City?* Harmondsworth, Penguin.

Pahl, R. (1984) *Divisions of Labour* Oxford, Basil Blackwell.

Pahl, R. and Wallace, C. (1985) Household work strategies in the recession, in N. Redclift and E. Mingione (eds) *Beyond Employment* Oxford, Basil Blackwell.

Painter, K., Lea, J., Woodhouse, T. and Young, J. (1989) *Hammersmith and Fulham Crime and Policy Survey, 1988* Middlesex, Centre for Criminology, Middlesex Polytechnic.

Parker, R. (1982) Family and social policy: an overview, in R. N. Rapoport, M. P. Fogarty and R. Rapoport (eds) *Families in Britain* London, Routledge and Kegan Paul.

Parkin, F. (1971) *Class Inequality and Political Order* London, MacGibbon and Kee.

Parry, N. and Parry, J. (1976) *The Rise of the Medical Profession* London, Croom Helm.

Parsons, T. (1956) The American family: its relations to personality and to the social structure, in T. Parsons and R. F. Bales (eds) *Family, Socialization and Interaction Process* London, Routledge and Kegan Paul.

Pearson, G. (1983) *Hooligan: a history of respectable fears* London, Macmillan.

Phizacklea, A. (1990) *Unpacking the Fashion Industry* London, Routledge.

Pierson, C. (1991) *Beyond the Welfare State?* Cambridge, Polity.

Poole, M., Mansfield, R. Blyton, P. and Frost, P. (1981) *Managers in Focus: the British manager in the early 1980s* Aldershot, Gower.

Popay, J., Rimmer, L. and Rossiter, C. (1983) *One Parent Families: parents, children and public policy* London, Study Commission on the Family.

Price, R. and Bain, G. S. (1988) The labour force, in A. H. Halsey (ed) *British Social Trends since 1900* London, Macmillan.

Raffe, D. (1990) The context of the Youth Training Scheme: an analysis of its strategy and development, in D. Gleeson (ed.) *Training and its Alternatives* Milton Keynes, Open University Press, 58–75.

Rapoport, R. N., Fogarty, M. P. and Rapoport, R. (eds) (1982) *Families in Britain* London, Routledge and Kegan Paul.

Reed, M. (1989) *The Sociology of Management* Hemel Hempstead, Harvester Wheatsheaf.

Reid, T. (1989) *Social Class Differences in Britain: life-chances and life-styles* 3rd edn, London, Fontana.

Reiner, R. (1985) *The Politics of the Police* Brighton, Wheatsheaf.

Rex, J. and Tomlinson, S. (1979) *Colonial Immigration in a British City* London, Routledge and Kegan Paul.

Rice, M. (1990) Challenging orthodoxies in feminist theory: a black feminist critique, in L. Gelsthorpe and A. Morris (eds) *Feminist Perspectives in Criminology* Milton Keynes, Open University Press.

Richardson, J. and Lambert, J. (1985) *The Sociology of Race* Ormskirk. Causeway Press.

Robbins, T. (1988) *Cults, Converts and Charisma: the sociology of new religious movements* London, Sage.

Roberts, K. (1989) Great Britain: socio-economic polarization and the implications for leisure, in A. Olszewska and K. Roberts (eds) *Leisure and Life-Style* London, Sage.

Roberts, K., Cook, F. G., Clark, S. C. and Semeonoff, E. (1977) *The Fragmentary Class Structure* London, Heinemann.

Robinson, J. (1984) Promiscuity isn't the cause *New Statesman* 30 March: 14.

Rojek, C. (1985) *Capitalism and Leisure Theory* London, Tavistock.

Routh, G. (1987) *Occupations of the People of Great Britain, 1801–1981* London, Macmillan.

Rowthorn, B. (1986) Deindustrialisation in Britain, in R. Martin and B. Rowthorn (eds) *The Geography of Deindustrialisation* London, Macmillan.

Royal Commission on the Distribution of Income and Wealth (1979) *Report no. 7* London, HMSO.

Runciman, W. G. (1983) *A Treatise on Social Theory* vol. 1 *The Methodology of Social Theory* Cambridge, Cambridge University Press.

Rutter, M., Maughan, B., Mortimore, P. and Ouston, J. (1979) *Fifteen Thousand Hours: secondary schools and their effects on children* London, Open Books.

Sarlvik, B. and Crewe, I. (1983) *Decade of Dealignment: the Conservative victory of 1979 and electoral trends in the 1970s* Cambridge, Cambridge University Press.

Saunders, P. (1979) *Urban Politics: a sociological interpretation* London, Hutchinson.

Saunders, P. (1990) *A Nation of Home Owners* London, Unwin Hyman.

Savage, M., Barlow, J., Dickens, P. and Fielding, T. (1992) *Property, Bureaucracy and Culture: middle-class formation in contemporary Britain* London, Routledge.

Savage, M. and Warde, A. (1993) *Urban Sociology, Capitalism and Modernity* London, Macmillan.

Scarman Report (1981) *The Brixton Disorders 10–12 April 1981* London, HMSO.

Scase, R. and Goffee, R. (1989) *Reluctant Managers: their work and lifestyles* London, Unwin Hyman.

Schieber, G. J. and Poullier, J. P. (1989) Overview of international comparisons of health care expenditures *Health Care Financing Review* annual supplement, 1–7.

Schieber, G., Poullier, J.-P. and Greenwald, L. (1992) US health expenditure performance: an international comparison and data update *Health Care Financing Review* 13(4): 1–87.

Scott, A. J. (1988) *New Industrial Spaces* London, Pion.

Scott, A. (1990) *Ideology and the New Social Movements* London, Unwin Hyman.

Scott, J. (1982) *The Upper Classes: property and privilege in Britain* London, Macmillan.

Scott, J. (1985) The British upper class, in D. Coates, G. Johnston and R. Bush (eds) *A Socialist Anatomy of Britain* Cambridge, Polity.

Scott, J. (1990) Corporate control and corporate rule: Britain in an international perspective, *British Journal of Sociology* 41(3).

Scott, J. (1991) *Who Rules Britain?* Cambridge, Polity.

SCPR (1988) *British Social Attitudes: the fifth report* Social and Community Planning Research, Aldershot, Gower.

Seabrook, J. (1978) *What Went Wrong? Working people and the ideals of the labour movement* London, Gollancz.

Seyd, P. and Whiteley, P. (1992) *Labour's Grass Roots: the politics of party membership* Oxford, Clarendon Press.

Sheldon, T.S. and Parker, H. (1992) Race and ethnicity in health research *Journal of Public Health Medicine* 14(2): 104–10.

Shilling, C. (1989) *Schooling for Work in Capitalist Britain* Brighton, Falmer.

Sinfield, A. (1981) *What Unemployment Means* Oxford, Martin Robertson.

Skellington, R. and Morris, P. (1992) *'Race' in Britain Today* London, Sage.

Smith, D. J. (1977) *Racial Disadvantage in Britain* Harmondsworth, Penguin.

Smith, D. J. and Gray, J. (1983) The police in action, in *Police and People in England* vol. 4, London, Policy Studies Institute.

Solomon, M. (1992) Public opinion and the National Health Service, in Harrison, A. (ed.) *Health Care UK 1991* King's Fund Institute.

Stacey, M. (1978) The sociology of health and illness: its present state, future prospects and potential for health research *Sociology* 12(2): 281–307.

Stacey, M. (1988) *The Sociology of Health and Healing: a textbook* London, Unwin Hyman.

Stanworth, M. (1983) *Gender and Schooling: a study of sexual divisions in the classroom* London, Hutchinson.

Stark, E. (1977) The epidemic as a social event *International Journal of Health Services* 7(4): 691–705.

Stewart, A., Prandy, K. and Blackburn, R. M. (1980) *Social Stratifications and Occupations* London, Macmillan.

Taylor, L. and Mullan, B. (1986) *Uninvited Guests* London, Chatto and Windus.

Taylor, L., Walton, P. and Young, J. (1973) *The New Criminology* London, Routledge and Kegan Paul.

Taylor, L., Walton, P. and Young, J. (eds) (1975) *Critical Criminology* London, Routledge and Kegan Paul.

Thane, P. (1989) Old age: burden or benefit?, in H. Joshi (ed.) *The Changing Population of Britain* Oxford, Blackwell.

Thompson, P. (1989) *The Nature of Work: an introduction to debates on the labour process* 2nd edn, London, Macmillan.

Thornes, B. and Collard, J. (1979) *Who Divorces?* London, Routledge and Kegan Paul.

Thorpe, D., Smith, D., Green., C. J. and Paley, J. H. (1980) *Out of Care* London, George Allen and Unwin.

Thunhurst, C. (1982) *It Makes You Sick* London, Pluto.

Tomlinson Report (1992) *Report of the Inquiry into London's Health Service, Medical Education, and Research* London, HMSO.

Townsend, P. (1979) *Poverty in the United Kingdom* Harmondsworth, Penguin.

Townsend, P. and Davidson, N. (1982) *Inequalities in Health* Harmondsworth, Penguin.

Townsend, P., Phillimore, P. and Beattie, A. (1988) *Health and Deprivation: inequality and the north* London, Croom Helm.

Turner, B. S. (1985) Knowledge, skill and occupational strategy: the professionalisation of paramedical groups *Community Health Studies* 9(1): 38–47.

Wagg, S. (1989) Politics and the popular press *Social Studies Review* 5(1): 17–22.

Walby, S. (1990) *Theorizing Patriarchy* Cambridge, Polity.

Wallis, R. (1984) *The Elementary Forms of the New Religious Life* London, Routledge and Kegan Paul.

Warde, A. (1990) The future of work, in J. Anderson and M. Ricci (eds) *Society and Social Science: a reader* Milton Keynes, Open University Press, 86–94.

Weber, M. (1968) *Economy and Society* Berkeley, University of California Press.

Westwood, S. (1984) *All Day, Every Day: factory and family in the making of women's lives* London, Pluto.

Wheelock, J. (1990) *Husbands at Home* London, Routledge.

White, M. (1991) *Against Unemployment* London, Policy Studies Institute.

Whitehead, M. (1988) *The Health Divide* in P. Townsend and N. Davidson (eds) *Inequalities in Health* Harmondsworth, Penguin.

Widgery, D. (1988) *The National Health: a radical perspective* London, Hogarth Press.

Williams, R. (1990) Paper presented to Annual Conference of the Society of Social Medicine, Glasgow.

Willis, P. (1977) *Learning to Labour* London, Saxon House.

Willis, P. (1990) *Common Culture* Milton Keynes, Open University Press.

Witz, A. (1991) *Professions and Patriarchy* London, Routledge.

Wood, S. (ed.) (1989) *The Transformation of Work?* London, Unwin Hyman.

Young, J. (1991) Ten principles of realism. Presented at the British Criminology Conference, York.

Young, M. and Willmott, P. (1957) *Family and Kinship in East London* London, Routledge and Kegan Paul.

Young, M. and Willmott, P. (1973) *The Symmetrical Family* London, Routledge and Kegan Paul.

Index